Toward the Making
of Thoreau's Modern Reputation

Toward the Making of Thoreau's Modern Reputation

SELECTED CORRESPONDENCE OF
S. A. JONES, A. W. HOSMER, H. S. SALT,
H. G. O. BLAKE, AND D. RICKETSON

Edited by Fritz Oehlschlaeger
and George Hendrick

UNIVERSITY OF ILLINOIS PRESS
Urbana Chicago London

*Publication of this work was made possible in part through
a grant from the National Endowment for the Humanities.*

© 1979 by the Board of Trustees of the University of Illinois
Manufactured in the United States of America

LIBRARY OF CONGRESS CATALOGING IN PUBLICATION DATA

Main entry under title:

Toward the making of Thoreau's modern reputation.

Includes bibliographical references and index.
1. Thoreau, Henry David, 1817-1862.   2. Literary
historians—United States—Correspondence.   3. Authors,
American—19th century—Biography.   I. Jones,
Samuel Arthur, 1834-1912.   II. Oehlschlaeger, Fritz.
III. Hendrick, George.
PS3053.T6   818'.3'09   79-12831
ISBN 0-252-00725-5

For
Paul Haller Jones
and
For Our Wives and Children

Contents

Acknowledgments

FOR PERMISSION to publish Dr. Jones's letters to Fred Hosmer and incidental quotations from sources in the Hosmer Collection, we are indebted to the Concord Free Public Library. We are indebted to the staff of that library for their efforts on our behalf.

For permission to publish materials in the Jones collection, we are indebted to the Rare Book Room at the University of Illinois at Urbana-Champaign. We are also indebted to the Rare Book Room of the University of Michigan for permission to publish sections of letters by Jones to Anna and Walton Ricketson, sections from George W. Cooke's letters to Jones, and brief quotations from the *Inlander*. Mrs. Harriet Jameson and her staff have been generous in their help.

For permission to publish letters from Jones to Salt, we wish to thank the editor of the *Thoreau Society Bulletin*. For permission to publish Salt's letters to Jones, we are indebted to Mrs. Henry Salt. Permission to publish pertinent sections of letters by Edward Emerson to Jones was generously given by the late Mr. Raymond Emerson.

We also wish to acknowledge the help that we received from the late Mrs. P. V. B. Jones, daughter-in-law of Dr. Jones, and from two of Dr. Jones's grandchildren—Mr. Paul Haller Jones and the late Miss Mary E. Cooley. Marcia Frizzell was of great assistance in typing the final draft.

Fritz Oehlschlaeger is indebted to the Research Board for funds which allowed him to carry out research in Concord. Parts of this work were submitted by Oehlschlaeger to the Graduate College of the University of Illinois at Urbana-Champaign in partial fulfillment of the requirements for the degree of Doctor of Philosophy. George Hendrick is indebted to the Research Board for funds which provided him, at several stages of this work, with a research assistant, and with typing and photocopying. Hendrick is also much indebted to Dean R. W. Rogers for helping arrange a leave of absence to edit the materials in the Jones collection.

⁂ Introduction

1

THE BEGINNING OF the last decade of the nineteenth century witnessed an unusual amount of literary activity concerning Henry David Thoreau, who had been dead for almost thirty years. Dr. Samuel Arthur Jones, a prominent homoeopathic physician in Ann Arbor, Michigan, read his first Thoreau paper, entitled "Thoreau: A Glimpse," to the Unity Club in his city on December 2, 1889. Only a few weeks earlier Henry S. Salt, a Cambridge man who had taught at Eton before giving up academic life, wrote Daniel Ricketson, a friend of Thoreau, asking for information to be included in a new biography of Thoreau. At about the same time Salt entered into correspondence with Thoreau's literary executor, H.G.O. Blake, with Emerson's son, Dr. Edward Emerson, and with several other Americans who could help with the biography.

Several months after delivering his Thoreau lecture, Dr. Jones issued it in pamphlet form, and it was read by Miss Eliza Hosmer, daughter of Thoreau's "long headed farmer," Edmund Hosmer.[1] She wrote to Dr. Jones about the essay, and from her he obtained the address of her relative Alfred Winslow Hosmer, an amateur photographer in Concord who specialized in "views" illustrating Thoreau's haunts. Jones wrote to Alfred Hosmer to inquire about obtaining some of the Concord views, and the two began a correspondence which was to continue until Hosmer died in 1903. Early in the spring of 1890 Jones sent copies of his lecture to Daniel Ricketson, H.G.O. Blake, and Henry Salt. All three wrote to Jones complimenting his essay, and Jones began to correspond with all three.

Raymond Adams has argued that Dr. Jones, Hosmer, and Salt were "to

---

1. For the circumstances which led to the beginning of correspondence between Hosmer and Jones, see letter 218 in the text which follows. Throughout this introduction we cite the appropriate letter only by number. For manuscript location, see "A Note on the Text," which follows the introduction.

1

lay the foundations for Thoreau's modern reputation,"[2] and we believe that publication of the correspondence concerning Thoreau contained in this volume will prove Professor Adams's contention. In another essay Adams has pointed to the last two decades of the nineteenth century as a critical period for Thoreau's reputation: this was the time that "Thoreau didn't die."[3] That Thoreau's reputation did not perish by the end of the last century is largely attributable to the efforts of Jones, Hosmer, and Salt.

During the late summer of 1890, Jones was to meet Blake and Fred Hosmer, for in August he left Ann Arbor with a delegation of the G.A.R. for a trip to Boston and Concord. Jones's chief interest was in Concord, where he visited the historical and literary shrines and met many others who had known Thoreau—Sam Staples, Miss Jane Hosmer, Cummings E. Davis, F. B. Sanborn, and Horace Hosmer, a former student in the school of John and Henry Thoreau. Horace Hosmer later supplied Jones with much valuable biographical information about the Thoreaus.[4] Jones never met Henry Salt or Daniel Ricketson; he did correspond actively with them. Fred Hosmer became his informant on matters Thoreauvian, and the information he received was then passed on to Salt, who kept Dr. Jones informed about Thoreau matters in England.

After Dr. Jones died in 1912, some of his Thoreau books, letters, and memorabilia were sold to meet pressing family needs; but part of his collection, including letters from Salt, Blake, and Ricketson, was saved and moved to Urbana, Illinois, by Jones's son, Professor P.V.B. Jones of the History Department of the University of Illinois. For over fifty years these letters remained in the attic of Professor Jones's home, apparently unread, until they were discovered by George Hendrick in the summer of 1974. The Jones collection was subsequently acquired by the library of the University of Illinois at Urbana-Champaign[5] and the many significant letters in that collection, including letters by Blake, Salt, and Hosmer, are being published now for the first time. In addition to the letters in the Jones collection, we have made selections from the letters of Jones to Hosmer, now at the Concord Free Public Library and, except in a few instances, also previously unpublished. The correspondence of Jones and

2. Raymond Adams, "Fred Hosmer, The 'Lerned Clerk,' " *Thoreau Society Bulletin* 36 (July 1951): 2.

3. Raymond Adams, "The Day Thoreau Didn't Die," *The Thoreau Centennial*, ed. Walter Harding (New York: New York University Press, 1964), p. 51.

4. Among Dr. Jones's private papers is a journal of his visit to Concord, in which he recorded meeting Miss Hosmer, Davis, Sanborn, and Horace Hosmer. Ms. The Collection of Dr. Samuel Arthur Jones, University of Illinois at Urbana-Champaign Library. (Referred to hereafter as Jones collection.) For Dr. Jones's 1890 meeting with Staples, see "Thoreau's Incarceration," *Inlander* 9 (December 1898):96–97.

5. For an incomplete listing of the materials in this collection see George Hendrick and Fritz Oehlschlaeger, *An Exhibition from the Collection of Dr. Samuel Arthur Jones* (Urbana-Champaign: University of Illinois Library Friends, 1974).

Ricketson has been reedited, and several letters not included in *Daniel Ricketson and His Friends*(Boston: Houghton, Mifflin and Co., 1902) have been added. We have not had available to us the original copies of letters between Ricketson and Salt and have used the versions published in *Daniel Ricketson and His Friends*. Unfortunately the letters of Jones to Salt are not available, though we do reprint three useful extracts which appeared in the *Thoreau Society Bulletin*.

Since Jones, Hosmer, Salt, Ricketson, Blake, and Franklin B. Sanborn (often mentioned in the letters) are known only to specialists in American Transcendental studies, we present biographical sketches of each before turning to an account of Thoreau criticism from 1849 to 1890.

Descended from the Hosmers who were among the original settlers of Concord in 1635, Alfred Winslow Hosmer was born in Concord in 1851. He worked for years as a clerk in a Concord dry goods store, which he bought in 1898. Hosmer never married, and the routine of his external life seems to have been consistent through his working years: six days devoted to work in the dry goods store, with Sunday reserved for walks through the woods and fields of Concord.[6]

Dressed in the clothes he made himself in protest against working conditions in the clothing industry, Hosmer used these Sundays to pursue his botanical and ornithological interests and to photograph Concord scenes. His photographs were used as illustrations in Margaret Sidney's *Old Concord: Her Highways and Byways* (1888), Annie Russell Marble's *Thoreau: His Home, Friends and Books* (1902), and the 1897 edition of *Walden*[7] published by Houghton, Mifflin. These photographs of Concord created a link between Hosmer and the major Thoreauvians of the period, for he also sent his "views" to John Burroughs, Dr. A. H. Japp, Daniel Gregory Mason, and many others. But more important for Jones and Salt, Hosmer was on the scene in Concord, seeing Concordians daily in the store and asking questions about Thoreau. Owing to his family connections, he also had entrée to homes throughout Middlesex County, a great advantage in his search for new information.[8]

Fred Hosmer published almost nothing on Thoreau, though he was certainly qualified to do so. Instead he preferred the private subordinate role of assisting Jones and Salt in their various biographical, critical, and bibliographical studies. He was also amassing one of the most important Thoreau collections in the United States. Hosmer's efforts to have

6. *Boston Transcript,* May 8, 1903. For the Hosmer family, see George Leonard Hosmer, *Hosmer Genealogy* (Cambridge: Technical Composition Co., 1928).

7. Harriet Mulford Lothrop (Margaret Sidney, pseud.), *Old Concord: Her Highways and Byways* (Boston: D. Lothrop Co., 1888); Annie Russell Marble, *Thoreau: His Home, Friends and Books* (New York: Thomas Y. Crowell & Co., 1902); Henry D. Thoreau, *Walden* (Boston: Houghton, Mifflin & Co., 1897).

8. Adams, "Fred Hosmer, The 'Lerned Clerk'," p. 1.

3

Thoreau better understood and appreciated were no less significant, however, because they were largely unrecognized in his own time. He was a curiously Thoreauvian man: private, independent, devoted to his own work—that of understanding the place in which he lived and of serving quietly the reputation of his predecessor.

Perhaps there could be no greater personal contrast than that between Fred Hosmer and his correspondent Dr. Samuel Arthur Jones. While Hosmer's Thoreauvian efforts were quiet and virtually anonymous, Dr. Jones enjoyed public combat with those who undervalued or willfully misconstrued Thoreau. Hosmer was characteristically temperate and genial; Jones was characteristically passionate and caustic, stern and uncompromising in assailing his and Thoreau's foes. Jones could, however, bring equal passion to the defense of those people and things that he valued.

The source of Dr. Jones's passionate nature may have been, as he liked to think, his Welsh blood. He was born of Welsh parents in Manchester, England, in 1834; and in 1842 he came with his parents to the United States. He studied at the Free Academy in Utica, New York, and then read medicine with a Dr. Watson. He studied medicine at the Homoeopathic Medical College in Philadelphia and was ready to receive his degree there in 1860 when he pointed out deficiencies in the abilities of some of his professors and was "blackballed." He did receive his M.D. that year from the Homoeopathic Medical College in St. Louis, and the next year the Philadelphia degree was issued. Jones's charges against the faculty were apparently well founded; but in this instance, as in many later ones, his devotion to principle was to cause him considerable difficulty.[9]

After service as a physician in the Union army, Jones practiced medicine in New Jersey and New York before being called to Ann Arbor as the first dean of the University of Michigan Homoeopathic Medical College. From the beginning of his tenure there in 1875 he was caught between rival political forces—the legislature, which supported the Homoeopathic College, and the university regents and "regular" medical professors, who opposed the new school. To the defense of his college Dr. Jones brought his characteristic passion; during one difficult struggle with the university administration, he told President Angell: "You don't have enough calcium in that backbone of yours to whitewash the bald spot on the top of your head."[10] His position was an impossible one, and he resigned the deanship in 1878 and his professorship in 1880, turning to private medical practice.

9. For sketches of Dr. Jones's life, see Hendrick and Oehlschlaeger, *An Exhibition from the Collection of Dr. Samuel Arthur Jones,* pp. 7–8; *Ann Arbor Daily News,* March 9, 1912; *University Homoeopathic Observer,* 10 (April 1912):33–34; Thomas Moore, "Prof. Jones Vindicated," unidentified clipping supplied by Hahnemann Medical College Library, Philadelphia.

10. Dr. Jones's remark is quoted in Walter Harding, "More Excerpts from the Alfred Hosmer Letter Files," *Thoreau Society Bulletin* 123 (spring 1973):6.

He continued to reside in Ann Arbor, where he wrote for medical journals, developed a large practice, reared a large family, and pursued his literary studies.

A believer in homoeopathy, Dr. Jones was an "irregular" among "regular" practitioners. He was fanatically devoted to Hahnemann's principles and theory—*let likes be cured by likes.*[11] Though Dr. Jones's belief in and defense of homoeopathy never wavered, during the 1880s he began to turn some of his awesome energies to literary studies, to Carlyle and the American Transcendentalists, especially the works of another irregular, Henry David Thoreau. Dr. Jones came to believe that the current interpretations of Thoreau were inadequate or unfair, and he set out, late in 1889, to set the record straight.

Personally Henry S. Salt was more like Fred Hosmer than Dr. Jones. Salt was a naturalist, a quiet soft-spoken man, kind and gentle to all creatures. He had a strong social conscience and, like Dr. Jones, a desire to have his views made known to the world.[12] Salt—the most literary of the three men involved in providing new information about Thoreau—was born in India in 1851. His father was an officer in the Royal Bengal Artillery, and his mother was from a prominent Shrewsbury family. Salt was returned to England at the age of one, and was largely reared by his mother and grandparents, for his father remained in India and seldom returned to England. Salt was educated at Eton and King's College, Cambridge, where he read classics; and he returned to Eton to teach. His life was entirely conventional until after he began to teach at Eton, when he was converted to Freethought, partly through reading Shelley, who also influenced his adoption of a vegetarian diet.[13]

Salt's brother-in-law, J. L. Joynes, Jr., also an Eton master, began to introduce the Salts to leading social reformers of the day—Shaw, the Webbs, Edward Carpenter, and many others. From reading Carpenter, much influenced by Thoreau and a devotee of the simple life, Salt decided to give up his respectable life at Eton, moving to a cottage and devoting himself to the causes in which he believed. In 1885 the Salts left Eton. Edward Carpenter, ethical socialist and almost an open homosexual, was the titular deity in the Salt household. The Salts soon found that they had

11. For the fundamental principles of homoeopathy, see Samuel Hahnemann, *Organon of Medicine,* trans. R. E. Dudgeon, M.D. (London: W. Headland, 1849) and Martin Kaufman, *Homeopathy in America: The Rise and Fall of a Medical Heresy* (Baltimore and London: Johns Hopkins, 1971).

12. For biographical information on Salt see his autobiographies *Seventy Years Among Savages* (London: Allen & Unwin, 1921) and *Company I Have Kept* (London: Allen & Unwin, 1930). See also Stephen Winsten, *Salt and His Circle* (London: Hutchinson & Co., 1951), and George Hendrick, *Henry Salt: Humanitarian Reformer and Man of Letters* (Urbana: University of Illinois Press, 1977).

13. See Bernard Shaw, Preface, *Salt and His Circle* (London: Hutchinson & Co., 1951), pp. 9–15, for Shaw's account of Salt's reform views.

to maintain rooms in London, as well as the country cottage, for London was the center for the causes for which Salt worked. At first Salt devoted himself to various socialist movements, usually those akin to ethical socialism, though he was also a Fabian; but within a few years he became more concerned with vegetarianism, the humane treatment of animals, prison reform, and world peace. Devoted to nature study, he wrote several books on the subject in a quiet yet Thoreauvian manner. In many ways Salt was ideally suited to write about Thoreau, for Salt had refined sensibilities, an excellent prose style, and an understanding of Thoreau's nature writings as well as his social criticism.

Henry Salt was a reformer with a sense of humor, a scholar with a social conscience, a visionary socialist. His friendship with Dr. Jones was a warm one. He provided Jones with invaluable information for Jones's Thoreau bibliography, but more important his own 1896 biography of Thoreau, to which Jones and Hosmer made significant contributions, was to remain the best Thoreau biography until Walter Harding published *The Days of Henry Thoreau* in 1965. The Salt biography of Thoreau was to have significant meaning to many who read it: the best known of its readers was M. K. Gandhi, who read it in South Africa when his *Satyagraha* campaign was being formulated and put into practice.

Salt was a man of many friendships (he knew future mahatmas and prime ministers), but for some reason his letters to Fred Hosmer were distant; although Salt admired Hosmer he did not warm to him as he did to Jones or to Ricketson.

Though the first world war destroyed the humanitarian movement, Salt served that cause well in his account of it in his autobiographies *Seventy Years Among Savages* and *Company I Have Kept,* autobiographies which have significant comments on Thoreau studies in England at the turn of the century. This private, sensitive humanitarian socialist was the leading English Thoreauvian until his death in 1939.

Toward the Making of Thoreau's Modern Reputation draws heavily on the correspondence of Samuel Jones, Fred Hosmer, and Henry Salt; but three other men are also particularly important: H.G.O. Blake, Daniel Ricketson, and Franklin Benjamin Sanborn. All three knew Thoreau, though Sanborn was more an acquaintance than friend. Blake and Ricketson were of special importance to Salt, Jones, and Hosmer, for these two friends of Thoreau were a living link to their dead hero. Blake and Ricketson could answer questions about Thoreau and provide new information. Blake was Thoreau's literary executor and many of Thoreau's manuscripts were in his possession. Sanborn, on the other hand, had staked his claim as the premier Thoreau scholar of the time, but Dr. Jones regarded Sanborn as a man without principle and wanted to rescue

Thoreau from such company. Hosmer had his doubts about Sanborn, and even Salt came to distrust him.

Harrison Gray Otis Blake was born in Worcester, Massachusetts, in 1816.[14] His father was a prominent lawyer and a state senator. Blake was graduated from Harvard in 1835 and then entered divinity school in Cambridge. He remained in the ministry only a short time, apparently, for in the words of the Worcester *Gazette* obituary, his religious views were "too far in advance of his time." He turned instead to teaching and conducted private classes for young ladies. His reticence, his stolidity, and his lack of a sense of humor perhaps contributed to his failure as a schoolmaster. According to Daniel Gregory Mason, Blake's classes "gradually disintegrated into single pupils."[15] When Blake had enough income for his frugal ways, he gave up teaching entirely. He died in 1898.

Blake was Thoreau's first disciple. As Daniel Gregory Mason has noted, Blake was perfect in that role: "He had the reverence for all that is good or great, the constant desire to spread its influence, and the lack of purely personal initiative, which combine to make an ideal follower."[16] Blake had known Thoreau casually, but when he came upon Thoreau's essay on Persius in the *Dial* he wrote Thoreau a long letter in March of 1848, and their friendship began. Blake's correspondence with Thoreau was extensive, and as was proper for a disciple, he attempted to spread Thoreau's fame. He arranged Thoreau's lectures in Worcester and brought together fellow admirers whenever Thoreau came there. Unfortunately Blake could also bring out the prudish vaporous side of Thoreau, but the best of Thoreau's letters to Blake contain some of Thoreau's major philosophic musings on Transcendentalism. The Blake-Thoreau friendship was purely an intellectual one and they seem not to have discussed personal matters.

Upon the death of Sophia Thoreau in 1876, Blake became Thoreau's literary executor, and he edited the following volumes from the journals: *Early Spring in Massachusetts* (1881), *Summer* (1884), *Winter* (1887), and *Autumn* (1892). In addition, he published in 1890 *Thoreau's Thoughts,* to which Dr. Jones's Thoreau bibliography was attached. Blake did make significant parts of the journals available for the first time, but unfortunately the material selected was concentrated on nature writing, and the seasonal approach was a mistake.

Not surprisingly other Thoreau students—less volatile than Jones—

14. Biographical details about Blake are drawn from Walter Harding, *The Days of Henry Thoreau* (New York: Knopf, 1965); Daniel Gregory Mason, "Harrison G. O. Blake, '35, and Thoreau," *Harvard Monthly* 26 (May 1898):87–95; and the obituary in the Worcester Mass., *Evening Gazette*, April 19, 1898.

15. Mason, p. 89.

16. Mason, p. 90.

were able to approach Blake for help and to stay on good terms with him, but the temperaments of Jones and Blake were such that it was inevitable that misunderstandings would arise almost immediately.

Daniel Ricketson, born in New Bedford, Massachusetts, in 1813, was a Quaker with a private income.[17] He studied law, was admitted to the bar, but practiced only a short time. His obituary in the New Bedford *Morning Mercury* explained why: "That sympathy for the oppressed, which was a prominent trait of his character, prompted him to undertake the cases of a class in whom there was more thankfulness than profit, and after conducting the trial of several causes in which he was finally called upon to pay the costs of court himself, Mr. Ricketson retired from the practice of law." He then turned to the writing of local history and verse. He did much of his writing in a shanty near his home. Thoreau wrote an excellent description of that hut in his journal on April 10, 1857. Walter Harding suggests in *The Days of Henry Thoreau* that Ricketson's marriage was not a happy one and that the shanty was a convenient retreat.[18]

Ricketson was a small man who had suffered several injuries and illnesses in his youth and was, when Thoreau knew him, overly concerned about his health. Thoreau noted in his journal that the quotations on the inner walls of Ricketson's hut expressed Ricketson's peculiarities well—"his fear of death, love of retirement, simplicity, etc." (9:324).

Ricketson first wrote to Thoreau after the appearance of *Walden*, but the response was not cordial. When Ricketson learned that Thoreau would lecture in New Bedford, he invited Thoreau to stay with the Ricketson family as a houseguest. That visit was a success, and many other visits in New Bedford and Concord followed. In spite of his hypochondria Ricketson seems to have brought out successfully the sociable side of Thoreau's nature.[19] After Thoreau's death Ricketson was generous in answering queries of Thoreau students, as his correspondence with Salt and Jones shows.

After Ricketson's death in 1898, Dr. Jones and Salt continued to correspond with two of Ricketson's children—Anna and Walton.[20] Walton was an artist of modest abilities; his bust of Thoreau is now in the Concord Free Public Library. The Ricketson children also corresponded occasionally with Fred Hosmer.

Franklin Benjamin Sanborn figures in many of the letters included in

17. Biographical details about Ricketson are drawn from Walter Harding, *The Days of Henry Thoreau,* and the New Bedford *Morning Mercury,* July 18, 1898.

18. Harding, *The Days of Henry Thoreau,* p. 344.

19. *Ibid.,* passim.

20. The letters of Anna and Walton Ricketson to Dr. Jones are located in the Jones collection and in the Rare Book Room of the University of Michigan.

this volume; more often than not he is presented as morally reprehensible, as one who knowingly distorted facts about the Thoreau family, most especially facts about the parents of Henry Thoreau.

Sanborn was born in New Hampshire in 1831 and prepared for Harvard at Phillips Exeter Academy. He was graduated from Harvard in 1855 and moved to Concord, where, following Emerson's suggestion, he had already opened a private school. For a time after he came to Concord, he took his dinner in the Thoreau home. He did, therefore, have a chance to observe the Thoreaus, but he was not a close friend of Henry Thoreau. Sanborn did know Emerson, the Alcotts, Channing, and other Concord writers and was to write about them all.

Sanborn was active in the abolitionist movement. In 1857 he met John Brown and became his New England agent; and he knew about the plans to raid Harper's Ferry. After the raid Sanborn refused to testify before a committee of the U.S. Senate in Washington and twice fled to Canada to escape arrest. In April of 1860, however, he was arrested in Concord but was soon released by Judge Hoar, and the arresting party was chased from town.

Although he was a young man when the Civil War began, he did not serve in it. Instead he turned to newspaper work and edited the Boston *Commonwealth* in the years 1863–1867. John W. Clarkson, Jr., has suggested that Sanborn stayed home from the war and "began a courtship of Edith Emerson." She refused his proposal and, Clarkson notes, Sanborn "wrote her a letter protesting strongly the treatment he had received at her hands—he felt that she had toyed with his affections. The result of this was a letter from Emerson himself that was, to quote its present owner, Mr. George Goodspeed, 'almost violent' in its content." Clarkson believes the incident did not permanently affect Sanborn's relations with Emerson, but Emerson *did* speak disparagingly of Sanborn's failure to serve in the war effort.[21] Dr. Jones knew nothing of the incident, but he had served in the Union army until ill health forced him home, and he clearly believed that a man of Sanborn's sympathies should have served in the army also.

Sanborn was to remain a journalist for much of the rest of his life: he was an editor of the Springfield *Republican* during 1868–1872 and was on the staff of that paper until 1914. In addition Sanborn was active in public service. In 1863 Governor John Andrew appointed him secretary of the State Board of Charities. He retired as secretary after five years but

21. Biographical details about Sanborn are drawn from the *Dictionary of American Biography* (New York: Charles Scribner's Sons, 1935), 16:326–327; Walter Harding, *A Thoreau Handbook* (New York: New York University Press, 1959); and Franklin Benjamin Sanborn, *Recollections of Seventy Years*, 2 Vols. (Boston: The Gorham Press, 1909); John W. Clarkson, Jr., "F. B. Sanborn, 1831–1917," *The Concord Saunterer* XII (Summer 1917), 3.

remained on the board, serving as chairman from 1874 through 1876. He was, as the *DAB* notes, "a founder and officer of the American Social Science Association, the National Prison Association, the National Conference of Charities, the Clarke School for the Deaf, and the Massachusetts Infant Asylum."[22]

His public service was exemplary, but the mistrust of Samuel Jones and Fred Hosmer was well founded. They did not know the worst about Sanborn as editor of Thoreau: his editorial principles were even more lax than those generally employed in the nineteenth century. Walter Harding has pointed out in *A Thoreau Handbook* that in Sanborn's 1894 edition of Thoreau's letters, he "revised the punctuation, spelling, and even the wording to suit his own taste and was extremely careless in dating and annotating the letters."[23] Walter Harding and Carl Bode, the modern editors of Thoreau's correspondence, found that in one letter Sanborn made over one hundred changes.[24] Speaking of Sanborn's 1882 biography of Thoreau, Harding remarks: "Sanborn apparently considered himself a better writer than Thoreau and did not hesitate to take liberties with his manuscript materials. Thus, his text can never be completely trusted."[25]

Francis H. Allen in *Thoreau's Editors* has much the same story to tell about Sanborn's 1917 biography of Thoreau: "As an editor for Houghton Mifflin Company I had the not unmixed pleasure of seeing this book through the press, and, finding that the author had followed his custom of using great freedom in the treatment of quoted matter, I asked him if he would not make some statement in his preface which would explain why his versions of matter already printed differed from the previous forms. To this he consented, apparently without reluctance and in writing, but the statement never came, and he died on the very day when the proof of his preface was mailed to him."[26] Neither Jones nor Hosmer had access to the manuscripts Sanborn was editing, but they would have been horrified at Sanborn's liberties.

Though they were not to discover Sanborn's perfidy as an editor, Jones and Hosmer did find that Sanborn's stories about the parents of Thoreau were suspect, and they used Horace Hosmer's testimony about the Thoreaus to present a more reliable account of Mr. and Mrs. Thoreau.

22. *DAB*, 16:326.
23. Harding, *A Thoreau Handbook*, p. 79.
24. Walter Harding and Carl Bode, eds., *The Correspondence of Henry David Thoreau* (New York: New York University Press, 1958), p. 14.
25. Harding, *A Thoreau Handbook* (New York: New York University Press, 1959), p. 18.
26. Francis H. Allen, *Thoreau's Editors*, p. 15; quoted in Harding, *A Thoreau Handbook*, p. 23.

Modern writers on Thoreau have tended to agonize over the careless editing of Sanborn but to praise Sanborn's collection of firsthand reports on the Thoreaus. One might well follow Jones and Hosmer and be skeptical about Sanborn's anecdotal and biographical material on the Thoreaus also.

2

BEFORE WE CAN DISCUSS the importance of the work of Henry Salt, Alfred W. Hosmer, and Samuel Arthur Jones to the growth of Thoreau's reputation, it is necessary to examine critical reception of Thoreau before 1890.[1] Thoreau appeared in early studies, with few exceptions, either as an unoriginal imitator of Emerson or as a hopelessly misanthropic egotist who attempted to declare, as Lowell put it, "an entire independency of mankind."[2] As Jones perceptively suggested, it was the Walden experiment that most frequently caused Thoreau to be misunderstood,[3] though Thoreau's sympathetic treatment of oriental religion also found little favor among American critics and reviewers. American critics who did treat Thoreau sympathetically generally focused on his nature writing rather than on the social criticism of *Walden* and the reform papers. Consequently Thoreau often seemed more nearly a sentimental "poet-naturalist" than a tough-minded critic of social institutions.

During his lifetime Thoreau received little critical notice. His first book, *A Week on the Concord and Merrimack Rivers* (1849), attracted two important American reviews: one by Horace Greeley, the other by James Russell Lowell. Greeley praised Thoreau's artistry and his observations of nature but spent nearly half of his review illustrating Thoreau's "misplaced Pantheistic attack on the Christian faith."[4] Lowell's review was similarly mixed: he objected to the book's apparent formlessness but found Thoreau "clearly the man we want ... both wise man and poet."[5] Perhaps

1. Important surveys of the rise of Thoreau's reputation are Randall Stewart, "The Growth of Thoreau's Reputation," *College English* 7 (1946):208–14, and Gilbert P. Coleman, "Thoreau and His Critics," *Dial* 40 (1906): 352–56. Wendell Glick's preface to *The Recognition of Henry David Thoreau* (Ann Arbor: University of Michigan Press, 1969) is also useful, as is Lewis Leary's chapter on Thoreau criticism and scholarship in *Eight American Authors*, ed. James Woodress, rev. ed. (New York: Norton, 1971), pp. 129–71. The best survey is Walter Harding's final chapter of *A Thoreau Handbook* (New York: New York University Press, 1959), pp. 175–213. We are particularly indebted to Harding's fine study. See also Harding's *Thoreau: A Century of Criticism* (Dallas: Southern Methodist University Press, 1954).

2. James Russell Lowell, "Thoreau," *My Study Windows* (Boston: James R. Osgood & Co., 1871), p. 208. The chapter on Thoreau is a reprint of Lowell's review of *Letters to Various Persons*, which appeared originally in *North American Review* 101 (October 1865):597–608.

3. Dr. Samuel A. Jones, "Thoreau's Inheritance," *Inlander* 3, no. 5 (February 1893):199.

4. "H. D. Thoreau's Book," *Pertaining to Thoreau*, ed. Dr. Samuel A. Jones (Detroit: E. B. Hill, 1901), p. 6. Reprinted from *New York Tribune* for June 13, 1849. Jones attributed the review to George Ripley, but it is now more commonly attributed to Horace Greeley.

5. James Russell Lowell, "Review of the *Week*," in *Pertaining to Thoreau*, p. 19. Reprinted from *Massachusetts Quarterly Review* 3 (December 1849):40–51.

the best indication of Thoreau's fame in 1849, however, was a review in *Godey's Lady's Book:* it attributed *A Week* to Whittier.[6]

Walden was more widely noticed than *A Week*, but once again the number of reviews was modest. As Walter Harding has pointed out, a number of important periodicals—including the *Southern Literary Messenger* and *North American Review*—gave it little more than passing mention.[7] Among the longer American reviews, the most favorable was that by Lydia Maria Child in the *National Anti-Slavery Standard* for December 16, 1854. Mrs. Child, reviewing both *A Week* and *Walden*, perceptively discussed the purposes of Thoreau's Walden experiment, defending him against charges of selfishness, and lamenting "that these books have received no more adequate notice in our Literary Journals."[8]

Gamaliel Bailey's review of *Walden* in the *National Era* (September 28, 1854), reveals many tendencies of early Thoreau criticism in this country. Bailey found the book's philosophy "quite Emersonian" and objected to Thoreau's economic experiment on the grounds that, if universally applied, his principles would lead to barbarism.[9]

Charles F. Briggs charged Thoreau with insincerity. Like Bailey, Briggs failed to consider the Walden experiment as Thoreau had presented it: "Although he paints his shanty-life in rose-colored tints, we do not believe he liked it, else why not stick to it?"[10] The *Knickerbocker* for March 1855 treated *Walden* more sympathetically, recommending its philosophy as a corrective to the views expressed in the autobiography of P. T. Barnum; this reviewer also failed to take Thoreau's experiment seriously. Both Barnum and Thoreau, he charged, were "humbugs."[11]

In 1855 Edwin Morton published an evaluation of *A Week* and *Walden* in *Harvard Magazine;* like Greeley, Morton objected to Thoreau's praise of the eastern scriptures in *A Week*, but he also commented very favorably on the artistry of both volumes, particularly that of *A Week.*[12] "The Forester" was a highly sympathetic treatment which Bronson Alcott published in the *Atlantic* for April 1862. Alcott praised Thoreau—whom he inexplicably failed to name in the essay—as "our best sample of an indigenous American" and a "son of Nature."[13]

6. *Godey's Lady's Book* 39 (September 1849):223.

7. Harding, *A Thoreau Handbook*, p. 176.

8. Lydia Maria Child, "Review of *A Week* and *Walden*," in *The Recognition of Henry David Thoreau*, pp. 9–12. The review has been attributed to Mrs. Child by Glick.

9. Gamaliel Bailey, "Review of *Walden*," in *The Recognition of Henry David Thoreau*, pp. 8–9. Following B. R. McElderry, Glick has assigned this unsigned review to Bailey.

10. Charles Frederick Briggs, "A Yankee Diogenes," in *Pertaining to Thoreau*, p. 36. Reprinted from *Putnam's Monthly* 4 (October 1854):443–48.

11. "Town and Rural Humbugs," in *Pertaining to Thoreau*, pp. 75–88.

12. Edwin Morton, "Thoreau and His Books," in *Pertaining to Thoreau*, pp. 51–72. Reprinted from *Harvard Magazine* 1 (January 1855):87–99

13. Bronson Alcott, "The Forester," in *Pertaining to Thoreau*, pp. 107–8.

By far the most important of Thoreau's obituaries was that which Emerson published in the *Atlantic* for August 1862. Though most of Emerson's essay was couched in highest praise, it also unfortunately reinforced the commonplace criticisms of Thoreau. Emerson labelled Thoreau a "hermit and stoic" and emphasized the antisocial aspects of Thoreau's character: "His virtues, of course, sometimes ran into extremes. It was easy to trace to the inexorable demand on all for exact truth that austerity which made this willing hermit more solitary even than he wished." Emerson further revealed his misconception of the Walden experiment in remarks which served those who thought Thoreau's retreat to Walden a mere absurdity: "I so much regret the loss of his rare powers of action, that I cannot help counting it a fault in him that he had no ambition. Wanting this, instead of engineering for all America, he was the captain of a huckleberry-party. Pounding beans is good to the end of pounding empires one of these days; but if, at the end of years, it is still only beans!"[14]

Emerson's obituary of Thoreau was one of several;[15] the long obituaries by Storrow Higginson in the *Harvard Magazine*[16] and by G. W. Curtis in *Harper's*[17] were generally favorable—though Curtis also thought Thoreau a stoic. These obituaries signified the beginning of a brief flurry of interest in Thoreau, which was also marked by the appearance of new volumes of Thoreau's works. *Excursions,* a volume of essays selected by Sophia Thoreau and introduced by Emerson's biographical sketch, became the first of these in 1863. *The Maine Woods* and *Cape Cod,* edited by Sophia Thoreau and Ellery Channing, were published in 1864 and 1865, and *A Yankee in Canada, with Anti-Slavery and Reform Papers* appeared in 1866. Biographical treatment of Thoreau also began, with Franklin B. Sanborn's publishing eight installments of Channing's reminiscences of Thoreau in the Boston *Commonwealth* (from December 25, 1863, until February 19, 1864). A first edition of Thoreau's letters, *Letters to Various Persons,* edited by Emerson, was published in 1865. Unfortunately, for Thoreau's subsequent reputation, Emerson again presented Thoreau as a "most perfect piece of stoicism" by deleting many of the most personal passages from the letters. Sophia Thoreau believed that Emerson's edition so badly misrepresented her brother that she complained to the publisher, James T. Fields; some of the deleted passages were restored,

14. Ralph Waldo Emerson, *Works* (Boston: Houghton Mifflin, 1903), 10:456, 478, 480. Subsequent references will be shown parenthetically.

15. Walter Harding has listed fourteen obituaries of Thoreau. See *A Thoreau Handbook,* p. 178.

16. Storrow Higginson, "Henry D. Thoreau," in *Pertaining to Thoreau,* pp.117–126. Reprinted from *Harvard Magazine* 8 (May 1862):313–18.

17. George William Curtis, *Harper's Monthly* 25 (July 1862):270–71.

but *Letters to Various Persons* still served to reinforce the conception of Thoreau as an unfeeling stoic.[18]

John Broderick has demonstrated that Thoreau's posthumous volumes received fairly wide notice in American periodicals and newspapers. Broderick has gathered together thirty-six American reviews, enough to justify a judgment that "Thoreau was not (as Hawthorne once claimed to be) 'the obscurest man of letters in America.' " Yet Broderick indicates that critical understanding of Thoreau by 1866 had not advanced notably since 1854: "Thoreau was recognized, to however limited an extent, chiefly as a writer on nature; other phases of his writing were considered at least extraneous." Reviewers repeatedly dismissed Thoreau as "eccentric," "idiosyncratic," or "morbid"; and they objected frequently to his religious unorthodoxy, particularly to the high value he accorded oriental scripture. Thoreau's social criticism fared no better: "His social and political doctrines were . . . 'heresies,' though a few writers accepted the championing of John Brown as significant."[19] Broderick also proves that Emerson's portrait of Thoreau as a stoic powerfully influenced the reviewers.

Thus the interpretation of Thoreau as an unfeeling hermit who sought, in the language of the *New York Times,* a "cold and selfish isolation from human cares and interests"[20] was commonplace in 1865. This view was reinforced by America's most highly respected critic, James Russell Lowell. In the *North American Review* for October 1865 Lowell published what was ostensibly a review of *Letters to Various Persons*; actually the essay was a general assessment of Thoreau's writings and character. The hostile tone of the review was markedly different from that of Lowell's earlier review of *A Week,* a change that resulted perhaps from the conflict between Thoreau and Lowell over Thoreau's "Chesuncook." In 1858 Lowell, then editor of the *Atlantic*, had accepted "Chesuncook" for publication and was bringing it out in the June, July, and August numbers of the magazine. From the July installment he deleted a sentence, probably considering it too pantheistic, without informing Thoreau in advance. Lowell's action drew an angry letter from Thoreau, which Lowell did not deign to answer. Lowell did not correct or note the omission in the following installment. Thoreau would never again submit work to the *Atlantic* while Lowell was editor.[21]

18. In a letter to Daniel Ricketson of July 17, 1865, Sophia Thoreau reported that Emerson "had *bragged* that the coming volume would be a most perfect piece of stoicism, and he feared that I had marred his classic statue." *Daniel Ricketson and His Friends,* ed. Anna and Walton Ricketson (Boston: Houghton, Mifflin & Co., 1902), p. 166.

19. John C. Broderick, "American Reviews of Thoreau's Posthumous Books," *University of Texas Studies in English* 34 (1955):136. Subsequent references are shown parenthetically.

20. *New York Times,* July 31, 1865, p. 5.

21. Walter Harding, *The Days of Henry Thoreau* (New York: Knopf, 1965), pp. 392–95. For

The first charge which Lowell made against Thoreau in his review of *Letters* was that which he had made in 1848 in *A Fable for Critics*—that Thoreau was an imitator of Emerson; in his satirical poem Lowell had written:

> There comes ———, for instance; to see him's rare sport,
> Tread in Emerson's tracks with legs painfully short;
> How he jumps, how he strains, and gets red in the face,
> To keep step with the mystagogue's natural pace!
> He follows as close as a stick to a rocket,
> His fingers exploring the prophet's each pocket.
> Fie, for shame, brother bard; with good fruit of your own,
> Can't you let Neighbor Emerson's orchards alone?
> Besides, 't is no use, you'll not find e'en a core,—
> ——— has picked up all the windfalls before.[22]

Critics have differed as to which of Lowell's blanks refers to Thoreau; the other presumably refers to Ellery Channing.[23] Exact identification hardly matters, for both men are charged with slavish imitation of Emerson. In his 1865 review Lowell again clearly asserted Thoreau's dependence on Emerson: "Among the pistillate plants kindled to fruitage by the Emersonian pollen, Thoreau is thus far the most remarkable; and it is something eminently fitting that his posthumous works should be offered us by Emerson, for they are strawberries from his own garden."[24]

Imitation of Emerson was not the only charge Lowell leveled against Thoreau. Lowell thought Thoreau excessively egotistic, lacking any "faculty of generalization from outside of himself" (p. 200). Thoreau's retreat to Walden was simply an expression of this egotism, a "morbid self-consciousness that pronounces the world of men empty and worthless before trying it." "Thoreau had not a healthy mind"; if he had had, "he would not have been so fond of prescribing" (p. 203). Still another charge that was

---

Thoreau's letter to Lowell, see *The Correspondence of Henry David Thoreau*, ed. Walter Harding and Carl Bode (New York: New York University Press, 1958), pp. 515–16. Emerson suggested that Lowell never forgave Thoreau for wounding his vanity; see Charles Woodbury, *Talks with Ralph Waldo Emerson* (London: Kegan Paul, 1890), p. 63. The omitted sentence referred to a pine: "It is as immortal as I am, and perchance will go to as high a heaven, there to tower above me still."

22. *The Poetical Works of James Russell Lowell* (Boston: Houghton, Mifflin & Co., 1890), 3:42.

23. F. B. Sanborn first argued that Lowell's first blank applied to Channing, while it was Thoreau who had picked up Emerson's windfalls. *The Personality of Thoreau* (Boston: Charles E. Goodspeed, 1901), pp. 2–3. Austin Warren, however, has argued that Thoreau's name is to be understood in Lowell's first blank; see *Studies in Philology* 27 (1930):442–61. While he does not assign specific names to either blank, E. J. Nichols argues cogently that Lowell's references are to Thoreau and Channing; see "Identification of Characters in Lowell's *A Fable for Critics*," *American Literature* 4 (1932):191–94.

24. *My Study Windows*, p. 199. Subsequent references are shown parenthetically.

long repeated by Thoreau's critics was Lowell's assertion that "Thoreau had no humor" (p. 204). Lowell also ignored Thoreau's antislavery essays; he even accused Thoreau of ignoring the movement for abolition.

Lowell did praise Thoreau's style highly: "There are sentences of his as perfect as anything in the language, and thoughts as clearly crystallized; his metaphors and images are always fresh from the soil" (p. 209)—though he thought that Thoreau lacked the ability to give imaginative unity to an entire work. Lowell also manifested some fundamental sympathy for Thoreauvian economics: "His whole life was a rebuke of the waste and aimlessness of our American luxury, which is an abject enslavement to tawdry upholstery." For the Walden experiment, however, he had only contempt: "Thoreau's experiment actually presupposed all that complicated civilization which it theoretically abjured" (pp. 208–9).

How much influence Lowell exerted on the early reputation of Thoreau is open to debate. His treatment of Thoreau was not accepted uncritically by later commentators; within a year Eugene Benson responded in the *Galaxy*, reproaching Lowell for acting "as prosecutor for the Boston public" with its self-satisfied philistine attitudes.[25] John Broderick is right, when he suggests that "the elements which composed Lowell's Thoreau were common property of the reviewers before Lowell fused them." Broderick argues that "the part Lowell played in fixing American opinion of Thoreau appears to have been exaggerated" (p. 137). Nevertheless Lowell was the most widely respected American critic of his time; his review, especially after it was reprinted in *My Study Windows* (1871), undoubtedly reached many more readers than any of the other early assessments of Thoreau—with the possible exception of Emerson's biographical sketch. It is hard to deny Walter Harding's judgment that Lowell's criticism "probably . . . postponed a true appreciation of Thoreau for a generation or more."[26]

In the decade and a half following Lowell's review, American critical interest in Thoreau declined noticeably. Little of interest or value was published in the years 1865–1880. W. R. Alger, a Unitarian clergyman, in *The Solitudes of Nature and of Man* (1866) showed the decisive influence of Lowell in his indictment of Thoreau's supposed egotism.[27] When Thoreau's work was treated appreciatively, as in Mrs. L. A. Millington's "Thoreau and Wilson Flagg" (1875), it was again his nature writing that received praise.[28] Bronson Alcott's reminiscences in *Concord Days* (1872)

25. Eugene Benson, "Reply to Lowell," in *The Recognition of Henry David Thoreau*, p. 47. Reprinted from *Galaxy* 2 (September 1866):80–81.

26. Harding, *A Thoreau Handbook*, p. 179.

27. W. R. Alger, *The Solitudes of Nature and of Man* (Boston: Roberts Brothers, 1866), pp. 329–38.

28. Mrs. L. A. Millington, "Thoreau and Wilson Flagg," *Old and New* 11 (April 1875):460–64.

similarly emphasized Thoreau's interest in and knowledge of the natural world.[29] While Alcott's pieces are sympathetic, they did not advance the critical interpretation of Thoreau.

The outstanding event of American Thoreau scholarship during this time was the publication of Ellery Channing's *Thoreau, the Poet-Naturalist* in 1873. Written by Thoreau's close friend, this first full-length biography contained many valuable anecdotes and included substantial quotations from Thoreau's unpublished writings. Its greatest service was that it made available many excerpts from Thoreau's journals, though Channing's editing was careless and he failed, in two chapters, to distinguish between excerpts from Thoreau's journals and those from his own and Emerson's. Channing's critical perspective was limited: he emphasized Thoreau's nature writings while largely ignoring the social criticism. Even "the Walden experiment and the jail experience," as Harding has noted, were "hardly more than mentioned."[30] Channing treated Thoreau almost entirely as a "poet-naturalist," a description which became commonplace in subsequent criticism.

American critical treatment of Thoreau in the 1880s continued to be dominated by studies which emphasized his abilities as a nature writer. This emphasis was undoubtedly reinforced as well by the method which H.G.O.Blake chose in publishing Thoreau's journals. In 1881 Blake brought out *Early Spring in Massachusetts,* the first of four volumes of excerpts from the journals, each organized around one of the seasons.[31]

While Thoreau's descriptions of nature were beginning to be honored, his social criticism—particularly that embodied in the Walden experiment—was still generally unpopular with American critics of the 1880s. Both J. E. Cabot and E. P. Whipple, for instance, accepted the now conventional characterization of Thoreau as a wayward and inflexible eccentric.[32] W. G. Barton was disturbed by Thoreau's "radical unconventionalism" and judged the Walden experiment a singular failure, though he did grant that "it was born of a high idea": "This experiment in living did not prove much. It provoked severe criticism, and has had to yield to much of it."[33] The continuing influence of Lowell's strictures was apparent, too, in Francis Underwood's "Henry David Thoreau," in *Good*

29. Bronson Alcott, *Concord Days* (Boston: Roberts Bros., 1872), pp. 11–20, 137–40, 259–64.

30. Harding, *A Thoreau Handbook,* pp. 16–17.

31. Blake followed *Early Spring in Massachusetts* with *Summer* (1884), *Winter* (1887), and *Autumn* (1892).

32. James E. Cabot, *A Memoir of Ralph Waldo Emerson* (Boston: Houghton, Mifflin & Co., 1887), 1:282; Edwin P. Whipple, *American Literature and Other Papers* (Boston: Ticknor & Co., 1887), pp. 111–12.

33. W. G. Barton, "Thoreau, Flagg, and Burroughs," Essex Institute *Historical Collections* 22 (1885):54–55.

Words (1888),[34] and in Oliver Wendell Holmes's biography of Emerson, in which Thoreau's life at Walden again suffered adverse criticism by a witty Brahmin. In Holmes's work Thoreau appeared as "that unique individual, half college-graduate and half Algonquin, the Robinson Crusoe of Walden Pond, who carried out a school-boy whim to its full proportions, and told the story of Nature in undress as only one who had hidden in her bedroom could have told it."[35]

There were signs in the 1880s, however, that Thoreau's stature in the American literary community was increasing. In 1880 William Sloane Kennedy published a highly favorable estimate in the *Penn Monthly.* Though Kennedy's essay was an appreciation rather than a critical assessment of Thoreau's ideas, it did effectively defend Thoreau against charges of misanthropy, and, perhaps most important, it stressed the significance of the antislavery essays.[36] In 1882 F. B. Sanborn's biography supplied a much fuller account of the details of Thoreau's life than Channing's earlier work, and it included many quotations from previously unpublished materials such as Horace Greeley's letters to Thoreau and Thoreau's college essays. Unfortunately Sanborn's work was seriously flawed: in addition to the carelessly edited texts and questionable interpretations, Sanborn included irrelevant material—including a full six pages devoted to Daniel Webster's affection for the young Louisa Dunbar, Thoreau's aunt. Furthermore Sanborn did little to advance critical understanding of Thoreau; as Lewis Leary has remarked, his work was "in no substantial sense critical."[37] Also important in this decade was *Emerson in Concord,* in which Dr. Edward Emerson argued that "the charge of imitating Emerson, too often made against Thoreau, is idle and untenable, though unfortunately it has received some degree of sanction in high quarters."[38]

Other defenses of Thoreau came from Thomas Wentworth Higginson and John Burroughs. In *Short Studies of American Authors* (1880) Higginson delineated a Thoreau who was much less eccentric than early writers suggested. Most important Higginson emphasized the value of *Walden,* judging it "the only book yet written in America . . . that bears an annual perusal."[39] Burroughs published several pieces on Thoreau during the

34. Francis Underwood, "Henry David Thoreau," *Good Words* 29 (July 1888):445–52.

35. Oliver Wendell Holmes, *Ralph Waldo Emerson* (Boston: Houghton, Mifflin & Co., 1885), p. 72.

36. William Sloane Kennedy, "A New Estimate of Thoreau," *Penn Monthly* 11 (October 1880):794–808.

37. Lewis Leary, "Henry David Thoreau," in *Eight American Authors,* p. 149.

38. Edward W. Emerson, *Emerson in Concord* (Boston: Houghton, Mifflin & Co., 1888), p. 114.

39. Thomas Wentworth Higginson, *Short Studies of American Authors* (Boston: Lee and Shepard, 1880), p. 26.

1880s[40] that were largely given to Thoreau's abilities as a naturalist, which Burroughs rated lower than most other commentators. But Burroughs also attempted to refute some of the most damaging misconceptions of Thoreau: the allegation, made by R. L. Stevenson, that Thoreau was a "skulker";[41] Emerson's lament that Thoreau lacked "ambition" and was content to be "captain of a huckleberry-party"; Lowell's claim that Thoreau's work was humorless. Burroughs also stressed Thoreau's "devotion to principle" and the significance of the John Brown affair to a proper understanding of Thoreau. Even Burroughs, however, accepted Emerson's portrayal of Thoreau as the great negator; in his essay in *Indoor Studies* Burroughs virtually echoed Emerson's biographical sketch: "He was, by nature, of the Opposition; he had a constitutional No in him that could not be tortured into Yes." He also presented Thoreau as the stern cold recluse, dominated by "the Puritan element in him—strong, grim, uncompromising, almost heartless." Burroughs also had little sympathy for Thoreau's act of civil disobedience: "his carrying his opposition to the state to the point of allowing himself to be put in jail rather than pay a paltry tax, savors a little bit of the grotesque and the melodramatic."[42]

By the year 1890, then, when Dr. Jones, Alfred W. Hosmer, and Henry Salt had begun to work on behalf of Thoreau's reputation, there were scattered indications of an American revaluation of Thoreau. Still the overwhelming mass of American criticism before 1890 reflects the interpretation of Thoreau fostered by Lowell and Emerson. Thoreau was a cold morbid misanthrope whose retreat to Walden was an attempt to disavow affiliation with humanity; predictably, the orthodox commentators asserted, his experiment was a failure. Moreover Thoreau was an imitator of Emerson, capable of brilliant descriptions of woods and fields but of little else; his social criticism and religious eclecticism were little short of heretical. These same interpretations appeared also in the histories of American literature and the anthologies of the period.[43] In 1890, in the United States, Henry Thoreau was still largely regarded as an eccentric poet-naturalist whose criticism of American society was, at best, unfortunate.

Students of Thoreau's reputation have generally agreed that the early English response to his work was marked by greater understanding and

40. Burroughs published "Thoreau's Wildness," *Critic* 1 (March 26, 1881):74–75; "Henry D. Thoreau," *Century Magazine* 2 (July 1882):368–79; and "Henry David Thoreau," *Chautauquan* 9 (June 1889):530–33.

41. Robert Louis Stevenson, "Henry David Thoreau: His Character and Opinions," in *The Recognition of Henry David Thoreau*, p. 66. Reprinted from *Cornhill Magazine* 41 (June 1880):665–82. Subsequent references are shown parenthetically.

42. John Burroughs, "Henry D. Thoreau," *Writings* (Boston: Houghton, Mifflin & Co., 1889), 8:13, 15, 9.

43. Harding, *A Thoreau Handbook*, pp. 187–88.

sympathy than that of American commentators.[44] Thoreau's first book, *A Week on the Concord and Merrimack Rivers,* was deemed an "agreeable book" by the *Westminster Review,*[45] and it elicited a letter of praise from James Anthony Froude, Carlyle's friend and biographer.[46] A review in the *Athenaeum* for October 27, 1849, though generally unfavorable, judged Thoreau "a man with an original habit of thinking" who in future might produce "a richer harvest."[47] More complimentary was a review in the London *People's Review.* The author of this piece, identified by Walter Harding as Sophia Dobson Collet, judged *A Week* more favorably than any other reviewer, English or American: "The writer describes the scenery of his voyage with the vividness of a painter, and the scrutiny of a naturalist. . . . The occasional digressions are . . . not unworthy to stand beside [the essays] of Emerson himself."[48] English reviewers of *A Week* were not unanimously enthusiastic, however: the *Spectator* for October 13, 1849, dismissed the book as of little worth.

Walden received less notice in England than *A Week* had; according to Walter Harding, Thoreau's most recent biographer, only two reviews appeared.[49] Yet one of these is particularly noteworthy, both for the enthusiastic reception it gave *Walden* and for its author herself. In the *Westminster Review* for January 1856, George Eliot found the book "a bit of pure American life . . . animated by that energetic, yet calm spirit of innovation, that practical as well as theoretic independence of formulae, which is peculiar to some of the finer American minds."[50] The reviewer for *Chambers's Journal* feared that Thoreau had as "his object . . . the exaltation of mankind by the utter extinction of civilisation."[51] Significantly, however, this review was cribbed almost entirely from two American reviews, those in *Putnam's Monthly* and the *Knickerbocker.*

English criticism of Thoreau, as James Wood has commented, "took an entirely ·different direction from the start." The English critics largely avoided invective and did not charge that Thoreau imitated Emerson: "It was Thoreau's thoughts and the actions by which he interpreted and

44. See Harding, *A Thoreau Handbook,* p. 192; Leary, *Eight American Authors,* p. 146; and especially James P. Wood, "English and American Criticism of Thoreau," *The New England Quarterly* 6 (December 1933):733–46. Subsequent references to Wood's article are shown parenthetically.

45. *Westminster Review* 52 (January 1850):309–10. Reprinted in *Thoreau Society Bulletin* 59 (spring 1957):2.

46. James Anthony Froude to Henry David Thoreau, September 3, 1849, *The Correspondence of Henry David Thoreau,* pp. 248–49.

47. Reprinted in *Thoreau Society Bulletin* 29 (October 1949):3.

48. Quoted in Walter Harding, *The Days of Henry Thoreau,* p. 252.

49. Harding, *The Days of Henry Thoreau,* pp. 337–38.

50. George Eliot, "Review of *Walden,*" in *The Recognition of Henry David Thoreau,* p. 12.

51. "An American Diogenes," *Pertaining to Thoreau,* p. 92. Reprinted from *Chambers's Journal* 8 (November 21, 1857):330–32.

extended them that really mattered" (p. 737). These critics tended to focus more on Thoreau's social criticism than their American counterparts. A review of Channing's *Thoreau, the Poet-Naturalist* in the *British Quarterly Review* for January 1874 praised Thoreau's "fiery hatred of wrong,"[52] and the *Spectator* (February 17, 1883) brought to the Walden experiment an understanding which was utterly lacking in most early American reviews: "The life of Thoreau during the two years he passed at Walden was liberty expressed in the clearest language. He could live gaily on what most men would call starvation. By this means he was able to reconcile his keen intellectual craving, and his still keener love of nature, with the law of existence."[53] English interest in Thoreau's social and economic thinking is demonstrated by his influence among factions of the socialist movement. Although Thoreau's influence upon the Fabians has been overstressed, it can be discerned in the works of the ethical socialist Edward Carpenter and the Independent Labour Party popularizer Robert Blatchford.[54] In *England's Ideal* (1887) Carpenter recommended Thoreauvian "simplification of life."[55] Blatchford's *Merrie England* (1895) included many quotations from Thoreau and similarly emphasized Thoreauvian economic principles. This book, which sold two million copies in a cheap edition, did much to popularize Thoreau in England; indeed H. M. Tomlinson has remembered hundreds of Blatchford's disciples carrying copies of *Walden* with them.[56] Particularly fortunate for Thoreau's subsequent fame was his influence upon Henry Salt, whose sympathies most closely matched those of the ethical socialists.

The early British criticism was not entirely free of invective against Thoreau. In 1880 Robert Louis Stevenson wrote an essay for *Cornhill Magazine* on Thoreau's "character and opinions" that indicted Thoreau as a "skulker" who "did not wish virtue to go out of him among his fellow-men, but slunk into a corner to hoard it for himself" (p. 66). Stevenson's essay again reveals the decisive influence that Emerson's biographical sketch and his edition *Letters to Various Persons* had upon early Thoreau criticism. Obviously swayed by Emerson's emphasis on

52. "Henry Thoreau, the Poet-Naturalist," *British Quarterly Review* 59 (January 1874): 100.

53. *Spectator* 56 (February 17, 1883):240.

54. In *The New England Quarterly* 50 (September 1977):409–22, George Hendrick has distinguished among the various factions of late nineteenth-century British socialism and assessed Thoreau's influence upon each. Hendrick's conclusion is that the "Social Democratic Federation, the Fabians, the Christian Socialist groups were not instrumental in spreading Thoreau's reputation"; instead the real Thoreauvians among the radicals were Salt and Carpenter, whom Hendrick terms (following G. B. Shaw) Regenerators, and the Independent Labour Party founder and popularizer Blatchford.

55. Edward Carpenter, *England's Ideal* (London: Swan Sonnenschein, Lowrey & Co., 1887), pp. 14–15.

56. H. M. Tomlinson, "Two Americans and a Whale," *Harper's* 152 (April 1926):620.

Thoreau's supposed negations, Stevenson argued: "So many negative superiorities begin to smack a little of the prig" (p. 65). The stoic Thoreau of Emerson's edition of the letters thus reappeared in Stevenson's treatment. To Stevenson Thoreau seemed the supreme egoist, incapable of ordinary human affection or emotion; of Thoreau's remarks on friendship, Stevenson commented: "Not one word about pleasure, or laughter, or kisses, or any quality of flesh and blood. It was not inappropriate, surely, that he had such close relations with the fish" (p. 82). Lowell also may have influenced Stevenson's essay, for Stevenson too found Thoreau "morbid," and he argued that Thoreau was humorless: "From his later works he was in the habit of cutting out the humorous passages, under the impression that they were beneath the dignity of his moral muse; and there we see the prig stand public and confessed" (p. 65).

Stevenson made little attempt to explain or evaluate Thoreau's ideas; he was obviously much more interested in assaulting Thoreau's character. He did show some sympathy, however, for Thoreau's economic principles, and he praised Thoreau's civil disobedience and his defense of John Brown. Stevenson also later retracted much of his indictment of Thoreau's "unhuman" character in *Familiar Studies of Men and Books*, after he had been rebuked by Dr. Alexander H. Japp.[57] Nevertheless Stevenson's writing on Thoreau again shows the limitations of the early criticism; his presentation of Thoreau was the familiar one of the American periodicals.

One of those who questioned the conventional interpretation of Thoreau was the British biographer and critic A. H. Japp, who in 1877 published *Thoreau: His Life and Aims* under the pseudonym H. A. Page. In the preface Japp rejected much of what he found in Thoreau's earlier critics. He discovered instead a Thoreau who was capable of affection and who was loved by his friends, who was a hater of "the artificial make believes of modern society," and who nevertheless "loved individual men, and most that which was individual in them."[58] Japp argued further that Thoreau's "love of Nature ... did not lead him to sour retreat from society, but rather to seek a new point of relation to it, by which a return might be possible and profitable"; he thus avoided one of the common failings of

57. For Stevenson's retraction, see the preface to his *Familiar Studies of Men and Books* (London: Chatto and Windus, 1882), pp. xix–xxiii. Stevenson explained that information he had received from Dr. Japp concerning Thoreau's being "once fairly and manfully in love" with a woman whom he "relinquished ... to his brother" provided "the explanation of the 'rarefied and freezing air' in which I complained that he had taught himself to breathe." Dr. Japp had also passed to Stevenson the erroneous information that the Walden house had been an Underground Railroad station, a fact which Stevenson thought helped to explain the purpose of the Walden experiment.

58. A. H. Japp (H. A. Page, pseud.), *Thoreau: His Life and Aims* (Boston: J. R. Osgood & Co., 1877), p. vii. Subsequent references are shown parenthetically.

Thoreau's early critics—the tendency to focus exclusively on the Walden experiment as the sole key to Thoreau's life and significance. Japp concluded that "the common view of Thoreau was quite wrong, or at any rate, needed many qualifications" (pp. vii–viii).

Dr. Japp suggested many qualifications to the "common view" of Thoreau. He rejected the claim that Thoreau was at odds with civilization; it was instead "the special evils induced by civilization which, he held, could be cured by a general or even an extensive return to simplicity of life and habit" (p. 114). Japp thought too that Thoreau had "considerable humor" (p. 149) and that he was no "mere disciple of Emerson" (p. 222). Perhaps Japp's most important insights concerned the significance of the Walden episode. For Dr. Japp, Thoreau's retreat to Walden was not the act of a misanthrope, a morbid solitary; instead even "amid all his *brusquerie*" Japp detected in Thoreau a steady "interest in humanity and human affairs" (p. 108). Of the Walden experiment he wrote: "Thoreau went to Walden not to escape men, but to prepare himself for them, and, as far as he could, for the artificial conventions on which society necessarily rests; not to brood, but to act—only to act in lines that would enable him to stand for ever after—free, vigorous, independent" (p. 109). Dr. Japp contended further that Thoreau did find significant ways in which to act for other men—in his act of civil disobedience, which "asserted that there was still a sphere where Government had no right to follow" (p. 110) the individual, in his antislavery action, and in his defense of John Brown.

A. H. Japp's insights into the Walden episode and Thoreau's social action were obscured by a fanciful comparison of Thoreau and St. Francis of Assisi which provided the central argument of his study. This comparison, which emphasized Thoreau's "wonderful sympathies and attractions for the lower creatures" (p. ix), undoubtedly served only to reconfirm the interpretation of Thoreau as a sentimental poet-naturalist of woods and fields. Despite its forced comparison of Thoreau with St. Francis, *Thoreau: His Life and Aims* presented an interpretation of Thoreau which differed significantly from that "common view" which Dr. Japp found inadequate.

The most important of the late nineteenth-century English critics of Thoreau was Henry Salt. Salt brought a particularly sympathetic perspective to his studies of Thoreau: prior to beginning his work, Salt had been studying and writing about such literary radicals as Shelley and James Thomson. Salt published his first essay on Thoreau in *Temple Bar* for November 1886.[59] Combining biography with an analysis of Thoreau's central philosophic ideas, this essay provided the basis for Salt's full biography, which appeared first in 1890 and, in revised form, in 1896.

It is in light of this critical reception of Thoreau up until 1890 that we must view the work of S. A. Jones, Henry Salt, and Fred Hosmer.

59. Henry Salt, "Henry D. Thoreau," *Temple Bar* 78 (November 1886):369–83.

3

HENRY SALT, in a letter of November 18, 1889, to Daniel Ricketson, declared that he intended in his biography to approach Thoreau as a sympathetic interpreter and to give a clear account of Thoreau's life as well as a serious "estimate of Thoreau's *doctrines.*" In order to accomplish his objectives, Salt used the published sources available to him at the British Museum and corresponded with those who could supply accurate information about Thoreau. Listed as contributors to the 1890 biography were F. B. Sanborn, H.G.O. Blake, Dr. Edward W. Emerson, Daniel Ricketson, Edward Hoar, Dr. Alexander Japp, Col. T. W. Higginson, John Burroughs, William Sloane Kennedy, and Dr. Samuel Arthur Jones.[1] Salt successfully fulfilled both the objectives outlined in his letter to Ricketson, and he did not ignore Thoreau's failings.[2] These failings, in Salt's judgment, included "his lack of geniality, his rusticity, his occasional littleness of tone and temper, his impatience of custom, degenerating sometimes into injustice, his too sensitive self-consciousness, his trick of over-statement" (p. 247). Salt did not "carp unduly" at Thoreau's personal limitations, as Lowell and Stevenson and many of Thoreau's other critics had done. Instead he presented a balanced assessment of Thoreau's character, one guided by his belief that Thoreau was a "genuine and distinctive" individual whose flaws were "incidental failings which did not mar the essential nobility of his nature." We must be willing, Salt asserted, to take Thoreau "just as he is" (p. 297).

Salt's evaluation of Thoreau's philosophic ideas and literary abilities, comprising the last three chapters of his biography, was the most comprehensive of its time. He began with the sensitive assertion that Thoreau was utterly without "a deliberate intent of advocating any particular class of doctrines." Salt's purpose was to clarify "certain important truths, intellectual and moral" which inform Thoreau's writing; but he proceeded with "reservation," fully aware that Thoreau possessed a "constitutional unwillingness to be trammelled by . . . any intellectual tenet." Fundamental to Thoreau's thinking was his idealism, though this idealism could be distinguished from that of Emerson and other transcendentalists

1. Henry Salt, *The Life of Henry David Thoreau* (London: Richard Bentley, 1890), p. v. Subsequent references are shown parenthetically.
2. See George Hendrick, "Henry Salt's Biography of Thoreau," *Festschrift Für Helmut Viebrock,* ed. Kuno Schuhmann, Wilhelm Hortman, and Armin Paul Frank (Munich: Pressler, 1974), p. 228.

by Thoreau's "distinctive quality"—"the resolute practicalness" which "had no taste for the subtleties of mere metaphysical abstractions, but made a strong actuality the basis of his reasoning." Salt concluded that Thoreau was not a mere follower of Emerson (pp. 217, 218, 219, 220–21).

Also central to Thoreau's writing, Salt maintained, was an optimistic belief in human freedom, a belief which largely determined his attitude toward orthodox religion, government, business, and social institutions. Thoreau's "first demand" was always "that each individual mind, instead of being crushed and warped in the struggle of life, may have space to develop its own distinctive qualities and follow the bent of its own natural temperament." All received values and institutional arrangements "must be examined" and must be discarded when they unnecessarily constrained the free development of the individual. Salt thus stressed the importance of the essay on civil disobedience with its radical individualist insistence that society is ultimately "to be reformed . . . by individual effort." Thoreau had proposed "simplification of life" because it lent "strength, courage, and self-reliance to the individual character, and so, in proportion to the extent of its practice, to the State." Salt was careful to add that Thoreau, in proposing simplification, was no mere "nullifier" of civilization. Neither was Thoreau simply opposed to humanitarian reforms, despite his attack on philanthropists in *Walden;* as evidence that he was "one of the humanest of writers," Salt cited Thoreau's denunciation of the Mexican war, his antislavery writing, his "humanity to animals," and the profession in *Walden* of his faith in "the humanities of diet" (pp. 231, 232, 236, 244–47).

Salt also analyzed Thoreau's nature writing, pointing out that his methods as a naturalist "were not those of the anatomist and man of science"; instead Thoreau saw the natural world with the inner faculty of the idealist, who sought "to transmute the mere facts and results of external observation into symbolical thoughts and images." Thoreau's genius was to have "in large measure what Emerson calls 'the philosopher's perception of identity'; the phenomena of time and space did not affect him—Walden Pond was to him an Atlantic Ocean, a moment was eternity" (pp. 248, 249, 252). Though Salt emphasized Thoreau's idealist approach to nature, he recognized that the real strength of Thoreau's writing derived from his careful observation of natural phenomena, his insistence on natural fact.

In his lengthy consideration of Thoreau's literary craft, Salt praised Thoreau's "unstudied freshness and wildness" of tone, his ability to idealize common and homely subjects in order "to bring to view the latent harmony and beauty of all existent things," and the boldness and novelty of his metaphors. Salt thought Thoreau's pungent epigrammatic style was "the appropriate expression of his keen thrifty nature," and he defended

Thoreau's oft-criticized use of paradox as a strategy calculated to surprise and challenge the reader, "to stimulate and awaken curiosity." With characteristic moderation, however, Salt did grant that the Thoreauvian paradox was sometimes the expression of its author's "wayward and contradictory nature." "Inexplicable" to Salt was the charge that Thoreau possessed no sense of humor, for Salt thought humor one of the consistent unmistakable features of Thoreau's style: "*Walden* is especially pervaded by this subtle sense of humour, grave, dry, pithy, sententious, almost saturnine in its tone, yet perhaps for that very reason the more racy and suggestive to those readers who have the faculty for appreciating it" (pp. 256–57, 259, 262, 263–64).

Thoreau made "the most vigorous protest ever raised against that artificiality in life and literature which constitutes one of the chief dangers of our complex civilisation" (p. 282). This was the strongest claim advanced for Thoreau by 1890, and Salt had devoted a careful critical biography to evincing it. On the one hand Salt's biography represents the culmination of early critical response to Thoreau in England, which had been generally more appreciative and far-sighted than that in America. On the other *The Life of Henry David Thoreau* was an indication that the revaluation of Thoreau was well underway, the revaluation that would free Thoreau from the narrow and ill-founded criticism which abounded during the three decades immediately following his death.

After the 1890 publication of his biography of Thoreau (which was largely complete before he began corresponding with Dr. Jones), Salt began revising it carefully, following information supplied by Jones, Fred Hosmer, and others; and in 1896 he published his much improved biography of Thoreau, a work which must be considered the most significant single piece of Thoreau scholarship of that decade.

Salt in the 1890s edited Thoreau's *Anti-Slavery and Reform Papers* with an introduction emphasizing Thoreau's philosophic anarchism. In 1895 he edited *Selections from Thoreau,* which covered the whole range of Thoreau's major works. He was intent upon bringing Thoreau to a large audience in England, even though he knew there would be little profit in it for him. In the same year he edited, with F. B. Sanborn, Thoreau's *Poems of Nature.* [3] Without access to the original manuscripts, Salt knew that the work would need to be done properly some time in the future. He also wrote about Thoreau in the humanitarian journals he edited, usually restating for the quite different English audience the conclusions first stated in the biography. Salt's active interest in Thoreau lasted from the 1880s until the 1930s, but the biography was to remain his greatest achievement.

3. *Anti-Slavery and Reform Papers* (London: Swan Sonnenschein, 1890); *Selections from Thoreau* (London: Macmillan, 1895); *Poems of Nature* (London: Lane; Boston: Houghton Mifflin, 1895).

Samuel Arthur Jones's Thoreau publications were more fragmented than Salt's but were nevertheless highly suggestive and useful. Dr. Jones's critical writings on Thoreau reveal two concerns which were similar to Salt's. First, Dr. Jones sought repeatedly to correct what he considered the misrepresentations of Thoreau by Lowell, Emerson, Holmes, Burroughs, and others. Second, he strived to present a complete interpretation of Thoreau, an interpretation which gave due consideration both to Thoreau's social criticism and to his nature writing. In this work he was influenced by Salt, whom Jones thought had "done more than any other writer, living or dead, to correct the errors that are current concerning Thoreau."[4] Still Dr. Jones's essays were thoroughly original, infused with a passionate spirit and sarcastic wit that were completely his own.

"Thoreau: A Glimpse," Jones's first Thoreau essay, set forth the major points of his interpretation. Jones dwelt at length on Thoreau's devotion to principle, as it was manifested in his experiment at Walden, his antislavery writings, his defense of John Brown, and his civil disobedience. Jones lashed out at Lowell, whose facile judgment of the Walden experiment he deemed a "pitiful ineptitude." The doctor also attacked John Burroughs, who had ridiculed Thoreau's refusal to pay "a paltry tax." Jones thought Burroughs's criticism only betrayed his own limitations: where Thoreau saw a principle to be affirmed, "Burroughs sees only a 'paltry tax'—so different the measure of men."[5] Jones did not ignore Thoreau's abiding interest in nature: several pages of "Thoreau: A Glimpse" were devoted to a discussion of Thoreau's search in nature for a revelation akin to religious truth.

In "Thoreau's Inheritance" (February 1893) Dr. Jones took both Lowell and Holmes to task for their criticism of Thoreau's Walden experiment. The genteel Lowell and Holmes were unsuited to understand Thoreau: "Men so different can never interpret, much less comprehend, each other." "Thoreau's Inheritance" presented Dr. Jones's own reading of the Walden episode, which he considered "a crucial experiment in the science and art of living." Thoreau had attempted, Dr. Jones maintained, to demonstrate that the mass of men need not live "lives of quiet desperation," that "such lives impugn the wisdom, the justice, and the compassion of the Divine Arbiter."[6] In a review of the 1897 edition of *Walden* he presented a similar interpretation, again denouncing Lowell and stressing the importance of Thoreau's simplification of life.[7]

4. Samuel A. Jones, "Thoreau and His Biographers," *Lippincott's Monthly Magazine* 48 (August 1891):224–28. For the text see the appendix.
5. Samuel A. Jones, *Thoreau: A Glimpse* (Concord, Mass.: Albert Lane, 1903), pp. 9–13. Reprinted from an 1890 edition that was privately printed in Ann Arbor. The 1890 edition was based on the *Unitarian* 5 (January, February, March 1890):18–20, 65–68, 124–28.
6. Samuel A. Jones, "Thoreau's Inheritance," *Inlander* 3, no. 5 (February 1893):199.
7. Samuel A. Jones, "Vox Clamantis in Deserto," *Inlander* 8, no. 6 (March 1898):222–30.

Two other essays of Dr. Jones's were substantially critical: "Thoreau and His Works," a review of the Riverside edition of Thoreau's writings, and "Thoreau and His Biographers," an assessment of the early biographical studies of Thoreau. In "Thoreau and His Works" (February 1894) Dr. Jones responded to those critics who portrayed Thoreau as a naturalist. Like Henry Salt before him, Dr. Jones rejected the idea that Thoreau was a naturalist in any scientific sense; neither was Thoreau the "fancy field-rambler" or "poet-naturalist" whom many early critics had presented. Instead Thoreau would be remembered "simply as one who 'did not wish to live what was not life.' "[8] Thoreau's value, Dr. Jones asserted, was as a "transcendental Puritan" who sought revelation in the natural world and who acted in accord with the higher laws of conscience.

In "Thoreau and His Biographers" Dr. Jones judiciously reviewed the works of Channing, Emerson, Japp, Sanborn, and Salt. He thought the chief value of Channing's *Thoreau, the Poet-Naturalist* lay in the extensive quotations from Thoreau's unpublished journal. For Emerson's obituary of Thoreau and his edition of Thoreau's letters Dr. Jones had severe criticism. Emerson was responsible for the idea that Thoreau was a stoic, the "conception of Thoreau which is at once the most general and the most unjust." Jones similarly pointed out deficiencies in the studies by Japp and Sanborn. Japp's *Thoreau: His Life and Aims* was written at "too great a distance from its subject" to be of value as biography; moreover Japp was the "chief disseminator of the figment that the shanty at Walden was a station of the underground railroad" (p. 120). Sanborn's *Henry D. Thoreau* drew Dr. Jones's heaviest fire. He criticized at length the biography's poor organization and its harsh characterization of Thoreau's parents. Salt's *The Life of Henry David Thoreau* drew Jones's praise, both for its biographical material and for its incisive interpretation of Thoreau's works.

"Thoreau and His Biographers" closed with a critical appraisal of Thoreau, in which the author reiterated the essentials of his interpretation: Thoreau's absolute sincerity, the importance of the philosophy tested at Walden, the moral heroism of Thoreau's defense of John Brown. Included, too, was one of Dr. Jones's favorite contentions—that Thoreau's importance would in future be greater even than that of Emerson (p. 124).

In the course of their Thoreau studies, Jones and Salt became acutely aware of the need for dependable biographical information about Thoreau. Jones thought that Salt's 1890 biography had done much to fulfill this need, but he did not consider it definitive.[9] A number of

8. Samuel A. Jones, "Thoreau and His Works," *Inlander* 4, no. 5 (February 1894): 238–40.
9. See letter 140, in which Jones remarks that "THE Life of Thoreau isn't written yet."

biographical questions still needed to be settled; as Dr. Jones was fond of telling Alfred Hosmer, the "readers of the future" would demand complete and accurate information. In his investigations of Thoreau's life Jones found his closest ally in Fred Hosmer. Hosmer had the inestimable advantage of being in Concord; he knew personally those who had been associated with Thoreau—Sam Staples, Mrs. Francis Edwin Bigelow, Parker Pillsbury—and whose reminiscences were an important remaining source of information. As Raymond Adams has aptly characterized him, Alfred Hosmer was "that indispensable man behind the first scholars, the resident amateur to whom doors are opened, confidences delivered, recollections told without reserve."[10] Certainly he was "indispensable" to Jones and to Salt.

Many of the letters in this collection deal with various Thoreau "problems" and their solution by S. A. Jones, Fred Hosmer, and Henry Salt. We see the slow process of gathering information and evaluating it. We see their successes and their failures as Thoreauvians, and we see the interplay of personalities.

One biographical problem which Dr. Jones thought to be of paramount importance involved the purpose of the Walden experiment itself. In the "Preface, By Way of Criticism" to his 1882 *Familiar Studies of Men and Books,* Robert Louis Stevenson, depending upon information supplied to him by A. H. Japp, contended that Thoreau's purpose in going to Walden "was not merely with designs of self-improvement, but to serve mankind in the highest sense. Hither came the fleeing slave; thence was he despatched along the road to freedom. That shanty in the woods was a station in the great Underground Railroad."[11] In his 1890 biography of Thoreau, Salt accepted the claim of Dr. Japp and Stevenson that the Walden house was a "station" on the Underground Railroad (pp. 97–98).

Dr. Jones doubted this claim, and he thought it extremely important that the point should be "definitely settled" (letter 40). To maintain, if it was not true, that Thoreau had gone to Walden to establish a station for fugitive slaves was to compromise the purpose of his experiment, to make it acceptable to critics like Stevenson who were offended by Thoreau's stated purpose.

On his trip to Concord during August 1890, Dr. Jones made the Underground Railroad question "the subject of special investigation."[12] He apparently discussed it with Alfred Hosmer, for Hosmer wrote the former abolitionist orator Parker Pillsbury for information. Pillsbury responded:

10. Raymond Adams, "Fred Hosmer, the 'Lerned Clerk,' " *Thoreau Society Bulletin* 36 (July 1951):2.

11. Robert Louis Stevenson, *Familiar Studies of Men and Books* (London: Chatto and Windus, 1882), pp. xix–xx.

12. Dr. Jones's lecture of February 9, 1891 (Hosmer collection).

"As to the Walden Cottage ever being in any sense, an *underground Railway Depot*. I must doubt it." Pillsbury thought that abolitionist lecturers, including Douglass, "would have called no doubt to see Thoreau at his Walden Cottage but no flying slave would ever have sought him there nor do I think Col. Whiting, or Mrs. Brooks, or Mr. & Mrs. Bigelow would ever have taken them there for concealment."[13] Hosmer immediately forwarded a copy of this letter to Dr. Jones, who used it in a lecture on February 9, 1891. Dr. Jones did not consider Pillsbury's testimony conclusive, however, particularly since Silas Hosmer, Alfred's uncle, had, when Dr. Jones interviewed him in Concord, expressed the opposite opinion. In his letter of January 10, 1891, to Hosmer, Dr. Jones reviewed the matter and suggested a means of solving it conclusively: inquire of Mrs. Francis Edwin Bigelow, who had known the Thoreaus well. Alfred Hosmer asked Mrs. Bigelow, whom Walter Harding has called "the acknowledged leader of Concord's participants in the Underground Railroad,"[14] for additional information; and she apparently concurred with Pillsbury, for in his letter to Hosmer of January 23, 1891, Dr. Jones remarked: "Between Mrs. Bigelow and Parker Pillsbury the fugitive slave question must be considered as definitely settled. Thanks to you!" (letter 42).

In August 1891 Jones published the results of his inquiries into the Underground Railroad question in "Thoreau and His Biographers," putting that story to rest, he must have believed. He did not reckon, however, with the tenacity of Dr. A. H. Japp, who delivered Dr. Jones a stinging rebuke in an English paper called *Old and Young*.[15] Dr. Japp argued that "Mr. Page," a pseudonym under which he published, had not based his contention on Channing's statement alone but also on *Walden*. This provoked an aroused reaction from Dr. Jones, who wrote Hosmer on September 29, 1891, urging the gathering of more corroborative information. On October 10, 1891, Jones again wrote to Fred Hosmer about the "Underground R.R. business"; by this time he had reviewed the Pillsbury letter and received "a rousing good letter from Horace Hosmer" (letters 84, 85), who thought it highly improbable that the Walden cabin had served as an Underground station.[16] Dr. Jones was not satisfied, however, either by Pillsbury's or Horace Hosmer's evidence, for both were only "conjectural." What was needed, he wrote Fred Hosmer, was "the evidence of someone who has positive knowledge, and, as you say, Mrs.

13. Parker Pillsbury to Alfred W. Hosmer, August 27, 1890 (Hosmer collection).

14. *The Days of Henry Thoreau* (New York: Knopf, 1965), p. 316.

15. Dr. Jones learned of Dr. Japp's paper in *Old and Young* from Salt, who sent him a copy. Unfortunately the clipping has not survived, and neither Salt nor Jones dated the paper. See letter 83.

16. Horace R. Hosmer to Samuel A. Jones, October 6, 1891 (Jones collection). For the text see *Remembrances of Concord and the Thoreaus*, ed. George Hendrick (University of Illinois Press, 1977), pp. 40–43.

Bigelow is the only one living who can supply *that*" (letter 85). Early in January 1892 Jones received the positive evidence he needed: Fred Hosmer had visited Mrs. Bigelow again and had new information which supported Jones. Hosmer noted, in concluding his account of the visit, "she referred a number of times to the 'mistaken notion that some people had, that the hut was used as an underground railroad station. I am well acquainted with the facts and I *know* it was *not*' " (letter 93). Later Dr. Jones received from Dr. Edward Emerson, whom he had also asked to inquire into the problem, the record of a conversation he had had with Mrs. Bigelow; Dr. Emerson's account corroborated the information from Alfred Hosmer.[17]

Dr. Jones did not publish anything on the Underground Railroad issue after "Thoreau and His Biographers"; perhaps he thought that account was authoritative enough. Nevertheless he did prevail upon Henry Salt to correct the error in the 1896 revised edition of his biography.[18] Several years later Dr. Jones included Dr. Japp's review for the *Spectator* and what is obviously the paper in *Old and Young* in the manuscript of his *Thoreau amongst Friends and Philistines*. Together with the pieces by Dr. Japp, Dr. Jones included some stinging annotations of his own and extensive quotations from the account of the Underground Railroad which he had obtained from Dr. Emerson. Unfortunately this highly interesting collection was not published.[19]

Henry Thoreau's night in Concord jail in July 1846 also moved Jones to initiate specific biographical investigation. He made his first inquiries into the facts surrounding this incident during his visit to Concord in 1890, when he was introduced to Sam Staples, the man who had arrested and jailed Thoreau.

Jones had little trouble inducing the garrulous Staples to reminisce about his famous prisoner. He remembered arresting Thoreau early in the evening, as Thoreau was "on his way to get a shoe that was being repaired preparatory to his piloting a huckleberry party on the morrow."[20] After locking Thoreau up, Staples "went up town on some business," during which time a "veiled young woman" came to his apartments and paid the tax to his daughter. Thus Thoreau could have been freed that night, but, as Staples remembered, "I had got my boots off and was sittin' by the fire when my daughter told me, and I was n't goin' to take

17. Dr. Emerson's account is included in the manuscript *Thoreau amongst Friends and Philistines* (Jones collection).

18. Henry Salt, *The Life of Henry David Thoreau* (London: Walter Scott, 1896), pp. 77–78. Subsequent references are shown parenthetically.

19. George Hendrick is currently editing this material for publication.

20. Samuel A. Jones, "Thoreau's Incarceration," *Inlander* 9 (December 1898):99. Subsequent references are shown parenthetically.

the trouble to unlock after I'd got the boys all fixed for the night, so I kep' him in 'till after breakfast next mornin' and then I let him go" (letter 99). Jones was careful to ask, too, if Staples knew who it was that paid the tax: "He replied that he did not know, but believed it was Judge Hoar—'the girl that brought the money had somethin' wrapped 'round her head so't you could n't see her face'; but he guessed it was Elizabeth Hoar" (letter 100).

During his visit Dr. Jones evidently made further inquiries in Concord concerning Thoreau's incarceration, but he received no conclusive information (letter 100). He seems, then, to have dropped his investigations until May 1894, when he read an article by Irving Allen in the *Boston Daily Advertiser* in which Allen contended that Aunt Jane Thoreau had paid the tax.[21] Recognizing the contradiction between Allen's information and that of Staples, Dr. Jones promptly wrote Allen. On May 7, 1894, Allen wrote that the "old ladies Jane and Maria Thoreau were intimate and valued friends of mine in my youth." He then contended that it was Aunt Jane who had paid Thoreau's tax, but admitted he was not entirely sure: "It seems to me that I have known for years that it was good old Aunt Jane who came to the relief of her eccentric nephew; yet I cannot prove that I was right."

Irving Allen also referred Dr. Jones to Professor Eben Loomis of Washington, D.C., whom he described as "a very intimate friend of the Thoreaus."[22] Dr. Jones immediately wrote Loomis, whose response gave a different account of the payment of Thoreau's tax: "I have always understood that it was paid by his Aunt, Miss *Maria* Thoreau, not Jane, who was very deaf, and all business matters concerning either of them, was attended to by Maria." Loomis, however, was not certain Maria Thoreau had told him she paid the tax, but he promised to write a "friend in Concord to find the fact and let me know." Loomis also mentioned a meeting between Thoreau and Emerson at the jail: "Mr. Emerson visited Thoreau at the jail, and the meeting between the two philosphers must have been interesting and somewhat dramatic. The account of the meeting was told me by Henry's Aunt Maria: 'Henry, why are you here?[']' 'Waldo, why are you *not* here?' "[23]

After reviewing the letters from Allen and Loomis, Dr. Jones wrote to Fred Hosmer, commenting on the contradictions in the various accounts of the tax payment: "All this shows how difficult it is becoming to fix these little events, and that the only chance of so doing is while the few survivors

21. Irving Allen, "Mr. Allen's Retort Courteous," *Boston Daily Advertiser*, May 3, 1894.
22. Irving Allen to Samuel A. Jones, May 7, 1894 (Jones collection).
23. Eben J. Loomis to Samuel A. Jones, May 12, 1894 (Jones collection).

are left." In order to resolve these contradictions, Dr. Jones asked Hosmer to call upon Sam Staples and to ask "if he remembers whether Emerson *visited Thoreau while he was in jail?* Ask him too *about time of the day he arrested* Thoreau and *about what time Emerson called*" (letter 176).

Soon after he received Dr. Jones's letter, Fred Hosmer visited Staples, who remembered, as he had in 1890, that he had committed Thoreau at sundown and that the tax had been paid later in the evening to his daughter while he was away from the house. Hosmer reported that "his daughter did not recognize the lady, as it was dark, and she had a veil on—he said he always thought it was Elizabeth Hoar" (letter 178). Pursuing Staples's conjecture that Elizabeth Hoar had paid the tax, Hosmer wrote to Judge Ebenezer Rockwood Hoar, brother of Elizabeth Hoar. Judge Hoar responded that he was out of town at the time of Thoreau's incarceration, but that he had always understood it was Aunt Maria Thoreau who paid the tax.[24] Hosmer, responding both to Dr. Jones's request and to the request of Professor Loomis, forwarded this information to Dr. Jones.

In the same letter, that of May 17, 1894, Hosmer reported Staples's opinion of the possibility that Emerson had met Thoreau at the jail: "Staples thinks that Emerson could not have seen Thoreau in jail—as while he was committed at sundown, or thereabouts, the jail was soon locked up, and the tax being paid that evening Thoreau was turned out immediately after breakfast, as Staples expressed it, 'mad as the devil.'" Hosmer expressed his own opinion concerning the meeting between Emerson and Thoreau: "If Prof Loomis says Aunt Maria told him Emerson visited Thoreau in jail, I should call it so—as the story told of their meeting is too good to lose, and also shows the difference between the men. 'Henry, I am sorry to find you here' 'Mr Emerson, why are you *not* here?' I repeated it to Staples, with the remark that Thoreau was ready to back up his principles, while Emerson was not, 'Yes, Fred, *that is so!* was his reply" (letter 178). Alfred Hosmer forwarded this information to Loomis, who wrote Jones to confirm that it "agrees with my own recollection of the story as told me." He offered a slightly different version of the conversation between Emerson and Thoreau; "'Henry, why are you here?' 'Waldo, why are you *not* here?'"[25] Professor Loomis had heard Maria Thoreau "tell the story several times, and always the same, never varying a word."[26]

Upon receipt of the information from Hosmer, Jones immediately made further inquiries of his Concord friend. He thought he had de-

24. Ebenezer Rockwood Hoar to Alfred W. Hosmer, undated (Hosmer collection). Hoar's reply is written on Hosmer's letter to him, May 16, 1894.

25. Eben J. Loomis to Samuel A. Jones, May 21, 1894 (Jones collection).

26. Eben J. Loomis to Samuel A. Jones, May 12, 1894 (Jones collection).

tected contradictions in Staples's testimony and was skeptical concerning the meeting between Emerson and Thoreau at the jail. In his letter of May 19, 1894, to Hosmer, Dr. Jones carefully sorted out the varying, often contradictory, information and posed more questions for Fred Hosmer to investigate (letter 179).

On May 22, 1894, Fred Hosmer responded, first making clear that Thoreau "was mad to think that someone should have paid the tax—when *he* refused to do it"; Hosmer reminded Dr. Jones, too, of one fact which he had overlooked in his last letter: "The payment was made to Mr. Staples' *daughter.*" He further suggested that perhaps Cynthia Thoreau and Aunt Jane had also been involved in paying the tax; this was the opinion of Miss Jane Hosmer. Hosmer argued, too, that "Emerson could readily have seen Thoreau, as the jail was easy of access, and he might have talked with him from the outside of the wall." He added that Jane Hosmer had "always heard" the story of Emerson's meeting with Thoreau; and "never heard it contradicted." Moreover Staples was notoriously "lax in his discipline at the jail." Fred Hosmer concluded: "I do not think there is any doubt, but what Emerson could have seen Thoreau, after his commitment and talked with him, without the jailer knowing about it" (letter 180).

In the *Inlander* for December 1898 Dr. Jones published "Thoreau's Incarceration," which has remained standard. He included the letter from Irving Allen, the two from Professor Eben Loomis, and the relevant parts of Alfred Hosmer's letter of May 17, 1894—though he concealed Hosmer's identity, referring to him only as X. Jones did not, however, include Hosmer's letter of May 22, 1894. This omission remains inexplicable, since Dr. Jones obviously thought this letter was of utmost importance; moreover it confirmed the possibility of a meeting between Emerson and Thoreau at the jail—a meeting which Dr. Jones, in his article, was disposed to accept as fact (pp. 102–3). The information which Jones had collected was relayed to Salt, who in the 1896 edition of his biography attributed payment of the tax to Maria Thoreau, recounted the meeting between Thoreau and Emerson at the jail, and quoted Staples's remark that Thoreau emerged from jail "mad as the devil" (pp. 78–80).

In 1895, the year after their collaborative investigation of Thoreau's incarceration, Jones and Hosmer attempted to clarify another issue of Thoreau biography, the brief "love affair" of Thoreau and Ellen Sewall. The impetus behind their efforts in this instance came from Henry Salt, who, in a letter to Dr. Jones, dated March 24, 1895, expressed his regrets that the name of the woman with whom Thoreau was in love was not known. Salt added that he had once inquired of F. B. Sanborn concerning Thoreau's brief "love affair," and that Sanborn had told him "the lady is still living." But Sanborn also felt "there would be no propriety in mention-ing her name," a propriety which Salt thought "might be sacrificed in such a matter, for the greater good of the greater number!" (letter 206). Dr. Jones wholeheartedly agreed with Salt "that the secrecy in regard to this matter is owing to a false and squeamish delicacy; as there was nothing dishonorable to either party in the affair" (letter 213). On June 5, 1895, Dr. Jones urged Fred Hosmer to "get permission to copy her picture, NOT for sale, BUT so that future generations may learn what her face was like, and then KNOW why Thoreau was so true to his one love" (letter 213).

Fred Hosmer soon succeeded in obtaining a photogravure of Ellen Sewall Osgood as an older woman; his source for the portrait was Annie J. Ward of Spencer, Massachusetts, a cousin of Mrs. Osgood's.[27] He evi-dently forwarded the names of Thoreau's beloved and her husband, the Rev. Joseph Osgood, to Dr. Jones as well, for Jones knew the names by June 23, 1895. Dr. Jones was particularly delighted by the photogravure of Mrs. Osgood, but he hoped that Hosmer might still be able to "get a picture of Miss Sewall as a *young* woman, for the readers of the future have a right to know to what a queen Thoreau was so loyal." Dr. Jones planned, provided he could learn more of "Miss Sewall's history," to "embalm that love affair in touching prose" (letter 215).

Jones's desire was frustrated, however, by the resistance of the Osgood family. Alfred Hosmer's request to interview members of the Osgood family and to gain access to the Sewall papers, though favored by Annie J. Ward, was denied by the children of the Rev. and Mrs. Osgood. Elizabeth Osgood Davenport, the daughter of Ellen Sewall Osgood, wrote to Fred Hosmer that she opposed the publication of any material pertaining to her mother's relationship with Thoreau; she added that if she should decide in future to give such information as she remembered, she would give it to a cousin to whom her mother had "told the story some years since," and not to Dr. Jones, as Hosmer had suggested.[28] Hosmer received a similar response from E.Q.T. Osgood, Mrs. Davenport's brother, who added, in response to Hosmer's request for an early picture of Ellen Sewall, that there was no picture of her prior to her marriage in 1844.[29] Nor was Fred Hosmer alone in being rebuffed by the Osgoods; Annie J. Ward apparently was rebuked severely by Mrs. Davenport for encourag-

27. See letter 215. See also Annie J. Ward to Alfred W. Hosmer; the letter is dated July 1895, apparently by Hosmer (Hosmer collection).
28. Elizabeth Osgood Davenport to Alfred W. Hosmer, July 24, 1895 (Hosmer collec-tion).
29. E.Q.T. Osgood to Alfred W. Hosmer, July 23, 1895 (Hosmer collection).

ing the Osgoods to aid Hosmer and Jones in their inquiries.[30] Miss Ward later suggested that Dr. Jones might find Edmund Sewall, Ellen Sewall's brother, willing to supply information about his sister's relationship with Thoreau, but Jones refused absolutely to "think of interfering between the relatives in regard to it."[31]

Dr. Jones was naturally disappointed in the failure of Fred Hosmer's approaches to the Osgoods, and he thought that "the statement that there is no picture of her in her younger days is a polite fiction."[32] The importance of this episode in Thoreau's life was clear; the "love affair" with Ellen did much "to redeem Thoreau's character from the reproach of being so cynical that he hardly seems to have belonged to the HUMAN race" (letter 216). It proved him "very human" and revealed "a side that he sedulously kept hidden from the world" (letter 217). Indeed Dr. Jones even granted that Stevenson's explanation in *Familiar Studies of Men and Books* (1882) "has more of truth in it than I at first supposed" (letter 216). Despite his conviction that Thoreau's "love affair" was of "profound interest . . . for the FUTURE" (letter 217), Dr. Jones could not be prevailed upon, either by his friend Fred Hosmer or by Annie J. Ward, to seek personally the private papers of the Osgood family. His first concern was for the rights of the family (letter 218).

Though Jones published nothing himself concerning Thoreau's love affair, he did apparently forward to Salt the material that he was able to collect; in the 1896 edition of his biography Salt referred to Ellen Sewall by name and gave an account of her 1839 visit to Prudence Ward and her mother Mrs. Ward, who were then living with the Thoreaus in Concord. During this visit Thoreau became attracted to her. At the end of his discussion of the affair, Salt again expressed his regret that "from a false notion of propriety, such extreme reticence has so long been maintained concerning the story of Thoreau's love, and that facts which have much interest for his readers, and can cause no pain to his survivors, should even now be very imperfectly known" (pp. 38–39). Considering the difficulties which he faced, Salt produced an admirably complete account of the romance; it was not until 1926 that T. M. Raysor added significantly to the facts surrounding Thoreau's brief involvement with Ellen Sewall. Henry S. Canby provided more information in his 1939 biography of

30. Annie J. Ward to Alfred W. Hosmer; the letter is dated July 1895, apparently by Hosmer (Hosmer collection).

31. Letter 218. See also Annie J. Ward to Alfred W. Hosmer, July 20, 1895 (Hosmer collection).

32. Letter 220. Dr. Jones's labelling E.Q.T. Osgood's statement a "polite fiction" was correct: Walter Harding has recently published a daguerreotype of Miss Sewall that was taken before her marriage. See *The Days of Henry Thoreau*, p. 141.

Thoreau, and Walter Harding in his 1965 biography gave a full account of the "affair."[33]

Of all the issues of Thoreau biography which Dr. Jones investigated, none engaged him as wholeheartedly as his attempts to redeem the characters of Mr. and Mrs. Thoreau from F. B. Sanborn's negative treatment of them in his 1882 biography. Sanborn had characterized John Thoreau, Sr., as a "small, deaf, and unobtrusive man"[34] who "led a plodding, unambitious, and respectable life in Concord village" (p. 27). Cynthia Thoreau, by contrast, appeared as an incessant talker who was given to "sharp and sudden flashes of gossip and malice" (p. 24) and who, "with her sister Louisa and her sisters-in-law, Sarah, Maria, and Jane Thoreau, took their share in the village bickerings" (p. 27). Before his trip to Concord in 1890, Dr. Jones accepted this portrayal of the elder Thoreaus. His "Thoreau: A Glimpse," delivered as a lecture and published before his trip, reveals a decisive Sanborn influence. Indeed, as he considered the sources of Thoreau's genius in this essay, Dr. Jones asserted: "In Thoreau's instance I feel obliged to eliminate largely the influence of heredity. Considering his ancestry, Thoreau is quite a psychological surprise" (pp. 2–3). Henry Salt similarly accepted Sanborn's account of the Thoreau family; his 1890 biography closely followed Sanborn's earlier work.

While in Concord Dr. Jones learned, probably from Fred Hosmer, of a letter to the *Boston Daily Advertiser* for February 14, 1883,[35] which sharply criticized Sanborn's characterizations of Cynthia Thoreau and the Thoreau aunts. The author of this letter, who described herself as knowing Cynthia Thoreau well, remembered Mrs. Thoreau as a woman who impressed others with "the activity of her mind and the wideness of her sympathy." The letter stressed Mrs. Thoreau's hospitality to the poor and her aid to fugitive slaves, and concluded that "she was never guilty of mean and petty gossip"[36] as Sanborn had alleged. Dr. Jones received a similarly favorable account of Cynthia and John Thoreau, Sr., from Horace Hosmer of Acton, whom he met during his Concord tour. Horace

33. T. M. Raysor, "The Love Story of Thoreau," *Studies in Philology* 23 (1926):457–63; H. S. Canby, *Thoreau* (Boston: Houghton Mifflin Co., 1939), pp. 111–27; Harding, *The Days of Henry Thoreau*, pp. 94–104.

34. Franklin B. Sanborn, *Henry D. Thoreau* (Boston: Houghton, Mifflin & Co., 1882), p. 25. Subsequent references will be shown parenthetically.

35. E.M.F., "Henry Thoreau's Mother," *Boston Daily Advertiser*, February 14, 1883. In 1897 Hosmer learned the identity of E.M.F.: she was Mrs. Jean Munroe LeBrun, a neighbor of Thoreau's. This name appears variously in the letters as Le Brun, LeBrun, and Lebrun; we have standardized the spelling as LeBrun, following Alfred Hosmer.

36. Quoted from Dr. Jones's lecture of February 9, 1891; the manuscript is dated January 19, 1891 (Hosmer collection).

Hosmer, who had been a pupil in the Thoreau school and sometimes took lunch in the Thoreau home, later wrote Dr. Jones a series of letters defending Thoreau's parents.[37]

Dr. Jones's faith in F. B. Sanborn's veracity as a biographer was also shaken by his meeting with Sanborn. While in Concord Dr. Jones called upon Sanborn at his home; he wished both to pay his respects to Sanborn and to catalogue the latter's file of the Boston *Commonwealth*.[38] Dr. Jones's letter of August 10, 1891, to Daniel Ricketson describes this awkward meeting of the two men and provides a partial explanation for the contempt which Jones felt for Sanborn: "On first seeing him, at his house, too, I told him that, for my father's sake, I was glad to meet him and to pay my respects to him *as an abolitionist*. A peculiar expression on his face told me that I had 'put my foot in it,' as the words go. . . . When I subsequently learned that Emerson had asked of the same Mr. S., 'Why does he not *participate* in the war he did so much to precipitate?', God's sunlight shone through all this man's disguises and I saw that he is a sham. . . . Such an one is not fit to deal with Henry Thoreau" (letter 77). Jones's dislike of Sanborn was undoubtedly strengthened by another exchange between the two men in Concord. At the time, 1890, Dr. Jones was very much concerned with the promotion of Henry Salt's biography in America. He hoped that a separate American edition could be published, perhaps by Houghton, Mifflin, who had brought out Sanborn's book in 1882. While in Concord Dr. Jones discussed the publication of Salt's life with Sanborn; later Dr. Jones wrote H.G.O. Blake an account of this discussion: "The same creature told Mr. Salt, when in London, that he could use his influence with Houghton, Mifflin and Co. to secure the publication of Thoreau's Life in America, and in consequence Mr. Salt forwarded to him advance sheets of the book. In Concord Library Mr. Sanborn showed me a letter fresh from Mr. Salt thereupon, and added: 'I do n't know about urging the publication of this book, as it may hurt the sale of my own' " (letter 75). Dr. Jones returned from Concord "with a lower regard for Mr. S. than anyone I met there" (letter 26). Certainly his contempt did not diminish through the years of his correspondence with Hosmer, Salt, Blake, and Ricketson; indeed Dr. Jones became increasingly adamant in his scorn of Sanborn as he came to regard the latter chiefly responsible for the interpretation which subordinated Thoreau to Emerson.

Upon his return to Ann Arbor, Dr. Jones set to work on a lecture, to be delivered before the Unity Club on February 9, 1891, which would correct

37. Horace Hosmer wrote more than thirty letters to Dr. Jones, beginning February 25, 1891. See *Remembrances of Concord and the Thoreaus*.

38. Dr. Jones's journal of his Concord trip contains bibliographical notes on Thoreauviana in the Boston *Commonwealth*, the files of which he had consulted in Sanborn's library (Jones collection).

current errors in Thoreau biography, chief among them being Sanborn's presentation of Thoreau's parents. In the first letter which he directed to Concord after returning home, Dr. Jones asked Alfred Hosmer to send him a copy of "Henry Thoreau's Mother," which appeared in the *Boston Daily Advertiser* (letter 18). He quoted this letter in its entirety in his lecture and also used a brief passage from his conversation with Horace Hosmer.[39] Within a month Dr. Jones began regular correspondence with Horace Hosmer, who devoted much of his letters to defending Thoreau's parents. Dr. Jones was delighted with his new correspondent; to Fred Hosmer he wrote, "Damn F.B.S.; but Horace Hosmer is making carpet rags of him at an alarming rate. —But it won't do to make carpet of those rags!!!" (letter 49).

Dr. Jones used material from Horace Hosmer to great advantage in his most extensive assessment of the Thoreau family, "Thoreau's Inheritance," published in the *Inlander* for February 1893. Throughout his letters Horace Hosmer placed particular emphasis on the virtues of John Thoreau, Sr.; Dr. Jones quoted Horace Hosmer in "Thoreau's Inheritance":

The father was a very cautious and secretive man, a close observer, methodical and deliberate in action, and he produced excellent results. His marbled paper and his pencils were the best in the market, while his stove polish and his plumbago for electrotyping have never, to my knowledge, been excelled. He was a French gentleman rather than a "yankee," and once having his confidence, you had a very shrewd and companionable friend to commune with. Then, when there were no unauthorized listeners about, the otherwise quiet man, who had such a faculty for "minding his own business" would sit with you by the stove in his little shop and chat most delightfully.[40]

In his recollections of Cynthia Thoreau, Horace Hosmer emphasized her love of nature, which Dr. Jones thought strongly influenced her son. On this point Jones again quoted his Acton correspondent: "There were good and sufficient reasons for the Thoreau children's love of, and marked taste for, Botany and Natural History. John Thoreau and his wife were to be seen, year after year, enjoying the pleasures of nature, in their various seasons, on the banks of the Assabet, at Fairhaven, Lee's Hill, Walden and elsewhere; and this too without neglecting the various duties of their humble sphere. Indeed, such was Mrs. Thoreau's passion for these rambles that one of her children narrowly escaped being born in a favorite haunt on Lee's Hill."[41] Jones concluded that no biographer had yet

39. Samuel A. Jones, lecture of February 9, 1891 (Hosmer collection).
40. Samuel A. Jones, "Thoreau's Inheritance," p. 201. Quoted from Horace Hosmer's letter to Dr. Jones, August 8, 1892 (Jones collection). Jones altered the text of the original letter, which appears in *Remembrances of Concord and the Thoreaus*, pp. 82–83.
41. "Thoreau's Inheritance," p. 200. This is the same letter referred to in note 40. Subsequent references to "Thoreau's Inheritance" will be shown parenthetically.

properly estimated the influence which Henry Thoreau's parents had upon him. He argued perceptively that Thoreau "most closely resembled" his mother, but stressed the importance of both parents to his development: "It is more than probable that Henry D. Thoreau's intense Nature-love caught its life-long fire from his mother's fervor; while the clear sanity of his genius is as distinctly attributable to the plain but solid virtues of his sire" (p. 202).

"Thoreau's Inheritance" contained sharp criticism of F. B. Sanborn. Dr. Jones noted the discrepancy between Sanborn's treatment of Thoreau's parents and the "high moral altitude" which he ascribed to the Thoreau children. "Such a discrepancy," Dr. Jones continued, "should not be left to disfigure and disgrace the *American Men of Letters* series" (p. 201). Dr. Jones had used similarly strong language to denounce Sanborn's book in "Thoreau and His Biographers." This article resulted in the end of correspondence between Dr. Jones and Thoreau's friend and literary executor, H.G.O. Blake.

Jones and Blake began to correspond in 1890 when Jones sent Blake a copy of "Thoreau: A Glimpse." Blake judged "Thoreau: A Glimpse" to be a highly significant work and encouraged Dr. Jones to continue his Thoreau studies (letter 14). When Blake published *Thoreau's Thoughts* in 1890, the volume included as an appendix the bibliography which Dr. Jones had previously published in "Thoreau: A Glimpse."[42] In August 1890 the two men met, when Dr. Jones travelled to Worcester to visit Blake at his home. Fairly regular correspondence between them continued until the publication of "Thoreau and His Biographers," to which Blake took exception in a letter to Jones of August 1, 1891. Blake's conclusion that he and Dr. Jones were "made differently" was an unintended masterpiece of understatement (letter 70). Dr. Jones strongly defended his published statements, and Blake responded with a conciliatory letter but referred again to what he regarded as "the severely critical spirit" of Jones's article (letter 81). With this letter Jones concluded that his friendship with Blake had ended; to Fred Hosmer he commented in a letter of September 16, 1891, on the irony of being condemned for defending Thoreau by Thoreau's friend and literary executor (letter 82).

Their exchange of letters in August 1891 did not conclude the relationship between S. A. Jones and H.G.O. Blake. In October 1892 Blake sent Jones an inscribed copy of *Autumn,* which Blake had edited from Thoreau's journal. Dr. Jones, however, sent Blake a copy in return, since he did not wish to be indebted to Blake (letter 121). Apparently this action evoked a letter of reconciliation from Blake (letter 124), a letter which led

42. *Thoreau's Thoughts,* ed. H.G.O. Blake (Boston: Houghton, Mifflin and Co., 1890). Pages 131–46 comprise "A Contribution toward a Bibliography of Henry David Thoreau" by Samuel A. Jones.

Dr. Jones to reconsider his judgment of Blake. Jones explained in a letter to Fred Hosmer dated October 16, 1892, the change in his feelings toward Blake: "It seems that I had misunderstood his letter and ascribed to him feelings which he did not entertain. I hope that I may be able to have a long visit with him before he is called away" (letter 125). Despite the reconciliation correspondence between the two men did not resume.

Jones did not retreat from his criticisms of Sanborn's biography. In addition to refuting Sanborn in "Thoreau's Inheritance," Dr. Jones ensured that Salt's revised edition of 1896 would include a fairer estimate of Thoreau's parents than had the original edition. Dr. Jones forwarded to Salt material he had gotten from Horace Hosmer and Mrs. Le Brun's paper "Henry Thoreau's Mother." Salt by his subtle changes in the 1896 edition drew a more honest portrait of the elder Thoreaus.[43] Salt also quoted both from "Thoreau's Inheritance," reproducing passages from Horace Hosmer's letters to Jones and from Mrs. LeBrun's paper. Salt virtually echoed the conclusion which Jones had reached in "Thoreau's Inheritance": "We see then that Thoreau was indebted to both his parents for some of his best qualities—to his mother for a quick-witted spirit and passionate love of Nature, to his father for the counter balance of a calm, sane, industrious temperament, with absolute honesty of purpose and performance" (pp. 21–22).

One of the most valuable studies which S. A. Jones and Alfred Hosmer undertook concerned the various portraits of Thoreau. Both Jones and Hosmer thought it important to determine the exact dates of Thoreau's portraits as well as the specific circumstances surrounding the making of each. This gathering of precise information was a difficult task since published accounts of the portraits were frequently contradictory. The *Critic* for March 26, 1881, for instance, published the New Bedford ambrotype of Thoreau, taken at Ricketson's request in 1861, with the assertion that it was the only portrait showing Thoreau with a beard (p. 73). In the next number of the *Critic* William Sloane Kennedy argued that there were two other portraits of Thoreau which pictured him with a beard: one was the daguerreotype taken in Worcester in 1856, and the other was a portrait taken a few years before Thoreau's death, also in Worcester.[44] John Burroughs inadvertently confused the issue further when he published in the July 1882 *Century Magazine* a woodcut of Thoreau, showing him with a beard, which was described as "from his last portrait, a tintype, taken by Critcherson, of Worcester, Mass., in 1861" (p. 368). In his 1890 life of Thoreau, Henry Salt contradicted Burroughs by dating the "Critcherson" portrait in 1857 or 1858 (p. 299). Jones himself

43. Hendrick, "Henry Salt's Biography of Thoreau," p. 227.
44. W.S.K., "Portraits of Thoreau with a Beard," *Critic* 1 (April 9, 1881):95.

best expressed the problems he and Hosmer faced as they attempted to sort out these conflicting accounts: "I am flabbergasted by this Thoreau picture business and begin to feel that we don't know much about it" (letter 105).

Alfred Hosmer proved invaluable to Dr. Jones in clarifying available information about Thoreau's portraits. Himself a photographer of considerable ability, Hosmer carefully compared the Blake daguerreotype with the "Critcherson" portrait and wrote his conclusion to Dr. Jones: *"That the Burroughs or Treadwell tintype is merely a copy of the Blake daguerreotype*—and if you write up an article on the pictures I should class it as such" (letter 106). Hosmer's judgment did much to resolve some of the contradictions surrounding the Thoreau portraits, but Dr. Jones was still dissatisfied with the imprecision of Salt's dating of the Blake daguerreotype. He asked Hosmer to inquire of Blake concerning the date and the name of the daguerreotypist. Hosmer wrote Blake, who responded that his daguerreotype had "the name B. D. Maxham attached to it"; Blake's memory was failing, however, and he could not date the daguerreotype more exactly than "abt. 1855 or 1856."[45] Nevertheless Blake's response made it clear that the daguerreotype which Thoreau had made in Worcester was done by Maxham, not by Critcherson. The "Critcherson" tintype was, as Hosmer had asserted, merely a reproduction of the daguerreotype made by B. D. Maxham.[46]

Jones was also interested in determining the circumstances surrounding the earliest portrait of Thoreau, the crayon drawing made by Samuel Worcester Rowse in 1854. He asked Alfred Hosmer to inquire of Dr. Edward Emerson whether Emerson had suggested that Thoreau sit for Rowse (letter 130). Hosmer apparently obtained information about the Rowse crayon from Miss Ellen Emerson, though it is difficult to establish exactly what account she gave from the scant reference in Dr. Jones's letters (letter 131). More important, when Dr. Jones was corresponding with Professor Eben J. Loomis in 1894 about Thoreau's incarceration, he learned that Loomis had been boarding in the Thoreau home when the Rowse crayon drawing was made.[47] Dr. Jones communicated this information to Alfred Hosmer, who later wrote to Loomis to inquire about the date of the Rowse crayon; on June 13, 1896, Loomis responded: "Give one credit mark to Mr. Sanborn! He is actually correct in assigning 1854 as the date of Rowse's crayon of Henry Thoreau."[48] The photographs and

45. H.G.O. Blake to Alfred W. Hosmer, March 1 and 2, 1893 (Hosmer collection).
46. Maxham has been identified as B. W. Maxham, in Harding, *The Days of Henry Thoreau*, p. 12, and as B. E. Maxham in Walter Harding and Carl Bode, eds., *The Correspondence of Henry David Thoreau* (New York University Press, 1958), frontispiece. Blake in his letter to Hosmer identified the man as B. D. Maxham.
47. Eben J. Loomis to Samuel A. Jones, May 12, 1894 (Jones collection).
48. Eben J. Loomis to Alfred W. Hosmer, June 13, 1896 (Hosmer collection).

letters which Hosmer sent also elicited from Loomis a highly interesting reminiscence of how he, Rowse, and Thoreau had stayed up late at nights during the summer of 1854 discussing " 'fate, free-will, foreknowledge absolute,' or other topics equally or more interesting."[49]

In February 1893 Hosmer wrote to Daniel Ricketson to inquire about still another portrait of Thoreau, the ambrotype made by E. S. Dunshee in New Bedford in 1861. Ricketson responded that the ambrotype was taken at his request on August 19, 1861, and that two impressions were made. Ricketson added that he had retained one of the ambrotypes and sent the other to Sophia Thoreau shortly after Thoreau's death.[50] Hosmer forwarded this information to Dr. Jones, who planned to include it in an article on the portraits of Thoreau, to be published first in the *Inlander* and then later sold as an explanatory note accompanying Hosmer's photographs of the Thoreau portraits.

Dr. Jones did not publish his article, but the results of the investigations which he and Hosmer had made did get into print. In 1899 Jones included photographs of each of the three distinct Thoreau portraits[51] in *Some Unpublished Letters of Henry D. and Sophia E. Thoreau*. He correctly dated each portrait and accurately identified the portraitists. The findings of Dr. Jones and Alfred Hosmer also indirectly benefited Francis Allen, whose *Bibliography of Henry D. Thoreau* included a note on the Thoreau portraits. Dr. Jones corrected the proofs of this volume, and corresponded as well with Allen while the bibliography was being compiled. It is virtually certain that Dr. Jones would have corrected errors in Allen's work, particularly since he was obviously interested in Allen's discussion of the portraits—as is suggested by Dr. Jones's allowing Allen to reproduce the daguerreotype of Thoreau which he had acquired from C. H. Greene as well as the letter to Greene in which Thoreau had sent his portrait.[52]

Jones, Salt, and Hosmer were all concerned with preserving Thoreau's letters. Henry Salt attempted to gain access to Thoreau's letters to

49. Eben J. Loomis to Alfred W. Hosmer, June 1896 (Hosmer collection).
50. Daniel Ricketson to Alfred W. Hosmer, February 23, 1893 (Hosmer collection).
51. The three distinct portraits are the crayon drawing that Samuel Worcester Rowse made in 1854, the daguerreotype made by Benjamin Maxham of Worcester in 1856, and the ambrotype made by E. S. Dunshee in New Bedford in 1861. Maxham actually made three daguerreotypes when Thoreau sat for him in 1856, but these can properly be characterized as a single portrait. The same is true of the 1861 ambrotype, of which two impressions were made. Dr. Jones does mention another portrait in his letters, of which he apparently learned from Hosmer. This "Emmons portrait" has never been located or described. See letter 132.
52. Thoreau had sent one of the 1856 daguerreotypes to Greene, from whom Dr. Jones acquired it in 1897. Thoreau had mailed it to Greene with a letter on June 21, 1856. Jones first published this letter in *Some Unpublished Letters of Henry D. and Sophia E. Thoreau* (1899). It appeared in Allen, *A Bibliography of Henry David Thoreau*, pp. xiii–xiv. (The Greene daguerreotype appeared on the frontispiece.) For a text of Thoreau's letter, see *The Correspondence of Henry David Thoreau*, p. 426.

Thomas Cholmondeley, but he was unable to secure them from the Cholmondeley family. Sanborn, a completely untrustworthy editor, was finally given permission to edit the letters for publication.

Dr. Jones was more successful than Salt in obtaining letters by Thoreau. Following up a reference in Sanborn's edition of Thoreau's *Familiar Letters*,[53] Dr. Jones wrote to the postmaster of Rochester, Michigan, in an effort to locate Calvin H. Greene, with whom Thoreau had corresponded.[54] The postmaster responded with Greene's address, and Dr. Jones hastily wrote to inquire about Greene's relationship with Thoreau. On April 28, 1897, Greene said that he was willing to furnish the Thoreau letters which Dr. Jones desired to publish; this was the first of some forty letters and cards which Greene wrote to Dr. Jones.[55] Greene also invited Jones to visit him, and Jones wrote to Fred Hosmer of his forthcoming interview with Greene: "I shall bring a patent pump to bear on him and drain him as dry as—well, as E.W.E.'s [Edward Emerson's] lecture on Thoreau" (letter 285).

Dr. Jones's visit was successful, for Greene gave Jones six letters which he had received from Henry Thoreau, three letters from Sophia Thoreau, and one each from Ellery Channing and Franklin B. Sanborn (letter 286). Greene also gave Jones the daguerreotype of Thoreau which he had received in 1856, copies of *A Week* and *Walden* which Thoreau had sent to Greene's brother (letter 317), and at least one book which Sophia Thoreau had given him (letter 320).

Jones first presented the materials he had received from Greene in a lecture at the University of Michigan on May 19, 1897 (letter 289). Early in 1898 he repeated the lecture in Pontiac, Michigan (letter 329), and he then turned to preparing a publishable manuscript. After a conflict with Greene in May 1898 over certain language in the manuscript,[56] he published *Some Unpublished Letters of Henry D. and Sophia E. Thoreau* in 1899. Jones first asked Salt to edit the letters, but Salt declined. In the book Jones recounted how Greene had first written to Thoreau after being greatly impressed by *Walden*. Jones printed full and generally accurate texts of Thoreau's six letters to Greene[57] and the four letters which Sophia

53. *Familiar Letters of Henry David Thoreau,* ed. F. B. Sanborn (Boston: Houghton, Mifflin & Co., 1894), p. 454.
54. Samuel A. Jones to the postmaster of Rochester, Michigan, April 24, 1897 (Jones collection).
55. Greene's letters to Dr. Jones are in the Jones collection.
56. Greene objected particularly to Dr. Jones's characterization of him as "lowly born and lowly bred"; Greene understood that Jones had used the phrase to contrast him with Froude and knew that the contrast was complimentary. Still Greene believed that he was being damned with faint praise. See Greene to Jones, May 13, 1898 (Jones collection). Jones's conflict with Greene may account for one peculiarity of *Some Unpublished Letters:* Greene is never mentioned by name in the book.
57. For texts of Thoreau's letters to Calvin H. Greene, see *The Correspondence of Henry David Thoreau,* pp. 406–7, 407–8, 425–26, 485, 566.

Thoreau had written Greene after he had visited Concord in 1863.[58] Also included were some reminiscences of Greene's meeting with Sophia Thoreau, material which clarified events in the final weeks of Thoreau's life. Ellery Channing's short note to Greene of March 4, 1863, appeared in the volume,[59] as did James Anthony Froude's letter to Thoreau of September 3, 1849,[60] a copy of which Alfred Hosmer had acquired from Jean Munroe Le Brun, the author of "Henry Thoreau's Mother" (letter 289). Included with Froude's letter was a letter of Mrs. Le Brun which explained how she had received the letter from Sophia Thoreau when Miss Thoreau was making a final disposition of her brother's papers.[61] Dr. Jones thought it particularly important that the Froude letter be printed, for it suggested that Thoreau's first edition of *A Week on the Concord and Merrimack Rivers* had elicited an enthusiastic response from at least one genuine scholar. Not included in *Some Unpublished Letters* was F. B. Sanborn's letter to Greene of June 11, 1862. This letter was, however, later reproduced in Dr. Jones's concluding note to *Emerson's Obituary*, a pamphlet published by E. B. Hill in 1904.[62]

Walter Harding and Carl Bode have remarked: "Dr. Jones established an important precedent in the editing of Thoreau's letters by printing a relatively accurate and literal transcription of the original manuscripts."[63] Accurate editions of Thoreau's letters were of major concern to Jones. Indeed one of the earliest indications of Dr. Jones's interest in Thoreau is a note in his reading log of March, 1887, in which he objects to Emerson's edition of Thoreau's letters, *Letters to Various Persons,* in which Emerson sought to portray a stoic Thoreau: "It has lowered Emerson in my esteem to learn that he could desire to alter Thoreau's letters from a purely artistic intent."[64] Dr. Jones's own editorial philosophy, which he practiced in *Some Unpublished Letters,* was uncompromising: "He who assumes to edit a dead man's writings should not forget his responsibility. Such an one should be above all things truthful."[65]

Jones and Hosmer pursued other leads in their search for letters by

58. Sophia's letters were dated June 24, 1862; October 20, 1862; March 4, 1863; and May 24, 1873. For texts see *Some Unpublished Letters of Henry D. and Sophia E. Thoreau,* ed. Samuel A. Jones (Jamaica, N. Y.: Marion Press, 1899), pp. 49–54, 60–63, 64–65, 68–69.

59. *Some Unpublished Letters,* p. 66.

60. For a text of Froude's letter see *The Correspondence of Henry David Thoreau,* pp. 248–49.

61. *Some Unpublished Letters,* pp. 6–8. Dr. Jones misdated the letter December 17, 1897; the original of Mrs. LeBrun's letter to Alfred W. Hosmer is dated December 27, 1897 (Hosmer collection).

62. *Collectanea Henry D. Thoreau: Emerson's Obituary* (Lakeland, Mich.: Edwin B. Hill, 1904).

63. *The Correspondence of Henry David Thoreau,* pp. xv–xvi.

64. Dr. Jones's reading log for March 1887 is in the Jones collection.

65. Ibid.

Thoreau, but it is the "find" of the letters to Greene and the supporting letters in the possession of Greene that was of the greatest importance.

When Henry Salt inscribed his 1896 biography to S. A. Jones, he praised Dr. Jones's many "labours full of sympathy and insight," but he singled out for specific mention the doctor's "invaluable Bibliography." Dr. Jones was truly the pioneer bibliographer of Thoreau; indeed, when Francis Allen described previous bibliographies in his own *Bibliography of Henry David Thoreau,* he wrote, "The only bibliographies of Thoreau of any interest or importance to the student or the collector are those by Dr. Samuel A. Jones."[66] The first of Jones's bibliographies was published in the *Unitarian* for March 1890 as "A Contribution toward a Bibliography of Thoreau." It was reprinted in Jones's *Thoreau: A Glimpse* (1890) and again in H.G.O. Blake's edition *Thoreau's Thoughts* (1890). Jones also contributed to the bibliography in Henry Salt's first biography of Thoreau.

Dr. Jones's most extensive work in this field was his *Bibliography of Henry David Thoreau,* published in 1894 in a limited edition of ninety copies by the Rowfant Club, an exclusive book-collecting club in Cleveland, Ohio. This edition included a chronology of Thoreau's life, listings of Thoreau's contributions to periodicals, information concerning early editions of the works, and a list of secondary works which included biography, ana, reviews, and critical articles. Reprinted in the volume was Dr. Jones's amusing sketch, "An Afternoon in the University Library," which gave a history of the first edition of Thoreau's ill-fated *A Week on the Concord and Merrimack Rivers.*[67] The frontispiece was a photograph of the 1856 daguerreotype which Thoreau had given to Blake, reproduced by Alfred Hosmer.

Jones received important aid in his bibliographic studies from both Henry Salt and Alfred Hosmer. Salt was particularly valuable as a source of English references to Thoreau, while Hosmer searched for items in sources that were often unavailable to Jones. Both Hosmer and Salt continued to send Jones items of interest even after the publication of the 1894 *Bibliography,* since Jones hoped to publish a revised popular edition of the bibliography, but he was unable to bring that project to completion.

Dr. Jones was, in connection with his bibliographic interests, intent upon republishing hard-to-find articles, recollections, and reviews concerning Thoreau. The first of these to be completed was the immensely useful *Pertaining to Thoreau,* printed by Jones's friend and patient E. B.

66. Francis Allen, *A Bibliography of Henry David Thoreau* (Boston: Houghton, Mifflin & Co., 1908), p. 88.
67. "An Afternoon in the University Library" had originally appeared in the *Inlander* 1 (June 1891):150–53.

Hill. The selections in the volume were well chosen, and *Pertaining to Thoreau* was a worthy forerunner of collections edited by Walter Harding and Wendell Glick. In addition Dr. Jones completed (except for one item) *Thoreau amongst Friends and Philistines,* a collection of English and American reviews from the 1890s. It was one of his most characteristic works, since he commented freely upon opinions of friends and detractors alike. Unfortunately he did not submit the manuscript for publication, for a deep depression settled over him in 1901 after the death of his son Carroll. The collection remained unfinished, finally to be discovered by George Hendrick in 1974, over seventy years after it was put aside. The manuscript has now been edited for publication.

How did Hosmer, Jones, and Salt help lay the foundations for Thoreau's modern reputation? For Hosmer the answer is relatively simple: in addition to being literary detective in Concord and making pioneer photographic studies of Thoreau country, his great claim to our attention is his magnificent grangerized *Life of Henry David Thoreau,* which forms the heart of his substantial Thoreau collection at the Concord Free Public Library. Into this grangerized or "extended" *Life* (Henry Salt's revised biography), Hosmer placed photographs, items of antiquarian interest, and manuscripts, both those of Thoreau and of early Thoreauvians—all of which he had painstakingly obtained and preserved through his many years of Thoreau study. Without the materials preserved in this *Life,* Thoreau scholarship would be far more incomplete than it is today.

Among the manuscripts in Hosmer's amplified edition of Salt's *Life* is Thoreau's boyhood composition "The Seasons," which Hosmer obtained in 1892 by finding Horatio Allen, the son of Phineas Allen, Thoreau's preceptor.[68] Also included are three letters of Thoreau's: to H.G.O. Blake, November 20, 1849; to Blake, June 1, 1858, and to Daniel Ricketson, September 23, 1856. This *Life* is rich, too, in letters to Thoreau: there are letters from Emerson, February 15, 1839, and February 12, 1843; from Horace Greeley, June 25, 1852; from Thomas Cholmondeley, Thoreau's English friend, "Tuesday 1855"; and two from Daniel Ricketson—one dated March 7, 1856, and the other inserted within the first without separate date. A copy of James Anthony Froude's letter of September 3, 1849, to Thoreau is another of the important items of Thoreau's correspondence.[69] There is also a Thoreau certificate of survey, dated September 22, 1857.

Alfred Hosmer preserved within the grangerized *Life* many manu-

68. Horatio Allen to Alfred W. Hosmer, May 14, 1892 (Hosmer collection).

69. For texts of the letters to and from Thoreau in the Hosmer *Life,* see *The Correspondence of Henry David Thoreau,* pp. 32, 85, 248–49, 250–52, 282, 364–66, 414–19, 432–33, 514–15.

scripts of those who were most closely associated with Thoreau—Blake, Theophilus Brown, Ellery Channing, Horace Hosmer, Eben J. Loomis, Parker Pillsbury, Ricketson, Maria Thoreau, Sophia Thoreau, and George Thatcher. Included among these materials are letters to Hosmer himself which bear significantly upon important issues of Thoreau biography—Pillsbury's letter arguing that the Walden hut was not used as a station on the Underground Railroad, Loomis's letter dating the Rowse crayon, Blake's letter explaining that Maxham had made the 1856 daguerreotype, Ricketson's letter dating the 1861 ambrotype, Jean Munroe Le Brun's letter explaining how she had received Froude's letter to Thoreau from Sophia Thoreau.

On November 20, 1895, Alfred Hosmer wrote Dr. Jones that he had obtained a picture of Maria Thoreau from Annie J. Ward and had made a copy of it. He intended "to see if I cannot obtain a picture of each of the family so as to get a copy of them" (letter 236). His efforts met with considerable success, and the copies he made of likenesses of the Thoreau and Dunbar family members are another important resource collected within the grangerized *Life*. To the photographs of the Thoreaus and Dunbars, Hosmer added photographs of Thoreau's friends, disciples, and acquaintances, including photographs of Daniel Ricketson, Theo Brown, H.G.O. Blake, Thomas Cholmondeley, Edmund Hosmer, Horace Hosmer, Joseph Hosmer, Parker Pillsbury, C. H. Greene, and Sam Staples, as well as those of Thoreau's better known associates in Concord—Emerson, Alcott, Channing, Hawthorne. Hosmer also included photographs of early Thoreau critics and scholars—S. A. Jones, Henry Salt, Moncure Conway, John Burroughs, T. W. Higginson, A. H. Japp, and F. B. Sanborn. He supplemented the personal portraits with many of his own photographs of places in the Concord area associated with Thoreau. The correspondence between Hosmer and Jones amply documents the slow careful process by which Hosmer put together his magnificent collection of photographs.

Of tremendous value and interest also in Hosmer's Thoreau collection is his two-volume scrapbook of reviews and criticism pertaining to Thoreau. These volumes, covering the years 1840–1903, include numerous items that are practically unobtainable elsewhere and are an indispensable resource to Thoreau bibliography and to the study of nineteenth-century criticism of Thoreau. Equally valuable are the Hosmer letter-files, which include the letters Hosmer received from numerous Thoreauvians, enthusiasts as well as scholars. Among the correspondents whose letters Hosmer preserved are Charles C. Abbott, H.G.O. Blake, the Rev. David Cronyn, Anna and Walton Ricketson, John Burroughs, Ebenezer Rockwood Hoar, F. B. Sanborn, Eben J. Loomis, Emily Lyman, Annie Russell Marble, Henry W. Rolfe, and Annie J. Ward.

Most important Hosmer saved the correspondence of his major collaborators in the work of revaluing Henry Thoreau—Henry S. Salt and Samuel A. Jones. These letter-files are, as Walter Harding has remarked, a "gold mine of information."[70]

Fred Hosmer also gathered together a substantial library of works by and about Thoreau. Well represented in this sizable collection are nineteenth-century editions of Thoreau's works, periodicals in which Thoreau's essays appeared, early volumes of selections from Thoreau, critical and biographical volumes devoted to Thoreau, and works in which Thoreau is given occasional mention. Although Hosmer's collection of Thoreau books is perhaps of less interest today than his letter-files or his grangerized *Life*, it was of immense value to early bibliographical study of Thoreau, benefiting Samuel A. Jones, Henry Salt, and Francis Allen.

Dr. Jones's contributions to Thoreau scholarship are particularly notable. He refused to accept without question biographical accounts or standard critical interpretations of Thoreau: he wanted to know the facts about Thoreau's night in jail, about the personal characteristics of Thoreau's parents, about many other biographical matters. He smote such "enemies" of Thoreau as Sanborn, Lowell, and Japp, using strong language in an age when decorum was expected. He supported Henry Salt at a time when Salt's biography of Thoreau was little known in America. Jones understood, as Blake did not, the importance of publishing Thoreau's letters; he understood why it was important to learn as much as possible about Thoreau's "love affair." He wanted a complete, accurate Thoreau bibliography, and he wanted to publish reviews of Thoreau's books and articles about Thoreau.

Dr. Jones did much for the Thoreau studies of several other critics. For instance he became acquainted in 1899 with E. B. Hill, then working as telegraph editor of the Detroit *Journal*. He became Hill's physician, and he began encouraging Hill to print small pamphlet editions of Thoreauvian interest, work that Hill was to continue for over forty years. In 1901 he published Jones's *Pertaining to Thoreau*, setting the type and printing the book in the hours he had free from his newspaper work. Among his other important publications was Thoreau's boyhood essay *The Seasons* (1916), a copy of which he probably received from Jones—who had himself acquired a copy of the essay from Alfred W. Hosmer. Another of Hill's editions to which Jones may have contributed was *Two Thoreau Letters* (1916), which reproduced Thoreau's letters to Charles Wyatt Rice of August 5, 1836, and to George Thatcher of July 11, 1857; Thoreau's letter to Thatcher was one of two Thoreau letters which Dr. Jones had

70. Walter Harding, "The Alfred Hosmer Letter Files," *Thoreau Society Bulletin* 119 (spring 1972):7.

received, in copies, from G. M. Williamson in 1901.[71] Other Hill publications included Louisa May Alcott's *Thoreau's Flute* (1899); Dr. Jones's poem *Thoreau*, reprinted from the *Inlander* for February, 1893; *Letters to Edwin B. Hill* (1944) by Edward W. Emerson; *Henry D. Thoreau: Emerson's Obituary* (1904) reprinted from the *Boston Daily Advertiser* for May 8, 1862, with a short appendix by Dr. Jones; *Henry Thoreau's Mother* (1908), the letter to the *Boston Daily Advertiser* for February 14, 1883, by Mrs. Jean Munroe Le Brun; *Henry D. Thoreau to Elizabeth Oakes Smith* (1942),[72] a letter of February 19, 1855; and *Henry D. Thoreau to George William Curtis* (1942),[73] a letter of March 11, 1853. Jones's influence is manifest in all of Hill's editions, for, as Harding and Bode have pointed out, "his texts were accurate."[74]

Dr. Jones also was helpful to Dr. Edward Emerson, Ralph Waldo Emerson's son, even though Jones did not always find Emerson agreeable. Early in 1891 Jones arranged for Emerson to give his Thoreau lecture at a Unitarian church in Detroit (letter 50). In October 1891 Jones sought to secure Emerson a hearing in Ann Arbor but without success (letter 90). In 1895, however, he was able to arrange two lectures for Emerson in Ann Arbor and one in Cleveland at the Rowfant Club.[75] Dr. Emerson's lecture later provided the basis for his fine reminiscence of Thoreau, *Henry Thoreau as Remembered by a Young Friend* (1917), which perhaps did more than any other single book to correct Ralph Waldo Emerson's interpretation of Thoreau as a stoic.

As the correspondence published here shows, Dr. Jones, in addition to carrying out his own extensive Thoreau studies, helped other Thoreau scholars and enthusiasts[76] over a long period of time, as did Henry Salt.

Not all of Jones's Thoreauvian plans were realized. After the Rowfant Club had published his Thoreau bibliography, he attempted to persuade the club to bring out an edition of Thoreau's poems (letter 191). To this end he approached F. B. Sanborn, who responded: "The decision would finally rest with Mr. H.G.O. Blake, who holds most of the MSS. —though I have some. I mean to print a few of them in the magazines, before including them in any book."[77] In 1895 Sanborn did collaborate with

71. G. M. Williamson to Samuel A. Jones, February 28, 1901 (Jones collection). For texts of the letters which Hill published, see *The Correspondence of Henry David Thoreau*, pp. 8–9, 485–86.

72. For the text see ibid., pp. 372–73.

73. For the text see ibid., p. 301.

74. Ibid., p. xv. For a more thorough list of Hill's Thoreau editions, see "In Memoriam: Edwin B. Hill," *Thoreau Society Bulletin* 28 (July 1949):1.

75. Letter 224. Although he worked to arrange the lectures, Dr. Jones was unimpressed by Dr. Emerson's performance. Apparently Jones found Emerson's delivery deficient, marred by "continual 'ahs' and pauses." During one lecture Jones "slid into a back room and read until the show was over." See letter 235.

76. Dr. Jones turned over his materials for an Emerson bibliography to George W. Cooke.

77. F. B. Sanborn to Samuel A. Jones, September 14, 1894 (Jones collection).

Henry Salt in editing *Poems of Nature,* but he was apparently of little assistance in this venture. In a letter to Dr. Jones of September 21, 1895, Salt commented on his difficulties with Sanborn: "I fear the joint Introduction is not a very lively affair, and there will be some other shortcomings. Sanborn has again got between me & Mr. Blake, & has not sent a scrap of new material. . . . The only advantage of his cooperation is the permission to publish in America" (letter 228).

Among Dr. Jones's other unrealized projects were two volumes of correspondence. In 1898, after the death of H.G.O. Blake, Dr. Jones attempted to regain possession of his own letters to Blake, for he wanted the letters published after his own death, feeling they would show much about Blake's character. Jones's efforts to retrieve his letters failed, but we do publish for the first time Blake's letters to Dr. Jones, which do illuminate Blake's character.

In 1900 Dr. Jones contemplated publishing Horace Hosmer's letters to him. He thought them of great value to the study of Thoreau and Concord, and he had quoted at length from them in his own Thoreau lectures and essays. He expressed his feeling to Alfred Hosmer that they were "worthy of preservation" since they contained "so much about Concord in the early days" (letter 395). He began a typescript of the letters, but he could not bring himself to publish them. Horace Hosmer had been more than a literary acquaintance, and his letters had moved Dr. Jones deeply. George Hendrick has edited these letters in a collection entitled *Remembrances of Concord and the Thoreaus,* published in 1977 by the University of Illinois Press.

Dr. Jones repeatedly contemplated publishing an illustrated volume, *Thoreau's Country,* which would include Hosmer's photographs with appropriate quotations from Thoreau. In 1894 he considered a far-sighted plan to establish a bibliographic society in Ann Arbor which could "get all the Concord authors bibliographed" (letter 195). Dr. Jones was indeed a victim of his many good ideas. After long hours of medical practice, he stayed up much of the night reading and writing, and eventually his health broke from overwork. The deaths of his son in 1901 and of Fred Hosmer in 1903 were terrible blows to him, and he ceased his literary work and his correspondence with Henry Salt.

Dr. Jones has been too little known, his articles on Thoreau were difficult to find, his books appeared in small editions, and some of his best work was put aside and never published. The correspondence in this collection will, we believe, show his importance as a scholar.

Henry Salt is better known as a Thoreau scholar than are Fred Hosmer and Dr. Jones, but unfortunately even Salt's *Life* did not have the large number of general readers it deserved. One reader of note, however, was

M. K. Gandhi who read "Civil Disobedience," *Walden,* and Salt's *Life* "with great pleasure and equal profit."[78] The influence on Gandhi alone would mark the importance of the Thoreau biography.

Throughout his long life Salt continued his efforts to have Thoreau recognized as writer and thinker. Salt made special efforts to reach readers in the Humanitarian League and in vegetarian societies. His efforts culminated in his two autobiographies—*Seventy Years Among Savages* and *Company I Have Kept*—both infused with a Thoreauvian spirit and both filled with references to Thoreau. In the latter volume he noted that "a common love for Thoreau has often become a link of personal friendship (as the present writer has reason to remember with gratitude) between lives that were otherwise far apart." Certainly Salt had in mind Samuel Jones and, to a lesser degree, Fred Hosmer. Salt went on to explain a characteristically generous act of his: "Of this I have had a recent example, in a correspondence with my newest and latest Thoreau-friend, Mr. Raymond Adams, of North Carolina, who is devoting himself to the preparation of a full and up-to-date biography of the author of *Walden*. To be able to help this project, in however small a degree, by sending across the water the various letters and papers concerning Thoreau, that have accumulated in my hands during the past forty years, has been a great and unexpected pleasure, coming, as it did, at a time when I am nearing the end of my own powers of rendering service to the memory of the writer who, next to Shelley, has moved me more than any other."[79]

Salt's generosity was in keeping with the kindnesses shown him by Blake, Ricketson, and others who had known Thoreau and shared their knowledge with him. Indeed Dr. Jones and Fred Hosmer also benefited greatly from information passed on by those who had known Thoreau; they valued highly the opinions and comments of Blake and Ricketson, whom they regarded as men of principle, though Jones did have some qualms about Blake; they disbelieved much of what Sanborn said and wrote, for they questioned his integrity.

How have the findings of Jones, Hosmer, and Salt influenced the course of Thoreau studies since their time? First, they resolved numerous issues concerning Thoreau biography, providing a body of knowledge which their successors could confidently assume. Their studies, embodied particularly in Salt's biographies of 1890 and 1896, stood as the major source of information about Thoreau for seventy-five years and were of value to Walter Harding in *The Days of Henry Thoreau* (1965). Moreover Salt's biography continues to be one of the best expositions of Thoreau's central ideas. Later studies, such as F. O. Matthiessen's *American Renaissance* and Sherman Paul's *The Shores of America,* have superseded Salt in specific

78. Salt, *Company I Have Kept,* p. 101.
79. Ibid., pp. 103–4.

areas of Thoreau criticism; but as a general assessment of Thoreau's thought and art Salt's work remains of great value.

Modern scholarship of Thoreau is indebted as well to the efforts of Jones, Hosmer, and Salt to locate and preserve the primary materials on which the study of Thoreau depends. They argued for the publication of the journals and set an important precedent for twentieth-century editing of Thoreau by publishing complete and generally accurate texts of letters. The three men's pioneering bibliographical work has provided the basis for continuing study of Thoreau, and it is responsible for the preservation of many early reviews and notices, without which the study of Thoreau's reception in his own time would be incomplete. In addition Fred Hosmer's photographs captured Concord and Walden largely as it was in Thoreau's time, while Hosmer's photographs of those persons associated with Thoreau add materially to our knowledge of his life. All three men saw the value of illustrating Thoreau's works with photographs and sketches.

The critical interpretation of Thoreau proposed by Jones and Salt has been of seminal importance to modern Thoreau criticism. They liberated Thoreau from Emersonian interpretations, making possible the consideration of Thoreau as a distinctive thinker and stylist. They similarly liberated Thoreau from the confining interpretation in which he was seen merely as a naturalist; both Jones and Salt presented Thoreau as a complex mind who faced the dilemma of individualism versus political engagement. In fighting against the tendency to read all of Thoreau's life from *Walden,* Jones and Salt served both Thoreau biography and criticism. They argued that Thoreau's retreat to Walden was not the act of a stoic egoist, as many early critics claimed; thus they cleared the ground for modern readings of *Walden* which interpret the book as Thoreau's artistic enactment of withdrawal and return. By scotching such major misconceptions, Jones and Salt performed an inestimable service to modern biography and criticism of Thoreau.

With the publication of this correspondence, the full extent of the contributions that Dr. Samuel Arthur Jones, Alfred W. Hosmer, and Henry Salt made to the growth of Thoreau's reputation and to the understanding of his life and work can now be appreciated.

A Note on the Text

UNTIL RECENTLY only a part of the correspondence presented here was known to be extant. In the summer of 1974, however, approximately two hundred letters by Henry Salt, Daniel Ricketson, H.G.O. Blake, and A. W. Hosmer were discovered in Urbana, Illinois, and acquired by the University of Illinois Library, Urbana-Champaign. For this edition the Concord Free Public Library has made available approximately 350 letters of Dr. Jones to Fred Hosmer and twelve letters from Salt to Hosmer. Because it would not be economically feasible to present complete texts of these 560 letters, we are publishing selections from the correspondence.

This text is a selection from the Jones-Hosmer-Salt-Blake-Ricketson correspondence. All sections of the Jones-Hosmer-Salt letters pertinent to Thoreau's reputation have been included, except when such information is repetitive. The entire body of the letters by Blake and Ricketson is used, for they were close friends of Thoreau and their letters had special significance to the other three, as they have to anyone interested in Thoreau. We have also used comments on other writers (Emerson, Alcott, Jefferies, et al.) when they contribute to an understanding of the correspondents' studies of Thoreau. Routine personal remarks about weather, family, health, and other trivia have been excluded, although we have retained personal information when it helps the reader to understand the Thoreau work of the correspondent. We have, for instance, retained many of Dr. Jones's comments about the demands of medical practice and his involvement in the homoeopathic controversy in Ann Arbor, since these statements reveal the trying circumstances under which he accomplished his Thoreau work. We have also included some of Salt's statements on his humanitarian activities, for there was a Thoreauvian aspect to this work.

In order to conserve space, we have standardized the dateline of each letter and omitted the notation of place. The dateline for each contains the correspondents' names, the date (in brackets if conjectural), and in rare instances a notation if the document is a postcard or fragment. All of Jones's letters, except one which has been identified in the annotations, are addressed from Ann Arbor, Michigan; all of Hosmer's, from Concord, Massachusetts; all of Blake's, from Worcester, Massachusetts; all of Ricketson's, from New Bedford, Massachusetts; and Salt's, from London or from country cottages within commuting distance of London; a few were written while Salt was vacationing in various spots in England and Wales. Nor have we included identification of manuscript repository with each letter. All of Jones's letters to Fred Hosmer are in the Thoreau Library of Alfred W. Hosmer, Concord Free Public Library, Concord, Massachusetts, as are the letters of Henry Salt to Fred Hosmer; all of Hosmer's letters to Jones are in the collection of Dr. Samuel Arthur Jones, University of Illinois at Urbana-Champaign Library, as are the letters of Blake, Ricketson, and Salt to Jones. The few available drafts of letters from Jones to Blake, Ricketson, and Salt are in the collection of Dr. S. A. Jones. We have been unable to locate the Salt-Ricketson correspondence and have used texts from *Daniel Ricketson and His Friends*. The letters of Jones and Hosmer to Salt are in a private collection and were not made available to us; we do present three extracts from Jones's letters to Salt, however, through the courtesy of the *Thoreau Society Bulletin,* in which they were first published.

To further save space, we have omitted formal salutations and closings; there is little variation in these. Jones addresses his early letters to Fred Hosmer "My dear Hosmer," and soon switches to the more familiar "My dear Fred"; he characteristically closes with "Sincerely yours." Hosmer's letters to Jones are addressed "My dear Doctor" throughout, and close "Yours very sincerely." Henry Salt, as the correspondence with Jones continued, changed from "My dear Sir" to "Dear Dr. Jones" to "My dear Friend"; he characteristically signed his letters "Yours sincerely." Salt addressed Hosmer "Dear Mr. Hosmer" and characteristically signed the letters "Yours sincerely." Salt began his correspondence with Ricketson addressing him "Dear Sir" but soon changed to "Dear Mr. Ricketson." Ricketson also began his first letters with the formal "Dear Sir" but changed to "Dear Mr. Salt." Ricketson's first letter to Jones began "My dear Sir," but he soon changed to "My dear Friend"; he generally closed with "I remain very truly yours." Blake addressed his letters to Dr. Jones first to "Dear sir," then "Dear Dr. Jones," then returned to "Dear sir" in his letter of October 12 and 13, 1892.

The original letters are in good condition and offer few problems in the way of legibility. Dr. Jones regularly used a typewriter; only a few of his letters are in holograph. To present a readable text, we have silently corrected obvious slips of the pen or the typewriter. We have endeavored to present a text which follows the original letters without being slavish in its reproduction of error or idiosyncrasy; we have silently altered punctuation in a few cases in which the reader might otherwise be misled. Since these letters are valuable primarily for the information they contain, we believe such modest changes to avoid ambiguity are justified. We have retained abbreviations, set superscripts in the line, and have included all editorial additions within brackets. All postscripts have been placed at the end of the letter, whether the material originally appeared there or, as is sometimes the case, at the top of the page. All letters are numbered, following chronological sequence, and cross-references in the annotations include the letter number. In the case of struck-over words or phrases, the authors' revisions are followed.

These are our principles of elision. Three asterisks centered in the page indicate the omission of one or more full paragraphs at the beginning of a letter. To indicate omissions within sentences, three-point ellipses are used; a three-point ellipsis at the beginning of a paragraph indicates the opening word, words, sentence, or sentences have been deleted. Four-point ellipses signify deletion of the last part of the sentence, the first part of the next sentence, a whole sentence or more, or a whole paragraph or more. Omission of only the complimentary close and the signature is not marked by ellipses.

Annotations in each case follow the letter. Within the annotations we have referred to the Collection of Dr. Samuel Arthur Jones, University of Illinois at Urbana-Champaign Library, simply as Jones collection. Similarly the Thoreau Library of Alfred W. Hosmer, Concord Free Public Library, Concord, Massachusetts, has been denoted simply as Hosmer collection. These are the two main repositories of primary documents cited in the notes. Other manuscript locations are fully identified.

The Letters

1. Daniel Ricketson to Henry Salt, November 5, 1889.

Yours of the 18th ult. was received on the 28th, finding me quite ill with acute bronchitis, from which I am slowly recovering, and take this my first opportunity to answer your letter.

Among the foreign essays on Thoreau, that of "H. A. Page," A. H. Japp, LL.D., 13 Albion Square, Dalston, London, which appeared several years ago, from his high appreciation and genial style, has met with much approval here. With Mr. J. I have passed several letters, the last informing me of his great bereavement in the loss of his wife. I do not know that he intends writing anything further about Thoreau, and I am willing to afford you any help in my power for your proposed work.

I have to-day found the letter written by Thoreau on his father's death, which is at your service, while in looking over a large number of letters from him I find many more interesting and characteristic of the writer than those few already published by Mr. Sanborn and others. It would be through his private correspondence to his intimate friends that he would be best known. I think that a letter or more from Thoreau to an admiring English friend, who spent some time with him in Concord, Thomas Cholmondeley,[1] afterwards Owen, who died in April, 1864, would be of interest. He and Thoreau made me a visit at Brooklawn, my country home, in the early part of December, 1858. After Mr. C. returned to England, some time after, I wrote to him, not knowing of his death, which was very melancholy, on his marriage tour in Italy, dying of malarial fever at Naples. My letter was answered very cordially by his brother, Reginald Cholmondeley, Esq., Condover Hall, near Shrewsbury, Shrops., and we corresponded for a year or two. As I have not heard from him for some thirty years, I fear he has long since passed on. Should he or any of his family be living, I doubt not they would meet your wishes in supplying any correspondence Thoreau may have had with his friend, as well as my letters. I could also supply the letters of R. C. to me.

Letters showing the strong personal admiration of a well-educated and travelled English gentleman like Mr. Thomas Cholmondeley would add much to your book.

I think Thoreau also corresponded with William Allingham,[2] poet, etc., Ballyshannon, Ireland.

I should like to know a little more of your *modus operandi.* I suppose you address me in your own and not a *nom de plume.* If so, I am pleasantly reminded of Charles Lamb's "Old Bencher," Mr. S.

I have just been reading the autobiography of Mary Howitt, giving occasional sketches of William Howitt.[3] It has occurred to me, if you are in the way of writing biographies, William Howitt would afford you an admirable opportunity for presenting to the American as well as the English public one of the truest and most loyal writers of our time. As a friend and correspondent of himself and family I have a number of letters from them all, also an admirable daguerreotype of William Howitt, taken in London in 1846, and an excellent engraving of Mrs. Howitt, done about the same time, with accompanying letters from both.

This is not, however, Thoreau. But I cannot promise to do much for you requiring writing, as it exhausts me much, and my correspondence is too large already for an old man of seventy-six years. So please excuse this hasty scrawl as a sort of rambling, desultory answer; being far from well and strong is my excuse.

1. Thomas Cholmondeley, whom Thoreau met when Cholmondeley came from England to visit Emerson in the autumn of 1854. When Cholmondeley returned to England, the "two started a correspondence that with some gaps was continued for the rest of Thoreau's life," and in 1855 Cholmondeley sent Thoreau a magnificent gift of forty-four oriental volumes. See Walter Harding, *The Days of Henry Thoreau* (New York: Knopf, 1965), pp. 346–47.
2. William Allingham (1824–1889), an Irish poet, corresponded with Emerson and is known to have read Thoreau. If Thoreau did write to Allingham, the letters have not been found.
3. William Howitt (1792–1879), an English Quaker, wrote poetry, histories, religious studies, books for children, books on spiritualism, and travelogues.

2. Henry Salt to Daniel Ricketson, November 18, 1889.

I am exceedingly obliged to you for your kind letter and the copy of Thoreau's most interesting account of the death of his father. Let me first answer your question about my *modus operandi* in this volume on Thoreau which I am now preparing. My object is to give (1) a clear and succinct account of Thoreau's life, gathering up and arranging in their due order all the scattered records of him to be found in periodicals, as well as the information given by Messrs. Channing, Sanborn, and Page. (2) A fuller and more serious estimate of Thoreau's *doctrines* than any hitherto published, and a critique of his literary qualities. The book will consist of about ten or twelve chapters, the first two thirds of it being biographical and the remaining third critical. I shall aim throughout at *interpreting* rather than criticising in the ordinary sense, it being my belief that in the case of such a real man of genius as Thoreau it is the duty of the critic to accept him thankfully, and not to carp unduly at his limitations, though of course not shutting his eyes to them.

My name is not, like H. A. Page, a *nom de plume,* though I do not know that I can claim kinship with the Mr. Salt whom Charles Lamb has immortalized. There are a great many Salts in Staffordshire and Shropshire, and Shrewsbury is my native place.

Oddly enough, I find that my relatives at Shrewsbury knew Mr. Cholmondeley; he spoke to some of them about Thoreau, and gave them copies of his books. Some weeks ago Mr. Reginald Cholmondeley (who is still living) kindly promised to look up his brother's papers, in the hope of finding Thoreau's letters, and to allow me the use of them if they are still in existence.[1]

He has, however, been away from home lately, so there is necessarily a delay. I agree with you that Mr. Cholmondeley's high opinion of Thoreau is an important and valuable point, especially as he was (if I mistake not) the only Englishman who saw much of Thoreau.

Dr. Japp ("H. A. Page") is a correspondent of mine, but we have never met. He has very kindly given me some assistance in my preparation of materials for this volume. He told me of the medallion portrait which your son sent him, and which he had engraved for a magazine article on Thoreau.

Speaking of myself, I may add that I was an assistant master at Eton College until a few years ago, when I gave up teaching and took to literary work. An article of mine on Thoreau, which appeared in *Temple Bar* in 1886, was reprinted in the New York *Critic,*[2] and may possibly have met your eye.

I have published books on Shelley, James Thomson, &c., and it has always been one of my desires to write a good life of Thoreau. It will be my own fault if I do not do this now, for I have received a great deal of kind help from America.

I need not say that if you will let me print any other characteristic letters of Thoreau which you have in your possession it will be a great assistance to my book, and will put me under a great obligation to you. I would, of course, gladly pay the cost of having them copied, if copyists are to be found, for I could not think of asking you to do such laborious work; indeed, I feel ashamed to see how much you have already written on my account.

P.S. I am interested in what you say of William Howitt.

1. The letters were eventually given to F. B. Sanborn for editing. For modern texts of the letters, see Walter Harding and Carl Bode, eds., *The Correspondence of Henry David Thoreau* (New York: New York University Press, 1958).

2. H. S. Salt, "Henry D. Thoreau," *Temple Bar* 78 (1886):369–83. Reprinted in *Critic* 11 (November 26 and December 3, 1887):276–78, 289–91.

3. Daniel Ricketson to Henry Salt, December 9, 1889.

Since I wrote you I have remembered that a volume of Thoreau's letters not now in my possession, containing several to me, was published some years ago by Mr. Sanborn,[1] which, with others he used in his biography of Thoreau, must include about all of interest of mine. These volumes I think you informed me of having. Unless you can obtain somewhat from Mr. Cholmondeley or the poet Allingham I hardly know where you will look for new matter, and that you will be obliged to depend upon your essay on his character. On this point I can bear my own testimony, that without any formality he was remarkable in his uprightness and honesty, industrious and frugal, simple and not fastidious in his tastes, whether in food, dress, or address; an admirable conversationalist, and a good story-teller, not wanting in humor. His full blue eye, aquiline nose, and peculiar pursed lips, which even his mustache did not entirely conceal, added much to the effect of his descriptive powers. He was a man of rare courage, physically and intellectually. In the way of the former, he arrested two young fellows with horse and wagon on the lonely road leading to his hermitage at Walden pond, who were endeavoring to entrap a young woman on her way home, and took them to the village; whether they were brought to court I do not remember, and may not have given an exact account of the affair, but it is circumstantially correct.

Intellectually, his strong and manly mind was enriched by a classical education and extensive knowledge of history, ancient and modern, and English literature—himself a good versifier, if not true poet—whose poetic character is often seen in his prose works. There are few finer passages in any author than the following, which doubtless you will remember:—

"The morning wind forever blows, the poem of creation is uninterrupted, but few are the ears that hear it. Olympus is but the outside of the earth everywhere." (Walden, page 92.)

I will conclude by making a copy of lines written by me soon after his death, from a volume of pieces privately published twenty years ago, entitled "The Autumn Sheaf," three copies of which I sent to England,— one each to my honored old friends and correspondents, the late William Howitt, Rev. William Barnes, the Dorset poet, late Rector of Winterborne-came, near Dorchester, and Reginald Cholmondeley, Esq., Shrewsbury, Shrops. I mention these in case you may wish to see the humble production of my rustic Muse, now out of print and no spare copies.

P.S. There were ten letters to me published by Mr. S. I find in my package several more which I would willingly put into your hands with other matter were you here. Still, your essay would hardly be improved there-from.

1. Ricketson is obviously thinking of *Letters to Various Persons,* edited by Emerson.

4. Henry Salt to Daniel Ricketson, December 22, 1889.

I am very much obliged to you for your kindness in sending me the extracts from the "Autumn Sheaf,"[1] from which I shall be glad to quote in my book on Thoreau. I will ask Mr. Cholmondeley to send me his copy of the volume, which I am sure will be full of interest to me.

I thank you also for your testimony to Thoreau's genius, which has especial value as coming from one who knew him so intimately.

The published letters to which you allude are, I presume, those printed at Boston, and edited by Emerson, in 1865. I have quoted passages from more than one of those addressed to you: for of course I recognized who Thoreau's correspondent was by the initials and context. If an opportunity should offer of having copies made of the few unpublished letters now in your possession, I need not say that I should be very grateful for them, though I think I now have sufficient material to rely upon if no more comes to hand. Colonel Wentworth Higginson has very kindly sent me copies of some letters he received from Thoreau, and there is the chance of finding those addressed to Thomas Cholmondeley.

I had intended to write to the poet Allingham, when I was shocked to hear of his death, news of which has I suppose by this time reached you. Perhaps his widow may by and by be able to find the papers which you mentioned.

1. Daniel Ricketson, *The Autumn Sheaf: A Collection of Miscellaneous Poems* (New Bedford: Privately published, 1869).

5. H.G.O. Blake to S. A. Jones, March 4, 1890.

I thank you much for your note & the 'Glimpse of Thoreau'[1] wh. you sent me the other day. Your deepest ground of interest in him seems very much like my own, viz. his life & character rather than his merits as a writer or as an observer of nature. The John Brown episode on wh. you dwell considerably, brought out strongly the manly & heroic side of him, but I think he felt, as I [see?] you feel, that it was largely a disturbing & painful circumstance in his career. He interests me most when, as is usually the case, he is not aroused by indignation, & this is the way you present him in the latter part of your 'Glimpse.' All you say of that " 'invisible spiritual result' for wh. Thoreau hungered & thirsted & ceaselessly sought, tho, he had lost hound, horse, & turtle dove," interests me very deeply. It is that wh. has held me fast to him, as to no other, now for more than 40 yrs., or since I became acquainted with him. It may interest you to know, if you do not already, that those letters in the vol. of 'Letters' addressed 'Mr. B.' were addressed to me. You can judge frm. them what it was that mainly drew me to him. Here was a man who did not go back in time or far away for his revelation, but found it in his own soul, the souls of others where he could get at them, & in nature, here & now, & made it clear that spiritual, divine things were steadily the predominant consideration with him. The more such a faith is held as he held it, the nearer shall we come to the solution of all our problems, social & other. It is a deep pleasure to me to learn of any new person who takes such a view of Thoreau as you do, & if opportunity shd. offer, I shd. be glad to meet you.

1. Samuel Arthur Jones, "Thoreau: A Glimpse," *Unitarian,* January, February, and March, 1890.

6. Daniel Ricketson to S. A. Jones, March 8, 1890.

Your kind note and your "Glimpse" of our good friend Thoreau came duly to hand, and have been read with much interest. It (the Glimpse) will, I trust, prove a valuable contribution to the Thoreauana, which is still increasing. A new work, entitled, "Thoreau, a Study," by H. S. Salt, a London literateur, with whom I am in correspondence, is expected to appear in May next, from the press of the Bentleys. I think Mr. Salt would be glad to have a copy of your article, as he is very desirous of presenting his subject more fully and fairly before the British public than it has hitherto been done, although Dr. Japp, (H. E. [A.] Page) has already done it so well. They are both highly educated gentlemen, & in *rapport* in their work. I will add their addresses:
H. S. Salt, 38 Gloucester Road Regents Park, London.
Alex. H. Japp, L.L.D. The Limes, Elmstead Colchester, Eng.
Our dear philosopher was much displeased at the time with Lowell's article; and it was an act of retributive justice on your part, to animadvert upon it. I suppose the great public success of our late Minister to the Court of St. James, will *tide him over* this and any other errors that his pen has made; but I would say, as some one has said relative to Macaulay's injustice to the great and good William Penn, "he had better the next time he writes on the subject, '*mend his pen.*' "

I think we met at the School of Philosophy in Concord in the season of 1879, since which time our beloved and venerated Emerson and Alcott have "passed on."

7. H.G.O. Blake to S. A. Jones, March 10, 1890.

I shd. not feel quite satisfied to let your cordial & earnest letter go unanswered, tho. I have nothing important to say, unless it be to thank you, & to express again to you my deep pleasure at finding a new person whose interest in Thoreau is so genuine. If we were to know each other better, our education & habits, our temperaments, our finite & superficial natures might prevent our harmonizing, but it is a great satisfaction to feel in our relation to each other conscious of touching that infinite common element wh. binds all creatures together.

As to editing my letters to Thoreau, in connexion with his to me, it wd. be a task to wh. I could hardly bring myself. I formerly had the letters in my possession, tho. Mr. Sanborn has them now. I sent them to him when he was preparing the Life of Thoreau, & have never recalled them. If he shd. ever be preparing a new edition of the Life, he might have occasion to use them. Judging by my feelings generally when I read old letters of my own, it wd. be a somewhat mortifying occupation to read them even, still more to edit them.

Perhaps the best definite service I ever performed for my fellow-men was, like our best services generally, the unintended one of simply recognizing Thoreau at a time when he was yet so little recognized, giving him, as he said, 'an opportunity to live' making by my letters an occasion for his, wh. doubtless have already exerted & must hereafter exert so profound an influence upon individual souls here & there among men.

'I thank you again & again for attending to me; that it is to say, I am glad that you hear me, & that you also are glad' Letters, p. 92. Such sentences as this one, written 37 years ago, sing more gratefully & significantly to my soul now, than they did the day I received them.

If you print anything more abt. Thoreau, I trust you will send it to me, & if you wish to ask me any question abt. him at any time, I shall be ready to give you what light I can.

8. S. A. Jones to Daniel Ricketson, March 10, 1890.

I am deeply touched by your kind letter of the 8th inst.—"AEt. 76 yrs. 7 mos."—*that* went to my heart. To write so long a letter at your age to an utter stranger shows your loving loyalty to Thoreau's memory. I had received an equally genial letter from Mr. Blake, and now, dear Sir, my Thoreau collection is rich indeed. You and Mr. B. were his favorite correspondents, and your joint letters make me feel as if I had almost touched Thoreau's hand.

I have never had the pleasure of meeting you in the flesh, nor is it probable that I ever shall have. My life has not been given to making money. I have nine children and an aged father and mother dependent on me, and I just live and honestly pay my way. God gave me a love of books that has been to me more than wealth, and from the day that I began to *study* Thoreau I have been rich enough. That dear man's life and example has done for me far more than my dear old mother's Bible could do. I do not *comprehend* Thoreau, but I revere his memory and have learned from him the way of life. This is why I sent *you* a copy of my poor paper.

I had already sent one to Mr. Salt, and I will this day mail one to Dr. Japp—for whose address I am grateful indeed. My *pamphlet* (not the original paper) was "printed but not published," and as I have some copies (100) I will gladly mail one to any friend of Thoreau's whom you think would care for one: tho' I well know its only value is in the "Bibliography."

Both Lowell and Thoreau are judged by me from their written utterances. Lowell's genius and culture receive my unstinted admiration; but when it comes to *absolute sincerity* Lowell is to Thoreau as a "tallow dip" to an electric light. Lowell's nature is wholly inadequate to take in Thoreau. Lowell thought Thoreau was *posing* for effect. I am satisfied that Thoreau could not possibly *play* a part. I rank Christ Jesus, Socrates, and Thoreau as the sincerest souls that ever walked the earth. Alas! I have forgotten one—John Woolman, on whom God's peace sat as a garment. Just here please let me ask a question, namely: Thoreau is generally regarded as a sour, crabbed cynic. Now I never saw any photograph of Thoreau, and no steel engraving can give the eyes as a photograph does, yet I feel in my heart that, if one were absolutely an earnest and sincere man, *he* would find in Thoreau an infinite depth of tenderness. Not the demonstrative kind, but that which you *see* in the eyes and feel warming your own heart. Am I right? I do not want to burden your age with writing a letter, but a reply from you, if only a word, will do my heart good, and I ask it from pure love for Thoreau.

I thank you for the "Standard." Lamb taught me to love John Woolman, and Woolman to love the Quakers. And now, dear Sir, may the Source of All Good fill your eveningtide with peace ineffable.

9. Henry Salt to S. A. Jones, March 12, 1890.

Permit me to thank you heartily for your kindness in sending me your "Thoreau: a Glimpse", which I have read with much interest and agreement. It is pleasant to find that Lowell's unjust depreciation of Thoreau is being so successfully combated.

The Bibliography[1] will be of *very great* service to me, and I thankfully accept your generous offer concerning it, though I certainly shall not appropriate any part of it without due acknowledgment. I had been compiling a short Bibliography myself, but there are several works mentioned in yours which have hitherto been unknown to me, while on the other hand I note a few omissions on your part, such as Higginson's "Short Studies of American Authors", Alger's "Solitudes of Nature and of Man", Curtis' "Homes of American Authors", &c.[2] With the aid of your compilation I hope to make a full and correct list, which I certainly could not have otherwise done.

It is encouraging to me to hear my Life of Thoreau may be of service at the Michigan University. My object is to collect all the various threads of information respecting Thoreau's life, character, and doctrines, and to present them in a more compact and lucid form than has been done in previous memoirs. I have myself long felt the need of some such volume, to set Thoreau in a true light before the public, and other students of his writings seem to have felt the same. I have received much kind help from American correspondents, and it will be my own fault if I am not successful.

The book is to be published by Messrs. Bentley & Son, but I am not quite sure whether it will appear in the spring or autumn. Of this however I will notify you later, and if you will allow me to send you a copy it will give me much pleasure.

1. A bibliography was attached to "Thoreau: A Glimpse." Salt acknowledged use of the bibliography in the prefatory note to *The Life of Henry David Thoreau* (London: Bentley, 1890).

2. Salt did add these three studies to the bibliography which concludes his biography.

10. Daniel Ricketson to S. A. Jones, March 12, 1890.

Your warm-hearted letter of the 10th inst. has just come to hand, and been read with much interest and reciprocal feelings. The characteristics you name, I have heard applied to our dear philosopher, many years ago, but they have so long been buried in the high estimation and praise he has received at home and abroad, that I was almost surprised at the appearance of their ghost, which I thought had been effectually laid long ago. While Thoreau had no one of the characters mentioned, he was wisely careful not to have his friends expect too much intimacy, and it was my good fortune to receive more from him than he had given me reason to expect. There was a dignity in his composition, that commanded respect, and a genuine benevolence and hospitality in his companionship, that ever inspired confidence in his sincerity.

The best likeness of him was an ambrotype I had taken on his last visit to me in 1861, the year before his death—there were two copies, one of which I sent to his sister Sophia soon after his decease, and the other is in the possession of my son Walton, who with his sister Anna, both unmarried, have resided together since their mother's death in 1877, mostly in Concord, Mass.

The fullness and tenderness of his (Thoreau's) eyes are largely wanting in the engraving made from it in Sanborn's Memoir. A number of his best and most characteristic letters of friendship to me have never been published—they were omitted by Emerson, and Sanborn. These did far more justice to the true man than one or more of those they selected. I conclude such to be the case in those to Mr. Blake, of whom Thoreau always spoke in terms of much esteem. But the state of my health just now, (as I am somewhat as sailors say, "under the weather,") reminds me that I must not enlarge further, although I have a great deal I could say were you at my side.

P.S. I think Mr. Salt will have some new & interesting matter in his "Study of Thoreau."

11. Henry Salt to S. A. Jones, April 12, 1890.

I have received your kind letter and the two books you were good enough to send me, for all of which please accept my hearty thanks. I am interested in Mr. Hubert's "Liberty and Living",[1] both for its references to Thoreau, and also for its treatment of a very important social subject. I trust the whole question of Simplification of Life will come to be more and more studied and understood, for I am sure the problem of human happiness will never be fully solved without it. I am sending you herewith an essay by Edward Carpenter—our English Thoreau—with whose writings I am sure you would largely sympathise, though he is at present only known to a comparatively small circle of friends and admirers. I owe much myself to his teaching, for it was through him that I first became acquainted wtih *Walden,* and furthermore was induced to give up my educational work at Eton College, where I was an assistant-master from 1875 to 1885, and adopt a simpler and more independent style of life. Carpenter is a friend of Walt Whitman's, and has been strongly influenced both by him and by Thoreau. If you would care to see more of his books, it would be a pleasure to me to send you his volume of Essays.

I am much gratified and encouraged by the kind things you say about my Thoreau article and the likelihood of the book being of service to American students. Is Mr. Hosmer still living?[2] Had I known that he was, I should have liked to ask him for some reminiscences or impressions of Thoreau, similar to those given me by Mr. Blake and Mr. Ricketson; but the greater part of the book is already in print, so it would not now be worth while to trouble him.

As to the *Letters,* it would, I think, have been a very good thing to issue an English Edition, supposing a publisher could be found willing to undertake it; but I understand from Mr. Sanborn that *he* proposes to issue a second volume at no distant period, which would presumably include the letters to which you refer, and would give prominence to the more *domestic* side of Thoreau's character. This being so, I could hardly offer to step in between him and his proposal, even if the manuscripts were not actually in his hands. I could of course reprint the *Letters* of 1865, but this would be of little value if the others are shortly forthcoming. I should think Mr. Sanborn would be willing to give the letters entire, if strong representations were made to him on this point. I agree with you as to the mistake made by Emerson in his capacity of Editor to Thoreau's works; intimate though he was with him, I am sure he only partly understood his true greatness. I am convinced that Thoreau, in the *highest* sense, was quite as great and original as Emerson, though it will probably be a century or two before the world realises it![3]

I do not think there is any great probability of my "Life of Thoreau" being issued before the autumn, as the printing progresses but slowly, and publishers are averse to sending out their books in the summer months. I have been corresponding with Mr. Bentley lately about a frontispiece portrait, and we have decided to reproduce that prefixed to the original edition of *Excursions.* I think this will be more interesting and characteristic than the bearded portrait, for the beard seems to me to hide the distinctive expression of the earlier likeness.

I may mention, by the bye, that Mr. Sanborn sent me a few extracts from Thoreau's unpublished letters which I have included in my book; I obtained from Mr. Ricketson[4] one complete letter of great interest, in which Thoreau describes his father's death. Colonel Higginson also sent me two or three letters, one of them containing a full account of the provisions, &c, carried by Thoreau on his camping-out excursions. I have not yet been successful in getting hold of his letters to Mr. Cholmondeley, though there is still some chance of their turning up, as they can hardly have been destroyed. But Mr. Cholmondeley's brother is now an elderly man, and I suppose the trouble of overhauling old papers is considerable.

The bibliography will, I feel sure, be of considerable use to students of Thoreau, and I have to thank *you* for enabling me to give anything like a complete one.

[P.S.] You may be interested to hear that an Edinburgh publisher, David Douglas,[5] has in preparation a small vol. of selections from Thoreau. I do not know who is editing it. Mr. Blake is preparing a similar work.[6] So I trust we shall have a "boom" in Thoreau before long!

1. Philip G. Hubert's *Liberty and a Living* (New York: G. P. Putnam's Sons, 1889), was a practical book on simplification of life. Salt wrote *Living and Liberty.*

2. Salt is apparently referring to Horace Hosmer, who had been a student of John and Henry Thoreau.

3. In a journal entry dated 24 March 1887, in a notebook labelled "Comments occasioned by some of the Books read nights in 1887," Dr. Jones expressed dissatisfaction with Emerson's editing of Thoreau's letters in *Letters to Various Persons* (1865), for Emerson omitted letters which did not indicate that Thoreau was a stoic. Dr. Jones correctly perceived that a new edition of Thoreau's correspondence was needed.

4. Salt is referring to Thoreau's letter to Ricketson, dated 12 February 1859 and reproduced in *The Life of Henry David Thoreau* (1890), pp. 190–92.

5. This edition apparently did not appear.

6. H.G.O. Blake edited *Thoreau's Thoughts* (Boston and New York: Houghton, Mifflin, 1890). Dr. Jones contributed a Thoreau bibliography.

12. H.G.O. Blake to S. A. Jones, May 9, 1890.

Very likely I informed you that I am abt. to publish a small pocket vol. of selections frm. Thoreau's printed works. It has been suggested to me by a correspondent that a bibliography of Thoreau shd. be printed with this. I at once thought of yours & wrote to Houghton, Mifflin & Co. on the subject. I have since sent them your pamphlet with the bibliography for examination, & this morning they have returned it with the note wh. I will enclose to you. It had not occurred to me that there might [be] some charge for the use of your work, till this was suggested by something they wrote. My own compensation will probably be so small that I am not ready to offer anything, but your work is so far done that I am confident you will be ready to contribute it to the cause. If so, perhaps you wd. better confer directly with Houghton, Mifflin & Co. on the subject, & forward them a copy of the bibliography with any additions or corrections you may see fit to make. But will you please inform me what course you will pursue, & return the enclosed note.

Houghton, Mifflin & Co. to H.G.O. Blake, May 8, 1890.[1]

We have your favor of 5th inst. together with Dr. Jones's little monograph. We might not have thought it expedient to print such a Bibliography at the end of the book if we had been called upon to secure its preparation, but if Dr. Jones is willing generously to allow us to copy what he has already done, we should be glad to add to the interest of your book, and should expect to make proper acknowledgment by giving Dr. Jones's name as the author of the bibliography.

Inasmuch as you have had the correspondence with the author, and the courtesy is especially shown to you as the compiler of the book, we think it best to accept your kind offer and to leave you to obtain Dr. Jones's consent and a copy for the printer's use.

We would call your attention to the fact that though Dr. Jones records four of Thoreau's contributions to the Atlantic he omits mention of eight others. If we have the copy, we will examine it with reference to any other possible omissions, and confer with the author before printing.

1. This copy of a letter from the Boston office of Houghton, Mifflin & Co. was signed S.

13. H.G.O. Blake to S. A. Jones, May 14, 1890.

Thank you very much for complying with my request, as I was confident you wd. do. But I am sorry to have pained you. As I said before, in substance, I had not even dreamed, there might be any charge till it was suggested by a note frm. H. M. & Co. After that suggestion, I felt it necessary to speak of the matter. —I was sorry also that you shd. think your letters wearied me, if that is what you meant. On the contrary they gave me a great deal of pleasure. But I am so slow & difficult a writer myself, & accomplish so little generally in what I undertake, that I fear I shd. not answer your letters at all adequately except at pretty long intervals. Please write, if you are at any time, moved to do so, & I will do the best I can, in reply.

[P.S.] If you visit Concord in July, please come & see me, if you can make it convenient.

14. H.G.O. Blake to S. A. Jones, May 26, 1890.

I shd. be ready to correct the proofs of your bibliography, so far as errors of the press are concerned, but shd. hardly feel free to strike out anything you may have seen fit to write. At the same time, I am very desirous that the book shd. be small, easily portable, adapted to the pocket, in short, a genuine 'vade mecum.'

It has occurred to me that, perhaps, you might like to rewrite & add to your 'Glimpse', for the public at large, expressing yourself as fully & forcibly as you can abt. Thoreau. Your view of his untiring devotion to & communion with Nature, including the calm contentment of animal life, as being to him a revelation of the Divine, close at hand, is deeply interesting to me & very important to be said. It lies at the very core of my admiration for Thoreau, as you may gather from my brief introductions to the volumes I have edited. I do not know that any other writer has laid the same emphasis on this point that you have. My personal acquaintance & intercourse with Thoreau, & my recollections of him, do not diminish my admiration for him in this respect. He was the same man in his life & in his books. No other human being living or dead has given me so deep a sense of the reality & value of spiritual things as he. Here was a man pervaded by religion through & through, but with very little of the language of religion, so that he could, as he says, fully declare himself on that subject, without its being known to an audience by his language what he was abt. Now you seem to take a very similar view of him. If you wd. set yourself to bringing it out more fully, what a service you might render! Shd. you be ready to do so, it wd. be proper that your bibliography shd. be attached to your own book, & not to my selections, so that you shd. have all the advantage pecuniary & other, that it might bring. I do not think it is too late to make this change. Houghton, Mifflin & Co. have sent me no definite word as to the time of printing. Perhaps they wd. enter into the scheme I have suggested, & themselves publish your essay. Still, shd. you prefer the other arrangement, of course I shall be glad of your bibliography, trusting that even with your additions, it will not make the book too large.

15. Henry Salt to S. A. Jones, June 30, 1890.

I have to thank you for your two letters, full of kind thoughts and friendly encouragement which I assure you I value very highly.

And first, about Thoreau. It is very kind of you to send me the proof of your new bibliography, which I shall read with much interest. But I am sorry to say it will be too late to enable me to make additions to mine, as the *Life* is already printed off, "with all its imperfections on its head"—like Hamlet's father! It strikes me, however, that I may still be able to help *you*, if I chance to have hit upon any mentions of Thoreau which may not have caught your attention; I therefore enclose one of the rough proofs of my own bibliography, or rather of that part of it in which there is likely to be any divergence. There are a good many things in it which are not included in your earlier bibliography, but I daresay you have filled up many of them ere now. Of course both your compilation and mine will very soon be out-of-date, as there will doubtless be a crop of Thoreau articles when these books make their appearance.

My book will be published by Bentley in the autumn. I am also editing (I forget whether I told you this) a volume of selected Essays from the "Anti-Slavery & Reform Papers" for Messrs. Sonnenschein's *Social Science Series* of half-crown volumes. The Essays included are "Civil Disobedience", "Plea for John Brown", "Last Days of John Brown", "Paradise (to be) Regained", and "Life without Principle"—I should have liked to include *all* the essays, but this could not be managed; I hope, however, the volume may serve to create more interest in Thoreau; and as it will be issued at the same time as the *Life,* the two books will help one another. Messrs. Sonnenschein think of following it up with another volume of "Excursions", if it is fairly successful. I may add that my introductory note, or part of it, to the "Anti-Slavery" reprint, is to appear in magazine form in the August number of *Lippincott* (English Edition).[1]

So you see there is to be quite a carnival of Thoreauism this autumn, which will be swelled still further by Mr. Blake's volume of selections, and possibly by yet another which an Edinburgh publisher has in preparation! It should be a worthy answer to the malignant criticism of Lowell and his followers.

As to the *Letters,* you will, I am sure, understand my position. Mr. Sanborn has been exceedingly courteous and kind to me in helping me with the *Life,* and I would not on any account do anything which could be construed into a slight on him. He has, I rather think, possession of the bulk of these letters, and may (justly, perhaps) consider himself the best person to edit them. *Prima facie* it would certainly appear desirable that they should be edited by someone on the *spot;* and I should be well content to help by trying to secure the letters, which I really believe are still extant in England, addressed by Thoreau to his English friend Thomas Cholmondeley. I had quite hoped to get them for my own book, but, owing to the illness and apparent dilatoriness of Mr. C's surviving brother, I was so far disappointed. On the whole, probably Mr. Blake will do wisely to wait and see my "Life of Thoreau" before coming to any decision; but you may feel sure that I shall be glad to help in any part, great or small, which is likely to be of service to Thoreau's memory.

I may here remark that I do not of course regard my "Life of Thoreau" as in any sense a full or *final* biography. I only aim at doing what really ought to have been done twenty years ago, viz—giving a clear and succinct account of the man and his writings, and gathering together all the fragmentary records of him. I hope it may form a stepping-stone to a final *Life,* which must be written on the spot, and by someone who has full use of all the manuscript diaries and letters.

And now I must thank you still further for your kindness in sending me the photographs in the charge of Dr. Carrow. It will be a great pleasure to me to see Dr. Carrow, and have some talk about Thoreau, and American friends, and I need not tell how much interested I shall be in the photographs. The reproduction of the earlier portrait has been done very nicely by Messrs. Bentley's artist, and will, I think, form a good frontispiece to my volume; but of course it would have been more satisfactory if we could have had *two* portraits of Thoreau, one before he wore the beard, and one after. This however was more than the publishers were prepared to do, as they are not at all certain of the pecuniary success of the volume. I confess I do not much care for the portrait prefixed to Mr. Sanborn's book;[2] the beard seems to hide the distinctive traits of Thoreau's features. But I must not express an opinion until I have seen your photograph, which is perhaps a different one.

Your kind suggestion about a possible opening for me at Harvard University makes me feel certain that I should at any rate find one good friend in America, were I to cross the Atlantic! But for various reasons it would be impossible for me to think of leaving this country—one alone would be imperative, that my wife and I have both relatives whom we could not leave at present. Otherwise I am not specially bound to England *as* England, and I have much faith in the greatness and greatheartedness of the American people, in spite of the truth of Thoreau's strictures. However I hope that you and I may manage to meet some day. Do you ever come on a visit to England?

I am glad to hear you feel an interest in Edward Carpenter's writings, and I will ask Messrs. Sonnenschein, his publishers, to forward his two volumes of essays to the address you name, in the most convenient way. Please accept them from me; and if you would afterwards like to see his "Towards Democracy", a strange, original sort of poem, in Whitmanese metre, that could follow later. He is a most remarkable personality, with much of the Thoreau element in him, and much too of Whitman. He was formerly curate to the great broad-churchman, Frederick Denison Maurice, at Cambridge; but under the stress of new convictions, gave up his College Fellowship, left the Church, and is now a Socialist and advocate of various reforms, especially of a simplification of life which is very like that of Thoreau.

It seems to me that the hope of society lies in finding the balance between the just claims of socialism, which certainly will be heard more and more loudly each year, and the equally just claims of an intellectual (not commercial) individualism, such as that which Thoreau preached so finely. The true individualism, as I understand it, consists not in the freedom to cheat one's neighbour, but in the freedom to develop one's own intellect. At present our so-called "freedom" is mostly of the former kind.

I was particularly glad to hear that my little book on Shelley had been of interest to you. Believe me that when Shelley is rightly understood (as he cannot be under our existing system of morality which is really *im*-morality), he will be recognised as one of the truly great characters of this century—the poet without an equal since Shakespeare, and one of the most clear-sighted prophets of social reform. Unlike as he is to Thoreau in many ways, they are alike in this, that both were champions of the great humanitarian movement which will be *the* religion of the future, and both have that unspeakable tenderness which is for ever misunderstood by the mere critic, but endears them beyond all expression to those who are in sympathy.

[P.S.] You will see that I have put Theodore Watts's name to two *Athenaeum* articles in 1877 and 1882 respectively.[3] I have his authority for this. He professes to be a great admirer of Thoreau, from the point of view of a lover of Nature, and he tells me he introduced Thoreau's works to George Borrow, who greatly relished them.

You mention Dr. Japp. I have corresponded with him at times, but have never met him personally, some obstacle having always unfortunately intervened when we had hoped to meet. I like the *tone* of his book on Thoreau, though the book itself is scarcely satisfactory. I have met Mr. Dircks, and know his Prefaces on Thoreau, but must confess I don't admire them—at the risk of appearing like a workman who abuses his predecessors! The Essays I do greatly admire are those by John Weiss, in the *Christian Examiner,* and by John Burroughs in the *Century;* also Higginson's chapter, in his *Short Studies.*

1. Salt's essay "Anti-Slavery and Reform Papers" appeared in the English edition of *Lippincott's Magazine,* August 1890, pp. 277–83.
2. Sanborn used the ambrotype of Thoreau made in 1861 by E. S. Dunshee in New Bedford.
3. [Theodore Watts], "Review of Page's *Thoreau, His Life and Aims,*" *Athenaeum,* November 3, 1877, 562–64. "Review of Early Spring in Massachusetts and Sanborn's Life of Thoreau," *Athenaeum* 2 (October 28, 1882):558–60.

16. S. A. Jones to A. W. Hosmer, July 15, 1890.

Returning from a brief sojourn in the woods, I find your tasteful "Thoreau Souvenir"[1] waiting on my desk. Why is it that a "Thank you!" always seems so tame on such an occasion? Well, we must imagine the light in the eye, and the fervor in the voice, and then the written thanks are all that we need.

I hope to leave here on the 10th of August for Concord: a pilgrimage that I shall never forget.

I shall come with the Michigan deputation of the G.A.R.,[2] and shall thus see Boston under unusually favorable auspices; yet, could I see only one of these places, Boston would not be the one.

I am sorry you went to the trouble of writing to Mr. Sanborn, because it is more than likely that Messrs. Houghton, Mifflin & Co. will consult him on his return.[3] At the same time, I understand and appreciate the kindness that prompted you.

It is singular that Mr. Sanborn should write to you as he did, when he himself says, in his life of Thoreau that Mr. Channing edited The Maine Woods.[4]

However, we have the book—a good, solid fact: let that suffice. . . .

1. Hosmer's "Thoreau Souvenir" was a selection of his Concord photographs, in miniature, mounted on board.

2. Dr. Jones served in the Union Army from September 17, 1862, when he was commissioned first assistant surgeon of the Twenty-second Regiment of New Jersey Volunteers, to June 25, 1863, when he was discharged for reasons of illness. Dr. Jones's commission and discharge are in the Jones collection.

3. Hosmer may have written Sanborn concerning the publication of an American edition of Salt's 1890 biography of Thoreau. It is clear that Dr. Jones was at this time attempting to arrange for an American edition, for he discussed the possibility with Sanborn. See Dr. Jones's letter to H.G.O. Blake of August 9, 1891 (letter 75).

4. Sanborn attributed the editing of *The Maine Woods* to W. E. Channing in his *Henry D. Thoreau* (Boston: Houghton, Mifflin & Co., 1882), p. 248.

17. Henry Salt to S. A. Jones, August 11, 1890.

How can I thank you sufficiently for the photographs which I found awaiting me on my return to London yesterday? It was indeed very good of you to take all this trouble on my behalf, and no present that I have received for years past has given me so much pleasure. The photos all arrived in excellent condition, and are altogether charming; the one which interests me most, I think, where all interests me so much, is that of the Walden furniture—I had no idea that it was still possible to see the likeness of those immortal chairs and table and desk! The photo. of Thoreau himself is very striking and pathetic. I told you, I fancy, that the one engraved for my book is the earlier portrait, without the beard; but I only wish I could have persuaded the publishers to have this also.[1]

Since I last wrote to you, I have had a pleasant surprise in meeting Mr. and Mrs. Sanborn in London, where they had come on a short visit. I had two or three long talks with Mr. S. about Thoreau, and heard much that interested me greatly. I liked both Mr. and Mrs. Sanborn very much, and I was pleased to find that Mr. S. was of the same mind as you and I are regarding the mistake made in suppressing so much of Thoreau's correspondence. I feel sure that a *full* edition of the letters will be published when Mr. S. takes it in hand, so I think we may feel less anxiety now on that point.

As to your kind idea of writing a notice of my book for the *Atlantic Monthly,* I should of course be extremely glad if it could be carried out. But, strange to say, I do not yet know what American publishers are cooperating with Messrs. Bentley in the issue of the book. I am at the present time awaiting a long-delayed answer from Bentley on this subject (publishers are so terribly slow to take authors into their confidence!), as Mr. Sanborn asked me the question some weeks back—I doubt if Bentley would advance sheets direct from *his* publishing office, but it might perhaps be done by Messrs. Scribner, or whoever publish it in America. Anyway, I will find out about it as soon as I can, and let you have a line of information.

I am truly glad to hear you are interested and impressed by Edward Carpenter's books, and I wish now I had sent you "Towards Democracy" as well, but I did not like at first to do anything which might seem like "rushing" them on you. He is of course in advance on Thoreau, in the sense that he treats of a more complex social problem which Thoreau could know little of, though he has not Thoreau's tremendous directness and force. I am going up to Derbyshire the day after tomorrow, to spend a week with Carpenter on the farm where he "does his simplification of life", as a lady visitor once naïvely expressed it, and I shall be glad to be able to tell him of your kindness in spreading his doctrines across the Atlantic. I have lately been writing a short article on his works, of which I will send you a copy, if I succeed in getting any editor to accept it—which is by no means certain, such are the prejudices which hedge round all these subjects! Talking of Carpenter and Thoreau reminds me of another kindred writer—Richard Jefferies. I wonder if you know his "Story of my Heart"; it is a rare work of genius, rare now even in the bibliopolist sense, as the first Edition, which was for years in the publishers' hands (like the *Week*), is now exhausted. I gave a copy which I picked up in a second-hand shop to Edward Carpenter, and he was immensely struck by it. You will be able to tell me whether Jefferies' fame has gone far in America. . . .

1. For an excellent discussion of the photographs of Thoreau, see Francis H. Allen, *A Bibliography of Henry David Thoreau* (Boston and New York: Houghton, Mifflin Company, 1908), pp. xiii–xviii.

18. S. A. Jones to A. W. Hosmer, August 31, 1890.
* * *

When I reached home I was rushed into work at once, as an epidemic of dysentery is raging and many were waiting for me. Yesterday I could not find a moment to write a line to anyone. I think it will be at least three weeks before there will be much change, if I may judge by the experience of former seasons.

I am greatly obliged for your kind promptness in sending the Pillsbury letter[1] so soon. All these bits of evidence will be of great value to me in my final summing-up. Your good-hearted librarian was in error when she told me that I could buy a copy of the Boston Daily Advertiser for Feb'y 14th, 1883, and I shall be obliged to have that paper of Miss Folsom's[2] copied for me. If you will hire it done for me you will add yet another to my countless obligations. Beg the copyist to do the work carefully and to omit not a word or a point. . . .

1. The abolitionist and orator Parker Pillsbury (1809–1898) had written Hosmer in response to inquiries about the role of Thoreau's Walden house in the

Underground Railroad: "As to the Walden Cottage ever being in any sense, an *underground Rail way Depot*. I must doubt it." Pillsbury thought that abolitionist lecturers, including Douglass, "would have called no doubt to see Thoreau at his Walden cottage but no flying slave would ever have sought him there nor do I think Col. Whiting, or Mrs. Brooks, or Mr. & Mrs. Bigelow would ever have taken them there for concealment." See Parker Pillsbury to Alfred W. Hosmer, August 27, 1890 (Hosmer Collection).

2. "Henry Thoreau's Mother," signed E.M.F., appeared first in the *Boston Daily Advertiser*, February 14, 1883. It was reprinted in *Concord Freeman*, February 23, 1883. The article defends Cynthia Thoreau against Sanborn's characterization of her in his 1882 biography.

19. H.G.O. Blake to S. A. Jones, September 4, 1890.

I found your package here on my return frm. a short excursion, & during the few days between that excursion & another, occupied myself considerably with copying what I wished to, frm. my vol. into the one you sent. It did not seem worth while to be sending books backwards & forwards much over such a long distance; besides I do not care for another copy of the earlier edition. Some of the errata I found corrected in the vol. you sent, wh. of course saved some copying. I have indicated such corrections by a c or cd. in the vol. I send.

I am glad you enjoyed your Concord visit so much, & trust I shall some time see your account of it, & its suggestions.

On my last return to Worcester, I found awaiting me the first proofs of the Selections, so, I suppose they will be published before very long.

While stopping in Boston a few days ago, I took up at the Corner Bookstore, a book wh. I suppose is new, Talks with Emerson, by a Mr. Woodbury. Some things in it said abt. Thoreau interested me exceedingly. I was hardly aware how highly E. estimated him. For instance he says substantially, He will have an increasing number of readers, & more deserves to be read than any other American. Again He better deserves to be translated than Epictetus or Marcus Antonius [Aurelius]. These are very nearly the words, tho perhaps not precisely. No doubt you will see the book soon, if you have not done so already.

It seems as if I might enjoy very much a meeting of the friends of Thoreau, such as you refer to, & hope you may succeed in bringing it about.

20. S. A. Jones to A. W. Hosmer, September 16, 1890.

* * *

The "Glimpse" was never for sale by me, and you are welcome to copies as long as they last: 18 being the residuum! Don't hesitate to let me know when you have any use for them. I do not like the fact that my attitude towards Emerson is misunderstood;[1] but it was my business to speak of and for Thoreau, and on that occasion I had no use for kid gloves.

I wish I lived in Concord if it were only to stir up some of the little gods there resident. A skillful use of a darning needle would do some of them real service . . . to the detriment of your pine-flavored atmosphere. . . .

1. Any misunderstanding in Concord about Dr. Jones's attitude toward Emerson probably arose from his attack upon Lowell in the *Glimpse:* "It seems to me as if Lowell gets on all fours whenever he mentions Emerson; he always writes of him as if all the gods of Olympus had put on clean linen when Emerson was moulded—an admiration that dwindles into adulation." Such exaggerated respect for Emerson pained Dr. Jones particularly, for he early perceived that Thoreau's reputation had suffered greatly at the hands of those, such as Lowell, who relegated Thoreau to the position of Emerson's imitator.

21. S. A. Jones to Henry Salt, September 16, 1890 [fragment].

On my return I found a letter of yours awaiting me, and today I received one post-marked 5th of September. I have been so driven with imperative work since getting home that some of Thoreau's "loafing" is to [be] envied. I am glad that the leaves reached you unbroken. They grew just in front of where his chimney stood, and are the only approach to a memento that the nearly-filled cellar afforded. As I sat there, oh, how I wished that you were beside me! It is by far the most delightful visit of my life, and it keeps coming back to me in flashes of radiance just like sun-bursts through rifts in the clouds. I had such a strange feeling when talking with men and women who had known Thoreau. Especially was this the case during an interview with a sun-browned farmer who had attended the school kept by John and Henry Thoreau.[1] He said that John was beloved, while, as a teacher, Henry "was merciless." John entered into the sports of the school children, while Henry kept aloof. By "merciless" he meant a precise exactingness, such as Burroughs means when he says: "He was always making the highest demands upon himself and upon others." It was a Thoreauly Thoreauness (I like to spell it in that manner) that would best equip him from whom it was exacted for thoroughly playing his part in life. Yet this witness said of Henry, with a quiet emphasis, "He had no enemies!" The Nature-love that was so intense in Henry was, in this old scholar's opinion originated by John and taken up by Henry as one architect might piously carry out the unfinished design of a beloved fellow-craftsman. And I was glad to be assured that this Nature-love was a direct transmission from the Thoreau father and mother to the children. The truth is Mr. Sanborn has done great injustice to the parents of Thoreau in his Life. They were poor; but they were moulded from an unusually fine clay. No matter how plain and poor the meal the gods sent, it was always served with a stately grace, the remembrance of which shone brightly in this old man's memory after the lapse of more than half a century. Said he to me, as old-time recollections swept over him, "Why, they (the father and mother) were twenty years ahead of the times!" Evidently, far very far from "common" people. Henry "took after" the mother, and heredity is a much more important factor in Thoreau's individuality than Mr. Sanborn's book would lead the reader to conclude. In a word, the Thoreau family bear a post mortem examination with as little loss as when a noble metal is tried by fire. I pushed my researches that I even found and talked with. . . . Whom do you think? None other than the very jailor who locked him up for not paying his taxes. I do wish you could see this worthy. You know Thoreau calls him "a good-natured fellow." Well, he veritably is "as mild a mannered man as ever cut a throat" or turned the key upon a fellow man whom Fortune had eclipsed. When I saw this ci devant "turnkey", a large diamond stud sparkled on his shirt front!!

Where on earth save in AMERICA could you duplicate that spectacle!???? I got from him a bit of history that aptly illustrates the happy-go-lucky, free- and easiness that is also peculiarly American. Here it is: after he had locked up his prisoners for the night, a little girl came to his door and rapped. (He resided in a part of the jail, as is customary here.) On opening the door, she said "Here is the money that Mr. Thoreau owes," putting the amount in his hand. (It was six shillings sterling.) How do you suppose I felt when that jailor went on to say, with a chuckle, "I was n't goin' to unlock after I'd locked up, so I kept him in all night and turned him out after breakfast." Did you ever hear the equal of that in all your life! I asked him particularly who the little girl was. He said he did not know. I think Miss Ellen Emerson could tell if she only would.[2]

1. Dr. Jones met Horace Hosmer (1830–1894), a distant cousin of Alfred Hosmer, during his trip to Concord in 1890. Horace Hosmer had been a student in the Concord Academy when it was taught by John and Henry Thoreau, and had boarded in the Thoreau home. During their meeting in Acton, Hosmer supplied Dr. Jones with information about the Academy and defended John Thoreau Sr. and Cynthia Thoreau against Sanborn's uncomplimentary treatment. (See Sanborn's *Henry D. Thoreau,* pp. 24–27). Later Horace Hosmer wrote more than thirty letters to Dr. Jones; these have been edited by George Hendrick and published by the University of Illinois Press under the title *Remembrances of Concord and the Thoreaus* (1977).
2. This fragment is in the Jones collection.

22. A. W. Hosmer to S. A. Jones, September 17, 1890.

I found a genuine "John Thoreau & Son" Pencil, that was given to a lady in town, by Sophia Thoreau. This lady says she has a number of their make, but not stamped.

Will you please accept it from me—there are only four or five of them left. I wish you might have seen this lady, as she lived neighbor to the Thoreaus for some time.

23. Henry Salt to S. A. Jones, [September 1890].

* * *

What an interesting time you have been spending at Concord—it makes me envy you for being that side of the Atlantic! I trust you will work up your discoveries into an essay, and publish it for the benefit of all who love Thoreau.

I am glad you had a talk with Mr. Sanborn. It is a wonderful thing to converse with someone who was really intimate with Thoreau, for there are always a lot of things to be learnt from such a person which do not get into books. I am afraid to think how many questions I asked Mr. Sanborn during our two or three interviews, and I have since remembered as many more which I omitted to ask him! . . .

I believe my *Thoreau* will be issued on, or about, Oct. 21st. Bentley has, after all, only printed a small edition of the book, but this may possibly be followed by a cheaper edition, if it goes off pretty well. I am not yet sure whether there will be a simultaneous American Edition, but the matter is in Mr. Sanborn's hands and I am expecting shortly to hear from him. He kindly offered, when I saw him, to try to arrange with Messrs. Houghton & Mifflin, or some Boston publishers, but at that time I was under the impression that Bentley had already arranged with Messrs. Scribner. I afterwards discovered that B. had done nothing; so had to write in haste to Mr. Sanborn and leave it all to him.

Whatever is finally arranged, I will take care that you are informed, and that a copy of the book is sent to you.

[P.S.] Ed Carpenter was much interested in the Thoreau photos which you so kindly sent me. He said the portrait of Thoreau (the bearded one) helped him to understand his character better than any he had seen.

24. S. A. Jones to A. W. Hosmer, September 23, 1890.

I wish words could convey feelings: as it is they are wholly inadequate. If you could have seen me with that Thoreau pencil in my hand you would have realized the influence of matter over mind. They generally put it "mind over matter," you know, but in this case it was reversed.

"John Thoreau & Son, Concord, Mass." Why, it seemed almost as if I should hear the old gentleman's voice telling me the price of his pencils! And your gift is all the dearer in the fact that Sophia's own hand has touched the very pencil which is now in mine. I am carried back to those six graves and I know that they are sleeping there; otherwise, this pencil is so real that I could easily imagine the quiet father still at work and the son feasting his soul at Conantum or the Cliffs. . . .

25. H.G.O. Blake to S. A. Jones, October 4, 1890.

I shd. have written before to thank you for the books you sent me, had I not been delayed abt. this photograph wh. I wished to give to you at the same time. It is printed frm. a negative taken not long ago frm. my daguerreotype wh. I lent to a friend here for that purpose. This friend gave me a copy so satisfactory, that I wished to send you one like it. My copy is a little more shaded, wh. circumstance to my eye makes a somewhat more attractive picture. But as the photographer says, the shading is apt to take something frm. the expression of the face, I feel that very likely you wd. prefer this one. Shd. you wish for any more copies, you can get them for 25 cts. a piece by addressing the photographer.

I have as yet only glanced at the books you sent, but mean to taste of them before long.

You speak of Thoreau's lecture on beans here. I remember hearing it. It was, I suppose, substantially the same as the chapter on beans in Walden, & the ms. of Walden, (very likely the whole of it,) is in my possession.

I do not know of the Charles Parker Rice you mention, tho. I remember indistinctly a Rice that may have been Thoreau's classmate. I shd. like very well a copy of the letter you mention, if it will not trouble you too much to make one. But wait till it is perfectly convenient.

I suggested to Houghton, Mifflin & Co. (and they assented) that they shd. send the proofs of your part of the book to me first, & I wd. forward them to you, because I remember you wished me to see them, & I desired you to have the final revision. The proofs are sent rather slowly, & yours have not come yet.

26. S. A. Jones to A. W. Hosmer, October 6, 1890.

I am glad that the small volumes fit the pocket and I envy you the rare pleasure of reading Walden "on the spot". That visit of mine has spoiled me for this life; that is if I have to live it in this no-god no-devil of a Michigan. There is an indescribable difference in the atmosphere of Concord and Ann Arbor. I feel it but cannot define it. It impresses me as a restlessness without cause; that is I feel a quietude in Concord that I do not enjoy now that I am again at work: and it is not because I am averse to Work. It may be that your atmosphere is denser and therefore better for an old "bloat" who tends too much to fat. Be it what it may, I have cast

84

longing eyes backwards ever since I turned my face westward. Perhaps, if I am good, when I die I shall go to Concord!

What you wrote about the effect of the Glimpse upon your lady friend has made me ask myself if I had better reprint it. I would surely do so if I thought it would call attention to Thoreau and thereby increase the number of his readers. If it is reprinted I shall use Miss Folsom's letter and thereby secure Mr. Sanborn's ill will forever. So be it, for I came from Concord with a lower regard for Mr. S. than anyone I met there.[1] I think the unexpressed contempt must have been mutual, for I wrote Mr. S. a letter from here on a matter of business that concerned him, a letter purely in his interest, but have had no word in reply. Could you find out if he received it? If he is at all offensive to you, don't mind it. . . .

1. For the causes of Dr. Jones's attitude toward Sanborn, see his letter to Daniel Ricketson of August 10, 1891 (letter 77).

27. S. A. Jones to A. W. Hosmer, October 8, 1890.

* * *

A gentleman from the Unity Club called on me to-day to ask if I would read a paper before them during the winter. I shall do so, and my topic will be "A New England Village."[1] Concord, "Old Concord," of course. Will you allow me to "tap" you if I find myself in need of some facts not otherwise to be had? I will try and do your favored spot justice, and you shall judge if I succeed. I do not mean that *I* can say all it deserves; only I shall do it all the justice I can. It is indeed a place of which to be proud. . . .

1. Whether Dr. Jones delivered this lecture is uncertain. He did read two papers before the club early in 1891; both were devoted to Thoreau.

28. H.G.O. Blake to S. A. Jones, October 17, 1890.

I enclose herewith the proofs of your preface wh. the printers sent to me. Very likely they have sent to you already the proofs of the bibliography itself. I have made no changes or marks on the proofs, as you will see, leaving that for you. I am glad to have such good, strong words spoken for Thoreau.

In looking at the bibliography appended to Mr. Salt's Life of Thoreau, I do not see the name of Karl Knortz,[1] wh. I think you may like to add to it, if not too late, when you see the article & correspondence wh. I will enclose Please return them to me when you shall have done with them.[2]

I have not read much of Mr. Salt's 'Life', but so far as I have looked at it, it seems to me very good, & the Introduction to the Anti-Slavery &

Reform Papers appeared to me a very powerful presentation of the humane side of Thoreau's character. I shd. think these books wd. have a great influence in making him better known & appreciated.

After seeing your bibliography appended to Mr. Salt's 'Life', it occurred to me that Houghton, Mifflin, & Co. might object to repeating it with the Selections, & so I wrote to them on the subject, adding that as the former book wd. not be likely to circulate much in this country, & as the bibliography in its latest form wd. be more nearly complete, there could be no serious objection to using it again, & they assented to this view, on giving reasons nearly like mine. Of course there will be an advantage in having it easily accessible on both sides of the water.

[P.S.] You will see that I got frm. Mr. Knortz the suggestion of a bibliography.

1. We are unable to determine what article by Karl Knortz is referred to; in 1899 Knortz published a pamphlet on Thoreau entitled *Ein amerikanischer Diogenes.*
2. The enclosures were apparently returned; they are not in the Jones collection.

Houghton, Mifflin & Co. to H.G.O. Blake, October 17, 1890.[1]

We are sending you proof of the *Bibliography.* In preparing it for the press, we found it desirable to work over the first division, but we doubt if it is desirable to follow the printers' suggestion and make the style of II and III agree. Be so good as to forward proof-copy to Dr. Jones, & to ask him to return both to us, as soon as possible, as every day counts.

1. This letter, signed S., was written from the Boston Office of Houghton, Mifflin.

29. S. A. Jones to A. W. Hosmer, October 28, 1890.

I think your desire to send Mr. Dircks a copy of your Thoreau souvenir perfectly proper, and if you tell him that you were led to do so by reading his essays in the WEEK and in WALDEN he can but be deeply pleased. He is one of a band of three young men, living at Newcastle-on-Tyne who are leading such a life as Thoreau would commend. Plain living and high thinking, as it is termed, and these three are derisively spoken of as "the philosophers". . . .

I am reading Mr. Salt's Life of Thoreau, a complimentary copy he sent me. As a "Life" it has not so much of incident as Mr. Sanborn's, as an exposition of Thoreau's doctrines and meanings, it is infinitely beyond anything that Mr. S. can ever do. I told my bookseller here to get me six copies of Mr. Salt's book; he sent the order long ago, but the books have not come. I know that only a limited edition was published, and it may have been all sold. If so, a new edition will follow, and then I can get my copies. I want to give you one and if there is not a copy in your Concord Library, I want to put one there. . . .

30. Henry Salt to S. A. Jones, November 3, 1890.

* * *

I trust you are well, and that your recent visit to Concord may bear fruit in some further articles from your pen. The photographs which you so kindly sent me from Concord are likely to be instrumental in still further spreading Thoreau's name in this country, for I hope to arrange for an article in the *English Illustrated Magazine* which will be written by Dr. Japp and accompanied by some reproductions of the photos.

My book has been very well received by the English press, with only one or two exceptions, and has been the subject of long notices in most of the leading papers. If you should chance to see any interesting mention of it in American periodicals, whether favourable or adverse, I should be much obliged by a word of information.

The attempt to arrange for a simultaneous American edition, by sending over "early sheets", was a failure. In the first place, the sheets were *not* early, but very late, owing to a piece of mismanagement on Bentley's part. Secondly, Messrs. Houghton & Mifflin kept the book under their consideration so long, that it was actually issued in England by the time they had decided not to reprint it. I am not one of those English authors who thirst for making profits out of American readers; and I shall be only too glad if the book is "pirated"—otherwise I don't see how it can ever be known on your side of the Atlantic. If you ever get an opportunity of suggesting a reprint of it to any American publisher, I shall be very glad if you will do so. . . .

31. H.G.O. Blake to S. A. Jones, November 11, 1890.

Thank you for taking the trouble to copy & send Thoreau's letter to his classmate, Rice in 1836.[1] It is, of course, interesting as related to Thoreau's development, & is, as you say, characteristic, but was a surprise to me for its immaturity. Not that he appears more immature than any other young men of 19, but I do not associate immaturity with Thoreau. It seemed as if he must always have lived in that realm wh. is both old & new, like the truths with wh. he dealt. He must, I think, have made a very sudden & great leap within the next 2 or 3 yrs.

I suppose you have received copies of 'Thoreau's Thoughts'. The publishers sent me a dozen, & I trust have sent you as many, at least. Please tell me, if they have not. The title is not mine. I suggested 2 others, at the publishers' request, but am inclined to prefer this to either, it is so unpretending. The vol. is, I think, a very pretty one. The word 'journals' on the cover I have objected to as incorrect, & am promised it shall be changed hereafter. I thank you again for the Bibliography, wh. will doubtless be an attraction to many who are much interested in Thoreau. The article called 'Prayers' is you know, perhaps, attributed to Emerson, I have supposed on good authority, but you may have investigated, & so may think otherwise.[2] If you find that Emerson was probably the author, of course you will not retain it hereafter.

1. Edwin B. Hill published the text of this letter in *Two Thoreau Letters* (Mesa, Arizona, 1916), probably from the text given him by Dr. Jones. The letter is reproduced in Walter Harding and Carl Bode, *The Correspondence of Henry David Thoreau*, pp. 8–9.

2. The article "Prayers" is by Emerson; it appeared in the *Dial* 3 (July 1842):77–81, and it was mistakenly included in Thoreau's posthumous *A Yankee in Canada, with Anti-Slavery and Reform Papers* (Boston: Ticknor and Fields, 1866).

32. Henry Salt to S. A. Jones, November 11, 1890.

I am afraid your kind estimate of my powers led you to expect too much in my *Life of Thoreau*. The fact is, my object from the first was not a more ambitious one than to do what ought to have been done long ago by Thoreau students, viz. simply put together the existing material in a clear and coherent manner. Until this was done, I despaired of seeing Thoreau understood & appreciated except by a very small body of enthusiasts, but when once his story is fully and unmistakably set forth, I don't see why a much wider appreciation should not follow.

Of course there can be no final biography, except by someone who is on the spot and has access to the Journal. Nor did I much hope to catch that rare "effluence" that you mention; indeed, I think I should rather try to catch it in some shorter essay than in a volume of this kind, which necessarily includes much that is ponderous. But it seemed to me that somehow a plain straightforward biography of this sort would have to be done, and the sooner the better. The result in England has really been very satisfactory,[1] the chief papers having given much prominence to the subject, and very favorable reviews in all but a few instances. I want to follow it up, a little later on, by an article in some English magazine on "Thoreau and his Critics", in which I mean *to get very near some of the critics,* whether I get near to Thoreau himself or not!! I especially wish to speak plainly about Lowell; and if you happen to be able to tell me what was the cause of Thoreau's "wounding Lowell's self-consciousness"—whether it was over that matter of Thoreau's contributing to the *Atlantic Monthly*, or what—it would be a great assistance. If they were at loggerheads, it is well the world should know it fully, & then Lowell's taste in writing that article will be more clearly understood![2]

I am sorry, by the bye, if I wronged Thoreau's parents in following Sanborn; but you see I was *quite* at the mercy of American writers in such matters, and Moncure Conway having written in much the same way of Thoreau *père* as Sanborn did, I never for a moment doubted that it was so.[3]

Farewell, for the present! I am sending you a copy of the *Anti-Slavery Papers*,[4] which please accept from me with all kind regards.

1. Salt in his later letter of January 30, 1891, to Dr. Jones (letter 43), lists only five reviews. In this statement he is perhaps being optimistic about the attention the biography received.
2. In the 1896 edition of his biography of Thoreau, Salt did assert that differences which arose from Lowell's editing of an article for the *Atlantic Monthly* explain Lowell's attitude toward Thoreau in *My Study Windows.* For corroboration see Walter Harding's *The Days of Henry Thoreau*, pp. 392–95.
3. Dr. Jones had undoubtedly written Salt about Horace Hosmer's favorable impression of Mr. and Mrs. Thoreau, refuting Sanborn's statements which would lead readers to believe that Mrs. Thoreau was the village gossip.
4. *Anti-Slavery and Reform Papers*, ed. H. S. Salt (London: Swan Sonnenschein & Co., 1890).

33. S. A. Jones to A. W. Hosmer, November 13, 1890.

* * *

Your statement that Edward Emerson[1] is to lecture on Thoreau on the 10th of Dec. has made me itch to be there on that date; but it can't be did. Do you know if Mr. Emerson is going to publish his lecture? If so I shall get it "you bet."

Since you wrote me Houghton, Mifflin & Co. have published Mr. Blake's little book called "Thoreau's Thoughts." It makes a handy volume for the pocket, and will enlarge the number of Thoreau's audience. The appended bibliography will enable anyone to "read up" on Thoreau as completely as possible up to date. H. M. & Co. have not paid me the compliment of giving me a single copy of the booklet, although it would have cost them at least a hundred and fifty dollars to have had the bibliography prepared. I purpose sending them a quiet reminder, and if they "come down" with a few copies you shall surely have one. . . .

1. The last of Emerson's children, Dr. Edward Waldo Emerson (1844–1930) is best known for his 1903 edition of his father's works (the Centennial Edition) and for his reminiscence of Thoreau, *Henry Thoreau as Remembered by a Young Friend* (Boston: Houghton, Mifflin & Co., 1917).

34. H.G.O. Blake to S. A. Jones, November 24, 1890.

Your letter dated Nov. 20 reached me this morning, & I was glad to learn frm. it that you had received the 12 copies of Thoreau's Thoughts. As you probably inferred, I feared, judging by your former letter, that you had not received any copies frm. the publishers, & so requested them to send these, not feeling easy that you shd. receive fewer than I did. Even with them, your bibliography might be considered largely a free gift. Still I understand somewhat your feeling, & if the publishers have sent you 6 copies, I am willing you shd. pay me for 5, after I have got their bill, wh. will not probably be till next May. The one that is presented to the University Library, of course, I shall not let you pay for, especially as I have received this morning, at the same time with your letter, one of 'grateful acknowledgment' frm. the Regents. I shd. be ready to have you make in my name & at my expense a similar disposition of any of the other 5 copies, one or more as you think best.

I sent a copy to Mr. Salt very soon after receiving my package frm. the publishers.

You notice that I took few passages frm. 'Winter.' Of course, I felt very much limited as to space, wishing to make a small book, & having more or less in mind a Calendar, so that I gave but 366 passages & one of those was omitted on account of a difficulty abt. indicating the page. As to the elision in the passage you refer to on the 280th p. of Winter, the first words wh. follow the printed ones, are 'I had better have retained the most inexperienced tyro who had straggled into the camp, & let go the heavenly alliance.' There is more before coming to the next words that were printed. Probably I wished to condense, & thought the idea was sufficiently expressed in the words I gave.

I was interested in what you say of the activity of Thoreau's mind in 1841 & 2. It has seemed to me heretofore that some of the most profound & beautiful of his work belongs to that period & a few years after.

I have not read more of Mr. Salt's book since I last wrote to you abt. it. I feel that if it corresponds to the Introduction to the other little book, it may do much to make Thoreau better appreciated. I shd. hardly think it wd. pay to republish it here at present, tho. I shd. be glad to see that done. I do not feel the interest that you seem to in knowing more of the incidents of Thoreau's life, perhaps owing mainly to my general familiarity with his outward life, since I do feel such a curiosity abt. some other lives. What he says in the Letters in nearly or quite the following language expressing my idea abt. him, 'Our thoughts are the epochs in our lives, all else is but a journal of the winds that blew while we were here.' This shd. have been the motto to my little book, & very likely might have been, if I had chosen the title myself, & so had known what it was to be before I selected the motto.

I cannot tell you whether the shanty at Walden was a station of the Underground R.R. Mr. Sanborn probably knows as much as anybody abt. that.

[P.S.] The title 'Thoreau's Thoughts' I rather preferred to two wh. I suggested as being more simple, as I very likely have told you.

35. S. A. Jones to A. W. Hosmer, December 5, 1890.

I did not mean that your letter should wait for an acknowledgement until I had received your transcript of Thoreau's Class History;[1] but here I am surprised by the arrival of that document.

I do not know how to adequately thank you for putting this valuable article in my hands. It is so characteristic of Thoreau, and it adds to one's knowledge of him. I wish I had known of this publication in time to have incorporated it in the bibliography. By the way, when you can readily spare the time, will you send me a copy of the full title-page of that Class History, and also the pages occupied by the account of Thoreau? Such details will enable me to enter it in a larger bibliography that I shall one day publish.

I know a relative of a member of that Harvard Class of '37, and I am going to make a big try for a copy of that History. If it could be bought I would have one at once; but, get it or not, I am grateful to you for sending the transcript. . . .

1. Henry Williams, *Memorials of the Class of 1837 of Harvard University* (Boston: Printed for the Class by George H. Ellis, 1887). Dr. Jones reprinted the sketch of Thoreau in *Pertaining to Thoreau* (Detroit: Edwin B. Hill, 1901), pp. 163–71.

36. Henry Salt to S. A. Jones, December 11, 1890.

I find myself indebted to you for so many favours that I hardly know where to begin! I postponed replying to your last letter until I should have received the box of relics; and now, on returning from a day or two in the country, I find this arrived, with the arrowhead, pencil, and Walden stone all safe inside. Many, many thanks for them! They are most interesting, and most precious to me—the arrowhead in particular, which sets one thinking of a strange and eventful history indeed! The photographs which you so kindly sent me some time back have been an object of much interest to many friends to whom I have exhibited them; and now, with these further relics, I shall really be the proprietor of a small Thoreau museum! It is *very* kind and generous of you thus to give away what must, I know, be of such great value to yourself.

The copy of *Thoreau's Thoughts* reached me from Mr. Blake about a week ago. It is a charming little volume, and both the manual and the bibliography will undoubtedly be a great boon to Thoreau students. The "Thoughts" seem to strike one with a new sense of their wonderful beauty and insight when thus arranged, and I think Mr. Blake has made an excellent selection. Your bibliography is a fuller and more exact one than mine, as it deserved to be; and on comparing the two I congratulate myself that the omissions in my compilation are not still more serious. As to the reviews that have appeared since the issue of my book, I will keep a careful account of them (I have cuttings sent me by an agency), and when they seem to have run their course, I will send you a list up to date. The *Athenaeum* has not yet had a review, but almost all the other papers have.

That letter which you so kindly copied from the Boston *Advertiser*[1] is most interesting & important; as indeed is all that you have told me respecting Thoreau's parents. If my book should ever reach a second edition, I would certainly modify what I said about John Thoreau and Cynthia Dunbar, and quote portions of this letter in a footnote or appendix. What I should especially *like* to see is an account from your pen, in some magazine, of the information recently collected by you in Concord, and the impressions of your visit. Such a record would be invaluable to future biographers. Could you not write some such article, with illustrations of Concord scenery and Thoreau relics, in one of the admirable American illustrated magazines? Do be persuaded to do this; it would be *most* welcome.

I am afraid the negotiations with the *English Illustrated* for an illustrated article on Thoreau are likely to break down; as the Editors, while not definitely declining, interpose such delays that it seems better to apply elsewhere. I asked Dr. Japp to write the paper, because it would be partly a review of my book, and so I could not do it myself. We are now in negotiation with Messrs. Cassell, and I hope may arrange successfully for a paper in one of their magazines. I think we shall have quite enough material for the illustrations, as Dr. Japp has also some photographs that might be used; but I will bear in mind your kind offer, if by any chance we should need more. I have written Dr. Japp your message, by the bye, about your letter relating to Carlyle, but have not yet had his answer.

I am going to read a paper in February on "Thoreau and his Critics" to the "New Fellowship", a society which advocates social reform much on Ed. Carpenter's lines. I shall then dwell on the Lowell incident, and on other misunderstandings of Thoreau such as R. L. Stevenson's essay, and a recent absurd article in the *Daily News* by the volatile Andrew Lang—of all flippant people the least competent to understand Thoreau.[2]

I hardly know what to think of what you tell me about Mr. Sanborn and the proposed American edition of my book.[3] That there should have been no edition is certainly a piece of bad management on my part; but the fault is really Bentley's, for it was entirely owing to their not keeping me informed of their arrangements that I did nothing all the summer. It had been fully arranged that *they* would settle matters in America with Scribner; they did nothing, and let me go on thinking they had done everything. I do not trouble about the matter now, as it is beyond my control; but of course if you ever get a chance of suggesting an issue of the book in America, I shall be very much obliged. . . .

1. Salt is referring to the article "Henry Thoreau's Mother" by E.M.F. (Mrs. Jean Munroe LeBrun) which appeared in the *Boston Daily Advertiser*, February 14, 1883. Salt did modify his 1890 statement on the elder Thoreaus in his 1896 edition of his biography of Thoreau, and he referred to Mrs. LeBrun's article on p. 21.

2. Salt's essay was not published.

3. Sanborn opposed publication of Salt's book in America because he feared it would reduce sale of his own book. See Dr. Jones's letter to H.G.O. Blake, August 9, 1891 (letter 75).

37. H.G.O. Blake to S. A. Jones, December 26, 1890.

I received your letter this morning, & hasten to reply. I have intended to be careful in making my selections, & have omitted a great deal. I have wished, in each case, to make an interesting book, & to present Thoreau in the way that most attracted me. I by no means recorded all under the Janry 1st; June 1st, &c., but omitted pretty carefully what seemed to me uninteresting matter, tho. to some people, careful students of natural history &c., it might be very interesting. —I see you have found many more entries for March than for any other month. 'Early Spring' was my first book, & as well as the Summer, covered little time, so that I was less ready to omit for them than for the Winter. This applies still more to the Autumn wh. I am now engaged upon, as I mean it shall cover more time than either of the others. Besides, I make it a point in general to omit what has been printed before, as in Channing's book & Sanborn's article, also in Autumnal Tints, Wild Apples, &c., tho. I am not very careful abt. this. Moreover, the 1st. vol. of the Journal, a small one, extending from Oct. 22, 1837 to Dec. 2, 1839, is headed in Thoreau's hand writing,

'Gleanings—
On what Time
Has not Reaped
Of my
Journal.'

For these & perhaps other reasons, I shd. think you wd. hardly be safe in drawing very definite inferences such as you refer to.

As to the price of the copies of the 'Thoughts,' I shd. rather wait till my account comes in, the 1st. of next May. If either of us shd. die before that time, let the debt be cancelled, if there is any. Meantime, you may like to present one or more copies as you did one before, & I shd. be ready to have you thus dispose of any of the remaining 5, in my name.

[P.S.] I wish you a happy new year.

Dec. 27. I have of late used the 'Thoughts' as a sort of calendar, & found great satisfaction in it, reading a page in a few minutes soon after break-fast, when I am most apt to be awake. For instance this morning, being the 27th of Dec., I read what was on the 27th page. See what noble & uplifting thoughts are these, as this, 'Money is not required to buy one necessary of the soul.' One might take a single thought for the day, as there are 365, I believe. I copied 366, but one was omitted because the proofreader did not find it in either edition of the 'Week.'

38. S. A. Jones to A. W. Hosmer, December 26, 1890.

What a deluge of kindness: first the album,[1] then the report of Emerson's lecture, then the N. E. Magazine—one treading on the heels of the other! I must cry halt, or you'll have me in debtors' prison.

I have got a copy of "Memorials of the '37 Class," and am in corre-spondence with its author. Am working him with a breast-pump for personal recollections; but expect to get only some skim milk.[2]

Your notes from Dr. E's lecture open some interesting questions. If you know Dr. E. well enough will you ask him if he will allow me to make some enquiries of him? Sanborn has been so disdainful that I am afraid to write to Dr. E. without permission.

Will you also beg Miss Hosmer to give you the *name* of the lady whom Thoreau loved.[3] Such things must be preserved for the future. . . .

Sanborn's paper in the New England Mag.[4] is decidedly sawdustish—the pictures are all that redeem it. Where *did* he get the sketch of Thoreau's birthplace?[5] Is it a *correct* sketch?

1. An album of photographs, entitled "In Thoreau's Haunts" by Hosmer. Now in the Jones collection.

2. Dr. Jones's correspondence with Williams did clarify one issue. In his 1882 biography of Thoreau, Sanborn had intimated that Thoreau took part in class "pranks" at Harvard (see pp. 54–57). In the class memorial volume Williams answered Sanborn: "It is very doubtful, however, whether Thoreau ever took part in any irregularities of the sort described, or any others calculated to excite the distrust of the Faculty." (See *Pertaining to Thoreau*, p. 165.) In a letter to Dr. Jones, Williams strengthened his statement: "The 'It is very doubtful' in my statement

might have been much stronger, I feel sure, with entire truthfulness" (quoted by Dr. Jones in an unpublished lecture, dated January 19, 1891, Hosmer collection).

3. Undoubtedly a reference to Ellen Sewall; for an account of Thoreau's "love affair" with her, see Walter Harding, *The Days of Henry Thoreau*, pp. 94–104.

4. Franklin B. Sanborn, "Emerson and His Friends in Concord," *New England Magazine* 3 (December 1890):413–31. Sanborn's relegation of Thoreau to the status of one of Emerson's "friends in Concord" probably accounted for Dr. Jones's objection to the article.

5. Sanborn's article included a sketch of the house on Virginia Road where Thoreau was born.

39. Henry Salt to Daniel Ricketson, December 30, 1890.

I was very glad to learn from your letter of October 9 that you thought well of my book on Thoreau. It has been very widely noticed in the English press, and I trust it will be the means of exciting a greater interest in Thoreau's character and writings.

What you told me of your correspondence with William Howitt, and of the letters in your possession, interested me very much. I much wish I were competent to undertake the work which you suggest; but I am ashamed to say that I am almost unacquainted with William Howitt's writings, though I have read the biography recently published, or rather edited, by his daughter. If I should ever hear of any worthy person meditating a volume on Howitt I will bear in mind the existence of these valuable letters.

I was touched by what you said respecting the loss of so many of your early friends—one of those most pathetic experiences of life which affect us in thought even before they come to us in reality. But it must cheer you to remember that you numbered among your friends so noble and notable a personality as Thoreau, for to have known a man of genius is indeed a rare and inestimable privilege.

With myself, change of opinion, rather than death, has hitherto been the cause of friends falling away; but as I am now in my fortieth year I have come to a time when I am not likely to make many new friends, and can ill afford to lose old ones. I forget whether I told you in former letters that I was an assistant master at our great classical school, Eton College, for ten years, but gave up my position owing to the adoption of views (such as those of Thoreau) which brought me into antagonism with the conservative tone of an old-fashioned institution.

If, as I hope may be the case, you should some day feel disposed to write to me again, there is one point in Thoreau's history on which I should be very glad to receive enlightenment. I have been told by an American correspondent that in following Mr. Sanborn's account of Thoreau's parents, I have done an injustice to John Thoreau, the elder, and Cynthia Dunbar. Mr. Sanborn (and I think also Moncure Conway) represents John

Thoreau as a somewhat dull, plodding person, and his wife as a lively gossip; but I am now assured that they were both persons of more than average sensibility and attainments, and possessed of a true love of nature and natural life. It would be interesting and valuable to have your reminiscences as to this point.

40. S. A. Jones to A. W. Hosmer, January 10, 1891.

To-night's mail brought your letter and it found me busy on a lecture on Thoreau which is to be given on the 9th of February and followed by another on the 16th.[1] I am not trying so much to give a history of Thoreau as to correct certain errors that are current about him. If the thing gets into print I will see that you get a copy. It will be only a small return for your valuable assistance in getting me many facts about him.

I love Thoreau so sincerely that I was deeply pleased to learn from you that Dr. Emerson regards me as "one who knew Thoreau." That, of course, is not literally true, but the Dr. means one who is in sympathy with Thoreau, and I am glad that he recognizes me as such. I shall be bold enough to write to him on the strength of his wife's opinion.

I note what you say of Sanborn's errors, and I well remember the Hosmer house[2] that you pointed out to me as the one that Thoreau used to visit. I think you would feel partly repaid for your kindness to me if you knew how fresh in my memory are the places that you showed me. Why, when I sit down to write, they come back to me so vividly that the pen stops and I am back there again. I knew that that house in Sanborn's picture of the Baker farm was an interpolation: it wasn't there when we saw the farm.

That he should use your photographs without one word of acknowledgement only shows the ingrained selfishness of the "fellow."[3] I sized him up for all he is worth after one short interview, and have not yet had occasion to change my opinion.

If I live to visit Concord again I will join you in getting up a book on Thoreau's Home and haunts that will beat all yet done in that line. Your negatives must be reproduced in photogravure, and the accompanying text must be in Thoreau's own words.

Such a work will sell in both England and America. By the way, did you ever see a copy of May Alcott's Concord Sketches?[4] I should like to see what she did in that line.

I suppose you have not yet learned the name of the lady with whom Thoreau was in love. Don't forget to get it from Miss Hosmer because all these things must be preserved for the readers of the future.

I often look at the Thoreau pencil you sent me and always with an increasing desire to know the name of the lady who furnished it.

Miss Hosmer took me to see a very venerable lady, Mrs. Bigelow,[5] who had known the Thoreaus intimately, and who had been very active in the anti-slavery movement. It occurs to me that she can help to clear up the question about "Walden" as a post in the "Under-ground Rail-Road." This point is by no means clear: You know Parker Pillsbury wrote you that it was not; but Mr. Silas Hosmer thought it highly probable that it had been. The English writers make a great point of this, and the question should be definitely settled. . . . [6]

1. Alfred Hosmer's handwritten copies of these lectures are in the Hosmer collection. The first refutes Sanborn's characterization of the Thoreau family, Sanborn's assertion that Thoreau was involved in class "pranks" at Harvard, and the claim advanced by Robert Louis Stevenson and Dr. A. H. Japp that the Walden hut was an Underground Railroad station. The second discusses the Walden period as Thoreau's experiment in simplification of life.

2. Probably the farm of Edmund Hosmer, a sketch of which appeared in Sanborn's article, "Emerson and His Friends in Concord." Dr. Jones acquired a photograph of the house, probably taken by Hosmer; the photograph is now in the Jones collection.

3. Sanborn's article included photographs of Emerson's house, Concord River, and Orchard House, for which no acknowledgment was given.

4. May Alcott, *Concord Sketches* (Boston: Fields, Osgood & Co., 1869).

5. Walter Harding has called Mrs. Francis Edwin Bigelow the "acknowledged leader of Concord's participants in the Underground Railroad." See *The Days of Henry Thoreau*, p. 316.

6. Relying upon information provided by Dr. A. H. Japp, Robert Louis Stevenson claimed that the Walden hut was an Underground Railroad station. See *Familiar Studies of Men and Books* (London: Chatto and Windus, 1882), pp. xx–xxi. Dr. Japp reiterated the claim in a review of Salt's *Life* for the *Spectator* 65 (October 18, 1890):527.

41. Daniel Ricketson to Henry Salt, January 19, 1891.

. . . Your welcome letter of the 30th ult. came duly to hand on the 10th inst. We are only eleven days apart, although over three thousand miles, and then, more wonderful still, within only a few hours by cable telegraph. We live truly in an age of wonderful scientific discovery.

I had been lately reading a very pleasant and well-written essay on Thomas Gray and his Friends, by D. C. Tovey of Trinity College, Cambridge, and as I sometimes do under like circumstances, wrote a letter of thanks to the author, in which I mentioned your life of Thoreau. I quote the following from his letter in reply to mine:—"Your correspondent, H. S. Salt, is one of my greatest friends. I have not yet seen his Thoreau, though I have heard much of it. Salt is a very able writer, I think. He was a master at Eton with me for some years. Though I don't suppose our opinions very much harmonize, I find Salt and Mrs. Salt very lovable people, and very much in earnest."

I trust I have made no breach of confidence, as the sentiments expressed are so friendly and appreciative, and such as should pass among Christian gentlemen and ladies.

I had addressed Mr. Tovey at Trinity College, from whence my letter was forwarded to him at his home, "Worpledon Rectory," Guilford, Surrey, in which he says,—"You will gather from my address, that I am a country parson."

The more I read of your Thoreau the more I am impressed with his rare excellence of character and the admirable manner you have set him forth to the British public. It seems remarkable to me, who knew him so intimately, that you should have been able to make so lifelike a portraiture of him. I do not know who your American correspondent may be that criticised Mr. Sanborn's representation of the good old couple, Mr. and Mrs. Thoreau. Mr. Sanborn was an inmate of their family for some length of time when a teacher in the Academy at Concord, and of course knew the parties well. You are aware that portraits of the same person by different artists are often very dissimilar, and yet good likenesses. Although the portraits of Mr. and Mrs. Thoreau which you have copied from Mr. Sanborn are readily recognized, I should never have spoken of them in any manner that could have been construed into any disrespect for their genuine worth. Our philosopher was indebted undoubtedly to both his parents for much of his rare qualities—to the father for a calm, patient, industrious spirit, with great honesty of purpose and performance. He was a man rather to be drawn out than to obtrude himself. He moved my respect for his genuine worth. On the other hand, Mrs. Thoreau was an unusually active, voluble person, rather tall, while her husband was short, a great talker, and strong delineator of character, but not unlike many other good housewives gifted in relating historical and domestic events. They lived harmoniously as husband and wife, and their children excelled in whatever is good and noble and therefore praiseworthy.

Had I your youth and high literary qualifications, I should feel strongly inclined to write the Life of William Howitt, one of England's truest sons, whose works stand high in America as well as at home. He had much of the character of the statesman, Hampden, and Sidney, etc., and would have graced the government of his country had he been called to parliament.

P.S. It will always give me pleasure to receive a letter from you.

42. S. A. Jones to A. W. Hosmer, January 23, 1891.

* * *

You ask if you "bore" me by sending such Thoreau material as your reading reveals to you. My dear man, I have welcomed that as an extra pair of friendly eyes doing me unexpected kindness. You put me on the track of the Class Memorial volume, and by Jupiter, the Class Secretary sent me one after reading the Glimpse.

If you could hear my paper in Feb'y next you would see that I am deeply indebted to you for most valuable aid. The only feature that "bores" me is how I can ever repay my obligations. I can't; there will be a large balance that you must charge to Thoreau's memory.

The notice of Thoreau's Thoughts is nice, but the skinning of F.B.S. is delicious. Thayer rakes his victim fore and aft, and is really guilty of "cruelty to animals."[1] But, self-conceit gives a man a thick skin, and I don't believe Mr. S. suffered much. When I was in Concord I thought I had gotten on the track of a map of a survey by Thoreau, but it failed to materialize. I envy you if you manage to capture the one you saw.

Between Mrs. Bigelow and Parker Pillsbury the fugitive slave question must be considered as definitely settled. Thanks to you! . . .

I received a letter from Mr. Emerson the other day from which I am led to hope that I may hear the Thoreau lecture. He will not be at liberty until April, and our Students' Lecture Association is out of the field late in February, but I think I can get him an invitation from one of our University societies, which will be more of a compliment. Don't mention this to him until I find out definitely. . . .

1. In the *Boston Daily Traveller* for December 27, 1890, Eli Thayer criticized an address which Sanborn had made "before the Abolition reunion in Boston on the 22nd of September last." Thayer wrote to defend the Emigrant Aid Company as it operated in Kansas and denounced Sanborn's praise of John Brown. Much of the article is bitter invective directed against Sanborn.

43. Henry Salt to S. A. Jones, January 30, 1891.

I yesterday received your kind letter, telling me of the offer of the firm at Cleveland respecting an American edition of the Thoreau—an offer which, it seemed to me, is well worth consideration. Today, lunching in a Vegetarian restaurant (we have many such in London now), I chanced to meet my friend Dr. Japp, and he strongly advises me to entertain the proposal, his experience being that a young firm is often better to deal with than an old-established one, because of the much greater interest and energy spent on the work.

So, if the offer still holds, and if you are really good enough to take such trouble on my behalf, I shall be very glad to have it thus arranged, and I am therefore not writing to Messrs. Harper. (Mr. G. W. Curtis, by the way, though answering courteously a letter of enquiry which I wrote him last year, did not seem disposed to be much interested in the Thoreau; so I have no particular reason to expect that the Harpers would care to publish for me.)

As to the "writing in", I shall be *very glad indeed* if you will be so kind as to do it, and it will be a real pleasure to me to have your name thus associated with mine in a subject where we have so much in common. There are doubtless a good many slips in the book, such as the one you mention about Curtis and Harvard,[1] and I should like to feel that you will not hesitate to correct where it seems advisable to you. You have my full authority to do what you think best in all such arrangements.

I presume a new *Preface* would be desirable, and perhaps the first two pages of the Appendix (on the Parentage & Portraits) are hardly worth preserving. Whether the Bibliography shd. be included or not, you will best judge.

One other point, as to the 10 per cent. offered by the firm. I could not think of letting you send this on to me, while *you* are having all the trouble of the edition. You, of course, must be paid by the publishers, if they issue the book, for your services as Editor and joint-author; if they like to give me an honorarium, (if the book sells), or to arrange for a royalty to be divided between you and me, well and good! But you will understand me, that I have never reckoned on getting further remuneration from America, and, if any comes, should count it pure gain. What I do primarily desire is that an edition of the book should be accessible to the American public. If you can secure this last point, I shall be greatly indebted to you, and shall be well pleased with whatever form the publication may take. It would certainly be a great boon to have some illustrations of Thoreau's haunts.

Of course, if the proposal should fall through, I can then make my offer to the Harpers or Messrs. Roberts. But I am inclined, in this case, to prefer the bird in the hand; and I trust it may be arranged on the lines indicated in your letter. If you will want another copy of the book, by the bye, I can send it at any time.

I read my paper on "Thoreau's Gospel of Simplicity" to the 'New Fellowship' Society a few evenings ago, and we had an interesting discussion, Lowell being severely handled on all sides! If, as is probable, the paper is printed in a magazine, I will forward a copy.[2] I subjoin a list of the chief reviews of my book which have so far appeared in English papers— *literary* papers only, for it scarcely seems worth while to chronicle the notices of the daily journals, except when the writer is a well-known Thoreau student.

The Academy, Oct. 25, 1890, by Walter Lewin.
The Speaker, Nov. 8, 1890. 'Thoreau'.
Newcastle Daily Chronicle, Nov. 25, 1890, by W. H. Dircks.
Spectator, Oct. 18, 1890. "Thoreau's Life".
Animal World, Dec. 1890. "Life of H. D. Thoreau".

The Athenaeum review has not yet appeared.

1. George William Curtis was not a Harvard graduate, as Salt had asserted on p. 87 of the 1890 biography of Thoreau. The mistake was corrected in the 1896 edition.

2. Salt's paper appeared in *Paternoster Review,* March 1891.

44. S. A. Jones to A. W. Hosmer, February 11, 1891.

As soon as I saw your hand-writing on the picture package I said to myself "It's Thoreau's portrait!" before I cut the strings. I was also sure that it was the Blake copy[1] enlarged. It was a clear divination. I am more than pleased; I have to spell it DELIGHTED. THANK YOU!

Miss Eliza Hosmer[2] does not like the Blake picture: I do. It gives me the best conception of the man that wrote *Walden.*

Now let me give you a pointer, namely, get Mr. Blake's permission to take a life-sized negative from the daguerreotype, and ask him to allow you to copyright it. You will then have a monopoly in the best picture of Thoreau extant. . . .

I was safely delivered of my "lecture" on Monday night, and though I thought it dry to those not well acquainted with the biographies of Thoreau, I was astonished at the marked attention with which my hearers listened. It was wholly devoted to correcting errors concerning Thoreau, and I "went for" F.B.S. without gloves. I used all Miss Folsom's letter which you so kindly copied for me; also facts gotten from Mr. Horace Hosmer and Mrs. Bigelow. The Class Memorial also furnished some effective ammunition. Thanks to your more than kindness my Concord visit enabled me to speak by the card, and the facts that I gleaned then must go on record in permanent shape. No fear but that you will get copies.

Next Monday night I am to speak of Thoreau's ideal life that is possible for all men. Of course, I mean as far as I am capable of understanding it, for one must be as tall as Thoreau to see as far, and as great to see as deep. I am only doing my little best, and only my sincerity can palliate my audacity. It is to me even as a religious exercise, and I assure you I feel my unfitness. But Thoreau is not popular, and somebody has got to assert him and assert him until the many begin to look into him for themselves. Then such as I must keep silent. . . .

By the way, if in those stores you can find a copy of Thoreau's "Excursions" with 1863 on the titlepage,[3] I wish you would secure it for me at any price. It is the only first edition of any of his books that I lack. You may find it and a copy of Channing's book[4] under the "Old South," but that is the dearest of all the old book places in Boston. Nevertheless, if you find the right edition of the Excursions there, pay the price and let me know. I am scanning such book stalls as I meet, and if I see a Channing, it will start for Concord pretty d.q. I assure you. . . .

1. The Blake portrait of Thoreau was a daguerreotype made in 1856 by Benjamin D. Maxham of Worcester, Massachusetts. Thoreau had three made at this sitting, one each for H.G.O. Blake, Theophilus Brown, and Calvin H. Greene. See Walter Harding, *The Days of Henry Thoreau*, p. 367.
2. A note in one of Dr. Jones's Concord scrapbooks identifies Eliza Hosmer as the daughter of Edmund Hosmer, Concord farmer and Thoreau's friend.
3. Henry D. Thoreau, *Excursions* (Boston: Ticknor and Fields, 1863).
4. Ellery Channing, *Thoreau, the Poet-Naturalist* (Boston: Roberts Bros., 1873).

45. S. A. Jones to A. W. Hosmer, February 23, 1891.

* * *

I am to edit an American edition of Mr. Salt's Life of Thoreau, and I propose to fill it with Concord scenery in photographs. I will arrange for you to be the artist, and will get you more than even with Mr. Sanborn and others who have not done you justice. . . .

46. S. A. Jones to A. W. Hosmer, February 23, 1891.

In the matter of illustrating the American edition of Salt's Life of Thoreau I want photographs, if they are not going to prove too costly.

I would like to present the three photographs of Thoreau.[1] Also any picture of his father, mother and Sophia, provided any are in existence and accessible. Then pictures of people who were intimate with him: as E. Hosmer, Edward Hoar,[2] Emerson, Alcott, Curtis, Ricketson, Blake & C. Channing—if the cuss can be had? Also John Brown,—Mr. Davis owns Thoreau's own picture of Capt. John Brown.

Of SCENERY, a good view on the ASSABET. The site of the Bean Field at Walden, Dr. Emerson can locate it. A good picture of the cliffs. A good scene on Concord River. A good view of the Hollowell Farm—that he didn't buy! . . .

I would also like to photograph some of Thoreau's manuscript which is in your Concord Library. And a photo of a map of his surveying would be a good card.

This edition, if carried out, will give me a good deal of work, but the book will be a famous one, as it will try hard to put the reader "on the spot." It is sure to please the English, for such of your photos as I have sent over have attracted marked attention. . . .

1. The Maxham daguerreotype of 1856, the crayon drawing made by Rowse in 1854, and the ambrotype made by E. S. Dunshee in 1861.
2. Son of Judge Samuel Hoar, brother of Senator George Frisbie Hoar and Judge Ebenezer Rockwood Hoar, Edward Sherman Hoar (1823–1893) was a frequent companion on excursions with Thoreau, whom he accompanied to the Maine woods in 1857 and to the White Mountains in 1858.

47. S. A. Jones to A. W. Hosmer, February 28, 1891.

* * *

Your reference to the "4 pictures" opens an interesting question about the ambrotype that Mr. Davis has. He is way off when he says "it is the picture that was put on Thoreau's coffin at the funeral." Look at Sanborn's "Life", page 265, and you will see that Sophia did not get possession of the ambrotype until after the funeral.[1] You will also learn from the same page that the very picture Mr. Davis has is the one that was engraved for Sanborn's book, and is beyond doubt the original of all the photographs that look like it. The engraver of Sanborn's steel plate undoubtedly worked from a negative of the ambrotype; as the original picture was too precious to be exposed to the risks of fire while in the engraver's hands. The ambrotype was photographed by Black, and the negatives from his plate were on sale at J. E. Pilton & Co's, 167 Washington St., Boston. I have one of these negatives: a carte visite, given me by Mrs. Hosmer of Chicago. So, Fred, we have knocked that "fourth picture" out of the field. As this is a matter of some importance, just ask Mr. Sanborn where he got the picture from which the steel engraving was made. Write to him the enquiry, and ask him to be kind enough to give you a written reply; for history should rest on documents as far as possible. On Monday next, if I am alive, I will look up a paper in the *Critic*,[2] on "Portraits of Thoreau with a Beard." That will give some more light. . . .

I am glad that you are reading Mr. Salt's book. I was at first disappointed in it, but a careful reading has made me change my opinion. It is much more coherent than Sanborn's, who seemed to think he must give the history of half of Concord as well as Thoreau's life.

I do not think it so strange that E. W. Emerson should go to Acton and "tap" Mr. Hosmer.[3] You see, "Ed." was only 18 years old when Thoreau died, and I am satisfied that Thoreau is a much larger man to E.W.E. and to F.B.S. than he was in the year that he died. And I'll bet a pan of cookies that E.W.E. has learned far more of Thoreau since his death than he knew during his life.[4]

His trips to Acton go to prove this; but, O Lordie, don't breathe a word of this to any save the Misses Hosmer—they can "size up" E.W.E. correctly!

I am glad you wrote me Horace Hosmer's remark about the "brains." If you meet him again, please give him my warmest regards. Send me his full name and post-office address: he must have a copy of "Thoreau's Thoughts."

If I thought it would not bore him, I would like very much to write to him, for he saw INTO the Thoreau family as not many have done. . . .

[P.S.] Last night I expressed my desire to write to Mr. Horace Hosmer, and the mail of this morning brings me a letter from him. I am struck by the vigor of his language. He is more like Thoreau than anyone I have yet found in your State. In fact I have not had so enjoyable a letter in a long time. If Mr. Hosmer was cut up into thin strips there would be the making of an E.W.E. in every piece.

Mr. Hosmer's letter makes me feel that even I have not sufficiently magnified Thoreau's father. I will copy that part of my lecture and send it to him for his comments. I shall also try and persuade him to write out his recollections of the Thoreau family; they are too precious to be lost, and the witnesses are too few to let the chance go by default.

His letter brought back vividly the ride we took to see him, and I wonder why it did not occur to me then to tell you how much the scenery about the school where we found him resembles Wales. I suppose I was too much preoccupied with what he was saying. . . .

1. Sanborn quoted a letter from Daniel Ricketson explaining that he had sent the Dunshee ambrotype of Thoreau to Sophia Thoreau "after her brother's death." See *Henry D. Thoreau,* p. 265. The ambrotype had been made in 1861 at Ricketson's request.

2. W.S.K. [William Sloane Kennedy], "Portraits of Thoreau with a Beard," *Critic* 1 (April 9, 1881):95.

3. Edward Emerson used information from Horace Hosmer in *Henry Thoreau as Remembered by a Young Friend* (1917).

4. Silas Hosmer, an uncle of Fred Hosmer to whom Dr. Jones had sent a copy of Salt's *Life,* expressed a similar judgment of some of Thoreau's Concord admirers: "There was many that did not understand him while he was with us but looking back they now see many noble traits in him that they did not appreciate at the time that he was with us" (Silas Hosmer to Dr. Jones, December 30, 1890, Jones collection).

48. S. A. Jones to A. W. Hosmer, March 7, 1891.

Your favor of the 5th instant makes me fear that F.B.S. will not keep long in your climate. His answers denote a far-advanced dry rot and you may as well summon the mourners.

At p. 265 of his Life of Thoreau you can read as follows: "The ambrotype of him, *which is engraved for your volume,* was taken for me by Dunshee, at New Bedford, August 21, 1861, on his last visit to me at Brooklawn. Of this portrait, Miss Sophia Thoreau, *to whom I sent it soon after her brother's death,* wrote me, May 26, 1862," &c &c.

Yet Mr. Sanborn is flippant enough to tell you that his engraving was from Mr. Ricketson's medallion!!![1]

The firm that proposed to publish Mr. Salt's Life of Thoreau has been changed into a Stock Company with the usual apparatus of President &c. and the new concern *does not propose to do any publishing.* As the proposition to publish came unsolicited from Taylor, Austin & Co., and as they are in the new combination, I should think they would feel a little cheap; but the lust for money destroys the better parts of our nature. I am only sorry for Mr. Salt's disappointment when he learns of this "Yankee trick," as the English will call it. . . .

1. A bas-relief medallion of Thoreau made by Walton Ricketson, son of Daniel Ricketson, a few years after Thoreau's death. See Walter Harding, *A Thoreau Handbook* (New York: New York University Press, 1959), p. 204.

49. S. A. Jones to A. W. Hosmer, March 17, 1891.

. . . I am having an undeserved feast from Mr. Horace Hosmer, who is indeed a TRUMP! His expressions are as fresh and bracing as the air of the Acton hills. He makes me realize that John Bull "bit off more than he could chaw" when he tackled the ancestors of such a man. I declare, his letters make me hungry for another talk with him. . . .

I prize much your pencil sketch of Thoreau's birthplace, and I shall mount it in Salt's Life of him. Damn F.B.S.; but Horace Hosmer is making carpet rags of him at an alarming rate. —But it won't do to make carpet of those rags!!! . . .

Never, NEVER, NEVER will "Edward" forget that he is the son of his father! BUT neither must he forget that he is NOT his father. That he declines my doggerel shows his good sense,[1] for it is not likely to be in the same key as his lecture, and it would mar his harmony.

I am very curious to hear him, and yet I am half afraid to go to Detroit, for he will find an audience that will be more critical than a Boston one because they will not swallow anything simply because it is an Emerson.

I sincerely hope that his matter will make ample amend for any falling-off in his manner.

Judging by his letters, he has a sublime self-confidence. If he has enough other traits of his father he'll "take the cake" or "bust the bakery." Success to him!

Morning, 18th March. On waking, almost the first thing I did was to indulge in a hearty laugh about Asa J.[2] and that makes me think about F.B.S.—he must not have liked the smell of me. I had sent him a "Glimpse" whilst he was in "Yurop," and he found it amongst his mail on his return. He learned that I was in Concord from Miss Hosmer, so he called at the Thoreau house and, not finding me, left his card and an invitation to take a walk with him. He, evidently, did not find me congenial: on which fact I must confess I have been disposed to congratulate myself as his traits have become more and more known to me. For one who flutters in society "disguised as a gentleman," I have no use, and I much regret that I went to Sanborn's for the sake of consulting his file of the Boston Commonwealth.[3] Still, it is not my fault that he is what he is. God mend us all?

It occurs to me that in ten days E.W.E. will be in Detroit, and it has "just struck me," as they say, that I may not go there to see and hear him. Whilst I was hunting up places for him to lecture in he was a prompt correspondent; since the list is filled he is an indifferent. Again I say, God mend us all!

This morning I shall drop into the mail for you a copy of White's history of Selborne.[4] You will see how much drier his observations are than Thoreau's.

By the way, Mr. Salt has much to say about Richard Jefferies, an English writer who lately died, and who is much like Thoreau as an observer.[5] I have none of his books, but have read some selections from him. I learn that Roberts Brothers, of Boston, have republished several of his best works, so take a peep at them when you are "in town."

When I was in Concord I felt keenly that my little knowledge of Nature was a great drawback. But it is now too late for me to make it up. It is a sad defect in anyone's education, and yet it is a part generally neglected.

Thoreau's life was a grand success when you think how filled it was with a perennial delight. "He quaffed the brimming cup of Life." There is a volume in that when you think it over a little.

But I must get into the harness and go to work. There is something tiresome in the practice of Medicine, and if I thought I should have to go about the golden streets prescribing for sick angels, I believe I should make for the woods! . . .

1. Dr. Jones had sent Dr. Emerson a short Thoreau poem with the suggestion that he might find it useful in his lecture on Thoreau:

He kept the temple as divine
  Wherein his soul abided;
He heard the Voice within the shrine
  And followed as it guided;
He found no bane of bitter strife,
  But laws of His designing;
He quaffed the brimming cup of Life
  And went forth unrepining.

O shaven crown and mitre-crowned,
  In court or cloister scheming,
Hath even meek à Kempis found
  In rapt ecstatic dreaming
A creed that swifter strips the Schools
  Of all their craven terrors,
And simply says, "The Maker rules:
  Who chargeth Him with errors!

"He gives unsought the boon of Life:
  When He shall will, resign it.
Vex not thyself in sinful strife
  With Fate, if He design it
That thou shalt drop thy task at noon
  And not when night is falling:
With Him is neither late nor soon,
  Nor, O my Soul, mis-calling!"

O heart so true, so strong, so brave,
  Teach us thy noble daring
That we may face the ruthless grave
  Thy dauntless courage sharing.
From vale and streamlet comes reply—
  "What doth this world of beauty
More plainly teach than that to die
  Is Life's supremest duty."

2. We have been unable to identify Asa J. specifically; he was obviously a member of the Concord G.A.R. whom Jones met in Concord in 1890. Perhaps he made the mistake of saying something disrespectful about Thoreau to Dr. Jones, for he figures repeatedly in Jones's letters as a representative of those in Concord who failed to appreciate Thoreau.

3. A notebook among Dr. Jones's papers records his meeting with Sanborn on August 23, 1890, at which time Dr. Jones catalogued the library of Sanborn for inclusion in his Thoreau bibliography.

4. Dr. Jones's gift was probably Gilbert White, *A Natural History of Selborne*.

5. Salt later published *Richard Jefferies: A Study* (London: Swan Sonnenschein & Co., 1893).

50. S. A. Jones to A. W. Hosmer, March 22, 1891.

I waited for the quiet of Sunday to acknowledge the receipt of the solar print of Thoreau, and lo, the morning's mail brings your letter.

I take hold of it hind end first, and reply to your query about E.W.E.'s prices for "orating." His largest figure was at St. Louis, where he was to be paid $50,00 and his hotel expenses. Many of his engagements were for $30,00, and he said he would not refuse an offer of $25,00. I managed the matter so as to get him $100,00 at Detroit, for, to tell you the truth, I did not think they would have him at the cheap rate.

If all his friends in the West have "worked" as hard for him as I have he is under a heavier load of obligations than I would like to carry; and if he could read all the correspondence I have had it would draw heavily on his "nerve" to stand up and speak his little piece. None are too ready to take him on account of his father; and some are ungodly enough to say "right out in meetin"—that if he is as dry a stick as his father was they would rather pay for the privilege of staying at home.

But, as I have said to you before, he has a sublime self-reliance, and if his matter is good and his manner not absolutely unbearable, he will achieve a position in the lecture field. If he does, he'll be "a bigger man than Grant," and don't you forget my prophecy!

It would gratify my literary curiosity to hear him, and I think I could predict his fate; but I feel that a decent self-respect forbids my going. You see, he ignores the rudiments of common politeness, and my non-appearance in his Detroit audience may be a positive benefit to him if it enters into his mind to consider why I am absent. He did not answer the first enquiry I made as one who is studying Thoreau. He promised to, but his own business has engrossed all his attention. This shows plainly that his interest in Thoreau is a commercial one: if he loved Thoreau's memory he would answer any enquiry that is calculated to make Thoreau better and more truly known. With E.W.E. "gratitude is a lively sense of favors to COME."

My last two letters to him were of a nature to evoke an instant reply from a generous man, and his neglect of them gives me a "Kodak" picture of his "true inwardness" that no microscopical examination could contradict.

Do you recollect my judgement of him when you first pointed him out to me? I called him a "snob," and my doing so gave you pain. Well, that impression flashed upon me by some occult influence, as such things do; and I do not know a single instance in which my instinct has been falsified by subsequent experience. Why Fred, you could cut Horace Hosmer into shoestrings and get more true man out of every strip than E.W.E. has got in his whole carcase.

When he practised as a physician, was he BELOVED? The answer to that will "size him up" correctly, for a doctor's demeanor reveals the inner man infallibly and unerringly. If the heart of him is mean, no device will hide the damning fact.

As is the fountain so is the stream, and you may depend upon it, R.W.E. had the tact to hide that which the son reveals.

But, let me be just and avow to you that, while I am warmer blooded than E.W.E., and therefore more emotional, my skin encloses fully as much meanness as his.

I know it, and in my better moments I abase myself, but as THE EMERSON says, "One cannot escape the black drop in the ancestral blood."[1] Alas, no!

After dinner I took a smoke and read the last number of the Athenaeum, a London paper, and in it I find this:

"Mr. Edward Emerson, whose little book concerning his father originated in a paper read to the Concord club, recently gave his boyish and youthful reminiscences of Thoreau. In this paper Thoreau appears as a veritable Pied Piper among the children of Concord, while to their scholarly fathers he was Pan. Mr. Emerson speaks with a charm that often recalls his father, and possesses a fine touch in personal and intellectual portraiture."

As "this paper" has not been published, how in the deuce did the Athenaeum get to know of it? I'll tell you my explanation of it: Moncure D. Conway[2] is living in London, and perhaps E.W.E. has "worked" him. . . .

1. The reference seems to be to Emerson's comments on heredity in "Fate" from *The Conduct of Life:* "How shall a man escape from his ancestors, or draw off from his veins the black drop which he drew from his father's or his mother's life?" See Emerson, *Works* (Boston: Houghton Mifflin Co., 1903), 6:9.

2. Moncure Daniel Conway (1832–1907), a friend of Emerson and an acquaintance of Thoreau, was for many years a liberal Unitarian clergyman in London.

51. Henry Salt to S. A. Jones, April 1, 1891.

* * *

It was extremely kind of you to take all that trouble about the projected Edition of the Life. Of course I should be very glad if an American Edition could be arranged, and if Dr. Emerson could be induced to cooperate in it. Before writing to Messrs. Harper, or any other firm, I will wait to hear again from you as to the result of Dr. Emerson's visit to Detroit.

I hear from W. H. Dircks that he is now at work on a third Thoreau volume (miscellaneous, I believe)[1] for the Camelot Series; so the English public are not going to be allowed to forget that Thoreau existed. I must try to induce some publisher to reprint *Cape Cod* and the *Excursions.* . . .

I think I have sent you a list of the chief English reviews of my book. The *Athenaeum* failed me, & ignored it, (rather comical this, considering what rubbish they review weekly at great length!), and I think there is now nothing more to be looked for, until new editions call forth new reviews.

By the way, did I ever suggest to you that a passage in Lowell's "Fable for Critics" should be entered in a Thoreau bibliography? You will doubtless know the ins and outs of it better than I do, but there is a reference to two friends and imitators of Emerson, one of whom (I don't know which) is apparently meant for Thoreau.

Also Allibone's Dict. of Eng. Lit. (London & Philadelphia, 1871) vol. III, pp. 2406, 2407, has a passage on Thoreau.

Also a Mr. Karl Knortz writes to me from 540 E. 155th St. New York to say that in his "Geschichte der Nordamerikanischen Litteratur", published just now at Berlin, he has devoted about 20 pages to Thoreau. But probably this is no news to you.

I am interested to learn that the William Sloane Kennedy portrait turns out to be a myth! I shall greatly value the one you kindly promise to send me. If, when you are next writing, you are able to send me one of yourself, it will be another favour to crown the many I have received from you. I have got quite to think of you as an old friend.

[P.S.] Do you collect the various reviews, &c, on Thoreau topics? If so, I will make a point of regularly sending you all that appears in England— also the late reviews of my book.

1. *Essays and Other Writings of Henry Thoreau* (London: Scott, [1891]).

52. S. A. Jones to A. W. Hosmer, April 3, 1891.

You owe this scribblement to the fact that I have just received a letter from the Duke of Concord written by his highness at Chicago on April the second.

He says, "Do not be too hard on me as negligent or ungrateful because you have not heard from me sooner. Thus far the days and nights have been so full that there have been no spare moments."

He closeth thusly: "I believe you and I shall yet meet, and if you ever march Eastward without the Army, or with it, be sure I shall welcome you at my house."[1]

Of that I shall by no means "be sure," for a veneered politeness is not the thing to rely upon. As a carpenter's son I know that much about furniture!

Last night's mail brought me a letter from that dear old simplicity, Cummings E. Davis,[2] and it warms my heart as nothing from E.W.E. can ever do. Give me honest homespun rather than broadcloth, forever for every day wear.

At the request of a lady in Philadelphia[3] I wrote a review of Mr. Salt's

"Life" which she wished to have published in "Lippincott's Magazine." The editor said he "wanted nothing on Thoreau." This makes me think that the son of his father isn't going around the country with the most taking topic, and it is quite probable that one sight of the son will be sufficient for each audience.

Our university boys have a monthly, "The Inlander," and, unless they "want nothing on Thoreau," I will publish my review in that. If so, I'll send you some copies for the sake of stirring up Mr. Sanborn—who gets "honorable mention" in it.

White's "Selborne" shows how fitly Channing called Thoreau the Poet-Naturalist. White is a naturalist; Thoreau is the naturalist *plus* the poet, and crowning these is the moralist. . . .

P.S. Since typing the above I have seen a report of E.W.E.'s lecture in a Cleveland paper which speaks highly of his effort. From what is quoted in this report it seems that the lecture is made up largely of selections from others. I recognized much of Mr. Blake's writing. A great deal is given as from Thoreau's "unpublished journal," but every word quoted has been published. I should like to have heard the "whole business," but I really could not go into his audience with my letters unanswered—and he would have despised me if I had.

I shall write him a letter to-night, and I shall be as plain with him as Thoreau would have been. If he is true stuff, he will appreciate it accordingly; and if he is n't, I shall appreciate him accordingly—and so we'll both be happy. One can see from the Cleveland that his father's "rep" is floating him.

Ann Arbor, 3rd April 1891.

Dear Mr. Emerson,

Your favor of the 2nd instant is at hand and most welcome. That old fellow was absent from the before-mentioned "back seat" because, as the Quakers say, he did not feel "free" to go to the lecture. There were expressions in his last letter to you which he remembered; and which, under the ambiguity of your silence, such a self-respect as is consistent with a becoming humility forbade his attendance. He had looked forward to that event with peculiarly pleasant anticipations, and if your "disappointment" equalled his own, you have his sincere commiseration.

My old schoolmate, Mr. Skinner, wrote me that your lecture "pleased the audience," and an editorial friend in Cleveland sent me a copy of his paper in which I see a long notice and a warm [notice] of your effort there. . . .

I sincerely trust that next year you will talk from our University platform with an appreciative audience to look you in the face.

As this may find you "on the wing" it shall be so brief as not to add materially to your fatigue. With every good wish, I am,

Sincerely yours,

* * *

(Writing of my chagrin at not being able to secure him a hearing in Ann Arbor, I said "if you see a dejected looking old fellow on a back seat at your lecture, you can say to yourself, "That's Jones, of Ann Arbor." His letter refers to his not seeing me on the "back seat."[4]

His letter also expresses his "real disappointment" at not seeing me on the said "back seat."

Reviewing the whole episode, I fancy it is he, not I, who will occupy that same "back seat;" at least, in such a contest I am not willing to take it.)

You may show this to the Misses Hosmer in confidence; then "mum's the word!"

1. Dr. Edward Emerson to Dr. Jones, April 2,1891 (Jones collection). On the envelope Dr. Jones wrote "Finis."
2. Dr. Jones met Cummings E. Davis, the Concord antiquarian, during his trip to Concord in 1890.
3. She was later identified by Dr. Jones as Emily Lyman, an early enthusiast of Thoreau.
4. Dr. Edward Emerson to Dr. Jones, April 2, 1891 (Jones collection).

53. S. A. Jones to A. W. Hosmer, April 12, 1891.

On Friday evening my son handed me your letter and also one from Mr. Emerson written at Quincey, Illinois. He disclaims any deliberate discourtesy, and writes, "I deeply regret to have seemed scant in courtesy towards you."[1]

The whole matter is just one of those nasty *little* disagreeabilities which are all the more vexing because it is as easy to avoid as to perpetrate them.

Ordinarily, I can put up with as much as anyone, and I don't go waltzing through this world with a chip on my shoulder; but on extra-ordinary occasions I spit out as any Welshman would. I am sorry that this "late unpleasantness" occurred, for one never forgets the flaw in the gem when once they have found it.

You ask about the lectures. At present, Miss Eliza Hosmer is reading them in the MSS. I do not know whether they will find their way into print or not.[2] If they are published, it must be at my expense. I should not hesitate at that were I at all assured of their deserving it; but I am not particularly "stuck" on my own performances, and I have no shekels to sacrifice at the shrine of my own vanity.

A bookseller in Cleveland, Ohio, proposed reprinting the "Glimpse" with the two subsequent lectures, but a change in partnership obliged him to "go back on me." (What a pity it is that slang is so expressive and yet so vulgar.) That is just where the matter rests. I believe I shall submit the lectures to a Professor in our University for his sincere criticism, and if he says they are worth publishing I shall forego my anticipated visit to Concord this summer, for I cannot both publish and visit. I should be sorry to lose the visit, because I believe I am prepared to profit more by it than I did by the first—and yet *that* visit will remain green in my memory so long as I live. By the way, Mr. Emerson wrote me from Chicago as follows: "I am sorry to say that after long waiting I cannot give you the information you asked for and I expected to bring you, about the Under-Ground Rail-Road, because the old lady who has all the facts, in addition to much deafness and blindness, had been sick a-bed for six weeks before I left home and could not see me."[3]

Can you tell me if this is a "blind," or the truth? If it is simple truth then E.W.E. is merely careless in some matters; if it is not the truth—then I want no more of *him*.

I ask you the question thinking that you may know to which old lady he refers, and I beg leave to assure you that I ask it for the sake of the truth. If the enquiry is one that you at all shrink from, please consider it a *blank*. . . .

1. Dr. Edward Emerson to Dr. Jones, April 8, 1891 (Jones collection).
2. These lectures, read before the Unity Club in February, were not published.
3. This material is in Emerson's earlier letter, that of April 2, 1891, to which Dr. Jones took such vigorous exception (Jones collection).

54. Henry Salt to S. A. Jones, April 15 [1891].

* * *

I will not write at length in answer to your last, as this may perhaps cross one from you. If Dr. E's visit led to no particular plan respecting the *Thoreau,* perhaps you will kindly let me know that I am free to write to Messrs. Harper.

Many thanks for the extracts from the Hosmer reminiscences which I found very interesting. That the work you have done, and are doing, in thus collecting & giving permanence to what might otherwise be fugitive records, is of the utmost value, there can be no question.

I am very pleased to hear that you liked my article in the *Paternoster Review.* I sent a copy to the *Eclectic,* in the hope they might reproduce it.

55. S. A. Jones to A. W. Hosmer, April 19, 1891.

* * *

The other day I received a letter, written from Concord, by E.W.E. in which he signs himself "Yours truly." All the preceeding were, "Sincerely yours."[1]

No more favors needed! I am obliged to put him side by side with my dear Asa in my cabinet of curious things.

I was glad to learn Mr. Hoar's testimony to the faithfulness of your Thoreau picture; from the first glance I had of dear Mr. Blake's daguerreotype I felt *this is the man!* . . .

1. In this letter Dr. Edward Emerson expressed his desire to end any disagreement with Dr. Jones: "So now that we have explained that there was nothing but good will in our thoughts, whatever misadventure chanced, I think that we can safely drop the subject and hope to prosper better another time" (Emerson to Jones, April 16, 1891, Jones collection).

56. S. A. Jones to A. W. Hosmer, April 28, 1891.

* * *

I also write at once because your suggestion about sending a Thoreau picture to Mr. Salt is peculiarly pleasing to me, and *your* doing it will give him an especial delight.

I have sent him a lot of your other pictures and a copy of your Ricketson-Thoreau photo. I had also promised to send one of the Blake-Thoreau pictures, and designed writing to you for it so soon as I had your letter—which I now have.

Please send him one of your largest—not the large one you had specially made for me—and let me share with you the expense of picture and mailing. Don't be foolish and "get your back up" at this proposition. You know how I mean it, and I have confidence enough in your good sense not to be afraid to make it.

Send it in your own name, but, as the Englishmen are a curious set, you had better mention that you are a friend of mine and that we are all three of us bound by the common tie of a love for Thoreau. I mention this because Englishmen are even more given to "smelling" a stranger than is our dear friend Asa—whose shadow, I sincerely trust, will never be *less*.

The address is, H. S. Salt, 38 Gloucester Road, London, N.W., England.

You will get a response from him that will do your heart good, "and do n't you forget it!"

O Fred, I *may* get into correspondence with Mr. Dircks, and if so I'll find out if he received your pictures, and if *so*, I'll find out why in he******h—ah, there!—he did n't acknowledge the gift. By the way, he is soon to put forth another Thoreau volume like the *Week* and *Walden,* and I'll see that one is on your shelves. . . .

57. Henry Salt to S. A. Jones, May 7, 1891.

I return Messrs. McClurg's letter herewith, and sincerely thank you for all your kind services in this, as in so many other matters. It is very disappointing, of course; and yet I suppose it is only what must be expected, while people in general are what they are![1] Oddly enough, a day or two after receiving your letter, Bentley sent me in his accounts for the first six months of the book's existence, which revealed the fact that he has only sold a bare three hundred copies out of the 750 printed! This is a strange proof that a book may be very widely noticed by the reviews, and even read rather widely by the more thoughtful class of readers, and yet fail altogether to *sell.* Bentley, however, seems pleased to have published the *Thoreau,* and, after all, he has sold enough copies to pay the expenses incurred by him, though not enough to pay *me* more than a few pounds. However, I presume it will continue to sell, albeit slowly.

So you see the two countries are about on a par in their appreciation of Thoreau!

I have written to Messrs. Harper, suggesting an American Edition, but I am not at all sanguine of the result. I hope, after this, you will not trouble yourself any further about it; though of course if at any time anything should chance to offer itself, I should be very grateful if you would bear me in mind. When we remember what Thoreau himself had to experience in the case of the *Week,* little disappointments of the present kind seem very trivial.

Thank you for telling me the genesis of the lines on Thoreau, and how they were spoken at the meeting. I have no doubt whatever they 'went home', for true and deep feeling, as yours for Thoreau, does not fail of its effect.[2]

I am sorry to hear what you tell me about Emerson's son. The sons of great men are too often, I fear, a clog upon their fathers' names; and the shock of finding them out is necessarily painful for their friends and acquaintances. It is better, perhaps, to get it over quickly, and think no more of them!

As to the reference to Thoreau in the "Fable for Critics", there is this further difficulty—that *two* Emersonian imitators are ridiculed, one at the beginning of the passage ("There comes . . . for instance") and one at the end ("—has picked up all the windfalls before", or something to that effect). The cadence of the lines wd. seem to indicate that Thoreau is the former; but I remember Mr. Sanborn quoted it to me the other way round. Perhaps, however, you know for certain who is indicated in the second allusion, and I suppose the shortness of limb points emphatically to Thoreau in the former case.[3] I shd. have thought that, being by Lowell, it *was* worth insertion in the bibliography, altho' so short.

I transmitted your message to W. H. Dircks, who will, I doubt not, be gratified by it. He asked me, some time back, to suggest passages for inclusion in his volume, and I have sent him a list of my special favorites. I am extremely glad that this new Camelot volume is forthcoming, as it will serve to give another impetus to the study of Thoreau in this country. I am sorry to say I have quite failed to get any illustrated magazine to accept the proposed article & illustrations of Thoreau's haunts. This is partly, perhaps, because there are so very few illustrated magazines on this side of the Atlantic. Could not *you* write such a paper for *Scribner* or *Harper* or the *Century,* and give the results of your recent researches at Concord? A Thoreau article of that kind, giving a series of illustrations, would be of immense interest and value. Do please feel that you are called upon to do this!

I have lately been somewhat unfortunate in another of my literary ventures, a fire at Messrs. Ballantynes', the Edinburgh printers, having destroyed all the unbound copies of my "Life of James Thomson", i.e. all but about 100 copies in the bookseller's hands. As they were uninsured, it is a loss both to the publisher and me. Do you know this book? If not, and if the pessimism of "B.V." does not repel you, I should like to send you a copy, to read yourself, and lend to anyone who would care for it.

Since I last wrote to you, I have had the privilege of spending an evening with George Meredith, the novelist, with whom I had corresponded several times on the subject of James Thomson. Meredith is a wonderful old man—his conversation a monologue of brilliant epigrams and apothegms as in his books. . . .

[P.S.] Dr. Japp's "De Quincey Memorials" is just published—an interesting book, but perhaps rather too bulky & spun out. Dr. Japp is a most hearty and good-natured soul. I lunch with him occasionally at one of the London vegetarian restaurants. He has a genuine feeling for Thoreau.

1. McClurg is undoubtedly the Cleveland publisher referred to in Salt's letter of January 30, 1891, to Dr. Jones.
2. For the text of these lines by Dr. Jones, see his letter to Hosmer, March 17, 1891 (letter 49).
3. For a discussion of this matter, see the introduction.

58. Henry Salt to A. W. Hosmer, May 16, 1891.

Please accept my warmest thanks for your great kindness in sending me the photographs of Thoreau, which arrived safely a day or two ago. I am sure all lovers of Thoreau owe you their gratitude for the skill with which you have added this admirable portrait to those already familiar to us. It is most interesting to see him in this intermediate state between *no* beard and *full* beard; and the portrait gives such a clear and life-like expression that I can well believe what you tell me of Mr. Edward Hoar's judgment on it. Of the two copies you sent me, I think I prefer the larger one; it is so wonderfully delicate and vivid; but I am glad to have both, for, as you say, there are certain points that are distinctive in each. I shall value them very highly, both on Thoreau's account, and as coming from the artist who took them, and one of a name so well known to readers of Thoreau's journal. . . .

Here, in England, there is of course nothing like a proper appreciation of Thoreau's wonderful genius, and one is constantly hearing a repetition of all the stupid old arguments that are brought out against him; but it is consoling to find a gradual increase in his admirers. I am very glad to hear that my book interested you. I hope it may be useful at any rate as helping to draw English readers to Thoreau, and paving the way for the full & final biography which can only be written by someone on the spot. . . .

59. Henry Salt to S. A. Jones, May 29, 1891.

I am sending you (by book post) two magazine articles of mine, one on Ed. Carpenter's writings, the other on Richd. Jefferies'.[1] As they contain allusions to Thoreau, they may perhaps interest you; perhaps, too, for Jefferies' and Carpenter's sake. All these "poet-naturalists" have a great attraction for me. (I hope, by the way, you have not to pay duty on packages of this kind? If you have, I fear I am doing you a doubtful compliment in thus transmitting my effusions to you!)

Also I sent, a few days ago, a pamphlet on "Humanitarianism", which, with the notices of the "Humanitarian League" subjoined, will explain why I am very busy at present, as hon. secretary of the new League. In this package I enclosed some press-cuttings with reviews of my *Thoreau.* I hope these will have arrived safely.

The day before yesterday we spent a pleasant evening in talk with Mr. McQuesten,[2] who came up here to see us by appointment, after calling once & missing me earlier in the week. I am obliged to you for introducing him to me, as I like him much; he is so frank, and genial, and thoroughly genuine in every way. We had much talk, you may be sure, about Thoreau, and Concord, and a certain Dr. Jones who seems to have the knack of making those who have met him only once (or not at all!) feel towards him as towards an old friend! A week or two ago, I had a letter from Mr. G. W. Curtis (to whom I had written) saying that he would much like to see my *Thoreau.* I also heard from Messrs. Harper to the same effect, saying that they would submit the book to their reader with a view to considering the publication of it. Copies have now gone to both of them; and though I do not expect a favorable answer from the Harpers, I hope Mr. Curtis may mention the book in his "Editor's Easy Chair" column.

I mention this because it strikes me that while Mr. Curtis has the subject before him you might take the opportunity of arranging something about an illustrated Thoreau article in *Harper's Magazine.* I don't know whether you have any such plan in mind; if not, excuse me for suggesting it; but you know I feel strongly that you might give us all a treat by an illustrated record of your Thoreau-studies and visit to Concord! . . .

1. These articles are not in the Jones collection.
2. Dr. Jones apparently met Mr. McQuesten in Concord in 1890 and gave him Salt's name. The Jones correspondence at the University of Illinois does not include McQuesten.

60. S. A. Jones to A. W. Hosmer, May 30, 1891.

* * *

. . . Now let me tickle you under the short ribs. Prepare to shout! Well, in the August number of Lippincott's Magazine there will be a paper of mine entitled "Thoreau in the hands of his Biographers," and when you have read it you'll conclude that no lover of Thoreau's memory owes Mr. Sanborn anything.[1] O Fred, it does my soul good to think of the delight with which the best of you Concord people will read that short paper; and I do sincerely hope that you all will see in it evidence that I am deeply grateful for the countless kindnesses that aided my Thoreau studies when I was the "stranger within your gates."

If F.B.S. attempts to "chaw" me up, you'll see a circus, and I rather "guess" he'll spit me out as a dog does a toad. You keep an eye on the Boston papers about that time, and if he says anything there, please let me know. I do not see the Springfield Republican, and as that is Sanborn's dunghill[2] he may throw a—pardon me—"stinkpot" from it. However, we'll see what comes of it. . . .

1. Samuel A. Jones, "Thoreau and His Biographers," *Lippincott's Monthly Magazine* 48 (August 1891):224–28. In this article Dr. Jones characterized Sanborn's biography as beginning "the era of personal misrepresentation" and again defended John and Cynthia Thoreau. See the appendix.
2. Sanborn was associated with the *Springfield Republican* from 1856 until 1914.

61. S. A. Jones to A. W. Hosmer, June 16, 1891.

* * *

That proof of Thoreau's survey of the Hosmer farm[1] made me knock one of the ten commandments all to smithereens. Thou shalt not covet! Good Lord, how can flesh and blood help it? As God is my judge I do declare that I had rather own that survey than the farm itself—yes, than any estate in your whole township. Such, dear Fred, is the shape my insanity takes, and I am even ready to thank Heaven for giving me the deflection in that direction. . . .

Do you remember the letter you got from Parker Pillsbury? It may become a piece of very needful evidence for me. Do you set an especial value upon it as an autograph? If so, I must borrow it should occasion come when I may need the original text of his statement to you.

It may be that I am needlessly magnifying my paper in Lippincott's and that Mr. Sanborn may despise a critic who is absolutely unknown; but if he replies I want my ammunition all at hand, and then "the devil take the hindmost!"

Mr. Salt is urging me to prepare an illustrated paper on Thoreau's Haunts, but I much question if any American magazine would care to publish it. It is a sad fact that Thoreau's admirers are few. Of Mr. Salt's *Life* only 300 copies were sold in a year!!! It makes me want to "puke" on the majority of mankind, or rather, fool-kind.

But if I were not such a "pismire" myself I should regard all these poor devils as calmly as Thoreau did. . . .

1. Probably the farm of Edmund Hosmer, which Thoreau surveyed on the 18th and 21st of June 1851. See Walter Harding, *The Days of Henry Thoreau*, p. 275.

62. Henry Salt to S. A. Jones, July 2, 1891.

* * *

I am of course delighted to hear of the forthcoming article in *Lippincott*. It will be a great advantage to my book to be thus made known to the American reading public, which at present must necessarily be almost ignorant of its existence. I shall look with interest, too, to see what you say of Mr. Sanborn! Harpers, by the way, have declined to issue an edition; so now I shall not trouble any further on that score, but leave the rest to time.

We had a most interesting time in Derbyshire with Edward Carpenter, walking daily with him through all his favorite haunts in wood and on moorland, and meeting most of his working-men friends from Sheffield and its neighborhood. He is preparing a third edition of his "Towards Democracy", and it is easy to see that he regards this book as *the* expression of whatever message he is charged to deliver. (He wrote it, after a period of long thought and trouble and mental perturbation at white heat, so to speak, almost without immediate thought of either matter or form. If ever a man was literally "inspired" to write a book, I believe this is a case in instance.) To know such a man on close and intimate terms is some compensation for *not* having known Shelley and Thoreau! . . .

63. S. A. Jones to A. W. Hosmer, July 7, 1891.

* * *

[P.S.] Will you please see Mr. F. B. Sanborn and tell him that a gentleman who is making a Thoreau Collection—to be presented to the University of Michigan when it is complete—authorizes you to offer him $125,00 for the copy of THE DIAL that belonged to Thoreau.[1]

Tell him also that the Library building of the University of Michigan is absolutely fire-proof, which insures the permanent safety of the said copy of THE DIAL.

For such a purpose he may be willing to part with it: under any other circumstances I do not for a moment think he would.

If he is willing to make such a sacrifice for the sake of erecting a perpetual memory-offering to Thoreau's genius, I will send you a draft for the money at once.

I do not consider this in the light of a sale—Mr. S. will simply sacrifice a treasured memento for the sake of doing honor to Thoreau's memory. . . .

1. The journal which Dr. Jones kept during his trip to Concord suggests that he saw Thoreau's copy of the *Dial* while visiting Sanborn. Walter Harding has suggested that Sanborn was probably given Thoreau's copy of the journal by Sophia Thoreau, who gave away many of her brother's books in the years following his death. See Harding, *Thoreau's Library* (Charlottesville: University of Virginia Press, 1957), p. 22. Thoreau's copy of the *Dial* is now in the Southern Illinois University Library.

64. Daniel Ricketson to S. A. Jones, July 7, 1891.

I am in receipt of a copy of the "Inlander" containing a short colloquy in which the parties thereto appear to be our late lamented friend Henry D. Thoreau and yourself, for which please accept my thanks. If our deceased friend could have received a tithe of the appreciation during his short life, that has been so liberally awarded him since his death, it would have been at least cheering to his great soul, which, however, so bravely fought out his struggle against opposition and unkind criticism. I perceive your name among the contributors to Mr. Salt's excellent tribute to the genuine worth of our dear Thoreau.

65. Henry Salt to S. A. Jones, July 10, 1891 [postcard].

Just a few lines to thank you sincerely for what the post has today brought me, a photograph that I have long wished to possess & which I shall value greatly.

Also for the copy of the *Inlander,* recd a few days ago. That 'Afternoon in the University Library'[1] is one of the most charming things I have read for some time; I can tell you its tender phantasy gave *me* a delightful afternoon, not in a University Library but in a Sussex hamlet! Looked at from another side also, the *poetry of bibliography* was never more happily manifested! I must try to get it reprinted in some English journal.

I will not write more now, as I lately sent a letter from here. I heard lately from Mr. McQuesten and Mr. A. W. Hosmer, both of whom very kindly sent me some photos. One of the 'Old Manse' sent by Mr. McQuesten is very interesting—still more so that of Thoreau's survey of the Hosmer farm.

1. "An Afternoon in the University Library" appeared in the *Inlander* 1 (June 1891):150–53.

66. S. A. Jones to Daniel Ricketson, July 11, 1891.

I sent you a copy of the "Inlander" solely for the purpose of giving so old a friend of Thoreau's the history of the 1862 edition of his *Week,* and, behold, you have been kind enough to delight me with a friendly note.

I beg leave to say that, as a bibliographical fragment, the paper in the Inlander is based on absolute fact. When preparing a bibliography of Thoreau I was not aware of the existence of the "1862 edition," and having found a copy thereof, the problem was to account for it. I therefore visited Concord last August, and to solve this puzzle was a part of my purpose. As I am the first to record this bit of history I am as pleased with my performance as is the young mother with her first baby—"for pride attends us still."

The manner in which the fact is presented may make the paper appear as a clumsy figment; but I have only allowed fancy to dress up the fact. I did wish to contrast Carlyle's famous *Sartor* with Thoreau's first book, and to declare my conviction that the stormy Scotchman must sit at Thoreau's feet—*as a philosopher.* I also wished to have that particular book in our University Library tenderly preserved, and I am glad to inform you that, from a little regard for me as an effete ex-professor, that book can now be *seen,* but no rude hand can harm it. A common copy is provided for *use.*

When I was in Concord I ached to go to New Bedford and see you; but when I learned what strange creatures the School of Philosophy had erstwhile attracted thither, I feared I might be taken by you for one of the same, and I had not the courage to knock at your door. Of course, Mr. Ricketson, such self-distrust is based on self-knowledge, and a consciousness of my own defects tends to make me shy in the presence of strangers. Nevertheless, I have many times repented that I did not call upon you; for your deepest scrutiny, while detecting my fallings-short, would have also found a sincere veneration for him whom it was your happiness to know. I am not worthy to even grease Thoreau's shoes—you know he wouldn't let me "black" them—but I am a truer man than I would have been had Thoreau never lived.

You refer to Mr. Salt's Life of Thoreau and to me as a contributor. I did put my bibliography at his service, and have ever since been in correspondence with him—a love for Thoreau being "the tie that binds." Let me add that when Houghton, Mifflin and Co. published an enlarged bibliography in Mr. Blake's "Thoreau's Thoughts," I reserved the right to publish another bibliography whenever I saw fit. I did this because I desire to see a bibliography that will give as complete a history of each of Thoreau's books as is possible at this late day. To this end I shall need the aid, here and there, of those who knew Thoreau. Therefore I beg leave to apply to you when need arises.

I am also collecting first editions of Thoreau's Works, and everything that I can find which in any way applies to him. It is already a large collection, and it will ultimately be deposited *en bloc* in some suitable place where they may fructify those who shall come to them after I am insensate dust.

From Mr. Salt's *Life* I learned for the first time of your *Autumn Sheaf,* and I am surprised that he did not include it in his bibliography. As I am collecting items of this nature for the larger edition of this bibliography, will you kindly copy the title-page of that volume, and state the pages therein in which Thoreau is mentioned? I know this is bold in me, but I ask it in his name.

In Lippincott's Magazine for the coming August I shall have a paper entitled *Thoreau in the Hands of his Biographers,* and if you would give me your plainest and most unsparing criticism you will help one who is most earnestly desirous of securing for Thoreau that audience which his life and work should have, but as yet, does not.

I most sincerely trust that the spirit which urges me to write will also lead you to pardon so long a letter.

67. S. A. Jones to A. W. Hosmer, July 12, 1891.

I have just time enough to throw off a line to say that I am "allfired glad" that you did not have that set of John Burroughs' *Works*.[1]

If you had n't them, I knew, of course, that his paper on Thoreau[2] would please you. Some consider it the best thing yet written about Thoreau.

My only criticism is that Burroughs is worldly-wise, and measures Thoreau accordingly. To do *that* justly one has to soar as high above the world as Thoreau did—then you get such a conception of Thoreau as you have the capacity for. Anyone will fall as far below the true conception of Thoreau as their nature is below his.[3]

I find myself so far below that I am not fit to grease Thoreau's boots. . . .

[P.S. 13th July.] Please tell Mr. Sanborn that he can forgive my audacity only by remembering that I wished the DIAL here to make it the capstone of such a monument to Thoreau as I shall place in the University Library. . . .

1. Dr. Jones had sent Alfred Hosmer an eight-volume set of the works of Burroughs.
2. Burroughs's fullest assessment of Thoreau was originally published as "Henry D. Thoreau," *Century Magazine* 2 (July 1882):368–79.
3. Dr. Jones had earlier argued in "Thoreau: A Glimpse" that Burroughs did not soar quite so high as Thoreau. In that essay Jones criticised Burroughs sharply for belittling Thoreau's act of civil disobedience. (See Burroughs's article in the *Century*, cited above.) Dr. Jones praised Thoreau for his willingness "to live up to a conviction," though to do so was to be "a minority of one with the universe against it." Where Thoreau saw a principle to be affirmed, "Burroughs sees only a 'paltry tax'—so different the measure of men." See *Thoreau: A Glimpse* (Concord: Albert Lane, 1903), p. 13. Reprinted from the 1890 edition.

68. Daniel Ricketson to S. A. Jones, July 15, 1891.

I received your kind letter of the 11th inst. in the same kind spirit, but I fear I shall hardly be able to answer your expectations in my response. I presume I am considerably older than you, as I was four years older than Thoreau, so that I shall reach my seventy-eighth year on the 30th of this month. Just now I am rather *poorly,* having had an "ill turn" a few days ago, and added thereto, I am afflicted with poison in my face and eyes, to which I have been subject for the past five or six years at this season whenever I go to visit my son and daughter at their summer resort, "Nonquit Beach," some six miles hence on the north shore of our beautiful Buzzard's bay, so full of historic interest from the days of the Northmen in the 10th, 11th, & 12th centuries, giving it the name "Straumfiord," stream currents, and the adjoining coast, Vineland. Afterwards, re-discovered by Bartholemew Gosnold in 1602, who gave the name of his queen to the Elizabeth islands that form its southern boundary. I crossed this bay with Thoreau in the summer of 1856, and landed on Naushon, the largest of the islands, and strolled with him along its shores and into the primitive woods, where the native deer are still found. Here we also heard the wood-thrush and other of our songbirds much to our delight. Days sacred in memory, so great the changes to me in common with other mortals.

But to return to your letter,—in my remembrance of Thoreau, I must repeat what I have so often written before to his biographers, but I must also caution you in its use.

I never felt that I was as near to him as some of his older friends whom he often mentioned to me in much respect, particularly Messrs Blake and Brown, who were I think more *loyal* than I, who being quite free, often too much so, in my expressions differed occasionally from our more learned and exacting Seer—Still I enjoyed and profited much in his companionship during the seven or eight years of his latter life. His strict honesty, veracity, justness &c. &c. somewhat, perhaps, lessened the warmth of his friendship, which those of more ardent natures like myself desire, but are usually doomed to disappointment. Of course Thoreau was by far the wiser and better man.

I shd. conclude that you & I were more alike than T. and ourselves, and that in an early friendship we should not have done so well together as with him.

My "Autumn Sheaf," to which you refer, was privately printed, and very limited number, all of which were exhausted many years ago. I shd. be glad had I a spare one to send it to you. As you wish for references therein to T., I send the following.

"The improvised dance," page 198
"In Memoriam" page 209

These I think are noticed in brief by Sanborn and Salt.

I fear I have hardly responded to your warm-hearted letter, but must plead as excuse my present *collapsed* condition, as Thoreau's eccentric & poetic friend, Ellery Channing, might say.

P.S. I obtained two or three copies of "The Autumn Sheaf" a few years ago by advertising in our papers, but hardly think any copy could now be found for sale. My published matters have usually been "out of pocket."

69. S. A. Jones to A. W. Hosmer, July 28, 1891.

I purposed writing you to-night, and here is your letter of yesterday to remind me of my purpose. It is a delight to learn that the paper[1] pleases those whom I love in Concord. It pains me to think that I forgot Mr. Davis. If you can spare one, please do give it to him in my name. The simple soul can not "take in" Thoreau, but he loves Thoreau's memory and that is enough.

It gives me a deep pleasure to learn that you sent a copy to Miss Folsom. Had I known that she was alive, she would have had one *hot* from me. As it is, if you know her you can tell her that I never remember her letter in the "Advertiser" without blessing her for having written it.

It is almost a certainty that the paper will be reprinted in England: if so, it will help to neutralize the venom in Mr. Sanbor's book. (I see the machine has spelled it "Sanbor;" if it had made it Sand bar, I should think the darned thing was a prophet!)

If the sand bar says anything, it will probably be in the Springfield Republican—and that I should like to see. I don't care so much for a "muss" with him—I can easily find more profitable employment—but if he tries to "do me up" it will eventuate in putting the Thoreaus *fairly* before the reading public, and to accomplish *that* I would toil for years.

As I have ranked Thoreau as a moral force higher than Emerson,[2] I wonder how "the son of his father" enjoys it. It will doubtless slide off his self-conceit like water from a duck; but it has already set some to thinking about the *life* of the two worthies. Tired, tired tired from a hard day's work. . . .

1. Dr. Jones had sent several copies of his article "Thoreau and His Biographers" to friends in Concord.
2. Of Emerson and Thoreau Dr. Jones had commented in "Thoreau and His Biographers": "When the latter-day mad race for wealth, only wealth, shall have brought us the inevitable result and a chastened people shall seek 'the better way,' it will be the 'hermit' of Walden, not the Sage of Concord, that will lead them."

70. H.G.O. Blake to S. A. Jones, August 1, 1891.

I shd. probably have replied to your letter of July 20 before, if I had not been out of town considerably, since receiving it. Your time & thoughts must have been much & sadly occupied with the care & loss of your aged parents.

As to the books, it was my wish in sending them that you shd. receive as many copies, at least, as I did. You said, I believe, that H. M. & Co. sent you 6. You gave away one to some institution; that I shd. like to account for. The remaining 5, at the rate of H. M. & Co. charged for the 12, including express charge, wd. amount to $3.31¼. But, if you pay me nothing, you will get but a very inadequate pecuniary return for your contribution to the book, so that, if you let the matter stand as it is, I shall be most truly satisfied.

Thank you for sending me the Lippincott. I shd. have seen it at our Reading Room, but it is pleasant to receive it directly frm. you. I have read the article pretty carefully, twice. The last page, beginning, 'That he was sincerity-incarnate' touches the heart of the matter, & interested me deeply. Your statement that 'his religion grew out of his philosophy' I like very much; scientific religion, using the word scientific in its longest and profoundest sense, equivalent to philosophic, knowing with the united action of all our faculties, our whole nature. Thoreau was a new revealer of divine truth, as every creature shd. be in his own way. But how dim it is in most of us.

You will, I trust, like to have me frank enough to say that I think some of the other parts of the article were somewhat quarrelsome & bitter, nor do I believe much in making comparisons, as between the 'hermit' & the 'sage', however I may be inclined to indulge in them. But, then, we are made differently.

71. Henry Salt to S. A. Jones, August 3, 1891.

* * *

I went down last spring (perhaps I have already told you this) to George Meredith's cottage in Surrey, to hear him talk about Thomson, and he told me that what most impressed him in the man was his whole-hearted courage and honesty. The day before yesterday I happened to be going a short journey, and at a railway book-stall I got an August *Lippincott* and there discovered and read your article on "Thoreau & his Biographers". My dear Dr. Jones, I do thank you most sincerely for what you have there written of my efforts to get justice done to Thoreau's genius; what you say of my desire to *live* the life, and not only to write of it, is the one word which I value above all "literary" appreciations whatsoever.

I enjoyed the whole article immensely (what does Sanborn think of it?!!); and of course I wholly agree with you in your recognition of Thoreau as *the* great figure of Concord for future generations. I was disposed to let Emerson alone in my *Life;* but what you say of him is true, and will have to be asserted and reasserted in the future.

Your correction of the errors about the "underground railway", and the character of Thoreau's parents, are very important, and will no doubt make their mark in future biographies—certainly if my book shd. ever be reprinted, I will correct what I have written. By the way, I may tell you in confidence that Dr. Japp wrote that review in the *Spectator* which I sent you. He would not like it to be known, on account of his remarks about himself (a nom-de-plume has its advantages, it appears!), and his criticism of Sanborn.[1]

1. "Thoreau's Life," *Spectator,* October 18, 1890, pp. 526–28.

72. H.G.O. Blake to S. A. Jones, August 6, 1891.

I write specially to acknowledge the receipt of your money order. I accept your views abt. that matter, tho. I was ready to be mulcted for the sake of doing something more towards an adequate pecuniary compensation for you.

I was deeply touched by your expression of attachment to me. You are, of course, no more unworthy of my friendship, for your aggressiveness, than I may be of yours, for want of it. As I grow older, I believe more & more in love & consideration for my fellow men, knowing how much I need them myself. At the same time, I know that the frankly aggressive man may have far more genuine love for his fellows than he who abstains frm. aggression frm. a cowardly & selfish regard for his own peace, wh. I fear is too much my fault.

Tho. Thoreau's attitude or view of life interests me more deeply than Emerson's, yet Emerson's character & genius & work appear to me so noble that the expression 'tact incarnate' seems harsh as applied to him.

[P.S.] We agree so well on what is deepest & most essential, that we must not dwell upon our differences. Thoreau, you know, warns us against that.

73. S. A. Jones to A. W. Hosmer, August 6, 1891.

* * *

If circumstances should prevent that Western trip this year, I shall feel as if there is a Providence in it. I'll tell you why: 1st. That trip should be made in July, because it grows cold sooner in the upper peninsula, and it isn't nice to be shivering nights as Edward Hoar did on a trip with Thoreau.[1] 2ndly. My friend, Dr. Rominger (for 14 years our State Geologist) has just returned from Europe, and next summer he will go with us as guide—for he not only knows the country but also the people. On such a trip we can take tents and food, and go and live right in the wilderness, as Thoreau used to go into the Maine Woods. I would take also a son and a live professor along, and we would do a month in primitive style. 3rdly. Between November and July I have lost both Father and

Mother; and, Fred, although they were ripe for the grave, I feel the blow through and through. I am shaken from head to foot, and weaker in body than I have been since Army days. At present, I certainly have not the strength for such a trip as I had planned. Nevertheless, if you can get away this year, we will have some sort of a trip. . . .

Oh, I mustn't forget to tell you that Mr. Blake thought some parts of my paper "quarrelsome and bitter," and he reproved for making a comparison between the "hermit" and the "sage." Some parts of it were as highly praised by him. The fact is, he has got a far higher opinion of F. B. S. than I have any room for. . . .

1. Edward Hoar shivered through the night of July 14, 1858, while on a trip to the White Mountains with Thoreau. See F. B. Sanborn, *Henry D. Thoreau,* p. 254.

74. Daniel Ricketson to S. A. Jones, August 7, 1891 [postcard].

I am indebted to you for a copy of Lippincott's Mag. for August. I have read with repeated interest your "Thoreau and his biographers." I am glad you have come to his defence, though late. I remember how badly Thoreau felt about Mr. Lowell's critique. I like Mr. S[anborn] but quite disagree with him in his representation of T's parents, for whom I entertain much respect. I have passed my 78th birthday since I wrote you last. Thoreau was 4 years younger.[1]

1. Anna and Walton Ricketson did not use this postcard in *Daniel Ricketson and His Friends* (Boston: Houghton, Mifflin, 1902), probably owing to the remarks about Sanborn.

75. S. A. Jones to H.G.O. Blake, August 9, 1891 [draft].

Your kind letter of the 6th instant reached me in the cool of the evening and I read it while sitting within a few feet of some young pine trees that began their life in the cellar of Thoreau's hut at Walden. Your words fell upon my heart like dew, and they were good for me.

While I am not fit to call myself a follower of Thoreau, I still apprehend enough of his teachings to know that absolute sincerity was the rock on which he rested; and I must tell you that I seek that rock myself as earnestly as a man of my composition can. Standing there, I wrote you that I deem Emerson "tact incarnate." To you the expression sounds harsh as applied to him.

Now my dear Mr. Blake I do not wish to "dwell upon our differences;" but I trust you will allow me to point out one reason for my different judgement.

You knew Emerson in the flesh; you came under the spell of that personality which captivated even the stormy Carlyle; which so strangely disarmed Henry Crabb Robinson: "It was with a feeling of predetermined dislike that I had the curiosity to look at Emerson at Lord Northampton's, a fortnight ago; when in an instant, all my dislike vanished. He has one of the most interesting countenances I ever beheld—a combination of intelligence and sweetness that quite disarmed me." Diary, Vol. 3, 317.

I know nothing of this glamour; I can only judge by his writings and his conduct of life. Now which is the more likely to be right: a *charmed* contemporary, or one who never succombed to that singularly seducing "sweetness?"

I must also be allowed to say that I have made Carlyle and Emerson the subjects of long and earnest critical investigation—such, indeed, as a biographer would, or *should*—and in calling Emerson "*tact* incarnate" I only render such judgement as my knowledge brought to me. It may, indeed, "sound harsh," but if his whole life affords no other conclusion, what then?

Now, however "harsh", or even offensive, this may sound, I fail to see why the statement of a critical judgement is "aggressive." A truth may be unwelcome; but in what moral latitude and longitude can any truth be *unwholesome*? I am too well aware that Society has agreed to forbid the utterance of certain verities at certain times and in certain places; but who goes to "Society" for those Tables of the Law by which alone the Soul should live?

As far as I can read, it appears that Socrates was "aggressive," and the Athenian remedy for *that* was not a place in the Prytaneum but a cup of hemlock; Society today approves of that heroic treatment.

The fact which neither you nor I can evade is that both Emerson and Mr. Sanborn have misrepresented their contemporary, Thoreau. An obscurer of Thoreau's Life and Writings makes public avowal of his recognition of the hard fact, impelled thereto by reverence for the dead, by gratitude to the dead, and in simple fealty to the Truth.

Emerson's false picture has not been corrected; Thoreau is to the majority a "stoic," but Edward Hoar can scarcely speak of anything other than Thoreau's infinite tenderness. Mr. Sanborn is by nature incapable of comprehending such a man as Thoreau. It was of him (Sanborn) that Emerson asked "Why does he not *participate* in the war he did so much to *precipitate*?"

One of the precipitants went to the gallows and the other went to Canada. One went to the gallows to save his soul; the other went to Canada to save his skin, and came safely back to eke out a miserable existence by writing lying biographies!

The same creature told Mr. Salt, when in London, that he would use his influence with Houghton, Mifflin and Co. to secure the publication of Thoreau's Life in America, and in consequence Mr. Salt forwarded to him advance sheets of the book. In Concord Library Mr. Sanborn showed me a letter fresh from Mr. Salt thereupon, and added: "I do n't know about urging the publication of this book, as it may hurt the sale of my own."

I tell you this that you may know why I wrote of Mr. Sanborn as I did. I want truthfulness, sincerity, manliness; or I want him in whom all these are lacking to keep his unhallowed hands from defiling the memory of a family whose reputation was for an instant at his mercy.

Such is the feeling that burns in the heart of me; such is the opinion I have of him; and now that you know all if you can condemn me, I can accept it even cheerfully for the truth's sake.

[P.S.] (I wrote the above under deep feeling. I have kept it until now in order to know if that feeling rests on conviction. It does and I must send what I had written.)[1]

1. This draft is in the Jones collection.

76. Henry Salt to S. A. Jones, August 9, 1891.

* * *

I have already told you how grateful I feel for that *Lippincott* article; it will be invaluable in making American readers aware of my Thoreau writings. Moreover (and you seem to be unaware of this) there is a flourishing English edition of *Lippincott;* so you have done me a benefit on both sides of the Atlantic.

I can well believe that a lover of Thoreau like Miss Hosmer would be moved to tears by that passage in your *Inlander* article.[1] A phantasy inspired by deep sympathy with the subject is, I think, one of the most moving and impressive of literary forms—and how different from the shocking stuff which "literary men" perpetrate when they go about to write phantasies *without* such inspiration! Julian Hawthorne's article about Poe, for example, in the August *Lippincott,* struck me as a monumental absurdity. I will see what can be done towards getting your "Afternoon in the University Library" reprinted in this country?

I am sending a line to W. H. Dircks, to draw his attention to that misprint in the *Week* ("*interrupt* the silence"). Some months back my brother-in-law suggested that it should be "interpret"; but I had no means of verifying it, or rather I did not think of referring to the original edition, & I was out of London at the time. . . .

As to Walter Besant, I do not know him personally, but friends of mine are also friends of his, and we have communicated in that way, by private messenger, so to speak. I ascertained from him, before I wrote that article on Jefferies, that, as far as he was aware Jefferies had no knowledge whatever of Thoreau's writings. I think this is probable, as J. was rather stand-aloof and contemptuous in his attitude towards other writers. . . .

1. Salt is referring to "An Afternoon in the University Library."

77. S. A. Jones to Daniel Ricketson, August 10, 1891.

Your kind postal card is just at hand, and you can little imagine what a comfort I have had from it. You see, Mr. Blake thought parts of the paper in Lippincott's "quarrelsome and bitter." And in his mild manner he deprecated making "comparisons," as he phrased it, between the "hermit" and the "sage."

I am willing to be considered "quarrelsome" if a defence of the dead merits such an interpretation; and I have long since learned that many a truth is "bitter" *per se*. I was, however, somewhat cast down to think that I had outraged the proprieties—in a friend's conception.

I am thankful for the expression of your respect for Thoreau's parents. I found so many in Concord whom Mr. Sanborn's *mis*representations had deeply, yes, *deeply*, wounded.

I have no personal feeling in regard to Mr. Sanborn, but I cannot say I like him, as you do. I met him in Concord with eager anticipations. On first seeing him, at his house, too, I told him that, for my father's sake, I was glad to meet him and to pay my respects to him *as an abolitionist*. A peculiar expression on his face told me that I had "put my foot in it," as the words go. Yet never in my life had I ever spoken more sincerely. When I subsequently learned that Emerson had asked of the same Mr. S., "Why does he not *participate* in the war he did so much to precipitate?", God's sunlight shone through all this man's disguises and I saw that he is a sham. He may *pose* in whatsoever attitude he can devise but he can *be* only and always an Insincerity. Such an one is not fit to deal with Henry Thoreau.

If this avowal leads you to despise me, I must silently accept your condemnation, for in my very soul I feel the truth of my conviction concerning this man. And when I remember that his Life of Thoreau has had by far the wider circulation, I wonder why the Infinite allows the living to traduce the dead!

When I recollect your years I feel ashamed to ask questions that take your time to reply; but your evidence belongs to the literary history of this century and you are paying the penalty of your environment. I must, then, ask if there is not a slip of the pen in the following sentence from your recent postal card: "I remember how badly Thoreau felt about Mr. Lowell's critique." As Lowell's severe criticism was published in 1865 and

Thoreau died in 1862, I suspect a slip of the pen; or was Lowell inimical before that date? Did you not mean to write "Emerson" instead of *Thoreau?*

I hope that the years are dealing kindly with you, and I breathe the wish because I lately buried my mother, (who was nearly ten years your senior), whom they had over-burdened. I have learned what a void a mother leaves, and yet I could but thank God for the beneficence of death.

[Dr. Jones added the following note in 1901:] Read, approved as *true* and publication authorized, and personal responsibility for every word, hereby assumed.[1]

1. Anna and Walton Ricketson did not use this letter in *Daniel Ricketson and Friends*, undoubtedly because of the statements about Sanborn.

78. Daniel Ricketson to S. A. Jones, August 12, 1891.

Your *type letter* of 10th inst. has just come to hand, and I hasten to make more clear my statement relative to Thoreau and Lowell. It was in reference to an article which Thoreau had sent to the "Atlantic Monthly Mag." some two or three years before his death, and which Lowell, if my memory serves me rightly, as editor, took the liberty of criticising. My use of the word *critique* led you to suppose & very justly, a subsequent production.

Our dear Thoreau stands now far beyond any reproach, and the unfair words said before or since his heroic life and death, are harmless ripples on the smooth surface of his fair name and fame.

I regret that you were so unfortunate in your interview with Mr. S. as I also regret his unfavorable portraits of the good old couple, the parents of our friend. My own painting of these worthies would be far different, and more to your own and the liking of other friends. Our friends largely reflect to us from the impression we make upon them. Many feel like you, very keenly the want of reciprocity in warmth of heart. I can sympathise with you herein.[1]

My daughter, who now in winter resides in Concord, and knew Thoreau & his sister Sophia well, was much pleased with your article in Lippincott, and took it with her to her sea-shore summer home, to read to her brother & other friends. We all meet with our rebuffs, but "time makes all things even," and the great problem of our own existence remains to be solved.

[P.S.] In a letter I have lately received from my friend Whittier, he says, "I am calmly waiting my call." He is in his 84th year.

1. This paragraph, with its comments on Sanborn, was not included in *Daniel Ricketson and His Friends*.

79. S. A. Jones to A. W. Hosmer, August 16, 1891.

* * *

Last night I received a letter from Mr. Salt. He is very much touched by the Thoreau paper. He says, "I wholly agree with you in your recognition of Thoreau as *the* great figure of Concord for future generations. I was disposed to let Emerson alone in my *Life;* but what you say of him is true, and will have to be asserted and re-asserted in the future." Do tell Horace, and the Misses Hosmer, that they may know that we have our feet on the solid rock in so believing.

My dear Friend, I have some heart symptoms of late that as a physician I know the meaning of and I wish to say to you quietly that I may cross the border suddenly some day. If so, all right, for He makes no mistakes; if I am not to go for awhile, all right, too, for He doeth all things WELL.

If I get strong, I am actually desirous of lecturing just once before the Concord Lyceum. I owe that as a tribute for what Concord Thinkers have done for my soul. But we will see what the Fates have in store; perhaps Concord may be spared such an *in*fliction and *af*fliction. . . .

80. H.G.O. Blake to S. A. Jones, August 28, 1891.

I hardly know what reply to make to your interesting letter, & yet it seems to demand one. This certainly I can say, that I greatly respect your sincerity & fidelity to your convictions, while I still dislike the tone of much that you say. It seems to me useless to prolong the discussion. My own view of Thoreau is no doubt very imperfect. Whose view of another is not? The 'infinite tenderness' in Thoreau wh. you say so appealed to Edward Hoar, did not appeal to me, yet it may well have been there. But enough. I greatly respect your sincerity & conscientiousness, & claim strong fellowship with you in your admiration of Thoreau. I trust you will not lose sight of what is best in me thru. contempt for my imperfections.

I have lately spent a pleasant week at a School of Literature & Philosophy at the Adirondacks, or on their borders. Among the pleasant people, I met there were Prof. Dewey frm. Ann Arbor & his brother frm. the Technological Institute in Boston. On Sunday evening, Aug. 16, I read there before a considerable audience frm. 'Thoreau's Thoughts', with some introductory remarks, & conversation interspersed. As far as I could judge frm. the expressions of individuals afterwards, the thing was pretty generally enjoyed.

81. H.G.O. Blake to S. A. Jones, September 14, 1891.

After your last letter, you may hardly expect another frm. me at present, & I doubted abt. writing, but I do not feel quite satisfied without telling you how that letter touched me, & that when I first read it, it was with moistened eyes. I hardly thought you knew enough of my faults & weaknesses *now,* to feel contempt for me, unworthy as I am of the deep regard you assure me of. My thought was that with what I cannot but regard as your severely critical spirit, if you saw me as I am, your gaze might be so fastened on what is poor in me, that you wd. lose sight of the good. That is the great danger in the relation of friends to each other. As I grow older, I believe more & more in our trying to find out & appreciate what is good in each other. I wd. extend this beyond the circle of friends to acquaintances & the world at large. It must have been in the direction of this principle that Jesus was looking, when he said, 'Love your enemies'.

I have hunted among my photographs for one I liked, wh. I could spare, but without success. Perhaps, at some time hereafter, I may send you one.

82. S. A. Jones to A. W. Hosmer, September 16, 1891.

I am in receipt of your two pictures and can but conclude that you are bound to bury me in gifts. The "Pond" picture helps one to realize Thoreau's description of Walden at low water. That 1727 house is a poser to me, as I can't find any recorded trace of Thoreaus living on Prince Street. The first American Thoreau had a store on Long Wharf, and later one on King Street, afterwards called State Street—but this picture says Prince Street.[1]

Perhaps there is some history here that Sanborn has overlooked—and *that* wouldn't be a strange proceeding on his part. What is the history of this picture, anyhow?

In regard to your enquiry about John Burroughs and the Blake daguerreotype—Burroughs knows all about it, as he had the daguerreotype engraved to illustrate a paper on Thoreau that he published in "Harpers"[2] long ago. You can get Burroughs's address from Houghton, Mifflin and Co., I do not know where he is. . . .

My paper on Thoreau in Lippincott's has cost me Mr. Blake's friendship. I held to what I had written of Sanborn and of Emerson, and backed it by solid reasons, but while Mr. Blake does not refute what I advance, he sticks to his friends and condemns what he terms my "severely critical spirit." He does not seem to consider that Justice to Thoreau demands that some one should write "severely." Well, I can bear all this and more for Thoreau's sake; but it shows plainly that Sanborn is so "solid" in Mr.

Blake's esteem that the chances are that all Thoreau's mss. will pass into Sanborn's custody after Mr. Blake's death—and then we will not have a true edition of Thoreau's Letters. If Fate will have it so, Amen!

I have not had courage to write to Edward Hoar, and shall give it up, for this Blake experience is all that I want. Still, I must remember that at Mr. Blake's age I might see things as he does; but it is rather peculiar to be reproved by Thoreau's oldest friend for defending Thoreau's parents from calumny!

I hear from Mr. Salt quite regularly and I must content my self by setting off his approval against Mr. Blake's condemnation. . . .

1. Jean Thoreau, Henry Thoreau's grandfather and the first of his family to emigrate to America, opened a shop on Long Wharf in Boston after the Revolutionary War. He later moved this store to Kings Street, which is now State. His private residence was, for many years, at 51–53 Prince Street. See Walter Harding, *The Days of Henry Thoreau*, pp. 4–5.

2. Dr. Jones is here in error regarding Burroughs's article, which appeared in *Century Magazine* 2 (July 1882):368–79. Included in the article is a woodcut of Thoreau, which Burroughs identified as being "from his last portrait, a tintype, taken by Critcherson, of Worcester, Mass., in 1861."

83. Henry Salt to S. A. Jones, September 16, 1891.

* * *

How kind & good of you to be still trying to arrange for an American Edition of my *Thoreau!* By the way, I lately sent the *Inlander* to Dircks, and asked him about the suggested inclusion of your article in the Camelot *Week.* He is a quite terribly bad correspondent, and it will probably take months to get a reply from him; not a word as yet! His selected *Essays* of Thoreau are just published, & he has sent me a copy.[1] If he has not sent you one, as I imagine he will have done, please let me know, & I will send one at once. I have not yet had time to examine it carefully, but his *Introduction* seems rather scrappy, though I ought not to quarrel with it, as he says kind things of me. In the last letter I had from him, he says: "I am afraid my selection is shocking bad, but I found that I really could not go into the thing exhaustively. Betwixt you and me, I find I have *not* your perennial enthusiasm about the subject. I have a great admiration for Thoreau, but it bores me excessively to have to write about him".

Perhaps I ought not to quote this: please consider it private. It is rather sad that Thoreau shd. be edited in this spirit; but I suppose Dircks is overworked, like so many literateurs. He did good service in his other volumes—and even this will do much to make Thoreau known. Scott's books circulate far more widely than Sonnenschein's, so I am glad Dircks has included a lot of the *Anti-Slavery Papers* that I edited.

I am afraid good old Dr. Japp took your *Lippincott* article rather to heart; see his reply in enclosed paragraphs from a weekly journal to which he contributes. I have informed him of your intention to do justice to his services in recognising Thoreau so early. He is a most kind warm-hearted old fellow, and a sincere admirer of Thoreau, so I know that in sending you these paragraphs it will not "make mischief" in any way, as you will allow for his feelings. Perhaps he sent you the paper, *Old & Young*, direct. . . .[2]

1. *Essays and other Writings of H. D. Thoreau* (London: Scott, 1891).
2. Dr. Jones did not list in his Thoreau bibliography the response of Dr. Japp in *Old and Young*.

84. S. A. Jones to A. W. Hosmer, September 29, 1891.

* * *

I shall be glad to know what you learn about the Thoreau house in Boston. I have thought that perhaps Mr. Sanborn pulled the string which set good Mr. Blake a-dancing, but, confound it, Mr. Blake is dancing to the wrong tune!

Mr. Blake put me in an entirely false position, but I know in my heart that I wrote in defense of those who are dead, and I do not care if the whole earth damned me for so doing. Of course it is painful to be misunderstood, but one must stand that if the truth demands it.

But I am getting H—in England, too. Dr. Japp is after me with a sharp stick for what I wrote about his Underground Rail Road myth. He calls in question all that I say on that point; so you can see why I was so anxious to own that letter which Parker Pillsbury wrote to you. It was not that I wished to deprive you of his autograph, but because I knew I should some day have sore need of that letter to make myself "solid" against all attacks. I wish you would go to work and get as much evidence as you can from those in Concord who are yet living, and who were interested in the Underground R.R. business. Mrs. Bigelow, Silas Hosmer, Horace Hosmer—all in fact who can know anything about it. The question is, Was the Walden hut used by Thoreau as a "station" of the said Rail Road?

I do not know the address of the Thatchers of Bangor, Maine;[1] so please send it and I'll send them some of my Thoreau work. I do not expect to get hold of any of Thoreau's manuscripts, but I would like to see the custody of them awarded to some one who will do justice to Thoreau in spite of all the great Concord names which at present overshadow his. . . .

On the 22nd I received a large lithograph of R. W. Emerson, and on the 24th a letter from E.W.E.—the first since our "onpleasantness." Can it be that he is going on a lecturing trip again and wants me to drum for him some more? I hope to God that such is not the motive that impelled him to write to me after all those long months of sullen silence.

He asked me to let him know if the picture was received, and I did so, at the same time asking him if he meant to enter the lecture field this winter. If he does I shall do all I can to get him a hearing in the University Lecture Course, as I want every one heard who is saying a word for Thoreau.

I would rather see Edward Waldo Emerson the custodian of Thoreau's MSS. than Sanborn, for I do believe he would be just to Thoreau. . . .

1. The Thatchers, relatives of the Thoreau family, lived in Bangor, Maine. No letters by the Thatchers are in the Jones collection.

85. S. A. Jones to A. W. Hosmer, October 10, 1891.

Your letter came duly, and the copy of P. Pillsbury's letter was read with interest—the previous copy you sent is mislaid amid a heap of your letters.

Pillsbury's testimony is only conjectural; he does n't *think* the shanty was used as a "station." But we need the evidence of someone who has positive knowledge, and, as you say, Mrs. Bigelow is the only one living who can supply *that*.

I received a rousing good letter from Horace Hosmer, and he makes some telling points; but the positive assertion *from knowledge* he can not make.[1] Of course his reasoning about the improbability of Dr. Japp's "figment" is perfectly satisfactory to one who has seen the location of Walden Pond; but it is men across the Atlantic that must now be convinced by witnesses.

I answered Mr. Emerson's on the 24th of September, and asked one or two questions of some importance to both him and to me, but up to date I have no word in return.

Edward S. Hoar very kindly answered some enquiries,[2] and if I thought it would not be presuming too much upon his courtesy, I would greatly like to trouble him once more.

Horace Hosmer says Edmund Hosmer was active in the Underground Railroad business:[3] please ask the Misses Hosmer if they have any knowledge bearing thereon. . . .

By the way, if there is anything in Thoreau's Journal about fugitive slaves it would be a good thing if Mr. Blake would allow it to be copied.

I will write to Mr. Blake about the matter,[4] and if he sees fit to repel me why, I must bear it as well as I can. Is n't it curious that, while I undoubtedly would do more for Thoreau's memory than he, he, of all others, should be "down on me" for my plainness of utterance in Thoreau's behalf. . . .

1. Horace Hosmer argued that the Walden hut was never used as an Underground Railroad station, for it was both poorly situated—and impractical since Thoreau had neither a team nor a suitable place to shelter fugitives. (Horace Hosmer to Dr. Jones, October 6, 1891, Jones collection.)

2. Edward Hoar wrote that he could not answer Dr. Jones's inquiry about the role of the Walden hut in the Underground Railroad. He did remember hearing Thoreau speak to him of John Brown but never of fugitive slaves. (Edward S. Hoar to Dr. Jones, October 4, 1891. Jones collection.)

3. Horace Hosmer to Dr. Jones, October 6, 1891 (Jones collection).

4. No response from Blake to these inquiries is included in the Jones papers.

86. S. A. Jones to A. W. Hosmer, October 11, 1891.

* * *

I hope it will not give you or Mrs. Bigelow undue trouble to settle that Underground Railroad business, but it has become extremely important to get her testimony. I am astonished at Dr. Japp's "cheek" in sticking up so boldly for what he must *know* to be an invention of his own; and as he reiterates the figment with such assurance, I want to knock his card house all to flinders "for keeps."

I wonder what led Sanborn to enquire about the republication of Mr. Salt's book—it cannot be from any interest that he takes in it, and as a Yankee never does anything without a purpose, what can be his object? But, pshaw! the conundrum is n't worth trying to answer.

I learn from Mr. Salt that Mr. Dircks is an exceedingly bad correspondent, and that will account for his not acknowledging your picture; but some Englishmen are no better than hedge-hogs. . . .

87. S. A. Jones to A. W. Hosmer, October 18, 1891.

In the same mail came your letter and one from E.W.E. He wrote in a friendly manner, and I am glad, for it is painful to be at any variance with one whom you wish to respect.

I would not disturb Mrs. Bigelow, for as you say, she has already given her testimony. Moreover, anyone who knows anything of the location of the shanty at Walden will see at once how foolish Dr. Japp's "notion" is. . . .

Fred, what you write of Sanborn's taking Channing into his house[1] gives me a feeling of gratitude to him that I cannot put into words. I do not know his motive, nor will I question it; I only know that Channing is old and near the end and it will cheer his soul to have a familiar face near him as the darkness deepens around him. From the depths of my heart I say

God Bless Mr. Sanborn! For this deed I will do him reverence as long as I live. Whatever of "toll" he may take I shall not see; that he has taken to his house a lonely old man who has been disappointed in life is the one fact for which I am glad.

Your friend "Gig-lamps" is the most procrastinatingest "cuss" you ever heard of. He has promised to sit for his photo times without number, and by Jupiter, he aint "sot" yit. Just now he has got too darned lazy to get shaved, and is lettin' his bristles sprout, and he looks like the very d****! (He looks much that way without bristles, too, but a trifle more so with.)

Gosh hang it, Fred, I'll brace up, get shaved, and have a picter takan: honest! I'll also send you one showing how I looked some fifteen years ago, for I found two the other day that were taken when I was a "live" professor, and covered with pin-feathers. Please look at it through smoked glass—I look best when viewed through that medium. Some folks do; I'm some folks. . . .

1. On September 8, 1891, Ellery Channing moved into the Sanborn house, where he resided until his death December 23, 1901. See Frederick T. McGill, Jr., *Channing of Concord* (New Brunswick, N.J.: Rutgers University Press, 1967), p. 177.

88. Henry Salt to S. A. Jones, October 18, 1891.

* * *

To turn to the subject of Thoreau, here also I have nothing but disappointment to report to you. Dircks writes that it is "physically impossible" to append your "Inlander" article to the *Week;*[1] and all other attempts to get it reprinted have been equally failures. The interest in Thoreau, and indeed in the whole *Nature* subject, is almost *nil* in "literary" circles; our literateurs feel instinctively, I suppose, that their whole position is an artificial one, & they therefore do their best to ignore the contrary principle. As an example of this, I find it practically impossible to get a publisher for my proposed volume of essays on *The Return to Nature:* i.e. a reprint of articles on Jefferies, Carpenter, Burroughs, Thoreau, Melville, &c, &c, most of which you have seen.[2]

I wonder whether you saw a little anecdote about Thoreau told by Bret Harte in the Sept. no. of the *New Review,* just at the close of an article on Lowell? Its point was that Thoreau used to hear Emerson's dinner-bell (rung for that very purpose), & come up from his Walden hermitage to dine; & Bret Harte tells the story as Emerson told it to him ("with a very peculiar smile", I think he describes E.), the object being to ridicule the Walden residence. Anyone who knows anything of Thoreau knows the value of the story; but it is in one way rather significant, as implying that E.

was not always the appreciative friend of Thoreau that he is usually supposed, and as lending force to your contention that the misunderstanding of Thoreau in great measure proceeds from Emerson himself. If you have not seen the *New Review,* I will procure a copy for you. . . .

I saw in a newspaper a day or two ago, with deep regret, that Herman Melville has lately died in New York. I regard him as one of the greatest writers America has produced. I have one or two interesting letters from him about James Thomson, whose works he much admired.

1. "An Afternoon in the University Library."
2. Salt was not able to find a publisher for such a volume.

89. Henry Salt to S. A. Jones, October 24, 1891.

* * *

To turn to Thoreau: I think your idea of a "Walden journal" volume a very good one, though (after recent experiences) I am not sanguine of its success in this country, or of its ready acceptance by publishers. I will try what can be done, & will write to Scott, Fisher Unwin, & one or two others, as soon as opportunity offers. Meantime will you ascertain Mr. Blake's feelings on the subject?[1] The only drawback that suggests itself to me is this—did not Thoreau to a great extent use up and embody the Walden diary in the volume *Walden?* I had always thought this must be the reason why Mr. Blake gave so few extracts for the years 1845–1847. Let me say that if such a volume as you suggest should ever appear, *you* would be the right person to edit & introduce it. Your personal knowledge of Thoreau's haunts at Concord would be invaluable in such a work. And why should it not be illustrated from some of Mr. Hosmer's & Mr. McQuesten's photographs? . . .

1. Dr. Jones did write to H.G.O. Blake about this proposed "Walden Journal." See Blake's response of October 12 and 13, 1892 (letter 124).

90. S. A. Jones to A. W. Hosmer, October 31, 1891.

How kind of you to think of me as the sending of 'Mandy Harris's book[1] shows that you did. Poor 'Mandy, according to her light she is just to Thoreau, but a tallow dip is n't enough to show up so large a specimen. However, her work must have a place in the bibliography, and it is worthier of it than much that is already there. . . .

E.W.E. does not take as a lion in these parts. I have failed in my endeavors to get him on the Students' Lecture Association List, and also I find Unity Club decidedly lukewarm. I don't believe he will have a chance to open his mouth in this burgh.

He purposes making two trips the coming winter; one South, and one in the North-west. It seems that he has some Emerson relations in Beloit, Wis., and they want to hear the noise of his chin. His voice is unfortunately so inefficient that he will have to win glory with the pen. . . .

Do you hear from Mr. Salt now-a-days; are you aware that his present address is Oxted, Surrey, England? He moved there a month or so ago, and I hear from him pretty regularly.

I am afraid he will never be a popular writer because he has cast his lot with the English Freethinkers, and I must say that some of them are a pretty rabid set. How often it is that when a man cuts loose from the Church he becomes one of the noisiest in barking at its heels. And it is curious to what an extent a man's religion, or no religion, is a clue to what he writes. But, I must n't begin a preachment at the tail end of a letter—if, indeed, this can be called a letter! . . .

1. Amanda Harris, *American Authors for Young Folks* (Boston: D. Lothrop Co., 1887).

91. S. A. Jones to A. W. Hosmer, November 15, 1891.

I have been very much impressed by Mr. Silas Hosmer's death,[1] and that event has made Concord much poorer to me. My intercourse with him was but brief but he grew into me deeply and quickly. I have many kindnesses to remember, and many visible tokens of his good will. I never go out of a night without taking the North Bridge cane that he gave me. It is a piece of work as quaint and solid as himself. And the faithful hand that fashioned it is at rest forever: may the peace of God be his!

Elsie will learn of his departure with real regret, for his manner won her as completely as it did me. I am very glad that she met him because she has, as well as I have, seen a specimen of the stuff that Concord was made of when Thoreau walked its streets and made friends of only the worthy. Alas! It can not be long before all those who knew Thoreau in the flesh will have gone to join him in the spirit, and the visiting stranger will be no longer thrilled, as I was, to find himself talking with one who "knew Henry."

He gave me two copies of the report of your celebration in 1875,[2] and in one he wrote his name. That copy I presented to the University Library, and there a memento of him will remain when you and I are also in the dust. If I live to see Concord again, I will do his memory reverence at his grave.

Do you know I often find myself thinking of Channing and wondering how he is getting on. He is the last one of the historical names associated with the transcendental period in Concord, and it almost seems as if the town will change its nature when he dies. Your arrow-head is quite a trophy, and it is really as good as if Thoreau *had* picked it up, for he and Channing were the most intimate of all in their day. How long Channing has lingered after his companion. . . .

1. Silas Hosmer died October 30, 1891. See George Leonard Hosmer, *Hosmer Genealogy* (Cambridge, Mass.: Technical Composition Co., 1928), p. 105. Dr. Jones's daughter Elsie met Silas Hosmer in Concord.

2. The Concord celebration of 1875, commemorating one hundred years of independence, featured a brief speech by Emerson, an oration by G. W. Curtis, and the unveiling of Daniel Chester French's statue of the Minute Man. For a full discussion, see Townsend Scudder, *Concord: American Town* (Boston: Little, Brown and Co., 1947), pp. 265–76.

92. S. A. Jones to A. W. Hosmer, November 30, 1891.

I was glad to learn from your last letter that Channing's Thoreau is to be reissued.[1] It is not much of a "life," but it contains so many selections from Thoreau's journals that are not printed elsewhere as to make it really a part of Thoreau's works. If it is put out with *notes* by Mr. Sanborn under Channing's direction it will find many buyers, for even those who have the first edition will get the new book. I saw a copy of the first edition advertised in a New York catalogue a little while ago at $2,00, but it was gone when I wrote for it.

I recently completed my set of first editions of Thoreau by the purchase of a copy of his *Excursions*[2] for $3,75. It was originally published at $1,50 so his fame is at a premium of 150 per cent. I hope the interest in him will increase until all his journals are published. I shall hail "Autumn"[3] with delight; but every one of Mr. Blake's volumes only makes me hungrier for the whole of the journals. By Mr. Blake's plan we only get Thoreau in pieces; I should like to see his thoughts in the order in which they came, not broken as they now are.

By the way, Fred, are copies of his first two books common in Concord? One can but wonder how his townsfolk appreciated him, and that makes me ask the question. I should hardly suppose you would find there many copies of his first book, the *Week*, but his *Walden* ought to have had many Concord buyers.

We have had two letters from Elsie, one from Gibraltar, and the other from Naples.[4] They are full of the usual wonder expressed by travellers; for instance, she says over and over again, "I never saw such a thing before in my life." Of course not, for if she had why in the devil did she go abroad? Nevertheless, the letters are interesting, for we can almost see what she is describing, and we can easily believe that she never saw the like before in her life. Let them enjoy it; but I would rather spend a month in Concord than a year in the old world. I suppose they have been in Rome for some time now, and a letter full of new wonders will be here before long. . . .

1. Ellery Channing's *Thoreau, the Poet-Naturalist* was not reissued until 1902 when an enlarged edition, edited by Sanborn, was published by Charles E. Goodspeed, Boston.
2. Henry D. Thoreau, *Excursions* (Boston: Ticknor and Fields, 1863).
3. Dr. Jones is referring to Blake's selections from Thoreau.
4. Dr. Jones's daughter was traveling with her husband, Charles Cooley, pioneer American sociologist, who had a distinguished career at the University of Michigan.

93. A. W. Hosmer to S. A. Jones, January 2, 1892.

I mail you today a copy of "John Brown"[1] and "Elliott"[2] by Channing. Have got on the track of one or two more, but find that it will be almost impossible to complete the list of his works. Have been interviewing Sanborn in regard to them and put me on the track of these books.

We are having a miserable open-warm winter—no snow—no ice—however it gives me a good chance to keep up my wood rambles.

Have just been up to see Mrs. Bigelow. She says "The hut was *never* used as a station, if Henry got word of one of the fugitives, he immediately took them to his mother's—he helped them with all they needed, money or what else, and then the organization would repay him, as they had money given them for that purpose. He took one to *West* Fitchburg, they never went to Fitchburg proper. His hut offered *no* place of concealment, it was open, the cellar was merely a hole in the ground reached by a trap door in the floor and only used for a storage room for his food.

"He built the house to show to the world that if a person wished to live a certain life, there was no reason why they could not, he was as fond of a good dinner as any one, or could go without, without any trouble, he merely gave the actual cost of his bean field and made his own bread, giving the cost of that, to show how cheaply a man might live if he so desired it.

"He did not build it for retirement, as Dr. Emerson says for he was as much retired at home—occupying a room in the third story, and was never visited there. He was one of the most truthful, pure of men. I do not believe that both the brothers were in love with the same lady. That Henry was very fond of a young lady who afterwards died in consumption, but it was merely a youthful attachment, for he was never well enough off to

143

support a wife, and he would not have asked any one to share his life unless able to support them.

"John was very much attached to Miss Martha Bartlett.[3] It was a rich blessing that my life was thrown in with the Thoreau's." This was about the drift of her conversation, but she referred a number of times to the "mistaken notion that some people had, that the hut was used as an underground railroad station. I am well acquainted with the facts and I *know* it was *not.*"

She has the pocket book carried by John Thoreau, until his death, with his autograph written in it, that she is going to hunt up, and give me. Hoping this is not too late and that it will help you. . . .

1. Ellery Channing, *John Brown, and the Heroes of Harpers Ferry: A Poem* (Boston: Cupples, Upham, 1886).

2. Ellery Channing, *Eliot: A Poem* (Boston: Cupples, Upham, 1885). Hosmer's spelling in the letter is incorrect.

3. Walter Harding lists Martha Bartlett among the pupils who attended the Concord academy in 1839 when it was taught by John and Henry Thoreau. See *The Days of Henry Thoreau,* p. 76.

94. S. A. Jones to A. W. Hosmer, January 4, 1892.

* * *

I am so glad that Mrs. Bigelow is able to testify for her dead friends as she does. How well she understood them, and how truly she defines the purpose of Thoreau's residence at Walden. Of course that foolish Underground Railroad business is settled by her statement. . . .

95. S. A. Jones to A. W. Hosmer, January 17, 1892.

* * *

It is now some little time since I received a letter from Edward Waldo informing me that he was going West, and stating that he would endeavor to drop in upon me on his homeward route. I have been in a cold sweat of apprehension ever since. I do not want to meet him because I should feel like a hypocrite all the time he was under my roof. It would mortify me too to think that he could not find an audience in Ann Arbor. But the fact is I could not get him a chance to appear even before the Unity Club—which is a Unitarian Church Society, where an Emerson, at least, should find an audience. There was no enthusiasm at all; they tried at my urging to raise a purse of $25,oo and couldn't do it. I do not know what Edward made last Winter, but he will make far less this, I warrant you.

From his letter I judge that he fully realized this before starting from home this time.[1] Golly! when I remember how I worked last Winter to get him his Detroit lecture I am glad that I did not have such another contract on my hands for this season.

He informed me in the same letter that he had seen the only one who knew and he was now prepared to tell me all about that Under-ground Railroad business. I am sorry that it will not do to tell him that another Concord friend had settled that long ago. Moreover, why couldn't he write, as then his testimony would be worth something. . . .[2]

1. In his letter of January 4, 1892, Emerson commented on the difficulties of arranging a successful lecture tour: "I have been forced to combine my South-western & North western trips to make up one good one, as the demand for lectures without stereopticon seems to be small; for my lectures at any rate" (Dr. E. W. Emerson to Dr. Jones, January 4, 1892, Jones collection).

2. The Jones papers do contain an extensive account of the Underground Railroad in Concord which Dr. Jones obtained from Edward Emerson; the account is in the manuscript of *Thoreau amongst Friends and Philistines,* a collection of early criticism of Thoreau which Dr. Jones prepared but never published. Emerson's information, gained from Mrs. Bigelow, substantially confirms that provided by Hosmer.

96. S. A. Jones to A. W. Hosmer, February 10, 1892.

* * *

Does Mr. Burroughs mention the fact that the Blake daguerreotype was engraved to illustrate his (Burroughs's) paper on Thoreau that appeared in Harper's Monthly? Subsequently Houghton, Mifflin and Company bought the cut and used it in their book catalogue.

I do not think I could write an article on Thoreau that the New England Magazine would accept. You see, I am an utter nobody in the literary world and it takes a *name* to get a paper accepted. That Lippincott paper was actually bullied into print by two ladies, one of whom is a contributor to the magazine.

You remember that Mr. Dircks to whom you sent some pictures; well, I learn from Mr. Salt that the cuss doesn't care a copper for Thoreau—writes about him solely as task work for pay.[1] No wonder he didn't acknowledge your gift! . . .

1. For Dircks's statement that writing about Thoreau bored him, see Henry Salt to Dr. S. A. Jones, September 16, 1891, letter 83.

97. Henry Salt to S. A. Jones, March 4, 1892.

* * *

I am interested to hear of your forthcoming new edition of the Bibliography. I hope you will mention Lowell's "Fable for Critics",[1] & clear up the doubt as to *which* verse alludes to Thoreau. There is a passing reference to Thoreau—I don't know whether it is worth chronicling—in John Burroughs' essay on "Touches of Nature", in *Birds & Poets*. And did you not omit Allibone's Dict. of Eng. Litre., and the Encyclopoedia Britannica, Edn. 9?

By the way, Dr. Japp told me, some little time ago that *he* wrote the article in the *British Quarterly*, 1874, and also (he thinks) those in the *Spectator*, 1883 & 1885. . . .

Thank you for Helen Thoreau's lines. They are true, & come from the heart; & I think the second & third stanzas have some literary merit.

I hear from Sanborn that he is going to publish some Emerson-Thoreau letters in the *Atlantic Monthly* for May & June. This will be a first step towards the volume of letters he has in contemplation. Let us hope he will some day secure, & publish, Ellery Channing's Thoreau-papers! . . .

1. Dr. Jones did include Lowell's *A Fable for Critics* in his *Bibliography of Henry David Thoreau*. He also included the Allibone entry on Thoreau.

98. S. A. Jones to A. W. Hosmer, March 6, 1892.

* * *

That poem—supposed to be Helen Thoreau's—interested me very much, and I send hearty thanks for it.[1]

In the first line of the third verse, "Through the eternal ages sounding," I think 'sounding' should be *bounding;* which, you see, makes sense—as 'sounding' does not. The verses were evidently written by a serious person who had duties that were recognized, but who was little used to writing poetry; and I should ascribe them to Helen much sooner than to Henry.

I am expecting daily a new English book called "Nature in Books, some studies in Biography,"[2] in which pages 66–93 are about Thoreau. Mr. Salt called my attention to it and I sent for it on account of the Bibliography which I am keeping up as new items occur. I do not believe that Thoreau ever dreamed that such an amount of writing would be done about him: but it is all writing and no practice, and I do not think he would have much minded the writing.

I learn from Mr. Salt's letter that he and Sanborn are in correspondence, for Mr. S. mentions that Channing is at Sanborn's house. How is that old crank? Channing I mean. Do you know how Sanborn is getting on with his book about Alcott, and when it will be published?

The mention of Sanborn's name reminds me that there is one point about Thoreau's pictures which Sanborn can settle, and that is whether the ambrotype now in the Antiquarian rooms is the one that Mr. Ricketson sent Sophia after Henry's death. You can settle this by asking Mr. Sanborn where he got the portrait of Thoreau that was engraved for his life of Thoreau. My belief is that the picture was engraved from that ambrotype. . . .

1. We have been unable to identify this poem.
2. P. Anderson Graham, *Nature in Books* (London: Methuen & Co., 1891).

99. S. A. Jones to A. W. Hosmer, March 19, 1892.

Well, you have straightened out the kinks in the matter of the portraits of Thoreau; but even your letter would help to perpetuate an error. You mention the Dunshee pictures as daguerreotypes: unless my memory deceives me Mr. Davis's picture is an ambrotype. The portrait that Mr. Blake has is the only daguerreotype. . . .

Mr. Salt informs me that, in the Atlantic for next May and June, Sanborn is going to publish some Emerson-Thoreau letters,[1] and Mr. Salt thinks this is the prelude to a new edition of Thoreau's letters by Sanborn.[2] I should be glad to welcome such a volume.

Fred, I wish you would watch for a good chance and SHOOT Channing—with a Kodak, of course. That venerable ancient is a part of the history of Concord and he should not be allowed to "peg out" without leaving his "picter."

I have often wondered where the Thoreau family lived when John and Henry started on the trip recorded in the Week.[3] Probably Mrs. Bigelow can tell. I think they then lived on the other side of the road from where the house is in which Henry died, for their garden reached to the river when the boys started on their trip.

All these little things are going to have an importance when the people who can give information are dead, and we who are the link between Thoreau's days and the future should attend to them.

I have never seen any picture of Ricketson's bust of Thoreau,[4] and if Mr. Ricketson is in Concord I wish you would find out what a copy of his medallion costs. . . .

[P.S.] The mail brought the two Advertisers with Sanborn's "Breakfast Table."[5] I wonder what pay he gets for such thin stuff, for it wouldn't stay long on a hungry man's stomach. He adds nothing to our knowledge of Thoreau, yet with Channing on tap in his house one would think that he would be getting points all the time.

I have been thinking of getting out a new edition of the bibliography of Thoreau, but I hesitate because I cannot get hold of Channing's books, and as Thoreau is mentioned in several of them I do not like to put out an incomplete bibliography, especially as it will be the last that I shall do.

There are several of Channing's books in your Concord Library; but one or two are in Sanborn's possession, and I much doubt if copies could be found elsewhere.

It is a bright sunshiny day, and I am wishing that I could take a leap to Concord and have a day's walk with you.

1. F. B. Sanborn, "The Emerson-Thoreau Correspondence," *Atlantic Monthly* 69 (May, June 1892):577–96, 736–53.

2. Henry D. Thoreau, *Familiar Letters of Henry David Thoreau,* ed. F. B. Sanborn (Boston: Houghton, Mifflin & Co., 1894).

3. John and Henry Thoreau set off on their voyage on August 31, 1839. At that time the Thoreaus were living in the Parkman house on Main Street near Sudbury Road. See Walter Harding, *The Days of Henry Thoreau,* pp. 44, 90.

4. The reference here is to a bas-relief medallion of Thoreau made by Walton Ricketson. For a photograph of the piece, see Walter Harding, *The Days of Henry Thoreau,* p. 45. Ricketson later did a bust of Thoreau as well; it was based on the Rowse crayon drawing of 1854. See letter 48.

5. Sanborn had published "Breakfast Table" columns devoted to Thoreau in the *Boston Daily Advertiser,* March 8 and March 18, 1892. The first was concerned with Thoreau's poems; the second, with his reading.

100. A. W. Hosmer to S. A. Jones, March 25, 1892.

You are right, that picture of Ricketson's is an ambrotype.

I send you today a photo of Ricketson's medallion, he says you keep it—price of medallion—life size—ivory finish—$25.00 with frame (broad plush frame) $35.00. The medallion was made a very few years after Thoreau's death, and was brought to Concord in the clay and criticized by Emerson, Channing and Sanborn, and changes made according to their criticisms.

Have not found out about the school but will just as soon as I can see Mrs Bigelow, I tried to see her today but could raise no one at the house.

You must be mistaken in regard to the house they lived in (Read that portion of the Week over. I do not see as it says the garden reached the river.) when Thoreau started on his "Week", for he says they lived about half a mile from the river.[1] I will ask Mrs B. about that too.

I have had in my hands today Thoreau's flute and his spy glass—and also Miss Alcotts autograph copy of her poem.[2] Mr. Ricketson kindly played two tunes on it for me—it is a *very* sweet sounding one—light colored wood and very few keys, and is quite a light weight one. He hopes you will call on him, if you come east again. I told him that if he had anything of Thoreau's it would be sure to bring you. He thought that Reginald Cholmondeley (is that the way to spell *Chumley*) the brother of Thoreau's friend might have some letters or other things that were once his. He lives, he thinks at Condover Hall Shropshire. Eng. Mr. Salt might help you out to the correct address.

Much obliged, but I have Higginson's[3] and about all the rest who have written about T.

I had *good* success in *hooking* a portion of the old shanty, have a piece about 3 × 6 and five feet long—rather worm eaten however.

There is a most excellent picture of Channing in existence, but it cannot be bought while he is alive—and Mr. R. tells me he goes along about every day into Boston. Let me know what books of Channing's you have and I will look up those in the library, and see if he speaks of Thoreau in any of them, and will ask Sanborn about the others, so as to help out your bibliography. Just ask for what you want and I will help you out all I can.

1. In the "Saturday" section of *A Week* Thoreau had described his boat as being "loaded the evening before at our door, half a mile from the river."

2. Thoreau's spyglass, flute, and the autograph of Louisa May Alcott's poem "Thoreau's Flute" were owned by Walton Ricketson, son of Daniel Ricketson.

3. Probably Storrow Higginson, "Henry D. Thoreau," *Harvard Magazine* 8 (May 1862):313–18. Dr. Jones later reprinted this paper in *Pertaining to Thoreau* (1901).

101. S. A. Jones to A. W. Hosmer, March 27, 1892.

I am in error about the location of the Thoreau residence when the boys started on their voyage. I must have had Channing's garden in my mind as the starting place, as C. lived at one time almost opposite your present Library, and his potato patch reached to the river bank. It is very clear that I know altogether too much for a fellow who was in Concord for only three weeks! (I have crawled into my hole and pulled the hole in after me.)

The medallion of Thoreau disappoints me, and I much prefer your photograph from the Blake picture—there we have *the* man. I am greatly obliged for the picture of the medallion as it has gratified my curiosity, but I really wouldn't care to own one of the casts.

Cholmondeley is pronounced Chumley, and you may tell Mr. Ricketson that Mr. Salt tried to get Thoreau's letters to him, but Cholmondeley's heir is an old man, and he did not care to take the trouble to look through piles of old mss. to find them. . . .[1]

1. For Salt's failure to obtain Thoreau's letters to Thomas Cholmondeley, see his letter to Dr. Jones of April 12, 1890, letter 11. Sanborn later published these letters in his edition of *Familiar Letters* (1894).

102. S. A. Jones to A. W. Hosmer, April 1, 1892.

It is on record that the Dunshee ambrotype was taken in 1861. And Mr. Salt says the Blake photo belongs to 1857 or 8.[1] He, doubtless, had his information from Mr. Blake, and evidently the very year is forgotten. . . .

1. For Salt's dating of the Blake daguerreotype of Thoreau, see *The Life of Henry David Thoreau*, p. 299. Salt erroneously attributed this portrait to Critcherson; the daguerreotype was made by B. D. Maxham of Worcester, Massachusetts, in 1856.

103. A. W. Hosmer to S. A. Jones, April 2, 1892.

I looked up the books by Channing in the library and in the "Wanderer," J. R. Osgood & Co. Boston 1871[1]—I find that it refers to Thoreau all through—the subjects of the book are "The Wood"—"The Hermit" (in this he speaks of "such an one who built a house by the borders of a lake &c. the whole poem being about Thoreau though he never mentions his name) "The Mountain"—"Henry's Camp"—"The Island"—"The Cape"—& "Hillside."

In "Near Home" Jas. Munroe & Co. Boston 1858[2]—there are only 2 poems. "To Henry" Pages 3–6 is to Thoreau while in "Near Home" the other one he brings in various Concord people—in notes written in in pencil. "Rudolpho" in one place and "Vernon" in another are given as being H.D.T.

I did not find Autumn Sheaves in the library, but am on the track of one and will let you know about it when I hear from my letter.

That letter to Sanborn on Thoreau's Mother was published in the Concord Freeman of Feb. 23, 1883.[3]

The picture of Thoreau in Burrough's article in the Century of 1882— is said to be "from last portrait, a tintype taken by Critcherson of Worcester in 1861, presented to John H. Treadwell by Ralph Waldo Emerson."[4] What picture can that be? It looks like the Blake picture only as it is a tintype, is just opposite from the photo—that is the right is left & visa versa. Hold either the photo or the print in front of a glass, and compare the reflection with the other one. . . .[5]

Warm spring day, and am looking forward to a good tramp tomorrow—can get down to bicycle suit and shall not have to lug round so much clothing.

1. Ellery Channing, *The Wanderer* (Boston: J. R. Osgood, 1871).
2. Ellery Channing, *Near Home* (Boston: James Munroe, 1858).
3. "Henry Thoreau's Mother," the letter by Jean Munroe LeBrun mentioned earlier.
4. John Burroughs, "Henry D. Thoreau," *Century Magazine* 2 (July 1882):368.

5. Alfred Hosmer concluded this letter with a catalogue of his Thoreau library, which is now in the Concord Free Public Library.

104. A. W. Hosmer to S. A. Jones, April 5, 1892.

Mr. Ricketson writes me the book[1] is out of print, and not to be had, so I send you a copy of the title page, and of those poems relating to Thoreau.[2]

The book was printed by L. Anthony & Sons. New Bedford, Mass.

1. *The Autumn Sheaf.*
2. "The Improvised Dance," "Walden," "In Memoriam. To H.D.T."

105. S. A. Jones to A. W. Hosmer, April 6, 1892.

I am flabbergasted by this Thoreau picture business and begin to feel that we don't know much about it.

Is the Emerson tintype a copy of the Blake daguerreotype? I am not enough of an artist to settle the question by the looking-glass business.

When it is convenient ask Mr. Walton Ricketson's opinion, as an artist he will be able to give a sound judgement. . . .

My son has just brought in your letter of yesterday. O Fred, you are taking too much trouble to copy the poems. I read them with much eagerness, and am glad to have seen Mr. Ricketson in a new light.

I knew that his book was out of print, and you are lucky in having had a glimpse of a copy. Evidently, Thoreau inspired a deep friendship as Mr. R's verses show.

The copy of Plutarch that I send with your books is for Horace Hosmer: will you hand it to him the first time he is in Concord? I am going to try and get you a copy of Mr. Salt's essay on Thoreau that was published in a volume of his called "Literary Sketches."[1] I like it even better than his Life.

I learned by a college paper last night that I have captured the $25 prize offered by the Inlander for the best literary article.[2] As this was open to all graduates, students, professors, and all who had ever been connected with the University, I feel a leetle proud of it.

The prize paper will be the leading article in this month's issue, and I will send you a copy. . . .

1. Henry Salt, *Literary Sketches* (London: Swan Sonnenschein, Lowrey & Co., 1888).
2. Samuel A. Jones, "Carlyle's Apprenticeship," *Inlander* 2, no. 7 (April 1892):289–96.

106. A. W. Hosmer to S. A. Jones, April 20, 1892.

. . . Sunday I started at 6 A.M. with Plutarch under my arm, and took a roundabout way for East Acton, climbing Strawberry hill &c—to use up time—then called at Horace Hosmer's about 9, spent an hour with him, then he put on his coat and walked back about two miles with me. Perhaps you have already heard from him in regard to the book.

Yesterday, being the day we celebrate, as long as the store was closed I took advantage of it and went down to Plymouth for the day—had a fine day and enjoyed the antiquities very much.

In regard to that portrait of Thoreau in the Century, that Burroughs wrote about—I do not think there is the slightest doubt, on comparing that and the Blake photo—that they were taken from the same picture, and that the Burroughs one was *not* taken from life—as considering that Thoreau died in 1862—and the Ricketson ambrotype was taken in Aug 1861—(while this Burroughs one is said to have been taken in 1861)—and that Thoreau wore a *full* beard the latter years of his life, it seems to bear out the statement I made in my other letter, *that the Burroughs or Treadwell tintype is merely a copy of the Blake daguerreotype*—and if you write up an article on the pictures I should class it as such—or if you wish, I will write Burroughs and find out more fully from him in regard to it, but I do not believe you will find but those three, (no beard—frill under the chin,— and full beard) of him.

Shall be glad to read that prize essay. . . .

107. Daniel Ricketson to Henry Salt, April 21, 1892.

I have by no means forgotten you and the generous as well as admirable work you have done for my dear friend Thoreau, as well as for the large and increasing circle of his admirers. I hope it has proved a pecuniary success—for most certainly the handsome manner in which the publishers as well as yourself have given it to the great republic of letters deserves the most cordial reception.

However much I love my own native land, I think we have reason to be proud of our mother country, who in thoroughness of scholarship is still ahead of us, as most of our best educated people are aware. Our more variable climate, even than yours, and still more unsettled state of public matters, keep the great mass of our people so constantly in a state of excitement that a retired, studious, and reflective mind, whether man or woman, is an exception. It is the great advantage of an old country, whose institutions are settled, that genius and merit find a readier sphere of action. I know the greed for wealth is the bane of the best lands, but a new country in some ways suffers the most therefrom. We have a few political-economists among our public men, and our *high,* so-called *protective* tariff has already created monopolies of wealth and a spurious aristocracy. Time, however, will rectify all this, and our hopes are still in the ascendant for a better future.

P.S. Please remember me, should it come in your way to do so, to Dr. Japp, with whom I had a pleasant correspondence a few years ago. He was then under affliction at the loss of his wife.

108. S. A. Jones to A. W. Hosmer, April 24, 1892.

Those two books—of which I happen to have duplicates—were sent to help fill out your Thoreau collection. Scudder's estimate of Thoreau[1] is that of a man of the world, while Alcott[2] writes with more warmth. . . .

The other day I bought a copy of Frank Leslie's Monthly for the sake of a paper on Thoreau. When I came to read it I found that the writer of it had stolen bodily from Emerson's Biographical Sketch in the *Excursions*.[3] I at once wrote to the editor, and I guess that unblushing thief will be called to account.

Fred, I think Mr. Blake will be better able than Burroughs to solve that tintype puzzle. If it was taken from Mr. Blake's daguerreotype for John H. Treadwell, Mr. Blake must have loaned it for that purpose, and he will be likely to remember it.[4]

I will write to John Burroughs, as I had a letter from him the other day which I meant to follow up by asking him about this picture. If we could compare the tintype with the daguerreotype the question could soon be settled; but I have just been looking at the engraving in Burroughs's paper and comparing it with an engraving from Mr. Blake's which was published in Houghton and Mifflin's catalogue. The expression in these two woodcuts is quite different, and if the engravers did their work faithfully, I should say they worked from different pictures.

However it may be I do not intend to take any conjectures so long as it is possible to "tap" Mr. Blake and know the facts. . . .

1. Horace E. Scudder, ed., *American Prose* (Boston: Houghton, Mifflin & Co., 1880).
2. Bronson Alcott, *Concord Days* (Boston: Roberts Brothers, 1872).
3. W. I. Lincoln Adams, "A Faithful Lover of Nature," *Frank Leslie's Popular Monthly* 33, no. 5 (May 1892):574–76. The article follows Emerson's sketch closely, without always giving adequate credit. Unfortunately no response from the editor to Dr. Jones has survived.
4. Alfred Hosmer evidently inquired of Blake regarding the "Critcherson" portrait of Thoreau, for Blake wrote Hosmer that the Critcherson tintype was taken either from his own or from Theophilus Brown's daguerreotype. See H.G.O. Blake to A. W. Hosmer, March 1 and 2, 1893 (Hosmer collection).

109. Henry Salt to S. A. Jones, April 26, 1892.

* * *

You will have received, I hope, ere this, the copy of Edward Carpenter's "Towards Democracy", first edition; and a photo (of myself) which I sent you a little time back. Carpenter's advent, in a third & enlarged edition, has been rather significant, coinciding, as it did, with the time of Whitman's exit. Some of the English papers have had good notices of "Towards Democracy"; & his kinship with Thoreau, as well as with Whitman, has not escaped observation. For my own part, I always think of Thoreau, Whitman, Carpenter, Jefferies, & Burroughs, as members of one school, the natural school. . . .

I am half inclined to print at my own expense an edition of my "Return to Nature" (essays) in America—say 500 only—& have half of them sent back to England. In case I should decide to do this in the course of the summer (I should not hurry about it, as I have only tried two English publishers as yet), can you give me any hints as to a reasonable publisher, or printer, to go to in the States? Of course I should not do this in any expectation of the book *selling;* but merely because I feel that the subjects of the essays are interesting, & that the interpretation (I won't say criticism) of these "natural" writers is the only literary work I have much at heart. . . .

Sanborn recently sent me copies of the first half of the batch of letters addressed by Thomas Cholmondeley to Thoreau. They are interesting—give good descriptions of what he saw in the Crimea & elsewhere, & contain references to the Oriental books he presented to Thoreau—but there is nothing in them of importance to the biographer. Cholmondeley writes in a philosophising tone, but I shd. judge him to have been rather a would-be philosopher than a real one.

110. S. A. Jones to A. W. Hosmer, May 1, 1892.

You caused an unusual ripple by the announcement that you were on the track of some of Thoreau's early writings. May you have the good fortune to make a "find." You know we have some specimens given in Sanborn's Life of him and what we read there makes me hungry for more. . . .

I struck a stinkpot the other day. You see, I wrote to the editor of Frank Leslie's Monthly,[1] calling his attention to the plagiarism in that paper on Thoreau, and, by Jupiter! the cuss wrote back telling me that my letter was "impertinent and wholly superfluous." I replied that it was decidedly pertinent to inform an editor when he was dealing in stolen goods, but that in his case it did seem to be "wholly superfluous." It is his turn to "say something," but up to date he hasn't.

Of course you've seen the "Emerson-Thoreau Correspondence" in the last "Atlantic." What a toady Sanborn is! Here are eleven letters by Thoreau and seven by Emerson, yet Sanborn terms it the Emerson-Thoreau instead of the Thoreau-Emerson as it by right should be. We shall have a second batch of these letters in June, and Mr. Salt thinks they will be followed by a new edition of Thoreau's letters.[2] I shall be glad to see it if Sanborn prints all that Thoreau wrote instead of cutting out as Emerson did.[3]

By the way, is there anything more about that new edition of Channing's book on Thoreau?

I was looking over my copy of that work this morning and it is a puzzle to know what Thoreau wrote and what Channing did. He had the thirty odd volumes of Thoreau's journals, and he appropriated therefrom without quotation marks. I wish I could find a copy of that book for you because seven-eighths of it is unmistakably Thoreau's. . . .

1. The editor was probably Miriam Florence Folline Leslie, who in 1882 took the name of her deceased husband Frank Leslie. She was editor and manager of the Frank Leslie publishing business from 1880 through 1895. See *DAB*, 11:187.

2. See Henry Salt to Dr. S. A. Jones, March 4, 1892, letter 97.

3. In order to emphasize Thoreau's supposed stoicism, Emerson deleted many personal references from his edition of Thoreau's letters, *Letters to Various Persons* (Boston: Ticknor and Fields, 1865). Dr. Jones had small patience with this kind of misrepresentation; of Emerson's editing he remarked in an unpublished journal: "It has lowered Emerson in my esteem to learn that he could desire to alter Thoreau's letters from a purely artistic intent." Dr. Jones's own editorial philosophy was stern and forthright: "He who assumes to edit a dead man's writings should not forget his responsibility. Such an one should be above all things truthful" (reading log of March, 1887, Jones collection). Unfortunately, as Walter Harding has pointed out, Sanborn's *Familiar Letters* (1894) was edited even less responsibly: "He revised the punctuation, spelling, and even the wording to suit his own taste and was extremely careless in dating and annotating the letters" (see *A Thoreau Handbook*, p. 79).

111. A. W. Hosmer to S. A. Jones, May 3, 1892.

* * *

Have not had time to read Sanborn's article through but it looks as though he felt obliged to follow out your remarks, from the way he writes on the top of the second column on the first page.[1]

I hear nothing new in regard to the republication of Channing's Thoreau.

I enclose quotations from the record of the C.A.D. Society[2] but it is not as full as I was in hopes it would be, however, I have got the line moving that will probably give me a chance at some early essays of Thoreau's. . . .[3]

1. "The Emerson-Thoreau Correspondence," *Atlantic Monthly* 69 (May 1892):577–96. At the top of the second column of the first page, Sanborn commented on the significance of these letters: "They will, I think, open a new view of Thoreau's character to those readers—perhaps the majority—who fancy him a reserved, stoical, and unsympathetic person. In editing the small collection of Thoreau's letters which he made in 1865, three years after the writer's death, Emerson included only one of the epistles to himself in the year 1843, though several of those addressed to Mrs. Emerson from Staten Island were published." Dr. Jones had earlier criticized Emerson's editing of Thoreau's letters in "Thoreau and His Biographers."

2. Included with this letter was more than a full page of quotation from the records of the Concord Academic Debating Society, which Thoreau participated in in 1829. Dr. Jones passed this information on to Salt, who later wrote that he thought it "very valuable." See Henry Salt to Dr. S. A. Jones, June 9, 1892, letter 114. Salt used part of the material in the revised edition of his biography; see *Life of Henry David Thoreau* (London: Walter Scott, 1896), p. 23. The material has been recently used by Walter Harding, *The Days of Henry Thoreau*, p. 28.

3. Alfred Hosmer was probably already in correspondence with Horatio Allen, the son of Phineas Allen, Thoreau's preceptor at the Concord Academy. Later in May 1892 Hosmer acquired Thoreau's boyhood composition, "The Seasons," from Horatio Allen.

112. S. A. Jones to A. W. Hosmer, May 8, 1892.

* * *

Of course I was much interested in the report of the Concord Academy Debating Society. It seems that Thoreau was "on deck" in the twelfth year of his age, but he had not then got down to business, according to the Secretary's report. I am writing to Mr. Salt to-day and I shall copy the "item" for him.

It is curious that the lady who defended the Thoreaus so ably should not have signed her true initials, and it explains your failure to find the Miss "Folsom" when you sent her a copy of Lippincott's Magazine.

Miss Jane Hosmer told me that the writer's name was Folsom, and she spake as if she knew her. Well, we'll have to leave the lady in her hiding place.

The books came duly and the package was opened with eagerness. The Emerson volume is a splendid copy of an early issue of the first edition, and I assure I prize it very much. The "Blithedale Romance" shows that it has been in appreciative hands. It may be poor taste, but it interests me more than any of his novels. I suppose it is because of the Brook Farm background that I am better pleased with it. I can't tell why it is, but I read a first edition with an extra relish. It seems rather tame to say "Thanks!" for so rare a present; and it is too bad that I have no chance of an auction to help me to a more tangible acknowledgement. Well, I can only wait *my* opportunity! . . .

Horace Hosmer is certainly "off" in regard to "Leaves of Grass." His copy was the second edition, 1856, and both Emerson and Thoreau had the first, 1855, so that the *Leaves* were in Concord before Horace sent his copy around.[1] Sanborn has both the Emerson and the Thoreau copy; he showed them to me when I was at his house. . . .

1. Under the pen name *Crayon* Horace Hosmer had written a piece for the *Concord Enterprise*, May 6, 1892, entitled "How 'Leaves of Grass' First Came to the Concord People," in which he described circulating the book among his Concord friends in 1856. Emerson's copy of *Leaves of Grass* is now at the University of Michigan Library.

113. A. W. Hosmer to S. A. Jones, May 14, 1892.

. . . I also find that in addition, for the Qr. ending Feb 25. 1829 Henry D. or as it is given David Henry Thoreau spoke "The death of Leonidas"—Qr ending Aug 22. 1829—"Lines written in 1821 on hearing that the Austrians had entered Naples, with scarcely a show of resistance on the part of the Neapolitans, who had declared their Independence & pledged themselves to maintain it."

Qr ending Feb 25 1830—"Extract from an oration delivered by E. Everett, at Plymouth Mass Dec 22. 1824"

Qr ending Aug 18, 1830 "Extract from a letter of the British Spy" and in a dialogue with Edw. W. Wright "Chas. II & Wm. Penn." He also at an examination gave "Buonaparte's address to his Army."[1]

The compositions have been mislaid, but will be sent to me as soon as they can be found.

That Mr Rolfe, the Advertiser spoke of, that is to deliver some lectures in Oxford this summer, was in looking for some views to take over with him. I think from the way he spoke, he intended to speak on *Emerson* more than any other Concord Author but I talked *Thoreau*—however he was very glad to get a chance to read Dircks essays and also Salts introduction to Antislavery papers.[2] By the way speaking of Salt, I wonder if there are any views connected with Thoreau that he does not own, you just find out for me and I will send them to him.

That article *was* supposed to be by Miss Folsom, but now I have an idea given me, that I think can be worked out, so I can find out who she was. It will probably take some little time for everything to come round all right, to locate her, but I think that with the help of the Misses Hosmer, I may find her yet. . . .

1. Here Hosmer is again quoting from the records of the Concord Academy. This material has appeared in Walter Harding, *The Days of Henry Thoreau*, pp. 27–28.

2. Henry W. Rolfe later wrote that his lectures at Oxford had been very well received. His letter to Hosmer of August 29, 1892, is interesting for its comments on the reception of Emerson, Thoreau, and Hawthorne in England: "I was amazed at the enthusiasm shown by so miscellaneous an audience for Emerson and Thoreau. Many persons had read them, but not from quite the right point of view, so that they were very glad to learn something about their lives and the conditions that their writings presupposed; while others were ignorant of them, but immediately awoke to the keenest interest. No better subject, I am sure, could have been found for just this company of earnest thoughtful people. . . . Hawthorne is fully appreciated too over here. I heard one of the most promising of the younger Oxford teachers declare that 'The Scarlet Letter' is the greatest tragedy in the language" (Henry W. Rolfe to A. W. Hosmer, August 29, 1892, Hosmer collection).

114. Henry Salt to S. A. Jones, June 9, 1892.

I have to thank you for two very interesting letters. The information about the Concord Academic discussion and the Harvard Class of 1837 is very valuable; I don't think I have seen anything to beat that letter of Thoreau's written in reply to the circular notice; it is so supremely Thoreauish throughout.[1] I was thinking the other day what a lot of biographical matter I have got in the letters I have had from you, & that I must some day go through it carefully & see where it all "comes in"! Unfortunately a second edition, or cheap edition, of my book is out of the question in this country, Bentley having only sold 8 copies in the past twelve months, & I doubt if there is much more chance for it in America. Otherwise I should indeed have liked to cooperate with you in a revised edition under our joint names.

I have just received the *Atlantic* for June from Sanborn with the further letters. What most strikes me is the immense superiority of Thoreau's letters, as compared with Emerson's, in this correspondence. But I suppose the young man was naturally more on his mettle than the elder. . . .

Carpenter has been here for about a week at Whitsuntide, & as a number of socialist friends have been in the neighborhood we have been quite gay. Bernard Shaw, whose name you may possibly have heard in connection with the Fabian Society, has also been here. He published a book on Ibsen ("The Quintessence of Ibsenism") a few months ago, which I believe was reprinted in America. He & Carpenter are as unlike as possible in temperament, & yet they seem to be arriving at the same conclusions by different routes. . . .

I get letters occasionally from Arthur Stedman, son of E.C.S., who is editing the new forthcoming edition of Herman Melville's works. Did you see my art. on Melville in the *Eclectic* for April? I wonder whether you are a Melville enthusiast? You *ought* to be. He was one of the very greatest of American writers. . . .[2]

I had a very kind & genial letter lately from old Mr. Ricketson. Do you correspond with him & Mr. Blake?

1. Dr. Jones was undoubtedly quoting the text of Thoreau's letter of September 30, 1847, to Henry Williams, which is reproduced in part in "Memorials of the Class of 1837 of Harvard University" (Boston: Geo. H. Ellis, 1887). Jones reprinted this article in *Pertaining to Thoreau*. For the full text of the letter see Walter Harding and Carl Bode's *The Correspondence of Henry David Thoreau*, pp. 185–86.

2. Dr. Jones first heard of Melville from Salt, and he soon began to collect Melville. The University of Illinois Library has acquired that collection.

115. S. A. Jones to A. W. Hosmer, July 3, 1892.

You have had a long rest so far as your Ann Arbor correspondent is concerned, and the Lord only knows how long I should have slept had not Horace Hosmer woke me up by sending me his copy of the *Leaves of Grass* as a present. He has had the book for thirty-two years, has read and read and read it, and it is full of his marks: is indeed so much a part of his life that I can not for a moment think of keeping it; so I braced up and wrote him at once, explaining why I cannot keep the book.[1] Having broken the dumb spell that has bound me so long, I finished his letter and put in a new sheet for you.

I much doubt if one of your good health can understand such a rickety existence as mine. I am seldom down sick, and there is never a day when I feel really well. I am either in a gale of good spirits, or way down in the dumps, and as I grow older I find that the bright spells grow less and less frequent.

It is two months since I have written a line to Mr. Salt, and I must try and send him a line tonight.

Your last letter contained a copy of Thoreau's "composition,"[2] and after it came a *traced* copy of the same composition. That was more trouble than you should have taken. Thoreau must have been very young when that essay was written, and of course it contains no trace of his future genius; at the same time it is by no means such a "composition" as the average small boy produces. The ideas in it are boyish but the literary expression is by no means that of an ordinary boy. It is noteworthy, too, that Nature engaged his attention at that early day.

Since I last wrote to you we have had both installments of the "Emerson-Thoreau Correspondence." The title shows what a toady Sanborn is. Thoreau wrote the greater number of the letters, and the title should have been Thoreau-Emerson. Mr. Salt wrote me when he had read all this correspondence, and he notes how much better Thoreau's letters are than Emerson's. The publication of these letters makes me hope that

Sanborn will follow them up by a new edition of Thoreau's correspondence. To print all that can be found and to print *all* of the letters would be to give us a most interesting book. . . .

1. Dr. Jones returned Horace Hosmer's *Leaves of Grass,* which was the 1860–61 edition of Thayer and Eldridge. It was later given again to Dr. Jones by Bertha Hosmer, daughter of Horace Hosmer, after her father's death (Bertha Hosmer to Dr. Jones, March 29, 1894, Jones collection). The volume is now in the Rare Book Room of the University of Michigan, the gift of Miss Mary Cooley, daughter of Charles and Elsie Cooley, the son-in-law and daughter of Dr. Jones.

2. Alfred Hosmer acquired Thoreau's schoolboy composition "The Seasons" from Horatio Allen, the son of Phineas Allen, Thoreau's preceptor (Horatio Allen to Alfred W. Hosmer, May 14, 1892, Hosmer collection). The manuscript of the composition is in the Hosmer collection.

116. Henry Salt to S. A. Jones, July 27, 1892.

Best thanks for your two very welcome letters, one of them containing a copy of that interesting document, Thoreau's schoolboy essay. The anecdote about Miss Howells' juvenile drama is extremely good, & withal so very credible & natural—a much better story, I should say, than any of the masterpieces which her literary papa has given to an admiring world. . . .

I hear from Ed. Carpenter sometimes. His "Notes on Ceylon & India" will, I think, be a very interesting book. He is also preparing a record of his friendship & talks with Walt Whitman, which will be valuable for the light it throws both on W.'s character & his own. . . .

117. S. A. Jones to A. W. Hosmer, July 29, 1892.

* * *

I am afraid your trip would have been pleasanter with a younger man, or with one of more energy; but I will hope that what you saw of Nature made up for any fallings short in me.

I am travelling the route over again in memory, and the narrow passage through the "Soo" is the part that lives freshest in my recollections.

The Indian cabins along the silent shore, and the shadows of those Canadian mountains come back to me like a picture, and to crown all, I again hear the "Kanuck" maiden with her "Ross bif, fresh fish, bacon."

The old geologist tells me that Mackinac Island is not of volcanic origin, but is a deposit, and that once the whole island was as high as the top of Sugar Loaf now is. The snows and rains of thousands upon thousands of years have worn it down, and the time will come when Sugar Loaf will have crumbled down.

What chiefly disappoints me in that island is that it is so wholly given up to frivolous pleasure seekers, and that the plain living of a sensible person is not to be had by the visitor. I am glad that I have seen it, though I think it extremely doubtful if my eyes ever behold it again.

The ideal trip there is to get away from the fashionable crowd and enjoy the solemn silence of those delightful evenings without the "gobble" of the hotels or the "gabble" of the fools.

I am glad that you have been under our humble roof, and that your face is henceforth one of our household memories; but I am sorry that a previously-arranged visit took my wife from home before your departure. However, you have seen us as we are, and if ever fate or fortune bring you this way again you will please remember that the latch string hangs out for you.[1]

If Horace Hosmer had been with us we could have defied the devil and any other fellow, and I am sure our enjoyment would have been trebled. The hope of yet seeing him here is one of my dearest anticipations.

Fred, I have been thinking of writing a paper upon Thoreau's mother to refute the injustice that Sanborn has done her. How many, now in Concord, beside Mrs. Bigelow remember her? Do you think you could enlist Miss Jane Hosmer to assist in gathering all obtainable facts? . . .

1. The Hosmer collection includes a brief journal of Hosmer's trip to Michigan. He left for Ann Arbor on July 14th, 1892, arrived on the 15th, and spent several days with Dr. Jones in and around Ann Arbor. On about the 19th they left for a tour of Mackinac Island and Sault Ste. Marie, from which they returned on July 25th. Hosmer then left Ann Arbor the next day and arrived in Concord on the 27th.

118. A. W. Hosmer to S. A. Jones, August 8, 1892.

I drove up to see Horace Hosmer yesterday—found him just getting over an attack of inflamation of the lungs. He was very glad to hear from you—and delighted to think you were going to write up Thoreau's parents.

I find that G. Wm. & Burrill Curtis—while with the Hosmers—at the place near Walden—(of which you have a photograph of Thoreau's survey) did not do much farming—merely cultivated a small plot of land, but spent their time in study.[1]

Miss Hosmer does not think that Mrs Thoreau had aid from the masons, as they were comparatively well off after Mr Thoreau died—the lead business helping them a great deal—as Miss H. says. The work was done very quietly—and the finer grinding was done at the house, and there was more of it done than the public had any idea of. This fine lead was all taken by the Harpers for electrotyping.

Chas. Dunbar[2] is probably buried in the Dunbar tomb on the Hill burying ground—(I will find out for sure and let you know later,) Louisa[3] is buried in the New burying ground (the first portion of Sleepy Hollow).

Thoreau's library, with the exception of that part that was given to Harvard College, is probably in the possession of Mr. Thatcher of Bangor Me. where Sophia died.

Judge E. R. Hoar,[4] Edward's brother, might give you points in regard to Mrs Thoreau.

Horace Hosmer in speaking of the great love of Nature that both Mr & Mrs Thoreau had—not only seeing them himself, but being told by others, of their walks abroad, quoted "The aspirations of the parents often become realizations in the children," and thought it was a truism in the case of Henry. He said his mother told him, that one of the Thoreau children came very near seeing the light for the first time, on Nashawtuc hill, or Lee's hill as it was then called. . . .

1. Horace Hosmer's remarks were perhaps made in refutation of Sanborn, who had reported in his biography of Thoreau that G. W. Curtis and his brother Burrill "hired land" from Edmund Hosmer "which they cultivated for a time." See Sanborn, *Henry D. Thoreau,* p. 118.
2. Charles Dunbar was the brother of Cynthia Thoreau. He was buried in the New Burying Ground (now part of Sleepy Hollow) and not in the Hill burying ground.
3. Louisa Dunbar was a sister of Cynthia Thoreau.
4. Judge Ebenezer Rockwood Hoar (1816–1895).

119. Henry Salt to S. A. Jones, September 2, 1892.

* * *

The other day, I came across a reference to a poem by Katherine Tynan (the Irishwoman) on "Thoreau at Walden". I have not seen the poem, but will look it up at the Museum Reading Room & copy it for you, if you wd. like it for the Bibliography & if it is not accessible to you at your library. . . .[1]

1. Katharine Tynan, "Thoreau at Walden," *Louise de la Vallière and Other Poems* (London: Kegan Paul, Trench & Co., 1885), pp. 90–91. Dr. Jones did not include the poem in his bibliography.

120. S. A. Jones to A. W. Hosmer, September 10, 1892.

Your letter and the "picters" came to-day. By gosh, the Jones family looks as if it had been in pickle and was about three-quarters dried-out! Old Jones is at least 89 and pretty damned sleepy at that. The young ones appear as if they had been hatched in an incubator and somewhat over-done.

We have looked at each other all day and asked, "Can this be thus?" It is the devilish thusness that overcomes us, and we are wishing that we had died young.

Finally Dot braced up and declared, "The sun should be sued for libel." Howell replied, "The sun isn't libel in the case." (The poor boy has lain insensible ever since.) . . .

Your own portrait is more than welcome. I did not take one on the day you offered it, in Concord, because I was all packed up, and I was afraid of breaking it if put into my handbag; but now I can see just how you look without drawing on my memory. Next week I shall be in a decent new suit of clothes and then you shall [see] a shadow of my seedy self as sure as I live. . . .

121. S. A. Jones to A. W. Hosmer, October 5, 1892.

* * *

I am glad if you liked Thoreau's Autumn. It did not please me so well as some of the other books of the series.

Mr. Blake sent me a copy with an inscription, but not wishing to be in his debt I sent him a copy in return. . . .

122. Henry Salt to S. A. Jones, October 6, 1892.

* * *

Those words of G. W. Curtis's quoted by you[1] are certainly very interesting. It seems strange—& a pity—that he did not write more fully about Thoreau than he has done.

The London papers of this afternoon contain the news of Tennyson's death. The older generation of poets is rapidly passing away—Whitman, Whittier, Browning, Tennyson—and it is not easy to see who are to be their successors. I trust the new democratic enthusiasm may inspire a new school of poetry, but it is likely enough there will be an *interregnum*. Any way, I do not believe there is anything good forthcoming on the old lines.

I have not as yet received a copy of "Autumn", but it is quite likely that Mr. Blake will be sending me one. If he does not do so, I will take you at your word & accept your kind offer to send me the book. I am glad the series is now complete. I wonder if you could tell me where to look for the original & authorised version (if such there be) of the John Brown marching song? If it would be at all suitable for my "Songs of Freedom", I should like to include it, but I have no clear idea as to its authorship, &c. Sanborn tells us nothing about it, I believe, in his ponderous Life of J. B. . . .

A great deal of my time is occupied now in the secretarial work of the Humanitarian League. As an organised society, it is not, & is not likely to be, either wealthy or powerful; but indirectly we are setting people thinking with some result. The Royal Buckhounds, which worry tame stags in the Windsor district, are likely to be discontinued at the end of this season, owing to the agitation we set going. I have today been "interviewed" by the representative of an American newspaper syndicate on this subject of the Buckhounds, & the English papers have been taking the matter up very warmly for some months past. A little book of mine, on "Animals' Rights", is just about to be issued by George Bell & Sons. (Let me know, if you would like me to send you a copy. But you would probably think it rather a fantastic production, so I hesitate to inflict it on you without due warning!) . . .

1. Dr. Jones sent Curtis an offprint, and Curtis replied:
"I am very much obliged to you for your 'Glimpse of Thoreau.' It always seemed to me one of the good fortunes of my life that I knew Concord when Emerson, Hawthorne and Thoreau, were citizens there, and that I personally knew them.
"I sympathize fully with the regard and admiration for Thoreau which inspire your paper, and if in personal intercourse he seemed to be, as Hawthorne said, a 'cast iron man,' he was after all no more rigid than the oak which holds fast by its own roots whatever betides.
"One of my most vivid recollections of my life in Concord is that of an evening upon the shallow river with Thoreau in his boat. We lighted a huge fire of fat pine in an iron crate beyond the bow of the boat and drifted slowly through an illuminated circle of the ever-changing aspect of the river bed. In that house beautiful you can imagine what an interpreter he was." Quoted in Dr. Jones's "A Belated Knight-Errant," *Inlander* 5 (January 1895):190–91.
From the context it is clear that Dr. Jones had sent extracts from Curtis's letter to Salt. The letter is not in the Jones collection.

123. S. A. Jones to A. W. Hosmer, October 11, 1892.

* * *

I am going to write an article for a new paper soon to be started in New York, on *Thoreau's Inheritance.*[1]

I shall endeavor to show that his intense love of Nature was inherited from his mother.[2]

Now, Sanborn says that John and Helen were "clear Thoreau," and Henry and Sophia "clear Dunbar."[3] Can you, then, find out from those left who knew Sophia if the love of Nature was strongly developed in her? If such is the fact it will make the paper all the stronger.

I shall have a chance to do justice to the character of Thoreau's parents, and that is a job I am ready for every day in the week, Sundays included. . . .

1. The New York paper rejected Dr. Jones's "Thoreau's Inheritance"; it later appeared in the *Inlander* 3, no. 5 (February 1893):199–204.

2. In "Thoreau's Inheritance" Dr. Jones argued that "Henry D. Thoreau's intense Nature-love caught its life-long fire from his mother's fervor." Cynthia Thoreau's love of nature was a favorite point of Horace Hosmer's as well.

3. Of the Thoreau children F. B. Sanborn wrote: "The two eldest, John and Helen, were said to be 'clear Thoreau,' and the others, Henry and Sophia, 'clear Dunbar;' though in fact the Thoreau traits were marked in Henry also" (see *Henry D. Thoreau*, p. 8).

124. H.G.O. Blake to S. A. Jones, October 12 and 13, 1892.

I wish to say that my sending a copy of 'Autumn' to you was by no means owing to any suggestion frm. your letter. It was my desire & purpose to send you an early copy, before receiving that letter.

As to your suggestion abt. a vol. frm. the Walden period, you have probably noticed that in the vols. already published, there are few or no dates frm. that period. In the little there is of the ms. journal relating to it, there are very few dates, & the passages to be found there are, so far as I have examined (rather cursorily,) very much the same as in Walden itself. Besides, if I go on with the work, as I mean to do, it seems to me my first business is to fill up the gaps wh. now exist, & make my representation of Thoreau's Year as complete as I may.

As to what you say of my displeasure, it was simply a difference of view & difference of temperament. If you are too much of a warrior, it may well be that I am too little. As to any superiority on my part & infirmities on yours, you can hardly be more conscious of infirmities than I am. Hence in criticising others, I am very apt to be brought soon to think of my own faults. As Thoreau said in substance, I barely make out to stand where I am, & tho. I am glad of your affection, you must not waste any admiration on my imagined superiority.

125. S. A. Jones to A. W. Hosmer, October 16, 1892.

It is very thoughtful and kind of you to send me from time to time those papers containing Sanborn's droppings. They contain, now and then, something that I find worth preserving; and only for your consideration I should not see them.

Did I tell you that some little time since Edward Emerson sent me the notes of his investigation of the shanty as an "underground R. R. station?"[1] It is an interesting paper, but your kindness had enabled me to settle that question long ago.

I have just mailed an article on Thoreau and his Inheritance to a New York magazine, and when it is published I think Horace Hosmer will be surprised to see what use I have made of some grist he sent me.[2] In my own opinion it is by far the best thing I have done for Thoreau's memory. There is a little poem[3] at the end of it that I hope will please you Concord folks. Last night I received a letter from Mr. Blake which is very pleasing to me as it shows that I had misunderstood him. He is an exceedingly fine and gentle old gentleman, and it grieved me to think that by my unworthiness I had forfeited his good opinion; but it seems that I had misunderstood his letter and had ascribed to him feelings which he did not entertain. I hope that I may be able to have a long visit with him before he is called away. . . .

1. Dr. Edward Emerson's account of the Underground Railroad in Concord was based on information supplied by Mrs. Francis Edwin Bigelow; it is very similar to the account which Hosmer had earlier sent Dr. Jones. (See Dr. Jones's notes in *Thoreau amongst Friends and Philistines*, unpublished ms, Jones collection.)
2. In "Thoreau's Inheritance" Dr. Jones quoted at considerable length from Horace Hosmer's sympathetic account of Thoreau's parents.
3. For the text see letter 49, footnote 1.

126. Henry Salt to S. A. Jones, November 11, 1892.

I am in fortune this week, for within a day or two I received the copy of Thoreau's *Autumn* which you so kindly sent me, and Melville's *Typee* and *Omoo* (new edition) from Arthur Stedman of New York. I have only glanced into *Autumn* as yet, but I see it is as full of fine things as its predecessors. I know one person, to wit Ed. Carpenter, who will be mightily pleased with the very first entry in the book, that for Sept. 21, '54.

I forget whether I told you that Mr. R. Cholmondeley has sent Mr. Sanborn a long letter addressed by Thoreau to Thomas Cholmondeley in Feb. 1855—"a very good letter" Sanborn says. It will probably appear in the *Atlantic*. I am glad that R. C. is at last making successful search for these letters; though I wish he had been more obliging about doing so when I was in correspondence with him three years ago.

I can't help thinking that you would greatly enjoy Herman Melville's works, if you once got started off on them, especially *Typee* and *The Whale*. They are so full of profound reflection & earnest humanity—I do not know any literature I more heartily enjoy reading. He is undoubtedly one of the great brotherhood of nature-writers. . . .

127. S. A. Jones to A. W. Hosmer, November 21, 1892.

* * *

You ask about that Thoreau paper. Well, I sent it to the editor of the New England Magazine in the last week of October, and I have not heard a word from him yet. As a rejected paper generally comes back at once, I thought this delay favorable.

However, I shall write and make enquiry about the end of this week. By the way, do you know anybody who goes into Boston that could make a personal enquiry of the editor of the N.E. Magazine, Mr. Edwin D. Mead.[1] He might think I was a little *some*body if a live Concordian asked about that paper. I enclosed stamps for its return in case he declined it, and should therefore expect him to send it back. . . .

So Mrs. Emerson has gone to join the great host who have gone before; well, she was ripe and ready. I trust that the consciousness of well-doing will make Miss Ellen's remaining life a joy to her.

1. Edwin Doak Mead (1849–1937), author and lecturer, was editor of the *New England Magazine* from 1889 through 1901.

128. S. A. Jones to A. W. Hosmer, December 12, 1892.

Your letter and the Advertiser[1] are just at hand and the matter referred to is soon settled. Mr. Salt has mentioned the fact that "Chumley's" heir had been more obliging to Sanborn than he was when he, Mr. S., applied for Thoreau's letters. It will be well if Sanborn can get all the letters to the Englishman, for no one else has so good a chance to obtain them, and in no other way that I can see will the general reader ever get hold of them. Sanborn can undoubtedly give us a better edition of Thoreau's Letters than any one now living, and we must be content to get them from that source. At all events, Mr. Salt will not move in the matter I am sure. . . .

After keeping my Thoreau paper over a month it was returned with thanks, but was not deemed appropriate for the New England Magazine. It is very probable that it was lacking in literary merit, but it hit Mr. Sanborn pretty hard, and it also had a crack at The American Men of Letters Series for defaming the parents of Thoreau,[2] and on the whole the editor had good reasons of *policy* for declining to publish it.

Horace Hosmer has a rough copy of the paper, and I also sent him the printed slip in which the editor declined it. I shall crawl into my hole and let such matters alone. Thoreau cared so little for men himself that he will never be popular; nor did he care to be. . . .

1. Probably refers to the *Boston Daily Advertiser* for September 14, 1892, which contained Sanborn's review of *Autumn*.

2. In the version of "Thoreau's Inheritance" which appeared in the *Inlander*, Dr. Jones wrote: "One biographer bears glowing testimony to the high moral altitude of the Thoreau children, but quite forgets to explain how they could possibly attain to such a lofty ethical grandeur in the atmosphere of a home that was moulded and managed by a gossip-loving mother. Such a discrepancy should not be left to disfigure and disgrace the *American Men of Letters* series."

129. S. A. Jones to A. W. Hosmer, January 1, 1893.

* * *

If Mr. Mead is a friend of Mr. Sanborn the fact helps to explain why Mead kept my paper a whole month before returning it: he must have sent it to Sanborn to read!

Of course, the Blake daguerreotype of Thoreau is by all odds the best picture of him, and I am glad you got a negative of it. It occurs to me to ask if it would pay you to issue a little tract on "The Portraits of Thoreau" giving a history of the Rowse, the Ricketson, and the Blake copies. The little tract should be small enough to put in the same envelope that carries the photo.

If you will look in the late Silas Hosmer's copy of Salt's Life, page 299, you will see that there is some error prevalent about them,[1] and you will know that the "fourth picture" mentioned by Mr. Kennedy,[2] is the one you photographed from—I believe, didn't you? I mean the Ambrotype that Mr. Davis had.

A short advertisement in one of the literary journals stating that you are prepared to furnish photos of Thoreau with an authentic history of The Portraits of Thoreau would no doubt increase your sales, and also oblige the many lovers of Thoreau who do not now know where such pictures are to be had. If you think such a thing desirable I'll write the tract for you with pleasure. . . .

1. In his 1890 biography Salt had erroneously referred to "a photograph by Critcherson, taken at Worcester, Massachusetts, in 1857 or 1858 (not in 1861, as has been wrongly stated). Thoreau here appears with a fringe of beard on his throat, but with lips and chin shaven." See Henry Salt, *The Life of Henry David Thoreau*, p. 299. This portrait was the daguerreotype made by B. D. Maxham of Worcester in 1856.

2. W.S.K. [William Sloane Kennedy], "Portraits of Thoreau with a Beard," *Critic* 1 (April 9, 1881):95. Kennedy mentioned three portraits which show Thoreau with a beard: the 1856 daguerreotype, the 1861 ambrotype, and another portrait taken in Worcester a few years before Thoreau's death. Here Dr. Jones speculates that this last portrait was simply another impression of the Dunshee ambrotype made in 1861 for Daniel Ricketson. Two impressions of the 1861 ambrotype were made; Ricketson kept one and sent the other to Sophia Thoreau after her brother's death. Apparently Cummings E. Davis, the Concord antiquarian, obtained the impression which Ricketson had sent to Sophia.

130. S. A. Jones to A. W. Hosmer, January 13, 1893.

As we are to do that portrait business, let us see that it is thoroughly done.

I began upon it to-day, with a most telling quotation from Carlyle as a text, and, by Thunder, I have struck a snag on the second page of my paper.

You see, we must give a history of each portrait, and as I begin, of course, with the crayon by Rowse, it suddenly occurred to me to ask myself: "How came Thoreau to have his picture drawn by so celebrated an artist as Rowse; did n't Emerson suggest the thing, or, bring it about?" It is important to settle this point, and Edward W. Emerson can help us definitely.

Will you, then, ask him if his father did not bring about the business? You see, Emerson had more than one portrait of himself drawn by Rowse,[1] and as it must have been a somewhat costly job, for those days, I am sure he had a hand in bringing about the making of the Thoreau portrait. There will most probably be something about it in Emerson's unpublished Journal, and Edward will know because he wrote me that he had been going through that journal to find what he could about Alcott for Sanborn's book.

Find out too *for whom* the portrait was made, and give me the history of it until it came into the possession of the Concord Library. *How* did the Library obtain it? Was it a gift; if so by whom? Or was it a purchase, and if *so,* from whom?

I want to make the history of the portraits so faithful and so true that it will be kept by the possessors.

Can you not get permission to take a negative from the Rowse crayon now in the Library; then, if you can also secure a negative from the Davis picture, *you* can furnish every picture I mention.

I will first publish my history in The Inlander, and it will look better when you say in your copy, "Republished from The Inlander." Or, if you prefer it at first hand, you shall most surely have it. But as an "Ad" I think it will be more effective as a reprint.

The Thoreau paper that Mead rejected will be published in The Inlander; so you Concord people will have a chance to read it in print, after all. The editor of The Inlander snapped at it at once, like a hungry dog at a bone.

As it is a safe plan, at least, not to christen a child until it has been "borned," so it will be well to leave unsettled the place of advertising the history until it is all written; but I think the "Critic" of New York will reach the greatest number of readers. It is so much easier to cook a rabbit after it is shot and skinned. . . .

1. See William James Stillman, "Rowse's Portraits of Emerson," *Atlantic Monthly* 3 (May 1859):653–54.

131. S. A. Jones to A. W. Hosmer, January 27, 1893.

That piece of information about the origin of Rowse's picture of Thoreau is just the thing. I am particularly pleased to learn that it was not any self pride on Thoreau's part that led to the taking of the portrait.

And Miss Emerson's explanation is such a natural one: you have got the facts beyond all doubt.[1]

One of these days when my liver is in good order I will write up the portraits. I must n't try it until I feel just like it. . . .

1. Unfortunately Hosmer's letter containing Ellen Emerson's account of the making of the Rowse crayon-drawing has not been found. Samuel Worcester Rowse did this crayon-sketch of Thoreau in the late summer of 1854 while boarding with the Thoreaus during a visit to Concord. The drawing was made at the request of Cynthia Thoreau. See Walter Harding, *The Days of Henry Thoreau*, p. 351.

132. S. A. Jones to A. W. Hosmer, February 19, 1893.

If the gods are good they will allow you to find that Emmons picture[1] and thus you will be inseparably connected with the history of "The Portraits of Thoreau."

I almost yelled when I read your letter. Put your nose to the ground and follow that daguerreotype to the ends of the earth—if necessary. Lord, to recover it will be the crown of the whole business! . . .

I struck a snag the other day of this shape: Mr. Salt says—"A photograph by Critcherson, taken at Worcester, Massachusetts, in 1857 or 1858." Did you ever learn from Mr. Blake when his "daguerreotype"—for *that* is what Mr. Salt means—was taken?[2] And do you know if Critcherson is the proper name?

These of course are little things, but it is in just these little things that the errors are found. We must get rid of them once for all.

I mail with this a copy of the INLANDER containing my last Thoreau paper. Can you tell me if the Concord Library is receiving the "Inlander" now? I ordered it sent, but the boys are careless, and if they have overlooked it, I will see that it is sent, for I want it *there* on Thoreau's account. If you would like some extra copies let me know quickly, as they are going off like the famous hot cakes.

Do you think Miss Ellen Emerson would think me impertinent if I sent her a copy through you? I shall send one to the Doctor, to Edward Hoar, and to the only HORACE R. HOSMER and one to the Sisters. . . .

1. The "Emmons" picture of Thoreau is unknown.
2. Alfred Hosmer evidently inquired of Blake concerning the date of his daguerreotype of Thoreau, for on March 1 and 2, 1893, Blake wrote: "My

daguerreotype of Thoreau has the name B. D. Maxham attached to it; but I cannot give you the date at wh. it was taken. I shd. think it might have been abt. 1855 or 1856" (H.G.O. Blake to Alfred W. Hosmer, March 1 and 2, 1893, Hosmer collection). For a discussion of the portraits of Thoreau, see Francis Allen, *A Bibliography of Henry David Thoreau,* pp. xiii–xviii.

133. S. A. Jones to A. W. Hosmer, February 25, 1893.

I waited for the quiet of to-day in order to acknowledge the receipt of the 2nd edition of "Old Concord."[1] I assure you that I deeply appreciate the kind thoughtfulness which led you to send me a volume so illustrative of the place that is of such lasting interest to me. I am glad to have the enlarged edition, and I am especially glad to see that justice is done to Miss Wheeler and yourself.[2] You forgot to put your name in my copy, and that was a large "forget." Now I want you to get from the publisher a second copy into which you will not forget to put your name, and *with which you will enclose the publisher's bill.* You see, I am going to send the first to Mr. Salt; and I shall call his attention to your share in the illustrating.

The notice of Mr. Hoar's death[3] was a shock. I had sent him a copy of "Thoreau's Inheritance," directing it to Concord—alas, too late!

Tomorrow I shall mail you three copies of the INLANDER—one of which you will kindly give to Miss Emerson,—if you are sure she will not deem me impertinent. It is out of place for you to write about "paying" for them, as I *have been amply paid long ago.*

I will see if I can get some more copies, so that when a friend of Thoreau's turns up in the future you and I can be in shape to send him, or her, one. I do not know what luck I'll have, for *that* "Inlander" sold like hot cakes.

I am going to send a copy to Houghton, Mifflin & Co., as a hint that they had better get Mr. Sanborn to change those parts of his Life that are so unjust. . . .

1. Harriet Mulford Lothrop (Margaret Sidney, pseud.), *Old Concord: Her Highways and Byways* (Boston: D. Lothrop Co., 1892). The first edition was published in 1888.
2. Among the illustrators of *Old Concord* were Alfred Hosmer and Mary Wheeler.
3. Edward Sherman Hoar.

134. S. A. Jones to A. W. Hosmer, March 8, 1893.

* * *

It goes without saying that the Two Thoreau portraits are from the "Davis" ambrotype. But, Fred, are you "darn" sure that the picture in Sanborn's Life[1] is *not* engraved from that ambrotype!!!! I'm NOT!!!!!!!!

I'll bet all my peanuts that Ricketson's picture is "not in it." I have compared it and the other cabinet photo of T. that I bought from you long ago, and I'll be hanged if I can see any difference. . . .

1. For this portrait of Thoreau, see the frontispiece to F. B. Sanborn, *Henry D. Thoreau.*

135. Henry Salt to S. A. Jones, March 9, 1893.

* * *

How I wish we were near enough to "collaborate" in this matter, & in other similar works! There is much that is valuable & interesting in your *Inlander*[1] article (for which many thanks!), & I still dream of an American edition of my *Life of Thoreau,* revised & annotated by you, & with our joint names on the title page. Surely Providence must somewhere be preparing a publisher for that epoch-making volume! But, for the present, I shall really be very grateful if I may incorporate your Jefferies notes in my *Study of Richard Jefferies* (for so I think I shall call it). Of course I shall give them as a quotation, & mention their source.

Those lines of yours in the *Inlander* are worthy of their subject.[2] The first stanza in particular, which I knew before, always moves me strongly; it is a profoundly true description of Thoreau. It was certainly very strange that you should have been jotting down those notes about Thoreau's "ecstasy", just as my enquiry was on its way to you. . . .

1. Dr. Jones had sent his "Thoreau's Inheritance," *Inlander* 3 (February 1893):199–204, to Salt.
2. For the text of the poem, see letter 49, footnote 1.

136. S. A. Jones to A. W. Hosmer, March 19, 1893.

* * *

You may tell the enthusiastic friend who likes the Thoreau paper[1] so unwisely that it was refused by the editor of the New England Magazine, and that Mr. Blake, Mr. Ricketson, and John Burroughs each and all ignored the copy that I sent them. I am not small boy enough to want to be patted on the head, but I feel that this Thoreau paper was not a success. That makes no difference, however, for I wrote what I thought and firmly believe, and there my duty ends. My humble testimony is also on file in the Concord Library, and may some day find its way into the heart of some Concord boy when I am snugly laid where praise and blame are of equal value. . . .

1. "Thoreau's Inheritance."

137. Daniel Ricketson to S. A. Jones, March 29, 1893 [postcard].

Please accept my thanks for a copy of "The Inlander," and more particularly for your excellent article on our dear Thoreau. I am slowly recovering from a severe bronchial illness, but am still confined with weakness to the house. I have passed my 79th winter and am close to the door of my 80th birthday. Excuse brevity.[1]

1. This postcard, acknowledging receipt of Dr. Jones's "Thoreau's Inheritance," was not included in *Daniel Ricketson and His Friends.*

138. S. A. Jones to A. W. Hosmer, April 6, 1893.

* * *

It is curious that the older a doctor gets, and the more need he has for rest, the harder they put it to him. But the winter was so darned healthy that my bank account looked as lean as a Presbyterian deacon. Well, if the dear public will only keep it up awhile at the present gait, that projected pilgrimage to Old Concord will get beautifully sure.

I hardly know "where I was at" when last I wrote to you, but I remember a proof of the house in which the Thoreau brothers taught school.[1] If you have a negative of it I shall be more than thankful for a copy. And more than that, Mr. Salt would get from it not only a picture of a house that has deep interest for every lover of Thoreau, but also such a conception of a New England winter as an Englishman would never even dream about. . . .

Will you kindly let me know if there is in that Library a copy of a book about some "MODERN HUMANISTS?"[2] It was published a year or two ago by SONNENSCHEIN AND COMPANY of London, England. If the library hasn't it, I want to send on a copy, as it contains the best summing up of Emerson that I have yet seen. When the book arrives let it be distinctly understood that no name is ever printed in regard to where it came from.

By the way, doesn't that Herman Mellville—darn it, I['m] afraid that name isn't spelled right!—isn't he a TRUMP.[3] Lord, Fred, if I had read those books when I was at school I should have "run away" and gone to sea as sure as shootin'. . . .

1. For a photograph of the Academy building, Middle Street, see Ruth R. Wheeler, *Concord: Climate for Freedom* (Concord: The Concord Antiquarian Society, 1967), p. 148. Henry Thoreau moved his private school from the family home to this building in the fall of 1838; in March 1839 John Thoreau joined his brother as instructor. The Thoreau brothers continued the academy until April 1841, when John's failing health forced its closing. For a full account of the Thoreau school, see Walter Harding, *The Days of Henry Thoreau,* pp. 75–87.

2. John M. Robertson, *Modern Humanists* (London: Swan Sonnenschein & Co., 1891).

3. Dr. Jones sent Hosmer *Omoo, Typee, Moby-Dick,* and *White Jacket.* Jones's own reading of Melville was encouraged by Salt; see Henry Salt to S. A. Jones, November 11, 1892, letter 126.

139. Henry Salt to S. A. Jones, April 9, 1893.

I am writing these lines to you as I sit by the sea on a Sunday morning while the good people are in church. (I have come down to Eastbourne, on our "south coast", for a couple of nights, to see my mother, who has been wintering here.) . . .

I have to thank you both for the revised notes on R. J. lately received by me,[1] and also for the very charming & interesting book on "Old Concord", which I ought to have acknowledged before now. It was very kind of you to send it, & I need not say that it contains much to attract me—I am somewhat of an enthusiast (in a literary way) about Hawthorne, so that it was not only the Thoreau passages that I "made for" on receipt of the book. (Emerson . . . shall I say it? I may venture to say it to *you.* . . . I have always found rather dull!)

The impression I have of present Concord society—you will be able to correct me if I am wrong in this—is that it is too *respectable,* that it suffers from a sort of moral, Emersonian superiority; just as Grasmere and the English lake district is virtuously but afflictingly Wordsworthian. What Concord would have become without the saving spice & tartness of Thoreau, is too terrible to conjecture! . . .

1. Salt used the notes on Richard Jefferies in his study of that writer.

140. S. A. Jones to A. W. Hosmer, April 24, 1893.

* * *

Let me try and pick up the broken ends of several of your last letters. First, I recollect you asked for Mr. Salt's address. Here it is: H. S. Salt, OXTED, SURREY, ENGLAND. He will more than thank you for a picture of the old Thoreau school, and if you can send him a copy of each of Horace Hosmer's Reminiscences of Thoreau[1]—Lord! I can't imagine what the effect will be. For God's sake, keep that Acton man ON TAP; pull out the spiggot and drain him dry of such recollections. You see, Fred, THE Life of Thoreau isn't written yet, and Horace's material is too precious to be BURIED WITH HIM. I am eternally in your debt for things innumerable, but these recollections, which I owe entirely to your thoughtful kindness, take the cake in biographical value. If you send them to Mr. Salt, cut them out, give the name and DATE of the paper from which you cut them, and send them to Mr. Salt in a LETTER. You'll see how it will stir him up!! I got a letter from him to-day in which he just shouts over the "old Concord" that YOU sent him through me—as I shall tell him when I write. I dare not break his confidence by telling you what a shrewd question he asks about Concord people of the "ASA" stripe, but I will get his permission to share it with you, and then you'll smile more than you did when you balanced accounts with THAT Pork. . . .

I have had the little book on "Modern Humanists" at the office a long while waiting for time enough to tie it up and mail it to Concord. It can't go to-night, as this letter will, but it'll go on tomorrow. Before you put it in the Library, just read Page 133 and see how he hits Emerson on the "slavery question."[2]

I am more than tired, and I feel in my bones the truth of Thoreau's philosophy about being the slave of work. But what would he have done had he been a doctor. You see, people get the foolish notion that only THEIR doctor can be trusted, and he's GOT to "git up and git" at their summons. It is white slavery, and it tickles me to know that once in my little earth bed they may call in vain.

I realize, too, that I'm getting nearer that place every year. WHERE has my old endurance gone to? Broken sleep, irregular meals, and contact with the "pure cussedness" of human nature—that's what kills. Well, I've had a better time than I deserve and I'll cheerfully "shove up" to make room for a better fellow. But, bless me! I'm talking like an undertaker— and I'm naturally shy of that breed. . . .

1. Under the pen name *Crayon* Horace Hosmer published two "Reminiscences of Thoreau" in the *Concord Enterprise* for April 13 and April 20, 1893.
2. Robertson argued that Thoreau had repaid his debt to Emerson "when he gave Emerson the right lead on the slavery question." See John M. Robertson, *Modern Humanists,* p. 133.

141. S. A. Jones to A. W. Hosmer, May 28, 1893.

I can only say that I must judge Alcott by the old adage that "A man is known by the company he keeps," and you may add, by the company that keeps *him* (in their company).

How came Alcott to be so highly esteemed by Emerson and by Thoreau? I cannot explain that intimacy from the standpoint of your estimation of Alcott and my own conception of the character of Emerson and of Thoreau. I think Emerson was politic, and I am *sure* Thoreau was honest, so that if I leave out of count Emerson's policy, I am met by the question, If Thoreau was honest, and if Alcott was all that Fred says, how came Thoreau to esteem a "dead beat" so highly?

I want to say to you, in all kindness, too, that just as you know that *all* Concord is not just in its estimation of Thoreau, neither is all Concord JUST in judgement of Alcott. Go to the right crowd and you hear Thoreau properly reverenced; go to another set of men and he is judged just as my esteemed friend "Asa" measures him. Of course, I do not for a moment design to set the opinion of an Asa against that of a Fred Hosmer, but I cannot dismiss from court a Thoreau and an Emerson as I am obliged to do an Asa.

I am led to one thing, however, and that is—I shall not write my notice of that book until I have read it over and over again. My mistakes as a critic are that I am often led by my sympathy rather than by my calm (and later) judgement.

Moreover, Fred, in reviewing such a book, it is my nature to keep a constant lookout over myself lest I should not be just to Sanborn. You see, I may and do despise him as a man, but if he has said the true thing I must not fail to recognize that true thing.

All this while, Fred, I have by no means forgotten that note of Alcott's which I saw at your house and which brought such a peculiar smile to your father's face.[1] In a word, I am going to "go slow," to weigh every consideration for and against, and perhaps, after all, to write—not a word.[2]

I have not written a word to Mr. Salt in a long while and simply because I have been almost wholly absorbed in a deadly struggle between the two schools here.[3] It has done me a great deal of bodily harm, for indignation is a most consuming passion, and the truest life is one as free from all passion as it is possible to us poor, erring mortals.

If I can regain some little nerve tone by resting *here* awhile, I shall be glad, but if I do not, I shall be obliged to go away for that purpose, and if I have to do that it will be out of all consideration for me to also visit Concord this year. I do not like to face that alternative, but it is facing me, just the same.

Horace Hosmer has sent to me papers pertaining to Thoreau that are the most entertaining reading because they were written by one who KNOWS what he is telling his reader. But I am not the proper custodian of such a treasure, nor do I desire to have a man whom writing affects so injuriously spending his strength in that work for me. I am satisfied with what little I already have learned about Thoreau and am very thankful to all those who have so generously taught me that which I could not have learned otherwise. I am NOT a literary man, and I am not much of a doctor, but I must stick to my trade and leave this Thoreau matter henceforth to purely literary men like Mr. Salt—IT is THEIR trade.

More than all, these papers of Mr. Hosmer's have a decided commercial value, and he should sell them to such papers as the NEW England Magazine. . . .

1. When in Concord in 1890, Dr. Jones had apparently seen an unpaid note of Alcott's to Hosmer's father Nathan. See Dr. S. A. Jones to A. W. Hosmer, July 23, 1893, letter 143.

2. Dr. Jones was reading F. B. Sanborn and William T. Harris, *A. Bronson Alcott: His Life and Philosophy* (2 vols.; Boston: Roberts Brothers, 1893). Dr. Jones later published a review of this volume, "A Pewter Plato," *Inlander* 4, no. 3 (December 1893):123–31.

3. Almost from the time of his appointment as dean in 1875, Dr. Jones was forced to defend the Homoeopathic Medical College of the University of Michigan against the university regents and the allopathic professors of the medical school. Dr. Jones resigned as dean in 1878, but his able and often passionate defense of the college continued far beyond that date. For a discussion of the beginnings of the "Ann Arbor Controversy," see Martin Kaufman, *Homeopathy in America: The Rise and Fall of a Medical Heresy* (Baltimore: Johns Hopkins, 1971).

142. Henry Salt to S. A. Jones, July 16, 1893.

A few weeks ago I received a delightful present of Thoreau photographs from Mr. Hosmer, of Concord, and this set me again attempting to induce some English publisher to issue an illustrated volume of Thoreau— whether *Walden* or one of the other works. But I have met with no success whatever up to the present; for publishers one & all seem afraid to venture on Thoreau, and I daresay they are right enough in a *commercial* view of the matter!

Mr. Sanborn has been in London lately, but only on a flying visit, as he was returning to America from the east of Europe, where he has been spending the winter and spring. I went up to London one afternoon and had an hour's talk with him. I had received, a week or so before I saw him, his new *Life of Alcott*, which doubtless you have read or looked through before now. I was rather disappointed at not finding more about Thoreau in the book, though one or two of the references are interesting. Sanborn talks of publishing another volume of Thoreau letters shortly. . . . [1]

1. Sanborn's *Familiar Letters of Henry David Thoreau* was published in 1894.

143. S. A. Jones to A. W. Hosmer, July 23, 1893.

* * *

There is something inexpressibly pathetic in that copy of Rowse's crayon drawing. To think that the LIVING Thoreau sat for the artist—it makes me feel as if Thoreau would speak if I waited long enough. But, after all, your Blake photo is the one that brings the real man before one: that is THE one to send to Walter Scott. I am glad you are in touch with him, for those pictures will add immensely to the "Camelot" WALDEN. . . .

I have been reading widely in order to review Sanborn's Life of Alcott. Only for you I should have "shot off my mouth" prematurely, but I have "gone slowly" and I hope to "size up" that "tedious archangel"[1]—as Emerson calls him—in a fair manner.

Of Sanborn as a biographer I get more and more tired the more I read of him: he can NOT stick to his legitimate subject but must drag in the most irrelevant matters. The fact is, he makes books for the money there is in them, and he uses up every RAG that he can find in order to swell out his pages.

I saw Mrs. Pratt's[2] death announced in the papers: now I suppose Sanborn will get out the whole of Alcott's life-long diary! . . .

I found a mention of "the carpenter Hosmer"[3] in Alcott's life, and I at once thought of the unpaid note that your father showed me. I wonder if "Plato" left many such reminders in Concord? Likely enough he did. . . .

1. Quoted by F. B. Sanborn and W. T. Harris from Emerson's *Journal;* see *A. Bronson Alcott: His Life and Philosophy,* 1:348.
2. Anna Bronson Alcott Pratt, daughter of A. Bronson Alcott.
3. The "carpenter Hosmer," Alfred Hosmer's father, Nathan Sumner Hosmer, is mentioned in a quotation from Alcott's journal for July, 1849: "I am at Hillside (now the Wayside), and sell my grass crop there to Hosmer the carpenter for the house repairs." See F. B. Sanborn and W. T. Harris, *A. Bronson Alcott,* 2:454.

144. S. A. Jones to A. W. Hosmer, August 4, 1893.

* * *

I learned the other day that Houghton, Mifflin & Co., are going to publish a new edition of Thoreau's writings.[1] My informant says it will be in 10 volumes and in the same style as the edition of Lowell's works. Mr. Salt wrote me recently that he had tried his best to get some English publisher to put out an illustrated edition of the "Week," or of "Walden," but in vain. All that can be done by us, so far as I can see, is this: to get up an illustrated work called "Thoreau's Country." As the pictures alone would not be intelligible to all who see them, I propose a written text gotten up by the guide, the artist, and the friend, and in a sort of dialogue form. For instance, as though Horace Hosmer (guide), you (artist), and I (friend) had made the pilgrimage together, camping out the while and having our talks in the different places pictured—drawing, of course, upon so much of the text of Thoreau as would be needed. Find out, please, what Horace Hosmer and the Misses Hosmer think of such a plan. . . .

1. The Riverside edition of 1893 in ten volumes, with an eleventh volume added in 1894.

145. S. A. Jones to A. W. Hosmer, September 5, 1893.

* * *

If those Thoreau papers gave anybody one moment's pleasure I am glad of it, but even if I had the money laying around loose, I have NOT the courage to do the printing act. I am greatly afraid that your audience were biased through their love for Thoreau. They felt my reverence for his memory, and from that standpoint judged the literary merit of the papers.

If you could get Mr. Blake's critical opinion of the SECOND paper,[1] I should be glad to gather from his criticism my own conclusion in regard to the real merit—if, indeed, there be any—of the attempt.

The fact is, the paper is only a fragment, although it is an hour long. It should go more into Thoreau as a whole: as it is it is fragmentary, dwelling upon only a part, and a small part of him.

As I wrote to you before, I was in the midst of a severe attack of "Concord Fever" when it was written, and I suspect that it did not take the audience as the "Glimpse" did. All that keeps me from feeling chagrined is the consciousness that I felt through and through all that I had written. . . .

1. This was probably the paper which Dr. Jones read in Ann Arbor on February 16, 1891. The Hosmer collection includes a copy, in Alfred Hosmer's hand, of this paper, which assesses and defends Thoreau's Walden experiment.

146. S. A. Jones to A. W. Hosmer, October 11, 1893.

* * *

It makes me grunt to think of your copying those two blamed papers, and of what a chore poor Mr. Blake has before him in the reading!! Poor man, I fancy he'll wish he had never been born.

I am preparing a new bibliography of Thoreau which a Book Club in Cleveland, Ohio is thinking of publishing.[1]

By the way, when have you heard from Mr. Salt? I wrote to him on the 27th of last July but have not heard a word from him since. In his last letter he wrote: "A few weeks ago I received a delightful present of Thoreau photographs from Mr. Hosmer, of Concord." He also informed me that he had gone up to London to see Mr. Sanborn who told him he was getting up a volume of Thoreau's Letters. I wish he would hurry it up.

I finally dropped the Alcott books; there was too much home criticism "founded on fact" for me to digest, so I leave Mr. Alcott to the Concord School of Philosophy—they'll take care of him. . . .

1. Samuel A. Jones, *Bibliography of Henry David Thoreau* (Cleveland: Rowfant Club, 1894).

147. Henry Salt to S. A. Jones, October 15, 1893.

* * *

What makes it so difficult for me to get away from England for any length of time (to mention one reason of several) is that the whole work of the Humanitarian League practically depends on me, and that work has lately become more important. There are a good many persons who lend a hand in the League's business, in one way or another; but no one else has time or inclination to do the *continuous* secretarial & organising work which is quite indispensable to the society's existence. I hope, after a year or two, that we shall have more workers—and *then!*

I was at Millthorpe (Ed. Carpenter's) with my wife & sister-in-law all August, living in a farmhouse close to E. C.'s. Olive Schreiner, who was over from South Africa for the summer only, was in a neighboring cottage; and all sorts and conditions of people kept flocking to the valley to see Carpenter—so we did not lack for company. E. C. is now thinking & writing on the sex question; and one of his essays on that subject which I saw in manuscripts seemed to me as beautiful as anything yet done by him. I don't know yet whether he will work them up into a volume.

Olive Schreiner (do you know her "Story of an African Farm"?) is just what one would imagine her from her writings—a keen, brilliant, intensely emotional & sensitive personality, all talk and vivacity one day, and plunged in the depths of moody pessimism the next. She is a great friend of C.'s, & a great admirer of his genius. . . .

148. S. A. Jones to A. W. Hosmer, October 22, 1893.

* * *

I hope I may be permitted to read a new edition of Thoreau's Letters one of these days, for it is plainly evident that Emerson culled severely when he edited the volume we have. I learned from Mr. Ricketson that Emerson did not begin to publish what Thoreau had written to him.[1] Some of Thoreau's strongest writing is in his letters; he wrote them in an extra serious strain as if he were on the witness stand.

I find my thoughts recurring again and again to old Alcott, and I take up Sanborn's book, but with little satisfaction from IT. He writes as if he was in fetters, and I rather think he was. Alcott is a puzzle. There are curious features about his life that make him hard to be understood; but the hardest thing to explain is the regard in which so many held him. On the whole, the only explanation for him will be found in his own Journals, and by restricting Sanborn, Mrs. Pratt has postponed the true estimate of her father.

We cannot rightly estimate Thoreau's philosophy because he was not married, and we cannot rightly estimate Alcott's because he was married.

The thing that perplexes me most of all in regard to Alcott is Thoreau's unswerving friendship for him. I cannot think that Thoreau was "sucked in" by him, and we know that Thoreau was mighty particular about his friendships. . . .

1. See Daniel Ricketson to S. A. Jones, March 12, 1890, letter 10.

149. S. A. Jones to A. W. Hosmer, November 5, 1893.

* * *

The Thoreau papers and the photo of Rowse's crayon picture of Emerson came duly. I was sorry to find that the photo was not one of your own; had I known that you would be obliged to buy it I should not have accepted your offer so glibly. The catalogue of your gifts is longer than the Thoreau bibliography and heavier than one can bear with comfort. As an evidence of a friendship that I can never forget I add it to the long list of your kindnesses.

It is by no means as good a picture as the one you took of Rowse's Thoreau, but it is the smooth, smiling Emerson that we all know. How that group is passing away: Channing is about the only one left. I have just finished Lowell's Letters as edited by Norton,[1] and they have given me far less satisfaction than anything that I have read in years. I found the two costly volumes prosy and of no human interest. As a letter writer he is not a success. However, these volumes leave a clear field for the next writer.

I have also received the first two volumes of the new edition of Thoreau. As I expected, they reprinted from the 1867 edition of the "Week" and have repeated two errors. Look at your edition of the "Week," p. 273, third line from the bottom: "Now he falls between two *souls*." Thoreau wrote "between two stools."

Again, p. 414, "It were vain for me to endeavor to inter*rupt* the Silence." The first edition reads "to interpret the Silence." These blemishes should not appear in so fine a book as they are now putting out. They have issued "Walden" without Thoreau's map of the survey of the Pond; this is too bad, as that showed how thoroughly he loved the Pond when he so faithfully gave its dimensions and its various depths. The books are most elegantly printed and they show that Thoreau is a fixture in our literature. They reproduce Rowse's picture of Thoreau in the "Week," and it is very well done. Did they get a photo from you for the copy? They promise two other likenesses, so that the Blake daguerreotype and the Ricketson ambrotype—both from you, I hope—will go down to Fame. . . .

1. James Russell Lowell, *Letters of James Russell Lowell*, ed. Charles Eliot Norton, 2 vols. (London: Osgood, McIlvaine & Co., 1894).

150. Henry Salt to S. A. Jones, November 9, 1893.

* * *

You shall have a copy of the Jefferies (large paper) forwarded to you at the earliest possible date. I hope you will like the book. I have had quite a free hand in it, & have used the freedom to speak of writers like Thoreau & Ed. Carpenter as the really great men they are, and of the orthodox literary critics as the idiots *they* are! In fact, it is a vindication of the nature-school, from Rousseau to Carpenter. I doubt if either the Jefferies family, or the literary critics, will enjoy it; for their present tendency is to whitewash Jefferies, by dwelling on his qualities as a "naturalist" (in the narrow technical sense), & ignoring his later utterances as a reformer on religious & social matters. I have shown the other side of his character with brutal frankness, & it will never more be possible to trot him out, & patronise him, as a sheep of the respectable fold! . . .

I can't stand *much* of Alcott at any time, though I like & respect his character. Sanborn's presentment of him is a terribly dry affair. How *does* the man manage to make his books so dull? He writes me that he is now editing the Thoreau-Cholmondeley correspondence for the *Atlantic Monthly*. He is a very sirocco of a biographer, parching up one hero after another (Thoreau, Brown, Alcott!), & burying them, like mighty cities of the past, under a flood of dry sand. Let us hope future ages will dig them out!

151. S. A. Jones to A. W. Hosmer, December 9, 1893.

* * *

Beside working my way through Sanborn's dry-as-dust account of Alcott I have read the two large volumes of Lowell's Letters. When I think how very flippantly Lowell wrote of Thoreau and compare the seriousness of Thoreau's life with the mere society existence of Lowell, I am struck by Thoreau's superiority. There was far more MAN in him who lived by Walden Pond than in the one who was minister to the Court of St. James.

Your thoughtful kindness enabled me to read the Thoreau "Chumley" correspondence[1] much sooner than I could have done had I been obliged to wait for the arrival of the "Atlantic" in Ann Arbor. The little that there is has made me like Cholmondeley.

There is a hearty tone about him that bespeaks his sincerity, and I can see why Thoreau liked him. I wish that his relatives, Cholmondeley's, would look up Thoreau's letters, so that Sanborn could give us as many as possible in the new edition, but you can't make an Englishman hurry up, and those letters will never come into Sanborn's hands. . . .

Are there any signs of the forthcoming of another brood of Concord writers? Just think of the list, Emerson, Thoreau, Hawthorne, Channing, Louisa Alcott, Plato Alcott, and SANBORNE!!! Pshaw! the town is bankrupt. Henceforth it must live on its memories. But in the literary history of this century, in America, it will figure more largely than any other one place in America. It can afford to rest now. . . .

1. F. B. Sanborn, "Thoreau and His English Friend Thomas Cholmondeley," *Atlantic Monthly* 72 (December 1893):741–56.

152. S. A. Jones to A. W. Hosmer, January 1, 1894.

* * *

Since I wrote you last, I have seen the new volume of Thoreau's as issued by Houghton, Mifflin & Co., and am disappointed in finding nothing new in it. They announced some material that "had not been published before," but they have only republished two papers that first appeared in The Dial, and a piece of his that Sanborn once read at the "Concord School of Philosophy," and which was published by the "School" in 1883.[1] Whatever we now get that is new will be in Sanborn's volume of Letters.

I have been at work lately on the new edition of Thoreau's bibliography, and am over seven-eights done. It has grown finely; the first issue[2] having only one hundred and twenty-one (121) items, while this last will contain two hundred and thirty (230).

As you know, William Ellery Channing's books are not accessible to me, and yet I am sorely in need of some definite items. He mentions Thoreau in his second series of Poems,[3] p. 157, and he must refer to him in his later publications. This was published in 1847; in 1849 "The Woodman, and other Poems;"[4] in 1858 "Near Home;"[5] and "The Wanderer" in 1871.[6] These last three I have not seen, and the lack of information as to the pages wherein Thoreau is referred to leaves an ugly gap in the Bibliography. I saw these books at Sanborn's but could not get the chance to examine them, nor did I then know that Thoreau is mentioned therein. In a letter of April 2nd., 1892, you mentioned "The Wanderer" and "Near Home," but did not include the pages. If you are not ill and can help me out with this it will be most gratefully received, I assure you.

Horace Hosmer sent me a newspaper, four pages, entitled "Thoreau Annex,"[7] and it was published by the "CONCORD FREEMAN", though my copy is headed "ACTON PATRIOT." It should be included in the bibliography, but I want the year, and DATE of publication if it is possible to get them.

I left my writing awhile to go and see [about] some poor men who were this day buried in a deep trench by the caving in of the walls. The accident occurred at 3 P.M., but at 10 o'clock they had not reached the bodies. It was a terrible sight to look into the yawning hole and think of the crushed humanity lying in it. They had arranged three arc electric lamps and the fellow-workmen of the buried ones were working away with a silent and dogged earnestness.

This job—that of building a drain for the city—was undertaken this winter for the sake of giving the poor employment, and doubtless the unfortunate workmen had congratulated themselves on their good luck in getting this deadly job.

There are places yet to be dug where the men must go down 30 feet, and this accident happening at only 18 feet will lead them to exercise more care.

What a New Year's day for the wives and children—God help them! . . .

1. *Miscellanies,* volume 10 of the Riverside edition, included Thoreau's translations, "The Prometheus Bound of Aeschylus," which had appeared originally in the *Dial* 3, no. 3 (January 1843), and "Translations from Pindar," *Dial* 4, no. 3 (January 1844). Also reprinted were extracts from *The Service* which Sanborn had read before the Concord School of Philosophy on August 2, 1882, and which had been published in *Concord Lectures on Philosophy* (Cambridge, Mass.: Moses King, 1883).

2. Dr. Jones's bibliography of Thoreau was first attached to "Thoreau: A Glimpse," and then appended to H.G.O. Blake's edition of *Thoreau's Thoughts* (1890).

3. Ellery Channing, *Poems: Second Series* (Boston: James Munroe, 1847).

4. Ellery Channing, *The Woodman, and Other Poems* (Boston: James Munroe, 1849).

5. Ellery Channing, *Near Home* (Boston: James Munroe, 1858).

6. Ellery Channing, *The Wanderer* (Boston: J. R. Osgood, 1871).

7. "Thoreau Annex," *Concord Freeman,* 1880. This paper contained a reminiscence of Thoreau by Joseph Hosmer, brother of Horace Hosmer. It has been reprinted as *Thoreau Society Booklet Number Ten* and in George Hendrick, *Remembrances of Concord and the Thoreaus* (Urbana: University of Illinois Press, 1977).

153. Henry Salt to S. A. Jones, January 6, 1894 [postcard].

There are one or two interesting references to Thoreau in the following book:

"Birds in a Village", by W. H. Hudson, C.M.Z.S. London, Chapman & Hall, 1893. pp. 153 & 190. Mr. Hudson is a humane naturalist, like Thoreau, & uses no gun. He is an immense admirer of *Walden,* which he calls "the one golden book in any century of best books". He is the author of "The Naturalist in La Plata", &c. . . .

154. S. A. Jones to A. W. Hosmer, January 9, 1894.

I am glad to learn that business kept you from writing rather than illness, and I shall bear in mind that possibility in future.

I have just received your letter of the 7th instant and I am more in your debt for the page references to Channing's books. I could not get these references elsewhere.

I had a letter from Horace Hosmer, and an enclosure from his daughter, Bertha, informing me of his paralysis. I wrote to him at once.

He mentions an excellent article in the Boston Herald, and one in Our Dumb Animals,[1] on Thoreau, and I want dates, if they can be had. As it is not at all likely that another bibliography of Thoreau will be published in a great while, I want to make my edition as inclusive as possible. I have not seen a single review of this last edition of Thoreau's writings, though the last volume of Emerson's has had the usual laudatory notices. . . .

1. "The Riverside Thoreau," *Boston Herald,* December 18, 1893. Horace Hosmer thought this review "far better than the ordinary 'puff and paid for.' " He also recommended George T. Angell's enthusiastic review of the Riverside edition in *Our Dumb Animals* for December, 1893 (Horace Hosmer to Dr. Jones, December 30, 1893, Jones collection).

155. S. A. Jones to A. W. Hosmer, January 10, 1894.

I had a sad surprise last night in a note from Miss Bertha Hosmer informing me of her father's sudden death.[1]

From the fact that he wrote me a line, in pencil, after his seizure, I had expected his recovery, and that I might meet him once more.

His daughter informs me that half an hour before he died she read to him the paper on the "Pewter Plato" and that he commented upon it. It invests that poor piece of writing with a peculiar solemnity for me now.

Isn't this life strange; I meet him in Acton and his recollections give me so much to think upon. A few years pass, and the last earthly communication that engages his mind is a few thoughts of mine about a Concord man.

I have quite a file of his letters, and they are precious now.

I have sent a line to Miss Hosmer, but I shall look to you for some more about his last days and the funeral.

Fred, if I get to Concord again I shall find it and its vicinity much poorer than when my wondering eyes first saw it. Well, we all must pass away as a dream. . . .

1. Horace Hosmer died January 7, 1894. Bertha Hosmer wrote that night to Dr. Jones, who had given her father "much pleasure with the books and friendly letters." Bertha Hosmer to Dr. S. A. Jones, January 7, 1894 (Jones collection).

156. S. A. Jones to A. W. Hosmer, January 15, 1894.

I send just a line to acknowledge the receipt of the note you received from Miss Bertha Hosmer, and also of the Boston Advertiser, that came to-day.

It seems that the last letter he wrote was one to me. It is dated Dec. 30th. On the morning of Jan'y 1st. he had his seizure; yet on the 2nd. he took a pencil and wrote under his pen-and-ink signature, "Good bye If I do not write again. Horace R."

It is very pathetic, and I shall treasure it while I live. In fact, all my relation to him is more like a dream than a reality.

I have all his letters and I am going through them with a view of writing a paper on "A Scholar of Thoreau's." His letters contain so much about Concord in the first quarter of this century, and also many of his recollections of Thoreau, and this material must be put into permanent shape. I will see if the Inlander boys will accept such a contribution. If they do, I will have it reprinted so that you and I will have a sufficient number of copies to distribute.

IF THERE IS ANY WAY OF GETTING ME A PHOTOGRAPH OF HIM, PLEASE DO SO. I always put off asking him for one—and now HE cannot hear me. . . .

157. S. A. Jones to A. W. Hosmer, January 26, 1894.

* * *

Will you look in the Concord library and see if they have a copy of the Massachusetts Quarterly Review. If so, I want to borrow Volume 3. It contains Lowell's review of Thoreau's "Week"[1] and I most AWFULLY want to read it.

I will give security for its safe and speedy return. I stretch out my arm so far to find it because I cannot get track of a copy anywhere.

Lowell's tone in it is so different to what it is in the later review that I can make a good point of that fact in my Inlander article.

If the Library hasn't it, it is very likely that Emerson had one, and I have gall enough to try and borrow that.

Anyhow, please make some enquiry amongst your Concord folks; some of them must have a copy. . . .

1. James Russell Lowell, "Review of the *Week*," *Massachusetts Quarterly Review* 3 (December 1849):40–51. Dr. Jones later reprinted this review in *Pertaining to Thoreau* (1901).

158. Henry Salt to S. A. Jones, January 31, 1894.

* * *

I duly received the copy of the *Inlander,* with your entertaining essay on Alcott,[1] which I enjoyed very much, though I won't deny that I think you are a little hard on him here & there! However, there is a serious & practical view of a man that has to be taken into consideration esply. in the case of one who set up to teach others as Alcott did; & examined by such a test Alcott's life is certainly far from satisfactory. Still, I feel with Browning in "Rabbi Ben Ezra" that the unaccomplished aspirations of a man have also to be taken into account in an estimate of him. . . .

1. "A Pewter Plato," *Inlander* 4, no. 3 (December 1893):123–31. Dr. Jones ended his essay thus: "He endeavored to live out of his sphere, and the deflection began when the glamour about those Virginia plantations bewitched the boy peddler's admiring eyes. He soared from peddling to Philosophy. Without knowing a word of Greek, he read Plato, Proclus, and Plotinus just as Don Quixote devoured the tomes that turned his head. He thought he was a philosopher, and he found those who confirmed him in his delusion. He was one, if his daughter's definition of a philosopher, as given to Dr. McCosh, is correct: 'A man up in a balloon, with his family and friends holding the ropes which confine him to earth and trying to haul him down!'

"To reform the human family he neglected his own family, and by that token the race will recognize a *pewter Plato.*"

159. S. A. Jones to A. W. Hosmer, February 9, 1894.

Your kindness has given me great pleasure on a rainy day. I went to the post office and found a notice requesting me to call for a registered letter. On seeing your superscription, I at once smelled a mice and hurried to the office to enjoy it. I have just finished reading Lowell's paper and I could but wish that he had always been as just to Thoreau. It is very plain that the personal element got into the review written after Thoreau's death, and it arose from the falling out about that Chesuncook article in the Atlantic.[1] But it was not the thing to inflict punishment upon a dead man, and Lowell's passion has injured his reputation.

There are some fine touches in this paper of Lowell's, and I shall not rest content until I own a copy of the journal containing it. Only yesterday I ordered a bookselling friend to find a copy of the four volumes of the Massachusetts Quarterly Review for me. He will advertise, and ultimately it will turn up.

My Inlander paper[2] is already in print, so this copy came too late, but as I read it I find that it did not come within the scope of the article that I had in hand. I may find future use for it, and then I can make it tell.

You have learned from my letter of the other day that the bibliography is to be published in fine style. It will be a rare book, as the Rowfant Club will not allow it to be reprinted. I shall get as many copies as possible, but it is only sure, now, to reach the few I mentioned in my last letter. . . .

1. See the discussion of "Chesuncook" in the introduction.
2. Samuel A. Jones, "Thoreau and His Works," *Inlander* 4, no. 5 (February 1894):234–40, a review of the Riverside edition.

160. Henry Salt to S. A. Jones, March 8, 1894.

You will, I am sure, be glad to know that I have (provisionally) arranged with Macmillan & Co, the chief London publishers, to bring out a five-shilling volume of Thoreau's writings. For a long time past I have been trying to induce some English publisher to take up Thoreau; but hitherto without success. A few days ago I thought I would try Macmillan, & I have just heard from them to the effect that if I will put into a single volume (of about 450 pages) what I consider the *best* of Thoreau, & write a short Preface for it, they will issue it in their "Eversley" series. So I shall now have the not very easy task of selection; and then if all goes well, & Macmillan does not back out of his offer, the English people will have another opportunity of studying Thoreau's masterpieces. Macmillan's circle of readers being in every way superior to Scott's, the book shd. really be of great use to Thoreau's reputation. I will let you know what is finally settled. For the present, please regard this as private; for of course the scheme *may* fall through, though, as far as I can judge, it is all safe.

I hope the Bibliography is going on prosperously. I suppose it will be published very shortly? I received your last letter safely, though I am not sure that I acknowledged it. I refer to the one in which you told me of the death of one of the Hosmer family,[1] who had known Thoreau & remembered the glow on his face when he had found the rare plant. That struck me as a very beautiful reminiscence. . . .

1. Horace Hosmer.

161. Henry Salt to A. W. Hosmer, March 14, 1894.

The two photographs and the pencil have arrived safely. How can I sufficiently thank you? The photos—especially the large one—are splendid, and give me a far better idea of the spot than any I have seen before. The view is so clear, & yet so tender; I don't think I have ever seen a forest photograph I admired so much—not to mention the special value of this one from the association. It is strange indeed to read the "John Thoreau & Son" on the pencil! Not many firms have a partner of that quality! . . .

162. S. A. Jones to A. W. Hosmer, March 15, 1894.

The Rowfant Club is not an Ann Arbor institution. Some booklovers in Cleveland organized it in 1892. It costs $50,00 to join it and the annual dues are $10,00. They elected me an honorary member for getting up the Thoreau bibliography that they are to publish—otherwise, I assure you, I should not be "in it." There are 55 members and two honorary members. A member is allowed to subscribe for a certain number of copies of every book that the Club publishes. In the case of the bibliography, 125 copies will be printed, but photos will be put in only the copies that go to actual members. This is in order to make the Club copies different from such as may get into outside circulation. The actual cost of each volume will be $2,75, so it will be a sumptuous volume.

Of course the volumes that are given to me will contain the photo, for I have concluded to have but one, namely, the Blake daguerreotype; so you will take the order for sixty-five (65) copies of it. . . .

I received a picture of Horace Hosmer a few days ago and it brings him to remembrance vividly. I am thankful for it. Death is making my Concord visit a tender memory, so many have gone forth whom I should now seek there in vain. Even my friend "Asa" is growing rosy from recollection and "F.B.S." isn't so very devilish, after all.

The thought of your "fine walk" on Sunday last makes my legs ache: am glad you enjoy it. I hope there are many of them in store for you.

163. Henry Salt to S. A. Jones, March 15, 1894.

I have today received your note of March 5, with the quotations from the *Critic,* which paper (by the chance kindness of an English friend) had been sent to me a day or two ago. The review can do the book nothing but good; and my only regret is that the writer should have been so exceedingly unfair & unfriendly in his remarks about your "Notes". My impression on reading it was that it must proceed from someone who wanted to have a tilt at you, but of course I am not sufficiently behind the scenes to judge.[1]

Certainly there is nothing in the review which at all changes my former opinion, that the citation of your Notes is a most valuable addition to the book. The opinion of Ed. Carpenter, & others who really appreciate Jefferies, is surely more weighty than that of an anonymous gentleman on the staff of the *Critic!* It was kind & generous of you to write to the *Critic* to exculpate me from responsibility; but as far as the insertion of your estimate of Jefferies implies responsibility, I shd. certainly commit the same crime again, were the book still to write. The critic seems to have distorted *your* meaning, as much as *my* purpose.

Since I wrote my last letter to you, a week ago, I have finally settled with Macmillan & Co. about the volume of Thoreau. It is to be pubd. early in October, & is to consist of selections, the limits of space precluding me from inserting one of the larger works complete; though this point is left quite at my discretion, & may be reconsidered if necessary. Macmillan is to give me "half profits" (i.e. half of the profits, *after* all expenses of printing, advertising, &c.) which probably will amount to £O–O–O. But as the work will not cost me much time, and as I was most anxious for various reasons to secure the issue of such a volume, I did not care to haggle over it; & of course there *may* be a good sale of the book under the auspices of a very powerful publishing house.

My present idea is to make the work consist of about 80 pages of "Walden", 60 of the "Week", 30 or 40 of "Cape Cod" & the "Maine Woods" (i.e. of each of them), & about six of the essays—say "Natural Hist. of Massts.", "Walking", "John Brown", "Civil Disobedience", & "Life without Principle".

In brief, I shd. try to put into the book the very best writing of Thoreau (exclusive of the Journals, Letters, & Poems); choosing passages, whole chapters wherever possible, which throw light on all sides of his character.

I need not say how grateful I shall be for any suggestions you may be disposed to make, either about the general scheme of the book, or about particular passages. The point is, how best to utilise some 400 or 450 pages, rather a smaller page than that in the (old) Riverside Thoreau.

I have not told Sanborn of this agreement with Macmillan, because I think it may be wiser not to let the Houghton, Mifflin & Co. party know so long before. So please consider the matter private for the present. Perhaps you can tell me whether Thoreau's works are still copyright in America?

I hear from Sanborn that his edition of the *Letters* is now printing, but may perhaps not appear till the autumn.

Yes—Ed. Carpenter's "Sex Love" is certainly rather a "staggerer" in its candour of speech. He is writing other pamphlets on the whole sex question, & will probably eventually collect them into a volume. I shall tell him of the German work mentioned by you.

The Bibliography will be very welcome. This Macmillan volume will have to stand over till yr. next edition. How endless is the bibliographer's task!

1. The reviewer of *Richard Jefferies* (*Critic* 24 [1894]:143) wrote: "In writing his book, Mr. Salt forgot that genius defies definition, and in striving to understand what we can only feel, he found in Dr. Samuel A. Jones's 'Notes on Richard Jefferies' the simple explanation—scrofula and hysteria—which he adopted, introducing thereby into his book the only discordant note it contains."

164. S. A. Jones to A. W. Hosmer, March 29, 1894.

* * *

I am sure that the Thoreau pencil would be a great delight to Mr. Salt. It is the next thing to shaking hands with Thoreau himself. I frequently gather my Thoreau relics about me, and between them and the photos it is almost as good as a visit to Concord.

I learn through Mr. Salt that Thoreau's Letters are even now being printed, though the book will not be published until next Fall. Do not mention this, as Sanborn does not want it to be generally known. Another secret is that Mr. Salt is getting up a Thoreau book[1] of some 450 pages which the Macmillan's will publish next autumn. It will contain an introductory chapter by Mr. Salt, and I am certain you can count upon receiving a copy. . . .

1. Henry D. Thoreau, *Selections from Thoreau,* ed. Henry S. Salt (London: Macmillan, 1895).

165. S. A. Jones to A. W. Hosmer, March 31, 1894.

* * *

The Club has decided to make it a decidedly rare book and so will publish only 90 copies. With this limited number I much question if I shall get ten copies; if so, you and I will have to be content with one copy apiece.

The Club, however, has taken out a copyright, and if there should arise any demand for the bibliography it will be reprinted in a cheaper manner. . . .

166. S. A. Jones to A. W. Hosmer, April 12, 1894.

I have just got hold of something that is too good to keep, so I must share it with you and the Misses Hosmer. You see, a friend in Cleveland has an assistant in the library under his charge who is intimately acquainted with

Sanborn, so at my friend's request she wrote to Mr. S. asking him point blank if he wrote the review in The Critic that scored me.

He replied on a postal card that is before me, and I send you an exact copy of it.

Concord Mass Ap 7 '94

Not only did I not write that notice in the *Critic*, but I have not even seen it. Mr. Salt writes me that *he* was let off easy, but that Dr Jones of Ann Arbor "caught it" from the *Critic*. I do not think anybody can hit Dr J. amiss

F. B. Sanborn

I intend to paste that postal in my copy of Lippincott's Magazine as a testimonial from F. B. Sanborn to the truth of my paper.

Notwithstanding his denial, I am more than ever disposed to regard S. as having written the Critic's review. What is the general opinion in Concord of his veracity, or don't you know?

1. Sanborn's card is in the Jones collection. Dr. Jones apparently did paste it into his copy of *Lippincott's Magazine*, where "Thoreau and His Biographers" appeared (August 1891). Unfortunately when the card was later removed, the name of Sanborn's correspondent was effaced. The review in the *Critic* was of Henry Salt's *Richard Jefferies: A Study (Critic* 24 [March 3, 1894]:143). The review was highly complimentary, except in its treatment of Jones. Dr. Jones later responded to this review in "The Pathological Element in Literature," *Inlander* 4, no. 9 (June 1894):405–11.

167. Henry Salt to S. A. Jones, April 16, 1894.

* * *

I don't wonder that the *Critic* shirked publishing that trouncing letter of yours. It was capital—the first sentence, about the turtle,[1] made me laugh immoderately! But I don't think any English editor wd. have inserted it; for the truth is editors, all the world over, are a feeble folk. There must be something enervating in the profession.

Here is a Thoreau item which perhaps you have already got—*New Review* no. 56. January, 1894. "Some Impressions of America", by Walter Crane. Reference to Thoreau on pp. 47, 48. There is nothing of importance in the article; only a passing reference to Thoreau & his work.

Macmillan does not intend to publish the "Selections from Thoreau" till the autumn. I have not yet done the selection or preface, but shall set about it next month. I shall probably put a good deal of my *Paternoster Review* article into the preface. I shall take the opportunity of doing justice to Thoreau's parents, & withdraw what I said in the *Life* on Sanborn's authority. At present I am looking up my various Shelley essays; as I am going to weld them together in a final form in the course of the year, & call them, "Percy Bysshe Shelley, Poet & Pioneer", or something of that sort. I feel more & more that Shelley & Thoreau are the two writers to whom I owe most in life. . . .

I have a feeling that the writer of that review in the *Critic* was *not* Sanborn. I don't think he rates Jefferies so highly as that writer did; can't see much in him, in fact, except the naturalist pure & simple (!).

1. Dr. Jones used the sentence in an article which was published: "It is recorded of the naturalist Le Valliant, that he removed the brains from a turtle and filled the cavity with cotton; incontinently, and as if nothing was missing, the reptile began to write reviews. This explains a great deal, and the reviewers kindly (or blindly) do the rest." See "The Pathological Element in Literature," *Inlander* 4, no. 9 (June 1894):405.

168. S. A. Jones to A. W. Hosmer, April 18, 1894.

* * *

If F.B.S. did not write that review, then I should ascribe it to no one in New England; certainly not to Mead.[1] It makes no difference, however, for the Critic excludes any reply to its reviewers, and they are as safe as a dog that barks from behind a locked gate. . . .

1. Edwin D. Mead, editor of the *New England Magazine.*

169. S. A. Jones to A. W. Hosmer, April 23, 1894.

* * *

The members of the Club are allowed to subscribe for as many copies as they see fit, but they make their subscriptions small so as to have a very limited edition, and therefore a "rare" book. Sixty-five copies will contain a photo and twenty-eight will be without one. You and I are really giving the illustrations, and solely on the condition that a copy is given to each actual member only. There is, then, no need for my writing to Mr. Hopkins,[1] as you suggest.

I should not like to live in Concord if a mob over runs it year after year on the 19th. It certainly destroys that quiet which I found so noticeable. I see they gave the Gov. a cane. How many canes did that old bridge contain, anyhow? They are getting to be as numerous as the furniture that came over in the Mayflower, and which would load a modern freight train. I am glad my cane was given me by one whose character puts its genuineness beyond all shadow of question, and I assure you I prize it accordingly. . . .[2]

1. Frank Hopkins was the printer for De Vinne Press, printers of Dr. Jones's bibliography.

2. Silas Hosmer had given Dr. Jones a cane made from wood of the Old North Bridge when Jones was in Concord in 1890.

170. S. A. Jones to A. W. Hosmer, April 25, 1894.

* * *

I sent the framed picture of the site of the shanty to the club the other day and I hope you may hear from some of them in the way of orders for some of your views. The Rowfant fellows are getting up quite a Thoreau enthuse and I shouldn't wonder if some of them turn up in Concord this summer. If I learn of any that are going to pilgrimage in that direction I shall give them letters to A. W. Hosmer.

171. S. A. Jones to A. W. Hosmer, April 27, 1894.

* * *

That article in the Boston Advertiser[1] is grand in bearing out all that Horace Hosmer said of Mrs. Thoreau, and it heaps the dirt on Sanborn so high that his corpse cannot be "dugged" out.

Can you possibly get a copy of that paper and send it to Mr. Salt? I ask because I have just had a letter from him in which he writes that in the introduction to the volume of Thoreau that Macmillan is to publish he "will take the opportunity of doing justice to Thoreau's parents, and will withdraw what I said in the Life on Sanborn's authority." You see, that paper in the Advertiser will give him some important testimony as to the intellectual quality of Mrs. Thoreau.[2] I am going to write to Mr. Salt to-night, and will inform him that you will send a paper if you can obtain one. I had pasted mine in my Thoreau scrap-book before his letter came or I would have sent it on at once. . . .

1. Irving Allen, "Of the Thoreaus," *Boston Daily Advertiser,* April 23, 1894.
2. Allen described Cynthia Thoreau as "one of the most remarkable and brilliant women I ever met"; to her Henry was "indebted for his intellectual preeminence."

172. S. A. Jones to A. W. Hosmer, April 29, 1894.

Yesterday I read the paper on Bronson Alcott with much pleasure, and this morning I read Sanborn's reply to Irving Allen with unusual interest.

I think it very likely that Mr. Scudder wrote the article on Alcott,[1] and I am led to this opinion because he handles Emerson's fondness for Alcott so tenderly, while, at the same time, he evidently estimates Alcott just as the majority does. I guess, Fred, that "pewter Plato" is about right, after all. Sanborn's pride was hurt by Mr. Allen's contempt for "schoolmasters" and that is the basis for Sanborn's rejoinder.[2] That Sanborn has a positive ill feeling towards Mrs. Thoreau is evident from what he now writes about her "Tory" ancestors.[3] Why didn't he mention that in the Life?

The passage that you marked with the pen is significant.[4] I am more and more convinced that Mrs. Thoreau must have "sat down" on some of Sanborn's self-conceit and blistered him with her flashing wit.

I am going to write an article to the Advertiser, though I am not sure it will be printed. . . .

1. "Bronson Alcott," *Atlantic Monthly* 73 (April 1894):549–55. A review of *A. Bronson Alcott* by Sanborn and Harris.

2. "Mr. Sanborn Corrects Mr. Allen," *Boston Daily Advertiser,* April 25, 1894. In his article Allen had remembered a sleighing party in Concord, "late in a February day of 1851," which included Emerson, Hawthorne, Alcott and one of his daughters, Rockwood and Elizabeth Hoar, Thoreau, and Channing. Sanborn wrote in his correction that such a gathering "would have been a little difficult to assemble there at that precise date." Sanborn also pointed out, in a derisively sarcastic tone, many errors which Allen had made in dating biographical facts about Hawthorne, Emerson, and Thoreau.

3. Of Mrs. Thoreau Sanborn wrote: "Mrs. Thoreau deserves to be remembered but her ancestry is not so well known as it might be. She could hardly take rank with 'Sons' or 'Daughters' of the Revolution—her grandfather, Col. Elisha Jones of Weston, being a tory, like Col. Watson of Plymouth; and several of her uncles having served in the British army against Washington. Her father, Rev. Asa Dunbar of Bridgewater, Salem and Keene, was also inclined to toryism."

4. Sanborn had pointed out that he dined daily "for three years or so" with the Thoreaus; he then claimed: "This intimacy has made me a little more careful of facts than Mr. Allen seems to be." Hosmer marked this statement in pen.

173. S. A. Jones to A. W. Hosmer, April 30, 1894.

I this morning mailed to the "Advertiser" a paper entitled "A Word for the Dead."[1] If they publish it Mr. Sanborn will be happy—for a little while, at least.

I enclosed a directed envelope, with the request that the paper be returned to me if it was not deemed worthy of publication.

Keep your eye out, and if it is printed, please send me a couple of copies so that I can keep Mr. Salt posted.

The occasion gave me a fine chance to show Sanborn's malice, and I made a strong point of his twitting Mrs. Thoreau with her tory ancestry. That matter makes his malice perfectly evident, and people ought to know him.

If Mrs. Bigelow is alive, Irving Allen's letter must have given her a great deal of pleasure; and I imagine other Concord folk did not feel bad over it.

It is possible that Sanborn's influence may restrain the "Advertiser" from printing my paper; if so, how does your home paper regard Sanborn?

It will be a real pity if the "cuss" is allowed to escape; but, will the "Advertiser" allow any man to traduce the dead without rebuke? I doubt it. . . .

1. This paper was not published; no manuscript has been found.

174. S. A. Jones to A. W. Hosmer, May 3, 1894.

I "tink" it would be well to send Mr. Salt a paper containing Mr. Sanborn's rejoinder to Mr. Allen, as it will show him how S. feels towards Mrs. Thoreau.

As Mr. Salt is going to write an introduction to the new volume of Thoreau's writings, in which he will change what he had written about Mrs. T., this fresh evidence of Sanborn's malice will make his correction all the stronger; it will also show him what kind of a chap Mr. Sanborn really is.

As I have not had my paper back from the Advertiser, it looks as if it might get into print. If so, Mr. Sanborn may think twice in future before he attacks the dead.

I read the proof of the bibliography the other day. It will make a volume of 85 or 90 pages, and will end with my paper to the Advertiser, *if* it is printed. . . .

175. S. A. Jones to A. W. Hosmer, May 8, 1894.

I consider that last picture the best I have yet seen. I like it because it shows more of the body, and especially because it has the coat buttoned in such a careless manner. That is very characteristic; it is indicative of the man who didn't care so much about having a patch on his breeches as he did about not having to have one on his character.

I have always felt that the Ricketson picture made Thoreau look too much "stuck up;" more of a clergyman than of a Henry Thoreau. Now I can see him as Blake did the day that photo was taken.

You will undoubtedly have given the Rowfant Club the best picture of H. D. Thoreau that has yet been published.

If you print any from that positive for your own trade I would surely include so much of the plate as will show below that button of the coat.

I conclude that the Advertiser is not going to publish my letter; probably because Mr. Allen's reply reached them first, and he was fully able to take care of himself.[1]

You noticed that he says *"Aunt Jane"*[2] paid Thoreau's tax. Thoreau says some *man* paid it. Mr. Staples told me he thought Judge Hoar was the one, but he was not sure. I took the liberty of writing to Mr. Allen asking if it was "Aunt Jane" who continued to pay that tax until Thoreau gave up his resistance.

I wish this matter could be definitely settled; it is a little thing, but these little things are important. If the aunt really paid the tax, it is evident that they did not let Thoreau know it. If I hear from Mr. Allen, I'll let you know what he says.

1. "Mr. Allen's Retort Courteous," *Boston Daily Advertiser,* May 3, 1894. Allen here acknowledged his debt to Sanborn for correcting errors in his original article, but took exception to "the discourteous tone of his communication." As a final note to the conflict between Allen and Sanborn, Eben J. Loomis wrote to the *Advertiser* on May 8 describing himself as a member of "that sleighing party of long ago" described by Allen in his first paper. Of Allen's description of the sleighing party, Loomis wrote: "The writer is strictly authentic in his description of events and persons"; but Loomis did add that some of Allen's dates were "erroneous."

2. Jane Thoreau, sister of John Thoreau Sr.

176. S. A. Jones to A. W. Hosmer, May 14, 1894.

I had a letter from Mr. Irving Allen in which he writes that he "thinks" it was Aunt Jane who paid Thoreau's tax, but is n't sure.[1] He referred me to Prof. Loomis, of Washington, D.C. He, Prof. L., writes that he "always understood that it was paid by Aunt Maria."[2] He adds that he has written to a friend in Concord to settle the fact, and will let me know when he has been heard from. He also writes, "the payment of the tax rests between two persons, Miss Maria and R. W. Emerson."

All this shows how difficult it is becoming to fix these little events, and that the only chance of so doing is while the few survivors are left.

Prof. Loomis says he was at Thoreau's house spending the summer when Rowse was there making Henry's portrait, so you see we will now be able to settle the year for that.[3]

When it is convenient, will you ask Mr. Staples if he remembers whether Emerson *visited Thoreau while he was in jail?* Ask him too *about time of the day he arrested* Thoreau, and *about what time Emerson called.*

I have been writing a paper called "Thoreau's Incarceration as told by his Jailer." It is the recollection of my talk with Mr. Staples, and the facts I ask about are necessary for accuracy in regard to the transaction. Miss

Maria Thoreau told Prof. Loomis that Emerson did call at the Jail, but Mr. Staples did not mention that fact to me.

Prof. L. says he yesterday received a photo of Thoreau which is quite different from Rowse's crayon likeness. Can it be one of your last?

1. Irving Allen to Dr. Jones, May 7, 1894 (Jones collection). Dr. Jones included this letter in his authoritative article on Thoreau's night in jail, "Thoreau's Incarceration," *Inlander* 9 (December 1898):96–103. Reprinted as *Thoreau Society Booklet* Number 4.

2. Eben J. Loomis to Dr. Jones, May 12, 1894 (Jones collection). Dr. Jones also included this letter in "Thoreau's Incarceration."

3. Hosmer did later write to Loomis to inquire about the circumstances surrounding the making of Rowse's crayon drawing of Thoreau. Loomis responded: "Give one credit mark to Mr. Sanborn! He is actually correct in assigning 1854 as the date of Rowse's crayon of Henry Thoreau." See Eben J. Loomis to Alfred W. Hosmer, June 13, 1896 (Hosmer collection).

177. S. A. Jones to A. W. Hosmer, May 15, 1894.

* * *

I find that only ninety (90) copies are to be printed—and, by Jove, the Club is not willing that any other edition shall be issued. I am disappointed in this, but all I can do is to wait a little while until additional items are found, and then the Rowfant Club will not be "in it."

I have hitherto forgotten to tell you that I also had heard from that fellow in Potsdam, N.Y.,[1] who is making inquiries about Thoreau. I guess he had the same questions to ask all his correspondents. I answered him at great length because I have had the same courtesy from those to whom I have written. . . .

1. Probably Edward W. Flagg, who apparently taught literature in Potsdam, New York. Flagg wrote to Hosmer to obtain information about Thoreau for a lecture he was to give to the school and townspeople. See Edward W. Flagg to A. W. Hosmer, April 23, 1894 (Hosmer collection).

178. A. W. Hosmer to S. A. Jones, May 17, 1894.

I had a letter from Prof. Loomis, after sending him one of the photos of Thoreau, in which he asked in regard to the payment of Thoreau's tax, "for a gentleman in Ann Arbor Mich."

I called on Mr. Staples, the jailer, last evening, and he told me that he committed Thoreau about sundown, that about 9 or half past, while he was away from the house, a lady called at his front door, and on his daughter's answering the bell, this lady handed her an envelope, with the remark that "that was to pay for Henry Thoreau's tax"—his daughter did not recognize the lady, as it was dark, and she had a veil on—he said he always thought it was Elizabeth Hoar, Edward Hoar's Sister, so I wrote to Judge Hoar in rega d to it, and his answer is, that he was out of town at the time but he always understood that it was Aunt Maria who paid it. He does not believe his sister did.[1] There is one sure thing about it. Emerson did *not*.

Staples thinks that Emerson could not have seen Thoreau in jail—as while he was committed at sundown, or thereabouts, the jail was soon locked up, and the tax being paid that evening Thoreau was turned out immediately after breakfast, as Staples expressed it, "mad as the devil." He says he always liked Henry Thoreau, that he was thrown in with him a great deal, in running the lines of different farms &c.

When I told him for whom I wished the information, he burst out laughing, "Oh, yes, that little fellow with the G.A.R. suit on!" Then he gave me a resume of the talk with you. Says, "tell him, he must not place too much dependence on what I say, for when I get to talking I am apt to say more than I mean."

If Prof. Loomis says Aunt Maria told him Emerson visited Thoreau in jail, I should call it so, as the story told of their meeting is too good to lose, and also shows the difference between the men. "Henry, I am sorry to find you here." "Mr. Emerson, why are you *not* here?" I repeated it to Staples, with the remark that Thoreau was ready to back up his principles, while Emerson was not, "Yes, Fred, *that is so!*" was his reply. . . .[2]

I am sorry the bibliography is not coming up to your expectations. I shall be glad to see it, however.

I had some wild flowers here at the store last week Saturday, when a lady & gentleman came in, and seeing them began asking about them, in the course of the talk I happened to mention what I expected to find in blossom the next day, and among other things mentioned the painted cup—the lady at once asked "are you going to Thoreau's painted cup meadow for it" and when I told her I was she turned to her husband with the remark, "Frank I think you better stop over one day and go with him."

I found they were both lovers of Thoreau's works, and we had a very pleasant chat about him, and his writings. . . .

1. Ebenezer R. Hoar to A. W. Hosmer (Hosmer collection). Hoar's response is written on Hosmer's letter to him of May 16, 1894.
2. Dr. Jones printed Hosmer's letter to this point in "Thoreau's Incarceration." Hosmer's name was concealed, however, as "X."

179. S. A. Jones to A. W. Hosmer, May 19, 1894.

I have just read your letter with much interest, and it makes me realize the difficulties that the biographer has to meet. The portrait matter was full of snags, the tax-paying business is no better, and the pretty story about Emerson's visit is hovering between fact and fiction.

As regards that visit, Prof. Loomis writes that Aunt Maria told him of it. Seemingly, that should settle it; but could Emerson make a visit to the jail and the jailer, if absent, not learn of it? Who could let him in to see the prisoner? And who would let him in and not inform the jailer of having done so?

I am led to doubt Mr. Staples's memory. He tells you that a *lady* came to pay the tax; he told me it was *"a young girl."* When he told me he thought it was Elizabeth Hoar, I at once wondered if she could have been "a young girl" *then.* Do you know if Miss Hoar was a small body?

He told me also that the visitor had something around her head so that *he* could not see her face. He farther said that he had his boots off and was reading the paper when she came, and that as the boys were "all fixed for the night" he wasn't going to unlock that night, so he kept Thoreau until after breakfast and then let him go. Nothing was mentioned about the "devilish mad."

But, please find out what the "devilish mad" was about; was it for *being put in jail,* or, as is most likely, because *somebody had paid a tax* that Thoreau had refused to do from principle. This is an important point to establish, because it will go to show that Thoreau did not know who paid it, and that the family had to keep it dark.

It seems, however, that Aunt Maria paid the tax. Prof. Loomis's direct statement and Judge Hoar's understanding of the matter ought to settle it. As regards the "visit" I must say I am dubious. Prof. Loomis declares that Aunt Maria told him of it; but Mr. Allen *thought* that Aunt Jane told him that *she* paid the tax—so memory is treacherous. The first mention that I have found of the visit is by G. W. Curtis, in Harper's magazine (1862),[1] and as it has not been contradicted, there must be a basis for it. It is against Emerson, and one would think would have been corrected at that time if it were not true. It is indeed characteristic of Thoreau to have made such a reply.

If you can ever lay hands on one of Mr. Staples's photographs I will be glad to also get hold of it. He surely ought to go down into history. . . .

1. G. W. Curtis, "The Editor's Easy Chair," *Harper's Monthly* 25 (July 1862):270–71.

Henry David Thoreau in 1854. *Crayon sketch by Rowse.*

Henry David Thoreau in 1861. Ambrotype by E. S. Dunshee.

Henry David Thoreau in 1856. *Daguerreotype by B. D. Maxham.*

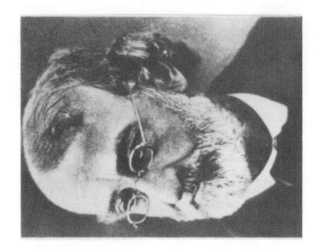

H. G. O. Blake

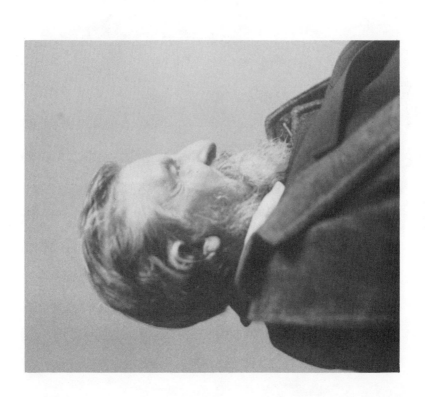

Daniel Ricketson

The house where Thoreau was born, Virginia Road, Concord. *Photograph by A. W. Hosmer.*

Site of Thoreau's cabin at Walden. *Photograph by A. W. Hosmer.*

Marlborough Road. *Photograph by A. W. Hosmer.*

Thoreau's Cove, Walden Pond. *Photograph by A. W. Hosmer.*

"Site of Irishman's house, Baker Farm, and Fairhaven bay." *Photograph by A. W. Hosmer.*

Concord Battle Ground. *Photograph by A. W. Hosmer.*

"Thoreau's belongings." *Photograph by A. W. Hosmer.*

The Main Street house in Concord where Thoreau died. *Photograph by A. W. Hosmer.*

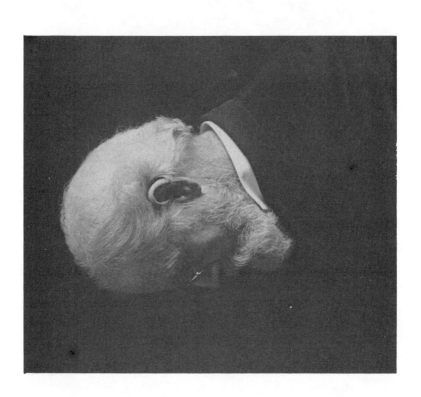

Dr. Samuel Arthur Jones

Alfred W. Hosmer

Henry Salt

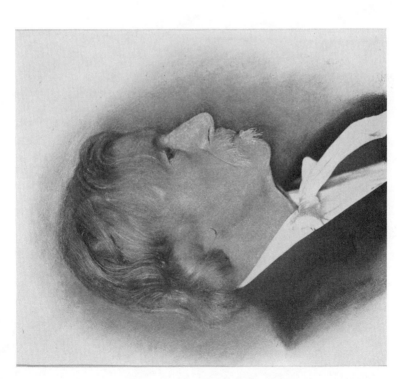

F. B. Sanborn

Sam Staples, Concord jailer. *Photograph by A. W. Hosmer.*

Ralph Waldo Emerson

180. A. W. Hosmer to S. A. Jones, May 22, 1894.

Did I not write what Thoreau was "mad as the devil" about? I surely meant to. He was mad to think that someone should have paid the tax—when *he* refused to do it.

Elizabeth Hoar was tall & slim. Jane Hosmer tells me that she always understood that Mrs Thoreau went down to the aunts, who were living in what is now the Thoreau House, and they were all concerned in the payment—Mrs.—Aunts Jane & Maria—though Maria was the one who went to the door, while the others waited near.

The payment was made to Mr. Staples' *daughter*.

Emerson could readily have seen Thoreau—as the jail was easy of access, and he might have talked with him from the outside of the wall. I do not think I gave Emerson's remark right—it should have been "Henry, why are you here" "Mr. Emerson, why are *you not* here!" Miss Hosmer says that story is about as old as Thoreau's imprisonment—she had always heard it—and never heard it contradicted. Staples was so lax in his discipline at the jail, that the story is told, and it is true, too—that when a case was called in court, the officer was sent over for the prisoner, and returned with the statement, that the court would have to wait until the prisoner was sent for, as he was helping Staples make hay, in a meadow some distance away.

As a boy I used to race in and out of the jail—the outside door (yard) was seldom locked, and once inside the yard, we had access to the whole building, with the exception of the cells that contained prisoners, and with those we could push open the slide, through which their food was passed, and look at the inmates.

I do not think there is any doubt, but what Emerson could have seen Thoreau, after his commitment and talked with him, without the jailer knowing about it.

I will get the address of Staples' daughter, and write her in regard to the payment of the tax, and see if she can throw any further light upon it.[1] Will ask Staples for one of his photos for you, the next time I see him. . . .[2]

1. We have been unable to find any response from Sam Staples's daughter. It is probable that she either did not respond to Hosmer's inquiries or that her response was inconsequential, since there is no further reference to her in the Jones-Hosmer correspondence.

2. Dr. Jones did not use this letter in his "Thoreau's Incarceration." The reason for its omission remains mysterious, since the letter clearly supports the conclusion which Dr. Jones reached in his article: that Emerson could indeed have seen Thoreau at the jail.

181. S. A. Jones to A. W. Hosmer, May 27, 1894.

That last letter about Thoreau's imprisonment caps the climax for information and settles the whole matter in the mind. One can imagine the consternation of those old maid aunts when they learned that "Henry" was in the coop, and how they flew around and raised the money, and Aunt Maria flung something over her head so that she would not be known and cut down the street to the jail to plank down the cold cash.

And yet the prodigal son (and nephew) was "mad as the devil" when delivered from durance vile!

If Mr. Staples' daughter can add anything to the facts, we may surely consider that matter as definitely settled.

The picture showing how devil-may-careish Thoreau buttoned his coat is the most esteemed one in my collection. It throws a flood of light on his character, and pronounces him the philosopher beyond question. . . .

182. Henry Salt to S. A. Jones, June 11, 1894.

I have, within the last day or two, received your welcome letter of May 28, with its further interesting Thoreau-ana. I think I shall soon prepare a revised copy of my Life of Thoreau & introduce in marginal or interleaved notes the many important additions & corrections which I owe to you. Then, if I bequeath this copy to the British Museum, nothing but the destruction of London by fire, or a Chinese invasion, can deprive this ungrateful country of the material for a second edition of a biography which it won't at present read! You have certainly done a great service to future Thoreau-students by the investigations you have made, on points which will be entirely beyond inquiry a generation hence. It amazes me that none of Thoreau's personal surviving friends have shown a similar industry. Mr. Blake, for example, seems to think that the *facts* of Thoreau's life are scarcely worth recording—surely a most mistaken idea, caused I suppose by the violent reaction from the contrary habit of over-minute biography.

I await the Bibliography with eagerness. Certainly I think a copy placed in the British Museum will, sooner or later, be most valuable. If you can ill spare one, out of so small a number, how would it be if I presented my copy to the Museum after a time, when I have thoroughly noted its contents? I am a socialist, you know, and I have often thought that valuable reference-books of this sort, ought *not* to remain permanently in private hands.

I have nearly finished the Selections for Macmillan. The Introduction will be to some extent a reprint of my article from the *Paternoster Review*. I believe the book will appear in the autumn. . . .

183. S. A. Jones to A. W. Hosmer, July 13, 1894.

* * *

That second paper on Thoreau[1] about which you write is so unsatisfactory to me that I myself would n't read it to an audience; but you may do as you see fit. If you read it to the Saturday Club,[2] please explain to them the circumstances under which it was written—and they were these: a large part of the audience for whom it was written were not in sympathy with Thoreau. They thought his love for Nature a mere "fad." Hence my citing so much from de Guerin[3] to show how intense a love of Nature is *perfectly natural* to some minds. I also wished them to know that they must not attempt to measure H. D. Thoreau with the ordinary little orthodox tape-line. He is of an entirely new species and must be considered as he is, not as they think he should be. If the paper is regarded as a fragment, it is passable; but it lacks the wholeness of a *literary* production.

Have you seen Sanborn's edition of Thoreau's Letters? He gives 128, instead of 65 letters from Thoreau, and much interesting information in between. As a letter writer I do not think Thoreau a success; but I am glad to get his thought in any shape. If you see any newspaper notices of the book please let me know for the sake of the bibliography, as I shall keep an eye on that so long as I live, and will try and leave it up to date when I die....

The value of that picture of "Sam" Staples is, that, after he has gone, the future readers of Thoreau will be glad to look at the likeness of Thoreau's jailer. The last letter I had from Mr. Salt contained some warm thanks for the little items pertaining to Thoreau's life that you and I have rescued from oblivion. He said that if he were preparing a new edition of the Life he could nearly fill it with Notes from my letters, and he wonders why Thoreau's professed friends, like Mr. Blake, for instance, have been so negligent in these matters....

1. This was probably the paper assessing Thoreau's Walden experience that Dr. Jones delivered to the Unity Club on February 16, 1891.
2. For a description of Concord's Saturday Club, a literary and social group founded in 1876 by Miss May Alcott, see George B. Bartlett, *Concord: Historic, Literary and Picturesque* (Boston: Lothrop, 1895), p. 165.
3. In his lecture Dr. Jones quoted extensively from the journals of Maurice de Guerin to clarify Thoreau's feeling for nature.

184. S. A. Jones to A. W. Hosmer, July 22, 1894.

This very morning I received a letter from Cleveland explaining why the book is not yet out, and adding that in 15 or 20 days it would probably be delivered. It seems that it is to be bound in such a "toney" style that only one man can attend to it, and as his wife was sick he had to go away with her for awhile.

It is decidedly rich to think of all this *style* being put on a book about Thoreau; but it will make some folks imagine he is somebody, after all.

It seems to me that it matters little what that Saturday Club thinks of the respective merits of Thoreau and Emerson. The world will doubtless settle the question without asking the opinion of the Saturday Club. Even that is quite possible, though the Saturday Club may not imagine it.

I bought the limited edition of Thoreau's Works (11 volumes and only 250 copies) and got the Familiar Letters as soon as the book was out. I can readily understand that the regular edition for the public is held back until the Fall trade opens. That will not be long.

What chiefly impressed me in this volume is this fact: Thoreau's plan of living had taken shape in his mind long before he went to Walden. On the day of his graduation, he held a "Conference" with some of his classmates, and the topic was "The Influence of the Commercial Spirit &c."[1] In his remarks Thoreau expresses the philosophy that he afterwards carried out in the Shanty. . . .

By the way, that old Channing has a firm grip on life! I could wish that Fate had ordered differently and taken him instead of Thoreau. But Thoreau was not from sound stock. In that last picture—the Ricketson one—I can see "consumption" in every line of the face. We may conjecture what he *would have done* as we like, but he *had* done his work or he would not have been called away.

I have lately been reading some of Lowell's early work, and it is very plain that he did n't mature as early as Thoreau. That is, his early writing reads so much "rawer" than does Thoreau's. Later, Lowell learned his trade by his devotion to literature; but on Thoreau's line, he is nothing to be compared to the man he so cavalierly criticised. His usual good judgement forsook him when he "went for" Thoreau; and his mistake remains to testify against him. . . .

I am coming last next week on purpose to shoot "Sam Staples" with a large—kodak!! Don't let that "cuss" escape you, for if I ever do get at a life of Thoreau, I am bound it shall have some good pictures in it. I never thought of doing his "Life", but I may experiment next winter, and if I think I can do the thing, I may leave a manuscript behind me of that nature. . . .

1. As a part of the Harvard commencement exercises in August 1837 Thoreau participated in a conference entitled "The Commercial Spirit of Modern Times, Considered in Its Influence on the Political, Moral, and Literary Character of a Nation." The paper which he delivered was published in part in *Familiar Letters*, pp. 7–9.

185. S. A. Jones to A. W. Hosmer, July 26, 1894.

I am not at all "stuck" on the inscription on Emerson's boulder.[1] Who in the deuce got it up? The echo of "passive" and "massive" isn't pleasing to my ear, and the idea of Ralph Waldo Emerson "lending a hand" to God Almighty is—well, it's immense, as the boys say. I am glad there is no such twaddle over Thoreau's grave!

I have read Howells's romance about Thoreau[2] and I don't believe he ever—saw Thoreau. What do you think of that? Mr. Howells is a novelist, you know, one in the romancing line—and he's romancing about Thoreau. The Thoreau that he saw had *short* legs and a "long trunk".[3] I rather think he's got things mixed!

And his talking to Emerson about William *Henry* Channing's poetry![4] He means that old mummy which is drying up by Sanborn's fireplace. Pshaw, I've no confidence in William D. Howells after this! His "First Visit to New England" may go whistling down the wind for all me. For a grain of truth, it has ten pounds of fiction, and such chaff will not catch this bird, you bet!

His reference to Thoreau will not make the beginning for the new edition of Thoreau's bibliography. . . .

1. On the pink quartz boulder that marks Emerson's grave there is a bronze tablet, bearing two lines from his poem "The Problem": "The passive master lent his hand / To the great soul, that o'er him planned." See George B. Bartlett, *Concord: Historic, Literary and Picturesque*, p. 43.

2. William Dean Howells, "My First Visit to New England," *Harper's Monthly* 89 (August 1894): 441–51.

3. Howells reported that he had gone to visit Thoreau in a spirit of "veneration" for the latter's "heroism" during the John Brown affair. But Howells found no saint, only Thoreau "in his insufficient person . . . a quaint, stump figure of a man, whose effect of long trunk and short limbs was heightened by his fashionless trousers being let down too low" (ibid., p. 447).

4. Howells wrote that Emerson "asked me if I knew the poems of Mr. William Henry Channing. I have known them since, and felt their quality, which I have gladly owned a genuine and original poetry; but I answered then truly that I knew them only from Poe's criticisms" (ibid, p. 449). Clearly Howells had confused W. H. Channing with William Ellery Channing II, as is suggested by the reference to Poe's criticism: Poe had published a severely critical review of W. E. Channing's work in *Graham's Magazine* for August 1843.

186. S. A. Jones to A. W. Hosmer, August 4, 1894.

I have just had the pleasure of sending you by Express a copy of the bibliography. It has just reached me and yours is the first one I have parted with. Mr. Salt's copy will go next.

It is a pretty book, and I believe an honest one, for I have tried to get in all up to the date of publication. I hope it may show you Concord folks that I am not unmindful of all the kindnesses I have had at your hands. You have helped me to do for Thoreau more than has yet been done for any American author in the bibliographical line: not even Emerson has been done so thoroughly.

I got your letter a day or two ago, and the paper with Mr. Sanborn's address[1] came this morning. I find it very dry reading, and think Sanborn has not done his best. He is evidently waking up to a sense of Thoreau's real importance, for he speaks of him in this address as he has never done before.[2] You are very kind in sending me a copy of the paper, for I should not have seen it otherwise, and it is valuable for bibliographical purposes.

Sanborn's staunch advocacy of Channing's claims[3] pleases me very much, and is greatly to his credit, for poor Channing has no other living man or woman to say a word for him. . . .

1. Probably "In Kossuth's Steps," *Boston Daily Advertiser,* July 12, 1894.
2. Sanborn closed his discussion of Concord's many shrines with these remarks: "Perhaps the whole township speaks most eloquently of Thoreau,—that pilgrim of nature, for whose fame nature herself takes care. When he died, Miss Elizabeth Hoar said,—'Concord is his monument, adorned with suitable inscriptions by his own hand.'"
3. In the article Sanborn quoted largely from Channing and described his poetry as moving "to a subtle intrinsic tune."

187. S. A. Jones to A. W. Hosmer, August 12, 1894.

I am glad if the book is any gratification to you, and I like your plan of letting Sanborn have just a smell at it. One of the Rowfant Club writes me that it has made a decided hit and they are proud of having published it. A great book-lover and collector, in Chicago, goes "wild", I am informed, over the history of that edition of 1862, as given in the sketch, "An Afternoon in the University Library."[1] That pleases me, as I am the coon who traced those books from Thoreau's garret to the book-shop of Ticknor & Fields.

I am very sorry that the copies are so scarce. Every one of the Club's is gone, and the demand for it is growing, but cannot be supplied. You see, it is the *limited* edition that makes these private publications so much in demand, and the Club prints but few so as to enhance their rarity. At the present, the Club is too much "stuck" on the book to think of allowing it to be printed in a popular edition; but when the novelty is worn off, I hope to see it republished. One of the Club wrote me that this book would increase the number of Thoreau's readers, and the man who wrote it is making a collection of first editions of Thoreau. He has found the "Week", both the

1849 and 1862 editions, and now he has a bad bellyache for "Walden." If you know of one for sale, I shall be glad to learn of it, for I will help anyone who is going to read Thoreau.

I have another immense scheme for a new book to be issued by the same Club. It is this: you remember that your Concord Library has the original manuscript of Thoreau's essay on "Walking." In it are all his *corrections:* what he struck out, and what he added. Well, I want to publish that with an introductory essay—giving the history of the preparing of that book when Death was drawing near him every day,[2] and he *knew it!* I was allowed to copy much of it, but not enough to edit an edition by. If the authorities will permit me to have every word of it copied, and one or more of the most significant pages photographed to put into my edition, I will make a beautiful monument to Thoreau, I tell you. Will you add yet another to all your bounties by finding out if I can be allowed to have a copy? Then I can make arrangements for procuring a conscientious and capable copyist. . . .

1. Dr. Jones reprinted his article "An Afternoon in the University Library" in his bibliography of Thoreau.
2. Thoreau submitted his essay "Walking" to the *Atlantic* in March 1862, less than two months before his death. It appeared in the June 1862 issue. See Walter Harding, *The Days of Henry Thoreau,* p. 458.

188. Henry Salt to S. A. Jones, August 17, 1894 [postcard].

This is just a line to acknowledge the receipt of the Bibliography today arrived—forwarded to me from Oxted to the English Lake District, where we are having a holiday. It is a beautiful book indeed, & I owe you hearty thanks for it. Shall write fully in a few days.

189. Henry Salt to S. A. Jones, August 25, 1894.

* * *

I admire the book greatly; and agree with you that it will be a hint to certain publishers that Thoreau's *commercial* value is not exactly the *full* value of his personality. More than this, it will be of the utmost service to present & future Thoreau-students; for the care & loving labour you have expended on it are unmistakable. I am particularly glad to see those very beautiful lines of yours prefixed. They have been often in my mind since I first saw them two or three years ago. I am sincerely obliged to you for sending me this copy of the Bibliography. When I have time to look it through carefully with my notes (which are at Oxted), I will send you any possible suggestions which may occur to me.

The proofs of my "Selections from Thoreau" are beginning to come in, but I suppose the book will not be ready before October. I am sadly restricted in space, and I fear I shall not be able to give much idea of Thoreau in the number of pages allotted to me. The portrait is being reproduced by a friend of mine who does a good deal of such work for Macmillan, and he is anxious to get a specially good one. He is I believe, in correspondence with Mr. Hosmer, of Concord, about obtaining a special photo for the purpose; but I have not yet heard with what result.

I have not seen the large-paper edition of the "Familiar Letters", but may be able to do so shortly at my Library, if I can induce that institution to expend a guinea on the book. If not, I shall get the small-paper edition when it appears. This plan of issuing the expensive edition *before* the other, instead of concurrently, seems rather an unworthy trick of the trade, does it not? . . .

190. S. A. Jones to A. W. Hosmer, August 26, 1894.

I have found some errors in the bibliography, and a sheet of errata is being printed. You will receive one in due time, and then you can paste it in and the book will be a true guide to the Thoreau literature.

I feel in my bones that Mr. Sanborn ought to have a copy, and I am thinking it over. He will appreciate it, and his editorship of Thoreau's Letters makes me feel that I owe him one in gratitude.

One bookseller in Cleveland got a few copies (as a member) and his price for them is $10,00 each. (This, of course, because they are so rare.) I am glad to be able to say that, as a book, it has made a decided hit. . . .

191. S. A. Jones to A. W. Hosmer, September 2, 1894.

Surely the beneficent gods granted me your friendship and it showers unnumbered kindnesses on my unworthy head. Here comes "Sam" Staples, smiling at me as he did that blessed afternoon when he chatted with me about Thoreau; and he has more than doubled his kindness to a stranger by enriching his picture with his autograph—the very "hand" that turned the key on Thoreau! Tell him I forgive him, from the bottom of my heart, and that ere he and I shall pass away I hope to shake hands with him in solemn token of my forgiveness. I know he'll die happier for this!

Really, Fred, please give Mr. Staples my more than thanks, for he has "done me proud."

I have just written Mr. Sanborn a long letter accompanying a copy of the book. I have also suggested that if he will collect and edit *all* Thoreau's poetry, I will get the Rowfant Club to publish it in as dainty a dress as the Bibliography. If he only will—O Lordy, words fail me, utterly!

Rub that bibliography right into the noses of Houghton, Mifflin & Co. Rub till the blood comes, and then tell them you hope they'll bleed to death if they don't republish it for the sake of facilitating the study of Thoreau. . . .

"The son of his father" has spoiled his father's monument. I wonder if "Edward" does n't SIT on the larger half of his own brains? There is that stone, a thing of beauty from the hand of God Almighty, disfigured and disgraced by a paltry bit of bronze from the puny hands of Man. Dash me, if I could not dissect Edward Waldo with an infinite relish!

But, Fred, I am comforted a little by that photo of David Scott's portrait.[1] I knew the light was poor, for I peered at the painting from every possible point of view, and only to feel that a really powerful portrait eluded me. . . .

1. David Scott's portrait of Emerson was made in Edinburgh in 1848. For a photograph of the painting, now in the Concord Free Public Library, see Ruth Wheeler, *Concord: Climate for Freedom,* p. 184.

192. S. A. Jones to A. W. Hosmer, October 3, 1894.

* * *

I sent a copy to your library, AND one to F.B.S. I received a short letter from him,[1] and answered it, asking some questions—which his lordship has not found either time or inclination to notice. You can't make anything out of a cur but a cur—a fact which his conduct recalls to me.

I am now engaged upon a bibliography of Emerson,[2] which will be a much larger book than the Thoreau. A Boston gentleman[3] has placed his immense collection at my service for that purpose; in fact, after seeing my Thoreau, he asked me to undertake the Emerson job. I shall probably have to spend a couple of months in Boston on this work; if so, you'll see me in Concord every Sunday, you bet! . . .

1. F. B. Sanborn had written to thank Dr. Jones for the "very welcome present of the Thoreau Bibliography" which he thought "well done, and by a lover of the man's genius." Sanborn responded, too, to Dr. Jones's suggestion that a volume of Thoreau's poems might be published through the Rowfant Club: "The decision would finally rest with Mr. H.G.O. Blake, who holds most of the MSS.—though I have some. I mean to print a few of them in the magazines, before including them in any book." (F. B. Sanborn to Dr. Jones, September 14, 1894, Jones collection).

2. Dr. Jones worked several years at a bibliography of Emerson, but he was unable to complete it. He later turned over his compilations to The Rev. George Willis Cooke, who acknowledged his debt to Dr. Jones in the preface to *A Bibliography of Ralph Waldo Emerson* (Boston: Houghton, Mifflin & Co., 1908), p. vii.

3. William T. Newton was the Boston collector of Emerson.

193. Henry Salt to S. A. Jones, October 3, 1894 [postcard].

... I have lately met Dr. Emerson. He gave a first-rate address on Thoreau last Sunday to a large audience in London. Through the kind help of Mr. A. W. Hosmer, Macmillan has got a beautiful copper-plate reproduction of the Worcester portrait of Thoreau. The vol. of Selections still in the press. Yes, thanks, I received the list of *errata* to Bibliography. Sanborn *is* sending copy of the Letters. . . .

194. S. A. Jones to A. W. Hosmer, October 19, 1894.

* * *

I learned from Mr. Salt that he had got a splendid picture of Thoreau for the Macmillan book, through your kind services.[1] The book is not yet published and I do not set much store by it, for Mr. Salt's introductory essay is only a patched up affair.

If you ever go to London, you can find a copy of the bibliography in the big library at the British Museum. That is something Thoreau did not dream about at Walden. . . .

The son of his father has lectured on Thoreau in London, and Mr. Salt writes that it was a good lecture. I should say that Mr. Salt is easily pleased, for those of the Rowfant Club who heard Edward Waldo thought him a sad dose to take.

That Emerson bibliography is a large job, but I get through so much of it day after day. The printing is almost as much work for one as the compiling.

I do not work on it in love, as I did on the Thoreau book, and that makes a vast difference, I tell you.

I can but wish that someone had collected Thoreau material as faithfully as Mr. Newton has done this Emerson work.

But, young man, there is yet one job waiting for you and me, namely, that illustrated book on *Thoreau's Country*.

Fred, that must be done; and if you can arrange a route that will make a day's walk, or more, if necessary, I will go through Thoreau's books and get the text to write up the journey as if he was the guide of a visiting party.

I have got on the trail of one or more Thoreau items, and I want to get hold of them correctly in order to get out another edition of the Bibliography for the students of Thoreau. Are you on good enough terms with Sanborn to ask him to let you consult his file of The Commonwealth?

He never saw fit to answer my second letter, yet I asked his advice in a very important matter. I should like to dissect him just to see how he is made; and, like as not, I should forget to put him together again! . . .

1. Salt's *Selections from Thoreau* included Hosmer's photograph of the 1856 daguerreotype of Thoreau.

195. S. A. Jones to A. W. Hosmer, October 31, 1894.

* * *

... I'll tell you what I propose doing, after the Emerson Bibliography is off my hands—it is to get every paper on Thoreau that can be bought and those that cannot be bought I will copy with the typewriter in uniform size for binding, and when all is done, put the collection in the Concord Free Library in memory of Thoreau.[1] Then the student of his writings can study him at full length by going to Concord.

The first step towards this will be to find out just what they have already of Thoreau's Writings, and what books referring to him, and what papers of the same nature are now there. Then you and I can work from that and complete the collection. AFTER I have learned what they have, I will make typewriter lists of what is wanted, and we will work together in procuring the lacking papers.

I do not imagine that any MSS. of Mr. Horace Hosmer's would help at all in our projected book, so I would n't bother Miss Hosmer; beside, it will be nearly a year before I can move in that matter. I had a letter from Mr. Sanborn the other day.[2] He apologizes for his long delay, and the *hatchet is out of sight!*

He can be of great assistance in aiding us in this Thoreau collection, and I shall make no bones in asking his services.

Please get the Misses Hosmer interested, and any others who are friendly to Thoreau's memory.

I am going to try and start a Bibliographical Society here, and if I succeed, I shall get all the Concord authors bibliographed; Hawthorne, Curtis, Channing, the Alcotts, father and daughter. . . .

1. The completed collection was given to the Concord Free Public Library.
2. This letter from F. B. Sanborn is not among Dr. Jones's papers.

196. Henry Salt to S. A. Jones, November 11, 1894.

Here we are, settled in a crazy old house [133 Cheyne Walk, Chelsea], but rather pleasant rooms, not far from Carlyle's dwelling place in Chelsea. My study looks right over the river, and the views are often very beautiful, especially at high tide, when boats and barges come up, and sea-gulls flap lazily overhead. We found the constant travelling up & down from Oxted was more than we could bear in winter; and for various reasons it suits us on the whole better to be in London; especially for my work in the Humanitarian League.

Our first visitor here was Dr. Emerson, who came for a long talk last Sunday. I liked him very well, and he seems to have considerable enthusiasm for Thoreau, though nothing particularly new to relate about him. He is possibly going to winter in England, so I may see him again.

Now about Thoreau publications. My volume of Selections is through the press, but it is quite likely that it will not be actually issued till after Xmas. I need not say that an early copy will be forwarded to Ann Arbor. The copper-plate reproduction of Mr. Hosmer's photo. of Thoreau is most successful, I think, altogether more tender & *human* than any of the photos I have seen.[1]

I am also in correspondence with two other publishers about an illustrated *Walden*, and a vol. of Thoreau's *Poems*. I don't know for certain that either idea will be realised, but I think it is quite possible they will. The *Walden* would be in two volumes (10/6 the two), with a number of illustrations taken from the photos sent me by yourself and Mr. Hosmer. The *Poems* would include all the complete ones that I can get hold of, but not all the fragmentary snatches of song from the *Week*, &c. (By the bye, have you noticed that "Independence", pubd. in the *Boston Commonwealth,* is an amplified form, with variations, of the "Black Knight", pubd. in the *Dial?* Also that there is a misprint in the poem "Haze", as reprinted in the Riverside edn. of *Letters.* In the first line it shd. be "Woof of the *sun*" (not *fen*).[2] I don't know how this stands in vol. X of the new edition; but I presume there is no doubt it is an error. It is *sun* in the *Dial*.) I shall ask Mr. Sanborn to send me copies of "The Funeral Bell", "Traveling", "The Departure", & "The Soul's Season"—which I suppose were contributed to the *Commonwealth* through his agency.

In your Bibliography I note the following misprints

p. 73 Joel Benton's article is in vol. xxxvii of Lippincott (not xxxxvii)

p. 75. line 8. Evening Post shd. be *Morning* Post

————line 11. My art. only appeared in the *English* edition of Lippincott's, not in the American. At least I think this was so.

I noticed with great surprise the other day that there is an English edn. of *Cape Cod,* dated 1865, & with (I think) the London publisher Low's name on the title-page. The copy at the London Library is of this edition, & the next time I get hold of it I will take down particulars & send them to you. I suppose sheets were sent over from Boston. It is odd that I never noticed this before. I hope Low won't set up any claim to copyright when Macmillan issues my *Selections,* for I have drawn largely from *Cape Cod.* This reminds me to ask you—do you know who, if anyone, holds the copyright of Thoreau's works in America. Is it Mr. Blake, or Mr. Sanborn, or Messrs. Houghton & Mifflin? In case any English publisher shd. want leave to sell in the States, I really don't know to whom he shd. apply! . . .

1. Salt used the 1856 daguerreotype, furnished by Alfred Hosmer. The copper-plate reproduction used by Salt was by Walker & Boutall.

2. In "Letters to Various Persons" Emerson does transcribe the first line of "Haze": "Woof of the fen, ethereal gauze." Carl Bode in *Collected Poems of Henry Thoreau* reads the line "Woof of the sun, ethereal gauze."

197. S. A. Jones to A. W. Hosmer, December 25, 1894.

* * *

. . . Fred, Providence is with us in our endeavor to get up a proper Thoreau collection. I am now in correspondence with the editor of a paper in New York City who is interested in Thoreau, and he is going to hunt for such old magazines as we need for the collection. Some friend of his in Cleveland made him a present of a copy of my bibliography, and the editor wrote to ask me if it was possible to obtain a copy of "Thoreau: A Glimpse."

Luckily, I had three left (have since found two more in an out of the way drawer!), and I sent him one. He lives in Englewood—where I lived before I came here—and, by Jinks, we are about as "chummy" as can be on the strength of my being an old-time Englewooder, and that editor[1] sails in with a will to further our desire! Now, my boy, we'll "get there with both feet!" as the elegant phrase is.

I really can't afford to die, Fred, until I stand with you and see a royal "THOREAU COLLECTION" on the shelves in Concord Free Library. . . .

1. The Englewood editor was Lewis Dawes.

198. Henry Salt to S. A. Jones, December 25, 1894.

* * *

I have heard no more of Dr. Emerson, and don't know whether he is still in England, or gone to the south of France, or returned to Concord. My volume of "Selections from Thoreau" is to be published early in January—so the publisher tells me—when it will be a pleasure to send a copy to a friend at Ann Arbor, & so add one more book to his Thoreau-library. The idea of an edition of Thoreau's Poems, perhaps illustrated, is still under negotiation; but the illustrated *Walden* has been abandoned. . . .

199. S. A. Jones to A. W. Hosmer, January 13, 1895.

I have just been itching all day long to have a chap of your size at my elbow while I read Thoreau's "Ktaadn, and the Maine Woods" in the UNION MAGAZINE!!!![1] That Mr. Dawes, whom I put into communication with you, found it in an old book-shop and sent it on. It is going into our Concord Collection, and this "find" is just a "daisy!" I sent Mr. Dawes a list of "Wants," and he has a dealer in such "truck" who will find what we are after. I did not expect to get the "Liberator," but I am in correspondence with Mr. Garrison, of Houghton, Mifflin and Co., and now we will have either the two original articles from the "Liberator," or typewriter copies to bind into our collection.[2] A little time, my friend, and that collection will come to you appropriately bound for the shelves of Concord Free Library! Whoop-la!

My Landor-Emerson book[3] is on the eve of publication, and proof-reading has kept me too busy—with my bread-and-butter work—to attend to my correspondence; but YOU will never mis-understand my silence. . . .

1. "Ktaadn and the Maine Woods." *Union Magazine* 3 (1848), appeared in five parts, beginning in July and running through November.
2. Francis J. Garrison, son of William Lloyd Garrison, had written January 3, 1895, to thank Dr. Jones for sending a copy of "Thoreau: A Glimpse"; Garrison also indicated his willingness to send Jones articles from the remaining files of the *Liberator.* See F. J. Garrison to S. A. Jones, January 3, 1895, Jones collection.
3. *Landor's Letter to Emerson,* ed. Samuel A. Jones (Cleveland: The Rowfant Club, 1895).

200. Henry Salt to S. A. Jones, January 27, 1895.

Your welcome letter and the copy of the "Familiar Letters" reached me together a few days ago. How kind it was of you to send me *that* book, and with *that* inscription! I don't know when I have been more touched than when I saw what you [had] written; for it made me feel keenly how one person's appreciation may more than counter-balance the non-appreciation of the many.

It is good news this that you tell me about the possibility of an American edition of my *Thoreau;* though, knowing the uncertainty that attends all dealings with publishers, I shall not be at all disappointed if the negotiations fall through. Some months ago I went carefully through the book, & made some corrections and additions, in case a second edition should ever be called for, so I shall be ready if the opportunity should arise; & if it does *not* arise, I shall be content. . . .

As it happens, I had a little correspondence, towards the close of 1894, on this very subject, with Messrs. Macmillan, of New York. They have lately published the new edition of "Animals' Rights", & the "Richard Jefferies" is in their hands, as far as American sales are concerned; and as both books have been rather well received in the States, and the London Macmillan firm is just issuing the volume of "Selections from Thoreau", I thought it might be well to try them with the *Life*. Their reply was to the effect that if a cheaper edition were ever published in England, they would take about 500 copies for the States; & so the matter rested. I understand that Bentley is now going to sell off the remainder (about 400) of the old edition at a reduced rate, and he is asking Macmillan (New York) to take some of these—I suppose to bind up anew, with a title-page of their own. So, if you should hear of an "edition" being announced by Macmillan, you will know what it means! I hope it won't complicate matters with Messrs. Houghton & Mifflin, but of course there is no copyright in the book. In case H. & M. don't take kindly to your suggestions, as is very probable (they being the publishers of Sanborn's book), you might turn your attention to Macmillan, who, for the various reasons above mentioned, are perhaps the most likely publishers to look on me with a favourable eye. I hope *in time* Bentley will publish a cheap edition in England, but naturally he wants to get rid of the old "remainder" first.

The "Selections from Thoreau" are not yet issued. I can't understand what is the matter with Macmillan about the book; some delay about the portrait, he says; but he does not give me any specific information. I don't see how it can be much longer delayed, for we must soon reach "the early autumn" (of 1894), even by a publisher's reckoning! That was the date that M. himself proposed for the publication!

This discovery of further news about the "Captain John Brown" lecture is indeed interesting. If future Thoreau students don't bless the labours of a certain Dr. S.A.J. they will be an ungrateful set. It makes one feel rather savage to think how much valuable matter must have been allowed to slip away by Thoreau's friends & contemporaries who survived him. Imagine, for example, what Sanborn's book might have been, if he had expended the same amount of research on genuine *Thoreau-ana,* that he devoted to raking the genealogical dust-heaps of Concord! . . .

201. S. A. Jones to A. W. Hosmer, January 29, 1895.

Your letter enclosing Thoreau's poems[1] is just at hand and the reading of the latter has filled me with regret that Emerson advised Thoreau to burn any of his poetry.[2] Thoreau did, indeed, lack the art of *rhythmical* writing, but he IS a poet, for all that. However, what is lost, is LOST and we can only make the best of what is left. Now give me a little breathing spell, and I'll have these poems that you have so religiously copied, put into print for our collection. I will write a sort of introduction for them. . . .

I learned from Mr. Dawes that you had got a whole lot of Atlantics, so that you have *duplicates*. Now, my dear fellow, you will make me more than happy if you will sell them to me, and for this purpose, namely: I will make another collection for the Library of the University here, and thus, Fred, secure more readers for that physician of the Soul, Henry D. Thoreau. I can not put my poor life to a better purpose, and I hope you can see your way to granting my request. IF I could pick up such things here, I would not dream of asking this favor; but I dare ask a great deal from YOU. . . .

1. These were copies of Thoreau's poems published in the *Commonwealth,* a Boston weekly edited by F. B. Sanborn, in 1863. For a list of these poems, see Francis Allen, *A Bibliography of Henry David Thoreau,* pp. 76–77.

2. Carl Bode has speculated that Thoreau's destruction of his poetry, "at the instance of Emerson," occurred about 1842 when Emerson was editing the *Dial.* See *Collected Poems of Henry Thoreau,* ed. Carl Bode (Baltimore: Johns Hopkins Press, 1964), p. vii.

202. S. A. Jones to A. W. Hosmer, February 17, 1895.

A typical New England winter with its impassable drifts and blinding storms and bitter winds and journeyings through fields and the devil to pay generally! Four hours in getting six miles, and having GOT, the serious question IF it was possible to get back. And the poor man died yesterday morning, after all!

Moreover, the old school doctors who have fought Homoeopathy in the university for the last twenty years are making one supreme effort to have the college that I founded ABOLISHED. To frustrate their machinations has kept my typewriter HOT in such moments as I could get from the drudgery of practice.

This will explain my silence even if it does not justify it; and, my dear friend, you are not the only sufferer. . . .

I hope to Heaven that you CAN find another Boston Miscellany,[1] and for this reason: the two numbers of the THIRD volume are VERY scarce, and this makes a complete lot of all the numbers of exceedingly great value for the purpose of writing the History of American Literature in this 19th century. So valuable is such a set that I am sure Thoreau would not allow one to be broken for the sake of such a collection as we are making. Mr. Dawes's finding a copy (in an ill-used shape, too) is almost a miracle. But the kindly gods may smile upon your efforts as they did on Mr. D's, so don't be discouraged. . . .

Mr. Salt's last book about Thoreau is not published yet, and he is getting a little impatient. He is also getting himself good and ready for a second edition of his Life of Thoreau with corrections and some additions! I hope it can be brought about so that H. M. & Co. will be the publishers. . . .

1. Thoreau's essay "A Walk to Wachusett" was first published in the *Boston Miscellany* 3 (January 1843).

203. S. A. Jones to A. W. Hosmer, March 3, 1895.

* * *

I groan inwardly whenever I think of your WORK on that "Walking." I do not believe I shall allow the Rowfant Club to "monkey" with it at all. I have a plan for getting up a Book publishing Club in the University of Michigan, and THEN we will not limit editions so that a good book is locked up. But I must first REST, for this winter has been hard on me, and I have felt the pecuniary stress as I never did in the world before.

Alcott's "Forester"[1] and Thoreau's poetry came all right. It was very thoughtful of you to send me the Scribner,[2] for with the Homoeopathic fight on hand, I should not have seen it. Mr. Sanborn has done himself "proud" in my opinion in his presentation of those few poems, and if his edition of Thoreau's Poetry is done as well it will make the last of the Thoreau volumes by long odds the best. There cannot be truer criticism than what he has written of Thoreau's "verse as melodious poetry." And that new letter of Thoreau's[3] ILLUSTRATES much of Thoreau as it has never been done before. Indeed, Fred, nothing that I have read in a long while has given me so much pleasure.

I cannot say that I like the picture in Salt's new book[4] better than the photo, but it is a FINE portrait, and I am proud that YOU have been the means of letting the English see what the REAL Thoreau looked like. The acknowledgement on p. xxii is a nice clean way of doing things, and is a marked contrast to our Yankee manner of doing business. Mr. Salt's Introduction is a splendid piece of writing. It PRESENTS Thoreau so justly, and it shows how clear a conception of him as a man and author is Mr. Salt's idea. It is the best piece of Thoreau writing that Mr. Salt has yet done. I can see how skillfully he has worked-in knowledge that I wrote him and which I picked up from Horace Hosmer (Oh, if *he* only could have lived to see this book!), and from you, and THROUGH you. Fred, our meeting has some curious things about it, for our joint endeavors have certainly done something towards making Thoreau better understood, by doing away with certain *mis*understandings concerning him. Even Mr. Sanborn will allow THAT.

Would I "like a photo of Mr. H.G.O. Blake?" Well, "I should smile" if I would not! Did n't I try to coax him to give me one; and did n't he crawl out of it in a decidedly ingenious shape, without saying either yes, or no![5] Of course he did, and I've been hankering for one ever since. Mr. Blake didn't like my mannner of dealing with the FACTS in Mr. Sanborn's case, and I would n't "back water" an inch. That really ended our correspondence.

It was only the fear of being rebuffed again that kept me from asking Mr. Ricketson for his photo, and IF you can ever coax one of 'em through his son the sculptor, you can swing on our gate, slide down our cellar door, and kiss our hired girl, and I swear I'll never tell! . . .

1. A. Bronson Alcott, "The Forester," *Atlantic Monthly* 9 (April 1862):443–45. Dr. Jones included this piece in *Pertaining to Thoreau* (1901).
2. F. B. Sanborn, "Thoreau's Poems of Nature," *Scribner's Magazine* 17 (March 1895):352–55.
3. Thoreau to Emerson, March 11, 1842. For a text of this letter, see *The Correspondence of Henry David Thoreau,* pp. 63–65.
4. Henry D. Thoreau, *Selections from Thoreau,* ed. Henry S. Salt (London: Macmillan & Co., 1895).
5. See letter of H.G.O. Blake to Dr. Jones, September 14, 1891, letter 81.

204. S. A. Jones to A. W. Hosmer, March 9, 1895.

* * *

The Essay came the other day, and, lo! right on the heels of it comes Mr. Blake's photo! Alas! I cannot see a shadow of the white-haired man whom I regarded with such veneration and awe when I visited him on that August morning which I shall never forget.

This photo that you so kindly send does not do the subject justice; that is, he looks more of a man in his latter-day appearance—to my notion!

Keep cool; we will yet stumble on one of his later pictures, and then I can recall him as I saw him. Of course, the photo you send is simply invaluable, for it IS the man at one time in his life. Can you get any information as to his age when it was taken? . . .

The fight is on in full fury; I am going to the capital on Monday next to argue the merits of the situation before the Legislature. The Governor and the majority of legislators are with us: the board of Regents stand in the way; but the Legislature holds the purse, and we can starve them into doing *justly*.

205. S. A. Jones to A. W. Hosmer, March 24, 1895.

* * *

Mr. Garrison wrote me expressing his enjoyment of the Landor-Emerson book, but saying that the house does not think it would sell to any other than Emerson collectors[1]—and H. M. and Co. know better than I do how many of them there are NOT. You see, Fred, they got "stuck" on the large paper edition of Emerson,[2] and a burnt child dreads the fire.

I shall not try any other publishers until I can get some valid opinions on the booklet. It would help me if I could know what Sanborn really thinks of it. It does n't matter what he thinks; it is plain truth, and it will be unpalatable only to those who are "stuck" on Emerson. If I knew that Sanborn DISAPPROVES of it, I should be all the more fierce for finding another publisher; but I'm in no hurry—the booklet will keep in this climate, even if it will not in Massachusetts!

The devilish fight is still on and we shall not know which is on top until the Legislature has made the money appropriations. I am not scaring myself to death at all, for when I've done my best I care little whether I am on top or not: if I'm with the Right, I am satisfied. Waiting is a great art!

1. This letter from F. J. Garrison is not among the Jones papers.
2. The large paper edition of Emerson's *Complete Works,* in twelve volumes, was printed from the Riverside edition, edited by J. E. Cabot.

206. Henry Salt to S. A. Jones, March 24, 1895.

Your appreciation of the "Selections from Thoreau", and my Introduction, gave me much pleasure and encouragement. You will have recognised that the Introduction is in great part the same as the article in the *Paternoster Review,* but I think improved, both in additions and omissions. I hope the book may do good; but though the press-notices have been very favorable, the sales (so far) are not what might have been hoped—only about 250 copies. I am afraid this will make Macmillan dubious about taking up the *Life.* Many thanks, all the same, for your kind thought in writing to him. . . .

I have not yet acknowledged the receipt of your *Landor.* Very many thanks for it. It is a charming little book in every way, and your Introduction seems to be in just the right spirit for the Letter—I don't know which I enjoyed the more. I wonder if Emerson received any other "straight" letters of that sort from outspoken correspondents! On the whole I think Landor was very merciful to him; large-hearted & generous, in fact, he always was. I am sorry that the edition of the "Conversations", which I was to edit for Messrs. Bell & Sons, has for the present fallen through; for, on thinking it over, they decided against the plan, though it was their own suggestion in the first place.

To return to Thoreau. You will be interested to hear that I have arranged for an edition of a select number of the Poems. The Publisher is Mr. John Lane, who is quite the best man in London for the purpose as he make[s] a speciality of books of that kind (small editions of about 350 copies), and takes very great pains with them. Our idea is to include only the *best* poems, perhaps about 1000 lines in all, & make it a small vol. of about 70 pages. It happens that Mr. Lane is going to America in a few days, and will be at Boston. I have therefore arranged for him to see Mr. Sanborn and Messrs. Houghton, with a view to coming to some agreement about the simultaneous issue of the book in America. Sanborn writes offering aid in getting permission to print such poems as are still copyright, and it is possible that he may actively cooperate in the book, as I have left Mr. Lane free to make whatever arrangement he judges best—a joint Preface, or an American Preface by Sanborn, & an English one by me. He is taking over a type-written selection of the Poems recently made by me. So, at last, I hope we are about to see a volume of Thoreau's verse.

Your list of *errata* in my *Life of Thoreau* will be most valuable. Please send it me without fail. There must of necessity be a lot of errors in the book. I have heard doubt freely expressed as to the truth of the story about Thoreau's love affair—Do you believe it? Sanborn once told me that the lady is still living; but, he added, "there would be no propriety in mentioning her name". Really, I think "propriety" might be sacrificed in such a matter, for the greater good of the greater number! I wish you would hunt her up! . . .

No, I never heard of Mr. McQuesten again. Have often wondered about him. . . .[1]

[P.S.] It is rather cruel, perhaps, to repeat it, but as I know you will regard it as *private,* I cannot resist quoting a sentence from Mr. Sanborn's last letter to me. Speaking of his interest in Greek curiousities, he mentions that some friend of his has possession of Byron's helmet, and adds, "I have often tried it on, and found it too small". Now don't you wish you had been present with a kodak, to get a photograph of *that* scene—the helmet of Byron on the head of F.B.S.? I think it was the word *"often"* that tickled my sense of humour most. It seemed to indicate a recurrent idea on S.'s part that he had some affinity to Ld. B.!

Is he *the Hon.* F.B.S., by the bye? I see he is so addressed by some people. Is he an officer in the State legislature, or what?

1. We have been unable to identify Mr. McQuesten.

207. S. A. Jones to A. W. Hosmer, April 7, 1895.

* * *

Between moving and attending to business I have really forgotten whether I wrote you in regard to Mr. Ricketson's projected BUST of Thoreau.[1] My stars! If he can reproduce the Blake daguerreotype from your photo and give us a bust, it will be a grand service to the lovers of Thoreau for which readers yet unborn will bless him. I AM A SUBSCRIBER from this moment and the filthy lucre shall be forthcoming in two shakes of a ram's tail. (Did you ever see a ram "shake", and if so, is the cuss particularly lively? I ask for information.)

I heard from Mr. Salt the day before yesterday, and he informs me that he is engaged upon an edition of Thoreau's Poems—not complete, but a selection of the best. It may be published simultaneously in England and America. F.B.S. will probably collaborate, and between the two we will have quite a book. And so the good work goes on, bravo! . . .

1. For a photograph of Walton Ricketson's bust, which is not based on the Blake daguerreotype, see Walter Harding, *The Days of Henry Thoreau*, p. 44. The bust is now in the Concord Free Public Library.

208. A. W. Hosmer to S. A. Jones, April 13, 1895.

Mr. Blake was born April 10, 1816 and the photograph I sent you a copy of was taken about 1872.

I am hard at my book of views of Thoreau's Country, hunting up quotations that will fit all right. I have it about half done.

For fear that you do not see "The Bookman" English edition I enclose a copy of a review that came out in the March number.

My opposite neighbor who is quite a well read woman, said she considered herself fortunate in having the privilege of reading "Landor's Letter" and enjoyed it very much—thought it quite an addition to the Emerson literature.

Am delighted to hear that there is a chance of your coming east this summer—the dredgers are now at work deepening the channel so that the boat with your added weight will be able to make its way up the river at low water. You just keep that partner of yours drumming up the delinquents, so that you will be *sure* to come—and we will try to make it pleasant for you.

You will miss one other Concordian, as Sam Staples died this week, in Altoona Florida, and his body has been brought home, and will be buried next Monday, he dropped dead out of his chair, had been troubled with heart disease for a year or more.

209. S. A. Jones to A. W. Hosmer, April 28, 1895.

I received the announcement of the death of Mr. Staples as if I had known him intimately, and I felt a real sense of loss when I learned from your letter that he had departed. I shall always feel grateful to Miss Hosmer for her thoughtfulness in introducing me to him. His genial manner and his frank openness pleased me, and I forgave him for locking up Thoreau. There is no use in dodging the fact that Concord grows poorer as each of its historic citizens goes Beyond, and the last great link of a distinguished chain will disappear when Channing departs to join his contemporaries. I should like to have seen him, but he has soured on humanity and I must not expect to ever see the face he wore among men.

I was more than glad to receive the paper containing the short account of Mr. Staples. He paddled his own canoe through life and made more out of himself than many with more advantages than he. Peace to his ashes!

I am glad to be able to send you the review of Thoreau's "Week" that Ripley wrote for the New York Tribune.[1] Mr. Dawes hunted it up and I paid a stenographer to typewrite it for me. I have enclosed you a better copy than he made for me, and yet mine is capable of great improvement. However, you can get a hint that goes to explain why Thoreau's first book did not sell. Ripley hits the bull's eye when he points out the flagrant and rudely defiant Pantheism. I can but ascribe THAT to Emerson's influence upon the YOUNG Thoreau.

I did not copy the passages quoted by Ripley as specimen bricks, but I have denoted the paging in the first edition, and you will have little trouble in finding Ripley's selections—which I consider very judicious and well adapted to show off the book to advantage. Ripley's short review is worth a cartload of such sky-rockets as Lowell's Mass. Quarterly Review paper[2]—which was written more to show off Lowell than to introduce Thoreau to readers. . . .

1. "H. D. Thoreau's Book," *New York Tribune*, June 13, 1849. Dr. Jones later reprinted this review in *Pertaining to Thoreau* (1901). The review is commonly attributed to Horace Greeley.

2. *Massachusetts Quarterly Review* 3 (December 1849):40–51. Also included in *Pertaining to Thoreau*.

210. Henry Salt to S. A. Jones, May 14, 1895.

* * *

I have just heard from Mr. Sanborn that he has seen Lane, the London publisher, who has been on a visit to America, and that all is amicably settled about the volume of Thoreau's Poems. It is to be issued in the autumn—a limited edition of 750 copies (250 for America)—published by Lane in England & Houghton in Boston. Sanborn and I are to contribute a joint Preface; and doubtless we shall entrance the readers of both hemispheres by the glories of our combined style? What do you think?

I am very glad to have got this settled, and to have pushed Houghton & Mifflin into what they ought to have done long ago. I don't like joint

Prefaces, but in this case the advantages of the arrangement are obvious, as it has smoothed away all possible difficulties with Messrs. H. & M.

It is a pity, as you say, that the *Selections* are kept out of America. I have a duplicate set of the press-notices that have appeared in England, which I am going to send to you. I do not want them returned. You may be interested to glance through them, for they show a very remarkable increase in English appreciation of Thoreau, though some of this may be due to the powerful influence of Macmillan.

Why on earth shd. you not write to Ed. Carpenter about that pamphlet? That is to say, if you will not be surprised if he does not answer, for he is what is called a "very bad correspondent". But he likes to hear criticisms, & he *ought* to hear them. Since the first excitement over the Wilde case, public feeling here has a good deal calmed down, and I think many people feel that, whatever one's opinion of Wilde and his swinish life may be, the *law* has made an awful mess of the matter. I doubt if any conviction will be obtained against him . . .

211. S. A. Jones to A. W. Hosmer, June 2, 1895.

Our Legislature has just adjourned. Both houses passed a bill to remove the Homoeopathic College to Detroit, but the citizens sent a committee of three of us to present a protesting memorial to the Governor, and by Thunder! he did n't sign the bill! I expect to return to civilization now, and to get acquainted with the good people I used to know before this struggle began. We have got the old school quieted once more, and their friends in the university have been made to realize that the rights of the homoeopathic taxpayers of Mich. are not to be trifled with.

I must now pick up the Thoreau work that I had to lay aside while the struggle was on. This will employ my spare hours for the next four months; and do you know I have got to go over the whole business again in order to piece the broken thread.

I found a new mention of Thoreau the other day, namely, a notice in the "Necrology of the Alumni of Harvard College, from 1851 to 1865."[1] The brief mention of Thoreau is very good considering the date at which it was written.

The other day Mr. Salt sent me some twenty odd press notices of his last Thoreau volume. It is good reading for a man who wants to learn of how little value criticism is, for the few that understand are so few. The author must be content with having put his very heart into his book. If he has done that he can leave his work to speak to those who can understand it—all the rest count for nothing. . . .

1. *Necrology of Alumni of Harvard College* (Boston, 1864).

212. Daniel Ricketson to Henry Salt, June 3, 1895.

I have been much interested in reading your late work, "Animals' Rights,"[1] a copy of which I received soon after its publication last autumn. It is a grand contribution to the cause of humanity, as well as the higher culture of a pure and practical religion, such as the diviner portions of the Old and New Testaments inculcate, but which too often, and perhaps generally, have been supplanted by creeds and dogmas quite at variance with the great doctrine of "Peace on Earth and Good Will towards men."

At the advanced age of nearly eighty-two years, I still find myself constantly required to increase my faith in the Great Power that overrules all things, as creeds and dogmas lose their significance. This is an age of deep inquiry, and much that was deemed sacred has been relegated with the exploded doctrines of our forefathers. Among the good Friends (Quakers) from whom in an unbroken line I trace my descent back to the time of Fox and Penn, I can say in the words of my friend Ralph Waldo Emerson, "If I am anything, I am a Quaker." I still cling to their simple ways of worship, their honesty and truthfulness. I heard nothing of doctrines in my own father's family, but by precept and example was taught the higher principles of Christianity.

The religion seen so often in the works of our truest New England poet, John Greenleaf Whittier, whom I also had as a friend and occasional correspondent, is that which I can most fully endorse, as the result of a long life of research and striving for the Truth.

I have lately also written a hasty letter to Rev. Duncan C. Tovey, who speaks of you in a letter I received from him Dec. 19, 1890, as "one of his greatest friends," also as a "Master at Eton with him some years." He styles himself a "country parson," and in my reply I mention, "holy Mr. Herbert," as old Isaac Walton called Reverend George Herbert, the sweet old poet-divine, William Gilpin, Prebendary of Salisbury, White of Selbourne (Rev. Gilbert), &c., &c., as confrères.

Well, I will draw this rambling note to a close, with my best wishes for your welfare and happiness.

1. In *Animals' Rights* Salt argued that animals as well as men should be "exempt from any unnecessary suffering or serfdom."

213. S. A. Jones to A. W. Hosmer, June 5, 1895.

Your letter of the 3rd instant is very valuable for information that the students of Thoreau will need when you and I are dead and in clover (I hope!).

Sanborn has evidently turned State's evidence, and now we know why his attack on Mrs. Thoreau was made. Of course, Fred, all this must be kept secret while Sanborn is alive, but Mr. Salt should know it now, so that the explanation may go on record at the right time.

To make the evidence as strong as possible, you should recall the exact DATE of that meeting of the Saturday Club; that, you know, gives precision to the statement.[1]

It is a little singular that, in the last letter I had from Mr. Salt he expressed a regret that the name of the lady with whom Thoreau was once in love was not known. He feels, as does every sensible person, that the secrecy in regard to this matter is owing to a false and squeamish delicacy; as there was nothing dishonorable to either party in the affair. Is she alive yet? If so, you should get permission to copy her picture, NOT for sale, BUT so that future generations may learn what her face was like, and then KNOW why Thoreau was so true to his one love.

Are you aware that Mr. Salt is going to bring out an edition of Thoreau's poems in conjunction with Mr. Sanborn? Can you, then, possibly get those ladies to allow those "unpublished sonnets"[2] to appear there for the first time and thus give an extra zest to Mr. Salt's book. It seems to me that if they care for Thoreau's reputation they can surely have no valid objection; or is Mr. Sanborn already on their trail for the same purpose. After the destruction of so much of Thoreau's poetical writings at Emerson's request, it seems a duty to save all that has escaped that fate.

Put on your armor and coax out of them the sonnets and the letters, and let them know that they are solely for the future—NOT for to-day. . . .

1. Unfortunately Hosmer's letter of the "3rd instant" is not available and it is thus impossible to reconstruct precisely what Sanborn may have revealed at the Saturday Club.

2. Henry D. Thoreau, *Poems of Nature*, ed. Henry S. Salt and F. B. Sanborn (Boston: Houghton, Mifflin; London: John Lane, 1895). This volume did include one previously unpublished poem, "Ding Dong," furnished by Annie J. Ward, a relative of Ellen Sewall. Miss Ward sent the poem to Salt through Alfred Hosmer.

214. Henry Salt to S. A. Jones, June 20, 1895.

Your letter of June 5th, with its news of the Ward family, interested me greatly. And now, strangely enough, I am able to send *you* some further news on the same subject, derived from Mr. Sanborn in a letter received since I had yours. (See enclosed extracts.) *He,* too, is on the track of the Thoreau letters & poems; so we shall see—what we shall see!

So the *inamorata* was Ellen Sewall! I wonder if you will set off in quest of her brother or husband. I remember that some years ago, before her death, Mr. Sanborn told me that it would be "improper" to mention her name, as she was living, and long ago happily married. But it certainly seems a pity that she was not "interviewed" on the subject of her youthful admirers. What an interesting reminiscence of the Thoreau household *hers* would have been!

It is strange, is it not?, about the poem "Sympathy". One does not know how to regard it. It looks as if Thoreau had used the brother as a cloak, while really expressing his feelings for the sister. But I don't know what to make of it. I always felt we had not got to the bottom of that subject.[1]

By the bye, Mr. Hosmer's informants, Miss Ward's nieces, were wrong about the couplet

> "In each dew drop of the morning
> Lies the promise of a day".

These lines are not unpublished. You will find them in the *Week,* on the first page of "Tuesday".

Let me now point out a few errors in your Bibliography (forgive me if I have mentioned any of them before). On p. 75, line 5. read '*Morning* Post.' line 11, read Lippincott's Mag., *English* edition. My article, I fancy, did not appear in the American ed.

p. 73. line 8 from bottom. Was not Joel Benton's article pubd. in 1886? (I may be wrong in this).

p. 48. *Cape Cod.* There was an Eng. edn. published simultaneously with the Boston one, by Messrs. Low, I believe. Perhaps I have sent you the title, &c. of this.

p. 51. *Summer.* There is an Eng. edn. of this, but I cannot send you details at the present moment. It is pubd. by Fisher Unwin, Paternoster Sqr., London.

p. 46. The Camelot *Walden* is *not* the first English edn. The first is *Walden,* by Henry D. Thoreau. Edinburgh. David Douglas. 1884. It has an engraving (frontispiece) of the shanty, but not the plan of the Pond. It looks as if it was printed from the same plates as the Riverside edn.—perhaps it was sent over in the sheets from Boston. Also, the Camelot Edn. of Walden appeared in 1886, not 1888. My copy is dated 1886. Edited by Will *H.* Dircks. (The *H.* is omitted in yr. note.)

p. 36, line 6 from bottom. Sanborn tells me that "The Departure" is reprinted in his *Life of Thoreau,* & that "Travelling: Greece" had already been pub. by Thoreau, though S. forgot this, & has since been included in the new edn. He does not say where.[2]

Extracts from F.B.S.'s letter

"I have lately made acquaintance with some nieces of the Miss Ward who is mentioned in Thoreau's *Familiar Letters*" (pp. 86, 87, 60.)

Mrs. Ward (the mother of Miss Ward) "lived until 1844, spending the last eleven years of her life with the Thoreaus. The grandchildren of Mrs.

Ward have a great collection of their aunt's letters. . . . and a short poem of Henry's".

"It seems that the daughters of Ellen Sewall (Mrs. J. Osgood, of Cohasset) have many letters from Sophia T. & some from Henry & John, who both made love to Ellen Sewall during her visits to her aunt, Mrs. Ward, in Concord; & perhaps they have some verses of H.'s "Sympathy" is believed (so Emerson told me) to relate to Ellen Sewall, but the Wards think it related to her brother Edmund Quincy Sewall, to whom the original *MS*, as they think, now belongs. He is a civil engineer, living somewhere in New York. In boyhood he was a pupil of J. & H. Thoreau."

(Ellen Sewall's father was the Rev. Edmund Sewall of Scituate. See *Life of Alcott*, vol. 1. The Sewalls were relations of Mrs. Alcott's.)

"The Rev. J. Osgood, husband of Ellen Sewall,[3] is still living, at a great age, in Cohasset; but his wife died nearly 3 years ago. There is a delicacy in mentioning the early loves of Mrs. O. and John Thoreau (it does not appear that she ever cared much for H., except as a friend) but of the fact there seems to be no doubt. She did not accept Mr. O. until after J. T.'s death. . . ."

1. Salt, who knew many homosexuals, obviously did not discern any homoerotic overtones in "Sympathy." Walter Harding in *The Days of Henry Thoreau* says Thoreau admired Edmund Sewall intellectually, not physically.

2. Thoreau published four lines of "Greece" in *A Week*. The poem is included in *Excursions and Poems* and in *Poems of Nature*. For a reliable text see Bode, *Collected Poems of Henry Thoreau* (1965), p. 218.

3. Ellen Sewall married the Reverend Joseph Osgood, pastor of the Unitarian church in Cohasset, Massachusetts, in 1844. See Walter Harding, *The Days of Henry Thoreau, p.* 103.

215. S. A. Jones to A. W. Hosmer, June 23, 1895.

I have sat in my little room up stairs a long while now looking at the photogravure of the woman whom Thoreau loved,[1] and, Fred, I have been filled with strange thoughts about destiny, fate, fortune, or whatever men choose to call it. I have realized what a pang Thoreau must have had in his heart; and I have tried to imagine what Thoreau might have been had this woman only cast her lot with him. The old duffer that she did marry looks like a piece of goody-goody stuff; he was no doubt "respectable" and he kept his flock together, and lived what they call "a useful life", but the world would have gone on just the same if the Rev. Dr. Osgood had died of the croup in his cradle.

I most earnestly hope that you can get a picture of Miss Sewall as a *young* woman, for the readers of the future have a right to know to what a queen

Thoreau was so loyal. But, just now I am too "dazed" to write about this matter. I must wait until fortune throws more of Miss Sewall's history in my way, and then I will embalm that love affair in touching prose, if I know myself. . . .

Is it too late for you to change your time for your vacation, if you deem it desirable to change? I ask for this reason: matters pertaining to the college have taken a strange change, and it is deemed necessary that I should resume my lectures. NOT in the college, but an independent course. This request is made because, in their endeavor to kill the college, the regents have appointed the poorest men they could find for the new faculty—I mean, of course, men of the poorest qualifications.

Of course, it is a compliment to be asked to resume teaching under such conditions, and the honor of Homoeopathy demands that I should take up the work once more; but it is 15 years since I lectured, and as knowledge has increased in that time, I must read like sin to be up to the times. If then, I accept the demand, for it IS a demand, I cannot have any vacation for myself; if I forego *that,* I can be ready for the work.

If you can change your vacation, so that you will not suffer by having made arrangements for the end of August, then I will give up my vacation for the sake of taking up teaching again; but if you cannot change your arrangements to a more advantageous time for your own enjoyment, THEN I will keep my engagement with you and urge that previous arrangements will prevent me from being able to take up the lectures. My course would be attended by both homoeopathic and "regular" students—in fact the petition asking me to resume teaching is signed largely by medical students of both schools. I have withheld my decision until I shall have heard from you.

If it was only disappointing myself, I should not care, for all my life has been a series of sacrifices for Homoeopathy, but I am not going to break my word with you.

1. The photogravure of Ellen Sewall was apparently obtained by Alfred Hosmer through Annie J. Ward. Miss Ward evidently felt that the facts regarding the "love affair" of Ellen Sewall and Thoreau ought to be published. Encouraged by Miss Ward, Alfred Hosmer made inquiries of the Osgood family. The fate of those inquiries is the subject of much of the next several letters. See the correspondence of Annie J. Ward to A. W. Hosmer (Hosmer collection).

216. S. A. Jones to A. W. Hosmer, June 28, 1895.

* * *

I inflict another sheet upon you to let you know how very earnestly I am hoping that you may succeed in your mission to Spencer.[1] I KNOW how the readers of Thoreau in the coming century will appreciate your services in the matter of the tenderest episode of Thoreau's life. It will shine in the eyes of readers yet unborn, and it goes far to redeem Thoreau's character from the reproach of being so cynical that he hardly seems to have belonged to the HUMAN race. I now see that Robert Louis Stevenson's explanation in his "Men and Books" has more of truth in it than I at first supposed.[2]

I can also plainly see that what must have been Miss Sewall's attitude towards "religion" was an insuperable obstacle to her marrying *Henry* Thoreau, at least. Is it known that she was at all "in love" with either John, or Henry? From such recollections as Horace Hosmer had of the Thoreau brothers, I fancy a young lady might have fallen in love with John; but did not Emerson say that he could "like" Thoreau but NOT "love" him?[3] I must confess that I find it difficult to imagine OUR Thoreau "in *love.*"

When you arrive in Spencer, put your ear on the ground and listen for all your worth; and, O Fred, don't shut both eyes until you have that early picture of Miss Sewall!!! Great God, how could poor Thoreau drag out his life with such a vision as Miss Sewall's maiden beauty haunting his memory? I tell you, Fred, the fact of learning the personality of his lady love and of seeing her portrait as she was in the autumn of life has made me full of tenderness of poor Thoreau. He wouldn't thank me for that "poor" but while he bore his awful disappointment as few men could have done, he, too, was flesh and blood, and other flesh and blood can feel for him.

If I reprint my poor Thoreau papers, I shall reproduce the Glimpse just as it is so as to show the growth of my conception of Thoreau. By reprinting my papers in the order in which they were written, I shall fully clear up any misunderstanding of Thoreau's ancestry, and it will at the same time show how misleading Sanborn has been. That paper read before the Unity Club[4]—which you read in the typewriter copy—will have to be included, and that will get Miss What's-her-name's LETTER before the readers; and THAT will show how she combed "F.B.S."

The Unity Club is making up its next winter's course of lectures and I am trying to make arrangements to get "the son of his father" out here.[5] I suppose a letter sent to Concord will reach him? . . .

1. Fred Hosmer was preparing to visit Annie J. Ward in Spencer, Massachusetts.
2. In his "Preface, by way of Criticism" to *Familiar Studies of Men and Books* (London: Chatto & Windus, 1882), Robert Louis Stevenson argued that the knowledge which he had gained from Dr. Japp concerning Thoreau's being "once fairly and manfully in love" with a woman whom he "relinquished . . . to his brother" provided "the explanation of the 'rarefied and freezing air' in which I complained that he had taught himself to breathe" (p. xxi). Stevenson had earlier maligned Thoreau as a cold priggish "skulker" in "Henry David Thoreau: His Character and Opinions," *Cornhill Magazine* 41 (June 1880):665–82.
3. In his obituary sketch for the *Atlantic,* Emerson quoted: " 'I love Henry,' said

one of his friends, 'but I cannot like him; and as for taking his arm, I should as soon think of taking the arm of an elm-tree.'" See "Thoreau," *Atlantic Monthly* 10 (August 1862):240. This remark has generally been attributed to Elizabeth Hoar.

4. Lecture dated January 19, 1891; there is a copy in Alfred Hosmer's hand in the Hosmer collection. Dr. Jones delivered the lecture on February 9, 1891.

5. Edward Emerson apparently lectured in Ann Arbor in November, 1895. On November 12, 1895, he wrote from Chicago, thanking Dr. Jones "for laying the keel, so to speak, of this lecturing venture by securing me the two engagements in Ann Arbor and one in Cleveland." See Edward W. Emerson to Dr. Jones, November 12, 1895 (Jones collection).

217. S. A. Jones to A. W. Hosmer, July 8, 1895.

Yours of the Fifth instant is just at hand, and it is very interesting. I should dearly like to have been with you at Spencer; how my ears would have gaped to hear the 'talk.' The story is beginning to take a tangible shape, and it needs only to be told with the tenderest feeling, and it will fairly glow in the hearts of those who are daily learning to love Thoreau more and more.

If I am entrusted with the editing of those precious papers you may depend upon my whole heart being put into it, and I really think that in the matter of 'heart' I can boast of and SHOW more than "F.B.S."

The truth is, Fred, that episode in Thoreau's life needs very tender handling; and so does Miss Ellen Sewall's. Hers especially. You see, Fred, a beautiful young girl is not responsible for the havoc that her fair face makes with the young man who happens to see it. I can easily imagine the shrinking delicacy of Miss Sewall's position. Henry was not lovable and John was. Horace Hosmer accidentally made THAT very plain to me.[1] But I am glad that Henry LOVED Miss S. for it proves him very human, and shows a side that he sedulously kept hidden from the world.

I hope that Miss Annie J. Ward may be successful in getting the *picture* if not the papers. I am afraid her immediate relatives may not realize what a profound interest this whole matter has for the FUTURE—and indeed, a matter so near at home will not have the romance in it for them that it has for others, but we must do our best to preserve this epoch in Thoreau's life for the readers of the future. At the same time the Wards and Sewalls must be made to understand clearly that the utmost delicacy will be preserved, for we are not only dealing with human hearts but with dead hearts THAT MUST NOT BE MIS-REPRESENTED. . . .

1. When Dr. Jones met Horace Hosmer in the summer of 1890, he made a record of their conversation, which included Hosmer's judgment that Thoreau "did not have the 'love-idea' in him: i.e. he did not appear to feel the *sex*-attraction" (Jones collection).

218. S. A. Jones to A. W. Hosmer, July 17, 1895.

Yours relating to the letter from Miss Ward is just at hand and I hasten to let you know how profoundly it appeals to me. But, my dear friend, I could not for the life of me think of interfering between the relatives in regard to it.[1]

I am also superstitious in regard to some of the transactions of life. For instance, I wrote the "Glimpse" at the earnest request of the Unity Club. The Rev. Mr. Sunderland insisted upon publishing it in "The Unitarian." It found favor in the eyes of the readers, and there came many requests that it should be re-issued in pamphlet form. Then Miss Eliza Hosmer got hold of a copy (for the whole town was talking about it), and through her I got your address for the sake of getting some Concord views—and from that day to this you and I have been of some little use to the readers of Thoreau. Now comes the superstition, for I have a feeling as if you and I were the appointed agents for however little or much we may have done. It has been our privilege to add somewhat to what was known of Thoreau, and we certainly have corrected very much of the error for which Mr. Sanborn is responsible. Moreover, we have kept "dinging" at the public in regard to Thoreau, and really Fred, the bibliography in Mr. Blake's volume of "Selections", led to the Riverside edition of Thoreau.

Now for some more "superstition." It is my belief that if that bit of editing is to be done in love, I shall have it to do; if not, then most assuredly, NOT.

If it falls to me I shall assume it as a solemn duty, for it will come—as all has come, through you: then I can but feel that I am the one who was to do it, and I shall be sustained in the hope that it will be done as tenderly, yes, as sacredly, as such a thing should be done.

It is all so unspeakably pathetic: the uncouth Henry Thoreau moved to the depths of even *his* imperturbable being by the vision of beauty that burst in upon that quiet Concord home. The more lovable brother, John, wounded too by the same divine arrow (for, Fred, old as I am, Love is still divine to me, and you may laugh at me if you like!), and Henry finds it out, and gives up his one shadow of the hope of succeeding for his brother's sake—and that terrible fate, awaiting John Thoreau from before his birth, comes unrelentingly, and the bright creature (who could, perhaps, have loved *him*) is married to another, and makes his home a quiet heaven of delight for fifty years. Meanwhile, the uncouth Henry, like a wounded animal, carries his "pang" (you remember he delicately calls it that) in his heart for more than twenty years,—and the Healer touches his aching heart and the peace ineffable falls upon even such a sorrow as his.

Dear me, it is all so strange; and to know that it is not a foolish romance but a veritable chapter of Life's strange history! Talk about the realistic novel—the realities of Life are staring us in the face every day; so I care but little for novels!

If it should please Him who orders our ways to move the heart of the "Gentle Boy" in regard to this sacred old memory, and if through his ministrations it should fall as a duty to me, I know not of any writing I ever did that would fairly *gush* warm from my heart; but 'May Wright Sewall'[2] has the right (must I say?), and nothing connected with the memory of Ellen Sewall and Henry Thoreau must have even the shadow of an aspersion upon it. Of course, I wish that I had the precious MSS. in my hands now; but Honor first, last, and all the time.

1. Annie J. Ward had apparently suggested to Alfred Hosmer that Dr. Jones might find Edmund Sewall, Ellen Sewall's brother and the "Gentle Boy" of Thoreau's poem "Sympathy," willing to discuss his sister's brief "love affair" with Thoreau. See Annie J. Ward to A. W. Hosmer, July 20, 1895 (Hosmer Collection).

2. May Wright Sewall was probably the niece of Ellen Sewall; the family preferred that she should have first right to publish the material pertaining to Ellen Sewall and Thoreau.

219. S. A. Jones to A. W. Hosmer, July 21, 1895.

Yours of the 19th instant is just at hand, and while I fully participate in your desire to have those letters and the sonnets[1] properly given to the world, nevertheless I absolutely can NOT bring myself to feel that I must in any manner whatsoever SEEK them.

In the first place, it impresses me as being indelicate for me to go seeking them; they are too sacred for that. And in the second, if I am to be the instrument for bringing them into literature, then the destinies will put them into my hands.

Remember, Fred, that Sanborn makes a trade of that which has been to little me a duty. Such trifles as I have been permitted to commit to the press have been the fruit of bye-hours, stolen, as it were, from one of the most time-exacting callings that ever was followed. What I have done, I have done in love; and if ever I have reached the heart of a single reader it is simply because I wrote in love.

I hope that you will not misunderstand this, and I have confidence that your good judgement will avert that.

It might secure the sacred privacy that such matters must have if, instead of a large edition for the coarse public, a limited one were issued, say by the ROWFANT CLUB. This would secure the finest printing that can be had in these United States, and only such intimate friends as Miss Ward might desire could get a copy.

Such privacy might also induce the Rev. J. Osgood to give his consent to the immediate publication. The book would embalm Ellen Sewall's memory for the future like a fly in amber. It should have her portraits in photo, or GOOD photogravures, one with all the bloom of young womanhood upon, and the other with the sweet gravity that her life brought to her. Ah, Fred, the dramas that these graves hold!

[P.S.] My "work" for to-day is critically reading that essay on Thoreau which is Miss Knapp's thesis for the degree of Doctor of Philosophy.[2]

I am going over it at the request of Professor Demmon, of the chair of English Literature, and am to give whatever suggestions I can, as they want to do Thoreau's memory justice.

My dear Fred, I do wish you were sitting with me! Miss Knapp has certainly presented Thoreau in a light that no one has yet attempted. She is just SOAKED with what he has written; she makes the most apt quotations to prove from his own pen whatever she says of him, and, Fred, she [sees] into him farther than anyone who has thus far *published* anything about him.

Better than all, she understands him; she even shows that he is not an "imitator" of Emerson—she even hints boldly that Emerson could not have written what Thoreau did, and it tickles me hugely to find a bright scholar holding the same opinion on this matter that I have had from "way back." I have been laughed at for expressing it, but that makes no difference with the hard *fact*.

You folks will be just delighted when I am able to send you some copies of this Thesis. One will drop into Concord Free Library with a whack that will wake up some of the dusty respectabilities of Concord to a realizing of what Henry Thoreau is—that is if they have brains enough to take it in! . . .

1. Hosmer had apparently suggested again, as Annie J. Ward had, that Dr. Jones visit Edmund Sewall in order to ascertain more about the Thoreau-Ellen Sewall relationship.
2. Lawrence F. McNamee lists Ella A. Knapp's *A Study of Thoreau* (University of Michigan, 1899) as the first American dissertation devoted to Thoreau. *See Dissertations in English and American Literature* (New York: Bowker, 1968), p. 740. The University of Michigan does not have a copy of this dissertation.

220. S. A. Jones to A. W. Hosmer, July 28, 1895.

It is very natural that the Sewalls should want that episode in their mother's life handled by some of their own flesh and blood, and my doctrine of the destinies is proving itself; and most heartily do I wish success for the niece who has the duty to discharge.[1]

I am afraid the statement that there is no picture of her in her younger days is a polite fiction,[2] for pretty girls find their ways to the "gallery" as naturally as they do to the lookin-glass! Make a note of that, my bachelor friend, if you please.

I could but be pleased to hear that Miss Ward felt confidence enough in me to be willing to entrust to me the writing of such a paper as the old time Prescription book would suggest.[3] I should, of course, need something of a history of its author, not necessarily for printing, but so that I could handle the old book intelligently. I say, Fred, would n't it be queer—a surgeon in one army writing-up the prescription book of the surgeon in the earlier war. I fancy I can make a good job of it when it comes this way. I shall take courage from Miss Ward's kindness to write to her, and PERHAPS through her I may come into correspondence with Ellen Sewall's son. If HE also trusts me I may learn more of Thoreau that I can put into use. Meanwhile, tell Miss Ward that I cannot for my life see why the sonnets are withheld from Mr. Sanborn for immediate publication.

I am really sorry that I cannot go east this summer, for I should dearly like to meet Miss Ward face to face. Has she ever seen the article in Lippincott's Magazine?

1. Ellen Sewall's daughter, Elizabeth Osgood Davenport, had written Hosmer that she was opposed to the publication of any material pertaining to her mother's relationship with Thoreau. Moreover, she added that if in future she should decide to give such information as she remembered, she would give it "to the cousin to whom my mother told the story some years since," and not to Dr. Jones, as Hosmer had suggested. See Elizabeth Osgood Davenport to A. W. Hosmer, July 24, 1895 (Hosmer collection).

2. E.Q.T. Osgood, son of Ellen Sewall, had written Hosmer that he was opposed to publication of anything pertaining to his mother's relationship with Thoreau and that there was no picture of her prior to her marriage in 1844. See E.Q.T. Osgood to A. W. Hosmer, July 23, 1895 (Hosmer collection). Dr. Jones's speculation that there was an early portrait of Ellen Sewall was correct; for a daguerreotype of Ellen taken about 1840, see Walter Harding, *The Days of Henry Thoreau*, p. 141.

3. Annie J. Ward had asked Dr. Jones to prepare an article on the prescription book of her grandfather, Col. Joseph Ward, who was evidently a physician in the Revolutionary War.

221. S. A. Jones to A. W. Hosmer, August 3, 1895.

I have lost the count and have really forgotten whether I answered your last letter, or not. I tell you, my friend, I am growing beautifully stupid of late; am in fact plunging headlong into my second childhood.

Your last informed me of your approach to Mr. Sewall and of the result. Well it is very natural; he knows who has the contract to do that bit of writing, and he does not know how lovingly an old chap out here in Michigan would have tried to do it. My chief regret is that he says there is no early picture of HER. By Jupiter! I remember now that I did answer your last letter, for I advanced a notion of mine about a pretty girl going to the Dauguerrean gallery as naturally as they get before the looking glass. (All right, I'm glad I didn't forget to pay my epistolary debt to you, after my poor fashion.)

By the way, I am trying to get E. W. Emerson a chance to talk here next winter, and it will pan out all right, too. He's coming IF he gets other calls out West. I expect to bed and board him while he is here, and perhaps I shall go to Cleveland with him if I can get a "job" for him there.

I was much pleased with one thing in one of his late letters, which I tell you in confidence. It is this: he wrote me that Sanborn's conduct had been such that he, E.W.E., felt obliged to refuse to recognize Sanborn.[1] Fred, I want you to make a note of the fact that Emerson stock took a sudden rise in my market. Edward wrote like one who, as he had it, did not like to treat a fellow townsman, and his old teacher, in this manner, but something that Sanborn has done *compelled it*. Fred, I feel rather pleased now that I got Sanborn "down on" me; especially as he proves to be such a—shall I say "shyster"?

I read Irving Allen's opinion of Mrs. and Sophia Thoreau,[2] and by Jinks! it did me good. I am going to drop a line to Mr. Allen asking about the editorship of Thoreau's posthumous books. I had credited them to Sophia, largely; now I'll ask Mr. Allen what he knows about the matter.

1. Edward Emerson had written of Sanborn: "I have lost respect for him so utterly that lately I had to refuse his greeting." See Edward W. Emerson to S. A. Jones, July 30, 1895 (Jones collection).
2. "American Women to whom the World is Indebted," *Independent* 47 (July 25, 1895):987–88.

222. S. A. Jones to A. W. Hosmer, August 11, 1895.

Yours of the 8th instant is at hand and the poem has been read over until I can sing it in the dark.[1] I don't think it's perzackly poetry, but it is rhymed prose that shows Thoreau's power of close observation.

Better than all, it is very interesting, and I am deeply indebted to your kind thoughtfulness for the copy.

Miss Ward may depend upon my executing her commission most religiously.[2] Why, I can hardly wait for her return, and am selfish enough to cut short her visit, were it in my power. I declare, Fred, I shall have to come East if only to talk with her.

I am also desirous to try if I cannot present the old letters so as to make them glow with human feeling; and I really want to cope with Sanborn on that line. He is so cold-blooded that he must be related to the clam species!

But, Phew! didn't your inside history of the reason for E.W.E.'s refusing to recognize Sanborn cool my young enthusiasm! I should say yes!

Poor Sanborn, it is rather hard to be cut for doing an honest man's duty. It will make me feel queer when I meet Edward; and I should like to tell him that I am not built in the way he seems to be—and he a pupil of Thoreau, too!

How pleased Mr. Salt will be at the evidence of your helpfulness. Dear me, how strange it all is—Salt and you and I in correspondence, and all because a certain man lived and hoped and wrought and died in Concord so long ago. Well, I hope we meet him when we pass on higher; but will he speak to such as I! there's the rub. Let me at least hope for it.

1. Hosmer had probably sent Dr. Jones a copy of Thoreau's poem "Ding Dong"; Annie J. Ward had sent Hosmer a copy to pass along to Salt for inclusion in *Poems of Nature,* where it did appear. See Annie J. Ward to A. W. Hosmer, August 7, 1895 (Hosmer collection).

2. Annie J. Ward had written Hosmer that she wanted Dr. Jones to use letters in her possession of Prudence Ward, Edmund Sewall, and Maria Thoreau. She wrote that Sanborn was coming to visit her to look at these materials but that she much preferred Jones to have the use of them. Jones, however, did not make the trip to Concord and Spencer which Miss Ward expected; nor did he publish anything from these papers. See Annie J. Ward to A. W. Hosmer, August 7, 1895 (Hosmer collection).

223. Henry Salt to S. A. Jones, August 16, 1895.

* * *

When I have got this off my hands,[1] I hope to turn my attention to my Thoreau biography, with a view to a second edition. My idea now is, to lighten the book considerably by omitting many of the very numerous quotations with which it is interspersed. I do not regret having included those quotations in the first edn., because they helped to fortify the opinions which I expressed, & were mostly from out-of-the-way sources & unknown to the general public; but I think it would be an advantage to make the second edn. a smaller & cheaper book. Also the omission of the quotations would tend to a more artistic unity & 'finish'. If Bentley is still unwilling to re-issue the book in cheap form, I shall ask him to waive any legal objection he may possess to my giving it to another English publisher, for I think Reeves would probably do it. Then, possibly, some arrangement might be made with an American house, for sending over a few hundred copies, in the 'sheets', to be issued as an American edition.

Any hints or suggestions you may kindly make as to this plan will be most welcome. . . .

1. Salt was reading proofs for a revised edition of his *Shelley.*

224. S. A. Jones to A. W. Hosmer, September 1, 1895.

In the last letter I had from you, I fancied you were a little mixed as to my age; or, better, you knew it better than I do. I am aware that Concord is a peculiar place, but I remember being "borned" so well that I'm not going to let you knock me out of my notion about it.

I came into this world of sin and misery on the eleventh of June, 1834. Now for the figures that will "knock you silly."

```
11th of June, 1844, 10 years old
  "    "    "  , 1854, 20   "     "
  "    "    "  , 1864, 30   "     "
  "    "    "  , 1874, 40   "     "
  "    "    "  , 1884, 50   "     "
  "    "    "  , 1894, 60   "     "
11th of June, 1895, 61 years old
```

When I sent you that photo I'll be blessed if I had not sojourned HERE SIXTY-ONE years. Now, confound you, figure straighter than that if you can.

It is expected that the son of his father will lecture here on the fourth and fifth of November, and from here he will probably go to Cleveland, where I have worked up a job for him. I shall board him here and go to Cleveland with him, where I believe he will be the guest of its President. I am wondering if I can be at ease with him, and I shall be in a terrible [fix] if I'm not. . . .

225. A. W. Hosmer to S. A. Jones, [undated].[1]

Stanzas:
Written to be sung at the funeral of Henry D. Thoreau,
of Concord, Massachusetts.
Friday, May 9th. 1862.

Hearest thou the sobbing breeze complain
　　How faint the sunbeams light the shore,—
His heart more fixed than earth or main,
　　Henry! that faithful heart is o'er.

O weep not thou thus vast a soul;
　　O do not mourn this lordly man,
As long as Walden's waters roll
　　And Concord river fills a span.

For thoughtful minds in Henry's page
　　Large welcome find and bless his verse
Drawn from the poet's heritage,
　　From wells of right and nature's source.

237

Fountains of hope and faith! inspire
Most stricken hearts to lift this cross,
His perfect trust shall keep the fire,
His glorious peace disarm all loss!

This sounds as though it might have been written by Channing.[2]

I find that Emerson's biographical sketch of Thoreau is republished in "Lectures and Biographical Sketches" by R. W. Emerson. Boston. Houghton Mifflin & Co. 1884. p. 419.

1. This material was almost certainly included with a letter from Hosmer, which has not been found. We have placed it here because Dr. Jones's next letter—September 11, 1895, number 227—refers to his having received the funeral poem.
2. This hymn by Channing was sung by the choir of the First Parish Church at Thoreau's funeral service.

226. Henry Salt to A. W. Hosmer, September 10, 1895.

I found your letter of Aug. 27 awaiting me on my return to London a day or two ago, and I have only time to send a hurried line by tomorrow's mail. I doubt if this will reach you by the date of the "Thoreau" meeting; but if it does, please let it express my heartiest wishes for the success of the gathering. There can be no doubt that there is in England (and I trust still more in America) a growing appreciation of Thoreau's work; and I am sure that it will be both pleasant and profitable for students of his writings to meet together for discussion. I greatly wish I could be present on the occasion. If there should be any record of the proceedings, might I suggest that a copy should be sent to the Editor of "Seed-Time", the journal of the New Fellowship, a society which numbers among its members many earnest Thoreau students? (The address is, Maurice Adams, 22 Beulah Rd., Thornton Heath, Eng.)

227. S. A. Jones to A. W. Hosmer, September 11, 1895.

I am delighted to learn that you are the possessor of one of Thoreau's letters;[1] it belongs to you for your devotion to his memory.

I received the old Doctor's receipt book the other day and will see what I can make out of it for some medical journal. It is a dry subject and the old book is by no means juicy!

This morning I am in receipt of your letter enclosing the funeral poem. I tell you what, Fred, it makes death more terrible to think what stuff may be fired off over a fellow's remains! . . .

1. Hosmer had acquired Thoreau's letter of June 1, 1858, to H.G.O. Blake, from Blake. See Blake to Hosmer, August 31, 1895. (Hosmer collection). For a text of Thoreau's letter, now in the Hosmer Collection, see *The Correspondence of Henry David Thoreau,* pp. 514–15.

228. Henry Salt to S. A. Jones, September 21, 1895.

* * *

I am extremely grateful to you for that list of *errata* in my *Life of Thoreau.* All the hints contained in it are most valuable, & shall be acted on, where they have not already been adopted. I daresay you are right in thinking that the Preface to Macmillan's *Selections* is the best thing I have done in Thoreau work. It is far more concise, more "succinct", than the *Life;* but this is a point in which I hope to make the second edition much better than the first. (By the bye, though, as you say, the *Selections* are excluded from the American market, the Preface itself is not copyright; so if ever a chance shd. occur of having it inserted as an article in an American journal or magazine, please remember that I shd. be only too pleased to see it so used. It was originally a magazine article, & could be made so again, by some very slight omissions.)

It stands in this way, now, about the *Life.* I wrote to Bentley, telling him I was anxious the book should not be "shelved", and asking him, point blank, whether, in case of his not caring to issue a second edition, he would waive his legal rights & allow me to get another publisher. He writes in a friendly way, declining to have a second edn., but giving me the freedom I desired. I feel greatly relieved by this, as I am now unfettered, and can make an attempt to come to some arrangement with a less aristocratic publisher. I think it is quite possible that Reeves will take the book, in which case I should probably be able to get Macmillan to take a small edition for their New York house. I should omit everything which would be copyright in America. Anyhow I am once more free for some sort of action, so hope to go ahead.

In revising the book, I shall certainly shorten it very greatly, and I think I shall be able to improve it thereby. All the important matter you have sent me from time to time will enable me to deal far more *confidently* with a number of topics than I could do five years ago. There is one thing about Reeves which is usually counted as a *dis*advantage, but may in this case be advantageous—that he will beyond doubt ensure my "taking time" over it! His dilatoriness in printing is awful; & I doubt if the *Shelley* which he has in hand will be done before Christmas.

The *Poems of Nature* will be ready for publication quite soon, I believe. They form a nice little volume of 120 pages; & though I fear the joint Introduction is not a very lively affair, and there will be some other shortcomings. Sanborn has again got between me & Mr. Blake, & has not sent a scrap of new material. *(This is strictly private!)* The only advantage of his cooperation is the permission to publish in America. I hope the book will not fail of its effect. I will send you an early copy, as soon as I possibly can. Through Mr. Hosmer's kind services (no doubt), I lately received from Miss Ward a copy of "The Blue Bird",[1] a poem by Thoreau, and I also had a kind note from her. I have written to ask her to try to get information from her cousin, Mr. E. Q. Sewall, about Thoreau's love affair, & the poem "Sympathy". Mr. Hosmer also sent me a poem, "Ding Dong",[2] which arrived in time to be included in the volume. . . .

1. This was "The Bluebirds," which Thoreau wrote for Master George W. Sewall, a brother of Ellen Sewall; Hosmer had acquired a copy of the poem from Annie J. Ward. Miss Ward's copy is in the Hosmer collection. For a text of the poem see *Collected Poems of Henry Thoreau,* pp. 93–96.

2. "Ding Dong" appeared in *Poems of Nature;* for a text see *Collected Poems of Henry Thoreau,* p. 111.

229. S. A. Jones to A. W. Hosmer, September 22, 1895.

I read that poem[1] with a great curiosity and finished it with fully as great a disappointment. Of course, one reads every fragment of Thoreau's writing with eagerness, but every thing that he wrote must not be published. This poem, for instance, is of the "machine made" order, and only real LOVERS of Thoreau should see it.

In the matter of that one sent to Mr. Salt, I must say I think Mr. Sanborn's taste and JUDGEMENT far superior to the Englishman's. Mr. Salt has no *genius*, but one can truthfully say that of Mr. Sanborn. Sanborn the writer and Sanborn the man are two entirely different considerations, and as a writer I must say Sanborn excells Salt.

Yesterday I expressed the Emerson books back to Boston. Was n't I glad to get the darned things out of my house? May be not! It is curious, but the more I see of Ralph Waldo the farther I get from him; and to make a Bibliography of an author whom you do not love is a piece of the primest drudgery I know anything about. I have got about half way through this task, and when I shall finish the other half I really cannot imagine.

It seems to me that since you and Miss Ward have "tapped" Mr. Salt my part of his overflow is getting limited; but, Fred, I am glad indeed that he is now in correspondence with Miss Ward and you, for the nearer he gets to original sources the better will his next Life of Thoreau be. That book must be printed in the United States, if possible, for it is a positive loss to our readers not to have easy access to Mr. Salt's last volume of "Selections." That book is best of all adapted to make readers of Thoreau, and I feel in my bones that if Sanborn were a real friend of Thoreau he would use every endeavor to get the book into the American market through Houghton, Mifflin & Co. . . .

1. Obviously Dr. Jones had also received copies of "The Bluebirds" and "Ding Dong."

230. S. A. Jones to A. W. Hosmer, October 3, 1895.

I have just finished arranging the Magazine articles by Thoreau that we collected some long time ago, and I have come to a halt on some points, namely, the fact that *two* papers are not to be had for any price. These are, 1. The article in the *Liberator* for March 28th., 1845.[1] 2. The paper in the New York Tribune for October 6th., 1860.[2] These are practically unobtainable, and we have got to face the fact that the collection MUST BE INCOMPLETE.

This unavoidable incompleteness goes far toward reconciling me to the leaving out of the first of Thoreau's publications: *The Walk to Wachusett.* You know that Mr. Dawes, by the merest chance, found an incomplete copy of the BOSTON MISCELLANY. The first two volumes of it were imperfect, but the last two numbers were complete. I already had the first two VOLUMES *complete,* and the finding of the two parts of volume 3 (all that were published of that volume) gave the opportunity for getting a complete set of one of the rarest of American Magazines.

Then came the question, Shall this chance to complete a set of the BOSTON MISCELLANY be sacrificed for the sake of the Thoreau Collection. I feel that the obligation to Literature is far greater than the making of the Thoreau collection, *especially* as that collection can not be made *complete.* I feel too, that, under the circumstances, the BOSTON MISCELLANY should be kept complete, and *that* I have concluded to do in this case. You see, I can learn of only *one other complete set* in the United States, and that one De Vinne's man found in the library of the New York Historical Society.

Now the question is, shall I bind up what we have gathered, or shall I *wait one more year* to try if the missing numbers of the Boston Miscellany will turn up? If you say, Bind, I'll bind; if you say, Wait, I'll wait.

As it is, the collection will make two volumes; one of the papers published while Thoreau was alive, and the other of the papers and selections from his Journal published after his death. It will be as well to finish what we have begun; but, really, I would not be foolish enough to start another such collection, for it seems to me now, that the game is n't worth the candle, as the phrase is. But, say the word, and I'll go on and finish the job.

I now turn to another matter, namely, the Rowfant Club has bought a building and is soon going to move into it. To-day the president wrote to me saying that each member was expected to give some relic to adorn the new club rooms and begging me to chip in. I purpose that my contribution shall be in memory of Thoreau, inasmuch as the Club published his bibliography. To this end I am ready to beg like a born devil.

I shall give one of the tiles you got for me, provided you give your consent to my parting with ONE. I should also like to get a piece of the Walden hut, a genuine Thoreau pencil, a bit of his manuscript (begged from Mr. Blake), in fact, any relics that can be had for love or money (if not too much for these hard times).

The Club has many and costly curiosities now, so that anything pertaining to Thoreau would be in the midst of somewhat distinguished surroundings; and I should like to see his memory perpetuated and duly honored in so distant a place as the stirring city of Cleveland.

I learn from the president's letter that I have got a paying job for Edward Emerson. He is to read before the Club and will pocket Fifty dollars beside having a royal good time. When he returns he can tell you what for club the Rowfant is. . . .

1. "Wendell Phillips Before the Concord Lyceum."
2. "The Succession of Forest Trees."

231. S. A. Jones to A. W. Hosmer, October 8, 1895.

I have just received yours of the 6th instant, and I am impelled to send you a line at once. I do not know what the "meeting" is to be *in detail,* nor who is to meet, but if it is something of the nature of a Thoreau Club I want to know more about it and its aims.[1]

If it is a purely local affair, I do not wish to interfere in the least, but if the "meeting" is to include outside heathen, I certainly want a seat somewhere in sight of the altar.

I presume that Thoreau has enough earnest lovers to justify the founding of a Thoreau Club, having its headquarters in Concord and its auxiliaries everywhere. Such a club might publish material relating to Thoreau that is not otherwise likely to get into print. This would be of great interest and value in the century that is about to dawn. These publications would of necessity appear irregularly, that is, as the material turns up. They should be issued in pamphlet form and be uniform, so that they could be bound when enough of them have been printed to make a volume.

That Essay on WALKING would be a good initial number; it might be followed by the history of Thoreau's Arrest and imprisonment, and the question as to who paid his tax definitely settled, and so on. Much pertaining to him could be rescued from oblivion if begun before all the witnesses are gone beyond; and this is what ought to be saved.

You can, at least, make a suggestion of something like this and see what the sense of the "meeting" will be. I should, of course, like to be near enough to take a hand, but as an outsider I might be of some little use. . . .

I had a letter from Mr. Salt the other day. He tells me, confidentially, that Sanborn has been of no help whatever in the new book of poems. He sent not a line of anything new, and Mr. Salt writes, "He has again got between Mr. Blake and me." Drat F.B.S., I'd like to pull his nose!

Do you know whether the poems from the Commonwealth were copied and sent to Mr. Salt? He says the "Poems of Nature"—for that it seems is the title—will make a book of some 120 pages, and he thinks it will soon be out. . . .

I have always been sorry that instead of giving a copy of the scarce bibliography to Sanborn, I had sent it to Mr. Blake; but Sanborn gave me to understand that Mr. B. did not really care for such things. He, wrote Mr. Sanborn, thinks more of Thoreau spiritually than in the literary sense. But what must Mr. Blake's spiritual instincts be when he is deluded by such a hollow friend to Thoreau as is Mr. Sanborn? That's a conundrum that you need n't try to answer. . . .

1. Alfred W. Hosmer published an account of the Thoreau meeting in Concord, October 25, 1895, as "An Evening with Thoreau," in *High School Voice* for November 15, 1895; this was later reprinted in London in *Seed-Time* for January 1896. The meeting, chaired by George B. Bartlett, was held at the studio of Daniel Chester French, where Mrs. Kate Tryon was then living. Alfred Hosmer played a considerable part in the affair: he presented each guest with a *Chronology of the Life of Henry D. Thoreau,* which he compiled and privately published, read selections from Thoreau's *Autumn,* and closed the meeting by reading a letter of greeting from Henry Salt and Dr. Jones's poem "He kept the temple as divine." Bartlett, Mrs. Tryon, F. B. Sanborn, Jane Hosmer, and Walton Ricketson also took part in the program.

232. Henry Salt to S. A. Jones, October 16, 1895.

A few lines, in haste for today's mail, to tell you that things are looking well—at last!—for a second edition of my *Life of Thoreau*. Messrs. Walter Scott have offered to put it in their eighteen-penny series, "Great Writers", and to publish it simultaneously in Eng. and America. The book will be shortened to 200 from 300 pages, on the plan which I described to you in my last letter.

This, you will see, is all, and more than all, that I had been hoping for, as it will give the book a wide circulation in both countries, and bring it within the purchasing powers of even the poorest of Thoreau's admirers.

The only danger of a hitch in the negotiations is that Scott might fear Bentley's possible interference at some later date, he (B.) having the prior "agreement" with me. But B. has behaved very nicely, and written me a letter which sets me free to enter in a new engagement; so I think the matter may be considered settled.

I have not told anyone of this as yet, so please dô not mention it until you hear from me again. But I should like Mr. Hosmer to know, if you chance to be writing to him. The editor of the Great Writers Series seems anxious to have the book out soon, but no date is as yet fixed. Still, it is possible it will be with the printers before this reaches you; so if you have any further hint or advice to give your biography-writing friend, I would just say, "Hurry up!"

Every volume in the series has a Bibliography at the end, and I made a suggestion to Scott that he should ask *you* to contribute one (though possibly the Rowfant Club would have said nay to this?). But it appears that they are all done, on a uniform system, by Mr. Anderson of the British Museum; so this too will have to be his work. I take it for granted he may be allowed to "exploit" your Bibliography, but I will ask him to make due acknowledgment thereof.

And this reminds me to ask you to send me any later items that you may have noted, if there is anything of importance *since* your Bibliog.

The *Poems of Nature* are not yet issued, but I imagine it can only be a question of a week or two. I am sorry to say Macmillan has done very badly with the *Selections;* only about 300 copies (less than that) sold. Really, under the circumstances, and in view of the fact that the British Public *will not* buy Thoreau, I think I am lucky to get so many volumes sent out! Whether I am morally justified in thus ruining one publisher after another with unsaleable Thoreau books, is a point of casuistry which I submit for your friendly consideration. Do the means justify the end?

233. Henry Salt to S. A. Jones, October 25, 1895.

It is now all settled with Messrs. Scott about the Life of Thoreau and they are going to put it in the printer's hands at once. Bentley has behaved very courteously, and has made the way smooth for a second edition. Scott is to give me £40 for the copyright of the book, in its shortened form, so I shall be "Passing rich on forty pounds a year",—(for *one* year, at any rate!) It is really a great relief to have got out of the *impasse* with Bentley, and to see the book started again, especially as it will be in a cheap popular series where it will have every chance.

I am working hard at the revision of the text, and introducing a lot of corrections; also cutting out a lot of superfluous stuff. I think it will be a much better book in its shortened form ("The half is greater than the whole", as the Greek proverb had it), but I must confess I don't see my way to altering the *general* form or tone of it. It is so extremely difficult to alter a book in that respect without entirely re-writing it. I am aware, on re-reading it, that it is as you said! too cold, too far-off, and (I think) considerably inferior to my study of Jefferies. Still we must hope for the best, and I shall do what I can! . . .

[P.S.] Mr. Anderson tells me that he has got yr. Bibliog. at the Museum. He does not go much into detail in his bibliogs. for this series, but is going to let me see a 'proof' in case I can suggest anything.

234. Henry Salt to S. A. Jones, November 2, 1895.

I am sending you today a copy of the *Poems of Nature,* which please accept. Copies have also been sent (by the publisher) to Mr. Hosmer & Miss Ward.

I hope you will like the book, and the designed title-page. I think the latter is beautiful, and also appropriate to the subject. Let me know of any errors you detect in the book. There probably are some. There are one or two points concerning the text, about which I must consult you, when I have time to write fully.

The *Life* has gone to the printer's today. I think I have adopted all the chief suggestions made by you; but I should like to ask you more particularly about one thing. You say, "Give an entirely new reading of the love affair, breaking the old idol". What do you mean precisely by this? I *have* re-written that passage; but I don't know that it now amounts to a *new* version, although it is much fuller in detail than before. What is the "old idol"? Was there any point in the story as previously told that was actually untrue?[1]

Perhaps I am seeing too much significance in your words; in which case don't trouble to reply to all this!

The only point which now troubles me about the new edition is the copyright in America. But I have taken very great trouble to omit all lengthy quotations which are copyright, & I hope it will be all right. I am drawing my quotations from the essays which were published before 1854 in magazines, & from the *Week,* as I understand the right has expired in these cases. I can't get much advice from Scott, although it really concerns him as closely as myself. Like all publishers, he seems to have so much to do that he can't do anything. . . .

1. Given all the Victorian reticences of the Sewall family, Salt's account of Thoreau's love affair with Ellen Sewall is as complete as was then possible. See chapter 6 of *The Days of Henry Thoreau* for an account of Thoreau's "love affair" with Miss Sewall; Harding had access to the family papers not available to Salt and Jones.

235. S. A. Jones to A. W. Hosmer, November 9, 1895.

Well, I have heard Mr. Emerson's lecture on Thoreau. I found so little that is new in it that I was not much interested. I was more curious to see the speaker's manner than I was about his matter, for I did not expect to hear anything new, nor did I. I do not think I should care to ever hear him again, for I think him the most uninteresting talker I ever heard. He does not put one solitary spark of enthusiasm into his hearers; but I was agreeably surprised at the number who turned out to hear his second lecture, which was on "Animal Structure as related to Art." He spoke for about an hour and a half and without manuscript, but his continual "ahs" and pauses affected me disagreeably, so I slid into a backroom and read until the show was over.

He made himself pleasantly at home with us and made us feel at home with him, so that I was much relieved on that score. For myself I found him decidedly uninteresting; he talked an infinite deal but it subsided and left no mark. I believe all I learned from him that I did not already know was the name of the Canadian wood-chopper whom Thoreau mentions in "Walden."[1] He happened to mention him, and I asked his name. He told me too of the wood-chopper's visit to Thoreau when the latter was ill, who, his visitor being drunk, Thoreau advised to go at once to the river and drown himself. It is so characteristic that *one* has no room for a shadow of doubt as to the verity of the story.

Your relics reached the Rowfant Club the very night he read his Thoreau paper to them. He told me he did not see the things, but saw the members crowding around them. I have not heard from the Club, but I know the treasures would be a great pleasure to the members. You had long before sent me a picture of the site of the shanty and it was already framed and in the Club-house; so I shall give the picture you sent me the other day to the University when it is suitably framed. It will be hung in the room where the students of American Literature read their papers about Thoreau and his works. Emerson told me that he was urging upon Mr. Ricketson that he should make a bust of Thoreau. I was glad to hear it, for a good bust is desirable. Good luck attend Mr. Ricketson's effort!

I should not be surprised any morning to find Mr. Salt's book of Thoreau's *Poems* in my mail box. He wrote me the other day that a new life of Thoreau is now assured. Walter Scott is going to publish it in the "Great Writers Series." This will secure for it a large circulation and a permanent place in literature. Mr. Salt expects that this life will be better than the first one he wrote. He says he will try to get nearer the man, and if he "gets there" it will give the book a flesh-and-blood warmth that I greatly missed in his first attempt. In fact, Mr. Salt says he will be able to write with a great deal more confidence than he felt at first. Between Horace Hosmer, you, and I he certainly has got much more precise information than he had, and he will use it to Thoreau's honor, I know.

I should like to have had a back seat at your Thoreau meeting, and I should have asked F.B.S. to place that stolen Thoreau manuscript[2] in the Free Library.

Edward Waldo and I talked a little about F.B.S., but he "fought shy" and hedged, for he tried to say all he could in defense of Sanborn. As he had once written so outspokenly about S. I did not understand his change of manner—nor did I care to understand it. I don't think he will ever "lecture" here again. . . .

1. Alek Therien was the French-Canadian woodchopper who appears in *Walden*.
2. We have been unable to identify this "stolen" manuscript.

236. A. W. Hosmer to S. A. Jones, November 20, 1895.

Yes, I received a copy of "Poems of Nature," with Mr. Salt's compliments, and a dainty little volume it is too, I have already purchased one, and shall one or two more for Christmas remembrances.

Miss Ward sent me a while ago, her picture of Maria Thoreau,[1] that I have had copied, and enclose one of the photos for you. I am trying to see if I cannot obtain a picture of each of the family so as to get a copy of them.

I was in one of the stores the other day, when a gentleman said, "Well, you are having quite a little to say about Henry Thoreau, did you know him?" "No" I replied, "I never even saw him, that I know of." "Well, I have, I used to work, when a boy at Sam Barrett's mill", (grist mill, near North branch on Spencer brook) "and Thoreau used to come in there quite often. He was in one day when some boys were there, and they asked me if I was going in swimming, I said, no, I was afraid of the water snakes. Thoreau said they would not hurt me, and asked if there was any chance of one being out, so I shut off the water, and we went up the brook, found one about three feet long, when Thoreau went up carefully, picked up the snake, and showed us that it had no sting in its tail, and no bones in its head, that would give it power to bite, & that it was perfectly harmless, and since that time," he added, "I lost all fear of the snakes."

The first chance I get I will see if he can give me any other bits of interest in regard to Thoreau.

1. Maria Thoreau was the sister of John Thoreau, Sr. For her picture see Walter Harding, *The Days of Henry Thoreau*, p. 140.

237. S. A. Jones to A. W. Hosmer, November 25, 1895.

I looked at Aunt Maria's features with a good deal of interest and I failed to find any trace of a "gossip-monger" there. On the contrary I see a quiet, mind-your-own-business sort of a woman. I fancied her standing on the steps at Sam Staples's house paying Thoreau's tax, thereby making him mad as the devil, though she was happily unaware of it.

I wish you could have the good luck to find pictures of other members of the family, for each picture that one sees seems to make one better acquainted with "Henry."

. . . I hope Mr. Emerson will have a good account to render of his Western trip. We were speaking of him yesterday at dinner. Charley Cooley said he liked both his talks, and really we all liked the way in which he carried himself while he was in our house. Tap that man who was cured of his fear of "snakes" for not many *are* left to give reports of the Concord "loafer." How is Salt's last book selling? Have any Concord folks bought copies beside you. Salt's new life will come next. . . .

238. Henry Salt to S. A. Jones, December 2, 1895.

I am glad you like the "Poems of Nature". I followed the text of Emerson in preference to that of the *Commonwealth* in "Inspiration", because I saw somewhere (I think in Sanborn's *Critic* article) that the changes introduced in the *Commonwealth* were by "another hand" than Thoreau's, presumably that of F.B.S. And I believe the scraps of the poem quoted in *Walden*, &c, bear this out. But of course this sort of editing, without access to the original *MSS*, is poor work at best; I can only hope someone will use the materials properly some day! What is wanted in all cases is what Thoreau wrote, not what his literary friends were good enough to write for him.

I confess there are a few things in the Poems that I can't understand. For example, the three last lines of the third stanza of "Sic Vita"—what *does* it mean? (the "rabble rout", &c). And then the 8th stanza of "Sympathy" may be read in two ways; viz (1) "What matters it, now that we are wise, if we are separated"—i.e. what does separation matter? or (2) What can even wisdom avail us *now,* since we are separated?

As punctuated by Emerson, with a comma after "avails it," the meaning must be the first one; but I have grave doubts whether Thoreau did not mean the second, & whether we do not owe that comma to Emerson's officious care! I have always forgotten to look it up in the *Dial;* in my copy of the *Week* there is no comma; and I fear I made a mistake in following Emerson's punctuation.[1]

248

The book is being favourably noticed in the reviews here. I sent for a copy of one—the *Daily Chronicle*, now the most powerful of the "advanced" London papers.

I have had an interesting letter from Miss Ward, with a photo. of Maria Thoreau, and a lot of information about Henry's "love affair"—nothing new, but some details which will be valuable for the *Life*. She insists that "Sympathy" was originally dedicated, under the title of "The Gentle Boy", to E. Q. Sewall, the brother of Ellen, & that the original *MS*. is now in Mr. Osgood's possession. She encloses, for my perusal, a letter written in 1839 by E.Q.S., then a boy of eleven, & one of Thoreau's pupils at Concord. He says, "I am going to school here now to a Mr. Thoreau, who is a very pleasant schoolmaster"; & proceeds to give an account of a trip in Thoreau's boat. It does not explain however whether Henry or John is primarily referred to, though "his brother" is mentioned. The whole question about the poem "Sympathy" is very puzzling. It seems incredible that Thoreau should have written it of a boy;[2] & yet it is unlike him to use that kind of "blind", if he meant it for the girl. Miss Ward says the boy was extremely like Ellen Sewall; so perhaps this was the attraction, & the compliment was meant somehow to be divided—But I confess I see no light in it!

I quite agree in what you say about Dr. Emerson. It is just what struck me in talking to him.

I have no more news of "The Life". No proofs have arrived yet from the printers, but I suppose they will begin to come before long.

1. Thoreau did not place a comma after "avails it." For a careful modern reading of Thoreau's poetry based on manuscripts, see Carl Bode, ed. *Collected Poems of Henry Thoreau* (Baltimore: Johns Hopkins Press, 1964), pp. 64–66.
2. Salt did not perceive any homoerotic overtones in the poem.

239. S. A. Jones to A. W. Hosmer, December 12, 1895.

* * *

I should not be surprised if the new life of Thoreau turned up any day, for Scott's press does not delay things a moment. I am very curious about the new life, for Mr. Salt has much to correct and I want to see how the truth about Thoreau looks.

The other night I was reading Horace Hosmer's letters and I think I shall typewrite the portions that have historical value so that they may be of use some day to someone. . . .

240. Henry Salt to S. A. Jones, January 4, 1896.

I am much vexed to find what a stupid blunder I have made about the text of "Inspiration". I see that it must have come about thus. Through careless reading of Sanborn's article in the *Critic,* I did not notice it was "Inspiration" which he copied from Miss Thoreau's *MS.,* but thought, presumably, it was the *other* unpublished page of verses ("Prayer", &c) that he was speaking of. Then I fixed my attention on the next sentence, in which he says that any differences in the *Commonwealth* version from Emerson's were caused by "another hand", and got the idea that the "other hand" was F.B.S.'s; especially as he goes on apologetically to say that Miss Thoreau did not object, &c. It is very tiresome; because I said in the Preface that we had returned to the original text!!!

Curiously enough my error was confirmed in my mind by this fact, that the fragments of "Inspiration" quoted in *The Week* (in "Monday") are the same as *Emerson's* text, not Sanborn's! viz:

> "Now chiefly is my natal hour,
> And only now my prime of life".

> "I will not doubt the love untold".

Does not this perhaps show that there must have been *two* authentic *MSS* of the poem? Evidently the differences in this case were not the work of "another hand". Anyhow it partly explains how I got fixed in a wrong impression about the text.[1]

As regards variations in punctuation generally, I do not feel quite so (excuse the unintended pun) compunctious. Each generation to some extent has its own method of punctuation, which renders bygone methods unintelligible. Thoreau seems to have gone in for almost unlimited commas—one at the end of each line, whether it makes sense or not! or perhaps he just let the printers have their way in the matter. The verse you quote from the top of p. 28 in my book is an instance; for how can it possibly be right to have a comma after "doles"? Again, the semi-colon seems now almost a necessity in some places where Thoreau has only the comma.

The only sense I can put on the 7th and 8th stanzas of "Sympathy" is this. When the lovers *were* actually together, all near approach was *(apparently)* nullified by the "stern respect". In reality they were at one, through Sympathy, but the very fact of this oneness prevented them "driving even the simplest bargain". Now they are wiser, & understand things better; but this wisdom is of no avail, because "absence" has separated them.

I think I see, dimly, what is meant; but probably I have quite failed to convey my meaning. The whole poem is very strange, because there is a note of despair in it which I don't remember elsewhere in Thoreau. The production of the original *MS* of "The Gentle Boy", if it exists, might perhaps throw light on the whole affair. At present it is dark indeed.

I have no news to tell you of the *Life*. Not a page of "proofs" has reached me yet, but I hope Scott will really get to work on it soon. I have heard nothing of Bentley's intentions about the remainder of the old edition. The copyright difficulties I feared were on account of Scott's edition clashing with Sanborn's *Life* in the States, but I daresay Messrs. H. & M. would not be disagreeable, especially as the book would help the sale of the Riverside Edn., as you suggest.

There are some references to Thoreau in W. H. Hudson's *Idle Days in Patagonia,* Chapman & Hall, London, 1893. See index. All Hudson's writings are notable, & the title "poet-naturalist" is fairly applicable to him.

There are two American books which I don't think I have ever heard you speak of, and yet you would surely, perhaps do, delight in (1) Herman Melville's "Whale" or "Moby Dick", which I verily believe to be one of *the* great works of American literature. (2) Joaquin Miller's "Life among the Modocs". If you don't know the "Whale", do please forget all the minnows and small fry of life, until you have read & digested him (inverting & avenging the case of Jonah), & tell me what you think! . . .

1. See Carl Bode's text of "Inspiration" in *Collected Poems of Henry Thoreau,* pp. 230–33.

241. S. A. Jones to A. W. Hosmer, February 9, 1896.

* * *

Jefferies interests me in an entirely different manner to Thoreau. As a delineator of farm life in England Jefferies is fearfully true, and he makes a terrible picture. When it comes to the actual *delineation* of Nature I deem him superior to Thoreau. His descriptions are like a rich painting, and he is more of an artist in words than Thoreau. In the ethical part, of course, he is not to be compared with the Concord "loafer." Jefferies' life is a pathetic story, and you should read Walter Besant's "Eulogy of Richard Jefferies"[1] in order to learn the touching story. Mr. Salt's "Study" of Jefferies[2] is also interesting. The mention of these Nature writers leads me to ask if you have read Gilbert White's "Natural History of Selbourne?"[3] Jefferies says it is a book that would have saved him a great deal of time if he had seen it sooner.[4] I have often thought it strange that Thoreau does not mention White, for the book is more than famous. . . .

1. Sir Walter Besant, *The Eulogy of Richard Jefferies* (London: Chatto and Windus, 1888).

2. Henry S. Salt, *Richard Jefferies: A Study* (London: Swan Sonnenschein & Co., 1893).

3. *Natural History and Antiquities of Selborne* (1789).

4. In his preface to the 1887 edition of *Natural History of Selborne,* Richard Jefferies wrote: "I did not come across Mr. White's book till late in the day, when it was, in fact, too late, else this Calendar would have been of the utmost advantage to me." See Gilbert White, *Natural History of Selborne* (London: Walter Scott, 1887), p. xii.

242. Henry Salt to S. A. Jones, March 10, 1896.

* * *

You will see from the enclosed proof that I have been "taking your name in vain" in my Prefatory Note.[1] You will probably indulge in a good swear at my audacity; but with the Atlantic between us I can afford to feel easy on that account. The last proofs—the index—have just passed through my hands, so I really hope the book will be out in two or three weeks at latest. I need not say that a copy will be on its way to you as soon as I can get hold of one.

Carpenter's sex pamphlets are just being reissued in volume form, under the rather fanciful title, "Love's Coming of Age". Bertram Dobell is to be the London publisher. The book consists, I believe, of the three published pamphlets & one new paper (*not* the privately printed one on Homogenic Love). . . .

1. Salt dedicated his 1896 *Life of Henry David Thoreau* to Dr. Jones. The presentation copy is in the University of Michigan Library.

243. S. A. Jones to A. W. Hosmer, March 20, 1896.

* * *

Mr. Salt wrote on the 10th instant and says that he thinks the book will be out in two or three weeks. I am quite anxious to see it, for I think it will be quite an improvement upon the first edition. By leaving out the quotations from Thoreau he will be less hampered in dealing wtih his subject and we will get a better picture of the man Thoreau than we had in the first attempt. Then, again, the errors will be corrected and justice done to the family at last. I am glad to think that owing to my visit to Concord I have been able to do a little towards bringing this about. You can share largely in the satisfaction which this result brings to all who love Thoreau. . . .

244. Henry Salt to S. A. Jones, April 1, 1896.

* * *

Your letter of March 20 arrives today, & is very welcome.

I am just off for a few days to Edward Carpenter's retreat among the Derbyshire hills, & only write this line to tell you that a copy of the new *Life of Thoreau* was sent off on Saturday last, so you should have received it ere this reaches you. I much hope it may meet your approval. Copies have also gone to Mr. Hosmer & Miss Ward.

My only further news is on the back of this sheet.[1]

1. A letter from the publisher John Lane to Salt, dated March 31, 1896: "I am glad to tell you that Houghton Mifflin Co. has sent for another hundred copies of Thoreau's poems, so that although the sales here have been so far from encouraging there is a prospect of the edition eventually selling out through the Boston publishing firm."

245. S. A. Jones to A. W. Hosmer, April 5, 1896.

* * *

I shall look at the bibliography in it [Salt's new Thoreau biography] pretty earnestly for new items, and I have a sneaking notion that I will try and get out one more edition without the errors of the last.

Alas! It will be much work, for I have not kept track of several additions that must be made, and I must go over the book carefully to "spot" the errors into which I fell. However, I will do the best I can: I surely can *omit the errors*, even if I do not get in every item up to date. This once done, and my Thoreau work will end. Poor enough it is, but it was done in love and is my poor best. . . .

I intend to get an extra copy of Salt's new Life of Thoreau to illustrate it with your photos. By the way, when Mr. Salt sends you your complimentary copy don't forget to let me know whether it is one of the "Library Edition." Scott publishes these books in two sizes and the "Library" one is just large enough in page to receive your pictures. I shall get several of them (by purchase, of course) and I will gladly send you one, for I can get them through my bookseller easier than you can. . . .[1]

1. Both Dr. Jones and Alfred Hosmer prepared grangerized editions of Salt's *Life*. The one made by Hosmer is perhaps the triumph of his Thoreau collection. Now in the Concord Free Public Library, it contains many Thoreau manuscripts, as well as those of his intimate friends and early students. Hosmer also collected photographs of almost all of those associated with Thoreau—family, friends, students. Many of the following letters refer specifically to Hosmer's efforts to secure the photographs needed for his volume. We have been unable to locate Dr. Jones's grangerized *Life*.

246. Henry Salt to S. A. Jones, April 19, 1896.

Your letter, received yesterday, with news of your reception and appreciation of the *Life,* gave me much pleasure. I shall look with interest for your further opinion of the book, when you have had more time to judge it, and I need not say how glad I shall be to have any criticisms that may strike you. It is, I believe, a great advance on the first edition, as it really contains more information in less compass; and if I can feel now that it will serviceably "stop the gap", until the arrival (a generation later?) of *the* biographer of Thoreau, who with all the facts and all the manuscripts at his disposal, and a less prejudiced public to write for, shall produce a full and really adequate biography, I am more than satisfied. At any rate we shall have saved *our* generation the reproach of having neglected to make a genuine and coherent study of Thoreau, as far as it was possible to do so. I say "we" because you are really as much responsible for this Life as I am. Not only am I indebted to you on almost every page, but I should probably have lost heart and given up Thoreau-work years ago, had it not been for your encouragement and assistance!

Now with regard to the publishers. Scott seems (very inopportunely) to have given up his New York office, and tells me that *Messrs. Scribner* are acting for him in the matter of this book. I shall be very glad to have any news of what they appear to be doing in the way of advertising and pushing the book in America, if you have means of ascertaining. Meantime Mr. Sanborn, on hearing that the new edition was forthcoming, but before receiving a copy, has written in a friendly way saying that *he* would have no objection to its coming to the States, though he is the author of two *Lives,* the *Familiar Letters* being counted as one. As a matter of fact I don't think the book can be prohibited by Messrs. Houghton, for the reasons which I told you previously (my choice of quotations from the earlier-published works), but we shall see what we shall see! You perhaps will hear something of what is going on, if there is any commotion in Boston and New York!

It happens that my other new book or new edition, *Percy Bysshe Shelley, Poet and Pioneer,* is also in Scribners' hands, so I hope they will try to push the two together. I have not sent you a copy of this, fearing to bore you with Shelley; but if you have the heart to read more of my outrageous insults to the flag of Respectability in art, religion, and morals, you have only to say the word!

If I get any interesting press-notices of the *Thoreau,* I will send you copies; but as the book is a second edition, I doubt if it will be much reviewed. A few notices have already come in.

Sanborn tells me there is to be a gathering in Concord on April 30, when he will act as leader to the shrines of Concord's heroes, and he has asked me to send a letter of greeting which accordingly I have done, taking as my text Emerson's absurd complaint about Thoreau not having ambition enough to "engineer for all America". Perhaps my letter will be printed somewhere, & so come to your notice. I should like you to see it.

I shall be interested to hear what you think of my remarks about Emerson's relations with Thoreau, in the concluding chapter. I suppose the Emersonian clique will not approve of what I said!

247. S. A. Jones to A. W. Hosmer, April 20, 1896.

I received my copy of Salt's Life of Thoreau just the day before you did yours, and I read mine "in a jiffey," if you can tell what a jiffey is. I am glad to see the important errors corrected, but I am disappointed in not seeing Mrs. Thoreau set right with a great deal more emphasis. The fact is, Mr. Salt's hands were tied by sundry literary obligations to F.B.S. I should have "busted" them like a cobweb—and F. B.'s head too, if he had put it in the way.

I touched up Mr. Salt a *leetle* for his tender handling of Sanborn;[1] just enough to let him know that I thought his forbearance a great deal kinder to the living Sanborn than to the injured—and *silent*—dead. I'll be damned twice over if I would use soft-soap when only sand-paper will clean up a dirty job.

But, somehow, the tone of this Life does not warm me up like Mr. Salt's introductory note to his volume of Selections from Thoreau. I wish he could have blown the same sonorous and defiant note in this last book. The truth is, there was such an up-and-downness about Thoreau himself that his every biographer should write of him without gloves. That style does not please Mr. Blake—as I found out, but a man should follow his nature, even if it does lead him to the devil: that's why *his* nature was given him. And, after all, going to the devil isn't a bad thing if that is where one *belongs*. Them's my sentiments, and I shall probably fetch up with the dear, old, much-abused devil one of these days. I don't believe that "cuss" *is* as black as he's painted. . . .

1. Salt did make changes in the 1896 edition to draw a more sympathetic portrait of the elder Thoreaus. For a comparison of Salt's treatments of the Thoreau family, see George Hendrick, "Henry Salt's Biography of Thoreau," *Festschrift Für Helmut Viebrock* (Munich: Karl Pressler, 1974), pp. 227–28. A later letter from Salt to Ernest Vickers reveals the difficulties Salt faced in balancing the estimates of the Thoreau family presented by Sanborn and by Dr. Jones: "I have thought it best to keep out of the fray; and indeed it is very difficult to judge at so great a distance. For example, Col. Higginson once, at my request, got an opinion about the rival pictures of Thoreau's parents—the picture drawn by Mr. Sanborn, & that drawn by Dr. Jones—from some one who had known them well, and the verdict was in Sanborn's favour! This made me feel that one must be careful, as the

same character impresses different minds so differently; though I certainly believe that the appreciative view of a character is more likely to be the true one than the depreciative." Henry Salt to Ernest Vickers, March 10, 1908. (Vickers's collection of correspondence about Thoreau has been acquired by the Rare Book Room of the University of Illinois Library.)

248. S. A. Jones to A. W. Hosmer, May 12, 1896.

* * *

I received the newspaper containing the account of the invasion of that *Cornucopoeia* Club—those boston folks beat the devil on names!—and I (By Thunder, I'm a dead man! I've spelled Boston with a small *b*. Do n't tell anyone for Mercy's sake!) I was glad to receive the paper so that I could see Mr. Salt's letter. He wrote to me that he had written one, and I think F.B.S. has added to his multitudinous shabbinesses by not printing it in full; but the hearers of a part of it found out that Thoreau did something more than engineer berrying parties.

Why in blazes does n't that old Osgood up and make a die of it? Here he is bobbing up from time to time at some anniversary or other when he should be sleeping quietly under the daisies! Confound him; if his sermons are as long-winded as he is, I do n't see how the people stand it: do you? . . .

Do you know how Mr. Blake is? If you have occasion to write to him please tell him that I remember him with the profoundest respect and loyal affection, and that I hope the burden of years may rest upon him as lightly as possible.

He and Mr. Ricketson are well on towards the night that cometh to all. How soon the last ties that bind us to Thoreau will have been broken and the old friends re-united! . . .

249. S. A. Jones to A. W. Hosmer, May 21, 1896.

* * *

The Rowfant Club has in hand a new volume of my editing; some lectures on English Poetry[1] that Lowell delivered in Jan'y and Feb'y, 1855, and which have never been published. A copy will fit on your shelf nicely, and I think you'll enjoy the reading of it. . . .

1. James Russell Lowell, *Lectures on English Poets* (Cleveland: The Rowfant Club, 1897).

250. Henry Salt to S. A. Jones, June 9, 1896 [postcard].

I am sending you some press-notices of the *Thoreau,* of which I have duplicates. If you think of bibliographing any of them (but I doubt if they are worth it), you might perhaps send me the names of those selected, that I may compare the list with mine & see that there are no important omissions. I notice with satisfaction the great advance in appreciation of Thoreau shown by the reviewers. Several of the papers that were most hostile in 1890 have quietly come round to the other view in 1896, especially the *National Observer,* a strong Tory paper. I trust you will have received copies of the *Vegetarian Review,* with an article of mine on Thoreau,[1] and the *British Friend,* a Quaker organ.

1. "Among the Authors: Henry David Thoreau," *Vegetarian Review,* May 1896, pp. 225–28.

251. Henry Salt to S. A. Jones, July 6, 1896.

* * *

I was much interested in what you told me of your plan of collecting Thoreau photographs, to illustrate the *Life.* Mr. Hosmer has very kindly been sending me some more photos. of Concord scenes, and I much wish I could get some illustrated magazine to reproduce them.

The only Thoreau item I have for you (and you probably have it) is this. "Idyllists of the Country-Side, being six commentaries concerning some of those who have apostrophised the Joys of the Open Air", by George H. Ellwanger—1896. (New York, Dodd, Mead, & Co—London, George Bell & Sons.) Chapter on "The Sphere of Thoreau", pp. 171–218. I can't say I find the book very interesting. There is also a chapter on "Afield with Jefferies".

How terrible must be Channing's death-in-life at Concord, of which you speak! Thirty-four years since Thoreau died, and he still there! If it be true, as Mr. Sanborn once told me, that C. still mourns constantly for his friend, surely it is one of the world's strangest instances of a pathetic though morbid faithfulness. One does not like to think harshly of *any* faithful love, when such love is all too rare; but there seems something very contrary to the spirit of Thoreau's teaching in this phantom flitting round scenes which belong to the past. However I suppose Channing's genius was always thus morbid and introspective. I cannot see the great things in his poetry that Mr. Sanborn sees; though some of the epigrams in his *Thoreau* are certainly wonderful.

I have once or twice lately run across Dr. Japp ("H. A. Page"), a kindly old man enough, who haunts the British Museum and such places. I don't think his interest in Thoreau nowadays is of a very volcanic nature, though I believe he *did* fire up a bit, did he not, at something you wrote! I rather wish some of the younger generation of writers, in this country, would rally to my aid, in the attempt to win Thoreau his due. I am afraid W. H. Dircks has lost his interest in the matter; but no doubt the time and the man will come. . . .

252. S. A. Jones to A. W. Hosmer, July 8, 1896.

I wonder if there is any end to your benefactions? It would seem not. Only the other day it was an invoice of views, and to-day there comes a likeness of Thoreau's aunt Jane. It made me feel sort of creepy to get so near to those who were with him daily. Do you know, I have so sort of soaked in Thoreau materials that I should open a new book about him with little expectation of finding out anything new. For the past six and a half years you and I have been "grubbing" so industriously that the subject is pretty well sifted. It makes me say to myself, 'After all, what a little of the really solid there is in life.' What I mean by solid is the few events that really stand out in one's life; such items as Thoreau's going to jail, and his defense of John Brown.

The mention of Thoreau's jailing makes me take a peep at "Aunt Maria." Poor Maria; paying the taxes and making Thoreau "mad as hell" because her doing that tended to make his 'imprisonment' ridiculous; he had n't suffered enough to make the deed sublime.

You must have observed that aunt Jane looks far more like Thoreau than does his aunt Maria. The nose is the feature wherein the family resemblance appears. I have always liked a man with a good hook to his face—and Thoreau's nose is just a triumph in that line. . . .

O Fred, I was much pleased to receive Edmund Hosmer's picture—though a larger one of him would give a better idea of the man: still, the one I have leaves me no longer to my own imagination. I can see from his strong face why Emerson took to him as he did; but a talk with 'the long-headed farmer' would be better than any number of pictures. This reminds me that in illustrating a Life of Thoreau it will be wise to include as many *likenesses of persons mentioned* as possible. It is the *human* that interests, after all. Scenery is nice, but the living, thinking man—that is what 'takes the cake.' . . .

Is there a picture of Edward Hoar; of his sister Elizabeth—she gave Thoreau his inkstand. Is Elizabeth Peabody to be had on paper? Parker Pillsbury figures in Thoreau's life, and O Fred, it would be a good thing to borrow that picture of John Brown that is (or was) in the Antiquarian Rooms. A copy of that marked, "Taken from the lithograph in Thoreau's possession" would give it unusual interest. When you are some day in Boston, please find me a good picture of J. R. Lowell—that must go into the book.

Mr. Salt recently sent me a lot of newspaper clippings—reviews of his life of T. and I tell you the English people are changing their opinion of Thoreau. The altered tone is very marked, and it must be gratifying to Mr. S. to think how much he has done towards bringing this about. . . .

253. S. A. Jones to A. W. Hosmer, July 16, 1896.

Yours of the 14th inst. is just at hand, and I am electrified at your last find. Wouldn't it be "bully" if you should also get the picture of Thoreau's mother? Look into the history of that supposed portrait of John Thoreau, Jr.[1] It will add greatly to the general interest if you have really got his portrait—the beloved brother!

I am delighted to learn that you have really "got" that old curmudgeon of a Channing. I shall look upon Elizabeth Hoar's shadow with a great deal of reverence, if you are able to obtain it. . . .

1. The only known portrait of John Thoreau, Jr., is that painted by his sister Sophia. It is now in the Concord Antiquarian Society. For a photograph of the portrait, see Walter Harding, *The Days of Henry Thoreau*, p. 109.

254. S. A. Jones to A. W. Hosmer, August 2, 1896.

Since you heard from me someone has sent me Pillsbury's photo, with his autograph, and "picters" of Emerson, Alcott, and Benjamin Franklin Sanborn. I know he writes it "F.B.S.," but I'll bet a cookie he was christened "Benjamin Franklin."[1]

If you know the chap who sent these things give him the thanks that I have no words to express.

It was a surprise to me that Abbott's book did not set you on fire. I mean, of course, the chapter on Thoreau.[2] Such a bold defense, and such a downright reproval of such dignities as Emerson and Lowell,[3] and you as quiet as a musquash in the Musketaquid!

I wonder what F.B.S. thought of it? I wonder if he begins to suspect that Thoreau is going to overshadow both R.W.E. and J.R.L.? It's coming, just the same, and I think Sanborn will trim his sails accordingly.

By the way, if you can find out what number of the "Independent"[4] contains the editor's condemnation of Abbott I would like to know it, for it would afford one a good chance to "go for" that toadying editor. . . .

1. Walter Harding writes on this point: "Dr. Jones should win his cookie. Sanborn was supposed to have been named 'Benjamin Franklin,' but his father was so excited when he registered the birth that he got the names down backward" (letter dated May 6, 1977).

2. Charles C. Abbott, *Notes of the Night, and Other Outdoor Sketches* (New York: Century Co., 1896).

3. Abbott answered at length Emerson's charge that Thoreau lacked ambition and contended that Lowell was temperamentally unfit to evaluate Thoreau.

4. A review in the *New York Independent* for July 19, 1896, praised Abbott's writing on nature but did not "rate him high as a literary critic. Lowell knew more about Thoreau than Dr. Abbott does and was far better equipped to estimate his character, his work, and his place in literature."

255. S. A. Jones to A. W. Hosmer, August 11, 1896.

I am very glad to get Louisa Dunbar's picture[1] despite the "false front" that offends Miss Hosmer. It shows very clearly that Thoreau resembled his mother's side of the house. He has a Dunbar nose beyond doubt.

I should say that Daniel Webster might have done worse than marrying Miss Dunbar.[2] Her bold profile gives me something of an idea of the source of Thoreau's independence, and I hope that Louisa resembled her sister, Mrs. Thoreau.

It was the fact that you mentioned having read Abbott's book, *without one word of comment* upon it, that made me wonder.

You are more fortunate than I in your dealings with Dr. Abbott.[3] I wrote him warmly about his book, but he never replied—perhaps he is too modest!

I envy Mr. Salt his feelings when he reads Abbott's chapter. I sent him a copy and shall be hearing whether it hit the mark, one of these days. . . .

1. Louisa Dunbar, sister of Cynthia Thoreau.

2. In his 1882 biography of Thoreau, F. B. Sanborn devoted several pages to the romantic affection which Webster supposedly felt for Louisa Dunbar before he married Grace Fletcher. See *Henry D. Thoreau*, pp. 13–18.

3. There are eight letters from Charles C. Abbott to Alfred Hosmer in the Hosmer collection. In the earliest of these, July 22, 1896, Abbott commented on Lowell's assessment of Thoreau: "Lowell's attitude was that of a spiteful child and he was utterly incompetent to deal sincerely with anything outside of his own aristocratic circle." See Charles C. Abbott to A. W. Hosmer, July 22, 1896 (Hosmer collection).

256. S. A. Jones to A. W. Hosmer, August 18, 1896.

Another invoice from Concord! By Thunder! What am I to do? Miss Peabody's picture makes one feel old to look at it; she reaches back into antiquity. Lowell's nose is the feature wherein he fails. No man with such a nose could comprehend Thoreau. John Thoreau(?). What is the history of that picture? Surely, Mrs. Bigelow could say if it at all resembles John Thoreau. The nose makes me suspect it. The Dunbars had good-sized noses, but were the Thoreaus ornamented in that way. John and Helen were said to be "clear Thoreau; Henry and Sophia clear Dunbar."[1] Now, to me, John's picture has the Louisa Dunbar type of nose. But I knows so little about this matter that I'll let it alone.

I received the "Transcript" this morning. My detestation of Sanborn is such that I could not read his paper[2] with any pleasure.

I do not believe Emerson and Thoreau quarrelled as Sanborn intimates.[3] Thoreau was not vulgar enough for that; and I think Emerson would have been a hard one to pick a quarrel with. He was n't built that way.

I should like to know what the son of his father thinks of Sanborn's paper. If Sanborn publishes his paper at full length it must be had for the bibliography.

I am daily expecting to hear of Blake's death, and then Sanborn will have the Thoreau journals to bedevil at his own sweet will. I wonder what he will make of them? . . .

1. Sanborn, *Henry D. Thoreau*, p. 8.
2. "The Greenacre School: Emerson Day," *Boston Transcript*, August 15, 1896. The article reports an address by Sanborn.
3. In his lecture Sanborn had contended that Emerson and Thoreau were so diametrically opposite in heredity and manner that conflict between them was unavoidable.

257. S. A. Jones to A. W. Hosmer, September 6, 1896.

At this writing I have two more invoices from Concord to acknowledge. I am glad Jonas Minott thought enough of his second-hand wife to have her face-outline cut in paper, and I am as glad that he added his to it.[1] I am quite taken with his outline. In the smaller nose of his wife I can see a promise of the vivacity that characterized Henry's mother.

I looked upon Sophia's picture with something of awe—the awe that is akin to reverence. She answers my expectations fully: that is, she looks as Thoreau's sister should look. The thought of her services during that last illness comes over me and I would much rather think about it than write. . . .

1. In 1798 Captain Jonas Minott married Thoreau's maternal grandmother Mary Jones Dunbar (1748–1830), whose husband Asa Dunbar had died in 1787. See Walter Harding, *The Days of Henry Thoreau*, pp. 6–7.

258. A. W. Hosmer to S. A. Jones, September 16, 1896.

I send you today a picture of Henry Thoreau's father, his likeness follows out Horace Hosmer's description rather more than it does Sanborn's. The one with her hand at her cheek is Helen Thoreau.[1]

Both of these are from daguerreotypes, that were loaned me by Miss Lowell of Bangor. I have not yet succeeded in finding a picture of Mrs. Thoreau, but am in hopes to some day.

The copy of a miniature is Mrs. Prudence Ward,[2] at the age of 21, and the fourth is Miss Prudence Ward. She was the one that Thoreau referred to in his "Week" as the friend he wished he was able to send word to of the blossoming of the Hibiscus; and it was through Ellen Sewall's visiting Mrs. Ward, while she was boarding with Thoreau's Aunts, that Henry lost his heart. . . .

1. For photographs of John Thoreau, Sr., and of Helen Thoreau, see Walter Harding, *The Days of Henry Thoreau*, p. 109.
2. Prudence Ward boarded for many years with the Thoreau family. Her sister was Caroline Sewall, the mother of Ellen and Edmund. It was while visiting Prudence and her mother Mrs. Joseph Ward in July, 1839, that Ellen Sewall became the object of Henry Thoreau's love. See Walter Harding, *The Days of Henry Thoreau*, pp. 73, 94–104. For a photograph of Prudence Ward, see Milton Meltzer and Walter Harding, *A Thoreau Profile* (Concord, Mass.: Thoreau Foundation, 1976), p. 6.

259. S. A. Jones to A. W. Hosmer, September 20, 1896.

How the picture of John Thoreau refutes Sanborn's mean estimate of him. Evidently a close-mouthed man both literally and figuratively, but not a common man. An open face, with thought in it: a good, capacious brow, and a general air of solidity—far different bit of flesh to that known amongst men as F.B.S.!

Helen's picture is disappointing in its plainness, but with her soul looking out of her eyes all may have been changed for those who knew her in the flesh.

Prudence Ward has no interest for me at all, other than to show how "solid" all Thoreau's friends were. There is no frivolity about the calm and serious face of the old lady, and it was the affinities that made her and Thoreau friends.

How I do hope that you will find a picture of Thoreau's mother in your net one of these days. I can't see Henry in his father's photo; but the Dunbar-Minot face may show it. . . .

260. S. A. Jones to A. W. Hosmer, October 4, 1896.

Philip G. Hubert, Jr., Esq., is splendidly misinformed about Thoreau, is n't he?[1]

When was the "cuss" in town, for he surely saw you, I judge. What leads him to say that James T. Fields bought the 700 sheets of the "Week" from Sophia Thoreau?[2]

Hubert gets all his knowledge of that "first edition" from my Bibliog. but why does he go on to contradict what I had written.

We do not learn that Thoreau made a will; or that any special bequest of the unbound sheets of the "Week" was made to Sophia. If not so transferred, of course the ownership of them vested in the then head of the Thoreau household.

But Mr. Hubert is so far "off" in other Thoreau matters that it is not worth while to contradict him.

No "pencils" were made after the death of the father,[3] for the stamp "John Thoreau and Son" would no longer apply. The business that Thoreau conducted after his father's death was the preparing of levigated plumbago; and I have always understood that Sophia continued operations on that line after her brother's death.

As Thoreau is happily mentioned in one of Mr. Hubert's books, "Liberty and a Living,"[4] I have almost a mind to write to him and gently correct his rampant errors. But it is likely he will resent having his corns filed and I should get only a Damn you! for my pains. . . .

1. "Thoreau's Concord," *New York Tribune,* September 13, 1896.
2. Hubert argued that Fields had written to Sophia in 1862, asking "if her brother had left copies of the book. Sophia sold him the lot."
3. Hubert had written: "As most readers will remember, Thoreau, after his father's death in 1857, took up the family trade, that of pencil making, and carried it on until failing health compelled him to stop work."
4. Phillip G. Hubert, *Liberty and a Living* (New York: G. P. Putnam's Sons, 1889).

261. A. W. Hosmer to S. A. Jones, October 8, 1896.

P. G. Hubert, Jr. *did* call on me, it was his first visit to Concord, and I only saw him for an hour or so—and finding him much interested in Thoreau, I, of course, began talking about him, and found that he only knew him from his readings. The consequence was that I gave him so many *new* items that he got badly mixed. I have corrected him on the plumbago question but said nothing of the others, so if you wish to write him, you will find him at Bellport, N.Y. Guess he will take it all right.[1]

My enlargement of Salt's "Life" will make 2 vols. I already have about 20 views or portraits ready to go in, quotations and all, and about as many more ready for the quotations. The books have not yet shown up, but I expect them this week.

I was speaking to Walton Ricketson, the son of Dan'l, and he is to get me a view of his father's shanty, and house in New Bedford. He also suggested that I come up to his studio and photograph Thoreau's flute, spy glass, and copy of Wilson's ornithology, which I shall be very much pleased to do.

Have just had a call from the lady with whom Blake boards. She says he gets out to walk every day, for a short distance, but is very feeble, and does but little on the Thoreau Mss.—says F.B.S. is in correspondence with him and supposes he will have the Mss. when Blake is through. I told [her] I hoped he would *not,* and gave my reasons for so hoping.

I only wish there were some way of keeping them out of Sanborn's hands. . . .

1. Hubert had used information from Hosmer in his article "Thoreau's Concord."

262. S. A. Jones to A. W. Hosmer, October 16, 1896.

Mr. Philip G. Hubert, Jr., is not the kind of man I want to correspond with. He is evidently an unscrupulous newspaper scribbler who regards not the proprieties of literature, and who as little concerns himself with the verities of life. More than one reader of Thoreau will cut out that newspaper article of his, and the misrepresentations will go down in their memories uncorrected.

It is no small offence to appropriate facts from another investigator without acknowledgement; but to mis-state the facts of another is even worse.

There is no other printed source for his information about those editions of the "Week" than my bibliography,[1] and the use Mr. Hubert has made of it is such that I should as soon think of associating with a common pickpocket as with him. I wish him better manners and whistle him down the wind. . . .

1. In his "Thoreau's Concord" Hubert gave a history of the first edition of *A Week,* which he prefaced with this comment: "In connection with 'The Week,' the following information has probably not yet appeared in print." Dr. Jones had originally published the history in "An Afternoon in the University Library," which he had reprinted in his 1894 bibliography.

263. A. W. Hosmer to S. A. Jones, October 20, 1896.

I mail you today a photograph of yourself, mounted on one of the sheets for my "Life of Thoreau" with illustrations—and would like very much if you would kindly add your autograph to it, and remail it to me. I have ready, about 50 views and portraits with, on the views quotations from Thoreau, and with the portraits a quotation from them, as to what they have written about Thoreau. In addition I have about as many more ready for the quotations.

In the view of Thoreau's grave I have quoted the whole of your poem from "Thoreau's Inheritance."[1]

Am glad to hear that Houghton Mifflin & Co are at last to issue an illustrated copy of Thoreau—but am sorry that they have taken Cape Cod.[2] Walden would have been much better. I think I ought to have the credit of their starting that work, for three years ago I offered, if they would illustrate some of his works, (and I then suggested Walden,) to *give* them the use of my negatives, and also to take such other pictures as they would need, and give the use of them—at that time "they had made all arrangements for their Christmas books—and did not care to take hold of the work just then, thanked me, & if they ever decided to illustrate would let me know &c. &c. &c."

Had a call yesterday from Mr. Dawes. He came just after I had left home (for I am having my vacation now) to go out & get a photo of Thoreau's Flute—Spy glass & copy of Wilson's Ornthology—but he called again at 1. and after a talk at home I went with him to Walden & Fairhaven Cliffs.

I shall not object in the least if you will add a few words about Thoreau to your autograph.[3]

1. For the text of Dr. Jones's poem, see note 1 to Jones's letter to Hosmer of March 17, 1891, letter 49.
2. Houghton, Mifflin issued a two-volume *Cape Cod* in 1896 with illustrations from sketches by Amelia M. Watson.
3. Dr. Jones signed his photograph "Thoreau-ly yours, Sam'l. A. Jones."

264. Henry Salt to S. A. Jones, October 21, 1896.

* * *

I am now sending you a cutting from the current *Athenaeum,* to wit, a belated review of the "Poems of Nature", which bears some internal evidence of being written by Theodore Watts, or Theodore Watts-Dunton, as he now calls himself. It is not a very generous notice, but it is at least a tribute to the recognition of Thoreau's greatness as writer, if not as poet.[1] I thought the recent notice in the N.Y. *Critic* also very satisfactory in that respect. Doubtless you saw the *Critic,*[2] & a paper in the October *Dial,*[3] of which a copy was sent me by the author. This, I thought, was written too much from the purely literary point of view, and thus failed of its effect, though showing a good deal of insight here and there.

Mr. Hosmer has written to me once or twice, and sent more photographs, some of them, such as those of John Thoreau senior, & junior, extremely interesting. I have not yet begun *my* illustrated copy of the Life. How does yours proceed? . . .

1. Salt sent "Review of Poems of Nature," *Athenaeum*, October 17, 1896, pp. 517–18; "American Diogenes," *Literary World*, July 7, 1896; and a brief review of *Life of Henry David Thoreau* from *Bookseller*.
2. "Life of Henry David Thoreau," *Critic* 29 (September 19, 1896):172.
3. Hiram M. Stanley, "Thoreau as a Prose Writer," *Dial* 21 (October 1, 1896):179–82.

265. S. A. Jones to A. W. Hosmer, October 25, 1896.

I duly sent back the picture of that homely cuss you forwarded, and I return the stamps because, as I told you once before, Massachusetts' stamps will not go in Michigan. Bear this in mind in future!

Your double-barrelled book will be a most interesting collection, and it should find its way to some large library when you have got done with books and other matters here below.

Beside my autograph, I put on your picture all that seemed to me appropriate. It has also the advantage of being the plain truth, for it tells that in two directions.

How were you impressed by Mr. Dawes? I should like to have gone 'round with you two. From his letters, I should say he is not one to "gush." He impressed me as a sensible, level-headed chap whose silent admiration for Thoreau is worth far more than the effervescent enthusiams of more demonstrative disciples.

Mr. Dawes was very useful, too, in getting up that volume of "first editions" that we put in the Concord Free Library.

I think I shall leave all my Thoreau gatherings to the University Library when I get through with earthly matters. Then I hope the writings of the Concord philosopher will find their way into many a young heart after mine is only insensate dust. . . .

266. A. W. Hosmer to S. A. Jones, November 2, 1896.

The *autograph* came back all right—much obliged to you for it. Mr. Blake & Mr. Ricketson kindly added theirs, and I have sent a sheet to Col. T. W. Higginson, and shall send one to Burroughs for theirs.

I will mail you in a day or two, a picture of Thoreau's "flute, spyglass and Wilson's Ornithology."[1] The white cloth, which is the flute case, was made by Lucretia Mott's daughter, out of cotton cloth, the cotton for which was raised on their place in Anti-Slavery times, as Mrs. Mott, objected to using any thing raised by unpaid, and slave labor.

I have lately had two notes from Mr. Blake, about a month apart, and they show a great change in the handwriting, the first very clear, while it was a task to decipher the latter. It looked as though he might have had another shock, though I have heard nothing to that effect.

I had a Thoreau lover here from Danbury Conn.[2] yesterday and took a drive around town with him—we called on a gentleman who was one of John Thoreau's scholars, and in the course of conversation, his wife said that he boarded with Mrs. Thoreau & was always quoting Mrs. T. to her & that he was very fond of her. I asked him if he ever saw any thing in Mrs. T. that would lead him to call her a "gossip and scandal monger," he looked at me half a minute, the tears came to his eyes, and he answered, No! The gentleman who was with me, in speaking of it after we left, said it was the *strongest* answer, he had ever heard made. Mr. Thoreau, this gentleman said, was rather quiet, but if he believed a thing was right, and others differed with him, he would discuss the question so with them, that he would soon convince them they were wrong.

Mr. Dawes sent me last week a copy of "Echoes from Harpers Ferry,"[3] it arrived on the 30*th*. the anniversary of Thoreau's delivering his "Plea for Capt. Brown," in the Church vestry, and we had that for our reading last night, Nov. 1*st*. . . .

1. For this photograph see Meltzer and Harding, *A Thoreau Profile,* p. 25.
2. We are unable to identify the Thoreau-lover from Danbury, Connecticut.
3. James Redpath, *Echoes of Harper's Ferry* (Boston: Thayer and Eldridge, 1860). This volume includes both "A Plea for Captain John Brown" and "Remarks at Concord on the Day of the Execution of John Brown" (later entitled "After the Death of John Brown").

267. A. W. Hosmer to S. A. Jones, November 28, 1896.

My book is getting on in great shape—I have lately had sent me a photograph of both Dr. A. H. Japp[1] & Moncure D. Conway[2]—and have written to see if I can get one of Cholmondeley. If it will be of any help to you I will give you a list of the views I have, with the quotations I have used. I sent to Ricketson, Higginson and Burroughs as I did to you, and each one returned the photo with their autograph & also a few words in regard to Thoreau. Sanborn & Blake gave their autographs.

The Rev. Geo. W. Cooke who wrote a life of Emerson,[3] wrote me today to make arrangements to call on me some evening and talk about Thoreau, and also to look over what papers I had about him, to use in a book he is to write.

Do you ever see the Atlantic Monthly, if not let me know and I will send you the Dec. number which has a very good article on Thoreau by Bradford Torrey.[4]

I hear Sanborn is to write for the New England Magazine on the same subject and it will be illustrated. I hear this from out of town and am rather interested to see whether he comes to me for views, or if he uses any of mine without giving me credit for them, which would be very much like him. . . .

1. Under the pseudonym H. A. Page, Dr. A. H. Japp (1837–1905) published *Thoreau: His Life and Aims* (Boston: J. R. Osgood & Co., 1877).

2. Moncure Daniel Conway had treated Thoreau sympathetically in *Emerson at Home and Abroad* (Boston: James R. Osgood & Co., 1882).

3. George Willis Cooke, *Ralph Waldo Emerson: His Life, Writings, and Philosophy* (Boston: J. R. Osgood & Co., 1881).

4. Bradford Torrey, "Thoreau," *Atlantic Monthly* 78 (December 1896):822–32.

268. S. A. Jones to A. W. Hosmer, December 3, 1896.

* * *

I should like to meet Cooke and have a laugh with him (and at him) for dropping me after a letter I wrote him soon after my "Glimpse" was published.

I do not see the "Atlantic," but a paper by Bradford Torrey must be interesting. And Sanborn is going to coin some more money out of his acquaintance with Thoreau! Just wait and see how much more respectfully he will treat Thoreau now that the tide of popularity is setting in his way! Faugh!

I bought a copy of "Cape Cod" for four dollars, and have ever since wished that "Walden" was the subject. They may get round to that before they have done with Thoreau. The "Maine Woods" would also lend itself finely to the artist.

Meanwhile, how Thoreau is coming to the front and Emerson going silently to the rear. I shall always be grateful that I was amongst the early ones who *saw* Thoreau, and that my visit to Concord helped to clear the cloud that false biographing had raised. By the way, Horace Hosmer's picture should go into your book labelled "One of Thoreau's pupils". . . .

269. A. W. Hosmer to S. A. Jones, December 10, 1896.

Cholmondeley's photograph arrived this week.[1]

I carried my books in to show to Garrison, at Houghton Mifflin & Co.—both he and another gentleman seemed much interested in it. G. suggested using some of the pictures to illustrate Walden, while the other one thought that a book of pictures with quotations as I have them, or else to take Salt's "Life" and use most all my illustrations. They are to think it over and let me know later in regard to it. One of them suggested my leaving the books there for a few days, but I was not willing, and G. remarked that he should not want to if he owned the books, on account of the autograph letters in it.

I mailed you an "Atlantic" yesterday. I was sorry to see that Torrey let that one paragraph in regard to Mrs. T. as a gossip, creep in,[2] and wrote to him at once; he "supposed Sanborn was authentic on that subject, and had never heard that his writing had been disputed—was sorry not to have known it before he wrote his article, as in that case he would not have allowed it to enter."[3] He is at Wellesley Hills.

I hear that Mr. Blake is failing fast, is losing his mind, and is very feeble. . . .

1. Cholmondeley's photograph has been published in Walter Harding, *The Days of Henry Thoreau,* p. 364.
2. Echoing Sanborn's earlier charges, Torrey wrote that Cynthia Thoreau "had some reputation as a gossip."
3. Hosmer's letter apparently had the desired effect, for Torrey characterized Mrs. Thoreau much more sympathetically in his introduction to the 1897 edition of *Walden.*

270. S. A. Jones to A. W. Hosmer, December 18, 1896.

I read Mr. Torrey's paper with the same regret that you felt. It is more than a pity that so fine an appreciation of Thoreau should be deformed by that slur upon his mother, which is not true. Alas! That lie of Sanborn's is long-lived and long-legged and it will deceive others as it has done Mr. Torrey.

If you ever get a chance show Mr. Torrey my Lippincott's paper, and tell him how it is backed by the Concord people who knew Mrs. Thoreau. Some day Mr. Torrey may have a chance to undo his perpetuation of so mean a libel.

You took my breath away when you wrote that you had secured Cholmondeley's photo. By Thunder! I believe you could get Father Adam's if you set out to do so.

Your book will knock mine out of sight, for you have obtained pictures that I can not hope to secure. The *human* pictures in your collection give the book a greater charm, to me, than all the landscapes, precious as those are.

Jerusalem! If Houghton, Mifflin & Co. would only reproduce Salt's "Life" with the illustrations that you have gotten it would make the "Cape Cod" book shrink into insignificance. And how it would both please and help Mr. Salt! The publishers could certainly count on quite a sale for that book among Thoreau's English readers—a body that is constantly on the increase.

I hope Mr. Blake may have an easy translation; the weight of years is a heavy burden and he has borne it for long. Peace to him and strength to hold up serenely until his release comes.

I am so glad that I met him, and if you will let me know of his demise I will write an obituary notice of him for our college paper. Find out if you can *some* facts of his life; his place of birth, anything that will help me. . . .

I say wouldn't my Bibliography make a "bully" book if it had a photo, as far as they can be had, of those who have written about Thoreau. By George! It makes me feel like going to work at the awful job of correcting the errors of the Rowfant edition, and of writing it up to date.

I will enquire tomorrow about a publisher, and if I can find one I believe that idea will be carried out, and not in a limited edition.

Tell me what you think of the "notion."

I am more and more convinced that Thoreau will continue to grow, while Emerson will become more and more of a back number. Thoreau's sincerity will wear longer than the charm of Emerson's personality. And how nice it is that Thoreau should have been born in Concord—the only one of the Concord group that has that distinction. . . .

271. Henry Salt to S. A. Jones, December 29, 1896.

* * *

You will have received, some time before this reaches you, an extract which I sent you from an English paper, recording a visit to Concord, and talks with Emerson's son, &c. I have forgotten the name of the writer—it was no one I knew—and have been wondering if it was Nicholson, as Mr. Hosmer tells me that he hears some Englishman of that name is writing a Life of Thoreau.[1] I have heard nothing of this, but shall be glad if it is true, as there is plenty of room at present for more "appreciations". I don't think there has been anything more in the Thoreau line, over here, since I last wrote; but the article in the *Atlantic Monthly*[2] was deserving of notice.

Mr. Sanborn informs me that Mr. Blake is now extremely feeble, & that his death may be expected at any time. He (Sanborn) had seen him on Dec. 3rd, and found him quite invalided. "The journals of Thoreau are in his room, on his bookshelves, as they have been for 20 years"; but he will be able to do no more work at them. I suppose Mr. Sanborn will have the journals at Mr. B.'s death, but he does not allude to this in his letter.

I am glad to learn from Mr. Hosmer that Messrs. Houghton are beginning to turn their attention to the need of *illustrating* Thoreau. I have long hoped for this.

My time is, as usual, mostly taken up with the work of the Humanitarian League, which is growing considerably year by year. In addition to that, I do a little journalism, mostly monthly book-notices for the *Vegetarian Review,* which is a convenient and not too laborious way of earning a few guineas. I have no book in hand at present, and no particular literary plans. I should be glad if I could do anything more to make Thoreau known in England, but it is no use trying to "force the pace", and the result of the volume of Prose Selections was not encouraging. By and bye there may be opportunities for more articles.

1. Salt sent a copy of W. Robertson Nicoll's "A Visit to Salem and Concord," *British Weekly,* December 10, 1896, p. 137. Nicoll (1851–1923), was a prolific writer, but he did not write a biography of Thoreau.
2. Undoubtedly Bradford Torrey, "Thoreau," *Atlantic Monthly* 78 (December 1896):822–32.

272. S. A. Jones to A. W. Hosmer, January 3, 1897.

* * *

How much more like "Sam" Staples the last picture looks! The bright sunlight made him shut his peepers, and that gives a quizzical look to him; but when I had my talk with him, his eyes were as wide open as any man's.

What chiefly attracted my notice was that, although his linen was none of the cleanest, he had a great diamond stud flashing on his shirt front!

As he talked with me I *felt* the qualities that had enabled him to feather his nest so comfortably,—'cuteness and thrift; an eye for the main chance, and a genius for a bargain. For these he had Emerson's esteem. I am certain that a kinship in these features made Emerson esteem him; and I feel quite assured that these qualities in Emerson made "Sam" Staples regard him as a "good fellow."

Well, peace to the ashes of Samuel Staples! He treated Thoreau kindly when he had him in the "coop": but little did Staples dream that the locking up of Henry Thoreau was his one chance for immortality.

I hope that the Houghton, Mifflin house may decide upon the illustrated book, and it's possible that the sale of their pictured "Cape Cod" may lead-insure it. Why, our bookseller told me with some surprise that twelve copies had been sold in Ann Arbor!

I don't for a moment suppose they would let an unknown writer prepare the sketch of Thoreau for it, nor do I think I am the fit one to do it. I would suggest that they get Mr. Salt, who has earned the *right* to do it, and who would be helped by doing it, as it would introduce him to the American people. Do put in a word for him. . . .

I am not surprised at what you write of Emerson's treatment of Sanborn. When he was here Mr. Emerson told me that he had to turn his back on Sanborn. He did not go into any details, but he gave me to understand that Sanborn had done something which was not to be overlooked. He expressed regret at having to "break" with a "fellow townsman," as he said, but he did it effectually.

From all that I have learned, it is likely that the name, "literary thief" is a good fit.

How much there is in Alcott's grandson's[1] forbidding Sanborn access to his library. It hints at papers that might be "borrowed" without the trouble of asking, and disclosures that would be damaging to "Plato Skimpole". . . .

1. Probably Frederick Alcott Pratt, son of Anna Bronson Alcott Pratt and John B. Pratt.

273. S. A. Jones to A. W. Hosmer, January 28, 1897.

Chamberlin's paper in the "Atlantic" denotes the slow but sure growth of Thoreau's reputation,[1] and I think the fulness of time will bring a monument of Thoreau's greatness into the Common at Concord. . . .

Dircks' picture will go appropriately into your "Thoreau", but I do not see any really deserved place for that of Mr. Carpenter. Mr. Salt is just "stuck" on him, but Carpenter's brief mention of Thoreau[2] does not justify placing him in your book. Your own photo most surely belongs there and you must not let any false modesty lead you to omit it. . . .

1. Joseph Edgar Chamberlin, "Memorials of American Authors," *Atlantic Monthly* 79 (January 1897):64–72.
2. Edward Carpenter mentioned Thoreau briefly in *England's Ideal* (London: Swan Sonnenschein, Lowrey & Co., 1887).

274. Henry Salt to S. A. Jones, February 5, 1897.

* * *

I have just received a copy of the illustrated *Cape Cod* from Messrs. Houghton & Mifflin, and have written to thank them for the gift. I don't know whether this is the same copy of the book as that to which you refer, or whether you intended to send me one from yourself; but anyhow I am convicted now of being already in possession of one, so *don't* send off another if you receive this warning in time! I am sure I have had enough presents from my friend at Ann Arbor, without his sending more; but for the kind thought, all thanks! It was the first time Messrs. H. & M. have done me a compliment of that sort, so I was duly flattered. I like the book and the illustrations very much, and hope, as you say, that it may lead to more illustrated volumes. I have been much interested in hearing of Mr. Hosmer's *magnum opus,* and have been trying to get him some English photographs for it. In asking W. H. Dircks for his portrait, I took the opportunity of enquiring about the sale of my *Life* (Mr. Dircks is one of Walter Scott's managers), but have had no reply from him as yet. I have heard of the *Life* in a good many places, but doubt its having sold very largely, as compared with most in the series.

In return for that remark about the savour of roast beef at your table, I am going to send you my pamphlet on the "Humanities of Diet". I would readily endure that savour, however,—yes, & the savour of a cannibal banquet à la Typee,—if I could have the luck to find my toes under your table (or yours under mine) as you picture it![1]

1. Dr. Jones was a convert to vegetarianism for a time, but he soon returned to eating meat.

275. S. A. Jones to A. W. Hosmer, February 15, 1897.

* * *

I am glad you have written that paper on the life pictures of Thoreau,[1] for it is done out of the fulness of knowledge, as all such matters should be. . . .

1. This paper has not been found.

276. S. A. Jones to A. W. Hosmer, March 15, 1897.

* * *

The brakes are on in the Salt-Jones correspondence, and the train is going very slowly. You see, he has so much to do with his "Humanitarian" business that I felt it a downright robbery to keep him writing to so useless a chap as yours truly. When anything of note comes within my ken I shall let him know of it D.Q.; but what you don't get is little likely to fall into my hands; so, between the both of us, he'll be apt to be kept posted on that line. . . .

277. S. A. Jones to A. W. Hosmer, March 22, 1897.

I have got the autograph; it reads like W. H. Ducks, don't it? I don't care much for ducks unless they are stuffed with sage and onions. I haven't cared at all for W. H. Ducks since I learned that what he has written about Thoreau was done solely for money. Pot-boilers they call such articles; but I'd rather his pot didn't boil![1]

What he writes about "Walden" is significant, isn't it? But John Bull is too much this-worldly to care for Thoreau's philosophy, and so much the worse for J. B. . . .

1. Dr. Jones probably drew his harsh conclusion from Dircks's statement that writing about Thoreau bored him. See Henry Salt to Dr. S. A. Jones, September 16, 1891, letter 83.

278. Henry Salt to S. A. Jones, April 1, 1897.

* * *

I have been reading John Woolman's Journal lately, and am much delighted with it. He seems in many respects to have been a worthy forerunner of Thoreau and the transcendentalist school. It is curious to find the following words written just a century before the writing of "Walden"—"I was learning to be content with real conveniences, that were not costly, so that a way of life free from much entanglement appeared best for me, though the income might be small. . . ."

279. S. A. Jones to A. W. Hosmer, April 11, 1897.

* * *

I wonder if Houghton, Mifflin & Co. would consider a proposition to publish a new, enlarged and corrected edition of the Bibliography?

Will you look over your copy and note what errors you can? I am asking the same favor from others, including Mr. Salt, and I am doing the same work myself, but two heads are better than one, especially when that one is my own!

I see that Sanborn has a paper in the "Forum" on "Emerson and Thoreau."[1] I have not had a chance to read it, but a glance at it to-day shows clearly that Sanborn has changed his tone decidedly since I knew him.

I shudder at the task of bringing the bibliography up to date, but it must be done, and the end is worth the toil.

It is quite an astonishment how the Thoreau literature has grown in the last ten years.

Just here I stopped for a moment to think about it, and the thought occurred to me that a book entitled *Thoreau and his Friends,* illustrated, would take finely! Think it over, please, and let me know your think. . . .

1. F. B. Sanborn, "Thoreau and Emerson," *Forum* 23 (April 1897):218-27.

280. A. W. Hosmer to S. A. Jones, April 12, 1897.

Hip! Hip!! Hurrah!!! Walden illustrated with portraits, and views in photogravure, 40 or more, bound in 2 vols. with flexible back &c. &c. &c.

Am just back from Boston where I held a two hour session with their art managers, who seemed very much interested in the scheme. He offers me $50.—for the use of my negatives and also gives me a number of copies of the work, of which the first one I receive will leave at once for Ann Arbor—the book will probably be out a month or so before Xmas. They are inclined to take my suggestions in regard to what pictures to use. For portraits I suggested the 3 of H.D.T.—Father—Brother—Helen & Sophia—Emerson—Salt—Hawthorne—Alcott—Edmund Hosmer—Blake—Channing—Sanborn (felt obliged to put him in, but they got my opinion of him—*straight*) & Sam. Staples.

Walden will be issued with footnotes, so that it will contain other pictures than just those that would really illustrate the book, as it now is.

Scudder told me today that it cost them $6.000, to bring out Cape Cod. Printing in color made an extra expense, as each picture had to be gone over a separate time for each color.

281. S. A. Jones to A. W. Hosmer, April 14, 1897.

I am glad to learn that the "Walden"[1] is an assured thing, but I am 'down on' inserting Sanborn's portrait. That will be nothing less than an insult to those who know how he has traduced Mrs. Thoreau. It can be got around by not inserting Mr. Salt's picture—which I feel to be out of place in that book. *He* did not know Thoreau, nor is he an object of interest to Thoreau readers in general. My regard for him you well know, but I still think his picture out of place in "Walden."

George William Curtis should have his portrait there. You know he helped to 'raise' the shanty.

Beg the publishers to reproduce *Thoreau's map* of his survey of the Pond, giving his soundings. . . .

Let the publishers know that Sanborn's photo will prejudice many against the illustrated "Walden," and bear down hard in your statement of the fact.

Have you seen Sanborn's article in the "Forum" for April? It is the greatest change of base I know of; he is beginning to see that Thoreau is coming out on top, and sneaking Sanborn wants to be on the winning side. . . .[2]

1. *Walden* (Boston: Houghton, Mifflin & Co., 1897). This edition was published in two volumes, with an introduction by Bradford Torrey and illustrations from the photographs of Alfred Hosmer.

2. "Thoreau and Emerson," *Forum* 23 (April 1897):218–27. Sanborn here refuted Lowell's "mistake of thinking that Thoreau imitated Emerson," and he noted that Thoreau's "younger readers" are raising the question "whether the fame of Emerson in literature and philosophy will be so permanent as that of his younger and more scientific contemporary."

282. S. A. Jones to A. W. Hosmer, April 19, 1897.

Houghton, Mifflin & Co. know the Thoreau *Bibliography,* for a copy of it was given them by the Rowfant Club in return for certain courtesies; so there will be no need for your 'toting' the book down there.

I am glad you sent me a list of the proposed photos to be used; but I must offer some suggestions. First, then, there is no single thing to suggest the immortal 'shanty.' Then, there should be a picture of his birthplace *with its original surroundings.* That India-ink sketch on my picture-mat will do.

I have just written to Mr. Scudder[1] about these items, and I also put in a hint about Sanborn's picture.

I guess you're in for it as regards Mr. Salt's photo; it's too late to back water, now.

The more I think of the work, Thoreau and his Friends, the more I am taken with it. You see, it allows the introduction of so many pictures that are not appropriate for "Walden."

All these things are attention to Thoreau and the result will be that, in the next century, he will be better known than R.W.E. What in the world will such fellows as "Asa" say to that? Sanborn's paper in the Forum shows which way the wind blows, and S. is just cute enough to see it. He is trimming his sails to catch the 'trade winds'. . . .

1. Horace Elisha Scudder (1838–1902) was editor of the *Atlantic* 1890–1898 and a long-time associate of Houghton, Mifflin.

283. S. A. Jones to A. W. Hosmer, April 23, 1897.

The same mail that brought your letter had in it also one from Mr. Scudder. He says: "No final list has been made of the subjects to be reproduced in the new *Walden,* and I am very much obliged to you for the suggestions contained in your favor of the 19th. inst. Mr. Sanborn's name was not on my list, but I am just as much obliged for the caution you give."[1]

The "caution" was a hint to the effect that Mr. Sanborn's portrait would give offense to those of Thoreau's lovers who know that Mr. S. has traduced Mrs. Thoreau. I shall be glad indeed, now, if F.B.S. is *left out* and Mr. Salt *put in*.

I am afraid that book on Thoreau and his Friends would cost altogether too much to get up. I have just gone through Thoreau's letters and I have 51 pictures of friends mentioned in that book alone!!!

I do not suppose that the subjects could all be found, but they would have to [be] sought for, and life is too short for such an interminable correspondence.

I fancy this list could be made up to 100, before the search is done, and I much doubt if the portraits would have enough interest for the great majority of the readers of Thoreau, and the question arises naturally if there are enough ENTHUSIASTS to pay for the book.

Of course, the value of such a book could be great in the middle of the next century, but the editors and publishers would be buried from the poorhouse long before that! . . .

1. The Jones collection does not include this letter of Scudder to Dr. Jones.

284. S. A. Jones to A. W. Hosmer, April 29, 1897.

Mr. Scudder has written to me to borrow that pen and ink sketch of the Thoreau birthplace *as it was in the olden days*.

Will you lend him your sketch, as mine is on the picture-mat and so clumsy to send. I believe you wrote me the other day that you had a copy and one in which the *trees* were as they should be;—my copy being 'off' in that respect.

Have you a copy of that issue of the "Acton Patriot" called the "Thoreau Annex"? It was published in 1880, and distributed amongst the schools. On the first page is a crude wood cut of the shanty and its surroundings as they were in Thoreau's time. On the third page is a letter from a correspondent certifying to the accuracy of the sketch.[1] This can be used by H.M. & Co's artist to present a view of Walden as it was.

I am loaning my copy to H.M. & Co. for the purpose of getting such a conception of the shanty and its environs as they were then.

I write this one day ahead of the letter to Mr. Scudder so that you can send your sketch of the birthplace before him by the time he will receive my note.

The said "Annex" contains a paper about Thoreau by Joseph Hosmer, of Chicago, which I shall shortly publish. Can you give me any information as to his family, birth &c.? I believe he was Horace Hosmer's brother, and will search Horace's letters to find out. . . .

1. See *Concord Freeman*, Thoreau Annex, 1880. Reprinted as *Thoreau Society Booklet Number Ten*. The paper includes a woodcut of Thoreau's shanty, which Walter Harding and Milton Meltzer have attributed to Joseph Hosmer, Horace Hosmer's brother. See *A Thoreau Profile*, p. 145. Apparently the special issue was published in the *Acton Patriot* as well as in the *Freeman*. The sketch is also reproduced in George Hendrick, *Remembrances of Concord and the Thoreaus*.

285. S. A. Jones to A. W. Hosmer, May 2, 1897.

Yesterday I started to copy Horace Hosmer's letters to me, and I am not sure but they will do to print. He has certainly given me quite a deal of curious information, and if it were put into shape, it would make interesting reading for a lover of Thoreau. He mentions a Concord newspaper to which his brother Joseph contributed some precious recollections of Thoreau.[1] I wonder if a file of that paper is yet in existence? It is worth looking into, any way.

What do you think? I'm going, next week, or rather this, for this is the first of the week, to visit a man who corresponded with Thoreau in the Fifties. He is the Mr. Calvin H. Green(e)[2] mentioned by Sanborn in his edition of Thoreau's Letters, p. 454.

I hunted him up by corresponding with the postmaster at Rochester, and he informed that Mr. G. was still alive and residing there. On writing to Mr. G., he informs me that he had received some half-a-dozen letters from Henry D. Thoreau, mostly on business (about the purchase of cedar wood, for pencils, is my surmise), but Mr. G. added that some of the letters contained such striking things that he copied them; and these copies he still has by him as something to be treasured so long as he lives. He says he will place this material at my service if I will call upon him. He also has a letter, or letters, from Sophia, written after Henry's death.

Greene visited Concord and the Thoreaus in 1863, and again in 1874. I shall bring a patent pump to bear on him and drain him as dry as—well, as E.W.E's lecture on Thoreau.

If the material and Mr. G's recollections are worth publishing, you'll hear of them when they are printed; if they do not justify putting into leaden type, I'll put them into typewriting for you. . . .

1. "Henry D. Thoreau, Some Recollections and Incidents Concerning Him, with Selections from his Works," *Concord Freeman*, Thoreau Annex, 1880.
2. Calvin H. Greene was among the few disciples whom Thoreau attracted during his lifetime. Greene learned of Thoreau by reading a notice of *Walden* in

the *New York Tribune,* and later, impressed by *Walden,* he wrote to Thoreau for a copy of *A Week.* Thoreau responded, sending a copy of *A Week*—the first of six letters from Thoreau to Greene.

286. S. A. Jones to A. W. Hosmer, May 11, 1897.

I just want you to know that I am sittin' on the front seat in the synagogue, and I'd like to have you observe that there are *no flies in my immediate vicinity!*

I'd like you, also, to put your ear to the ground and listen to this child for a few minutes. Thusly:

I,—did you get that correctly? *I* am the owner of SIX autograph letters written by Henry D. Thoreau, of THREE written by Miss Sophia E. Thoreau, of ONE by W. E. Channing, and one written by Sanborn[1] *before* he degenerated!!!!!!!!! (I advise you to crawl into your hole and to pull the hole in after you!)

There; my friend if I hadn't let off just that much steam I should have 'bust'—and that would be unpleasant, you know.

I am just home from a hundred mile trip and have not cooled off enough to be able by any possibility to tell you about the grandest Thoreau hunt I've had since my ever-remembered Concord days.

You shall know all so soon as I get my breath; meanwhile hold your mouth wide open for some anecdotes of Thoreau that have never been in print, and one of which alone is worth a journey around the earth, by the way of the North pole, *and barefooted, at that!* Good Lord! if I was in the sitting room with them Hosmer girls I'd dance a hornpipe that would beat Thoreau's all to pieces. You have GOT to visit Michigan this summer.

P.S. Tell Mr. Sanborn that I have gotten all the Thoreau correspondence with C. H. Greene, Rochester, Mich. Years 1856–59.

1. Dr. Jones published Thoreau's six letters to Greene in *Some Unpublished Letters of Henry D. and Sophia E. Thoreau* (Jamaica, Queensborough, N.Y.: The Marion Press, 1899). Also included in this volume were Sophia Thoreau's four letters to Greene, William Ellery Channing's short note to Greene of March 4, 1863, and James A. Froude's letter to Thoreau. Sanborn's letter to Greene of June 11, 1862, was later published in Dr. Jones's closing note to *Collectanea Henry D. Thoreau: Emerson's Obituary* (Lakeland, Michigan: E. B. Hill, 1904).

287. Henry Salt to S. A. Jones, May 18, 1897.

I am sending you by this mail a copy of my short article on John Woolman.[1] It is really not worthy of the subject, and written only for a limited vegetarian audience (limited in sympathies, as in numbers, I fear); but I hope it may at any rate widen the circle of Woolman's readers. It is most kind of you to offer to give me your own copy of the *Journal*, but I can't let you do so, because I have access to one or two editions in the London Library, and really I think it is time your altruistic tendencies should be curbed! What do your family say, when they see you posting your library to the four corners of the globe? . . .

I had not seen Sanborn's *Forum* article when your letter came, but I have now looked it up and read it.[2] I agree with you entirely in what you say of it. In itself it is not much of a production, but decidedly significant as showing how the writer has been influenced by the progress of new ideas. Depend upon it, in fifty or a hundred years hence, Emerson will be a *curiosity*, and Thoreau a living force; and F.B.S. is shrewd enough to suspect what is coming, and adjust his criticism accordingly.

Mr. Hosmer seems to be doing a fine work in getting Houghton & Mifflin to have an illustrated *Walden*. I hope the book may be financially successful, so as to induce them to go on to more.

Since I last wrote to you I have made the acquaintance of Dr. Haig, of "uric acid" celebrity. He is evidently a one-idea man, and too much immersed (if I may use so realistic a metaphor) in uric acid to think much of anything else; but he has come to be a believer in the humanitarian aspect of the food-question, though he approached it from the scientific. He has a terrible predilection for testing the blood of vegetarians, in order to show how the absence of uric acid purifies it; and I had an uneasy feeling that if we got very intimate he would produce a lancet and ask leave to "sample" me—and somehow I did *not* feel ready to "bleed for the Cause" in that way. I suppose I have not in me the stuff that martyrs are made of.

We are going to have an awful summer in London this year, with the celebration of the Queen's absurd Diamond Jubilee. Already scaffoldings and "grand stands" are being built in every available place along the route of the "procession"; snobbery is rampant; "shopping" ladies are roaming about in hordes, and tradesmen preparing for "a good season". You can imagine my feelings, as I walk office-wards each morning through St. James's Park, the centre of this mummery, and think of Thoreau's "I would not run round a corner to see the world blow up". You have some bad things in American society, I dare say; but you may be thankful that you have nothing *quite* so sordid and snobbish as this Royalty humbug of ours!

It has lately struck me as curious that, though I occasionally see Moncure Conway at South Place Ethical Society, of which he is still the Pastor, I never seem to feel the interest in him which one would naturally feel in a surviving acquaintance of Thoreau's. He never impresses me as a man who *really* knew Thoreau at all, though those old Fraser articles of his were far from uninteresting. Did you ever come across Conway, and have you any feeling with regard to him? Seeing that a few years hence it will be impossible to find anyone who has walked and talked with Thoreau, why don't I hurry off to Conway and ask him to tell me all he knows? I can't say; but somehow I don't feel at all disposed to take this precaution! Conway's latest exploit at South Place, I hear, has been to speak in favour of vivisection in a debate on that subject; which does not look as if he had inherited a large share of the Thoreau-spirit! I hear that Wentworth Higginson is going to be in London this summer; so it is possible I may see him. He has always written very cordially, but I know nothing of him personally.

1. "The Journal of John Woolman" appeared in the *Vegetarian Review,* May 1897, pp. 229–31.
2. F. B. Sanborn, "Thoreau and Emerson," *Forum* 23 (April 1897):218–27.

288. A. W. Hosmer to S. A. Jones, May 25, 1897.

Do you happen to have an extra copy of Lippincott's with "Thoreau's Biographers" and the Inlander with "Thoreau's Inheritance" that you could spare me. I want to send them to *E.M.F.* who wrote that letter to the Advertiser in 1883[1] scorching Sanborn for his treatment of the Thoreaus. Mrs. Jennie M. LeBrun was the writer. She used to live here—neighbor to the Thoreaus and said she waited awhile to see if some one would answer Sanborn, but as no one else did, she wrote the article & signed it with the first initials that came to mind.

Its rather queer my finding out about it. I (Alfred W.) wrote her some time ago to see if she could help me to a picture of Mrs. T.—then she wrote to (Fred) me about some flowers, then came in to see me in regard to them—as she was leaving the store I said I was sorry she could not help me about the picture, and much to her surprise she found that Alfred W. H. was the one she always supposed was *Frederick*—she expressed a wish to see the other pictures of the Thoreau family, so I loaned her my extended "Life" to look over. On her way to the train she stopped in to thank me for it, and said she saw I had quoted her in the book. I could not recall any place until she mentioned that it was in relation to Mrs. Thoreau when I at once asked if she was the E.M.F. which proved to be the case.

She has a number of letters to Sophia Thoreau from M. D. Conway & others that she will look up and let me take.

So if you have a copy of those magazines to spare I should like to send them to her.

[P.S.] It was through Mrs. LeBrun that Sanborn got that letter from Maria Thoreau that he published in the "Life".[2]

1. "Henry Thoreau's Mother," *Boston Daily Advertiser,* February 14, 1883.

2. In his biography of 1882 Sanborn quoted a long letter by Maria Thoreau, dated March 18, 1878, in which she discussed her family's history. See *Henry D. Thoreau,* pp. 5–8.

289. S. A. Jones to A. W. Hosmer, May 29, 1897.

Your letters of the 25th and 27th respectively have interested me as much as you can well imagine, but an unusual amount of sickness has kept me too busy (and sickness must be attended to, you know) to reply at once, as I always like to do. So, if I ever delay, you will know that I'm 'tendin' to my knittin' like a good boy.

Isn't it queer how that "E.M.F." business should drop right "onto you!"

It is a question if I can find a copy of "Thoreau's Inheritance" as the Inlander is not kept on hand by the editors, the unsold copies being made away with to save the expense of storage. I shall have to try and find some one who has a copy that is not particularly cared for, in which case, Mrs. LeBrun shall certainly have one. The "Lippincott's" I will write to a dealer in New York to 'pick up' for me. So soon as he finds one I will have it sent directly to you. Mrs. LeBrun, however, might be more interested to see that unpublished lecture in which her whole letter is quoted. I will send it to you for her reading, if you like.

I consider the FROUDE letter[1] as the most important 'find' you have yet made, knowing what I do of Froude's religious life at the time it was written.[2]

When I see the copy I will 'post you up' if it is on the topic which I suspect it must be. As Froude is now *dead,* Mrs. LeBrun *must* consent to its publication, and I will make an article for the "Atlantic Monthly" of it and the correspondence that I got from Mr. Greene. Damn it, I'll make Scudder see with both eyes that Thoreau IS far more than he has yet been able to dream.

Strangely enough, the man who is to read the proof of the new edition of "Walden"[3] has, through Mr. Miller,[4] applied to me for information. I shall do my best to have him more than hint that the illustrations must not be cut down.

I wish you could visit us again just to see Mr. Greene. He is worthy of the letters that Thoreau sent him. I could gladly lick the dust off his shoes. He is old and poor, but great God what a MAN!!

I am writing at the office, after 11 P.M., and a hard day's work; but tired as I am I could not go home without sending you a line.

On the 19th I lectured in the University on the Thoreau correspondence. A short-hand writer took it down and it is to be printed so you are in for some copies. I talked off hand for an hour and twenty minutes, and I'll be danged if the hearers didn't tell me they "thought it was n't more than half an hour." That is a good sign that Thoreau interested them. . . .

1. Alfred Hosmer had learned that Mrs. LeBrun was the possessor of James Anthony Froude's letter to Thoreau of September 3, 1849. For a text of this letter, in which Froude praised *A Week,* see *The Correspondence of Henry David Thoreau,* pp. 248–49.
2. In 1849 Froude published *The Nemisis of Faith,* which marked his break with religious orthodoxy in England.
3. Dr. Jones in his next letter (292) identifies Mr. Stickney as the proofreader for *Walden.*
4. Wilhelm Miller was an editor of the *Inlander* and a friend of Dr. Jones's.

290. A. W. Hosmer to S. A. Jones, June 5, 1897.

The two magazines received O.K. and have started them for Germany— after Mrs. LeBrun—have also written her for permission to allow you to have a copy of the Froude letter to publish. I will report to you as soon as I hear from her. How much are the magazines, as I want to pay for them.

That proofreader of Walden ought to come to Concord for a day so as to get thoroughly filled with his subject, and in that way he might be able to suggest various foot notes. I should be pleased to show him around.

In this letter of Froude's—he speaks of his love & honor for Thoreau, at first on account of what Emerson had said, but then because of his having read Week I should say, and through a letter Thoreau had written him. That there is no one whose friendship or notice he values so much as that of Thoreau's. He had almost despaired there was so little truth among the writers & thinkers and had Thoreau to thank for a helping hand—signing his letter "God bless you, your friend (if you will let him call you so) J. A. Froude."

My negatives have gone into Houghton Mifflin & Co—the list now stands—3 portraits of Thoreau and a copy of the Ricketson medallion (4)—Emerson (5)—Hawthorne (6)—Curtis (7)—Edmund Hosmer (8)— Sam'l Staples (9)—Alcott (10)—view from Bristers hill (11)—Bristers spring (12)—Channing (13)—River from Nashawtuc (14)—Emerson house (15)—Fairhaven from Baker Farm (16)—Great meadows (17)— Old Marlboro road (18)—Pleasant Meadow (19)—Flute (20)—Birthplace (21)—house Main St. (22)—Walden showing sand bar (23)—site of House (24)—Pines (25)—Furniture (26)—Survey of pond (27)—Cairn (28)— White Pond (29)—Shanty (30)—Pond in winter (31).

It has called for more work than I expected when they first talked with me, as they have left more to me than I had any idea they would from the way they talked then.

I had a talk with one of the boys Thoreau whipped, the other day, he said there were 13 punished—that Thoreau had kept school only a couple of weeks, and resigned the same day he punished the scholars.[1] Said he always considered he had had an unjust whipping—but found of late years the cause for it.

1. When Nehemiah Ball of the Concord school committee visited Thoreau at the Center School in the fall of 1837, he was disturbed that the new teacher was using no corporal punishment. Ball told Thoreau that "it was his duty to flog the students on occasion"—to which Thoreau responded by arbitrarily feruling several pupils. That evening Thoreau resigned his position, which he had held for only two weeks. See Walter Harding, *The Days of Henry Thoreau*, pp. 52–53.

291. A. W. Hosmer to S. A. Jones, June 9, 1897.

I enclose photos of Emerson's summer house & the stairway in it. This is the one that Alcott built & Thoreau laughed at him about.[1]

I had a letter from a Mr. Stickney—(friend of Miller's) who is in Houghton Mifflin & Co.—who wishes to come out next Sunday for a tramp in Thoreau-land. Is he to be the proof reader?

1. In the summer of 1846 Alcott undertook the building of a summer-house for Emerson. He was assisted in the carpentry by Thoreau, who seems to have been both amused and dismayed by Alcott's fantastic plans for adorning the structure with gables and columns. The summerhouse was completed the following summer and promptly dubbed "The Ruin" by Emerson's mother. See Harding, *The Days of Henry Thoreau*, pp. 216–19. For Abby May Alcott's sketch of the gazebo, see Odell Shepard, *Pedlar's Progress* (Boston: Little, Brown, 1937), p. 414.

292. S. A. Jones to A. W. Hosmer, June 11, 1897.

* * *

I ended my sixty-third year in sickness, but am feeling better to-day, and I want to acknowledge the receipt of two letters from you, one announcing that H. M. & Co have finally selected the illustrations for "Walden," though too few for my notion, and the other asking about Mr. Stickney and bringing the picture of Alcott's Fool's Paradise,—which was enough to make Thoreau laugh.

Thoreau not only laughed: he flung up his share of the job: he didn't tell Alcott to go on and be damned (as we would to-day) but he was very sure Alcott would meet that fate, "just the same."

That Mr. Stickney is the "proof-reader" whom Miller wrote would be likely to make some enquiries of me. Let him come on; the more the better—for the book.

I mentioned being sick: *it was a malarial attack,* brought on by too much work and by riding too far through marshy lands in pursuit of some poor devils who don't want to go to the devil quite yet. I would rather have less to do, for I recognize that my harvest means loss to the sufferer. But, what is worse, I cannot get time to do the work I want to do in other directions; for instance, finish my last Thoreau talk for the press. I was disappointed when the reporter brought me his short-hand report. You see, I find it *too* short, for he reserves the right to defend his shortcomings by pleading that he couldn't help stopping to listen himself—but why did he stop his short-hand work! However, I shall do the best I can with his notes so soon as I get time. *** I must say, Fred, that I consider the last photo—Alcott's architectural mare's-nest—as, perhaps the most characteristic thing your kindness has yet sent me. It has thrown a flood of light on Alcott's character; he had a love for and a sense of the Beautiful but was wholly devoid of the Practical. It is a wonder Thoreau didn't borrow the axe once more to knock Alcott's useless brains out!

O Fred, my visit to Mr. Greene has enabled me to be born again. I am taking lessons from Thoreau's Michigan correspondent, and I am going to place all my Thoreau relics into the library of the University of Michigan. The authorities are even now preparing the glass case that will retain them. Tell your most ungodly brother that even the "brick" at which he mocked will SHINE in that collection. I hope, dear Fred, that you will approve of this movement of mine; but, really, Mr. Greene's making me the depository of all his treasures *before* he dies, set me to thinking that it would not do to keep these relics as mere curiosities in my own house; no, I must put them where they can *enthuse* many a young heart. The library is a fire-proof building, and so the letters, books and all will be safe. I shall be very bold in asking for your precious aid as I have had it all along, for what would I have been able to do without you—simply nothing. As it is, I shall go to my grave gladdened with the knowledge that you and I joined hands in doing honor to the memory of Henry D. Thoreau. . . .

293. Henry Salt to S. A. Jones, June 16, 1897.

This is great news about your "find" of the Thoreau letters.[1] Future students of Thoreau, who will be many, will owe much to your labours in this field. I shall anxiously await further details, for the quotations you have given show that the letters are of the true Thoreau quality. I wish indeed *I* could have been present at that lecture in Tappan Hall!

It is very interesting also to know that this letter of Froude's has turned up;[2] though I can't say that I ever discovered in Froude himself anything more than a learned man of decent ability. It would be through Carlyle, I suppose, that he heard of the "Week"; and all that can be added to

Thoreau memorials in that connection will be of value. With Mrs. LeBrun's self-revelation, events seem to be following each other in rapid succession; and I can only stand on the other side of the Atlantic and devoutly hope for a further shower of discoveries!

Yes, I think you are quite right about Conway. It is just the impression I have of him, and I feel a little sorry to have quoted him so largely. I hear he is about to leave South Place Institute in London, and return to America. The opinion of him here is that he is hopelessly out of date; that is, he has stood still during the past quarter century, and is now practically *opposed* to the party of progress, instead of a pioneer. His late championship of vivisection has damned him utterly with the best class of "ethical" folk.

I had an hour's talk with Wentworth Higginson about a fortnight ago. He is a fine soldierlike old man, with a humorous way of telling a story; very friendly & courteous, but a look that suggests a power of saying sharp things if need be. He has done good service, I imagine, in counteracting the false impression of Thoreau which Lowell so studiously fostered. Mrs. Higginson has just notified me that she will be "at home" on June 23rd, and not far from here; but I never go to such polite functions, because I always feel very much *not* at home in them. Higginson talked more about Whitman than Thoreau, and also told me a good deal about our friend F.B.S., and his (H.'s) kinsman Ellery Channing.

If you ever have time, and are in the mood for it, I wish you would tell me more about Mr. Hosmer. (Do you mean A.W.H. by "Fred"?) From something Sanborn said about him (in an indifferent but not unfriendly way), and from Mr. Hosmer's own letters, I have got the idea that he is really the person at Concord who is most akin to Thoreau in his life & thought; and I should be much more interested to see him, if it ever were my luck to come over, than all the Emersonian survivals! There is something rather oppressive to me in these polite personages who once "knew Thoreau", but are now living in such a very different sphere!

Here is a Thoreau item for the Bibliography, if you have not already got it: "Henry D. Thoreau, ein amerikanischer naturschilderer". by A. Prinzinger, pubd. at Salzburg, 1895, 8vo. I saw it lately in the catalogue at the Museum, but did not get it out, as I can't read German. It is a pamphlet, apparently, as it is bound up with other things. I will have it examined by someone who reads German, if you think it worth while. . . .

1. Salt is referring to Dr. Jones's finding Thoreau's letters to Calvin Greene.
2. Dr. Jones included Froude's letter to Thoreau, dated September 3, 1849, in *Some Unpublished Letters of Henry D. and Sophia E. Thoreau*, pp. 11–13.

294. S. A. Jones to A. W. Hosmer, June 18, 1897.

* * *

As regards the autograph letters that were given me, I feel that I have no right to keep them in a *private collection*. Thoreau's life and work are too sacred to be hidden in any illustrated book, or any private library; nor must one make a "dime museum" of these sacred relics. They must be put where they may happily inspire some fresh, young heart with his divine enthusiasm.

To that end, I am giving all I have gotten together to the LIBRARY of the University of Michigan; and if my life is spared long enough, Thoreau shall have such a monument in the university as Harvard, his own *alma mater,* has neglected to erect to the noblest of all her sons. Perhaps, dear Fred, when the aristocrats find how he is honored abroad, it may dawn upon them that HE is, indeed, "such a man as it takes ages to make, and ages *to understand.*" That is what he said of John Brown; and thank God! it is as true of himself.

You have given me many precious relics and pictures: for Thoreau's sake, please allow me to give them all to the purpose mentioned. Please answer this request so that I may go on with the good work.

295. A. W. Hosmer to S. A. Jones, June 21, 1897.

What else could I do but approve of your gift to the Library, and *what* a gift it will be. Not many, if any authors will be so well represented as Thoreau must be from what I know of your collections.

I shall continue to send you what I get hold of just the same. Have just had a new sketch of the birthplace made, so as to have one with the pine tree in full in it, for the Walden[1]—shall send the negative at once to Houghton M. & Co. and after it comes back shall make up some prints from it and will then send you one. . . .

1. See page 20 of the 1897 *Walden* for Mary Wheeler's sketch of the Thoreau birthplace.

296. S. A. Jones to Henry Salt, June 27, 1897.

And you want to know about "Fred." There is only one "Fred," and I do most certainly mean "A.W.H." when I write "Fred."

Sir Humphrey Davy was once asked which he considered his greatest discovery, and he promptly answered: "Michael Faraday." Well, when I went to Concord in 1890 my richest "find" was Fred Hosmer: so called from cutting the Alfred W. in two. He is but distantly related to the Edmund Hosmer of some renown as "the long-headed farmer" mentioned by Emerson and sneeringly referred to by Hawthorne's son in his Life of his father and mother. "Fred" carries in his heart some of the best blood that any "Mayflower" can ever carry from dear old England anywhere. His father was a carpenter, and a sturdy representative of all that can make Concord attractive to him who doesn't admire the frills more than the frock. (A distinction which too many of Emerson's "admirers" fail to make.)

Fred is about thirty-five years of age; a bachelor; a salesman in a little variety shop in Concord; an amateur photographer, and better informed about Thoreau's haunts than any man living or dead. *W. E. Channing not excepted.* Fred is also a botanist; an early riser; a member of that high caste erstwhile known as the "Sunday Walkers"—an unregenerate set who firmly believe "The groves were God's first temples".

Fred Hosmer makes his own clothes, and this from a desire to be independent of "sweating shops". But the night would fail me to tell you all about him. What do I say! All about him! God forgive me! when a pint cup can comprehend a gallon, I shall know "all about" a nature so infinitely superior to my own.

I am struck by the depth of your insight as shown in what you have written about "Fred" as contrasted with those polite personages who once "knew Thoreau" but are now living in such a different sphere. Those are your own words, and you have struck the nail right on the head.

I, poor miserable I, *admire* Thoreau; Fred *lives* him! Don't despise me now; I despise myself when I think of Fred and remember myself. That's punishment enough, for the Nemesis is neither myth, nor dead; no, not even sleeping. You can afford to come to America if only to look for a moment into Fred's clear grey eyes—after that, a tramp through "Thoreau's country" with him for guide is enough to make one's memory radiant forever.

Fred is not "literate", as Lamb's friend said of the servant girl with whom a Christ Church scholar elected to walk through life; but Fred shames all the "Humanities" that are known to any scholastic cloister. O, Mr. Salt, when God Almighty sets out to make a MAN, He always makes a success of it: Fred is the divine Q.E.D. of that proposition.[1]

1. This letter appeared in number 30 (January 1950) of the *Thoreau Society Bulletin* and is reproduced with permission. We give the text as it was presented by Raymond Adams.

297. A. W. Hosmer to S. A. Jones, July 6, 1897.

If you will send your article on the letters of Thoreau to Walter H. Page—Care Houghton Mifflin & Co. Boston, and say they are the ones I wrote him about, I think they will make use of them.[1] From what Scudder (W. S.) has said I do not think they hanker much after Sanborn.

There is nothing I should like better than helping you in that Thoreau matter, but I have to take my vacation the latter part of this month (19th to Aug 1st) and as I have not been feeling very bunkum[2] this spring I do not know as I shall feel much like taking so long a trip, more especially as this hot weather we now have is taking hold of me.

The last call I made on my doctor (Braley) last week he told me he had a dream about me the night after I was in before—he thought Dr. Jones of Mich. was calling on him when I came in and after talking awhile Dr. J. remarked "that's the remedy for him, you want to use that remedy," but Braley waked up before you gave him the name of the medicine. . . .

1. Walter Hines Page (1855–1918), an associate of Houghton, Mifflin and editor of the *Atlantic* (1896–1899), had written Alfred W. Hosmer to thank him for his letter of inquiry regarding publication of the Thoreau-Greene letters; Page thought the letters would probably be publishable in the *Atlantic* but desired to see them before making a final decision. See Walter H. Page to A. W. Hosmer, July 3, 1897 (Hosmer collection).
2. From Canadian French, meaning in good health.

298. S. A. Jones to A. W. Hosmer, [July] 9, 1897.

I am much obliged for the trouble you have taken in the matter of the Thoreau Letters, but I much doubt if such simple writing as mine would find a place in the scholarly "Atlantic." I shall most likely save my few pennies and publish a limited edition of the letters in fac-simile (zinco-photographs) and tell the story of them in between. The "Atlantic" is no place for so heartful a paper as I shall write. . . .

299. S. A. Jones to A. W. Hosmer, July 12, 1897.

Sunday's mail had in it the photo reproduction of Miss Wheeler's sketch of Thoreau's birthplace as it was when he was born. The picture afforded me infinite delight, for this kind of illustration is work done for the Thoreau readers of the future that will bless your memory when you are under the turf and insensate dust.

I am also more than thankful to Messrs. Houghton, Mifflin & Co., for their interest in that dear "loafer" whose fame is so steadily growing as the world is surely finding him out as a benefactor of the race. I am sanguine that they will have their reward in a pecuniary sense, and that is the "sense" in which it MUST come if business houses are to keep on with their high mission of raising readers to higher and better things. . . .

I wrote to Mr. Page, yesterday stating, that I was afraid my simple style would not be suitable for the "Atlantic", but expressing a desire to have him look over what I may write and make criticisms, suggestions, etc., *freely*.

There was something in the tone of his letter that found its way to my heart at once; I do not for the life of me know what it was that "fetched" me but something DID, and I was filled with a desire to live where, once in a while, I might talk with such a man. Well, we must live out our lives where we are placed by Fate; perhaps we can select our company, Fred, OVER THERE!! . . .

300. Henry Salt to S. A. Jones, July 20, 1897.

I was very glad to receive your delightful letter of June 27, with copies of two Thoreau letters enclosed. You have indeed made a rare "find" in that long-buried correspondence. There is something so impressive, I always think, in the discovery & resurrection of letters, bringing us in very fact a further speech and message from one supposed to be gone. It was generous, & like you, to wish *me* to do the editing of the Thoreau-Greene correspondence, but from every point of view it is better & fitter that it should be done by you on the spot. I do not mean so much that Mr. Greene shd. get the money, because it is so evident that, whether you or I did the editing, it *ought* to go to none but him, and of course it would go to him from me if it ever came to me—but I mean that you are in a position, knowing all the circumstances, to do the work much better than I can at this great distance. In short, you are obviously the proper person to do it, & do it you must. You are the chief actor in the drama of these letters, & the world unmistakably calls you before the curtain.

Thanks—many thanks—for what you tell me about Mr. Hosmer, which exactly fills out the picture outlined in my mind by a rather patronising but not unkindly word about him which I had heard from another quarter—you can guess whence. This report was of the "worthy-young-man" order; but my trigonometrical estimate, based on (1) the information itself, and (2) the character of my informant, seems to have been very accurate.

Still more thanks for what you say about your friendship with myself, & none the less because you so largely invert our obligations! That you should crown the pile of help you have given me—help by information, suggestion, sympathy, encouragement, such as I suppose few unknown workers like myself have received—by thanking *me* for our intercourse, is really too altruistic! We must not appear on the Day of Judgment with such a fanciful statement of our relations, or the Almighty will lose temper with us & ask us *both* to step down.

And this reminds me of another possible favour that you *may* be asked to do me. A friend of mine—not an intimate friend, but one whom I have met from time to time in a friendly way in connection with "Causes" in which we both sympathise—is coming over to the States in August with his wife, for a few weeks' study of social questions, and I am giving him a card of introduction to you in case he visits Michigan. His name is James R. Macdonald,[1] & he is a young Scotchman of a particularly honest manly nature which I am sure you will like. He is well known in the Socialist movement, & likely to become a prominent leader in it; also he belongs to the "New Fellowship", who go in for simplification of life & are great students of Thoreau. I am sending him to Sanborn, if he goes to Concord, & also mentioning A. W. Hosmer to him, & *vice versa*. But as he probably has a great number of introductions & lecture engagements, I don't know exactly where or when he will make his stoppages. So now you will understand if you hear from him.

I enclose a scrap which I cut out of a paper respecting Moncure D. C. You will appreciate the "deep emotion" & the "general emotion" of himself & his audience. By the bye, I wonder if his "Life of Paine" is constructed on the same principles as his articles on Thoreau. I see he has been "discovering the missing picture" of P., which sounds suspicious!

My visit to Concord! When is *that* to be? I sometimes have dreams of running over in the summer of 1898 for a few weeks, *to Concord only* (I should have no time or temper for the "sights" of America, never having yet seen our English "sights"); and if Dr. S.A.J. could be there, and I could somehow be saved from the polite society of the place, all would be perfect. We must think if it is feasible!

1. James Ramsay MacDonald (1866–1937), British politician and later prime minister, paid his first visit to the United States in 1897.

301. S. A. Jones to A. W. Hosmer, July 26, 1897.[1]

Just a line—Had an awful collapse. Taken into wilderness—shanty like Thoreau's, only *awful* mosquitoes. Wife & two sons with me. All I need is REST. Shall not leave here until *head* is *cured*—if that is possible. Writing *wearies* me soon—hence this scrawl.

Sick or well, yours dear Fred to the end of the *road* and *Beyond!*

1. This letter was written from Turtle Bay, Michigan.

302. S. A. Jones to A. W. Hosmer, August 28, 1897.

I am sorry to be obliged to write that I do not improve as I should like to do. My break-down was in the nervous system, entailing loss of memory, terrible insomnia, low spirits—in fact, a prostration that alarmed my family, and they took charge of me just as they would have done with any irresponsible person. My sojourn in the wilderness did me great bodily good, but my head repairs so slowly that I suppose I am knocked out of active business for at least a year. If I recover something of my old self in that time, I shall deem myself a lucky man. I ascribe my break-down to loss of sleep, from a wicked habit of LATE reading, and to this add a decidedly wicked ABUSE of tobacco.

Tobacco smoking helps to keep one awake; that is WHY I could stand such late hours a-reading as long and as well as I did. But, Fred, one can NOT insult Nature with impunity, as I have found out for myself. Here I had a stub-and-twist, A1, Welsh constitution, but I have "busted" it by unpardonable folly—unpardonable in anyone, and doubly so in a so-called physician. . . .

The Thoreau Collection has taken this shape, namely, to set apart a room in our university library to contain everything I can get pertaining to Thoreau, but to be known as "The Concord Room."

The reason for this is that American Literature—that which is *distinctively American*—really began at Concord, Mass., and with the movement that began to take shape in the "Dial". . . .

[P.S.] Fred: E.W.E.'s paper[1] in the Atlantic for July is worthy of the R.W.E., and the son has risen vastly in my regard. Is Edward in Concord now? I have some business to write to him about if he is.

1. Edward Emerson, "John Sterling, and a Correspondence between Sterling and Emerson," *Atlantic Monthly* 80 (July 1897):14–35.

303. A. W. Hosmer to S. A. Jones, September 14, 1897.

In a letter from Mrs. LeBrun received this morning, she says, after thanking me for the two magazines, and saying how much she was interested in them, in relation to the Froude letter that she had not written sooner because she could not make up her mind about it—to quote—"I have always thought I might sometime use it myself but very likely I never should and it seems ungracious to refuse to let Dr. Jones publish it with the six letters he has found. He is certainly a most appreciative biographer and deserves encouragement and help. I am sure Sophia would approve of him. I should be inclined to let you send him a copy to use in the way you mention if I could be sure that that would not give him a right to use it in any other way and that he would not give other people the right to publish it in some other volume. I wish it to remain my property but am willing he should get any benefit to be derived from the use you mention provided that does not deprive me of all after claim to it." I wrote her that you wished to use it in connection with those six letters.

I enclose a copy of the letter and will let you govern yourself by what Mrs. LeBrun writes.

[P.S.] I think Mrs. LeBrun is afraid Sanborn may get his clutches on the Froude letter.

304. S. A. Jones to A. W. Hosmer, September 19, 1897.

* * *

The Froude letter is a striking tribute to Thoreau, and it is just of the nature I had expected it to be.

I am sorry Mrs. LeBrun is so far off, for I want to use the letter soon, and I would feel freer to act if I could first communicate with her.

If she can trust to my honor, I can protect her from ten thousand Sanborns by copyrighting the BOOK in which the Froude letter SHOULD first appear. Then no one but Mrs. LeBrun dare reprint it without her consent.

If she will assent to this, I shall want a history of how she became possessed of the Froude letter so that the reading world will know to whom they are indebted for the pleasure of reading it.[1]

Fred, I was never in my life more deeply touched than when I read Mrs. LeBrun's words: "I am sure Sophia would approve of him." I will try and make that opinion true to the letter; and I send you a tearful thankfulness for writing it to me. Now that I am sick and depressed, it has been as a precious cordial. I hope to God that I deserve such a trust!

I will copyright all the letters and will protect Mrs. LeBrun by inserting "All rights reserved." Then, Fred, not even a foreigner can translate the Froude letter without her consent. There will be no surrender of property right on her part in all this matter. THAT IS AS TRUE AS DEATH.

If you write to her again, please tell the lady that her generous permission will enable me to pay the best of all tributes to the genius of him that was Henry D. Thoreau. My own thankfulness is beyond words. . . .

1. Dr. Jones included in *Some Unpublished Letters* a letter of December 27, 1897, from Mrs. LeBrun to Alfred Hosmer in which Mrs. LeBrun explained how she had received Froude's letter from Sophia Thoreau when Miss Thoreau was making a final disposition of Thoreau's papers before her death. Mrs. LeBrun felt that Sophia "feared people would think it too flattering and for that, or some other reason, did not at that time care to have it published" (Hosmer collection). Dr. Jones concealed the identities of both Hosmer and Mrs. LeBrun.

305. S. A. Jones to A. W. Hosmer, October 15, 1897.

I had a long correspondence with Miss Lyman,[1] beginning soon after the publication of "Thoreau: A Glimpse." She is a subscriber to "The Unitarian," the paper in which it was first published, and reading it there, she got my address from the editor and wrote to me herself.

It was through her influence that the Lippincott's Magazine article was written and finally published.

I have the highest regard for Miss Lyman, but I had to cease writing for the simple reason that I could not SPARE the time. As she is an old maid, I guess she took umbrage at my abrupt manner of breaking off a correspondence that was certainly as enjoyable to me as any I ever had; but I thought that abrupt way better than writing to tell her: "I have no time."

It gives me as much pleasure to learn that she has made the Concord visit as if I had myself made it; and I can tell you her letters stimulated me to do much of whatever little I may have done for Thoreau's memory.

I am slowly learning in some degree to be as blunt as Thoreau, and I am finding that the bluntest truth, if it is truth, is the best. Therefore if you will send me Miss Lyman's present address, I will write to her; her devotion to Thoreau's memory DESERVES that.

Houghton & Mifflin's enquiry, through you, about that paper on the Thoreau Letters is something I cannot understand. I wrote to Mr. Walter H. Page some time since, explaining to him that I would like to be released from my *implied obligation* to write a paper for the "Atlantic Monthly" on that subject and allow him the "refusal" of it. My letter was entitled to a reply, but I have not received one. I told him plainly that I am not in sympathy with the spirit of the "Atlantic." I feel that it is put forth solely in the interest of highly cultured scholarship, and that is the privilege of only a few of the sons of men; while my sympathies go out to all mankind. I told Mr. Page that I did not feel "in the spirit" to write the paper for the "Atlantic," feeling as I do to-day.

The situation is just this: the "Atlantic's" interest is a purely monied one; mine isn't. I feel that all the house of H.M. & Co. wants is the letters, and I do not dare to let the copyright of them pass into the hands of *any publishing house whatever.*

The long and short of it is, Mr. Page holds the key to the whole situation, in the letter I wrote to him and which he has not answered. If he feels that I am in honor bound to submit a paper for his "refusal" (provided he didn't like it), I feel myself in honor bound to do so, and will do so just as soon as I can.

I wrote to Mr. Page about my break down, (and he can get quite a conception of the nature and extent of it from my letters), and the fact is I have by no means recovered. I am at work BECAUSE I MUST WORK TO

SUSTAIN MY FAMILY. It would greatly enhance my chance for ultimate recovery if I could have absolute rest for a time.

Greatly against my own sense of prudence I have been forced into the lecture course at Unity Club's season of 1897–8, as you will see by the enclosed preliminary announcement. I do this simply to present Thoreau in yet a new aspect. My topic will be, "Froude and Thoreau: A Comparison and a Contrast."

Mrs. LeBrun's copy of Froude's letter to Thoreau is the basis of it all and I am doing it in reverence for Thoreau's memory. . . .

I lent Mr. Scudder a rude woodcut of the Shanty at Walden;[2] it was given me by Horace Hosmer; it is very dear to me; I hope it has not been thrown aside so as to be irrecoverable.

If you can find out what has become of it, please do so; but IF it has been lost, do not let Mr. Scudder know that I made any enquiry about it. If it is lost, it IS lost, and there is no need that he should THEN experience any chagrin. . . .

1. Emily Lyman, a friend of Alfred Hosmer, published *Extracts from Thoreau* (Philadelphia: J. B. Lippincott, 1899); and *Thoreau* (Concord, Mass.: Privately published for Alfred W. Hosmer, 1902).

2. The woodcut of the shanty was included in the "Thoreau Annex" published in the *Concord Freeman* in 1880.

306. S. A. Jones to A. W. Hosmer, October 22, 1897.

* * *

I did hope to put out one more edition of the Thoreau bibliography, but I must be in a very different condition before I can think of it. I could add so much to the Rowfant edition that is of great interest. Worse than all, I have no child to whom I can leave their father's unfinished work. However, Fred, I did my poor best, under adverse circumstances, and it has been my privilege to at least call attention to Thoreau to a degree that did not exist when you and I began our joint labor of love.

If I ever get the strength, your collection will be of great assistance. . . .

307. S.A. Jones to A. W. Hosmer, October 24, 1897.

Your two letters and the "Acton Sentinel" are at hand. It is a pity we had to "poke up" H.M. & Co. in order to get the latter!

I regret that they have used the old picture of the "shanty." It was criticised at the time of its publication as being incorrect,[1] while the rude cut in the "Sentinel" was praised by Horace Hosmer's brother for its fidelity.[2]

Two considerations have brought this about: First. Mr. S. doesn't care "a damn" for Thoreau farther than his selling qualities go, and, secondly, it was easier to follow the old cut AND cheaper.

I am glad that I do not have to write a line for the "Atlantic." But I am sorry I ever wrote a word to you about doing a paper for it; my zeal ran away with my discretion that time. Alas, that isn't the only time it has done me a similar trick.

Do you know Mr. Walter H. Page, the literary editor of the "Atlantic?" He has probably put me down for an "enthusiast" (as Mr. Scudder did some years since in a letter to Lyman). He meant it disparagingly, and Miss Lyman called him down for it; so you see, I had Scudder's measure taken long ago, and he didn't know it.

This is a rare old world, Fred, full of in-sincerities, and that is why it is so hard for the Scudders and the like of him to understand Thoreau. They'll have to be born again to be able to do it; meanwhile, the world goes on, and these insincerities eat their pudding and thank GOD they are not "enthusiasts." I prefer to be at the "enthusiast's" end of the rope.

1. The old sketch was the one drawn by Sophia Thoreau that appeared on the title page of the first edition of *Walden*. Thoreau himself was apparently dissatisfied with this sketch, for in correcting the proofs he wrote the printer: "I would suggest a little alteration, chiefly in the door, in the wide projection of the roof at the front; and that the bank more immediately about the house be brought out more distinctly." See F. B. Sanborn, *The Life of Henry David Thoreau* (Boston: Houghton Mifflin Co., 1917), p. 338.

2. The rude woodcut was in "Thoreau Annex"; Walter Harding and Milton Meltzer have attributed it to Joseph Hosmer. See *A Thoreau Profile*, p. 145.

308. S. A. Jones to A. W. Hosmer, November 14, 1897.

* * *

On Thursday last I received a complimentary copy of the new edition of "Walden" from the publishers. It was not pleasing to find no word of mention of *your* part, and I am more pleased than ever with myself for declining to write a line for the "Atlantic." I sized up the whole "shooting match" pretty accurately, and I despise the whole crowd of 'em.

I was greatly vexed at the conceit of Mr. Bradford Torrey in HIS patting on the back such a moral giant as Henry D. Thoreau![1] I am actually amazed at the bad taste of Mr. Scudder in allowing such a desecration of a book that is hardly in need of the "approval" of any of the Torrey stamp.

It must have tickled Houghton, Mifflin AND Co. to read my letter acknowledging their gift. It ended with this "sugar tit:" "I read Mr. Torrey's introduction with great interest, and am happy to be able to say that when Mr. Torrey is not original, he is quite entertaining."

I have been hugging myself for that touch, ever since.

I have finally got at work on "Some Unpublished Letters of Henry D. and Sophia E. Thoreau: a Chapter in the History of a Still-born Book." It has taken me a great while to get started, for I had not got back what I had lost by my illness, but I am warming up to the work, and I hope I may not disgrace my subject.

I can introduce the Froude Letter with immense advantage to the interest of the book, and as I understand Mrs. LeBrun's letter, I am at liberty to do so. I shall be obliged to copyright my book, to keep it out of H.M. and Co's hands, for one thing; but every right and interest of Mrs. LeBrun will THEN be as safe as if the copyright were in her own name. I have no "business" in me, Fred, but enough of old-fashioned honor to satisfy all demands.

I shall probably reproduce every one of the Thoreau letters in photolithograph—Sophia's as well as Henry's.

The book will be published at the very finest printing press in these U.S.[2]

I am thinking it would be well to introduce a photo of every picture of Thoreau himself, including one from my daguerreotype—which I consider a better one than Mr. Blake's. I am satisfied it was taken on the same day, AND *before* the Blake copy.

I think this because the eyes are better in mine; they were tired when Thoreau sat the second time, for Mr. Blake's picture.[3]

I have forgotten whether you sent me a picture of Sophia—though I am of the "notion" that you did. I cannot tell, for all my photos are in the University. But if her picture is to be had, I shall consider the propriety of passing her likeness down to posterity. THEN, Fred, there will [be] no failure of mentioning the faithful lover of Thoreau whose patient research made these photos possible. . . .

1. In his introduction Torrey had written patronizingly of *Walden:* "It is to be remembered always that 'Walden' is a young man's book. A philosopher of thirty may be pardoned for holding the truth somewhat stiffly; finding the ideal truer than the actual, and his own faith a surer guide than other people's experience. At that age the earnest soul still believes it possible to live according to one's inner light. With added years, of course, there come wisdom and a tempering of desire" (pp. xxxviii–xxxix).

2. Marion Press of Jamaica, Queensborough, New York.

3. The Greene daguerreotype was one of the three made by B. D. Maxham in Worcester in 1856. Which of the three was made first is not known. See Harding, *Days of Henry Thoreau,* p. 367. *Some Unpublished Letters* did include a photograph of the 1856 daguerreotype, but it was apparently a copy of Blake's rather than of Greene's. The Greene daguerreotype was first published in Francis Allen, *A Bibliography of Henry David Thoreau* (Boston: Houghton Mifflin Co., 1908).

309. A. W. Hosmer to S. A. Jones, November 15, 1897.

I have mailed you today a copy of "Walden" Illustrated—folded in sheets & unbound, as you wished for, which please accept with my regards.

Bradford Torrey has given a very good introduction, but I am rather disappointed in the book. When they first spoke of it, they talked of making more of a book of it, enlarging it with footnotes, but they finally— (to save expense?) used the old plates with the exception of the headings for the chapters, to which they added the scroll work. . . .

I had given me last week a receipt signed by *John Thoreau* "for 12 weeks board—$24.00," one signed by *John Thoreau Jr.* "for Instruction one term $4.00," and one by the *Irishman James Quinn*—to whom Mr. "Maynerd" was "dettor" for "pasterned two heffers" "for Driving and fetching," and "three ouers My oxen and A hand."[1] All the schooling Quinn had was what his wife taught him after he was married.

[P.S.] Both the Thoreaus' hand writing is as clear and regular as the old style writing book copies.

1. These items are in the grangerized *Life of Henry David Thoreau* (Hosmer collection).

310. S. A. Jones to A. W. Hosmer, November 18, 1897.

* * *

I have thought often lately that it might be well if you and I started *republishing* the rarest of the printed material that pertains to Thoreau.[1]

I believe it would sell if put out in pamphlet form, well printed but not so as to be foolishly dear. I would like to SIFT the stuff that has been already published and print it so that the students of Thoreau could have the material CHEAPLY at their hands. It would be a service to literature and it would not be without some pecuniary recompense—for "the laborer is worthy of his hire."

Talk this over with the level-headed Misses Hosmer. Their judgment would go far with me. . . .

1. Dr. Jones republished many early critical reviews and studies of Thoreau in *Pertaining to Thoreau* (Detroit: Edwin B. Hill, 1901).

311. A. W. Hosmer to S. A. Jones, November 18, 1897.

When and where did you get hold of a daguerreotype of Thoreau. Is it the Theo Brown one taken by Maxham of Worcester? For I have been trying for some time to find out where it was. If it is different from the negative that I have, I should like to get a negative from it.

I think I must have sent you a photograph of Sophia Thoreau, but if not let me know and I will send at once. . . .

You probably received my letter the same day that I got yours, which tells you about "where I am at"—and growls somewhat at H. M. & Co. They agreed to send me six copies but only sent two, and I have written them for the others and also touched them up on their not giving me credit as they agreed to do. . . .

312. A. W. Hosmer to S. A. Jones, November 20, 1897.

Just a word before the mail closes. H. M. & Co. omitted my name through an oversight but are printing up some more copies and will have it put in—so if you will return me the copy in sheets I sent you I will return it to them and get one with credit to me, in it. . . .

313. S. A. Jones to A. W. Hosmer, November 22, 1897.

The daguerreotype that was given me is mentioned in the letters that were presented to me by Mr. Greene. It was taken in Worcester and cost fifty cents. The clothing is the same as that worn by T. when the Blake picture was taken. The eyes in my picture are both equally wide open, which makes me think that Thoreau sat for the Greene daguerreotype *first*. The sitting for a daguerreotype was long and fatiguing, and the Blake picture shows that one eyelid drooped from weariness. I distinctly remember the daguerreotype artists used to caution a sitter not to "wink" until he absolutely couldn't help it. . . .

314. A. W. Hosmer to S. A. Jones, November 22, 1897.

* * *

I wrote H. M. & Co in regard to their not having given me credit for the negatives as they agreed to do and had a reply saying, that the one to whom I first spoke *(H. E. Scudder)* had turned the matter over to *W. S. Scudder,* who did not understand it, but on my touching him up, he found out that I should have had credit, so the next lot will have a note in it under "illustrations" that "with a few exceptions the illustrations in this edition of Walden are from photographs taken by Mr. A. W. Hosmer, of Concord, to whom the publishers are indebted for friendly assistance in its preparation". . . .

I wish you would kindly let up on your talk of *any* obligations that I am placing you under—for I feel that it is all the other way. It is entirely through you that I have been brought to know one of the few *Men* in the world, and through him the many good friends I have found.

The Misses Hosmer think that is a very good idea of republishing the best of the reviews on Thoreau.

I read them a week ago Torrey's article in the "Walden" and Jane remarked a number of times that he had drawn a good part of his article from what *Dr. Jones* had written!!!

315. S. A. Jones to A. W. Hosmer, November 24, 1897.

* * *

THANKS again for the copy of Ripley's last page.[1] I paid a good round sum for the original copy, and by some misadventure lost the last sheet. I will now prepare a clean copy for printing.

Ripley also reviewed Thoreau's "Walden" in the New York Tribune[2] and a copy of that must be had for the THOREAUIANA[3]—*as our reprints should be called.*

You can learn through Houghton, Mifflin and Co. just WHEN "Walden" was published, and then a file of the New York Tribune will give us Ripley's review.

The Boston Athenaeum Library or Harvard College will have the N.Y. Tribune on file, and I do not know where else to look for such a file.

It was this particular review that led to Mr. Greene's acquaintance (epistolary) with Thoreau, and I can give a most interesting history of the whole business.

At Harvard College we can also get that paper on Thoreau mentioned in my bibliography of Thoreau. *I mean Morton's paper.*[4] I have been at much trouble to get a paper published in the same magazine *just after Thoreau's death,*[5] and these two would be "stunners" for the lovers of Thoreau to read. Some time when you are in Boston call on Mr. Lane at the Athenaeum Library and tell him Dr. Jones of Ann Arbor, asked you to call on him and enquire how you shall proceed to get a sight of that Harvard Magazine. Mr. Lane has had favors at my hand, and I from his, so he will do all he can for you.

The more I think of this enterprise the more I am made to feel how desirable a matter it will be for the future students of Thoreau. It will also aid in the development of his fame, and I do not know any better purpose to which I can devote the remainder of my life. Do you suppose Houghton, Mifflin and Co. dream how much is owing to what you and I have already been permitted to do in that line? The Thoreau of 1890 and him of 1897 are not the same in public esteem, eh? Even Mr. Bradford Torrey knows that!

Mr. Torrey is a toady; he got his knowledge from Lippincott's Magazine and not from Dr. Emerson's letter, as he pretends.[6] However, that he has

GOT it is the all important fact; no matter where he found it if he will only go on stating it so plainly that the *"Asas"* of not only Concord can have it dinged into their long and hairy ears!

My plan for these reprints takes shape somewhat as follows: 1. They should be "Published by Alfred W. Hosmer. Concord, Mass." 2. They should be printed in uniform shape so that they can be bound in volumes of uniform size, according to the year in which each was published. They should also be for sale *singly*.

I will edit each paper, giving an introduction thereto so that we can copyright the series.

I have a great number of book-loving friends who will no doubt become interested in the movement: for instance, I should not wonder if every member of the Rowfant Club would be purchasers; and the librarians of the colleges will want these publications for the *study of Thoreau* in the courses upon American Literature. Indeed I do not wonder if the project led to my moving to Concord to reside until I turn up my toes to the daisies.

This looks dreamy now, doesn't it? And dreams go by contraries;—but, bless you, this only *looks* like a dream; so I ain't a whit discouraged. . . .

1. "H. D. Thoreau's Book," *New York Tribune*, June 13, 1849. The review is now attributed to Horace Greeley rather than to Ripley.

2. A review of *Walden*, with copious extracts, appeared as "A Massachusetts Hermit" in *New York Tribune*, July 29, 1854. Walter Harding has attributed this review, however, to Horace Greeley rather than to George Ripley. See Harding, *The Days of Henry Thoreau*, p. 332.

3. Dr. Jones did publish a collection of early Thoreau criticism as *Pertaining to Thoreau* (Detroit: Edwin B. Hill, 1901).

4. Edwin Morton, "Thoreau and his Books," *Harvard Magazine* 1 (January 1855):87–99. Reprinted in *Pertaining to Thoreau* (1901).

5. Storrow Higginson, "Henry D. Thoreau," *Harvard Magazine* 8 (May 1862):313–18. Reprinted in *Pertaining to Thoreau* (1901).

6. In his introduction to the 1897 edition of *Walden*, Torrey drew a sympathetic portrait of Mrs. Thoreau, with "quotations made by permission from a letter of Dr. Emerson's" (pp. xiv–xv).

316. Henry Salt to S. A. Jones, November 30, 1897.

* * *

Not a scrap of Thoreau news has reached me for weeks, except a few references in a book presented to me by the author, Wm. Sloan Kennedy of Belmont, Mass., whom perhaps you know by name. This book is "In Portia's Gardens" (Whidden & Co, Boston), and has a foolish comparison of Thoreau with John Burroughs, much to the advantage of the latter. One reads with amazement that "Burroughs has abundance of humor,

Thoreau had very little. . . . He makes you in love with life, Thoreau makes you dissatisfied with it". Is not this astonishing, from a man who supposes himself to be a great admirer of Thoreau! What sort of life must he be living, one wonders, that Thoreau should make him dissatisfied with it?

This will reach you about the time your Christmas Dinner is beginning to be thought of, I suppose. It is well you cannot attend a meeting we are going to hold on Dec. 10, on the subject of "Christmas Cruelties", else I am sure we should succeed in spoiling your appetite for the good fare, and what would Mrs. Jones say to us, *then?* I intend to contribute to the occasion a horrible speech on the Christmas combination of guzzling and church-going, pig's-fat and piety, lard and laud—a sort of "Te Deum *lard*-amus", in fact. So be glad there is an ocean between us!

317. S. A. Jones to A. W. Hosmer, December 5, 1897.

Hoop-de-doodle-doo!!! The daguerreotype of Thoreau is FOUND and at this moment is safe under lock and key in a handsome case of glass and silver plate—never again to roam. I myself had put it away so "darned" safely that I had forgotten where and when I did it. The wife discovered it, and she has put on the most insufferable airs ever since. I have to sneak about the house meeker than Moses. (I pity Mose!)

"Concord Saturday, June 21st '56.

Dear Sir:

On the 12 ult I forwarded the two books to California, observing your directions in every particular, and I trust that Uncle Sam will discharge his duty faithfully. While in Worcester this week I obtained the accompanying daguerreotype—which my friends think is pretty good—though better looking than I.

Books and postage	$2.64
Daguerreotype	.50
Postage	.16
	3.30

	5.00	You will accordingly
	3.30	
find	1.70	enclosed with my shadow. Yrs

Henry D. Thoreau."

That, my dear Fred, is as nearly a facsimile as I can make of the letter Thoreau sent Mr. Greene with the likeness—which was taken at Mr. G's special request; so, you see, Thoreau wasn't so VERY disobliging, after all!

The "two books" are copies of the "Week" and "Walden", sent to Greene's brother in California by order. These volumes are now in my possession. . . .

During the next year the "Marian Press" will issue a "swell," small edition of "Some Unpublished Letters of Henry D. and Sophia E. Thoreau: a Chapter in the History of a Still-Born Book." I shall retain the copyright so that it can be reprinted in a larger edition later; meanwhile keep room on your shelf for a copy of the RARE first edition.

I am pulling a string in New York City with a view to printing, or rather reprinting those early critical essays to show up what gooseberry fools some critics are. If the editor to whom I have written gives a favorable opinion, the thing is a sure go.

If you have got a copy of "Walden" in sheets with your name duly honored in it, THAT IS FOR SALE, I want to buy it—but on no other condition will I touch it.

Oh, another thing: I am getting ready for another edition of the Thoreau Bibliography; so be ready to help me all you can in the matter of correcting the errors and making the due additions. It means a "heap" of work, but it is for HIM.

Can you possibly get from Mrs. LeBrun her history of the Froude letter. I want to surprise Mrs. LeBrun with a copy of the Marian Press book, wherein she will find her letter embalmed, with most grateful recollection of herself. All to be done with due delicacy, for she certainly deserves to live in the gratitude of all lovers of Thoreau.

Let me know whatever you can of Mrs. LeBrun herself so that I may be prepared at all points for my gracious duty.

Take care of yourself; and, O Fred, tell your sacrilegious brother I just took a loving squint at my Baker Farm brick, and I forgive him all his sins, if he won't do so "no more." Ah, how that one visit shines in my memory. I often live it over, and I am thankful for its delights. Oh, for one more!

318. A. W. Hosmer to S. A. Jones, December 17, 1897.

As you are at work on the enlarged bibliography may I make one suggestion, that, in my hunt for the articles I find would be a great help to others who might want to secure the articles, and that is to give the *month* as far as can be in addition to page, number and volume.

Dealers in old magazines do not take readily to hunting them up by page.

In checking up the list by the copies I have I find a few errors, which I will note for your benefit as soon as our Christmas rush is over. . . .

I have started quite a correspondence with Mr. Greene, shall have a photograph of him to add to my book. . . .

319. A. W. Hosmer to S. A. Jones, December 18, 1897.

* * *

Sanborn brought in and gave me some 20 Commonwealth's of '63 & '64, containing poems by Thoreau[1] and Channing's Articles on Thoreau[2]—which were afterwards reprinted in "The Poet-Naturalist"!!!!!!

1. For a complete list of Thoreau's poems which appeared in the Boston *Commonwealth* from June 19 to November 6, 1863, see Francis Allen, *A Bibliography of Henry David Thoreau*, pp. 76–77.
2. Channing's reminiscences appeared serially in the *Commonwealth*, December 25, 1863–February 19, 1864.

320. S. A. Jones to A. W. Hosmer, December 22, 1897.

You make me both pleased and ashamed; pleased to have a copy of "Walden" in which you have the simple justice of 'honorable mention,' and ashamed of finding myself hopelessly on the wrong side of the ledger.

I shall have to write myself: "Dr. S. A. Jones, *Dr.,* to Alfred W. Hosmer, etc." Just look at it a moment—"Dr. S. A. Jones, Dr." Isn't that most deucedly like a hog with a tail at both ends of him? Did you mean to decorate me in that way? Do you think so much "style" becomes me? If you were within reach, I'll be darned if I wouldn't break dear Silas Hosmer's Concord Bridge cane over your back. There! young man, come West and get your basting. . . .

I am delighted to learn what Mr. Sanborn has given you. The value of the first appearance of Channing's tribute to Thoreau is "immense" in a bibliographical sense; but equally valuable is the evidence that Sanborn recognizes what you are doing on the Thoreau line. You should put all those "Commonwealth" articles into a separate scrap-book, as the fittest and safest way of preserving them; in that shape they are also handier for reference and study.

I find in one of Mr. Greene's books a note to the effect that Sophia Thoreau told Mr. G. the poem "Sympathy" *referred to John Thoreau.*[1] This I can readily believe from the internal evidence of the poem itself. The ascription of it to the lady is a pure figment of Emerson's imagination.[2]

Now that you are "in" with Mr. Sanborn, try and find out for me if Mr. S. can say that he ever saw a copy of Froude's "Nemesis of Faith" in the possession of either Emerson or Thoreau. In view of the book I am to make from the Thoreau-Greene letters, it is Very Important for me to Know this Point. (Don't tell him *I* want to know this.) . . .[3]

1. The poem "Sympathy" is generally considered to be Thoreau's tribute to Ellen Sewall's brother Edmund. See Walter Harding, *The Days of Henry Thoreau,*

pp. 77–78. Miss Thoreau's comment to Greene suggests that perhaps the Thoreau family was disturbed by the poem's homoerotic overtones.

2. Dr. Jones marked this paragraph with an exclamation mark.

3. Dr. Jones marked this paragraph with double exclamation points.

321. A. W. Hosmer to S. A. Jones, January 5, 1898.

I have gone over my collections of reviews &c. and enclose a list of where they differ from your bibliography. All the words and dates *underlined* are different from yours or else it is the *month* added. The first chance I get I will go through my books that have references to Thoreau and see if I have any different from your list.

The list I send you is not quite all I have, but with some of them your record and my papers correspond. I have sent to England for some of the English articles and will report on them as soon as received.

Am quite busy at the store as Brown is closing out his business and with the goods marked way down it brings in a rush of customers. Last week I was too tired when I got out of the store to do anything but rest. . . .

322. S. A. Jones to A. W. Hosmer, January 10, 1898.

* * *

That note of yours about Froude and his "Nemesis of Faith" is valuable as *Sanborn's testimony;* but the information is dreadfully incomplete as it is.

How does he KNOW that "a copy was sent to Thoreau"? Sanborn did not know the Thoreau family until long after the publication of Froude's unfortunate "Nemesis," and it is n't likely that Thoreau would brag to Sanborn of having "had a letter from Froude."

When you GET TIME, pump Sanborn for MINUTE details; how he knew about the Froude letter; whether the "Nemesis of Faith" was published *before* or AFTER Thoreau's "Week."[1]

It is curious that Froude should "send a copy of the book to Thoreau", when there is no trace of his sending one to Emerson—at least, neither Edward nor Ellen recall anything about seeing one.[2] It was hardly a book for a young person to read, and I wonder if the prudent Ralph Waldo kept, or put, his copy out of sight. . . .

1. *The Nemesis of Faith* appeared either at the very end of February or in the first few days of March, 1849. *A Week* appeared on May 30, 1849.

2. Edward W. Emerson had written that he knew "nothing whatever of my Father's relations to Froude." Emerson to Dr. Jones, October 22, 1897 (Jones collection). Later, however, Edward added: "My Father evidently had the Nemesis for he refers to it . . . in a Journal which extends from Nov. 1849 until the end of the following year." Edward W. Emerson to Dr. Jones, November 14, 1897 (Jones collection). Emerson's copy of *The Nemesis of Faith* is still extant. See Walter

Harding, *Emerson's Library* (Charlottesville: University Press of Virginia, 1967), p. 111.

323. S. A. Jones to A. W. Hosmer, January 12, 1898.

I have this moment finished copying Mrs. LeBrun's letter and I enclose the original. It is singularly interesting as explanatory of the Froude letter, but it is even more valuable for its testimony to the superior quality of the "women of the Thoreau family." I shall incorporate the evidence it affords in a re-written text of that first unpublished lecture, delivered after my return from Concord in 1890. We will bury Sanborn for the dirty work he did in Thoreau's Life.

Last night I received your three sheets of bibliographical items; books this time. I shall incorporate so much of the list as should be preserved in a bibliography. Many of them I must SEE before including them, for in bibliography one has to do some *weeding*.

I should like a copy of the Proceedings at the Concord Celebration.[1] It will fit into the Thoreau Collection for the University nicely.

I learned in a very curious manner that there is a fine paper on Thoreau in the "Harvard Monthly" for December, 1897.[2] Of course that does n't find place in our far distant newspaper shops, so if it is convenient, look it up and see if it is a real addition to what we have so far found.

Miss Lyman's judgement is decidedly sound in regard to Mr. Bradford Torrey's inability to appreciate Thoreau.[3] Torrey is of the earth earthy, and I much question if Thoreau would have admitted him to one of his 'walks.'

Miss Lyman is an acute reader of Thoreau, and a woman's instinct goes further with me than heaps of the twaddle of the so-called 'critics'. . . .

1. The 1875 centennial of independence celebration.
2. Daniel Gregory Mason, "The Idealistic Basis of Thoreau's Genius," *Harvard Monthly* 25 (December 1897):82–93.
3. When Dr. Jones later published a review of the 1897 *Walden* which sharply criticized Torrey, Emily Lyman wrote Hosmer: "The criticism is a *correct* one, but it is severe, and Mr. Torrey will not be likely to misunderstand what Dr J——— means!" Emily Lyman to A. W. Hosmer, April 5, 1898 (Hosmer collection).

324. Henry Salt to S. A. Jones, January 18, 1898.

* * *

I was much entertained by your account of your dealings with Mr. Bradford Torrey. It is sad to think how many Mr. Bradford Torreys there are in literature. This particular Mr. B. T. must be a terrible blot on the new *Walden,* and it angers one that Houghton & M. should have been such fools as to let him in.[1] I have not yet seen the book, but shall doubtless do so before long, and if I should get a chance of doing a review of it will perhaps have a word to say about the "Introduction". . . .

I had a very pleasant letter from Mr. E. M. Macdonald, and hope he and I may keep each other in sight. We have a common interest in free-thought, as well as in Thoreau.

About the poem "Sympathy". I am much interested in what you tell me, but am not quite sure that I apprehend you rightly! Do you mean that Henry Thoreau in that poem speaks in the person of John, and that it is John's "affair" with Ellen Sewall that is referred to? That may be so, but would still leave unexplained the difficulty of the girl being described as a gentle boy. Or do you mean that John himself was the gentle boy of the poem? . . .[2]

1. For a more generous assessment of Bradford Torrey, see Francis H. Allen, *Thoreau's Editors: History and Reminiscence (Thoreau Society Booklet Number Seven,* 1950).

2. Dr. Jones was undoubtedly expounding this thesis which he entered in his copy of *Poems of Nature:* "In Mr. Greene's copy of the 'Week,' edition of 1868, he had written that Sophia Thoreau told him that this poem ["Sympathy"] referred to *John Thoreau, Jr.*" (p. 21).

325. S. A. Jones to A. W. Hosmer, January 25, 1898.

* * *

How do you like Mr. Mason's paper in the "Harvard Monthly?" He has taken a fanciful name for his title, and he is "off" in his notion that Thoreau is hardly appreciated as a profound philosopher; but it is a good sign when young men in college turn as seriously towards Thoreau as he has done. . . .

Your letter of Saturday last confirms my conjecture concerning the occasion of Thoreau's writing to Froude.[1] Take the "Week" and read the chapter named "Sunday." There are the *thoughts* for which Froude expresses his gratitude.

On the coming Friday night I am to read a paper on "Some Unpublished Letters of Henry D. and Sophia E. Thoreau: A Chapter in the History of a Stillborn Book." I am reading it for the pecuniary benefit of the Ladies' Gymnasium Aid Association and shall have to repeat it in other parts of the State; but so soon as possible I will send it on for you to read at the Hosmers some Sunday night.

How I do wish I were with you to read "The Nemesis of Faith." Does Miss

Emerson know anything about the Froude letter? I hope not, for if Sanborn gets "on to" it Mrs. LeBrun will be a much disappointed woman. . . .

1. Thoreau sent Froude a copy of *A Week,* perhaps at the suggestion of Emerson.

326. A. W. Hosmer to S. A. Jones, January 28, 1898.

I returned the "Nemesis" today and find that Miss Emerson had never read it. I enjoyed reading it, the first part better than the closing. I did not like the idea of bringing in the love of the man for another man's wife. Froude ought to have been able to carry out his ideas without that. To my idea it weakens the whole book.

We enjoyed Omar last sunday evening.[1] I read the whole of it, have read it to myself and also to the young lady in the store. Miss Jane thinks that after hearing Omar's ideas that the body turned to clay shall be worked again by the potter, turned out into vases, &c, he will cause her to have an added veneration for her china. To portions of it, it was "I do not like that," while to others it was "read that over again."

I wish I were going to hear you read that article. However I shall have to take it out in reading it myself—and to the Misses Hosmer. After trying my best at various old book stores to get a copy of the Jour. of Spec. Phil. with Cooke's article on "The Dial," with no success I wrote to Prof. W. T. Harris,[2] and he kindly sent me one.[3]

1. Dr. Jones had sent Hosmer a translation of *The Stanzas of Omar Khayyam.*
2. George Willis Cooke, " 'The Dial': An Historical and Biographical Introduction, with a List of the Contributors," *Journal of Speculative Philosophy* 19 (July 1885):225–65. W. T. Harris was William Torrey Harris, founder of the *Journal of Speculative Philosophy.*
3. With this letter Hosmer apparently sent a copy of a letter from Sophia Thoreau to Miss Ward. A text, from Hosmer's copy, follows:

Concord May 12, 1862

My Dear Miss Ward

I send you a copy of some mottoes placed in dear Henry's coffin by his friend W. E. Channing.

"Hail to thee, O man, who art come from the transitory place to the imperishable."

"Gazed on the Heavens for what he missed on Earth."

"I thynke for to touch also
The world whiche neweth everie daie,
So as I can so as I maie."

Your sorrow stricken friend
Sophia

Thoreau prefaced the second and third of these mottoes to the "Monday" section of *A Week*. The second is from William Browne, "The Shepherd's Pipe," Eclogue 4, line 170, although Thoreau in *A Week* incorrectly attributed it to "Britania's Pastorals." The third is from Gower, Prologue to *Confessio Amantis*, ll. 58–60. These have been identified by Walter Harding in his edition of *A Week* (New York: Holt, Rinehart & Winston, 1963), pp. 335–36. We have been unable to identify the first motto.

327. S. A. Jones to A. W. Hosmer, January 31, 1898.

I have received the letter Sophia wrote, but find nothing in it that I could use in my talk. I also have the account of the celebration of the anniversary. I am so glad your father's signature is on it; and I have often thought how fortunate I have been to have seen both him and Silas Hosmer. Depend upon it, Fred, they belong to a race of men that is disappearing; and God only knows what sort of stuff is taking their places. . . .

I had a letter from Mr. Salt the other day, and it led me to spend last night in reading his last Life of Thoreau. It is a book that grows upon me with every reading, and little more can be said about Thoreau. I have bought an extra copy for interleaving so that I can put in such notes as occur to me from time to time.

I am just crazy to read that "Nemesis of Faith," and crazier still to own a book that was once Emerson's. Of course the idea is preposterous; but I suppose that is the very reason the darned "notion" sticks so persistently to me. There are things that one cannot offer to purchase because that is so coarse a transaction; but I would wear the same old coat half a century if such a saving would enable me to get any book whatever for which I feel heart hungry. Dear me! *what* would my life have been only for the solace and the precious companionship. I never feel poor when I shut the door of my dingy little "den" and see the books around me—nearly every one of which is the silent witness of some privation in order that I might get it. . . .

328. A. W. Hosmer to S. A. Jones, February 11, 1898.

I send you today a few pictures taken by a friend of mine that I thought might be of interest to you. I shall probably get the same over later with my larger camera. Thoreau's description of Gowing's "Swamp—in Winter" p. 307 answers as well for the Ledum or C. Miles Swamp.

In the one from Hubbard's bridge, the Hollowell farm is on the left and about as far *off* the picture as the willows are from the edge of it—and in about the same line.

In the view from the cliffs—you are looking across the river, over Conantum to Nine Acre Corner. The cleared land is a portion of the *second* division of land that came to the first of our name here, and was in the family until about 50 years ago, it passed down through another branch of it and so went out of the name. The old front door step is still there, (the house must have been built in the latter part of 1600), but it will not stay through this winter as I have bought it, and it will be delivered to me before the snow leaves. Have just written Mr. Greene, and at his request have sent him one of my photos.

329. S. A. Jones to A. W. Hosmer, February [13?], 1898.

According to my promise, I send for your reading the paper I read here and at Pontiac. The Ann Arbor audience was one that had some knowledge of Thoreau, but I could not expect *that* in so worldly a city as Pontiac; so I did not venture to deliver the talk on the "Letters" to the Pontiac audience which gathered in the Lyceum Theatre. I read one hurriedly written for the occasion, giving some account of Thoreau's parentage, surroundings, education, life at Walden Pond, and the purpose of that episode in his life. I assured them that it was not a "whim," as Lowell and Holmes[1] more than insinuate (and I did "go for" Lowell in defiance of the worship of him by the la-de-da family). I told them that Thoreau was carrying out a design formed in his under-graduate days, etc.

The audience didn't agree with me, and THAT is what I liked; so I fired into them regardless of THEIR opinions. However, I held them earnest listeners for an hour. At the close, a lady announced that Dr. J. would give the "lecture" on the "LETTERS" at the residence of Dr. A. in the afternoon of the following day and that the members of the Library Association were invited. The following day it rained and was awfully slushy; but, by Jove! how the ladies did pile into that large parlor. The paper takes me over an hour to deliver, but they sat as quietly as if I were reading a will whose every devisement was for them, making them rich.

They saw and FELT the human side of Thoreau, and they were red-hot to read him and about him. I hate this public reading; I can understand how Thoreau disliked it; but I melted them, overcame the polite repugnance they had inherited (from hearsay), and they said my enthusiasm for Thoreau was sustained by what they had heard.

As the pulpit pounders put it, they were "under conviction" and I hope a genuine "conversion" will follow. . . .

[P.S.] (So soon as you return the "Letters" I shall go to work to put them into shape for publication. This paper will need to be entirely recast, for a "book" is n't a "talk." I want the Hosmers to put on their critical spectacles and tell me "honestly" if they think there interest enough in the "business" to justify making them public. They were written to a simple man and THEY are simple.)

1. In his biography of Emerson, Dr. Holmes flippantly characterized Thoreau as "that unique individual, half college-graduate and half Algonquin, the Robinson Crusoe of Walden Pond, who carried out a school-boy whim to its full proportions." See *Ralph Waldo Emerson* (Boston: Houghton, Mifflin and Co., 1885), p. 72.

330. A. W. Hosmer to S. A. Jones, February 21, 1898.

I read the papers[1] over to myself, then to the young lady in the store, and last evening to Jane Hosmer. Abby being sick abed, did not hear it.

Jane was very much taken with it, and wants me to read it over again so Abby can hear what you have to say. The only criticism she has made is: the suggestion that you leave out the "carcasses—that stink"[2] and that you change the "45 below-zero notelet"[3] to some other phrase.

She takes the other view, that Channing used those quotations to show his thanks, (this of course without knowing what they are—) the reading of them might change these ideas.[4]

After reading it to Abby, I will report again on it. For myself I have thoroughly enjoyed it, and if the book is published I shall want three or four copies. . . .

1. The lecture on the Thoreau-Greene correspondence which Dr. Jones read in Ann Arbor, January 23, 1898. A copy of this lecture, in Alfred Hosmer's hand, is in the Hosmer collection.
2. In his lecture Dr. Jones had commented that Sophia Thoreau could be "prouder of her brother dead than of all the countless carcasses strutting in the sunlight, alive, but kept from stinking only by the cheap salt of civilization."
3. In 1863 Calvin H. Greene had sent Sophia Thoreau a cane which his brother had designed especially for Thoreau; Sophia gave the cane to Channing, who wrote Greene a short note, which Dr. Jones characterized as a "forty-five-below-zero-notelet" containing "just sixteen words, not one of which will spell 'Thanks.'"
4. Channing included with his note to Greene some three pages of mottoes selected from Thoreau's writings. Of these Dr. Jones wrote sarcastically: "This is the manner in which a transcendentalist expresses one of the tenderest emotions of the non-transcendental heart."

331. S. A. Jones to A. W. Hosmer, February 28, 1898.

* * *

It does n't much matter whether Thoreau had a likeness taken for Brown or not; he certainly had one taken for Mr. Greene. But I do not know how I am to send a copy of it for Mr. Ricketson. If I get it photographed here the photographer will be reproducing it for sale, and I don't propose to allow that. The fellow has already been at me to copy the picture; but I know he can't be trusted, and I have invariably refused him the privilege.

I should not like to trust the picture to an Express company, for IF it was lost what would replace it? . . .

332. S. A. Jones to A. W. Hosmer, March 1, 1898.

Although I wrote to you this morning, I am giving up my afternoon snooze (I take one before supper, to rest after work hours) to get some things clearly settled in the matter of Thoreau's lectures before the Concord Lyceum.

In the list of lectures that you got from the Lyceum records you make no mention of any lecture in 1848. Now turn to page 19 of my Bibliography. Thoreau's letter to Emerson shows that he read a lecture that year, for he mentions how much Alcott liked it.[1] That lecture was subsequently published by Miss Peabody in "Aesthetic Papers."[2] See also *Letters*, p. 173, bottom of page, also p. 180 "Ktaadn."

Look, too, on page 18, at the mention of a lecture on "Friendship."[3] Perhaps he never read that, but it furnished material that he used in the "Week."

I consider this "record" find as the biggest thing you have done in a long time, and I have been working on the thing at every moment I could snatch today. I tell you, Fred, [it] will be a vast improvement, for between the two of us, it will have many additions and many needful corrections.

I was also so full of this lecture business that the Ricketson bust faded "out of sight." It is just like you to be so thoughtful as to send me proofs as soon as you could lay hands on the camera; and it was indeed a gratification to see what Mr. Ricketson has done; but, Fred, it is NOT Thoreau. Sanborn has hit the very word when he says it is not sufficiently "aggressive." The bust is a fine work of art, but it is not Thoreau. It looks like some promising young "theological" student. Was Thoreau *that!*? Not by a d. s.! Then, just see how deuced "slick" Mr. Ricketson has got him up! Thoreau couldn't WOULDN'T have tied his cravat so jauntily; and the collar—that is altogether too darned "proper" for Henry Thoreau.

In my daguerreotype, if I may so call it from holding it, the lower lip pouts in its fullness. There is none of that in the bust. Moreover, Thoreau's chin receded, and that would be a defect 'from an art point' in the bust; but we want the man as he WAS.

Thoreau is the last man for an artist to idealize, and that is just what Mr. R. has done; but it is a mistake.

To reproduce Thoreau exactly as he is in the daguerreotype I have been examining for the last five minutes would not be to make a "caricature." Unless, indeed, Thoreau, as God made him, is one.

If I admired Thoreau for the mere physical beauty in him, I should like Mr. Ricketson's presentment exceedingly; it represents a very "nice" man.

But we have abundant evidence that Thoreau was remarkable homely, and it won't do to palm off any sculptor's "improvements." The world does not want counterfeits; no, not even for "art's" sake.

But let me turn to the pleasanter work of writing up the "Chronology of Thoreau" with such new light as you have so happily afforded.

[P.S.] I forgot that the proofs were not "fixed" and so left one thoughtlessly exposed to daylight for an hour while I made some visits. During my absence Thoreau got awfully brown—sunburnt. I've got him in cold cream.

1. Thoreau to Emerson, February 23, 1848, *The Correspondence of Henry David Thoreau*, pp. 207–9.
2. On January 26, 1848, and again three weeks later Thoreau gave the lecture at the Concord Lyceum, which was published as "Resistance to Civil Government" in Elizabeth Peabody's *Aesthetic Papers* (1849). See Walter Harding, *The Days of Henry Thoreau*, p. 206.
3. There is no record of Thoreau's presenting "Friendship" as a lecture.

333. A. W. Hosmer to S. A. Jones, March 1, 1898.

I reread your article to the Misses Hosmer last Sunday evening, and they were both very much interested in it. Jane said she enjoyed it much more than she did the first time hearing it, and thought it a *very strong* article.

She offers a few suggestions, but those she says she would not have made, only you wanted them to criticize it.

In publishing the article she thinks that the *whole* of Channing's letter should be printed, that those quotations of his would be very interesting reading.[1]

That you are wrong in speaking of C. as being a "pensioner in the home of a friend,"[2] for he pays board, has quite an annuity, (thinks it about $1200. a year but is not positive). This money was left him in this way. The giver knowing the unpracticalness of the man, preferred to leave it in that way.

And that she should not use the word humble in connection with Mr. Greene—not but what in its *best* meaning it would be the word to use, but in the general use of the word it takes too low a meaning. That Mr. Greene showed himself anything but *low* in being able to grasp Thoreau's meaning, even if he is modest and retiring.[3]

I do *not* like to try and write this kind of a letter, wish I might *talk* with you instead—it is so much easier to say than to write, and it looks so stiff and cold on paper.

I read those letters to my cousins a week ago, and they wanted to know if I did not have some more of Dr. Jones' articles to read to them, so I read them one of your lectures of 1891 last night, and next week will read the other one.

1. Dr. Jones did not include in *Some Unpublished Letters* the mottoes which Channing sent Greene with his note of March 4, 1863.
2. Dr. Jones had referred to Channing thus in his lecture on the Thoreau-Greene correspondence; in 1898 Channing was living with F. B. Sanborn.
3. In his lecture Jones included some cutting remarks aimed at his "extra select" audience in Ann Arbor, whom he contrasted with Greene: "This lowly born and lowly bred man, who owes little to the school and less to the college, had vouchsafed unto him the divine gift of insight."

334. S. A. Jones to A. W. Hosmer, March 14, 1898.

* * *

I read your account of your visit to the Athenaeum with interest. Would n't it make a grand paper to reprint those newspaper reports with the editorial comments just to show Thoreau's moral courage? Ah, if I only lived where I had access to the Athenaeum I would do that bit of work. Mr. Garrison, of H. M. and Co., wrote to me some three years ago that he heard Thoreau deliver that Plea for John Brown.[1]

We of to-day do not begin to half realize what "nerve" it required to do what Thoreau did, and *so bravely*. It is the crowning act of his life, and to understand him rightly, it is necessary to know all that can be learned from the daily papers of the time.

I thought Mr. Blake was ill and near his end, and now I learn that he is well enough for you to write to him. If you will send me his address, I will also send him a letter. I feel that I should do so before he goes from us. Please bear in mind to give me his present address when you write.

I am struck by what Sanborn says about the lack of "aggressiveness" in the new bust. It is a defect and a deficiency, if HE notices it; and it should be corrected, for those who are poorly informed about Thoreau are apt to consider him something of a milk-sop—and THAT is just what he was NOT. . . .

H. M. and Company sent the INLANDER a copy of the illustrated "Walden" and the editor got me to do the "notice" of the book.[2] I have written pretty sharply about Mr. Bradford Torrey, and I have given one Fred Hosmer a dose about his pictures.[3] It is a strong paper FOR Thoreau; it gives Lowell a wipe that will do some of his admirers service in opening their eyes; and it occurs to me that you might like to have some extra copies. . . .

1. Francis J. Garrison, son of William Lloyd Garrison, wrote Dr. Jones that he had seen Thoreau deliver "A Plea for Captain John Brown" at Tremont Temple on November 1, 1859, (January 3, 1895, Jones collection).

2. "Vox Clamantis in Deserto," *Inlander* 8, no. 6 (March 1898):222–30.

3. Dr. Jones criticized Torrey sharply for the latter's condescending statement in his introduction that "it is to be remembered always that 'Walden' is a young man's book." Such comment, Jones retorted, "is only Mr. Bradford Torrey 'reconciling' Thoreau's 'sentiments' to the charitable consideration of the 'modern reader.'" For Hosmer's illustrations, though, Jones had nothing but praise: "'Fred' Hosmer's camera has done faithful work; doing it as for very love of Thoreau's memory."

335. A. W. Hosmer to S. A. Jones, March 16, 1898.

* * *

I will send you on some *proofs* from the Ricketson bust as soon as there is sun to print them. For my part, I like the bust *better* than any of the pictures. The beard under the chin makes too much of a caricature. . . .

I should like half a dozen copies of the Inlander, with your review of "Walden" and will remit on receipt of the same. Dec 14. 1853 Lectured—Journey to Moosehead Lake Feb 14 1855 What shall it profit a man, if he gain the whole world and lose his own soul, Feb 25. 1858 "Lectured or told the story of his excursion into Maine last summer" March 2. 1859 Autumn Tints Feb 8, 1860 Wild Apples.[1]

I will ask Sanborn in regard to Storms Higginson[2] the first time I see him, but perhaps you may find out about him from T. W. Higginson.

P.M.—I managed to print up some proofs this noon and so send them along. I should not bank too much on Sanborn's ideas on the bust, as he is such a kantankerous old cuss that he would find fault with anything but just what *he* did *himself*.

1. These were lectures which Thoreau delivered before the Concord Lyceum.
2. S. A. Jones and Alfred W. Hosmer incorrectly identified Samuel Storrow Higginson as "Storms" Higginson. Higginson was the author of "Henry D. Thoreau," *Harvard Magazine* 8 (May 1862):313–18. Dr. Jones later reprinted this essay in *Pertaining to Thoreau* (1901).

336. S. A. Jones to A. W. Hosmer, March 18, 1898.

I am more than obliged for the respective addresses of Col. Higginson and Mr. Blake. I shall make use of them speedily. I hope to get information from Mr. Higginson regarding Storms Higginson, but Sanborn's recollections would also be of real value for my purpose in editing S. Higginson's sympathetic paper on *Thoreau.* It would cost but little more to include that other paper: "On Thoreau and His Books,"[1] in the First volume and second number of the *Harvard Magazine.* It was written, you know, by Edwin Morton.

Can you get that Harvard student who is writing on Thoreau to obtain for me a *carefully collated* copy of Morton's review? Let him get a *reliable* typewriter to do it; I'll cheerfully "whack up" for the expense, because I would dearly like to reprint this paper with Higginson's.

It occurs to me that I can do better; I can get the University to borrow that volume of the *Harvard Magazine* from Harvard University, and I will copy it.

So don't bother that student until I try if this borrowing can be done.

I wonder if you dreamed how much your reading of the Lyceum records would be worth to the new edition of the Thoreau Bibliography? I guess not.

Now, please, help me to this information,—First, How was that debate on Jan'y 27th, 1841, settled? Did the Thoreau boys come out ahead, or did Alcott knock 'em out? This is a really significant item, for it is a matter of course that the Thoreaus would take the AFFIRMATIVE and old Alcott the negative; but *which party carried the day*?????[2]

Again: You write as follows—

> "Feb. 8, 1843. Lectured (no subject given).[3]
> Nov. 29, " . " "Ancient Poets"

Does this mean that Thoreau lectured *twice* in 1843; or should the date of the lecture on "Ancient Poets" be 1844?

In 1843 Thoreau left Concord to teach in Staten Island, and he returned to Concord in 1844. I do not see how he could have lectured in Concord in *November 1843*.[4] Please straighten out this snarl for me. . . .

You see, Fred, so many people turn up in Concord and find *you*, that you are in the most favorable position for making known anything that is written in defence, as it were, of Thoreau's memory; and as my review touches up Mr. Bradford Torrey so nicely that I am desirous of having the right people get hold of the INLANDER having that "tickler" in it. You will be able to place many copies in the right hands to bring Mr. Torrey to account—and that's what I'm after. . . .

1. Edwin Morton, "Thoreau and his Books," *Harvard Magazine* 1 (January 1855):87–99.

2. The subject of the debate of January 27, 1841, was "Is it ever proper to offer forcible resistance?" John and Henry took the affirmative position, Alcott the negative. See Walter Harding, *The Days of Henry Thoreau*, p. 142.

3. Thoreau's subject on February 8, 1843, was Sir Walter Raleigh. See Walter Harding, *The Days of Henry Thoreau*, p. 143.

4. Thoreau did lecture at the Concord Lyceum on November 29, 1843; he had come home from Staten Island for a Thanksgiving visit. His subject was "The Ancient Poets." He had gone to Staten Island in May, 1843, to serve as tutor to William Emerson's children. The experiment was an utter failure, and Thoreau

returned to Concord for good in December of the same year. See Walter Harding, *The Days of Henry Thoreau*, pp. 145–56.

337. Henry Salt to S. A. Jones, March 22, 1898.

I owe you thanks for your welcome letter of Jan. 30th, which I ought to have acknowledged ere now. I was glad to hear that your Thoreau lecture had gone off so successfully, and hope you will repeat it many times. It is certain that lectures often "find the spot" more effectually than books; and I wish I had the courage to *talk* about Thoreau as you have done. But I have always felt an insuperable repugnance to committing myself to a *lecture*, though I don't mind joining in a *discussion*, a weakness which has lost me many valuable opportunities of spreading the views I wish to see spread.

I don't know what to think of your interpretation of the poem "Sympathy". It seems to be open to as grave difficulties as the other solutions of the problem. For at the date when the poem was written—long before John Thoreau's death—what separation could there have been between the brothers, & what was the "bliss irrevocably gone"? Do you think it refers to some temporary misunderstanding, arising out of the Ellen Sewall affair? I confess I feel no conviction in *any* of the explanations that have been offered. I am becoming a prey to agnosticism of the worst kind! . . .[1]

1. Salt is apparently referring, as in the letter of January 18, 1898, to Calvin Greene's statement that John Thoreau was the "gentle boy."

338. S. A. Jones to A. W. Hosmer, April 1, 1898.

* * *

I am exceedingly sorry to hear that Miss Jane Hosmer "objects" to my mentioning Thoreau as being "homely". He was more than that: he was superlatively homely, and we have Emerson's word for it.[1] As Emerson was a full-grown man and Miss Hosmer somewhat younger than she is now, I feel it infinitely safer to take Emerson's word. I imagine that intelligent readers will do likewise. I am sorry to be obliged to write you that my dauguerreotype of Thoreau sʜows him to have been exceeding "uncouth in dress." Perhaps he was "disguised" when he had that picture taken: tried to make himself appear as "uncouth" as possible. Oh, yes, that explains it, of course!

Miss Jane Hosmer is not aware that she is tampering with actual history in her mistaken course of trying to make out Thoreau to be other than he

WAS; which fact—Thoreau's appearance—is safely established beyond all the devices of over-aesthetic ladies whatever.

I believe Miss Hosmer has taught school before to-day; then she should certainly know that a man in the CLEANEST of clothes can still be most uncouthly dressed. Is there such a thing as a dictionary in the Hosmer house?

I presume I ought not to let a little finicky nonsense disturb me—but, somehow, it always [does], and particularly when it comes from such a source. . . .

Our town is suffering from an eruption of pedagogues. It makes me think of your notorious "School of Philosophy," but I'll be danged if such a crowd of hang-dog looking creatures can be found outside of a gathering of clergymen. What IS there about schoolteaching that knocks the common humanity clean out of any man or woman who goes into it? Of course, I except such superior specimens as the Thoreau children. The ordinary run, however, are those of which I am making "honorable mention."

[P.S.] "He is as ugly as sin, long-nosed, queer-mouthed, and with uncouth and somewhat rustic though courteous manners."[2] Who wrote that of Thoreau!

By Jinks, Fred, Thoreau himself would laugh at the wax figure you latter-day Concord folks are trying so hard to make of him.

1. See Charles Woodbury, *Talks with Ralph Waldo Emerson* (London: Kegan Paul & Co., 1890), p. 79.
2. See *The American Notebooks by Nathaniel Hawthorne. Based Upon the Original Manuscripts in the Pierpont Morgan Library,* ed. Randall Stewart (New Haven: Yale University Press, 1932), pp. 166–67.

339. S. A. Jones to A. W. Hosmer, April 15, 1898.

* * *

We will not quarrel about the word "uncouth." "Uncouth in dress," does not mean what you ascribe to the word. The "style of fifty years ago" might appear odd to-day; it is not, therefore, "uncouth." Take two men wearing the garb of fifty years ago: one man puts it on in such manner that he looks "dressy," another's manner of wearing it makes that very garb appear uncouth because he wears it in a peculiar manner. What I wished to convey in my letter is that I am not prepared to go to school, at least in the matter of using the English language, and the exhibitions of false taste on the part of Miss Jane Hosmer made me "tired."

You see, Fred, I am so built that I go for any pretence as a bull does for a red rag, and Miss Hosmer's pretensions do not "cut any ice" with me. I tell you her APPRECIATION of Thoreau does not go very far beneath her skin.

Having said this to make my position clear to you, I have done with that topic forever.

I am so glad you sent a copy of the Inlander to Miss Lyman. I esteem her highly; but I dropped correspondence with her simply because I had not time for it. I did not care to hurt her feelings by telling the plain truth; I was willing to be considered a barbarian for breaking off as I did—but I have given the time that was taken up in writing to her, for such work as I have done on the Thoreau line. She may misjudge me NOW, but in Eternity she will know the truth, and if she really esteems Thoreau, all will be well.

I write amid much confusion, for I am far from settled and I am feeling old. My army life has made me play out early, but as I am, failing, stupid, pig-headed and I know not what, I still am, dear Fred, as truly yours as such a shabby old "seed" can be. Bear with my short-comings as well as you can, I shall not try your patience and forbearance very long.

340. Henry Salt to S. A. Jones, April 22, 1898.

Very many thanks for the copy of *Walden*, which reached me two or three days ago, and added another to the many visible proofs of your kind thought and friendship. I am as delighted with Mr. Hosmer's share in the book as I am amazed and disgusted with Mr. Torrey's—or rather with the publishers who could allow that inept gentleman to write his twaddle *there!* In reading the earlier & colourless pages of the "Introduction", I felt sure that some real impertinence would crop out later on, and when I came to pp. xxxviii, xxxix, I found my presentiment verified. So *Walden* is "a young man's book", and "with added years, of course, there come *(to a Mr. Bradford Torrey)* added wisdom", &c, &c. But "whether Thoreau would ever have arrived at this pitch of catholicity *(Torrey's pitch)* is more than any one can say". I wonder how it is that literary men grow up, in all parts of the world evidently, to such inconceivable silliness!

However I try not to think of Mr. Bradford Torrey, but turn to Mr. Hosmer's illustrations, and recover my serenity of mind. Many of them are familiar to me from the photographs he has sent me from time to time, and I am very pleased to see them in this permanent form, and so well reproduced. I must try to get some English paper to take an article about the illustrated *Walden* and *Cape Cod*.

You have done me yet another "good turn" in enabling Mr. D. G. Mason to write to me, and send me his *Harvard Monthly* article. On looking into it carefully, I see it is a very able piece of writing, and I am much struck both by his insight and vigorous phrases. If, as I gather from his letter, he is a young man, he should do some exceedingly valuable Thoreau-work in his time. . . .[1]

1. Daniel Gregory Mason (1873–1953) later became a composer and professor of music at Columbia from 1910 to 1938. In 1926 he composed a "Chanticleer Overture," which took its title from the epigraph to *Walden*. Mason also was the author of a biography of Thoreau, which unfortunately was never published.

341. Henry Salt to A. W. Hosmer, April 22, 1898.

Many thanks for forwarding the *Walden,* which reached me safely a day or two ago. I can sincerely congratulate *you* on your work in connection with it, for I think the illustrations are a great success and make the book a most interesting one. Mr. Torrey's inane introduction is certainly a drawback, and one marvels how the publishers could have let him disport himself in such a place in such a manner; but, even *with* Mr. Torrey, it is very gratifying to see an illustrated *Walden* at last! . . .

342. S. A. Jones to A. W. Hosmer, April 23, 1898.

* * *

It was surely the fulness of time for Mr. Blake;[1] yet I feel the world to be poorer for me now that he has gone hence. Only think, Fred, Mr. Blake was graduated the year (1835) after I was born. That makes him seem very old to me.

I thank you for the copy of the Boston Advertiser. I cut out the notice, corrected the error in the year of Mr. B's graduation, and pasted the slip in the very copy of "Early Spring" that Mr. Blake gave me: it is the copy the publishers sent him—presumably the first bound one.

If the Worcester papers have any mention of him, let me know the gist of the matter, for I must write up my visit to Mr. B in 1890, and all facts will aid greatly in doing him justice.

I can't write, Fred. Two of my sons start for the war tomorrow, and I am sitting in the dark shadow of the old war. They are all enthusiasm. Alas! I know what it MEANS. Nevertheless, it is a righteous war if the politicians keep their unholy hands off. A war for humanity must not be made a war for an inch of territory. Pardon my abruptness: I can neither write nor do anything else. I shall be a poor correspondent, Fred, henceforth, but you will know the reason and pardon me.

1. H.G.O. Blake died April 18, 1898.

343. S. A. Jones to A. W. Hosmer, May 1, 1898.

* * *

I am particularly pleased with the final disposition of such Thoreau material as was in Mr. Blake's keeping. Now we can only hope that Mr. Russell[1] will make a wise disposition of the sacred trust committed to him.

In a literary sense, Mr. Sanborn is well qualified to edit Thoreau, but he is not the man Thoreau would have appointed for that purpose. In my opinion, he lacks that high principle without which no one should touch anything pertaining to Thoreau. . . .

A letter from Dr. Emerson sides with me in regard to my utterances concerning Mr. Torrey.[2] Dr. E. would n't have written as I did, but he sees that I am one who writes what he thinks, and I know he respects my convictions as to the dead man Thoreau. . . .

1. Blake left Thoreau's papers to E. Harlow Russell.
2. Edward Emerson wrote to thank Dr. Jones for a copy of "Vox Clamantis in Deserto" and commented that "Mr Torrey's introduction is certainly open to the criticism you make in it." Emerson also reported that he had to "smile" at Torrey's apology for Thoreau, but that he liked "much of what he wrote, and especially that he was anxious to straighten out the misconception of Mrs Thoreau spread abroad by Sanborn." Dr. Edward Emerson to Dr. Jones, postmarked April 25, 1898 (Jones collection).

344. Henry Salt to S. A. Jones, May 1, 1898.

* * *

I enjoy your "Inlander" article very much. It expresses about Mr. Torrey just what I felt in reading his "Introduction".[1] I hope you sent him a copy.

When I mentioned the war, it had not struck me that you might have sons engaged in it. It must indeed be an anxious time for you; but there seems ground for hope that the war will be a short one, and I earnestly trust Spain may be speedily worsted with as little bloodshed as possible. You have probably heard that English "Society", now as always, has its sympathies on the wrong side, and is in love with the "gentlemanly" qualities of the picturesque scoundrels who have robbed and murdered the Cubans; but, in this case, Society is somewhat afraid of *proclaiming* its sympathies, so contents itself by expressing them in dinner-parties and clubs. Fortunately the mass of the English people takes the opposite view.

I am surprised at what you tell me about T. W. Higginson. I should have thought, from what I saw of him, that he would be punctilious in matters of courtesy; though, as I think I hinted to you, I did not feel very favourably impressed by him. I have had a letter from Dr. Emerson lately, with a warm invitation to stay with him when—*when!*—I visit Concord. But the problem of how to visit Concord is becoming doubly difficult for me; because, in addition to the difficulty of getting there at all, there is the question of satisfying the standard of respectability in Concord society. It is fourteen years since I gave away my dress coat, and turned my "top hat" into a shade for young cucumbers. Shall I have to go back to these insignia of propriety, *when I visit Thoreau's birth-place!* I could not quite bring myself to *that;* it would be better to be taken for a pedlar, like Thoreau himself!

1. "Vox Clamantis in Deserto," *Inlander* 8, no. 6 (March 1898):222–30.

345. S. A. Jones to A. W. Hosmer, May 15, 1898.

* * *

Mr. Daniel Gregory Mason—the author of that paper in the "Harvard Magazine"—has been writing to me. I have asked him to call and see you and your Thoreau Collection of writings. Mr. Salt is much taken with Mr. Gregory, and he will certainly be heard from in Thoreau literature. Please help him all you can for the sake of the good cause. . . .

346. S. A. Jones to A. W. Hosmer, May 17, 1898.

I send just a line to convey bad news, namely, the insufferable egotism and self-conceit of Thoreau's Michigan correspondent have obliged me to throw up the projected edition of the Letters.

There is not a statement in it that is not true and that is not based on Mr. G's own voluntary statements; but he has found so much fault that I am disgusted, and have dropped him and his conceit.

He has been sulking for some time, but his last two letters are such that only his years keep me from answering them as they deserve.

He is as full of whims as Channing, and while I have done him every honor consistent with the truth, and had kept my own name wholly out of sight in the whole book—he has as good as slapped me in the face.

He "kicks" at the "contrast" drawn between himself and FROUDE, and the old gentleman cannot see that the CONTRAST IS WHOLLY TO HIS HONOR.[1]

Inside of two months I hoped to have placed a copy of the little book—which was wholly re-written—in your hands. You will now know why it does n't come. I'll be darned if I have n't found a bigger *live* crank than even Yours truly.

[P.S.] He is so whimsical that I shall see that he never gets hold of the Thoreau relics again. I have a paper that will hold him, and they shall go where they [are] promised—to the UNIVERSITY.

1. Greene had three major objections to Dr. Jones's lecture on the Thoreau-Greene correspondence, which he had read in manuscript. He first objected to Dr. Jones's characterization of his brother-in-law as a "wry-necked member of some disorder"—a comment of the doctor's which was elicited by Greene's brother-in-law's failure to appreciate a copy of *A Week* which Greene had given him. Greene also felt that he did not have what Dr. Jones had called "Clerico-phobia," though he was not aligned with any religious orthodoxy. Finally Greene, like the Hosmers, objected to his being described as "lowly born & lowly bred"; Greene understood that Dr. Jones had meant to compliment him by using the phrase to contrast him both with the "extra select" crowd who failed to understand Thoreau and with Froude, but thought too that "with even a slight amount of analysis the expression would seem to damn one with quite a slight amount of praise." C. H. Greene to Dr. Jones, May 13, 1898 (Jones collection).

347. A. W. Hosmer to S. A. Jones, May 17, 1898.

I have just written you today, but if you will send me Mr. Mason's address I will write him and ask him to call.

You speak of Mr. Mason's knowing the present custodian of the Thoreau Mss. *So do I*—and have known him for five years or more. It was through his son, Philip Russell, that I tried to get the father to influence Mr. Blake to leave the Mss to some one else than Sanborn. Both Mr. R. & Philip knew my opinion of Sanborn, Philip, I corresponded with for some three years or more. Poor fellow—he got despondent, had been unwell for a number of years, and shot himself. His photo, sent me by his father, after his death, is on my desk, where it has been for the past two years. I had seen him a number of times and grew very fond of him.

348. S. A. Jones to A. W. Hosmer, May 24, 1898.

* * *

I am glad to learn how Sanborn got knocked out;[1] but, really, it is more than I dared to hope for at one time.

That Mr. Mason will call on you some of these days, and it will be better to wait for him than to go towards him.

I must give you a bit of private information about him. I wrote to him asking if he would join me in some editing work in the Thoreau line; and I asked him because he could be of great assistance in looking up some literary matters in the libraries to which I have not access. I thought he would like to do it for Thoreau's sake. He replied at once—to say "Yes?"

NIT; but to ask if there was any money in it; adding that he would not like to leave some "more congenial work" unless he could make something out of it.[2]

That some little pittance might eventually be made out of the Thoreau reprints is, of course BARELY possible, and as a co-editor he would have his editorial share; but his first thought being whether he COULD make anything out of Thoreau gave me a shock that was, to say the least, disagreeable.

Mr. M. may turn out to be all right, but I felt that you should know this little experience before he turns up in your neighborhood.

I want to give you a pointer, namely, that Theo. Brown, of Worcester, Thoreau's friend (and Blake's) was a fine letter writer and his family have *privately* published them.[3] Now I feel that you and I have done enough in the Thoreau line, and by our collections, to be worthy of a copy of that interesting addition to our Thoreau literature. Now will Prof. Russell think it improper to make such representations to the family of Theo. Brown as would secure a copy for you and I? Of course, I would willingly PAY for a copy—though I do not consider such sacred things as *merchandise;* and I would certainly reciprocate in the line of such Thoreau publications as I may in future have a part in putting forth.

I TRUST YOU WILL NOT ALLOW Mr. Mason TO SEE THE THOREAU LETTERS. There is an unfortunate stop put to their publication just now, but Mr. G. will not be an obstacle *forever.* I have reason to think Mr. M. would soon "make" something out of the publication of them. . . .

1. H.G.O. Blake left the Thoreau manuscripts to E. Harlow Russell rather than to Sanborn, as Jones and Hosmer had expected. Even Russell, the principal of the state normal school in Worcester, was surprised by Blake's bequest. He, too, had "supposed they would go to Mr. Sanborn." E. Harlow Russell to A. W. Hosmer, April 28, 1898 (Hosmer collection).
2. This letter of Mason's is not among the Jones papers.
3. *Letters of Theo. Brown*, 3rd ed. (Worcester: Putnam, Davis & Co., 1898).

349. S. A. Jones to A. W. Hosmer, May 29, 1898.

* * *

Fred I have been putting my letters from Mr. Blake in a docket—sixteen of them—and I wish I had copies of my letters to him. I would arrange them for publication after I am dead; and it would make a curious chapter as showing some interesting traits in Mr. B's character. I should write an account of my one interview with him—and, By Jove! he took me on that *afternoon walk* with him. (You know Mr. Mason mentions his custom of taking *that* walk in particular.)[1] Had it not been for the loss of my trunk, I should have remained in Worcester for at least a week; but I had to go to Boston to buy clean clothes, and I never got back to Worcester.

Now, in England it is the custom to return a man's letters when the person to whom they were written is dead; so I wonder if Mr. Blake saved them; and if so, whether they, or copies of them, could be got from Mr. Russell.[2]

You see, Fred, Mr. Blake and I almost fell out on account of the manner in which I made mention of Mr. Sanborn both in *Lippincott's Magazine* and in my letters—defending my position in the letters. I remembered Mr. Blake's years and his nobler nature than my own, but I did n't change an iota of my opinion of Sanborn, and that broke off my correspondence with Thoreau's friend.

Nevertheless, he did me justice, for he sent me a complimentary copy of his last edited book, "Autumn," and his *inscription* makes it very dear to me. How singular it is that I owe some of my life's rarest friendships to Thoreau!

I do not wish to put a straw extra upon your back, for your business will demand all your care and time, but if it is ever convenient to make enquiry of Mr. Russell, I perhaps can repay it by letting you read the double-correspondence after I have written it. Dear me, Fred, I must n't die until I have done all the Thoreau work that is before me.

I am re-writing all the Thoreau-Greene matter; so that it can be printed after Greene and I are under the daisies. I should not have allowed his conceit to 'rile' me so; but when I had paid him the highest compliment that truth would warrant, it was deuced hard to be so ignorantly mis-understood. He made the same mistake that the Hosmers did in mak-ing "lowly born and lowly bred" MEAN "low born and low bred." That is unpardonable ignorance in any person pretending to have been educated in English.

This afternoon I was reading Salt's last Life of Thoreau, and the more I read that biography the more I admire Mr. Salt as a biographer. But, Fred, how much of the facts in that book were supplied by you and me! We have been of some little use—and the thought comforts me. . . .

1. Mason had published "Harrison G. O. Blake, '35, and Thoreau," *Harvard Monthly* 26 (May 1898):87–95.
2. Dr. Jones apparently did not succeed in obtaining his letters to H.G.O. Blake.

350. S. A. Jones to A. W. Hosmer, June 10, 1898.

* * *

Since last writing to you I have entirely recast the manuscript of the Thoreau Letters—some 12,000 words! I felt in my bones that I had worked too hard and too faithfully on the thing to allow Mr. Greene's unreasonableness to cast it all aside. *He* cannot edit those letters; I am the *only man* who has the history of them, and I felt that my injured feeling should not be allowed to deprive the Thoreau readers of the future of them. Well, the printer now has the copy, all ready for printing. ONLY 120 copies will be printed,—so long as Mr. G. is alive, and of these he will not receive one.

The Hosmer Thoreau Collection will make room for a copy; the University of Mich. will get one; the British Museum will have one, Harvard College will NOT.

But, let me wait until the chickens are hatched!

I should be greatly obliged for a chance to READ Mr. Blake's letters to you.[1] I would typewrite whatever I wanted of them, for I can read typewriting better than I can anyone's hand-writing; so, at your leisure, send them on. I'll take precious care of them and speedily return them.

In regard to my own letters to Mr. Blake, I should be glad if you would make application for them—IF Mr. Blake thought them worth keeping. By law, they *belong to me* after his death.

I have just finished a letter to Mr. Mason; and, Fred, I am at a loss to PLACE him. Sometimes I think I do not do him justice; then comes a letter of his that makes me hesitate. He is young; has his living to earn, etc., but he shows signs of *policy* that I can not understand, because I am not "built that way." For instance, he would not say a word about Lowell's treatment of Thoreau because Lowell is a *famous man,* etc., etc.[2] What does it matter how famous, if he has been unjust to Thoreau! Must n't *he* take the consequences just as a "common" man would have to do? I reckon!

That is the line on which we differ; but you'll see him soon, so set me right if I am doing him wrong.

1. Dr. Jones's letter of July 10, 1898, makes clear that Hosmer did send the letters he received from Blake (letter 352).
2. This letter of Mason's is not among Jones's papers.

351. S. A. Jones to A. W. Hosmer, July 4, 1898.

On the 17th of June some curious codger of Worcester, Mass., wrote to the Librarian of the University that he had a valuable book for sale, namely, an unbound copy of Thoreau's "Week." The Librarian sent the letter to me stating that he knew I would attend to it. I at once wrote to the Worcester man offering Ten dollars for the unbound copy, if it was complete.

I wrote on the 22nd of June, and as I have had no reply (I presume somebody else offered more), I write to you about another phase of the matter, to wit, the same Worcester man says he has some *autograph letters of*

Thoreau, "as well as some of the most noted men of Concord. These came to me from my grand-mother, who was near friend of the Thoreau family."[1]

I wrote to the present owner that if these Thoreau letters were for sale, I would like to be informed of it.

It is evident from his letter that the Worcester man is very ignorant, and that will explain his not making any reply to my communication; but THOSE THOREAU LETTERS MUST BE COPIED. How can it be accomplished?

The owner's name and address I give from his letter: *Josiah Walter, 46 William Street, Worcester, Mass.*

His copy of the "Week," unbound, is no doubt one of those Thoreau carried to his garret, and it is a relic of value to an admirer; but I have no bellyache from not capturing that particular copy. I am, however, more than anxious that the letters shall be copied.

Josiah Walter is doubtless a Yankee of the bluest blood, and a Welshman is *no* match for any Yankee whatsoever; but if you get on his trail, it will be Yankee against Yankee, and I'm betting on the *Concord species.*

If you think it worth while to look into this matter, and can make out to see the letters, I will pay Mr. Walter a fair price for a copy of his letters: PROVIDED they have in them anything of literary value. It is hard to imagine anything from Thoreau's pen LACKING this element. . . .

1. Josiah Walter to R. C. Davis, June 17, 1898 (Jones collection). We have been unable to identify these Thoreau letters.

352. S. A. Jones to A. W. Hosmer, July 10, 1898.

You ask: "Were the Blake letters of any use." Did n't you receive a letter stating just how much of each I had copied of them and telling how much I coveted possession of the last he wrote to you, and this because it makes mention of the dauguerreotype I have? I wrote and personally mailed such a letter, and as we have now got a "stinker" for a postmaster, I want to punch him up if that letter did not reach you. Please let me know about this, will you?

My oldest son is in Company A., 31st. Reg't Mich. Vols; stationed as yet at Camp Thomas, Chickamauga.

You had not mentioned anything about the Brown letters, but the outlook does not seem to be very encouraging.

I did not suppose you could "see much" of Mr. Mason in one short interview, but his personality would make its impression darned quick. That's what I wished to hear of.

If Sanborn or Mr. Russell were "ahead" of anybody, why did Mr. Walker write all over the country to peddle his copy of the "Week?" That's what sticks me.

Besides, Mr. Walker did not say that the letters were for sale. A copy of them is well worth the attempt to GET, and I'd give a five dollar William for an accurate copy, attested as such.

My letters to Mr. Blake would throw such a side light on his peculiar character (as well as on my own!) that I should be glad if they can be had; but the world will go on just the same if they do not turn up. Nevertheless, the return of such letters would be the first DUTY of a literary executor in England. . . .

353. S. A. Jones to A. W. Hosmer, August 4, 1898.

I see by your report of your 'finds' that you are on the trail as eagerly as ever while I have taken a back seat so as to dodge the deacon's contribution-box.

Of course, the 'circular'[1] brings you a little nearer to the Thoreau's, but the great world cares more for Thoreau's thought than for all his pencils—good as they were. Nevertheless, go on with your collection; it will be more than appreciated when you are under the daisies. . . .

I imagine that Worcester man is off his base: if he is rich why in the deuce is he peddling rare books in that eccentric manner? . . .

1. For a photograph of a Thoreau pencil-circular, see Walter Harding and Milton Meltzer, *A Thoreau Profile,* p. 138.

354. Henry Salt to S. A. Jones, August 5, 1898.

* * *

I was much interested to hear that you are again on the track of Thoreau letters. What a genius you have for all that pertains to Thoreau! It is true in literary matters, as in other matters, that (as Scott says)—

> "Lovers' eyes are sharp to see,
> And lovers' ears in hearing";

and these discoveries of yours, with all the various services you have done for Thoreau's memory, make one feel how much more might have been done *at head-quarters,* had there been, among those in charge of the manuscripts, &c. anyone gifted with this keen instinct and outlook, & the love that is better than all. (I know Mr. Blake had this affection, but the impracticality of his nature seems to me to have somewhat marred its effect). I hope that with the assistance of "Fred" Hosmer, you will succeed in wheedling the grim possessor of the letters into letting you have them—or a copy. If there has been a further delay in the printing of the first lot of letters discovered by you, possibly you may be able to get the whole of them printed together. . . .

I offered a prospective article on the illustrated "Walden" to two English papers, but both declined it; so I have as yet written nothing on the subject. This sort of thing proves how very slowly the interest in Thoreau grows in this country; and yet I am convinced it *does* grow. . . .

355. S. A. Jones to A. W. Hosmer, August 6, 1898.

* * *

Certainly, that "Mr. Walker" is a curious duck; but I don't think he is worth the trouble you are taking on his account. Put in your spare time on the trail that Dr. Osgood's death has thrown open.[1] A picture of Thoreau's first and only love—as she looked when he was captured—that is something to strive for to the end of the road. . . .

1. The Reverend Joseph Osgood, husband of Ellen Sewall.

356. S. A. Jones to A. W. Hosmer, August 14, 1898.

While it was to be expected, I am still grieved to learn that Mr. Ricketson has gone beyond.[1] I always hoped to meet him, and should have done so when I was at Concord had not that railroad strike deranged all my plans.

I should like to get the date of his death and any newspaper articles thereon. If you can give me his son's address I will write to him direct.

Although I never met Mr. Ricketson, I feel from his letters that he was much warmer-blooded than Mr. Blake. You felt a palpitating human heart all through them, and while one respected Mr. Blake, one loved Mr. Ricketson. Blake was too much of a spiritual abstraction for earthly wear and tear, and I certainly had a feeling of out-of-placedness when I was with him. But, the peace of God be with them both! . . .

I had just finished a letter to Mr. Salt when I began upon this. He is summering in a fine part of England. Dang it, Fred, why ain't we blessed (?) with a fat purse so that we could go sky-larking 'round the globe. But I should n't be a success at that business; it's all right as it is. . . .

1. Daniel Ricketson died in New Bedford on July 16, 1898.

357. Henry Salt to S. A. Jones, September 4, 1898.

* * *

I shall look out for those Letters of Thoreau when winter approaches. I fear the owner of the rumoured new letters will turn out to be a fraud, unless, as you suspect, he is something more positive—, a scoundrel,—and has stolen the letters from Mr. Blake. I had heard of Mr. Blake's death some little time ago, but not of Mr. Ricketson's until you wrote. The contrast between the two men must certainly have been striking—the colourless piety of the one against the strongly-marked partialities of the other. It is a great testimony to the strength of Thoreau's character that he attracted such different minds. I have on several occasions received very friendly & genial letters from Mr. Ricketson, and indeed, as far as friendliness goes, from Mr. Blake also. Who is Prof. Russell? And is he likely, in your opinion, to do well by Thoreau's memory?

I have just seen a provoking reference to Thoreau in Havelock Ellis's volume of essays, "Affirmations" (W. Scott, 1898). In the essay on Nietzsche, referring to the way in which men seek their opposites, he says, "He grew to worship cruel strength, as the consumptive Keats, the sickly Thoreau, loved beauty and health, with 'the desire of the moth for the star'." The *sickly* Thoreau! Granting that Thoreau's constitution was not a strong one, and that his health was so to speak, self-made, would it be possible to find a more inappropriate epithet for him than *sickly!*

A few days ago I had a meeting with William Sloane Kennedy, of Belmont, Mass., author of the little book entitled "In Portia's Gardens", which I think you have seen. He is a very good fellow, natural and simple in life (though perhaps hardly so in writing), and a sincere lover of Whitman and to a lesser extent of Thoreau. Your countrymen buzz around Ed. Carpenter in considerable numbers in the summer! Your mention of young Mr. Mason reminds me that I owe him a reply to a long letter received from him in May. I thought he showed very great promise in that article about Thoreau, though one has to make allowance for a certain complacency of tone which is perhaps the accident of youth. Far from feeling vexed at your setting him in correspondence with me, I was very glad to get into touch with him. I wish I knew any such young man in this country, likely to carry on the Thoreau work with ability. . . .

358. S. A. Jones to A. W. Hosmer, September 11, 1898.

* * *

So good Mrs. Bigelow has joined the "Grand Army" and met those who had gone before. How true it is that our loss is their gain. I dimly remember her, and I am glad to have seen her. Fred, it will be a long time before Concord knows again the like of the breed of sterling people it has had. And how they are melting away! And how that old Channing holds out. The grave will not be solitude to him; here and now is the solitude for him. . . .

359. S. A. Jones to A. W. Hosmer, October 2, 1898.

Can you possibly leave home for a week or two? I believe I can get the malaria out of you, for one thing, and a change of air is always good in such cases. I can put you on your feet so that you can go to work with vigor, and you will *stay well,* too. You will be more than welcome here, and I am sure the results will pay.

If you do not feel that you can get away, then do let your doctor write to me your present symptoms; then he and I will put our heads together and pull you out of the slough. I have had so much experience with chronic malaria that I do hope you will let me try and be of some service to you. I had the pleasure of helping Miss Eliza Hosmer when she had failed elsewhere, and as you are a Hosmer, I think I can help you.

But, don't think of disposing of your Thoreau collection. Heavens! you have only begun upon it; stick to it and make the monument higher yet. . . .

360. Henry Salt to A. W. Hosmer, October 15, 1898.

It was very kind of you to send me the beautiful photograph of the bust of Thoreau. Mr. Walton Ricketson's work must be a fine one; the head and expression are very impressive, I think. What surprises me in it is that it gives one a *new* idea of Thoreau, with less, it seems, of the rough out-of-door look, and more of the polished student. For this reason I do not like it so well, at a first sight, as the portraits that I am familiar with; but this may be only a prejudice that will pass off. I should like to know what your feeling is on the point. A friend to whom I showed it yesterday, on its arrival, said, "Too much of the *gentleman!*" A short time back there was some reference to Thoreau in the London *Echo,* a half-penny evening newspaper, in which something was said of his simplicity of living and vegetarianism—at least I judge that was the case from a letter which was inserted later. This purported to come from someone of the name of Thoreau, speaking of "my illustrious relative", but pooh-poohing his hygienic ideas, & explaining that so far from being a vegetarian he killed a wood-chuck, &c., &c. *No address* was given with this letter, and I believe there is no doubt it was a hoax. The family has long been extinct in the Channel Isles, I was informed, as well as in America. . . .

361. S. A. Jones to A. W. Hosmer, October 26, 1898.

* * *

I sent some proof to Mr. Hopkins[1] to-day and also my notion about the illustrations he has selected. I have advised him to use the three pictures of Thoreau, that of Sophia, and instead of one of the house, one of the burial spot.

The end of the book proper, mentions Sophia's death as a "family reunion", and a picture of the burial plot in Sleepy Hollow will be exceedingly touching and appropriate.

I believe you have one showing distinctly the grave of Henry and that of Sophia, beside him. Indeed, I think this one picture would go to the heart of every reader of the little book. . . .

1. Hopkins was publishing *Some Unpublished Letters of Henry D. and Sophia E. Thoreau.*

362. S. A. Jones to A. W. Hosmer, November 1, 1898.

Mr. Greene was buried to-day. I received the word that he was dead yesterday, but was not able to attend the funeral, owing chiefly to the poor railroad connections. He must have died suddenly, for I had a letter from him only a few days before his passing away. It is pleasant to think that he and Thoreau may meet now.

I fancy Miss Lyman must have money to burn; but it is hers and she can publish as many selections as she pleases.[1] But why take a sample when the whole of Thoreau can be had? . . .

1. Emily Lyman edited *Extracts from Thoreau* (Philadelphia: J. B. Lippincott, 1899).

363. S. A. Jones to A. W. Hosmer, November 13, 1898.

* * *

The other day the editor of the "Inlander" handed me a book to review. It is entitled, "American Prose: Selections with Critical Introductions and a general Introduction. Edited by George Rice Carpenter. New York: The Macmillan Company."[1] The introductory article on Thoreau is by T. W. Higginson and it is very good. Higginson has a sly dig at Lowell and at Judge Hoar. It is a good sign to see Thoreau selected as a representative of American prose; but as Higginson says, "There has been in America no such instance of posthumous reputation as in the case of Thoreau. . . ."

1. Carpenter edited *American Prose* (New York: Macmillan Co., 1898). Pages 338–42 are by T. W. Higginson on Thoreau. Higginson recalled asking Judge Hoar, whom he characterized as "then lord of the manor in Concord," for support in his endeavor to gain Sophia's permission to edit Thoreau's journal. Higginson quoted Judge Hoar's response: "Whereunto? You have not established the preliminary point. Why should anyone wish to have Thoreau's journals printed?" Higginson also pointed out the irony involved in Lowell's criticism of Thoreau's renunciation of public life: "To complain of him as waiving all interest in public

affairs when the great crisis of John Brown's execution had found him far more awake to it than Lowell was,—this was only explainable by the lingering tradition of that savage period of criticism."

364. S. A. Jones to A. W. Hosmer, December 18, 1898.

* * *

Do you know whether anything is being done with Thoreau's Journals? I had hoped that Houghton, Mifflin and Company would have the courage to publish them in full and in the order they were written. You see, Channing's book—the Poet-Naturalist—shows that some of the best things are to be found only in it.

By the way, if you can readily lay your hand on that schoolboy composition by Thoreau[1] (you once sent me a copy which I have sought for in vain and more than once) I should be more than obliged for a transcript. I want to put it into the next bibliography with one other unpublished letter. . . .

1. "The Seasons."

365. A. W. Hosmer to S. A. Jones, December 21, 1898.

I enclose a copy of *the* composition, have copied it in division of lines, punctuation, spelling, capitals &c. . . .

Have heard nothing yet from Mr. Russell in regard to the publication of the Thoreau Diaries. Nor has he written me what he found out, if anything, about that fellow who had Thoreau letters to sell.

366. S. A. Jones to A. W. Hosmer, December 28, 1898.

The other day there came to me from Worcester a copy of "Theo. Brown's Letters." No word or bill accompanied the volume, so as it was ordered through you, I think it best to send the enclosed postal order [to] you, and if you will pay Mrs. Brown I shall be much obliged.

Something about the letters reminds me of Thoreau, or at least, something in the tone of the letters makes me understand how Thoreau would take to such a man as Mr. Brown. . . .

367. S. A. Jones to A. W. Hosmer, January 8, 1899.

* * *

. . . Did it ever occur to you that a new life of Thoreau would have little in it for you and me? We have gone over the ground so fully that only some minor items in his life are likely to be "news" to us. All that we can expect of the "new" is to be sought in the unpublished journals; and Higginson thinks there is a chance of their being published.[1] But their custodian makes no sign, and so long as the "Works" are called for, I don't suppose H. M. and Co., will be in any hurry to print more.

But, think of the difference between Thoreau's fame now and what it was the year he died. Fred, we have helped in that development, and the great "boost" came to Houghton, Mifflin and Company when they first saw the Rowfant edition of the bibliography. The elegance of that book, as a book, set them a-thinking—and, behold, they found out all at once that Thoreau was somebody.

I see by a circular Hopkins sent me that the price of the book[2] is $6.00. So much for a fancy press and acquaintance with a lot of bookish cranks. It is ridiculous to think of Thoreau's plainness, and then of a book about him pranked out in all the finery imaginable. But that's the way in this rare old world, and for Mr. Hopkins's sake I hope there are lots of six dollar cranks: it may encourage him to go on with the new bibliography. . . .

1. T. W. Higginson had mentioned that "it is a question whether the whole [journal] may not yet be published" in his sketch of Thoreau for George Rice Carpenter's *American Prose.*
2. *Some Unpublished Letters of Henry D. and Sophia E. Thoreau.*

368. Henry Salt to S. A. Jones, January 10, 1899.

* * *

I had a letter from Sanborn a few weeks ago in which he told me that Mr. Channing, after a somewhat alarming illness, had rallied, and was going to dine with the Emersons on Christmas Day, as he has done for years. It must, as you say, be a strange & solitary life for Channing, now that he has survived all that circle of friends. I shall look out for him as X.Y.Z. in the Letters. . . .

369. S. A. Jones to A. W. Hosmer, January 26, 1899.

* * *

The University Library has been enlarged to twice its size, and they have built a special room, 10 × 14, to be known as the "Concord Room." There are to be cases that lock for the preservation of the choicest articles, book-cases, etc.

I shall be sorely put to it to fill the room, but I shall do my best and hope to elicit the support of all lovers of Thoreau and of Concord.

There will be wall room for plenty of pictures and I hope to make Concord visible here in Michigan. If necessary, I shall sacrifice everything I have in the Thoreau line.

Now that the Rev. Osgood is dead, is there the hope of learning anything more in that direction? If there are any letters that could be had it were exceedingly desirable that a move be made in that direction. . . .

I feel now as if my Thoreau work had ended; and be it what it may, I did my poor best. Little did I think in 1890 that I should do what has been done, and now I can but wish that every line was better for Thoreau's sake. . . .

370. Henry Salt to S. A. Jones, January 27, 1899.

I have come to the conclusion that in all that pertains to the publication of a volume you are a consummate artist![1] For months you have been steadily infecting my mind with the belief that this volume of Thoreau Letters was a somewhat small and trivial affair, on which no great stress need be laid—and now what is the result? Two days ago the book duly arrived, and the whole of that evening was spent by me in the reading of it, with (literally) alternate tears and laughter at the pathos and humour which that "ex-professor", "editor", and what-not, had so craftily placed between the covers. Why, it is done in a *masterly* manner; that is the real truth of it! I can't answer for its effect on those who are indifferent to Thoreau; but I can't imagine that any lover of Thoreau can fail to find it a most precious addition to his book-shelf. I congratulate you heartily on the skill with which you have framed the letters in that excellent "setting" of your own. I don't know when I have enjoyed reading anything so much.

Your treatment of Lowell, X.Y.Z. and the twice-slain Sanborn, amused me greatly, and I thought all the description of the lecture to the fashionable audience first-class. Froude's letter to Thoreau shows the writer in a better light than I was aware of, and has a sincere ring. I must try to get it printed in some English papers, with a small notice of the book. Strange, is it not? that a letter from Froude to Thoreau is much more likely to be quoted for the interest in the *sender* than in the receiver!

I think the book is extremely well got-up, both as to print and illustrations. If the printer has been slow over it, he has done his work well. How very true & touching was Mr. Green's affection for Thoreau! The "old diary" is very effective as it strikes the closing note. I rather regret that you could not give the *names* throughout of the persons referred to, but I suppose the objections were serious. . . .

1. *Some Unpublished Letters of Henry D. and Sophia E. Thoreau.*

371. S. A. Jones to A. W. Hosmer, February 8, 1899.

Mr. Greene's photo has found its place in the booklet. I wish the old man could have seen the book before he departed.

Sanborn's notice was characteristic of the man;[1] and I wish you could read Mr. Salt's opinion of the book, as expressed in a letter I received the other night. I am sorry you showed Sanborn the book; he did n't deserve a sight of it.

I don't believe anybody wrote a word to him about the book; he made up the statement.

If he cared to insert the letters in his edition, why did n't he write to Mr. Greene for them? The fact is he had forgotten, or did not care about so humble a correspondent. He had written to Mr. Greene, yet he spells the name "Green" instead of Greene.[2]

I have been pushing the sale of the Ricketson copy of the "Dial" all I could, but the librarian has been down with the grippe and I do not know if the sale was consummated.

The Ricketson copy had been closely cropped by the binder and this took off from its value greatly. However, I hope the University may secure that particular copy because it was Ricketson's. . . .

1. Sanborn reviewed Dr. Jones's *Some Unpublished Letters of Henry D. and Sophia E. Thoreau* in the *Springfield Republican* for January 25, 1899.
2. In his review for the *Springfield Republican* Sanborn described *Some Unpublished Letters* as a "slender contribution to the increasing Thoreau literature"; he also mistakenly referred throughout to C. H. Greene as "Mr. Green." Sanborn was apparently piqued at not being able to include these letters in his own volume, for he remarked that "Mr. Sanborn . . . would gladly have included these brief epistles of Thoreau in his volume of 'Familiar Letters,' had they been furnished." The tone of Sanborn's closing remarks reveal much about his feeling toward Dr. Jones: "They have a value now, though hardly enough to warrant charging $6 for the booklet; for I do not agree with one purchaser who wrote me that he had paid that price for what is 'not worth six cents.' A curious youthful letter from Froude, relating to his 'Nemesis of Faith,' written to Thoreau in 1849, also appears,—but it is incorrect to say that Sophia Thoreau did not wish it published. She once showed it to me, and I could then have printed it; but that involved writing to Froude, which the importance of the letter hardly seemed to warrant."

372. S. A. Jones to A. W. Hosmer, March 12, 1899.

It is so long since I have bothered you with a letter that you can afford to let me have a shy at you. First, then, the University has bought Miss Ricketson's copy of the "Dial,"[1] and the son expresses himself as pleased that it has found a place in a Western college. I am surprised at their selling it. I had supposed Mr. Ricketson was rich; but I am glad we got that copy of so rare a publication. . . .

Mr. Hopkins wrote to me the other day that he had disposed of the remainder of the Thoreau Letters to Dodd, Mead and Co. They deal in such limited editions of out of the way books, and I am curious to see what the "Bookman" will have to say about the little booklet. I am content; the letters are in permanent book shape—the last of my poor Thoreau work. . . .

1. The *Dial* which the Ricketsons, encouraged by Dr. Jones, sold to the University of Michigan was an original subscriber's copy which had belonged to James Thornton, an uncle of Anna and Walton Ricketson. Dr. Jones to Walton Ricketson, undated letter—probably early 1901 (University of Michigan library).

373. A. W. Hosmer to S. A. Jones, March 20, 1899.

You have said nothing yet as to whether you had the photos of Thoreau and of the Cairn at Walden for the Concord Room. If you have not I should like very much to send you some for it.

I had a note from a friend of mine, saying she had met a gentleman from Lowell Mass, who boarded at the same place in Haverhill Mass, in 1852 or 3, when T. was working to pay for the publication of "The Week." He had often walked with T. and told her many things about him. Said he did not believe he ever in all his life did a wrong thing. He was all "purity and goodness personified." "He was a loving man, the moisture would come to his eyes whenever he spoke of his mother." He also said that Thoreau made the remark that "Fifty years from now the majority of people will believe as I do now." That looks as though Thoreau himself felt, as Horace Hosmer remarked about him.

This boarding house mistress, was a stiff, old fashioned Methodist and tried her best to convert Thoreau, but she said "he was too hard a nut for her to crack."[1] I shall try and see this gentleman when he comes back east, as he is to come to Concord to see about having some stones set in some lot in Sleepy Hollow.

1. Hosmer's notes here are from a letter to him of Henrietta M. Daniels of March 11, 1899 (Hosmer collection). The man whom Henrietta Daniels had met was Samuel A. Chase of Lowell, Mass., who had been a fellow boarder of Thoreau's with Mrs. Webster in Haverhill in the spring of 1850. See Harding, *The Days of Henry Thoreau*, p. 274.

374. S. A. Jones to A. W. Hosmer, May 16, 1899.

It is a long time since I have bothered you with any of my inanities. Having nothing to write about, I did n't write. There is a good deal of philosophy in that, if you only think of it!

Lately I have come into some correspondence with a Mr. Hill (telegraph editor of the Detroit Journal).[1] He is an admirer of Thoreau and he is also a practical printer who works with his own types after hours. He made me a visit lately, and proposed a matter that will have some interest for you, I am sure. It is this: he proposes that he and I reprint the best of the papers about Thoreau.

I enclose three sheets of his reprint of Ripley's review of the "Week"[2]— (which you will please return at your leisure).

I am to write an introductory note to each paper, and we are to follow the chronological order in reprinting them.

It seems to me that this is a useful work; republishing papers that are not easily got at, and many of them not generally known.

I believe you collected many of these papers, and I wish to ask if you will loan such as I have not for the purpose under consideration.

I am to write a prospectus, stating what we are about to undertake, and we propose to make Concord and Boston the centers from which we will distribute the reprints. Let me know what you think of the proposition. . . .

1. Edwin Bliss Hill (1866–1949) was for ten years a news editor for the Detroit *Journal*. A Thoreau enthusiast, Hill met Dr. Jones about 1899 and the two became close friends, as the following correspondence shows. Trained as a printer, Hill turned in 1899 to publishing small pamphlets devoted to Thoreauviana. In 1901 he printed *Pertaining to Thoreau,* the important collection of nineteenth-century criticism of Thoreau which Dr. Jones edited. After 1908 Hill continued to publish pamphlets, many of which were devoted to Thoreau, from Ysleta, Texas, and Mesa, Arizona, where he had moved. See Raymond Adams, "In Memoriam: Edwin B. Hill," *Thoreau Society Bulletin* 28 (July 1949). This article contains a partial list of Hill's Thoreau publications.

2. "H. D. Thoreau's Book," *New York Tribune,* June 13, 1849. Reprinted in *Pertaining to Thoreau* (1901). The review is attributed now to Horace Greeley rather than to Ripley.

375. Henry Salt to S. A. Jones, May 18, 1899.

* * *

You will have received the little notice of your Thoreau *Letters* which I wrote for the *Academy*. Its balance was somewhat spoiled by some editorial omissions; among them a mention which I made of Mr. Hosmer's services with the camera.[1] I see Mr. Bradford Torrey has been at it again, in the *Atlantic Monthly* (?).[2] I did not see the article itself, but a quotation in some newspaper, from which I judged it to be no better than that unlucky "Introduction" of his, which defaces the illustrated *Walden*.

I wish you would tell me, when you next chance to be writing, in what way, or variety of ways, the name Thoreau is pronounced on your side, and which is the right one. An American lately told a friend of mine that it should be *Thorōw*, with accent strongly on the *second* syllable, as I presume Lowell meant it to be pronounced in his poetical satire. But I suppose the usual fashion is to pronounce it as if it rhymed with "bórrow", is it not? . . .

I hope you are well, and happy in your sons' return by this time. You must not talk of your Thoreau work being ended, while Bradford-Torrey-ism still invites your sword! . . .

1. "Froude to Thoreau," *Academy* 56 (March 11, 1899): 305–6.
2. Bradford Torrey, "Writers that are Quotable," *Atlantic Monthly* 83 (March 1899):407–11.

376. S. A. Jones to A. W. Hosmer, June 25, 1899.

Mr. Hill was up from Detroit to-day with some proof of the Lowell paper and it put me in mind of you, as it is printed from the copy of the "Massachusetts Quarterly" that you sent me. When Mr. Hill has done there will be a book of some two hundred or more pages that will have considerable interest for Thoreau students. I shall be glad to see Storms Higginson's paper reproduced, for it is a fine tribute to Thoreau, and it is too little known, being buried in an old number of the *Harvard Magazine*. I think it will be well also to reprint Mr. Williams's paper from the *Memorial of the Class of '37*. The book will be of considerable interest, for the views of Thoreau's earliest critics will be gathered into one handy volume. . . .

The other day I gave a letter of introduction to Professor Gray, of Oberlin College (Ohio), who is going to Concord to study Emerson in his den.[1] Prof. G. was a student here, and you will find him a gentleman in all respects. His coming to me made me feel like jumping into an envelope and addressing it to Concord, so that I could walk around there with him and you; but I must stay at home this year.

1. Henry Gray later published *Emerson: A Statement of New England Transcendentalism as Expressed in the Philosophy of its Chief Exponent* (Stanford University Press, 1917).

377. S. A. Jones to A. W. Hosmer, July 5, 1899.

My venture with Mr. Hopkins did not turn out very well for me. He sent me an account regarding the book[1] lately and his cheque for $50.00. Beside this there are 24 copies on hand of the book, which he wrote he would divide with me, or if I would wait until he had sold them he would divide the proceeds with me.

As a bird in hand is better than no books (and no cash) I wrote him to send on my twelve copies; and so soon as they come I will send you one.

Mr. Mason wrote to me the other day from Worcester, where he had a peep at Thoreau's Journals and also at a box full of Thoreau's papers, odds and ends of all sorts.

Of the latter, Mr. Russell gave him some sheets to keep and he is the most delighted man you can imagine.

The printing of the Thoreau reviews goes on slowly, but Mr. Hill is pegging away, and you will get the Higginson paper in due time. I am sure it will please you better than all the rest.

We contemplate reprinting all my papers on Thoreau, which will make a volume by themselves. When this is done I shall sweep up my shop floor and dry up. . . .

1. *Some Unpublished Letters of Henry D. and Sophia E. Thoreau.*

378. S. A. Jones to A. W. Hosmer, July 16, 1899.

The book[1] came in this morning's mail and I have been eyeing it all morning. As a piece of printing, it is not as beautiful as I had expected. The moment I saw the cover I knew it was not from Mr. Hopkins' press—and I think Miss Lyman did wisely in selecting a more reasonable printer, for I was sure the Marion Press would "stick" her nicely for its work.

I am particularly pleased with her selection of illustrations, and I think the reproductions are better done than those in the "Letters."

She has written a very quiet and modest preface, one which shows how completely she is absorbed in Thoreau. Her selections are not like Mr. Blake's, nor can that be expected, for they show *her* individuality and taste. It is plain, however, that she sees Thoreau more as a "naturalist" than does Mr. Blake.

Do you know whether Miss Lyman got a copy of the "Letters." If not she must have one WHEN that dilatory Hopkins sends me the copies he promised.

Mr. Hill keeps pegging away at the reprints. He has the Lowell paper nearly all in type and when it is stricken off, he will take up the next, following the order of the bibliography. I am anxious to have the Higginson paper in print, as you will find that the most valuable of all for an insight into Thoreau's real character as a "sociable" man. The paper by Mr. Williams in the "Class Memorial" is also of great interest. Take them all together, they will be handy to have in one small volume. These Thoreau books are growing in value—just think, I was offered 15.00 dollars the other day for a copy of the Bibliography. . . .

You have repeatedly mentioned pictures for the "Concord Room," and I as repeatedly have forgotten to make any reply. The fact is, the University authorities are so careless in regard to such treasures as the Thoreau relics that I cannot trust them with such precious things. I shall reclaim what they already have and see that they go into appreciative hands when they leave my own.

By the way, do you think you could find a copy of the First Series of Channing's Poems[2] for me in your country? Mr. Greene gave me some rare volumes of Channing's and it has made me desirous of getting the above book to complete the odd fellow's writings. In spite of Emerson, Channing is not a poet, and I don't suppose anyone in Concord is "stuck" enough on Channing to set any great store by his "pomes". . . .

1. *Extracts from Thoreau* (Philadelphia: J. B. Lippincott Co., 1899).
2. Ellery Channing, *Poems* (Boston: Little, Brown, 1843).

379. S. A. Jones to A. W. Hosmer, July 23, 1899.

I am glad to learn that Prof. Gray has "struck it rich," as the Californians used to say. Surely, between yourself, the Misses Hosmer, and the incomparable Sanborn he has all he could ask for in reason, unless he "wants the whole earth."

I trust that the outcome of his work will repay you for the valuable aid you are giving him.

The more I look at Miss Lyman's "Extracts" the more do I feel that she is not to be compared as an extract*er* (or *or*) with Mr. Blake. But I value the book for its illustrations, and that picture of the "Old Elm" leads me to ask if there is any photo of the church in which Thoreau first delivered his famous Plea for Capt. John Brown?[1] That picture should be taken, and one of the Vestry room, if that place is n't much changed. That spot is connected with the most heroic action in Thoreau's life and a picture should be preserved for future generations.

You will be glad to learn that Mr. Mason is going to write a life of Thoreau for a Boston house.[2] It will be a volume of some 20,000 words and will deal more especially with Thoreau's intellectual (or literary) development. Mr. Mason believes that Emerson's influence, so far as he had any over Thoreau, was to the detriment of the latter. This is a good point and it will refute the foolish notion that some have of Thoreau's being an "imitator" of Emerson.

I wrote Mr. Mason a long letter to-day calling his attention to the FACT that Sanborn underrated Thoreau's family and that Thoreau's greatness is largely the outcome of the real "stuff" in both his father and mother.[3] I shall await Mr. Mason's book with much impatience. . . .

1. Thoreau delivered "A Plea for Captain John Brown" in the Concord town hall on October 30, 1859.

2. Mason's biography of Thoreau was never published.

3. Daniel Gregory Mason later wrote Dr. Jones that he disagreed "about the heredity question": "As for Thoreau, I do not know how his father could have contributed to his genius anything more essential than the faculty of minding his own business, or his mother anything more valuable than his irrepressible sprightliness of wit." Mason to Jones, July 30, 1899 (Jones collection).

380. S. A. Jones to A. W. Hosmer, October 29, 1899.

* * *

Did I ever write to you that the reprints which Mr. Hill is putting into type are to be called "Pertaining to Thoreau"? Well, he is doing something at that labor of love in his every spare moment, and eventually students of Thoreau will have ready to their hand material that has cost you and I many an hour's search—to say nothing of the incidental shekels. The book will be useful as showing how Thoreau was regarded by his contemporaries, and also the slow but sure growth of his fame.

I can but regret that the Thoreau MSS. has fallen into such hands as those of the present custodian. I should like to see Mr. Blake's letters to Thoreau printed. I really think that Sanborn would have made better use of the material than Prof. Russell is doing, and yet one sort of squirms to think of Thoreau left to Sanborn's tender mercies. . . .

381. S. A. Jones to A. W. Hosmer, November 5, 1899.

That letter[1] is certainly a prize. Perhaps the corrections that you mention were made by Emerson when he edited the "Letters." When Thoreau wrote "yogin" he did not know much about Hindoo literature, and the change to "yogi" is correct. I am however somewhat surprised that Thoreau should have written "in vacuum." If he had put it "in a vacuum" it would be correct English, but without the "a" it must be "in vacuo," which is correct Latin. . . .

That Mr. Hill is a curious fish: quiet, unassuming, sensible and a lover of books. He comes up here very often to talk Thoreau. You see, the electric car line runs just in front of our door, so he can jump on in Detroit and be dumped within twenty steps of my den.

He is to come up some Sunday and bring that paper from "Chambers' Journal."[2] I shall decide if it is worth reprinting. If it is a plagiarism or an adaptation, it will only go to show how little the English knew of Thoreau at that early day. . . .

1. This letter, from Thoreau to Blake, November 20, 1849, was sent to Alfred Hosmer by E. H. Russell, executor of Thoreau's manuscripts, on September 26, 1899. E. H. Russell to A. W. Hosmer, September 26, 1899 (Hosmer collection). For a text of the letter see *The Correspondence of Henry David Thoreau*, pp. 250–52.

2. "An American Diogenes," *Chambers's Journal* 8 (November 21, 1857):330–32. Reprinted in *Pertaining to Thoreau*.

382. S. A. Jones to A. W. Hosmer, December 18, 1899.

* * *

The omitted passage about which you enquire occurs on P. 396 of the first edition. (Same page in yours, for *it* is a first edition.) It is as follows: "winter, before any thought will subside. We are sensible that behind the rustling leaves, and the stacks of grain, and the bare clusters of the grape, there is a field of a". To such copies as Thoreau sold, he added this, in pencil, at the bottom of the page. When Ticknor and Fields put out the edition of 1868 they corrected this omission. You will find it on P. 399.

I know of one copy of the WEEK that Thoreau gave to a friend in which the addition in pencil does not occur. It was doubtless because Thoreau had not then discovered the omission.

It is not generally known that the pencilled addition denotes a copy that Thoreau had sold from the supply in his garret, and it is just as well that it should not be generally known for it will put up the price of such copies as are found to have it. It might also lead to the counterfeiting of Thoreau's pencil writing. . . .

383. Henry Salt to S. A. Jones, December 22, 1899.

Your letter of October 29 was very welcome. But you must not begin to talk of yourself as "played out". You have got to have a look into a new century yet, and write a good many more letters to cheer your friend over here.

I can sympathise with you in your sufferings from insomnia—not that I have myself had experience of it, for I sleep even too well, but my late assistant secretary, Miss Baker, has been a martyr to it for some time past, and indeed has been obliged to give up her post in consequence, so that I have heard much of its evils. But why can't you doctors invent a cure for such maladies? You ought to "sit up" at night with one of your own patients, and then, if wakefulness were indispensable, you would probably get a sound sleep!

What you tell me of the pronunciation of Thōreaū's name is very interesting. It explains that reference to him in Lowell's satire, which I never quite understood: "Thōreaū has picked up all the windfalls before". (I forget whether I quote rightly.)

I fear I have no news to tell you from this side. All our energies seem to have gone into this iniquitous war in South Africa, and it is a bitter thought that the last two years of the century will have been spent in overthrowing the independence of a brave nation whom we had already shamefully wronged. The organised lying of the London press, in their determination to blacken the character of the Boers, is one of the most shocking pages in our history. It would serve us only right if we lost the whole of South Africa.

You will get this about the time of the New Year, I expect.

384. S. A. Jones to A. W. Hosmer, January 7, 1900.

* * *

But, Fred, how the fame of that shanty is spreading! Here I received a letter last night from an utter stranger[1] telling me of a "find" he had made in the book line. He had bought a copy of the first edition of the WEEK containing this inscription: "This volume was bought by Miss Sarah E. Sanborn from Thoreau himself in April 1855 for $1,25. He was selling his own books from a stock of several hundred copies in his house just across the street in Concord from where Miss S. was keeping house for me. (signed) F. B. Sanborn."

The present owner lives at Sparkill, N.Y., and how in the deuce the book got into that part of the world puzzles me.

The same person also asks me, "Did you ever know of a pencil being found that Thoreau made?" I referred him to you for the chance of getting a pencil, and I also informed him that he could get Concord views, etc., from you.

Sparkill is in the South-Eastern corner of New York just at the boundary of New Jersey. I once lived within twenty miles of it, and if you knew the place as well as I do, you would wonder how Thoreau's fame ever penetrated into such a benighted region. . . .

Some time since I learned from Mr. Foley[2] that Mr. Mason's book about Thoreau was soon to be published. I have heard nothing of it further, but I do not think it is out, or Mr. F. would have let me know. . . .

1. The Sparkill book collector was G. M. Williamson.
2. Patrick Kevin Foley, Boston book-seller and bibliographer.

385. Henry Salt to A. W. Hosmer, January 11, 1900.

* * *

I am today posting to you a copy of *Nature Notes*, the journal of the Selborne Society, which is an association for the study of Natural History, &c. You will find in it an article on "Literature of Field & Hedgerow"[1] in which scant justice is done to Thoreau, as compared with Jefferies and Gilbert White. I have written a short letter of remonstrance, but I do not know whether it will appear.

1. "Literature of Field and Hedgerow," *Nature Notes* 11 (January 1900):5–11.

386. S. A. Jones to A. W. Hosmer, January 21, 1900.

I have waited to hear from Mr. Williamson, so that I could answer your enquiry about the price he paid for his copy of the "Week". He writes to me on the 18th, "This book came from F. B. Sanborn to me through a book dealer in N. Y. and I paid $20,00 for it." The book dealer has worked him nicely, and made a fine profit. I shall undeceive Mr. Williamson about his book coming from Sanborn! This is the highest price yet paid for Thoreau's still-born book, but I doubt if it is the highest the price to which that book will go.

I looked at the picture of the Parkman house[1] with a great deal of interest. It is a lucky chance that put that old time picture in your hands. What a contrast between the humble dwelling of the Thoreau family and the big house on their right; but the folks in that large house are forgotten, while folks are paying twenty dollars for the account of the journey made by those Thoreau boys.

Is there any picture extant of the jail in which Thoreau was confined? It would be quite an addition to Thoreau's account of his imprisonment.

It is [a] pity that no portrait of Mrs. Thoreau has been found. She gives the "go" that is in Henry, and the independence, and one would like to look upon her face. . . .

Am I correct in believing that Mrs. Bigelow is dead? It is my impression that I read an obituary notice of her. I was fortunate in seeing her before her departure; and I shall never forget how she rebuked Sanborn's lies about the Thoreau women. Dear me, that Sleepy Hollow of yours has some precious dust in it. . . .

1. The Thoreaus moved into the Parkman house on Main Street in the spring of 1837 and lived there until 1844.

387. S. A. Jones to A. W. Hosmer, April 12, 1900.

* * *

Mr. Hill is getting on slowly with the book which is to be called "Pertaining to Thoreau." He now has 114 pages printed, and he wishes to issue it at once and to complete the papers in another volume. I do not approve of this, for the papers should be together; there is less chance of their being separated if so published.

I have not seen the paper you mention, in the Dial, but it is a good topic, and a good paper on it will correct the notion, expressed by several writers, that "Thoreau had no humor. . . ."[1]

1. George Beardsley, "Thoreau as a Humorist," *Dial* (Chicago) 28 (April 1, 1900):241–43. That Thoreau was humorless was one of the criticisms Lowell advanced in his review of *Letters to Various Persons*.

388. S. A. Jones to A. W. Hosmer, May 18, 1900.

I can let you know that I am still on the turf and give you a Thoreau item in one shot; so here goes. The other day I received a letter from A BOSTON bookseller, reading to this effect: "In my forthcoming catalogue will appear first editions of Thoreau's "Week" & "Walden." Price $75,00 for the two. The "Week" has the following inscription on fly leaf, in Thoreau's autograph—"Sophia E. Thoreau, from her brother Henry." It also contains a few pencilled notes in Miss Thoreau's hand.

"The Walden has Thoreau's autograph in full on fly leaf, and a few pencilled memoranda in his hand throughout the book."

The bookseller writes that these volumes were bought from the family of one of Thoreau's classmates.

Of course, these copies have an extra value from the fact of their former owners, but "$75,00" for two of Thoreau's books—which some one will no doubt gladly pay for them—is an item to make a note of. . . .

389. S. A. Jones to A. W. Hosmer, May 25, 1900.

I received a letter from a book-loving friend, in Cleveland, Ohio, the other day informing me that he has bought those two Thoreau books that I mentioned in my last letter to you.

He wrote that if I would like to see them he would send them on. Of course I wrote for him to forward.

The copy of "Walden" is said to contain some marginal notes by Thoreau. These I shall copy if they are of any special interest, and you shall have a copy of them.[1]

I did not know of Mrs. Marble's projected book,[2] but shall now be on the lookout for it.

Do you mean that Mr. Sewall is the "gentle boy",[3] or how am I to understand your reference to him and the said "boy"?

I am saddened and yet gladdened to learn of the deaths of the remainder of Horace Hosmer's family. I hope in my heart that they are reunited. I remember him very vividly and I treasure the letters I had from him. Some day Mr. Hill may put them into type, for they have some Thoreau material of interest, and much of real interest pertaining to life in Concord in the first half of this century. . . .

1. Dr. Jones's book-collecting friend in Cleveland was Paul Lemperly. For a complete list of Thoreau's corrections, see Reginald Cook, "Thoreau's Annotations and Corrections in the First Edition of *Walden*," *Thoreau Society Bulletin* 42 (winter 1953):1.

2. Annie Russell Marble, *Thoreau: His Home, Friends and Books* (New York: Thomas Y. Crowell & Co., 1902). Alfred Hosmer provided the photogravures for this volume.

3. Ellen Sewall's younger brother, Edmund, is usually identified as the "gentle boy" of Thoreau's poem "Sympathy."

390. S. A. Jones to A. W. Hosmer, June 26, 1900.

* * *

Well, I have had those Thoreau books in my hands. All there is in Thoreau's copy of "Walden" are a few corrections of errors of the press. The only one of any importance is on p. 24, line 20: "it is a good *post*" should be "it is a good *port*". As the word "post" was used in regard to the stations on the Underground railroad, the correction is valuable.

On p. 277 Thoreau puts this note: "Surveying for Cyrus Jarvis, Dec., 23, '56, he shows me a deed for this lot containing 6 A, 52 rod abt., on the W. of the Warford Road, & 'consisting of plowland, orcharding & wood land,' sold by Joseph Stratton to Samuel Swan of Concord Inholder Aug 11th 1777."

On p. 198, opposite the lines "while they were thus engaged the hill shook and suddenly sank," he writes: "This is told of Alexander's Lake in Killingby, Ct., by Barber, v(ide) his Con. Hist. Col."

At the bottom of the next page, he adds, to the list of fish caught in Walden, "Pomotis obesus (Nov. 25, '58.) One trout weighing a little over 5 lbs (v. Nov. 14, '57)."

These days refer, no doubt, to the page in his Journal where these items are recorded.

These are but fragments, but we prize them just the same.

It was a large price to pay for the two books, but my friend holds them as fully worth it. . . .

391. Henry Salt to S. A. Jones, July 13, 1900.

* * *

What you tell me of the personality of Thoreau's "Gentle Boy" is extremely interesting, and I shall await further developments with expectation. Mrs. Marble's book should be good reading. I hope she will be in a position to clear up the "Gentle Boy" problem once for all,[1] and thoroughly, and not leave any part of it unexplained, to be a trouble to posterity—like the "Harriet problem" in Shelley's case! Why, for instance, should Thoreau have written thus of the brother, if it was the sister he loved?

It was a lucky chance that brought those copies of the *Week* and *Walden* into your hands, if only for inspection. The correction on p. 24 of Walden is interesting, and I think I must tell Dr. Japp of it, though he is a rather fussy and irascible old man-of-letters (I won't call him anything worse), when he thinks he is being impeached in any way.

Well, I don't know that I have any news to give you of myself. I am going on much as usual, but more and more in the humanitarian line, perhaps, and less in the literary. I wonder whether I sent you a copy of the *Humane Review,* a quarterly magazine we started in the spring; I meant to do so, but may have overlooked it, so will now post one. We get some good contributions for it; but of course it cannot be "successful", in the popular sense.

This disgraceful and blackguardly war in South Africa is having a very bad effect on all social improvement at home. Your affair in the Philippines is bad enough; but really the English attack on these free Dutch States takes the record in modern history for meanness and hypocrisy. The conspiracy of the press in this country, to blacken the character of the Boers, and delude the idiotic average Englishman into thinking he is fighting for a just cause, surpasses anything I have ever witnessed or believed possible. The century will go out under a cloud of disgrace and disappointment. . . .

1. Mrs. Marble in *Thoreau: His Home, Friends and Books* (New York: Thomas Y. Crowell, 1902), asserted that "Sympathy" was written to the brother of Ellen (Mrs. Marble could not bring herself to divulge the young lady's family name).

392. Henry Salt to A. W. Hosmer, September 12, 1900 [postcard].

I ought to have written before now to thank you for the interesting photograph of Thoreau, which reached me while I was away on holiday in the north of England. The two books that you speak of as forthcoming in the autumn should be valuable, especially Mrs. Marble's. Dr. Jones has also told me something of them. I have not much news to send you from here, as we are all too much taken up with killing our fellow-beings to think of anything that is sane or wholesome. I heard the other day from a friend who knows Tolstoy well that he (Tolstoy) is a great admirer of Thoreau's Anti-Slavery papers. I had sometimes wondered whether he knew of them.

393. S. A. Jones to A. W. Hosmer, September 24, 1900.

I am in receipt of your pretty booklet[1] and am admiring the tasteful ingenuity of its make-up; but to be very frank with you, I wish the matter was worthy of the setting you have given it.

Mr. C's letters add nothing to what was already known of Thoreau, and his bungling references to "the spirits of some pine trees" shows that he had not *read* Thoreau very carefully, or he would have found Thoreau's own words.[2]

However, there is not enough in or of Mr. C. to quarrel about. . . .

Is that Worcester man, Mr. Russell, doing anything with Thoreau's Journals? Poor Mr. Blake did not anticipate that they would fall into such inappreciative hands, I am sure.

Has that Worcester woman[3] put out that book she promised, or is she also as dilatory as Mr. R.?

Mr. Hill's book is crawling along and will be done sometime next century. He is contemplating printing Mr. Horace Hosmer's letters to me, as well as reprinting such of my Thoreau papers as have appeared in "The Inlander." At the rate of his progress, I shall never live to see these projections of his in print. . . .

1. *Three Letters* (Concord, Mass.: Privately published for Alfred W. Hosmer, 1900). A limited edition of forty copies of three letters to Hosmer of the Rev. David Cronyn of Bernardston, Mass. The letters recall a visit with Sophia and Mrs. Thoreau and give impressions of Thoreau's work and character.

2. Cronyn referred to Lowell's objection "to Thoreau's humorous passage that 'the spirits (of turpentine, I have it) of some pine trees ascend higher than some men's.'" Recently published by Walter Harding in "The Alfred Hosmer Letter Files," *Thoreau Society Bulletin* 119 (spring 1972):7. Cronyn's reference is to the sentence Lowell struck from Thoreau's "Chesuncook": "It is as immortal as I am, and perchance will go to as high a heaven, there to tower above me still."

3. Mrs. Annie Russell Marble.

394. Henry Salt to A. W. Hosmer, October 10, 1900.

It was extremely kind of you to send me a copy of the Letters. The book has arrived today, and I have just read it with very great interest. "C's" letters are very well & suggestively written, I think; and the binding is charming. The case against Lowell, as I daresay you pointed out to "C", is stronger than he supposes; as his praise of the *Week, before* the quarrel with Thoreau, makes his subsequent criticism the more suspicious.

With many thanks for this valuable addition to Thoreau literature.

395. S. A. Jones to A. W. Hosmer, October 28, 1900.

I can readily understand what an enormous task Mr. Russell has before him in collating Thoreau's Journal with the text of Mr. Blake's books, yet the *dates* which Blake gives will make the labor much less. I wonder what title Mr. Russell intends to give to his publication?

I am sure I wish that Mrs. Marble would hurry up her work. If she had her first proofs in July, three months should be long enough time to have brought forth the completed book.

I have written to Mr. Salt but once this year and have heard from him but once. There is nothing to write about in the Thoreau line, and as that was the link that bound us, there is nothing but silence until something turns up.

I should be delighted to see Salt's Life in an illustrated edition, and I do hope Crowell and Company may see their way to publishing such a book.

Did I write you that Mr. Hill is very desirous of printing Horace Hosmer's letters to me. There can be no objection now, as all his kin are dead; but his personality need not be made known. There is so much about Concord in the early days that I think the letters are worthy of preservation. . . .

Mr. Hill talks of visiting Concord, perhaps next year. When he goes I shall send my daguerreotype of Thoreau for you to copy and copyright in your own name. I can trust it in his keeping, while I dare not send it by express.

Did you ever get that expected picture of Thoreau's only love? I have often thought that pictures of Thoreau's friends would make an interesting collection for purposes of illustrating his writings, but so many are missing of the people he mentions that any possible collection would be very incomplete.

I must turn the bibliography over to Mr. Hill. I cannot finish it, as my memory is not what it was, and without a good memory the work cannot be done. It is really wonderful how long Mr. Blake was able to [do] what he did. I must rest content with knowing that I gave the bibliography its start. . . .

396. S. A. Jones to A. W. Hosmer, November 4, 1900.

* * *

After I had written to you last Sunday, I read over all Horace Hosmer's letters and I was blinded with tears. The last letter he wrote was in ink, and after he had written it he had that stroke. With strange prescience, he added, in pencil: "Good bye, if I do not write again."[1] I wrote to him on the spot, but before my letter reached Acton he had gone beyond.

I have had no experience in all my life like this; meeting the man but once and the impression lasting for my whole life.

There is much of interest in his letters, but I must ponder long before I conclude if they shall be printed. . . .

1. Horace Hosmer to Dr. Jones, December 30, 1893 (Jones collection).

397. S. A. Jones to A. W. Hosmer, December 11, 1900.

Are you weary of Thoreau service, or are you ready to help settle another problem?

In the bibliography of Thoreau, you will find that I have ascribed to him the following papers, published in The Dial: "The Laws of Menu," vol. 3, p. 331; "Ethnical Scriptures, Chinese Four Books," vol. 4, p. 205; "The Preaching of Buddha," vol. 4, p. 391, and "Ethnical Scriptures, Hermes Trismegistus," vol. 4, p. 402.

Now a correspondent, in The New York Times, says his copy of the DIAL has Emerson's *own initials to the papers that he wrote,* and according to them, all the papers that I have ascribed to Thoreau are really by Emerson.

Mr. Sanborn has Thoreau's own copy of The Dial, and perhaps Thoreau marked the papers that he wrote in it.

Can you possibly get a sight of Sanborn's copy of The Dial and look up this matter?

As it is nearing the holiday season, you may be too busy in the store to attend to this now, but there is no hurry; so take all the time you need.

It might be well to ask Edward Emerson if his father's copy of The Dial is marked. I feel that it is worth while to sift this matter, because if these papers are really Thoreau's, no one must be allowed to throw a shadow upon his claim to them. . . .[1]

1. Dr. Jones later corresponded with George Willis Cooke, who prepared the introduction to the Rowfant Club's reprint of the *Dial.* Concerning the "Ethnical Scriptures" Cooke wrote, apparently in response to an inquiry by Jones: "I am now inclined to think the Ethnical Scriptures were nearly all compiled by Thoreau. The evidence seems to go rather strongly that way, from two or three quite independent sources." Dr. Jones apparently assisted Cooke in identifying the

contributors to the *Dial* by collating Cooke's original listing—published in "*The Dial:* An Historical and Biographical Introduction, with a List of the Contributors," *Journal of Speculative Philosophy* 19 (July 1885):225–65—against the names written into the set owned by the University of Michigan Library, presumably that acquired from the Ricketsons. George Willis Cooke to Dr. Jones, April 30, 1901 (University of Michigan Library). The four selections of Ethnical Scriptures mentioned here have recently been attributed to Thoreau by Walter Harding, *The Days of Henry Thoreau,* pp. 117, 119.

398. S. A. Jones to A. W. Hosmer, January 6, 1901.

* * *

In the matter of my inquiry about those papers in the "Dial", I am making no progress. You referred me to Cooke's statement that Emerson had marked his own copy with contributors' names.[1] True, but Emerson had *not marked all.* If it is found that Thoreau's copy is marked, the fact will be decisive; but I am strongly of the opinion that the Bibliography is correct in this matter.

When I was at work on the bibliography, I had some correspondence with Cooke,[2] but he had forgotten so many things that he could only assure me of the general correctness of his published paper. . . .

1. In the article for the *Journal of Speculative Philosophy,* 1885, Cooke acknowledged using Emerson's own copy of the *Dial,* "in which some of the names of the writers had been written by his hand."
2. This correspondence is not included in the Jones collection.

399. Henry Salt to S. A. Jones, January 18, 1901.

I have had it in mind for some time past to write to you, but the profession of humanitarian seems likely to swallow entire those unlucky persons who tamper with it. One little message you will have received from me (I hope), viz. a copy of the *New Age,* containing a letter of mine on Thoreau, or rather on one of his traducers. The author of "My Favorite Books", Robert Blatchford, is a well-known socialist writer in this country, one of whose works, "Merrie England", had a sale of over a million copies. Why he should have spoiled an otherwise rather pleasant work by his stupid attack on Thoreau, is a mystery; apparently, he was nettled at Lowell's preference of Thoreau to old Gilbert White, so that one of the few just things said by Lowell in his venomous essay was the cause of *another* venomous utterance from the other side! Blatchford did not reply to my letter; so I presume he felt that he stood on insecure ground, for he is usually pugnacious. If you care to read his "My Favorite Books" (it has some good chapters), it is at your service.

Have you any news for me from your side? I wonder if Mrs. Marble's book has seen the light yet. I heard lately from Mr. D. G. Mason, of Boston, who is doubtless known to you as one of the younger generation of Thoreau students, and he tells me that he has written a Life of Thoreau for the series of Beacon Biographies (I think that is the title), but it is standing over at present unpublished, for some cause or other. I thought Mr. Mason's essay on Thoreau was very good, and he seemed inclined a year or two ago to give considerable time to a study of Thoreau; but now he is "going in" hard for music. . . .[1]

1. Mason's 1926 "Chanticleer Overture" takes its title from the epigraph to *Walden:* "I do not propose to write an ode to dejection, but to brag as lustily as chanticleer in the morning, standing on his roost, if only to wake my neighbors up."

400. S. A. Jones to A. W. Hosmer, February 2, 1901.

* * *

If Thoreau's copy of the DIAL does not contain his *name to his contributions* we can only fall back on the authority of Cooke's paper— which I used in making my bibliography.

In a notable book sale in New York, on Jan'y 30th, Thoreau's WEEK brought fifty-two dollars and fifty cents, and thirty dollars was paid for a copy of WALDEN. I also saw in a catalogue of autograph letters, one of Emerson's for five dollars; one of Thoreau's called for twelve dollars and a half. This is a striking feature.

We are in deep tribulation, for my son Carroll is seriously ill, and the chance for recovery is so small that it is full of heartache. It appears to me as if he was going just as Thoreau did. I cannot write about it, for it kills to think of it.

This, dear Fred, will explain the brevity of my letter, and perhaps its incoherence. Bear with me if I shall prove a poorer correspondent than usual.

401. Henry Salt to S. A. Jones, March 1, 1901.

I am posting you Mr. Blatchford's "My favourite Books". Blatchford was a soldier who turned writer and socialist, and has a great vogue among a certain section of workingmen for a sort of serio-jocose journalistic style which he has elaborated in his weekly paper *The Clarion.* I do not like either his philosophy or his physiognomy.

I shall be interested to read Mrs. Marble's book when it is published; also Mr. Hill's volume of the early reviews of Thoreau, of which you spoke.

I must have a Thoreau article before long in the *Humane Review,* which I am editing; but I will wait until some of these books make their appearance to give me a peg to hang it on.

Yes, I had at the moment forgotten that Mr. D. G. Mason had been put into communication with me by yourself—like some other of my American friends! I thought that article he wrote on Thoreau was good; but he seems now to be running on other lines, and in that case little more is to be looked for from him, for as you say, Thoreau is not to be studied in odd moments, by one "stans pede in uno" . . . .

402. S. A. Jones to A. W. Hosmer, March 10, 1901.

You have sent me a glorious piece of news in the statement that Thoreau's Journals are to be printed entire.[1] I hope my life may be prolonged until I have read every page.

I learn from Mr. Hill that you have had advance sheets of "Pertaining to Thoreau." (How I wish Horace Hosmer could have seen it!) Of course, the sole merit of this booklet is that somewhat remote and hard-to-be-got-at papers are made accessible. Thoreau students will be thankful, at least.

I have just received the New York Times Saturday Review for March 9th., and in it I find a very pleasant mention of you as well as mention of My Thoreau book—the "Unpublished Letters". . . .[2]

1. Thoreau's journal, edited by Bradford Torrey and Francis Allen, was first printed in its entirety in the Manuscript Edition of Houghton, Mifflin & Co. in 1906. The Walden Edition, also including the full journals, was printed from the same plates; it too appeared in 1906. Neither of these editions included the "lost" journal for 1840–1841 which Perry Miller edited under the title *Consciousness in Concord* (Boston: Houghton Mifflin, 1958).

2. An unsigned review, "Unpublished Letters of Thoreau," appeared in the *New York Times,* March 9, 1901. The review praised Dr. Jones's book, though it unfortunately identified Calvin Greene throughout as "Mr. Ricketson." The piece ended with high praise for the book-making and for Alfred Hosmer, "the excellence of whose photographs and interest in and knowledge of the Concord group will be remembered by all who have had the pleasure of meeting him."

403. S. A. Jones to A. W. Hosmer, April 8, 1901.

* * *

If Mr. Salt finds his way to America next summer, I shall make an effort to meet him and you in Concord. We will have to eat a meal in the cellar of Thoreau's hut for one thing and for the rest of the programme suggestions are in order. . . .

404. Henry Salt to S. A. Jones, April 14, 1901.

* * *

I thank you heartily for the "Pertaining to Thoreau". I have never seen a more *pertinent* piece of work. It was a happy idea of yours, for the book will be invaluable to Thoreau students; and what you tell me of Mr. Hill's printing of it makes me value it the more. How much truer a tribute to Thoreau's memory, than some of the more pretentious volumes that have been published!

And very sincere thanks, too, for that kindly inscription to myself. There is no honour I could appreciate more.[1]

I am delighted with your summing up of Mr. Blatchford's personality; and am even tempted of the devil to drop it in some journalists's way, so that it might see the light in print. It is more true of him than you know—as many who are versed in the *ins* and *outs* of the English social movement could assure you. . . .

1. The dedication read, "To / Henry S. Salt / Thoreau's Most Sympathetic Biographer." In a special insert in Dr. Jones's copy of *Pertaining to Thoreau,* Salt is quoted as saying, "the type of this little book was set up, after business hours, by a working printer, who had conceived the idea of thus rendering a service to Thoreau's memory" (Jones collection).

405. S. A. Jones to A. W. Hosmer, May 19, 1901.

I had learned from Mr. Hill that you had been at Worcester on some photographic business. It must have been a rare experience to be actually handling Thoreau's diaries! I saw the books when I called upon Mr. Blake but I did not have the chance to hold any of them in my hands.

It will be a great treat to see the photos of the pages that you have been so good as to offer me. I think, Fred, that mounted copies will be the best for me. I have facilities for mounting and the unmounted are harder to keep in good shape.

I am surprised that Mr. Russell is going to publish, not the whole diaries but only excerpts from them. What we want is Thoreau's Journals just as he wrote from day to day. Of course trivial matters might be excluded, but there cannot be much of such writing in Thoreau's pages.

How is that Mrs. Marble getting on with her Thoreau book? She is slower than molasses in cold weather. I hope Death will not overtake her with her book not done.

Alas! Fred, we do not hear good tidings from my son. Our days and nights are filled with wordless misery; we cling desperately to hope, but I am afraid the disappointment of all disappointments is to be ours. How hard it is to say "Thy will be done." The strain on my wife is dreadful; but I try and be patient when I remember how many have had to drink the same bitter cup. Pardon my infrequent writing; my heart is too full for it. At the same time, I am glad to hear from my friends—and, Fred, you cannot imagine how near to one his friends seem to be at such a time. Every now and then Mr. Hill comes up from Detroit on a Sunday and his visit keeps me from devouring my own heart.

In spite of many appeals, the publishing committee of the Rowfant Club has decided to limit the issue of the "Dial" to the members of the club. I suppose their aim is to make their edition scarcer than even the original "Dial." I am out of all patience with such a spirit, but I am powerless and must submit to the inevitable. 125 copies of four volumes—five with Mr. Cooke's supplementary history of the "Dial"—$40,00 is the subscription. As the members get the books at actual cost, this edition will cost $5000,00. That is a goodly sum to "blow in" for a magazine that could not support itself only fifty years ago.

406. S. A. Jones to A. W. Hosmer, June 19, 1901.

* * *

I was lately reading Mr. Blake's letters to me and I feel more and more assured that if I could get those I wrote to him it would be an accession to Thoreau literature to have them printed. Mr. Hill is strongly of the same opinion. Do you know whether Prof. Russell ever found them? They must have been left amongst Mr. Blake's effects, for he would not destroy them.

I received the copy of the "Atlantic" which you so kindly sent me, but Fred, that man's bogus "hermit" notes[1] didn't enable me to see Thoreau at all. I did see the shadow of Paul Elmer More *darkening* the page, but that was all. It seems to me that he writes of Thoreau as if he were telling of a very superficial postmortem examination made upon a very curious "specimen;" and to my mind that is not the way to write of Thoreau. . . .

1. "A Hermit's Notes on Thoreau," *Atlantic Monthly* 87 (June 1901):857–64.

407. S. A. Jones to A. W. Hosmer, June 23, 1901.

I enclose a copy of two of Thoreau's unpublished letters. The originals are now owned by Mr. G. M. Williamson,[1] Sparkill, Rockland Co., N.Y. You will remember that I gave him your address some time ago; and I believe he got some pictures from you. He bought them from the Mr. Arnold who had the celebrated book sale towards the end of last December.

You will see that the first letter refers to a journey to Maine after Henry had published his first paper, "Ktaadn," in *The Union Magazine,* (1848).

By turning to the *Maine Woods,* page 161, you will see that the journey mentioned in the second letter was begun on Monday, July 20th., "with one companion."

It is noteworthy that, at the time of writing the second letter, Thoreau did [not know] the proper name of the *Allegash* river, for in his letter he spells it "Allegatt." (The two ts are written plainly enough and they are crossed.)[2]

You will see from the page of the *Maine Woods* cited that "Mr. Loomis" did not go but that his cousin is probably the one that did,[3] and that the "Indian" was Joseph Polis—who died not so many years ago.

The first letter also informs us about the prices paid to Lyceum lecturers in the early days. Thoreau evidently thought his "25,00" a "big thing." Fancy a man of any note going from Concord to Bangor, Maine, for that sum to-day! Ten times that is the more likely price to-day for a first-rate man. However, Thoreau was not "on the make," as we well know. . . .

1. G. M. Williamson sent copies of Thoreau's letters of February 16, 1849, and July 11, 1857, to George Thatcher. For texts of the letters see *The Correspondence of Henry David Thoreau,* pp. 236–37, 485–86. G. M. Williamson to Dr. Jones, February 28, 1901 (Jones collection).

2. "Allegatt" was perhaps Williamson's error, for the Harding and Bode text, read from the manuscript, reads "Allegash."

3. The excursion was made with Edward Hoar, not with George Thatcher. See *The Correspondence of Henry David Thoreau,* p. 486.

408. Henry Salt to S. A. Jones, August 30, 1901.

I was indeed grieved to hear yr. sad news.[1] It is just such occasions that make one wish one could send some word of cheer other than the commonplaces of condolence, and yet—there is nothing more to be said! *There* is just the pathos of it. I had thought from your former letter that there was some good ground for hopefulness.

You are wise to occupy your thoughts with congenial work, such as that "pertaining to Thoreau". If you have the idea of printing a selection from the press-cuttings, would you like me to look up any that I may have and send them over? There may be, & probably are, a good many not included in those I have already sent you. The worst of it is that in these journalistic outpourings there is so much chaff to a small amount of wheat.

Your discovery of Mr. Greene's pencilled note about the Gentle Boy is very interesting, though I have a feeling that the same explanation of the poem "Sympathy" was once made to me—conjecturally—by yourself or some other Thoreau student. I certainly think there are fewer difficulties in the acceptance of that explanation than of the others—though of course there still are some. It seems more *like* Thoreau, I think, to write so of his brother than of the other persons suggested.

By the way, what of Mrs. Marble's (?) volume of letters, &c? Is it forthcoming this year, or is there any hitch in its publication? Was not that to throw light on the same subject of the poem "Sympathy"? . . .

1. Dr. Jones's favorite son, Carroll, died of tuberculosis in 1901.

409. S. A. Jones to A. W. Hosmer, September 7, 1901.

I am glad enough to hear from you again. I learned you were ill, but as you are on deck, I am relieved.

I have carried Miss Ricketson's letter in my letter-book (it is in my coat pocket) ever since I received it last April. When it came, we were under the terrible strain of Carroll's illness, but my wife and I tried to find Mr. R's letters, and could not. I knew they were not lost, so I did not reply to her request because I was hoping for the hour when I could send her faithful copies of them.[1]

The doom came, and the wordless anguish; and all of life's duties were forgotten.

My wife is away for a short visit, but on her return both of us will have a "right down smart" hunt for the missing papers, and Miss Ricketson shall hear from me in less than the time vaguely specified by the phrase, "two shakes of a sheep's tail." (I don't precisely know what that is, but I suppose the movement is something frisky!)

I wish you great joy of your new acquisitions in the Thoreau line.[2] I must have the next best thing, namely, copies of the letters—when you have no other use for your time.

If you care to have me call you a "daisy," send on that Harvard Mag. for May, 1862.[3] You could n't possibly [be] in better business (I put in the double *s* for emphasis!)

As you hope for sound sleep and good digestion, see that Goodspeed sends me a copy of Sanborn on "Thoreau's Personality."[4] I've got the postage stamps all ready, so that Goodspeed need only say how much filthy lucre he wants.

The mention of Goodspeed has given me a desirable hint, and thusly: I have prepared the "copy" for a book to be called "Thoreau amongst Friends, and Philistines."[5] It is "Inscribed (without express permission) to that respectable majority which thinks by proxy—when it thinks at all." It is as plucky and as "sassy" as any friend of Thoreau could desire, and it will make more noise than the small boy's firecracker on the "glorious Fourth."

It consists of ten reviews of Salt's various Thoreau publications from English papers, and six American estimations of Thoreau. Interspersed throughout the text are comments of my own, which are warranted "all wool, yard wide, and fast colors."

A limited edition of it will surely prepare the way for a second and cheaper one. . . .

1. Anna Ricketson had asked Dr. Jones to send copies of her father's letters for inclusion in *Daniel Ricketson and His Friends*. (Boston: Houghton, Mifflin & Co., 1902). Anna Ricketson to Dr. Jones, April 12, 1901 (Jones collection). For selections from the Jones-Ricketson correspondence, see that volume, pp. 265–74.

2. We are unable to identify these acquisitions.

3. Storrow Higginson, "Henry D. Thoreau," *Harvard Magazine* 8 (May 1862):313–18. Reprinted by Dr. Jones in *Pertaining to Thoreau*, 1901.

4. F. B. Sanborn, *The Personality of Thoreau* (Boston: Charles E. Goodspeed, 1901).

5. This volume was not published; the manuscript is in the Jones collection, and it is being edited for publication by George Hendrick in a collection entitled *Thoreau amongst Friends and Philistines and Other Thoreauviana by Dr. S. A. Jones*.

410. S. A. Jones to A. W. Hosmer, September 21, 1901.

* * *

It [*Thoreau amongst Friends and Philistines*] is not quite ready; I have found a criticism of Thoreau by Julian Hawthorne[1] that makes me "mad all over." I have not yet been able to learn where it first appeared; but when I get the facts of it, my, but I'll try and answer him as he deserves. I have done his sister to the queen's taste, especially if she likes "hot stuff," and I want to tickle Julian in even better style.

If you find yourself some day in Boston, will you ask Goodspeed if he would care to see the manuscript, with a view to publishing? Once in print, I am not at all afraid that the book will not be heard from in many quarters, for it handles some folks without gloves and in a manner that will gratify those who love Thoreau.

By the way, can you give me the date, or any approximation thereto, of that Schoolboy composition by Thoreau, on "The Seasons." I should like to write a paper on it. About how old was he when it was written? . . .

1. Dr. Jones had probably learned of the textbook which Julian Hawthorne had prepared with Leonard Lemmon: *American Literature: A Text-Book for the Use of Schools and Colleges* (Boston: D. C. Heath & Co., 1891). Pages 145–48 are a sketch of Thoreau which is largely personal invective: "He was bilious in constitution and in temper, with a disposition somewhat prone to suspicion and jealousy, and defiant, rather than truly independent, in spirit. . . . His heart was neither warm nor large, and he certainly did not share that 'enthusiasm for humanity' which was the fashionable profession in his day" (p. 146). Dr. Jones apparently did not locate Julian Hawthorne's criticism, for it is not included in the manuscript of *Thoreau amongst Friends and Philistines*.

411. S. A. Jones to A. W. Hosmer, September 29, 1901.

* * *

I note what you say about Goodspeed's reading the MSS. of "Thoreau amongst Friends, and Philistines."

I cannot send it on right off, because I am on the trail of Julian Hawthorne, who has published the most shameful thing about Thoreau I ever read. I wish to learn where it appeared—for I have only an extract from it—and to get the original paper, and *then!!!*

If you know Goodspeed's *name,* I wish you would let me know what it is, for I will write to him telling him what the book is, etc., etc.

The book is sure to please Thoreau's admirers, and it is as sure to make a noise, for I am going to handle the Hawthorne family—the father, "rose" and Julian—without gloves.[1]

The book also adds something to our knowledge of Thoreau; corrects some prevalent errors concerning him, and it shows up the critics in fine style.

I shall want Goodspeed to put it out in a limited edition, sold by subscription; but a second issue is sure to be called for, or I do not know how strong the love of a Thoreauite is—which I am not ready to allow.

I am disposed to place that Thoreau "composition" in the doings of his Eleventh year: certainly not any later. You know Mr. Blake expressed his surprise at its extreme boyishness.[2] It certainly is an early performance. I wonder if the four lines of verse at the beginning are his. That were a nice point to settle!

1. Included in *Thoreau amongst Friends and Philistines* was Rose Hawthorne Lathrop's "Glimpses of Force: Thoreau" from *Weekly Inter-Ocean,* July 1891. The annotation is in the best Jonesian style:

"This frail creature of the *transfixed pulses,* American born but exported to England in recognition of a prostitution of the paternal pen is, by a veering of the political pen 'transferred from English homelikeness to American sandbanks;' but she absolutely can not become reconciled to the exchange of 'British daisies and robins' for American golden-rod and Bobolinks. Fresh from the fogs of Liverpool, she brings to her native land 'a mind pining for gem-like blue heavens': British skies being so much 'bluer'. Is there a Nemesis that harries the *H's?*

"Long after the time when ordinary folk have reached the years of discretion, this creature of curious pulses becomes tempted of the Devil to let the readers of the *Inter-Ocean* know her estimate of Henry D. Thoreau. With the very eyes that a Liverpool fog failed to faze, she detects in him 'an affectation of a new outward bearing and manner of thought.' Surely, it is the reader now who has the 'transfixed pulses.'"

2. Alfred Hosmer had sent a copy of "The Seasons" to H.G.O. Blake, who found it "rather surprising . . . that he appears in that composition so much like other boys at that age." H.G.O. Blake to A. W. Hosmer, September 8, 1895 (Hosmer collection). For a text of the composition, which Walter Harding places in Thoreau's eleventh or twelfth year, see *The Days of Henry Thoreau,* pp. 26–27.

412. Henry Salt to S. A. Jones, October 6, 1901.

* * *

Yes, it is an advantage, as you say, to be so near Eden Bridge; but I fear it will detract somewhat from the beatitude of the idea when I tell you that the Eden river is but a tributary of the Thames, and that Edenbridge is (in prosaic language) my "post-town" and "railway-station". It lies in fact on the lowlands, some two miles from where I live, and my pleasure is to go as little near it as possible. My steps are only bent Edenwards when I have to go to my office in the modern Babylon. Crockham Hill is far more Edenic than Edenbridge.

Now with regard to your proposed volume of Press-Notices of Thoreau. Your Preface is so characteristic and so lively that I cannot find it in me to suggest any alterations, unless perhaps it be the omission of the rather trite Shakespearian quotation at the end.[1] In looking up the passages selected by you for insertion in the book, it strikes me that the articles in the "Standard" and "*Morning* Post" (not *Evening* Post, if it is the English Post that you are quoting) are rather colourless and dull—that is, they are just the ordinary newspaper article and no more. I think you would find some better game among the press-cuttings I am sending you, unless it is now too late to make changes. The extract from the *Star* I do not appear to have, unless I have overlooked it in my cuttings; but I remember that I thought at the time, judging from the style, that it was written by Richard Le Gallienne.[2]

I am going to send you, by the same mail as this letter, three sets of press-cuttings, viz: those that relate to (1) the first edition of my "Life" and the Anti-Slavery papers, 1890, (2) the "Selections from Thoreau", 1895, and (3) the second edition of the "Life", 1896. Among the 1890 criticisms, I would draw your attention to one in the *Daily News,* which, on internal evidence, is almost certainly the work of Andrew Lang, and exhibits well the inability of the elegant literary trifler to understand Thoreau. Lang is so well known that it might be good policy to pillory him, and you could justifiably say that the article was attributed to his pen. (He was a regular leader-writer on the *Daily News* at that time).

Notice also the *gradations* of criticism in the extracts from W. E. Henley's paper, the *National Observer* (now fortunately extinct). You will find no less than four notices from the *National Observer,* two in 1890, one in 1895, & one in 1896. It is amusing to see how the insolent brutality of the earlier articles is replaced in 1895 & 1896 by a quite different tone. The same sort of change is noticeable in some of the other papers.

Anyhow I hope you may find it interesting to glance through the cuttings; and if you do not think any of them worth reprinting, they may furnish some entertaining bits of impudence & mendacity for your lash.

The *Great Thoughts* article, with which you are commencing your volume, was written by a friend of mine, Mr. W. J. Jupp, one of Thoreau's truest admirers in this country.

The date of the *Inquirer* extract is July 18, 1896. I see that number 5 on your list is the *Newcastle Daily Leader* of Nov. 25, 1890; but the extract of that date in my collection is headed *Newcastle Daily Chronicle*. I don't know which is right. Perhaps both the papers (there is a Newcastle *Leader* and a Newcastle *Chronicle*) had articles on the same day.

Altogether your scheme seems a very good one, and I am sure it will result in another volume for which you will earn the gratitude of future Thoreau-students.

Keep the press-cuttings as long as you need them; after that, I shall be glad to have them back for possible reference in the future. I have just had a very kind letter from the daughter of Mr. Daniel Ricketson. She is going to write a Life of her father, and asks me to lend her what letters I received from him. I have hunted up several, all full of valuable matter about Thoreau.

1. The "Introductory Note" to *Thoreau amongst Friends and Philistines* ends with *Hamlet* III. ii. 376–82 (the Riverside Shakespeare).

2 Dr. Jones completed a draft but did not publish *Thoreau amongst Friends and Philistines*. The contents were: Introduction; "Thoreau," *Great Thoughts*, January 19, 1895, by W. J. Jupp; "The Life of Thoreau," *Standard*, October 16, 1890; "Thoreau's Life," *Spectator*, October 18, 1890; "Thoreau," *Academy*, October 25, 1890; "The Life of Thoreau," *Newcastle Daily Leader*, November 25, 1890; "Thoreau," *The Speaker*, November 8, 1890; "Henry David Thoreau," *The Morning Post*, January 9, 1891; "Henry David Thoreau," *The National Observer*, 1895, by W. E. Henley; "Thoreau," *The Inquirer*, July 18, 1896; "Thoreau's Poems," *The Star*, January, 1896; "Glimpses of Force: Thoreau," *Weekly Inter-Ocean*, July 7, 1891; "Glimpses of the son of his father" (this was the only section unfinished; it was to reprint, with comments, the essay on Thoreau in Julian Hawthorne and Leonard Lemmon, *American Literature*, 1891); "Reminiscences of Thoreau," *Concord Enterprise*, April 13, 22, 1892; "Memories of the Thoreaus," *Boston Daily Advertiser*, April 23, 1894; "Thoreau's Works," *Boston Herald*, December 18, 1893.

413. S. A. Jones to A. W. Hosmer, December 2, 1901.

* * *

I send but a line to let you know that Mr. Hill was here yesterday, bringing your remarkable catalogue.[1] Ah, Fred, once I had nearly as much energy as you have; but I fear it is buried in a grave I know.

However, my friend, Mr. Hill copied your catalogue and on reading it I said "God permitting me, I will prepare the new edition of the Bibliography." Without the aid of your catalogue, I could not possibly do it, for, Fred, I have grown prematurely old. I shall make due acknowledgement of my obligations to you. And when the book is ready, I shall deem my Thoreau work finished. . . .

1. This was a catalogue of Hosmer's Thoreau collection; it is now in the Jones collection.

414. S. A. Jones to A. W. Hosmer, December 16, 1901.

While I am not strong enough for continuous letter-writing, yet the reading of "The Personality of Thoreau" moves me to send you a line.

You can see plainly enough that our work FOR Thoreau's memory is not without fruit.

F.B.S. has *gone down on his belly* to write "The Personality" of not only Thoreau, but of the women whom he once called gossip-mongers![1]

You and I can correct Mr. Sanborn in many of his latest statements regarding Thoreau; but Mr. S. has so evidently had a *change of heart* that we will only pray that he may continue to grow in grace.

I am sending you a little book of mine on a subject foreign to Thoreau, but at the same [time] defending a dead man's memory,—just as we have in our poor way done for that of Thoreau. "The Porcelain Painter's Son" is really made from actual incidents in the life of Hahnemann, the founder of Homoeopathy. The only fiction in the book is the occasion when the old schoolmaster is said to have got over "full" from delight at his scholar's little triumph. . . .[2]

1. Sanborn softened his treatment of Mrs. Thoreau and the Thoreau aunts considerably from that which he presented in 1882. See *The Personality of Thoreau,* especially pp. 12–16.
2. *The Porcelain Painter's Son* (Philadelphia: Boericke & Tafel, 1898). After the young Hahnemann has delivered his thesis upon graduation from the *"Fuersten Schule,"* his schoolmaster, Herr Mueller, gets overfull from delight at the local *"Wirtshaus"* and must be escorted to bed.

415. S. A. Jones to A. W. Hosmer, December 25, 1901.

Your hearty damning of F.B.S. was so enjoyable that I have pasted your letter in my copy of "The Personality of Thoreau." Nevertheless, the value of Sanborn's book to Thoreau's REPUTATION is simply *in*valuable; but I could ask Sanborn some very nasty questions. This, for instance: Knowing Thoreau to have been a better scholar than Emerson and KNOWING IT ALL THESE YEARS, why did n't Sanborn SAY SO LONG YEARS AGO?!?![1] Because, when he wrote that detestable Life of Thoreau, "Henry" was not RECOG-NIZED AS HE IS TO-DAY!!!

Are you unable to see that this recognition of Thoreau is in great degree owing to what YOU have done since the Autumn of 1890. Somebody asserted that Thoreau was REALLY "somebody," despite Mr. Sanborn's cheap patronage. This was said in season and out of season, and at last the damn fools of creation began to think there was really "something in it." Of course, Fred, Thoreau had the stuff in him to back the proud statement made for him; and NOW folks are beginning to *see it*. . . .

I had a newspaper notice of Channing's departure, before your letter came.[2] I hope you are saving all the newspaper notices of the event, for Channing's life and Thoreau's are singularly intertwined and these notices will HELP the understanding of THOREAU VASTLY. I am on the lookout for all I can find; but alas! there is n't much to be had in these parts. It is quite likely that Boston papers will have lengthy notices, for Channing was a "part of history," though he himself was a poor stick, in my opinion.

Mr. Walton Ricketson has sent me an unpublished poem by Louisa M. Alcott,[3] with permission to print in THE INLANDER. In order to do it well, I ought to know more about his (Ricketson's) life, both at home and *in Concord*. Of course, I cannot ask HIM for this, so if you will help me out so far as you can, I shall be able, I hope, to do him and the poem something like justice.

Miss Anna Ricketson has invited me to visit them next summer, but I am not at ease with "grand" people and I shall not intrude upon them. . . .

1. Of Thoreau's college scholarship Sanborn had remarked: "He was a much better scholar, in the classical sense, than Emerson, Channing, or Hawthorne, and could have competed with Lowell at the same age." See *The Personality of Thoreau*, p. 37.

2. Ellery Channing died on December 23, 1901, in Concord.

3. Walton Ricketson's copy of Louisa May Alcott's poem is in the Jones collection; we give here the text of the poem from Ricketson's copy:

To W. R. ———.
Philosophers sit in their Sylvan Hall,
And talk of the duties of man.
Of Chaos and Cosmos, Haegel and Kant,
With the over-soul well in the van.

All on their hobbies they amble away,
And a terrible dust they make,
While devout disciples gase and adore,
As they daily listen and bake.

Our neighbor makes of his quiet life,
As he walks the path of duty,
A wiser sermon than many they preach,
A truer lesson of beauty,

Patient and faithful, tender and true,
A loyal Knight to woman-kind,

With a thousand little acts and words,
The hearts of his friends to bind.

The little cot by the River side
Where the summer air is fresh and cool
And genial natures welcome us all,
Is to me a better sort of School—

For Art and music, heaven-born twins,
Add beauty grace and simple mirth,
While the human pair add faith & love,
To warm and brighten their hearth.

With the poem Walton Ricketson included a note explaining the circumstances surrounding its composition: "Sent to me on my 45th birth day May 27th 1884. Then living with my sister Anna in a little cottage near the River in Concord."

416. Henry Salt to S. A. Jones, December 31, 1901.

* * *

Your letter of Nov. 14 came duly to hand. It struck me as very curious, and an example of how the unforeseen always happens, that those neglected old press-cuttings, which I had rolled up and stored away so untidily, should be undergoing the process of arrangement and classification in another continent, and at the hands of a Detroit journalist! What right have I to reap where I have not strawed, by receiving back a *book* where I sent but a *bundle?* But if they are really useful to you in your work, I am indeed glad I sent them. Keep them as long as ever you like, and altogether, if you wish it.

I am looking forward to your volume of "Friends and Philistines", and must write a special article for the spring number of the *Humane Review* on that and other forthcoming Thoreau literature. Mr. Sanborn's book on "The Personality of Thoreau" appears to be just forthcoming (he writes that a copy will be sent to me); and I suppose Mrs. Marble's volume is also nearing completion? There will be quite a "boom" in Thoreau again! And it will give me another opportunity for a hit at Robert Blatchford, for that gratuitously impertinent reference to Thoreau in "My Favourite Books". (How charitable and forgiving we journalists are towards each other, are we not?)

There was a foolish passage about Thoreau in the literary columns of the *Daily News* (London) lately, in connection with vegetarianism. The writer said that Thoreau was the most "successful" of all literary vegetarians, & then went on to assert that he was not a "convinced" vegetarian at all,—the old trick of exalting your man in order to demolish him the more effectually. In a short letter which appeared a day or two later, I disposed of the critic by quoting a sentence from "Walden"—"Whatever my own practice may be, I have no doubt". . . . &c, &c., which showed that there was not much question as to what Thoreau's *"convictions"* were on that subject. . . .

417. S. A. Jones to A. W. Hosmer, January 1, 1902.

You can scarcely imagine the eagerness with which I have read the papers you so thoughtfully sent me and the letter in which you describe the Channing-Sanborn circus.[1] It cured me of the regret I had felt that I could not be present at the planting of Concord's last curiosity.

If it is not putting you to too much trouble, I should more than like to SEE that copy of the Springfield Republican wherein Sanborn puffs his own book.[2] You see, Fred, it is time that he was shown up IN HIS OWN WORDS, for he uses the Springfield Republican to vent his personal spite, and does not criticise a book on its real merits or demerits—and that is just the sort of man one should SHOW UP.

I wrote for Mr. Goodspeed a first-class "puff" for Sanborn's "Personality of Thoreau." I did it in the hope that it might *help the sale of the book and thereby induce G. to publish Thoreau material FREELY* (not for nothing, of course, but so as to get all such material into print). In my letter *I flattered S. hugely in the hope of so "tickling" both him and Goodspeed that S. might be led on to publish ALL of Thoreau's under-graduate papers*—which I presume Sanborn "borrowed" from Sophia. *By flattering S. this matter can be printed;* if he is made angry he might make way with it from revenge. You see what I am after, and I hope the "end justifies the means" employed.

Now, I suppose S. will begin to coin old Channing into dollars. A nice friend is F.B.S.!

---

1. Channing's funeral included "Remarks" by Sanborn, which consisted of a long biographical sketch of Channing and an assessment of his poetry. Sanborn then apparently read three of Channing's poems, after which letters from Julia Ward Howe and Mary Russell Watson of Plymouth were read. The services then concluded with another selection from Channing's work, read by the Rev. Abraham Jackson. See the *Middlesex Patriot,* December 27, 1901.

2. "About Lowell and Thoreau," *Springfield Republican,* December 11, 1901. Sanborn quotes at length from *The Personality of Thoreau* and praises the illustrations by Mr. Gleason.

418. S. A. Jones to A. W. Hosmer, January 13, 1902.

And yet another of your unceasing kindnesses: as if I could [carry] a world of obligations upon my back and not be crushed!

And at last I am permitted to look upon the likeness of one who has occasioned me much conjecture, for it is really hard to rightly make an estimate of him.

Looking into his face; seeing the decidedly artistic pose for it; remembering his "personally conducted"[1] funeral, I am inclined to say that this Channing was one whose conceit far exceeded his capacity. His aspirations fell far short of accomplishment; the grapes were so sour because they were so far out [of] his reach. Worse than all, the grapes that he never tasted set his teeth on edge!

He made a tragedy of his life, and a foolish friend made his funeral a farce—and a farce at the graveside is the sorriest spectacle on earth. Only an insincerity could plan such a performance, and only a long-eared ass could carry it into execution. For such products, it now appears that Concord "takes the cake."

It should have been expected that the expiration of the "School of Philosophy" had ended the "monkeyings" which "old Concord" was called upon to endure; but there must be one more funeral in Concord before it can be delivered from the bondage of such fantastic folly as makes a friend to its people weep.

1. Dr. Jones's allusion is to the obituary of Channing which appeared in the *Patriot* for December 27, 1901; the notice referred to the services being "personally conducted by Mr. Sanborn."

419. S. A. Jones to A. W. Hosmer, January 20, 1902.

Your confidential statement in regard to the conduct of S. is not a surprise. When I first learned that Channing had been taken into S's house, I said to myself: "Yes and the "taking in" won't end there!" I "caught on to" the little game; and I have had to wait only eleven years to see it carried out to the letter. While I am sorry that S. is such a human "stinker," I still feel thankful that my condemnation of him *(as a man)* when I first met him, is justified by the "true inwardness" which he is revealing daily. I am wickedly inclined to say as you did: "Damn him!" But, Fred, that is just a waste of time, for he is very successfully damning himself.

If he were not the custodian of papers of Thoreau's writing which he might destroy IN revenge, I would skin him alive in the public press.

Don't vex *yourself* about him or his talk. You don't need to defend yourself against a skunk. It is not cowardness to give every skunk the "right of way," for you will only get pissed on if you stop to talk with the THING.

There are those who know WHO "discovered" the poetic value of

Thoreau's haunts WHEN F. B. Sanborn could only *defame Thoreau's mother.* Mr. Sanborn has learned to SEE Thoreau AFTER Thoreau's fame was seen by the world. Mr. Sanborn is not an "F.B.S.," but he is dreadfully like a F.A.R.T.!

Get permission to photograph that Cranch portrait of Channing[1] IF YOU CAN, and get it copyrighted. That is an historical picture on account of both artist and subject: THERE WILL BE A GROWING DEMAND FOR IT. (Make a note of that!) . . .

1. We are unable to identify the Cranch portrait of Channing.

420. S. A. Jones to A. W. Hosmer, March 10, 1902.

* * *

Of course Sanborn and Goodspeed are working Thoreau as they would a gold mine (for what there is "in it"), but I am glad to get all I can of Thoreau's writing, at any price within my reach; and I hope Sanborn can be flattered into publishing all Thoreau's under-graduate writings—which are very valuable for the proper appreciation of him. (Thoreau, of course, for one only needs KNOW S. to "properly" appreciate HIM!)

I hope, my dear Fred, that you are not feeling too much dejected about your health; and I am the more ready to believe your ominous reference to your Thoreau collection is to be traced to the despondency that attends dyspeptic ills. As I have successfully treated people as far off as California, I am asking myself why I cannot be of some service to you.

From what I remember of your father, I feel that you should be a long-lifer, and if you are not too much confined to the store your indigestion is certainly susceptible to suitable medication and dietetic measures.

At all events I am sending you some medicine that will relieve you in regard to the gas in your stomach, and if you will give the information wanted in regard to your habits in the matter of food, time for taking meals, amount of fluid drank, etc., I am confident you can be entirely relieved.

I feel a little embarrassed at FORCING my services upon a person who is in the hands of another physician, but I am presuming upon the fact that my forty odd years of study and experience may enable me to do a thing or two that your home physicker has not yet grown up to. If you feel that I am intruding do not hesitate to tell me so; but I am IMPELLED to offer you the best that a friend can do. . . .[1]

1. Many of the remaining letters of Dr. Jones to Hosmer are devoted largely to discussion of Hosmer's physical condition. We have deleted these letters.

421. S. A. Jones to A. W. Hosmer, March 31, 1902.

* * *

I am convinced that Goodspeed and Sanborn are a precious pair of DISINTERESTED dealers in Thoreau materials. Goodspeed knows that I am "onto" his tricks and he does not send me his catalogues!! It is a shame that Sanborn has got the Thoreau MSS. in his possession, for he does not care a tinker's dam for anything more than the money he can coin out of them. Goodspeed is also after the money ONLY. I am waiting for a reply to a *hint* that he had sold Mr. Hill a copy of the "Week" in which the pencilled writing (purporting to be Thoreau's) *is a forgery.* He said he would write when he got time, and he has NOT YET "got time."

In your dealings with him, KEEP YOUR KEENEST "YANKEE" EYES WIDE OPEN!!!!!! At the same time, be wary, for if Sanborn gets angry, the chance is sadly large that he will suppress the Thoreau under-graduate papers.

Do not hesitate to let Goodspeed KNOW that you are "onto Sanborn's curves" and that the best people in Concord are fully convinced of Sanborn's DISINTERESTEDNESS and incorruptible integrity. . . .

422. S. A. Jones to A. W. Hosmer, May 15, 1902.

* * *

I am particularly struck by Miss Lyman's deep sense of the religiousness of Thoreau.[1] A deeper and deeper recognition of his devout religiousness is growing upon me. George Ripley never made so utter a mistake as when he regarded Thoreau as being sacrilegious.[2]

The truth is, Thoreau is just beginning to be rightly interpreted. His life and his thoughts were so completely beyond the comprehension of his contemporaries that he was as completely misunderstood.

I have for many years now considered Thoreau as infinitely Emerson's superior in all respects—especially in SINCERITY—and every day of my life but deepens the conviction. Emerson could write "nice" things; Thoreau could LIVE them—and there you have the difference in a nutshell.

Miss Lyman is right: the last word has not been spoken of Thoreau. Never can the "last" word be said of such a man. He must remain the inexhaustible source of inspiration for every true soul so long as men sojourn in the mists that we call "Life". . . .

1. Emily Lyman, *Thoreau* (Concord, Mass.: Privately printed for Alfred W. Hosmer, 1902).
2. Dr. Jones refers here to the review of *A Week* in the *New York Tribune*, June 13, 1849, which criticized Thoreau's pantheism. The review is now considered to be the work of Horace Greeley.

423. S. A. Jones to A. W. Hosmer, June 21, 1902.

* * *

Mrs. Marble's paper[1] interested me far more for your illustrations than for her writing. You are thoughtful in remembering me and you will keep piling on obligations that I can never return.

I learned from Mr. Hill lately that when Sanborn was "chinning" at the pow-wow held in Detroit, he was repeatedly told to sit down, cut it short, etc., by the weary audience; but he was so "stuck" on his own mouth that he kept right on. He surely is "personally conducted"!

1. Annie Russell Marble, "Where Thoreau Worked and Wandered," *Critic* 40 (June 1902):509–16. The article is illustrated by A. W. Hosmer, including a reproduction of two pages of Thoreau's manuscript journal.

424. S. A. Jones to A. W. Hosmer, June 26, 1902.

* * *

Fred, do you know that you get actually poetical every time you "go for" F.B.S. As a sorry specimen of a "man" I probably despise him as heartily as you do; but, Fred, I cannot but admire the literary ability displayed by the "cuss" in his late Thoreau work. Frankly, I consider his "Personality of Thoreau" to be a purely *made up* article,—but, recollect how differently he HAS to write of Thoreau NOW compared with his writing 1882!! And in the Introduction to the "Service"[1] Sanborn is actually crawling on his belly before the majestic stature of Thoreau as the world is seeing him in 1902. I do not know any writer who could put Henry D. Thoreau more exquisitely and at the same time truthfully before the reader than F.B.S. has therein done; and while I can and heartily do despise S. as a *man,* I can but admire the *artist* in him; and this is the standpoint from which I wrote the brief review of the "Service" for the "Detroit Journal."[2]

Do not forget another thing, namely, Sanborn MUST be flattered into publishing Thoreau's under-graduate papers. WHEN *that* is done, you'll hear from "dis yere niggah," if he is still alive! Those college essays are necessary to show the splendid consistency of Thoreau's life; they will prove that the Walden episode was NOT a whim, and if that is shown before I die, I shall be content to "lay me down and sleep."

I have been the recipient of some presents from the Ricketsons that almost made me insane with delirious delight.[3] I am absolutely unworthy of such more than kindnesses, for I am sure if they knew what a good-for-nothing old seed I am they would despise me. I have not been well enough to do justice to my feelings in writing, acknowledging their munificence but I shall try and do so as soon as I am a little firmer on my pins.

1. *The Service,* ed. F. B. Sanborn (Boston: Charles E. Goodspeed, 1902).

2. "A Notable New Book," *Detroit Journal,* May 22, 1902. In this review Dr. Jones praised Sanborn's introduction to *The Service* for its "true critical insight" and commended Goodspeed for being an "appreciative" publisher.

3. Miss Ricketson sent Dr. Jones a piece of plaster from the Walden cabin which she and Walton had picked up while walking at the pond with Ellery Channing in 1868. Anna Ricketson to Jones, May 18, 1902 (Jones collection). Later the Ricketsons sent Dr. Jones photographs and a cane which Walton had cut in 1868 from the site of the Walden hut. Walton Ricketson to Jones, June 12, 1902 (Jones collection).

425. S. A. Jones to A. W. Hosmer, July 1, 1902.

* * *

Horace Hosmer's letter comes "pat" after Mr. Wood's fine paper; but I am chiefly desirous to have it printed for the sake of the "wipe" it gives F.B.S.[1]

If you think Mr. Albert Lane will publish it, you may give it to him: if you think NOT, then do with it whatever you see fit.

Mr. Hill sent me the other day an obituary notice of Henry Thoreau's paternal grandfather's second wife—the one who "brought up" Thoreau's father.[2] It is worthy of being reprinted, with notes to illustrate it: and it is the best possible manner of showing that "little" John Thoreau came from better stock than Emerson—whose American ancestor was a common baker—and even F. B. Sanborn, whose ancestors were—the devil knows who, for I'm sure I don't.

However, do what you like with the Hosmer letter.

1. Dr. Jones did publish one of Horace Hosmer's letters to him, with explanatory comment, as "How Our Great-Grandfathers Drank," in the *Middlesex Patriot,* July 11, 1902. The letter, of March 17, 1891, described the widespread drinking in Concord during the 1840s and included a highly favorable account of Thoreau's parents. Dr. Jones's reference here to Mr. Wood's paper contains an error; in his article he prefaced Horace Hosmer's letter with the remarks: "I beg leave to quote a letter bearing upon the subject treated of by Mr. Albert E. Wood in his most interesting paper, published in your issue for June 27." That paper, "Where Thoreau Worked and Wandered," was by Albert E. Lane, not Albert E. Wood.

2. Jean Thoreau's second wife was Rebecca Kettell, sister of Charlestown merchant Joseph Hurd and relative of Dr. Hurd, described by Sanborn as a "respectable physician" of Concord. See F. B. Sanborn, *The Life of Henry D. Thoreau* (Boston: Houghton Mifflin, 1917), pp. 29–30.

426. S. A. Jones to A. W. Hosmer, July 7, 1902.

* * *

Fred, to give the Devil his due, is n't Sanborn just "a peach"? I'll be damned if I don't have to admire him as an *artist at self-puffing;* and in spite of my contempt for his methods, I find myself obliged to admire his "nerve."[1]

What do you know about the editor of the Concord paper that you sent me? Is he a "brick" or is he a shyster??

I'll tell you why I ask. I am "spoiling for a fight," and I'd like to measure swords with F.B.S. himself.

My plot is this: to write a series of papers for the Concord man's paper entitled *"How others see us."* I shall not fall short of doing honor to all that is worthy in Concord—so far as so insignificant a man can see it—but, by Jerusalem, I'll tickle your fads immensely,—as Horace Hosmer would were he alive.[2]

If the bright Concord editor will keep me *incognito* I promise to give his paper some interesting material for the dog-days. Let me know what you think of the scheme—of course, Sanborn is the son of a gun that I'm after.

1. Hosmer had sent Dr. Jones "Emerson, Thoreau, Channing" from the *Springfield Republican* for July 2, 1902, in which Sanborn publicized his own books *The Personality of Thoreau, The Personality of Emerson,* and the enlarged edition of Channing's *Thoreau, the Poet-Naturalist.*
2. In "How Our Great-Grandfathers Drank," *Middlesex Patriot,* July 11, 1902, Dr. Jones did some tickling of Concord's fads: "Perhaps, long after all the 'gig respectability' of Concord is buried in its merited oblivion, the site of the Walden shanty will be the shrine to which the pilgrim will wend his way to worship."

427. S. A. Jones to A. W. Hosmer, July 12, 1902.

I have just sent off the "copy" for a Carlyle book[1] and I am as thoroughly done up as if I had had a baby—not that I have "labor pains," but labor weariness. . . .

Give my compliments to Mr. Albert Lane and tell him that when I get my "second wind" he'll wish I had n't!

Before he gets his "double columns" ready for me, he had better wait until he sees what kind of a honeysuckle I am, anyway.

I am afraid the Horace Hosmer Letters would prove too voluminous for a newspaper; they must go into a book if I am spared and gain enough strength to edit them fitly. If I do not do it, I shall see that they are left for the proper one to do it. . . .

1. *Collectanea Thomas Carlyle, 1821–1855* (Canton, Pa.: The Kirgate Press, 1903).

428. Henry Salt to S. A. Jones, July 13, 1902.

* * *

I hear from Mr. Hosmer from time to time; and from him and Mr. Sanborn I seem to receive most of the Concord news that concerns Thoreau. I did not think Miss Lyman's brochure on Thoreau very good;[1] it seems almost a pity to burden Thoreau's memory with goody-goody stuff of that sickly kind. Mrs. Marble's article was better; though even in that there seemed to be rather a want of what the literary folk call "distinction". . . .

1. Emily R. Lyman, *Thoreau* (Concord: Privately printed for Alfred W. Hosmer, 1902).

429. S. A. Jones to A. W. Hosmer, July 17, 1902.

* * *

I am reading the Antiquarian Society's monographs with as much interest as if I had a birthright in Concord. Perhaps I have, for I see from the records that they could n't start Concord *without* a JONES. (I cannot say that I *distinctly* recollect the Rev. John Jones,[1] but as he had the good sense to help start Concord he must have been a "peach" of a Jones. "John Jones" is a popular spectacle,—in Wales, especially; and I have often wondered why in the deuce the name "John" did n't wear out! It is such a handy name, and it hooks on—particularly to "Jones"—so easily. It is well known *in Wales* that the first man was a Jones; but his name was n't "John": it was Adam. You can the more readily believe this when you consider how natural it is that the pitiful things called men should have derived their origin from a damn Jones.

(It was not until the early Y.M.C.A. folks "got in their work" that the "a damn" was softened into "Adam." I must confess, Fred, that I have heard this genealogical FACT disputed by certain evil-minded people who were "hell bent" on figuring in the "first families"; but that does n't cut any ice.)

I believe it: the Joneses are always "in it." I'll be darned if the Concord cranks could get up even "The Concord School of Philosophy" without a Jones to give it a flavor; and old Alcott went all the way to Illinois for a Jones,[2] when the real thing, yard wide, all wool, fast colors and all that was as near Concord as New Jersey. *I know this to be the case for* I was living in Jersey at the time. I do n't care a cuss whether Alcott knew beans or not, but he certainly did n't know Welshmen, or he would never have over-looked me—that goes without saying!

I bite off this interesting Jones topic to just say that I shall claim a brevet citizenship in "old Concord" on the strength of the Rev. John Jones. I wish he had n't moved to Connecticut; but he shared the family weakness, for the Joneses are noted for their "wind" and for the craving for onions. THAT CONNECTICUT ONION "fetched" the Rev. John Jones just as an apple did his ancient ancestress! . . .

1. The Reverend John Jones was among the original settlers of Concord. He later removed with his congregation to Fairfield. Connecticut.

2. Dr. H. K. Jones, a Platonist from Jacksonville, Illinois, was one of the principal lecturers of the Concord School of Philosophy.

430. S. A. Jones to A. W. Hosmer, July 25, 1902.

* * *

Your mention of Channing's Poems as put out by Sanborn[1] leads me to tell you that I got a copy as soon as it was out. I had to pay the long price, but I enjoyed the cute "Yankeeism" of Sanborn which makes a mint of his departed friends.

The dear old devil will get his hands full when Sanborn ARRIVES, "and don't you forget it"! . . .

1. Ellery Channing, *Poems of Sixty-Five Years,* ed. Franklin B. Sanborn (Philadelphia and Concord: James H. Bentley, 1902).

431. S. A. Jones to A. W. Hosmer, August 4, 1902.

The photos of the bust are here and I got an artist in photography to touch out the few white spots so that I could see the departed "poet" at his best.

I suppose this bust job[1] was also "personally conducted;" it shows signs of it, I fancy. The pedestal and the lettering assure me that the "artist" has mistaken his calling. As a stone mason or a sign painter he would prove a howling success, but he should n't sculpt any more,—unless it is on Sanborn's pocket-book: he may *carve* that as much as he can. (If he gets ahead of its owner, I should like to hear of it, for I hardly think that can be done.)

I have the three views of *C.* that you so kindly sent me, and after a careful study of them and of the "bust," I must say death has a new terror in it: suppose Sanborn took it into his head to have all his admirers sculpted! Dear me!!!

Can't the Concord people persuade Mr. S. to have himself sculpted, first being *scalped* to add to the effect? Not that I for one moment imagine Mr. S. will be "beautiful in death," but that it would be a really cheerful sight. Suggest it, won't you. I'll gladly chip in to help pay the artist! . . .

374

1. This was probably the bust of Channing made by Frank Edwin Elwell (1858–1922), who was born in Concord and befriended by the Alcotts and by Daniel Chester French. The Jones collection includes Hosmer's photographs of the bust.

432. S. A. Jones to A. W. Hosmer, August 11, 1902.

The "Monitors"[1] you gave me contain the eight numbers you mention, though No. 8 lacks the cover. Of course, it is n't "complete," but the purely literary part is there, and that suffices. It is a pity, though, that more is not known of the history of the "Monitor"—*that* part should be looked up and recorded. . . .

1. For items of Thoreauvian interest in the *Monitor,* a short-lived Concord paper begun in 1862, see Francis Allen, *A Bibliography of Henry David Thoreau,* p. 120.

433. S. A. Jones to A. W. Hosmer, August 31, 1902.

* * *

Perhaps the following items of a recent correspondence between C. E. Goodspeed and me may interest you for a moment:

"Mr. Sanborn, however, says that you are wrong in your statement that the book (Channing's 'Poet-Naturalist') originally was *due to his* (Sanborn's) suggestion."
Goodspeed. Letter to Jones.

"If Mr. Sanborn says I am wrong in my statement that the book was due originally to his statement, of course he knows; but as Mr. Sanborn *made that statement to me in his own library, at Concord in 1890*, he can tell whether he told the truth or not.
According to the experience of many Concord people, Mr. Sanborn has one quality in which the Father of his Country is said to have been lacking!
For Mr. Sanborn as a literary man, especially as an editor, I trust I have all that regard for him which his qualities deserve; for Mr. Sanborn as a *man* I have only a contempt which is as profound as his conduct proves it to be merited."
Jones. Letter to Goodspeed. (Aug. 25th.)

I have not since heard from Goodspeed—a good 'running mate' for S.!

434. S. A. Jones to A. W. Hosmer, September 9, 1902.

Only for your thoughtful kindness it is a question whether I had seen Mr. Russell's paper in the "Atlantic."[1] You can scarcely imagine the interest with which I read the correspondence, for I was aware that Thoreau and Hecker had once come within touch, and knowing something of Hecker's career, I was curious to learn how Thoreau came out of the contact. His sweet SANITY shines out clearer than ever. Of a truth, Fred, he is not Emerson's "second best" by a long sight! (Indeed, when I look over my whole life, it is a small comfort to me to know that I was permitted to discern the splendid stuff in Thoreau long before he had "got to the front." But, even with this, I find that I "builded better than I knew," for I am finding more and more in Thoreau with every day of my life.)

Mr. Russell's presentation of the Hecker-Thoreau letters has made me regret that he has not published anything of the holy work Mr. Blake committed to his hands, and this, too, from learning by this Hecker-Thoreau correspondence how exceedingly well he is qualified to present Thoreau to us.

Broken as I am by the blows of Fate, I cannot expect to read that presentation of Thoreau's Journals for which, in these degenerate days, there is so much need.

But I shall escape the responsibility that will fall heavily upon those who DO read Thoreau and do NOT live up to his high teachings. Alas! I cannot do that; I am made of too shabby stuff.

1. E. H. Russell, "A Bit of Unpublished Correspondence between Henry Thoreau and Isaac Hecker," *Atlantic Monthly* 90 (September 1902):370–76. Hecker (1819–1888), a member of the Brook Farm community and briefly a resident at Fruitlands, became friendly with Thoreau in 1844 while he was boarding with the Thoreau family. That same year Hecker converted to Roman Catholicism, after which he tried unsuccessfully to persuade Thoreau to make a pilgrimage to Rome with him. Hecker later founded the Paulist fathers and the *Catholic World* (1865), which he edited until his death. For a full discussion of the Thoreau-Hecker relationship, see Walter Harding, *The Days of Henry Thoreau,* pp. 162–68.

435. S. A. Jones to A. W. Hosmer, September 26, 1902.

* * *

Did you know that I have been long hankering for just the Alcott school reports[1] that you have sent me—I read them late last night, and I should like to ask a heap of questions about them,—but who is now alive that can tell me!

If there is any one in Concord to-day who can enlighten a Michigan pagan, for sweet charity's sake do let me know. I want especially to learn what "songs" Louisa Alcott wrote: in fact, to learn, if I can, how much of a hand she had in the getting up of her "Daddy's" REPORT. Lord, how Alcottish it is!

I am beside myself with delight that at last you have "lit on" a semblance of Thoreau's mother. The fact that the *tornado in petticoats,* Mary Moody Emerson, presented it makes it all the more precious in my esteem. . . .[2]

1. As superintendent of the Concord schools, Bronson Alcott contributed yearly reports in 1860, 1861, and 1862 to the official records of Concord. Though he was superintendent from 1859 through 1865, only three of his reports were printed. These have been reprinted by Walter Harding in a Scholars' Facsimile edition, *Essays on Education* (Gainesville, Fla., 1960). One set of the copies Hosmer sent Dr. Jones has now been acquired by the University of Illinois Library.

2. Alfred Hosmer obtained a reproduction of a silhouette of Cynthia Thoreau from the granddaughter of Mrs. Leander Gage of Waterford, Maine. Mrs. Gage had apparently received the silhouette from Mary Moody Emerson.

436. Henry Salt to S. A. Jones, October 3, 1902.

* * *

I have not yet thanked you for your letter of July 25, which I read with much sympathy. You have indeed had heavy bereavements[1] to bear; but I rejoice that you still show the old courage and persevere so bravely in your literary and other work. I am sure the volume dealing with the press-notices of Thoreau will be a real boon to students.

I shall send you, in a few days, the October number of the *Humane Review,* in which you will find, *inter alia,* an article on the "Secret of the Mountains", in which I have tried to express some of my feelings about the mountain scenery of Wales and Cumberland. I don't know whether the article will appeal to you at all—I don't think it will be intelligible to many readers—but it is at least a record of real experience which has been very valuable to the writer. We are just back from our autumnal fortnight in the Lake District, and a very cold, wet, inclement time we have had there. . . .

I am looking forward to the appearance of the Ricketson book,[2] a copy of which Miss Ricketson has kindly promised to send me. I must try to do something to make it known in this country.

By the way, who is Frank E. Elwell, who perpetrated the "Bust of Sanborn for Kansas"?[3] Is he a bitter foe of F.B.S., and paying off "old scores" by taking so terrible a revenge on our Concord friend? Even *your* pity must be moved for Sanborn when you see what Elwell has made of him!

1. Carroll Dunham Jones, Dr. Jones's favorite son, had died of tuberculosis.
2. *Daniel Ricketson and His Friends.*
3. The Concord Free Public Library has a picture of Elwell's bust of Sanborn.

437. Henry Salt to A. W. Hosmer, October 3, 1902.

* * *

Many thanks for the copy lately received of the *Atlantic Monthly*. I think Thoreau's contribution to the correspondence with Hecker is very good and characteristic; but I am surprised that Mr. Russell, in editing the letters, should write as if "these two remarkable men" were about *equally* remarkable! A good many promising young aspirants have ended by joining the Catholic church; but it is less common to find them ending as Thoreau did. . . .

438. S. A. Jones to A. W. Hosmer, October 8, 1902.

* * *

You can hardly imagine how much I thank you—that is how earnestly—for those old School reports. One set is already in our University Library, and another will soon be in the library of our State Normal School. Poor old Alcott's ideal in matters educational is to be reverently recognized; and one must forget all about poor, impractical Alcott, the "dead beat."

439. S. A. Jones to A. W. Hosmer, October 12, 1902.

I have just finished cutting the leaves of the "Walden."[1] It came on Friday night, but had to be lain aside until the Sunday's quiet could enable me to look it over and enjoy it. I can't taste a book if I am at all hurried by anything else.

Only for your thoughtful kindness I should not have seen this edition, for my youngest son is now in the university and I have to count my pennies! It is a pleasure to see the publishers' note made so prominent in this reprint when one remembers how shamefully forgetful they were in the very first issue.

I prefer this one-volume book to the earlier issue, in two. The thin paper enables the compression into one book, and that is easily held in the hand for the slow reading that "Walden" should always have. I like to dip into its pages and to stop and chew on a Thoreau thought so as to get as much of the juice out of it as I possibly can; and the peculiar thing about Thoreau is that you can never chew any of his veracities until you have exhausted it. You may chew until you are tired; but when you take up the book again, the very same pregnant thought shall set you a-chewing again—and, Lo! it is as full of juice as ever.

This *lastingness* is what ties me to Thoreau. . . .

1. Hosmer had sent Houghton Mifflin's 1902 one-volume reprint of the 1897 *Walden*.

440. S. A. Jones to A. W. Hosmer, October 15, 1902.

* * *

It is six P.M., and Mrs. Jones has just handed me my afternoon's mail, and, Lo! here are the beautiful photogravures. I shall surely wipe my "specs" for a feast to-night!

I am not capable of critically judging, but it seems to me that the illustrations to Mrs. Marble's book are the better art of the two sets.[1] But, Fred, I could have hugged you for sheer delight when I saw Blake's picture. I have no words to express my deepest thanks for this particular picture. He was older and whiter when I saw him, but the picture brings him back as I saw him in Worcester in 1890. . . .

1. Hosmer had sent copies of his photographs for the illustrated *Walden* of 1897 and 1902 and for Annie Russell Marble's *Thoreau: His Home, Friends and Books* (New York: Thomas Y. Crowell, 1902).

441. S. A. Jones to A. W. Hosmer, November 3, 1902.

* * *

I am inclined to think that Mrs. Marble has not mentioned the aid she has had from free access to your Thoreau collection. Did you not lend her your "Inlander" papers! I imagine so, and she should surely have given you "honorable mention."

I am disappointed in my expectation concerning the revelations I had been led to expect she was going to be able to make. I do not know one iota more about Thoreau than I did before; and I KNOW she is in error in regard to many of her statements. She is not a success as a writer and the reviews will possibly convince her of it.

442. S. A. Jones to A. W. Hosmer, November 17, 1902.

* * *

Tell your editor friend[1] that I meant well when I proposed sending some "sheet music" for his Concord paper, but I am literary adviser for a publishing house, and also a rather over-worked consulting physician—

with an extravagant family—and the little time I have for writing must be for base lucre.

If I were only a dozen years younger! Then I could write for half the night and "come up smiling", as the "fancy" say, the next morning; but, alas! the glory has departed not only from Israel but from Samuel as well, and left just an effete semi-respectable ex-professor.

Alas! Fred, for *time* to review Mrs. Marble, Stinker Sanborn, and Saint Anna R. as I could "with one arm tied behind my back" if I could *make* the time. As it is, I suppose I must die with a skinful of unborn Thoreau material,—of a certain kind. However, it's all right!

1. Albert Lane of the *Middlesex Patriot*.

443. S. A. Jones to A. W. Hosmer, November 28, 1902.

* * *

Mrs. Marble is a good specimen of the American hysterical female—the very last creature on earth that should be allowed to lay unholy hands upon so sincere a soul as Thoreau.

Mrs. Marble has given the world a new style of writing, the Marbleese! It is the result of an illicit intercourse between a semi-intelligent school-ma'am and a Century Dictionary—and the dictionary gets the worst of it.

And it is dedicated to her husband! Poor devil, [if] he can stand it, I suppose the reader must. I sympathise with him, profoundly, and I hope my sympathy is n't thrown away upon one who can not comprehend his need for it.

I am disposed to regard Mrs. Marble's "soul-uplift"[1] as an experience of anything but a lifting-up; unless she refers to "shop-lifting!"

From my own researches, in which you have the larger part, she has *lifted* with disgraceful industry, and of all who have in any manner written of Thoreau, there is not one from whom she has so largely appropriated as from myself. And I do not think I am at all improved by going through the Marble mill.

Mrs. M. is not an honest woman in her literary work. She makes mention of Channing, Sanborn and Salt because they are so widely known that her stealings from any of them would be detected, but her indebtedness to such work as I have done in "The Inlander," in the "Bibliography of Thoreau," in *Lippincott's Magazine* and in "Some Unpublished Letters of Henry D. and Sophia E. Thoreau" is not acknowledged. Some of her appropriations in this line are put forth as if she was the original authority for whatever of Thoreau information they convey.

But she has forgotten that future students of Thoreau will also use my bibliography for reference to the sources of information concerning

380

Thoreau, and then *the date of publication will* reveal Mrs. Marble's unacknowledged appropriations in a manner that will most effectually show her up in all her "true inwardness."

The picture of Mrs. Cynthia Dunbar Thoreau is the most triumphant reply to Sanborn's defamations of herself. I am inexpressibly thankful that I have been permitted to see this likeness before I die. I can not thank you for it, because the words are utterly inadequate to express my feelings.

If I can find all my Thoreau family pictures I shall do so; and if you will give me little histories of each picture—how and where you found them—I will write you a small booklet on "The Thoreau Family" to be illustrated by the photos and sold only by you; copyrighted, of course.[2] You are fully entitled to the honor and gratitude of all Thoreau students for your zeal in finding them.

1. Mrs. Marble closed the foreword to her volume thus: "With full recognition of the inadequacy of the result, this study has yet proved a stimulant to research and soul-uplift unequaled in many years of literary work."
2. Dr. Jones did not write this booklet.

444. Henry Salt to S. A. Jones, November 30, 1902.

You see I omit the "Eden Bridge" from my address. I find that it is, postally speaking, "not necessary"; so with the stern practicalness of a disciple of Thoreau I am discarding even paradise rather than carry the superfluous. Also I began to fear that *you* were getting a bit jealous of the superior blissfulness of my residence's title over your own; though, as you live in an *Arbor* (do you not?), I suppose you also are by way of inhabiting the Edenic, in spite of the prosaic "Ann". . . .

I was amused at your account of Mrs. Marble's "soul-lift". I fear she has come a cropper like those unfortunate persons who sometimes (there was a fatal case lately) step out into what they *think* is the lift at the top of a high building, when unfortunately the lift is not there. I have not seen her book; and after what you say, I think I shall be lucky *not* to see its mangled *dissecta membra*.

But I have lately received copies of the new edition of Channing's *Thoreau* and the Daniel Ricketson volume, and I am writing to Miss Anna Ricketson to thank her and her brother for the good work they have done. The book is very true and satisfying, I think, in everything except that meagre and utterly insufficient "sketch" of D. R. by friend Sanborn! It is a pity that F.B.S. should be taking the edge off so much otherwise good Thoreau literature by his devastating dulness; but, to be just to him, the Preface to Channing's book throws some light on what was previously obscure. I note that Daniel Ricketson's views about Henry Thoreau's parents bear out all that you have said; though he would not express himself quite so clearly to me, when I asked him.

In some of the later letters (e.g. Dr. Japp's and mine) there should have been more rejection of what is superfluous; for example, it makes me feel rather unhappy to see that the fact of my having once been a master at a public school is impressed on the mind of the American public no less than three times! Still, I think the book is on the whole a model of careful workmanship; and though I would personally have preferred my own letters to be omitted, it is well to be in good company sometimes even if one cuts a poor figure by comparison.

Though Crockham Hill is only a small village, it contains some other queer literary folk beside myself, and among them some people (Americans, I believe) who live quite close to me—though I don't know them personally—and have lately started a periodical called "The Protest" published "at the Sign of the Hop-pole, Crockham Hill". What it protests against I don't know, for I have never had the curiosity to get it; but now I am told that they are publishing a reprint of Thoreau's "Life without Principle", with Emerson's memoir prefixed—also from the Sign of the Hop-pole! I shall have to get this, I think, as *I* shall very possibly be credited with their doings. I will send it along, if it is worth sending; meantime don't identify *me* with this accursed Hop-pole if you see mention of it.[1]

1. The volume was published, but it is not in the Jones collection and was perhaps not sent by Salt. The British Museum Catalogue description is as follows: "Life without Principle. With a short biography of the author by R. W. Emerson. Published for Subscribers: Eden Bridge, 1902." Salt was a teetotaler, and he clearly did not wish to be associated with the hop-pole.

445. S. A. Jones to A. W. Hosmer, December 20, 1902.

* * *

Mr. Salt's last letter suggests the first thing I should mention, namely, the fact that Mrs. Marble should in *common courtesy have sent him a complimentary copy of her book.* If she really cares a "single damn" for Thoreau's memory—the which I question—she would have needed no outside suggestion of this nature; by which token her "soul-uplift" has never hoisted her above the ground floor!

As you know the madame, you could easily do a worse thing than to casually ask if she had sent a copy of her book to Thoreau's English biographer, &c., &c.

If she does n't send one, I shall ask you to have one sent from the publishers direct, and I'll pay the shot gladly, for I am ashamed of Mrs. M's lack of delicacy, in this instance, especially.

Another inquiry that is interesting me is, what is the matter with the Ricketsons?? Do you know whether F.B.S. is particularly intimate with them? If so, that may serve to explain a great deal. You see, the sister had been quite profuse and emphatic in inviting me to pay them a visit. I had excused myself in various ways; but happening to send her a photograph of my semi-respectable self (and you know that a good photograph will flatter the very devil) Miss R. becomes rather sarcastic in a letter, intimating that I am too "high toned" to visit, "sich" as they, and so forth, and so forth.[1] It touched me on a raw spot, for although she knew I had suffered the greatest bereavement of my life, it did n't enter her mind to even dream that I was not in the mood for visiting even Daniel Ricketson's children, or anybody else's for that!

Well, they sent me a copy of their book and I acknowledged the gift in a note; but I have n't heard a word from either of 'em,—and she was owing me the courtesy of a reply to a previous letter, too. Now, if F.B.S. has their ears, there is no telling what he has been pouring into them! And that's my only explanation for their peculiar conduct. I rather think they have been accustomed to being toadied to, and that is n't in my line. I am willing to be deservedly damned for all my deficiencies of character and derelictions of conduct, but I'll be doubly damned if I like to be *mis*-understood. However, I guess the grass will grow next summer all the same; and if F.B.S. is the malignant devil in the back-ground, I have no fear but that they will find *him* out in due time.

(I wish they could read what Mr. Salt wrote me about Sanborn's presentation of their father in their book!)

Mr. Salt's last letter is peculiarly gratifying to me, for he confesses that Mr. Ricketson's evasions of some of my questions have convinced him (Mr. Salt) that what *I* had *bluntly and plainly written about Sanborn's treatment of the older Thoreau folks* was strictly true. How true, you and I well know! . . .

1. Anna Ricketson had written that Dr. Jones did not appear so "dilapidated" in his photograph as he had represented himself in his letters to her; to which she added, "if anything you are too elegant to travel to No 10 Anthony St." Anna Ricketson to S. A. Jones, October 22, 1902 (Jones collection).

446. S. A. Jones to A. W. Hosmer, December 21, 1902.

At last I've found out what's the matter with you and you can hardly imagine with what painful reluctance I write it: It's just "original sin," and you're full of it! . . .

Meanwhile, you just make your arrangements to spend two weeks with us next summer or as soon as you like!!! I can be of service to you IF I CAN SEE YOU; and what in the world am I here for if not to help a friend. I will not take "No" for an answer. I can put you so solidly on your feet that the trip will more than "pay." MAKE A NOTE OF THE FACT THAT YOU ARE DUE HERE JUST SO SOON AS YOU CAN BEST GET AWAY FROM YOUR BUSINESS. Don't disappoint me!

I have just had a letter from Miss Ricketson; so my apprehensions were baseless; but how easy is it to suspect such a slimy creature as F.B.S. . . .

447. S. A. Jones to A. W. Hosmer, January 31, 1903.

I have just sent a letter to Mr. G. that will close the chapter between him and me.[1] I informed him that I had forwarded his letters to you, and that I had received one from him *to you* of December 29th., 1902. I have written to him that in the face of this letter and the fact that "No. 82" of the Channing-Thoreau volume has no "slip," it is perfectly plain that you were justified in returning the copy he sent to you.

I did not directly accuse him of double-dealing, but I did tell him that he *was,* perhaps unknowingly, *the victim of sinister influences.*

Your statement is so transparently true that no one can fail to discern Sanborn's malignant work in this dirty matter; and while I do not rejoice at a fellow-man's discomfiture, as a rule, I do rejoice to learn that Sanborn is to be excluded from the Emerson anniversary. I know from what Edward Emerson said to me in a quiet, gentlemanly way, that Sanborn is beneath the notice of any self-respecting man.

I also told Mr. G. that the pirated picture was procured only through your zeal *in* and knowledge *of* matters pertaining to Thoreau, and that it had also been a matter of much expense; and that he (Mr. G.) had no more moral right to use it than he would have legal right, had the picture been copyrighted. I did not tell him in so many words that he was a party to a disgraceful theft, *but I did not leave him any room for doubt about it!* . . .

1. The conflict with Goodspeed concerned Goodspeed's failure to give Alfred Hosmer credit for photographs of a drawing of Thoreau's birthplace and of the Rowse crayon portrait which were included in the limited edition (250 copies) of Channing's *Thoreau, the Poet-Naturalist* (1902). In a letter to Hosmer of December 29, 1902, Goodspeed explained: "It had quite slipped my mind that the original of the photograph which Mr. Sanborn brought me for this illustration was owned by you. In fact, I did not know this when Mr. Sanborn gave it to me. It would have been impossible to have referred to this or the portrait of Thoreau in the book without entirely resetting a considerable portion of it for the reason that these illustrations were only used in the limited edition." Goodspeed also indicated that he had instructed the publisher, Updike, to "prepare a slip which will give full

credit to you" to be sent to purchasers of the limited edition. Charles Goodspeed to
A. W. Hosmer, December 29, 1902 (Hosmer collection).

448. Henry Salt to A. W. Hosmer, February 1, 1903.

I have to thank you for quite a number of good things which you have
been so kind as to send me—the silhouette of Mrs. Thoreau, the copy of
the Concord Calendar, and (quite recently to hand) the "Thoreau, his
Home, Friends and Books".

With regard to the last-named, I have a letter from Mrs. Marble in
which she says that the book is sent with joint compliments from you and
herself; and as I understood from Dr. Jones that *he* too was concerned in
the gift, I conclude that there has been a triple alliance for my benefit.
Really I don't quite know how I can sufficiently thank you and Dr. Jones
for all your many kindnesses. And I have just been saying to Mrs. Marble,
in thanking her for the book, that I wish the public understood better how
much your labours, and Dr. Jones's, have done during the past ten years
for Thoreau's memory.

449. S. A. Jones to A. W. Hosmer, February 3, 1903.

* * *

Don't lose any sleep over Goodspeed. I have intimated plainly enough
that Sanborn's hand is plainly detectable.

Why in the name of common decency do not your respectable Concordians join hands and repudiate the skunk? The public health demands
that sanitary measures shall be strictly carried out.

Don't worry about the New Bedford people. Evidently they have lost
the sense of smell, or Sanborn had stank them out long ago.

450. S. A. Jones to A. W. Hosmer, February 19, 1903.

* * *

When you write to Mr. Salt be sure and let him know that Sanborn is not
"in it" for the Emersonian picnic of 1903.

How have you come out with the Ricketsons? And how is the American
hysterical female coming on with her "second edition"?[1] I wish you could
read what Mr. Salt has written to me about her "cribbings." Surely, Fred,
she is as fond as a tailor of cabbage. Were any of her ancestors of that trade?

1. Mrs. Marble.

451. S. A. Jones to A. W. Hosmer, March 20, 1903.

I do not know if I ever told you that I got a game leg in the army; but whether I did or not, I know it, and as I get older it gives me more fun than I care for. I am nursing it now and have been since you last heard from me.

To-day I got out of bed and limped to this typewriter, and nothing in the world but that photo of yourself could have moved me.

So soon as I can get out to "sit" for a camera I shall send you one of my old self so that you can see what Time has done to me since we ate "ros-bif-fried-fish-bakon" in the long-ago.

The photo has made me hungry to see you, and if you were within fifty miles I'll be darned if I would n't "hoof it" to shake hands with you. Is it among the possibilities for you to get a rest this summer and let an old fellow see you once before he goes into the darkness?

I recently received an announcement of "The Personality of Emerson"[1] from Goodspeed; by F.B.S., of course. I dictated a letter to Goodspeed letting him know that I had had enough of Sanborn's "personalities" and wished to be excused.

I see that F.B.S. has wormed himself into a sort of Emerson celebration, after all.[2] He is a daisy, is F.B.S., and his shadow will never be less. He certainly has as much "gall" as any critter I ever met. . . .

1. F. B. Sanborn, *The Personality of Emerson* (Boston: Goodspeed, 1903).
2. Franklin B. Sanborn did participate in the Emerson centennial as a member of the special committee of the Free Religious Association that planned the Memorial School, which held a series of lectures in Boston and in Concord during July 1903. Sanborn also delivered one of the lectures, "Emerson and the Concord School of Philosophy." See George Willis Cooke, "The Emerson Centennial," *New England Magazine* 28, no. 3 (May 1903):255–64.

452. S. A. Jones to A. W. Hosmer, April 6, 1903.

It is with something akin to a shock that I learn from your letter of Mr. Lane's sending a letter to me, which I assure you I never received. Why, Fred, I could no more have refused to write an introduction to anything of Thoreau's writing[1] than I could fly without wings "especially adapted for the occasion." Had I received Mr. Lane's letter I should have written an introduction the like of which I have never read, for I should have gone back to that visit to Concord in 1890 and what has come from it bearing upon the genius and character of Thoreau. In the course of the introduction I should also have put *somebody* in the pillory in a delicate but I hope indelible manner. I should tell him some things about "The Personality of *Sham*born" that would interest *him,* to say the least. . . .

1. Albert Lane had seemingly asked Dr. Jones to write an introduction to a reprint of Thoreau's essay "Friendship." The volume was apparently not published.

453. S. A. Jones to A. W. Hosmer, April 16, 1903.

* * *

To tell you the truth, Mr. Merwin's "Books about Nature"[1] did n't do me any particular good. Nature study is a cheap fad of the latter-days and from John Burroughs up and down the line I do find some very "fine writing", but I can live without it.

I can enjoy only so much of "Nature" as comes to me through my own old eyes. I can't see through the other fellows, and when people declare *they* can, I am inclined to think they can beat the immortal George at some things.

Thoreau did n't *pose* and tell us how like the devil he enjoyed Nature; as if *his* enjoyment meant anything to *us,* unless we were "built" precisely as he was—which we are *not* by a d . . . . d sight!

The fact is, there is too much tweedledum and tweedledee about all this Nature and "Art" business! Who would give a tinker's dam for a description of a sunset that *he* had n't seen? Damn it, it's like kissing a pretty girl by proxy; it's all very well for the proxy, but WE are "not in it!"

I sent Mr. Lane a brief introduction for Thoreau's "Friendship" the other day. I am better pleased with it than with anything I ever wrote about Thoreau.

If I can only stir up F.B.S. to make any sort of reply to it, I shall try and show him up for the benefit of all true lovers of Thoreau—who, unhappily don't *know* "Benjamin Franklin" as well as we do. . . .

1. Henry Childs Merwin, "Books about Nature," *Scribner's Magazine* 33 (April 1903):430–37.

454. S. A. Jones to A. W. Hosmer, April 19, 1903.

* * *

It struck me as curious, to say the least, that just as I am contemplating a new "and revised" edition of the "Glimpse" that curious account of the origin of Thoreau's cairn should drop into my hand.[1]

For the benefit of F.B.S. I am going to put an appendix to the new edition of the "Glimpse" and I grant you I shall try to do him to a turn. . . .[2]

If you have seen the proposed introductory note to Mr. Lane's edition of "Friendship" let me ask what you think of it? I could n't for the life write any other and I am rather pleased with it. What say you? You did not answer my enquiry about illustrations for the "Glimpse." Was I asking too much? Speak out, we are surely acquainted long enough to be able to "talk with naked hearts together". . . .

1. Alfred Hosmer had received from Edward Bigelow an account by Annabel Adams Goan of the beginning of the cairn at Walden:

"This is as I remember it, as Mr. Alcott told me about it afterwards when he took me to Walden to add my stone, and as I recall it from one of mother's lively letters.

"She was visiting the Emersons. Both Mr. Emerson and Mr. Alcott had spent many a winter's evening at our fireside in our far away Western home discussing philosophy and poetry with my father and mother for they were kindred spirits.

"On this day Mr. Alcott called at the Emerson's for mother to take a walk in Walden Woods. She was almost as devoted a lover of Nature as you Dr. Bigelow and you know that is saying a great deal. She was of course delighted to go and when they reached the spot where Thoreau's little house used to stand, mother said it was a pity there was nothing to mark the place so strangers might know it. 'Well,' said Mr. Alcott, 'a cut stone would hardly be appropriate would it for Thoreau?' She suggested building a cairn and then let every one who loved Thoreau add a stone and said she was going to start it right then. She got a stone and with a little improvised ceremony laid it down in her own name. Then Mr. Alcott got one for himself and one for Mrs. Alcott. Then mother laid a stone for my father. She was a poetical, original sort of a person, with a musical expressive voice and a radiant face. Mr. Alcott stood by half amused at the blessings his young friend was invoking, half in fun—but also half in earnest upon the future memorial to his friend.

"Suddenly they noticed down through the bushes some eyes looking at them. There was a Unitarian picnic somewhere in the grounds and a party of gentlemen had strolled over to the spot. Noticing something unusual going on and recognizing Mr. Alcott, they had slipped behind the bushes to see what it all meant. They now came forward introduced themselves and asked what they were doing. When it was explained they wished to add their stone and brought some friends.

"The next morning Mr. Emerson went up and added his stone.

"That was in June 1872. I remember there was a pressed wild rose in the letter, that told of this, which mother said grew close to the hole where the little foundations had been.

"Mother's name was Mrs. Mary Newbury Adams, and my father was Austin Adams, Chief-justice of Iowa. We lived on one of the high bluffs over looking the Mississippi at Dubuque." Annabel Adams Goan to Edward F. Bigelow, March 21, 1903, sent to Alfred W. Hosmer by Bigelow with letter of April 16, 1903 (Hosmer collection).

2. Dr. Jones appended his paper "Thoreau's Inheritance" to *Thoreau: A Glimpse* (Concord: Albert Lane, 1903).

455. S. A. Jones to A. W. Hosmer, April 25, 1903.

I was with your folks on the 19th in spirit and I celebrated all alone, for I had the whole house to myself that day. Indeed, you have sent me so many mementoes of Concord that I am almost ready to claim citizenship. If you

Concordians will let in such a *stinker* as F.B.S., you certainly could tolerate ME, for I don't stink quite as "loud."

Yes, Fred, I need a cane, and the one you see in the picture was given me by Walton Ricketson. He cut it at "Walden" (meaning THE Pond) on Oct. 28, 1868. Channing had piloted Walton and his sister to visit the site of the shanty. On it is cut "Walden" and the monogram "WAR." He sent it to me so that it arrived on my birthday, June 11th., and I shall carry it so long as I "poke around" this side the grave. (The fact is, Fred, after my boy's departure, I grew suddenly old. He was my staff, and I have a *silent* substitute).

I am under obligations to you for the information about the cost of photogravures; but they are wholly beyond my means. I do not care a copper about reprinting the "Glimpse" on my own account. I do not pose as an "author" and I long since happily recovered from what Tom Hood calls the "type us fever." I am responsible for some dozen books and ten children, and I must rest from me labors in both the book and baby line. . . .

456. S. A. Jones to A. W. Hosmer, April 30, 1903.

I have your letters of the 27th and 28th,—the latter enclosing the sample pages of the Roycroft "Friendship."[1] I am so taken with the solid appearance of the work that if the book comes anywhere within my means I must have one. I feel that Thoreau himself could but be pleased to see the honor paid to his genius by this beautiful reprinting from his rejected book.

Please let me know whatever you can about the cost and the manner of getting a copy.

I have lost all track of Hubbard,[2] for when I learned his real character, I dropped him. If the projected book were about any other man than Thoreau, I could not be hired to touch anything that is of "Roycroft" origin.

In regard to republishing the "Glimpse." So many have sought for copies that a desire to make Thoreau accessible—to some extent, as far as the "Glimpse" could—aroused a desire to republish. But, Fred, since my boy's departure, I am no longer the man you knew ten years ago. My spirit is broken; my strength is gone and I am little short of an imbecile.

My circumstances will not enable me to do what my heart would delight to do; so the reprinting must remain a vain desire.

I could not possibly sink anything for the sake of reprinting the "Glimpse," for it would be a straight "sink", as I know no more how to dispose of a book, commercially, than a sucking child. This is why I dropped the "notion" of reprinting.

Has it ever occurred to you that the "Glimpse" is really the beginning of the Thoreau revival? It was the "Glimpse" that got me the acquaintance with Miss Eliza Hosmer; through her I got to know of you; a desire to see Concord took me there; and from that day you and I have done our duty to Thoreau's memory—far the smaller part being mine. Then came the Rowfant Club's "Bibliography", which, by the way, fetches $25,oo readily now. The Rowfanters got Horace E. Scudder to read a paper before the Club—paying him handsomely therefor. When he saw what the Rowfant Club is, he suddenly woke up to the fact that Thoreau might be a far bigger pumpkin than any in the pile,—and, lo! "The Riverside Edition of Thoreau's COLLECTED WORKS" appeared! This is history, and my dear Fred, we had a hand in it.

What kind of a hairpin is your Mr. Lane, anyhow? I have had no reply to my letter asking to let me read my own proof, and I do not know what to make of it.

Friendly letters can be kept waiting without offending or violating the proprieties; but letters pertaining to what may be called "business" matters are entitled to speedy attention.

Moreover, as I so readily prepared and GAVE Mr. Lane the desired introductory paper, one would have imagined that I should have had the courtesy of prompt attention.

I can tell YOU why I am the more desirous of reading my own proof: because I shall then know if I have been printed as I WROTE. As my initials are to be appended to the paper, I naturally do not want anything that I did NOT write put in nor do I want anything that I did write left out—*without my consent.*

If Mr. Lane has any sort of valid reason, his discourtesy can be overlooked, if not, then the less I have to do with such a man the better.

I believe in the straight up-and-downness that characterized Thoreau; and if Mr. Lane is n't "built that way," he may rest assured that I shall prefer his room to his company.

The one thing about your Mr. L. that has made me slightly suspicious of his "true inwardness" is that he is so "stuck" on that creature Hubbard. Birds of a feather, you know, go in flocks. Now I am a poor enough specimen, I know, but by Jupiter, there is a broad line between me and the Hubbard fellows.

I shall be glad to learn that Mr. Lane's apparent rudeness is owing to a constitutional neglectfulness; but he should mend his ways nevertheless.

I note that you dodge my repeated enquiries about YOUR condition. Well, you are not obliged to testify and doubtless have good reasons for declining; but if you were a physician you would understand my pertinacity.

We had the first real breath of Spring yesterday; and I kept thinking how I would like to have taken a stroll with you—not in Michigan, however![3]

1. The Roycroft Press of East Aurora, New York, published Thoreau's essay "Friendship" from *A Week* as *The Essay on Friendship* in 1903.
2. Elbert Hubbard (1856–1915) was proprietor of the Roycroft Press and editor of the inspirational magazine *Philistine* (1895–1915).
3. This was apparently Dr. Jones's last letter to Alfred Hosmer. Hosmer died May 7, 1903.

457. S. A. Jones to Henry Salt, [May 1903].[1]

Fred Hosmer died suddenly on the afternoon of May 7th of angina pectoris. The world has grown very lonely. I cannot write. I can only sit and think of the great mystery of death.

1. Quoted in Raymond Adams, "Fred Hosmer, the 'Lerned Clerk,'" *Thoreau Society Bulletin* 36 (July 1951):2. Mr. Adams says of this letter: "Great-hearted Doctor Jones, whose feelings usually gushed out in a flood of words, wrote but a four-sentence note to Henry Salt." Adams does not date the letter.

458. Henry Salt to S. A. Jones, May 26, 1903.

I am indeed grieved to hear of the death of our friend Hosmer. Not many weeks ago he sent me his portrait, and I greatly wish *now* that I had written at once to thank him and tell him how much I value it. I waited,—for the same reason as that which caused me to postpone writing to you,—because I have been hoping to know positively whether our proposed visit to America is to be realised or not. I have received so many kindnesses from Mr. Hosmer, that I hardly feel Concord would now have the attraction for me that I anticipated. To yourself, who have been in such close sympathy and touch with Mr. Hosmer, the loss must be an acute one.

Our friends the Curtises have been in London (in March), and are now on the Continent. They are still, I believe, anxious to take us back with them; but their own affairs are in somewhat of a tangle, owing to illness of friends and other troubles, and the date of their return is very uncertain. This reacts, of course, on *our* plans; and I think it is very doubtful if we shall come after all. But if we *do* come, I will write to you the very day it is settled, so that I may lose no chance of seeing you.

It was curious that in your last letter (dated, I see to my shame, as long ago as February 17) you referred to the possible inconveniences of being entertained at Concord by F.B.S. The subject has been in my mind often, as I should unspeakably dread being hedged round, as a guest, by any tiresome formalities, "living in style", &c. I can only breathe freely among simple people who *don't* live in style; and I should not like, for other reasons, to be "pocketed" by F.B.S. At the same time I should not like to appear ungrateful for his hospitable offers; and in fact I don't know what I *should* have done in the event of a visit!

However, it is useless at present to speculate on that, as I do not know that I am coming, and Concord without Hosmer would be a sad place for me, and still more for yourself. . . .

[P.S.] I lately posted to you (and to A.W.H.) a small, abbreviated, reprint of "Civil Disobedience". In some talk I had with Prince Kropotkin, the Russian exile, at Easter, I found that he did not know Thoreau's works. I lent him some of them & he is much taken by them, especially those bearing on anarchism.

459. Henry Salt to S. A. Jones, May 28, 1903.

Since I wrote to you, only two days ago, we have heard from our friends Mr. & Mrs. Curtis, and our visit to America is now definitely abandoned. The Cs. are in great distress and perplexity about certain troubles which have arisen at their home in N.Y. since they came on visit to Europe; and though they still hospitably press us to return with them, the circumstances are such as to make a contrary decision almost inevitable—even if *we* were certain of our ability to go, which is far from being the case.

It is a great disappointment nevertheless, in so far as it further lessens the chance of my ever meeting *you* personally; but if not *here*—well, we must hope to meet somehow or somewhere, or that we *have* met already in the best & truest sense!

I had always associated my hope of seeing you with the hope of seeing Concord & Fred Hosmer at the same time; and now where is all *that* plan gone!

This reminds me to ask you a question which I had meant to ask in my last letter, but in the hurry forgot—whether there are any relatives of Mr. Hosmer (I do not even know whether he was married) to whom it would be a satisfaction to hear from me how much I valued his friendship, in spite of the many miles that divided us personally. Perhaps if there are such relatives, and if you are in communication with them, you could kindly convey a message of sympathy; or I would write myself, if you advise it. Mr. Hosmer was so modest, and so silent about himself in his letters, that I seemed just to take him for granted as a kind friend, without knowledge of his surroundings. . . .

460. S. A. Jones to Henry Salt, [undated].

Professor Adams quotes in "Fred Hosmer, the 'Lerned Clerk' " this letter, with his own appropriate comments: "Mr. Salt gave up his plan to come to Concord, and Doctor Jones gave up his idea to meet with them [Mr. and Mrs. Salt] there, writing, 'In the desolation that death makes it was not hard for me to give up the thought of meeting even you. . . . Thoreau has written, "The universal content of the animal comes of resting quietly in God's palm." There we are, and it cannot but be well, come what may. Entsagen, entsagen, entsagen: that is the only "balm in Gilead".' What resignations must be made in the name of friendship and of love such as drew these three Thoreau pioneers together in the 1890's."

Adams does not date the letter.

461. Henry Salt to S. A. Jones, September 6, 1903.

I shall shortly be sending you a copy of the *Humane Review* (for October), containing a short article of mine on "Thoreau and the Humane Study of Natural History". It is not much more than a few quotations strung together, but I think it will help to show how much the humane naturalist school of the present day owes to Thoreau, a fact which some admirers of that school are, to my knowledge, very unwilling to recognize.

I now enclose two small cuttings from the correspondence columns of the *Daily News,* the chief Liberal paper in London. Dr. Clifford, who figures in the letters, is, as I daresay you know, the most distinguished of English nonconformists now living, and he has made a great fight lately against the Government's Education Bill. I don't know who Mr. Morris Hudson is, but he certainly has the reverend gentleman "on toast" as regards his allusions to Thoreau. It is encouraging, though, to find a leading Dissenter avowing such admiration for "the skulker".

I was grateful to you for giving me the address of "Fred" Hosmer's brother, and I wrote to tell him how I felt about his loss. I am mentioning A.W.H. in this article in the *Humane Review*. . . .

462. Henry Salt to S. A. Jones, July 13, 1904.

* * *

[P.S.] I think *you* once had a "brush" with that good-natured old fire-brand Dr. A. H. Japp, did you not? You may be amused to hear that *I* am now in his black books, I believe because I refuse to damn *Darwin* as he does! . . .

463. Henry Salt to S. A. Jones, November 10, 1904.

I am much concerned at your long & unaccountable silence. I sincerely hope you are not ill. Please let me have some news of yourself; for, now our friend Hosmer is gone, I know of no one from whom I can get tidings of you.

You will have received letters, &c, from me at intervals during the past year—the last, I think, was an extract from the *Times* newspaper, in which some foolish scribe wrote nonsense about Thoreau. My reply to him, which to my great surprise was inserted, would have been much severer, but for the fact that it was necessary, in order to obtain insertion at all, to avoid ruffling the feelings of the reviewer too violently. So, as it seemed essential that *some* answer should be attempted, I had to moderate my contempt for the fellow—at least in that letter. . . .

I have often wondered how the collection of extracts from press-criticisms of Thoreau is getting on. You have not abandoned the scheme, I hope?

464. Henry Salt to Mrs. S. A. Jones, November 12, 1905.

It has been a great grief to me that my dear old friend Dr. Jones is unable to write; for his letters used to be one of the greatest pleasures of the post. Would it be troubling you too much, if I ask for a few lines to tell me how he is? I owe so many kindnesses to him in the past that I wish I could do something to cheer him now.

We had a visit in the summer from Mr. Walton Ricketson, and were very pleased to make his acquaintance.

Dr. Jones may be interested to hear that we have lost the first of our English students of Thoreau, Dr. A. H. Japp, who died very suddenly a few weeks ago. He came to see me in May last together with Mr. Ricketson, who was then his guest, and we three had much talk about Thoreau and other literary matters. . . .

Dr. Jones will perhaps remember that I sent him some press-cuttings of a number of reviews concerning my book on Thoreau. If he has quite done with these, I would be glad to have them again, but there is no hurry. I would rather have some news of *him*.

465. Henry Salt to Mrs. S. A. Jones, March 15, 1907.

So long a time has passed since I received your kind letter, in answer to my inquiries about Dr. Jones, that I feel I ought to have written again; yet I can truly say that I have *thought* very often indeed about you both, and have wondered how my dear old friend, Dr. Jones, is getting on. I have sent him papers occasionally, as you said that he reads a good deal; but I have not liked to trouble him further with letters.

If he cares to receive messages, I daresay you will tell him that he is often in my thoughts, and that in regard to my Thoreau studies I feel more and more how much I owe to him. Just now I am busy with Thoreau again, because I am to write an article for the "Fortnightly Review" (of London) with reference to the new edition of Thoreau's Works brought out by Messrs. Houghton, who have been so kind as to offer to *present* me with a set—a handsome present which took me quite by surprise.

The doctor may be interested to hear that cheap "Waldens" continue to be published by various firms in this country, but we get nothing like a collected edition of Thoreau—so low are our tastes and intelligence! One of these "Waldens", issued by the Oxford University Press, has a most insufferably bumptious preface by Mr. Theodore Watts-Dunton, a critic who evidently thinks Thoreau a very minor personage as compared with himself; but *per contra* there is another "Walden" published by Blackie & Son of London, to which Mr. Richard Whiteing has contributed a really sympathetic introduction. If you think the Doctor would like me to send him any or all of these books dealing with Thoreau (and there are others), I need not say how glad I shall be to do so.

As to those press clippings from English papers (mentioned in your letter), I am in no hurry for them, as I know they are safe with you; so anytime when Dr. Jones has done with them will do for their return.

I have had some correspondence lately with Mr. Vickers,[1] of Ellsworth Station, Ohio, who seems a very sincere admirer of Thoreau. . . .

1. The University of Illinois Library has recently acquired the Thoreauvian correspondence of Ernest Vickers. For a description of the Vickers collection, see Fritz Oehlschlaeger, "The Thoreau Collection of Ernest W. Vickers," *Thoreau Society Bulletin* 140 (summer 1977):7–8.

❧ Appendix

Thoreau and His Biographers*

SAMUEL ARTHUR JONES

Lippincott's Monthly Magazine 48 (August 1891):224–28.

WHAT MORE DELIGHTFUL ANTICIPATION is there than when we cut the leaves of a new life of an author whom we have long loved? And if the reading prove only a "bootless bene," how absurdly inefficacious do we find dear Mary Lamb's "shoeless pea"! Beyond question there is a special limbo for the inept biographer.

It is Thoreau's good fortune to have biographers who improve upon each other. The initiatory endeavor, by Channing, though published eleven years after Thoreau's death, was still too near that event to allow his chosen companion to write anything other than a rhapsody. For a more satisfactory glimpse of Thoreau the student was obliged to have recourse to Emerson's calmer obituary sketch. From it and the subsequent volume of "Letters," edited by Emerson, has been derived that conception of Thoreau which is at once the most general and the most unjust. It was Emerson's desire to display Thoreau as "a most perfect piece of stoicism." He elided from the letters the evidences of Thoreau's human tenderness so unsparingly that Sophia Thoreau remonstrated: "it did not seem quite honest to Henry." Mr. James T. Fields seconded her protest, and a few passages which evinced "some tokens of natural affection" were retained.

---

* Thoreau, the Poet Naturalist. By Wm. Ellery Channing. Boston, 1873.
  Thoreau: his Life and Aims. By H. A. Page. Boston, 1877.
  Henry D. Thoreau. By F. B. Sanborn. Boston, 1883.
  The Life of Henry David Thoreau. By H. S. Salt. London, 1890.

Emerson, we are told, "fancied" that this pious interference of a bereaved sister "had marred his classic statue."

Channing's book is valuable as containing much of Thoreau's "Journal" that has not been published elsewhere; and many of his selections are of singular beauty. For instance, Thoreau is at Clematis Brook watching the dispersion of milk-weed seeds as the summer breeze catches their silken wings, and he derives this corollary from so commonplace an incident: "Who could believe in the prophecies of a Daniel or of Miller, that the world would end this summer, while one milk-weed with faith matured its seed?"

The succeeding Life by H. A. Page, now known as Dr. A. H. Japp, was written at too great a distance from its subject and too near Thoreau's books to be of any other use than to whet the reader's curiosity and make him eager for a more extended knowledge of its hero. Dr. Japp is the introducer and chief disseminator of the figment that the shanty at Walden was a station of the underground railroad. He infers this from a cursory statement of Channing's: "Not one slave alone was expedited to Canada by Thoreau's personal assistance." R. L. Stevenson accepts this myth as the *raison d'être* for Thoreau's abode in Walden woods, and even Mr. Salt repeats the story in his excellent Life. The writer has made this a matter of special investigation, and the truth is that there were specially-prepared houses in "Old Concord" which afforded infinitely more secure resting- and hiding-places for the fugitive slave. Moreover, the survivors who managed Concord "station" declare that Thoreau's hut was not used for such a purpose.

With Mr. Sanborn's Life began the era of personal misrepresentation; and soon after its publication a highly-incensed lady called its unfortunate author to account in the Boston *Daily Advertiser.* We have not been able to learn the whereabouts of Mr. Sanborn's reply. Living in Concord, and having known Thoreau personally, Mr. Sanborn had at hand the materials for an interesting book; but it appears that he felt called upon to write at once Thoreau's biography, and a history of Concord, and at the same time to make "honorable mention" of all its worthies, living or dead, past, present, and to come. It is, however, an entertaining volume if you possess the patience to unravel it and the skill to follow an often-hidden trail. Lacking these qualities yourself, the book is still deserving of the encomium that Dr. John Brown says a Scotch shepherd awarded to a boiled sheep's-head: "There's a deal o' confused eatin' aboot it." But this Life has left a smart in the hearts of those who knew and loved the Thoreaus that needs only to be known to nullify the false witness.

Mr. Salt's Life is purely a labor of love. To him Thoreau's "gospel of simplicity" is both chart and compass: he is not so much an "admirer" as an earnest follower of the sincere man whose life he both writes and lives.

When precept and practice go hand in hand and love walks with them, the printed page becomes refulgent. Mr. Salt has done more than any other writer, living or dead, to correct the errors that are current concerning Thoreau and to enable a just conception of his character to be made. Preceding this Life is an essay on Thoreau, *Temple Bar,* No. 78, p. 369, so felicitous that all students of Thoreau should read it; and since the appearance of the more formal Life Mr. Salt has published an "Introductory Note"° and a paper on "Thoreau's Gospel of Simplicity"† which form an all-sufficient reply to certain objections by Professor Nichol and James Russell Lowell. Writing in a foreign country, with only a scholar's access to his materials, and, of all who had known Thoreau personally, having met only Mr. Sanborn, Mr. Salt's Life is singularly correct. A few trivial misstatements are found: its one great blemish is owing solely to his having accepted Mr. Sanborn's estimate of Thoreau's parents and their relatives as trustworthy. It is to be feared that Mr. Sanborn has judged Thoreau's father from the exterior alone,—a shallow judgment! John Thoreau had in his veins the blood of Huguenot, Covenanter, and Quaker,—an ancestral blending to be coveted; Mr. Sanborn could discern only a "little," "deaf," "plainly-clad," "unobtrusive," "unambitious," "plodding" man whose shrug and snuff-box were the only reminiscences of his French extraction. They who knew him believe that John Thoreau is to Mr. Sanborn like the cathedral window described by Hawthorne: "Standing without, you see no glory, nor can possibly imagine any; standing within, every ray of light reveals a harmony of unspeakable splendors." But it isn't the window's fault!

That Mrs. Thoreau, her sister, and her sisters-in-law were vilified, after every one of the name Thoreau was dead, the best blood in and of Concord will this day testify. *De mortuis nil nisi bonum* should also be read *nil nisi verum.* Alas that the printed page should still be able to reiterate the lie that has been branded in the market-place!

There is another feature of Mr. Sanborn's Life that perplexes the thoughtful reader,—namely, the exalted character which he ascribes to the Thoreau children. Not that their moral status is to be questioned: the puzzle is to explain the phenomenon. The fountain, according to Mr. Sanborn, rises *so* much higher than its source. A "plodding, unambitious" father, but children living up to the highest ideals. A mother given to "flashes of gossip and malice," yet growing up around her hearth-stone sons and daughters whom such an atmosphere would have stifled! The problem darkens when Mr. Sanborn says, "Perpetuity, indeed, and hereditary transmission of everything that by nature and good sense can be inherited, are among the characteristics of Concord." (Life, p. 38.)

° *Anti-Slavery and Reform Papers* (London: Swan, Sonnenschein & Co., 1890).
† *Paternoster Review,* March 1891.

The whole household—father, mother, Helen, John, Henry, Sophia: the last of their name in America—are gathered together on that little hill-top in Sleepy Hollow which the morning sun is the first to visit and the last to leave; and if the reader shall ever stand a pious pilgrim there in the solemn silence of a summer's night, shadows below and starlight above, he will be devoutly thankful that nothing of earth can break their peace.

No man's life can be fully written by a contemporary. *Pace tua,* James Boswell. If thine angry shade shall threaten vengeance, then shalt thou be referred to Dr. Birkbeck Hill, whose editorship has made old Ursus Major better known to us than ever he was to those who supped with him at the Mitre or helped him to beguile the nights he so dreaded. Death and time break the seals of reticences that are sacred to coevals, and posterity is permitted to make the most searching post-mortem examinations. Meanwhile, the falsities that for a time batten on a dead man's memory one by one drop into oblivion, shrivelled by the light of Truth. Time is doing its kindliest offices for Thoreau. One after the other misrepresentations are being brought to judgment, and there is "reversal with costs." Lowell, the chief offender, is already condemned by all but the vulgar. Thoreau is no longer considered a "misanthrope," nor is he deemed a "hermit" who masqueraded at Walden Pond. The seriousness of his life is being recognized, his earnestness is seldom questioned, and the wisdom of his philosophy is more than suspected. Before the end of Plato's year he may find disciples in very deed.

That he was sincerity incarnate is the first necessary lesson to be learned concerning him. That he studied the problem of life as profoundly and as continually as did Marcus Aurelius, and that he lived it as regally, will soon be seen. Then it will be time to consider what was to him the outcome of his philosophy. It will be found that his religion grew out of his philosophy; not the philosophy from the religion. This reversal of the sacerdotal order produced precious fruit. He learned that life is not from the Divine *design* a soul-wearying struggle, but, truly lived, a pastime worthy of the soul. His spiritual ear discovered the source of the discords that mar the harmony of the psalm of life: "When we are weary with travel, we lay down our load and rest by the wayside. So, when we are weary with the burden of life, why do we not lay down this load of falsehoods which we have volunteered to sustain, and be refreshed as never mortal was? Let the beautiful laws prevail. Let us not weary ourselves by resisting them."

Volunteered to sustain. There is the hammer-stroke that buries the nail. The Eternal Unspeakable One is *not* the bungler: it is WE who will not "let the beautiful laws prevail." Thus devoutly doth he justify the ways of God to man.

He inculcated the supremest care of the body: "A man is never inspired unless his body is also." He insisted that man should accept his "genius"—

the voice within—as the unerring guide: not Socrates was more obedient to his daemon. He declares "that if one advances confidently in the direction of his dreams, and endeavors to live the life which he has imagined, he will meet with a success unexpected in common hours." Ay, more, "in proportion as he simplifies his life, the laws of the universe will appear less complex, and solitude will not be solitude, nor poverty poverty, nor weakness weakness. If you have built castles in the air, your work need not be lost; that is where they should be. Now put the foundations under them."

When our latter-day mad race for wealth, only wealth, shall have brought to us the inevitable result and a chastened people shall seek "the better way," it will be the "hermit" of Walden, not the Sage of Concord, that will lead them.

Though called away when his capabilities were at their highest and his cherished work undone, it is difficult to think of Thoreau's life as incomplete; still harder to believe with his distinguished friend that it was only "pounding beans." His end was presaged by that sublime outburst of supreme manhood, his defence of Captain John Brown "sick and in prison." When all other lips were sealed, Thoreau's flamed with living fire, for even God had touched them.

After that came the slow decay, and the sleep for one whom the grandest occasion in his life had found sufficient. But every vouchsafed moment was piously husbanded: manuscripts were arranged and essays revised before the hand had forever lost its cunning. One of these may be seen in Concord Library, and three handwritings are found in it,—his own with pen and ink, and, when he wearied, with the more convenient pencil, and, when too weak for even that, his sister Sophia wrote at his dictation.

He went forth at his prime, having "much to report on natural history," but obliged to take it all into the inexorable grave. Yet no repining; instead, the declaration from lips that were never sullied by a lie, "I am enjoying existence as much as ever, and regret nothing."

"A man's religion is the chief fact with regard to him." What was Thoreau's? He "rested quietly in God's palm." He was so filled with confidence in the Unspeakable One that he asked no curious questions; and, in our ignorance, perhaps that is the wisest attitude for any soul. Better than all, the moral grandeur of his exit shows that he had not only the courage but also the comfort of his convictions.

※ Index

Emerson, Edith, 9

Emerson, Dr. Edward, 1, 19, 25, 32, 43, 45,
51, 89, 90n, 94, 96, 99, 102, 103–4,
105–6, 108–9, 110, 111, 112, 113, 114,
115, 125, 136–37, 138, 140–41, 143,
144–45, 165, 166n, 169, 209, 210, 212,
213, 229, 230n, 235, 236, 237, 242, 246,
247, 248, 249, 261, 270, 272, 278, 292n,
300, 301n, 305, 321, 322, 334, 351, 384;
*Henry Thoreau as Remembered by a Young
Friend,* 51, 90n, 104n

Emerson, Ellen, 43, 82, 167, 170, 171, 305,
307–8

Emerson, Lidian, 156n, 167

Emerson, Mary Moody, 377

Emerson, Ralph Waldo, 9, 12, 13, 14, 15,
16, 17, 18, 19, 20, 21, 22–23, 24, 25, 26,
28, 29, 33, 34, 35, 39, 46, 48, 49, 51, 54,
55, 62n, 65, 66, 70, 71, 72n, 80, 81, 88,
90n, 95n, 97n, 102, 105–6, 108, 109,
110, 111, 115, 125, 126, 127, 128, 129,
131, 132, 133, 134, 136–37, 139–40,
142n, 146, 147, 148, 150, 151, 153, 155,
156, 157, 158, 159, 169, 173, 174, 175,
176, 178, 180, 181, 183, 185, 187, 194–
95, 197–98, 199, 200, 201, 204, 205, 206,
209, 210, 211, 213n, 214, 215, 217, 218,
219, 221, 222, 224, 225, 227, 229–30,
233, 237, 238, 240, 248, 250, 255, 258,
259, 260n, 261, 268, 270, 271, 274, 275,
276, 280, 283, 284, 286, 288, 292, 304,
305, 308n, 309, 311n, 312, 317, 339,
341, 342, 351, 352, 353, 363, 364n, 369,
371, 372n, 376, 382, 384, 385, 386,
397–98

Emerson, William, 316n

Emmons portrait, 44n, 170

Epictetus, 80

Everett, E., 157

F., E. M. *See* LeBrun, Jean Munroe

Faraday, Michael, 287

Fields, James T., 14, 263, 397

Flagg, Edward W., 198

Fletcher, Grace, 260n

Foley, Patrick Kevin, 344

Folsom, Miss. *See* LeBrun, Jean Munroe

Fox, George, 224

Francis, of Assisi, Saint, 24

French, Daniel Chester, 142n, 243n, 375n

Froude, James Anthony, 21, 45n, 46, 48,
49, 279n, 282, 283, 285–86, 292–93, 295,
297, 303, 304, 305, 306, 307, 308, 309,
322, 323n, 335, 336n

Gage, Mrs. Leander, 377n

Gandhi, M. K., 6, 53

Garrison, Francis J., 214, 218, 269, 314

Garrison, William Lloyd, 214n, 314n

Gilpin, William, 224

Gleason, Mr. (illustrator), 366n

Glick, Wendell, 13n, 48

Goan, Annabel Adams, 388n

Goodspeed, Charles (publisher), 358, 359,
360, 366, 368, 369, 371n, 375, 384, 385,
386

Goodspeed, George, 9

Gosnold, Bartholemew, 124

Gower, John, 309n

Graham, P. Anderson, 146

Gray, Henry, 339, 341

Greeley, Horace, 12, 13, 19, 48, 222n,
301n, 338n, 369n

Greene, Calvin H., 44, 45, 46, 47, 49,
102n, 278, 279, 282, 285, 286n, 289n,
290, 297n, 299, 300, 303, 304, 305n,
307, 310, 311, 313, 314n, 317, 322–23,
324, 325, 326, 332, 335, 336, 341, 354n,
357

Greene, Mr. (Calvin Greene's brother),
45n, 302, 311n

de Guerin, Maurice, 203

Hahnemann, Samuel, 5, 363

Haig, Dr., 280

Harding, Walter, 6, 8, 10, 13, 14n, 17, 18,
21, 31, 37n, 38, 43n, 46, 48, 50, 51, 53,
62n, 63n, 88n, 95n, 97n, 120n, 144n,
148n, 155n, 227n, 245n, 260n, 278n,
296n, 301n, 309n, 352n, 357n, 360n

Harper & Brothers (publisher), 100, 115,
116, 117, 118, 119, 161

Harris, Amanda, 140

Harris, William T., 176, 177n, 308

Harte, Bret, 139

Hawthorne, Julian, 130, 288, 359, 360,
362n

Hawthorne, Nathaniel, 15, 49, 156, 158n,
164n, 174, 183, 195n, 211, 275, 283,
288, 318, 360, 364n, 399

Hurd, Dr., 371n
Hurd, Joseph, 371n

Ibsen, Henrik, 158
Inlander, 35, 40, 47n, 111, 120, 121, 130,
135, 151, 165n, 167n, 169, 170, 171,
172, 173, 186, 187, 188, 314, 316, 319,
321, 332, 364, 379

J., Asa, 106, 107n, 114, 175, 176, 189, 276,
301
Jackson, Rev. Abraham, 366n
Japp, Dr. Alexander H., 3, 23, 24, 25, 29,
30, 31, 32, 49, 50, 61, 62, 63, 66, 68, 77,
87, 92, 97n, 99, 116, 127, 136, 137, 138,
146, 153, 229n, 257–58, 267, 348, 382,
393; *Thoreau: His Life and Aims,* 23, 24,
29, 77, 268n, 397–401
Jarvis, Cyrus, 347
Jefferies, Richard, 55, 79, 106, 117, 131,
139, 154, 172, 174, 182, 189, 190, 191n,
192n, 193, 215, 245, 251, 252n, 345
Jones, Carroll, 48, 52, 353, 355–56, 357,
358, 377, 383, 389
Jones, Elisha, 195n
Jones, H. K., 373, 374n
Jones, Rev. John, 373, 374
Jones, P. V. B., 2
Jones, Dr. Samuel Arthur, 2, 3, 4, 6, 8, 9,
10–11, 12, 20, 24, 25, 27, 28, 29, 30, 31,
32, 33, 34, 35, 36, 37, 38, 39, 40, 41, 42,
43, 44, 45, 46, 47, 48, 49, 50, 51, 52, 53,
54, 55, 56, 57, 68, 72, 78n, 81n, 82n,
85n, 86, 88n, 89n, 93n, 94n–95n, 97n,
102n, 104n, 106n, 107n, 112, 113n,
114n, 116n, 117, 118n, 120, 123n, 125n,
130n, 132, 135n, 137n, 138n, 139, 140n,
143n, 145n, 146n, 149n, 151, 153n,
155n, 159n, 160n, 161n, 162, 164n,
165n, 166n, 168n, 172n, 174n, 177n,
179n, 186, 187, 189, 190, 191, 192,
193n, 194n, 198n, 199n, 201n, 203,
207n, 209, 211n, 214, 215, 218, 219n,
230n, 232n, 233n, 234n, 236n, 238n,
240, 241n, 243n, 245n, 252n, 253n,
255n, 260n, 265n, 273, 274n, 277n,
283n, 286n, 289, 291, 292, 298n, 300,
301n, 304, 305n, 306n, 307n, 308n, 310,
311n, 313, 314n, 315n, 324n, 325n,
326n, 337n, 338n, 342n, 347n, 348,
351n–52n, 354n, 359n, 360n, 362n,
363n, 364n, 367n, 368n, 369n, 371n,
372, 375, 377n, 381n, 382n, 383n, 385,
387n, 388n, 391n, 393, 394, 395,
397–401; Homeopathy, 1, 4–5, 52, 55,
176, 177n, 216, 217, 218, 219, 223, 228,
363; as a Thoreau bibliographer, 50, 91,
107n, 116, 121, 136, 148, 149, 162, 184,
185, 223, 244, 257, 274, 286, 295, 303,
306, 316, 333, 350, 362–63
Jones, Dr. Samuel Arthur, Works of, "An
Afternoon in the University Library,"47,
120, 121, 130, 133, 139, 206, 207n,
264n; *Bibliography of Henry David
Thoreau,* 47, 51, 146, 162n, 179, 181,
183–84, 185, 188, 189, 191, 193, 194n,
196, 198, 199, 202, 203–04, 205, 206–07,
208, 209, 210, 211, 212, 213, 226, 242,
243, 253, 261, 263, 264, 270, 276, 295,
300, 305, 312, 334, 340, 351, 352,
380–81, 390; *Collectanea Henry D.
Thoreau: Emerson's Obituary,* 46, 279n;
"He kept the temple as divine," 107n;
Pertaining to Thoreau, 47–48, 50, 91,
149n, 159n, 187n, 218n, 222n, 298, 300,
301n, 303, 315n, 324, 338, 339, 342,
346, 349, 353, 354, 355, 357; "Thoreau:
A Glimpse," 1, 28, 38, 41, 47, 65, 66, 68,
69n, 73–74, 80, 81n, 85, 99, 106, 113,
123n, 164n, 179, 184n, 213, 214n, 229,
231, 268, 294, 387–88, 389, 390;
"Thoreau: A Glimpse" (Thoreau
bibliography in), 41, 68–69, 71, 72, 86,
184n; *Thoreau amongst Friends and
Philistines,* 32, 48, 145n, 358–59, 360,
361–62, 365, 377, 394; "Thoreau and
His Biographers," 29, 31, 32, 41, 118,
119, 122, 125, 126, 128, 130, 131, 132,
134, 135, 136, 145, 156n, 192n, 269,
281, 282, 283, 292, 294, 300, 325, 380,
397–401; "Thoreau and His Works," 29,
188; Thoreau bibliography in H. G. O.
Blake's *Thoreau's Thoughts,* 7, 41, 68–69,
72, 73, 74, 84, 85, 86, 88, 89, 90, 92,
122, 184n, 231; "Thoreau's Incarceration," 35, 197, 198n, 199n, 201n;
"Thoreau's Inheritance," 28, 40, 41, 42,
164, 165–66, 167, 168, 169, 170, 171,
172, 173, 265, 281, 282, 283, 288n, 292;
"Vox Clamantis in Deserto," 28, 314,
315, 316, 319, 321